The Mennonites in
Indiana and Michigan

Studies in

Anabaptist and Mennonite History

Edited by
Harold S. Bender, Ernst Correll,
Melvin Gingerich, Guy F. Hershberger, John S. Oyer, and John C. Wenger

1. TWO CENTURIES OF AMERICAN MENNONITE LITERATURE, 1727-1928.
   By Harold S. Bender. 1929.

2. THE HUTTERIAN BRETHREN, 1528-1931.
   By John Horsch. 1931.

3. CENTENNIAL HISTORY OF THE MENNONITES IN ILLINOIS.
   By Harry F. Weber. 1931.

4. FOR CONSCIENCE SAKE.
   By Sanford Calvin Yoder. 1940.

5. OHIO MENNONITE SUNDAY SCHOOLS.
   By John Umble. 1941.

6. CONRAD GREBEL, FOUNDER OF THE SWISS BRETHREN.
   By Harold S. Bender. 1950.

7. MENNONITE PIETY THROUGH THE CENTURIES.
   By Robert Friedmann. 1949.

8. BERNESE ANABAPTISTS AND THEIR AMERICAN DESCENDANTS.
   By Delbert L. Gratz. 1953.

9. ANABAPTISM IN FLANDERS, 1530-1650.
   By A. L. E. Verheyden. 1961.

10. THE MENNONITES IN INDIANA AND MICHIGAN.
    By John Christian Wenger. 1961.

STUDIES IN ANABAPTIST AND MENNONITE HISTORY

No. 10

THE MENNONITES IN INDIANA AND MICHIGAN

By John Christian Wenger

Professor of Theology
Goshen College Biblical Seminary

HERALD PRESS

SCOTTDALE, PENNSYLVANIA

The Herald Press, Scottdale, Pa., in co-operation with the Mennonite Historical Society, Goshen College, Goshen, Indiana, is publisher of the series, Studies in Anabaptist and Mennonite History. The Mennonite Historical Society is primarily responsible for the content of the Studies, and the Herald Press for publication of the Studies.

THE MENNONITES IN INDIANA AND MICHIGAN

By

John Christian Wenger

Professor of Theology
Goshen College Biblical Seminary

HERALD PRESS
SCOTTDALE, PENNSYLVANIA

Preface

Mennonites constitute but a small portion of Christendom today, numbering only about 400,000 baptized members around the globe. They are the spiritual descendants of the sixteenth-century Anabaptists, those brave pioneers who rejected the state church system, who set up free churches in Switzerland, Germany, and the Netherlands, and who earnestly sought to be faithful disciples of the Lord Jesus, converted from sin to Christ, and baptized upon the confession of their faith. They thought of themselves as holy pilgrims, separated from the sin of the world, and actively witnessing to all men of the saving grace and love of God. They insisted on the practice of church discipline, being compelled by their understanding of the New Testament to reject an "inclusivist" church. For them the church was a brotherhood of warm Christian love, a holy society in which Christian mutual aid, temporal and spiritual, was rendered. They took at face value the commands of the New Testament not to resist the evildoer, but to suffer wrong rather than to injure anyone. They believed that this "nonresistance" was demanded by both the spirit and the letter of the New Testament.

The Anabaptists were strongly evangelistic and missionary in the first decades of the movement, but this urgent sense of mission was crushed out by the bloody hands of executioners and by those who served in the torture chambers. The consequence was that for several centuries the flame of missionary endeavor burned low. Mennonites came to feel that "outsiders" could seldom be brought to the high vision of Christian discipleship to which they held, and which they were satisfied merely to pass on to their children. Only in the last few generations of American Mennonitism has the fire of missionary endeavor begun to burn brightly again. As far as "home missions" are concerned, it is only since 1935 that a host of mission churches have been planted in many regions in numerous states of the Union.

For many years Mennonites, Brethren, and Friends were known as "plain people," because many of the members of those churches wore a religious garb. These groups, the Mennonites in particular, isolated themselves from the larger American society by the use of the Pennsylvania German dialect rather than English in their home and church life, by marrying only within the ranks of their own congregations, by living in rather compact rural settlements, and by a strong in-group feeling. In recent decades these cultural differences have been breaking down, and the result has been some distress and inner tension in the congregations. This was particularly acute in the 1920's, but the problems associated with cultural accommodation and "worldliness" are not yet fully resolved. Fortunately, the evangelistic concern of the early Anabaptists has been partially recovered, and many members of the church now have a strong and compelling sense of mission in a spiritually needy world. A vigorous interest in Anabaptism has also brought to the group an awareness of its rich spiritual heritage. Goshen College and its Biblical Seminary have played a major role in nurturing and developing this missionary awakening and this awareness of a glorious Christian heritage. This awakening has led not only to the adoption of many new agencies of Christian education and nurture, such as the young people's Bible meeting and the summer Bible school, but also to a deeper desire to minister to human needs "In the Name of Christ" through such projects as disaster units (to render aid to those who suffer from fires, floods, and storms) and the building of mental hospitals. I have tried to summarize and interpret this working of the Spirit of God, particularly in chapters one and four.

It was in the year 1945 that the Executive Committee of the Indiana-Michigan Mennonite Conference commissioned me to write this book. For sixteen years I have worked at the assignment intermittently, during which time my wife and I have watched our children grow into young adulthood.

As to the order of the congregational histories in chapters 2-5, the counties in which these congregations are located are arranged in the approximate order in which Mennonites settled in those counties, or established mission stations in them; and within the counties the congregations are also arranged in the approximate chronological order in which they were established.

I am deeply grateful to a large number of people who have kindly helped me in numerous ways in the course of the years. It is impossible to list more than a mere sampling of those who generously gave of their time to answer questionnaires and queries. But I must mention H. S. Bender, president of the Mennonite Historical Society and chairman of the Historical and Research Committee of Mennonite General Conference; Melvin Gingerich, archivist of the Archives of the Mennonite Church; N. P. Springer, curator of the Mennonite Historical Library; Ivan Nunemaker; Joseph E. Martin, bishop in the Wisler Mennonite Church; and Wilmer D. Swope. Barbara Coffman helped immensely by making available information from the diaries of her grandfather, John S. Coffman. The Indiana-Michigan Mennonite Christian Workers' Conference granted me a stipend one summer to enable me to concentrate on the task. Goshen College made possible the rental of a dictaphone for the preparation of the first draft of the manuscript. Ben Cutrell,

Publishing Agent of the Mennonite Publication Board, Ellrose D. Zook, Executive Editor of Mennonite Publishing House, and Paul Erb, chairman of the Publishing Committee of Mennonite Publication Board, have each extended many kindnesses to me. Roberta (Mrs. Harold) Kreider rendered excellent typing service in transcribing my dictation. The conference historian's Advisory Committee, Russell Krabill, Malvin P. Miller, and Daniel Slabaugh, have been generous and kind. And throughout the project my wife, Ruth Detweiler Wenger, was my constant counselor and the one who did the most to encourage me to bring the work to completion. Mine has been the pleasure of working many hours in libraries and in courthouse records, and of exploring a vast number of cemeteries for birth and death dates of many of the 475 ordained men who have served as preachers, deacons, and bishops in the conference.

Now as this volume is released to the church and to the public, may God be pleased to use it to bring to Christendom a glimpse of that earnest discipleship to the Lord Jesus for which Mennonites stand, and may Mennonites themselves catch a fresh vision of the dynamic Christianity for which thousands of their forebears languished in prisons and died at the stake. *Soli Deo Gloria!*

April 1, 1961   J. C. WENGER

Introduction

It is in the local congregations and district conferences of the Mennonite brotherhood that the heart of the life of the church is to be found. The General Conference has served well as an advisory body since its beginning in 1897-98, and the general boards of Missions, Education, and Publication, founded in 1892 (1906), 1905, and 1908 respectively, with the schools and institutions they operate, have played an increasingly productive role in the life of the denomination. But it is what happens in the district conferences, which are authoritative governing bodies over the congregations, and in the congregations themselves, that determines the character and destiny of the church as a whole. For this reason carefully prepared, thorough, interpretative regional histories are basic to understanding the history of the total brotherhood in America.

It is such a history that John C. Wenger has given us in his unusually comprehensive account of the Mennonites in Indiana and Michigan, covering one hundred and twenty years of life and witness in this key Midwestern area since 1841. It is a thorough and accurate history, based upon the primary sources. Only prodigious labor and unflagging zeal combined with the seasoned judgment and research competence of a trained scholar could have made the volume possible. In addition to the general survey, the almost endless details of the over one hundred congregational histories and the 475 ministerial biographies of the main body alone, plus those of other smaller bodies, fill out with the stuff of life what might otherwise have remained a vaguely general account. The brief summary accounts of related groups are an added bonus.

The Mennonites of Indiana and Michigan depicted here can see themselves mirrored as they actually have been and are; they may be both inspired and instructed if they understand aright what they read. And since Indiana Mennonitism, with its large population, progressive movements, and influential institutions, has made a major contribution to the denomination as a whole, the entire brotherhood can profit by this historical review. Others who wish to become acquainted with American Mennonite life and work in a major area will find here much of real value.

The Indiana-Michigan Mennonite Conference is to be commended for making possible the publication of this very substantial volume, and the author is to be congratulated upon the happy completion of a long and arduous task, which has been carried along with his many other duties as a bishop and leader in the church in Indiana and at large, and as a professor in the Goshen College Biblical Seminary. May he be rewarded by a wide reading of the book, not only in the families of the conference district but also across the brotherhood.

April 1, 1961   Harold S. Bender

Contents

Illustrations

The pictures appear in the following order
and are in one section following page 256.

The Older Mennonite Ministers.

The Older Amish Mennonite Ministers.

Ministers Ordained Since the Merger of 1916.

Mennonite Meetinghouses in Indiana and Michigan.

Conservative Mennonite Church Buildings.

Wisler Meetinghouses.

Other Meetinghouses.

I

Historical and Interpretative Survey

I. EUROPEAN BACKGROUND

1. The Swiss Brethren

The Mennonites take their name from an early elder or bishop named *Menno Simons, ca. 1496-1561,* who united with a Dutch group of so-called Anabaptists in 1536. But Menno was not the founder of the church. He is not related to the Mennonites as Luther, for example, is related to the Lutherans of the world. No one man originated Anabaptism—as the movement was first called by its opponents. The chief founder of the Swiss Brethren (the proper name of the first Anabaptists) was *Conrad Grebel.* This young Swiss patrician was born at Zurich about the year 1498, studied at the Universities of Basel, Vienna, and Paris, for a total of six years, and was for many years a close friend of Ulrich Zwingli, the reformer and founder of the Swiss Reformed Church. It was Zwingli who led Grebel to an evangelical faith, and at first Grebel was one of Zwingli's warmest and staunchest supporters. But toward the end of 1523 and all through 1524 Grebel was becoming increasingly uneasy about Zwingli's evident unwillingness actually to set up a truly reformed and evangelical church. The fact is that Zwingli was slowly coming to the conclusion that it was not possible, or at least not advisable, to create the type of free church (a church not established by law, a church dissociated from the state) in which Grebel had come to believe. Zwingli sincerely wished to set up a Swiss Church which was wholly true to the New Testament. But he decided to attempt to do this without breaking the unity of the established church if possible, and without abolishing either the State Church or infant baptism. It is true that early in 1523 Zwingli had taught that it was prudent to delay the baptism of children until they were mature enough to understand the commitments of baptism. But by 1525 he had decided not to disturb the practice of infant baptism. Rather, he had concluded that it was about time to put to silence those who were minded to cast doubt on the practice.

In December of 1524 Zwingli met with Grebel and his party in a vain attempt to come to a satisfactory agreement on baptism. More discussions were held in January 1525, the most important being the great disputation before the Zurich Council on January 17, 1525, a Tuesday. Four days later, on Saturday, January 21, following mandates that Grebel

1

and his supporters were to desist from holding any further meetings for Bible study, and demanding that all children be baptized forthwith on pain of exile for defiance of the order, Conred Grebel, Felix Manz, George Blaurock, and possibly a dozen other defiant men met in Zurich for counsel and prayer. When they gathered together, they had no thought of inaugurating believers' baptism and creating a new church. But as they prayed, they believed that the Spirit of God led them to take both steps. Consequently George of the house of Jacob (commonly called *Blaurock*, from his blue coat), a priest from the canton known as Grisons, presented himself to Conrad Grebel, the natural leader of the group, and asked for baptism. Grebel performed the rite with no other authorization than that which he felt was given him by God through the Holy Scriptures. By so doing Conrad Grebel became the founder of the Mennonite Church. George in turn baptized the others who were present. The birthday of the church is therefore Saturday, January 21, 1525, at Zurich, Switzerland.

The movement spread rapidly over German-speaking Europe as a brief examination of the following articles in the *Mennonite Encyclopedia* will reveal: Alsace, Austria, Baden, Bavaria, Galicia, Germany, Lorraine, and Palatinate. Persecution was also not slow in coming, and soon the death penalty began to be employed against these devout disciples of Christ who wished only to follow the New Testament as closely as they possibly could. Several thousand of these "heretics" were put to death by water, fire, and the sword, although their chief "heresy" consisted of believing in separation of church and state, and believers' baptism. It is also true, of course, that they were critical of the state churchmen for not practicing a Biblical church discipline, for not requiring holiness of life for church membership. The Swiss Brethren also took seriously the New Testament command to love one's enemies, and not to take revenge under any circumstances. They therefore renounced the use of force and violence in all human relations, including the waging of warfare. But sixteenth-century Europe was not minded to tolerate such "foolishness" as the principle of voluntarism in matters of faith, a free church, believers' baptism, a disciplined church, and New Testament nonresistance. When the theologians found themselves unable to crush the movement by argument and persuasion, they called upon the state to lay violent hands upon the brethren and put them to death. The state was usually willing thus to oblige its spiritual "watchmen."

2. The Dutch Anabaptists

There was also a second cradle of Mennonitism in addition to Zurich. It was in the Netherlands. A man who carried the concept of believers' baptism to the Netherlands was, oddly enough, not himself a member of the Swiss Brethren, but a sort of free-lance reformer who happened to hold in part various doctrines in common with the Anabaptists, although he also held to other notions, especially as to prophecy which they vigorously repudiated. The name of this man was *Melchior Hofmann* (which see in *The Mennonite Encyclopedia*). Hofmann was a Swabian, an earnest reformer, a powerful preacher, a devoted student of the Scriptures. Nevertheless he was a rather unbalanced student of prophecy, and much given to apocalypticism. He was very sure that the end of the age was about to come upon the race, and that only his little band of followers would be ready to meet the Lord. He spent the last decade of his life in prison in Strasbourg, 1533-43. In the long run his followers, known as Melchiorites or *Bondgenoten* (Covenanters), did not amount to much as far as numbers are concerned. By 1560 the Melchiorite movement had about run its course.

In the meanwhile, however, a new development took place among some of the Melchiorites of Friesland in the Netherlands. Led by *Obbe Philips* and his brother *Dirk,* a peaceful, nonrevolutionary, and nonapocalyptic type of Anabaptism began to flourish, 1533-34. These peaceful Dutch Anabaptists were sometimes called Obbenites, from their chief leader Obbe. They were quite similar to their "half brothers" in the faith, the Swiss Brethren, although there was no organic connection with them. Indeed, the Obbenites differed from the Swiss Brethren on only two points: (1) They developed a religious practice known as *shunning* (which means breaking all social fellowship with apostates) in order to protect themselves from the revolutionary fanatics of Münster in Westphalia. (2) They held to a strange and non-Biblical theory of the incarnation which was meant to safeguard the true deity of Jesus, and to insure His sinlessness, while admitting His full humanity. According to this theory Jesus was conceived *in* Mary by the Holy Spirit, but He was not *of* Mary as far as His nature was concerned. He was rather a new Man, the Lord who came down from heaven. This theory rests on the assumption which Menno Simons himself often harped on, that a human mother receives seed from a man, but does not produce seed of her own. Therefore since Jesus had no human father, He was not able to inherit a sinful human nature from Mary. Thus His sinlessness was certain! It is too bad that the Dutch Melchiorites and Obbenites did not simply accept the Biblical statement that Christ was conceived of the Holy Spirit, born of the Virgin Mary, and in view of His Holy Spirit conception was a holy and sinless Man.

3. The Story of Menno Simons

Conrad Grebel was a young man of about twenty-eight when he died of the plague the summer of 1526, leaving no significant books to edify and guide his church. Obbe Philips lost heart by 1540 and withdrew into a life of retirement, perhaps because he was more inclined to cultivate a life of inner piety than to set up congregations kept pure by church discipline. The man who stepped into the place of leadership in the Dutch and North German Anabaptist brotherhood was a former priest named Menno Simons. Menno was born in Witmarsum, Friesland, about the year 1496, educated for the Roman Catholic priesthood, consecrated a priest in 1524, and served as a priest in his father's Friesland village of Pingjum, 1524-31, and in his own place of birth, Witmarsum, 1531-36. As a priest Menno had a rather tender conscience, yet engaged in the usual frivolities of his office at the time, cardplaying and the like. Three incidents had far-reaching consequences for the young Dutch priest; indeed they ultimately led to his renunciation of Roman Catholicism. The first was this. During the first year of his priesthood, as he was one day engaging in the service of the Mass, a doubt as to whether the consecrated wafers really became Christ, suddenly disturbed the young priest. Transubstantiation is a major pillar of truth in the Catholic doctrine of the Mass. Menno was therefore deeply troubled by this assault, as he then regarded it, of the devil. But he proved unable to shake it off, even through the use of the confessional. Ultimately he decided to read the New Testament. He was soon convinced that the doctrine was unscriptural, a rather fearful discovery for. one who believed that the church had the keys which could bar him from heaven. But within a few years he was helped by Luther's writings to see that the rejection of human doctrines could not be the occasion of one's damnation. Yet Menno remained a priest. Indeed he accepted a promotion in connection with his return to Witmarsum and its parish in 1531.

Menno's second jolt also came in 1531. He heard of the execution of a man named Sicke, sometimes called Sicke Snijder (Tailor) and sometimes Sicke Freerks (Frederick's son), for family names were not yet established in The Netherlands in this period. (Menno Simonsz, or Simons, means Menno Simon's son.) Sicke was executed for being rebaptized. Menno himself reports that he had never heard of rebaptism before this time. This incident troubled Menno afresh. Was another Catholic pillar of truth to be broken down? First of all Menno had learned that the Catholic doctrine of the Mass was not sound. Could the church also be wrong as to its doctrine of baptism? Ultimately he decided that the church was in error. Yet he shrank from a hasty withdrawal from the church. Perhaps he hoped to effect an evangelical reformation in his Witmarsum congregation.

And then religious fanaticism struck The Netherlands. Some misguided souls became obsessed with the idea of a theocracy in which people with "new light" should take over the government of cities or provinces and inaugurate the kingdom of Christ in advance of His return. (The most infamous of these attempts was made at Münster in Westphalia, in Northwest Germany, in 1534 by a Dutchman named Jan Matthijsz of Haarlem, a city in which polygyny was practiced by many of the "believers.") Menno's own brother was swept along into one of these unbalanced movements and died resisting civil authorities in the rebellion at Olde Klooster near Bolsward in Friesland. The death of his poor misguided brother was the third and final factor in Menno's conversion to an evangelical faith. The spring of 1535 he made an utter surrender of himself to Christ, entreating the Lord with sighs and tears to hear him, to forgive him, and to cleanse him. Menno's conversion was deep and genuine. He seems to have remained in the Catholic Church for an additional nine months, evidently with the hope that he could lead many of his congregation to conversion and faith. But on or about Sunday, January 30, 1536, Menno renounced Roman Catholicism, "without constraint, of a sudden," as he himself describes this step. About a year later, after a delegation of brethren had begged him in vain to take up the eldership in the church of Obbe Philips, Menno yielded to the desires of the group, and was formally installed into the office of elder (bishop) by Obbe Philips. This ceremony took place in the Dutch province of Groningen. Menno served almost a quarter of a century, mostly in North Germany. He died twenty-five years and one day after his renunciation of Roman Catholicism, on January 31, 1561.

As in the south, so here in The Netherlands the movement spread rapidly. One index to the numerical success of Dutch Anabaptism is the list of converts baptized by Leenaert Bouwens—no less than 10,252 between 1551 and 1582. Other active bishops besides Menno Simons and Leenaert Bouwens were Gillis of Aachen and Dirk Philips. One of the elders named Roelof Martens (also called Adam Pastor) had to be excommunicated for his unsound view of Christ in 1547; he denied the true deity of Jesus. The sad task of excommunication fell to Dirk and Menno. To gain some appreciation of the spread of Dutch Anabaptism one should read such articles in *The Mennonite Encyclopedia* as: Aachen, Belgium, Cologne, Crefeld, Danzig, East Friesland, Eifel, Emden, Friesland, Germany, Goch, Hamburg, Imgenbroich, Jülich, and Netherlands. Persecution was extremely severe in the Netherlands in the sixteenth century for the "Menists" as the peaceful Dutch Anabaptists began to be called as early as 1535. At least 2,500 men, women, and youths died valiant martyr deaths in that century. By the grace of God, Menno, Dirk, and Leenaert escaped the executioner. Gillis of Aachen was beheaded, however. The story of many of these martyrdoms is told in the great Anabaptist tome, *The Martyrs Mirror*, 1660, by T. J. van Braght.

II. AMERICAN MENNONITE BACKGROUND

1. In Search of Peace and Security

Abatement came in the severe persecution of the Mennonites in the low countries soon after 1600, but in Switzerland, especially in the canton of Bern, the persecution of the Mennonites continued by means of fines, imprisonment, exile, and at times even galley slavery on Mediterranean vessels, until the eighteenth century and beyond. The consequence was that some of the Swiss *Taufgesinnten* (the name given the Swiss Mennonites) began to cross over into South Germany, into Alsace, and especially into the Palatinate, to escape the severe persecution of the Bernese authorities. These severe measures seemed to have been instigated in many cases by the Swiss clergy. Toleration had not yet come to Switzerland. In 1664 the Count Palatine was good enough to grant limited asylum to a stipulated number of Mennonite families, although the restricted number seemed not to have been enforced. The act of Count Palatine was at least partially the result of a letter of intercession in behalf of the persecuted *Menisten*, written by an English Quaker, John P. Hilley. In the Palatinate the Swiss *Taufgesinnten* soon lost their Swiss German, the Bernese dialect, and adopted the German dialect of the Palatinate, a language which is known in Southeastern Pennsylvania and elsewhere in America as Pennsylvania Dutch.

But conditions in the Palatinate were also far from ideal. The Mennonites there suffered all sorts of restrictions and indignities. Not more than twenty persons were supposed to gather together at one place for divine worship. Each family had to pay six florins per year as a toleration fee. All through the eighteenth century the Mennonites of the Palatinate had to avoid city residence, they could not go into business, they could not become apprentices and learn trades, young people found it difficult to secure legal permission to marry, and there was a weary struggle as between the Swiss *Taufgesinnten* and the Palatine government. Consequently, when the English Quaker, William Penn, opened up Pennsylvania to people of all faiths in 1682, it was not long until Mennonites from various parts of Europe began to turn their eyes toward the new world. A group of Crefeld, Germany, Quakers and Mennonites located at Germantown, then seven miles north of Philadelphia, in 1683. By 1702 these *Taufgesinnten* had started a new settlement twenty miles north of Germantown at a location called Skippack (perhaps from the Swiss village Schüpbach), now in Montgomery County. Beginning in 1710 thousands of Mennonites of Swiss extraction, some directly from Switzerland and some from the Palatinate, poured into Southeastern Pennsylvania, all alike called Pfälzer (Palatines) by the colonial record keepers. The two chief centers of Pennsylvania Mennonitism became an area surrounding the modern borough of Souderton in Montgomery County, but close to the Bucks County line, and Lancaster in Lancaster County. These two settlements or groups of settlements had by 1960 developed into the strong Franconia Conference of 5,500 baptized members, and its bigger brother, the Lancaster Conference with over 15,000 members, plus the other Mennonite groups which seceded. The Swiss Mennonites—an estimated 2,500 of them—crossed the Atlantic for the most part from 1710 until the Revolutionary War, 1775. They came to escape the poverty and the persecution of Europe, as well as its wars.

In Pennsylvania the Mennonites thrived, along with their Lutheran and Reformed neighbors, with whom they enjoyed the best of relations. In some cases the three groups even united to build a union house of worship. But more commonly it was the Lutherans and Reformed who together built such union places of worship, while the Mennonites erected simple log structures in the colonial period to serve as schoolhouses during the week for their patrons' schools in which associations of parents hired and paid the teacher, and in many cases gave him room and board in turn. In later decades stone and brick meetinghouses commonly displaced the original log building.

The Mennonites of the Franconia and Lancaster conferences gradually pushed out in three main directions, especially after the Revolutionary War had ended. (1) Settlements were made farther west in Pennsylvania, especially in the counties of York, Lebanon, Dauphin, Adams, Franklin, Somerset, and Westmoreland. (2) Some families pressed on down the Shenandoah Valley in Virginia and settled first in Shenandoah and Page counties, while the more prosperous settlements were made later in Rockingham and Augusta counties. (3) Other families made the trek to Ontario to remain under the British Crown, a government which had granted the peace churches, both Friends and Mennonites (later the German Baptists, now Church of the Brethren, also), full liberty as conscientious objectors to participation in the military.

Soon after 1800 the state of Ohio began to attract Mennonite settlers, beginning with Fairfield County in 1803. Here the first bishop was Henry Stemen, 1775-1855, who traveled by horseback over the state of

Ohio visiting the little flocks of Mennonites which were scattered far and wide, preaching, baptizing, and giving communion. Stemen became a preacher in 1809 and a bishop in 1820. His successor was the outstanding leader of the Ohio Conference for many years, indeed the real shepherd of the Indiana congregations as well, John M. Brenneman, 1816-1895, ordained preacher in 1844 and bishop in 1849. The second settlement of Mennonites in Ohio was the Rowland congregation, east of Canton in Stark County. The Columbiana County Mennonite settlement was made in 1807, with Jacob Nold (preacher from 1794 in the Franconia Conference) as the first bishop; he lived 1765-1834, and settled in Ohio in 1817. A colony of Mennonites direct from Switzerland began to settle in Wayne County, Ohio, in 1817. This is the origin of the Sonnenberg and Kidron congregations. Mennonites began to move into Medina County from Bucks County, Pennsylvania, in 1829. And so the settlement spread westward across Ohio in such northern counties as Ashland, Crawford, Seneca, Wood, and Williams, as well as the more southern settlements in Holmes, Clark-Greene-Montgomery, Allen, and Putnam counties.

2. The Amish

It is not only the Mennonites who belong to the story which is here being told. It is also necessary to say a few words about the Amish. The name Amish comes from a young elder or bishop in Switzerland named Jacob Ammann who in 1693 led a schism from the Swiss Mennonites. Ammann wanted a stricter discipline than then obtained among the Swiss Mennonites, and most of all he wished to introduce the Dutch practice of shunning which Obbe Philips had inaugurated. The leader of the mother body which resisted Ammann was Jacob Reist, an older elder. After the division Ammann also introduced the washing of the saints' feet (John 13:1-17) as a religious rite in his group.

Several dozen Amish families came to America before the Revolutionary War and settled in Southeastern Pennsylvania where their picturesque and quaint garb and simple manner of life have attracted the attention of the American public. After the time of Napoleon some 1,500 Amish Mennonites of Swiss ethnic origin came to America and settled in Garrett County, Maryland; Somerset County, Pennsylvania; Fulton County, Ohio; Waterloo County, Ontario; Johnson and Henry counties, Iowa; and Bureau, Woodford, Tazewell, Champaign, and Livingston counties, Illinois. After the Revolutionary War Amish families from Eastern Pennsylvania began settling in the beautiful Kishacoquillas Valley in Mifflin County, Pennsylvania. Others located in Somerset County, Pennsylvania. By 1809 the Amish had also reached what is now

Holmes County, Ohio. And this was just the beginning of a westward trek of the Amish: from Lancaster County to Central or Western Pennsylvania, to Eastern Ohio, and then on to Elkhart County, Indiana, or to Johnson County, Iowa.

There were two immigrations of Amish to the Midwest, including Indiana: (1) those who came to Pennsylvania in the eighteenth century, and (2) those who migrated to America after the time of Napoleon. The former group had its own names, such as Beiler, Eash, Fisher, Glick, Hooley, Kauffman, King, Lapp, Riehl, Smucker, Stoltzfus, and Zook. The nineteenth-century Amish immigrants had such names as Albrecht, Augsburger, Bachman, Bechler, Berkey, Camp (Kemp), Egli, Eicher, Gascho, Gerig, Gunden, Heiser, Imhoff, Jantzi, Klopfenstein, Litwiller, Nafziger, Oesch, Oyer, Raber, Ramseyer, Ropp, Schertz, Slagel, Springer, Stahley, Stuckey, Sutter, Wagler, Wyse, Yordy, and Zehr. The Amish who settled in Pennsylvania in the eighteenth century tended to have more conservative standards of discipline than did the nineteenth-century Amish immigrants who settled farther west; that is, they had stricter regulations on dress and other matters.

3. Mennonite Family Names

It may be of interest to note that for the most part the Franconia and Lancaster settlements in Pennsylvania each had their list of distinctive family names. Typical *Franconia* names are: Alderfer, Allebach, Bechtel, Beidler, Bergey, Bishop, Clemens, Clemmer, Derstine, Detweiler, Freed, Fretz, Funk, Gehman, Godshalk, Gross, Haldeman, Hiestand, Hunsberger, Hunsicker, Johnson, Keyser, Kolb, Kratz, Krupp, Kulp, Landes, Lapp, Leatherman, Lederach, Mack, Mininger, Moyer—Myers, Nice, Oberholtzer, Rittenhouse, Rosenberger, Rush, Ruth, Shaddinger, Souder, Stauffer—Stover, Swartley, Tyson, Wisler, Wismer, Yoder—Yothers, and Ziegler.

Typical *Lancaster* Conference names are: Bare, Bomberger, Bowman, Brackbill, Brubaker, Bucher, Buckwalter, Burkholder, Charles (Karli), Ebersole, Eby, Erb, Eshleman, Garber—Garver, Good, Grabill—Krabill, Greider—Kreider, Groff, Herr, Hershey, Hess, Hoover—Huber, Horning, Horst, Hostetter, Kauffman, Landis, Leaman—Lehman, Lefever, Longenecker, Lutz, Martin, Mellinger, Metzler, Miller, Mosemann, Mumaw, Musser, Neff, Newcomer, Nissley, Ressler, Risser, Rohrer, Roth, Rutt, Sauder, Sensenig—Sensenich, Shirk, Snavely, Stauffer, Weaver—Weber, Wenger, Witmer, and Zimmerman.

Most of the families of the *Virginia* Mennonite Conference moved there from the Lancaster Conference area. Some of the names were Anglicized in the course of time. Roth, for example, became Rhodes, Kauffman became Coffman, and Groff became Grove. Other common names in Virginia Mennonite circles are Beery, Blosser, Brenneman, Brunk, Burkholder, Driver, Geil, Good, Heatwole, Hildebrand, Martin, Shank–Shenk, Showalter, Weaver, and Wenger. Mennonite families came from all the above areas: Franconia, Lancaster, and Virginia, into the state of Indiana.

Other Mennonites came from *Ontario* where we find such typical names as: Baer, Bechtel, Bergey, Biehn, Bowman, Brubacher, Burkhart, Burkholder, Clemens, Coffman, Cressman, Detweiler, Eby, Fretz, Gehman, Gingerich, Good, Gross, Grove, Hagey, Hallman, Hershey, Hoover, Hunsberger, Kolb, Lehman, Martin, Moyer, Oberholtzer, Rittenhouse, Schmitt, Shantz, Sherk, Snider, Weaver–Weber, Wideman, Wismer, and Witmer.

III. INDIANA

1. Mennonite Settlers

For the most part the Mennonites of Indiana are descendants of Mennonite families who migrated from Pennsylvania, Ohio, and Ontario, beginning about twenty years before the Civil War. Three congregations, however, were largely or wholly composed at first of people who came directly from Europe: (1) In 1838 a large number of families from Switzerland began to make a Mennonite settlement in Adams County, Indiana. The present center of the group is Berne. Included in this group were both Mennonites and Amish. (2) In 1853 a group of Dutch Mennonite families migrated from Balk in Friesland to Elkhart County, Indiana. (3) The Leo congregation was initially made up largely of Amish immigrants from Alsace and their families. (4) Beginning in 1916 a number of Amish Mennonite families largely from Illinois and Nebraska began to settle in Porter County, Indiana, thus forming a fourth group which did not come from Ohio and Pennsylvania to Indiana. (5) The Bethel congregation at Ashley, Michigan, is also composed largely of Amish Mennonites from the state of Illinois.

Besides these five special exceptions to the general rule that the Mennonites of Indiana moved to this state from Ohio, Pennsylvania, and Ontario, a few individuals introduced new names into the church. Examples would be Bishop Jacob A. Beutler, 1833-1886, of the Holdeman congregation, whose father John was a German immigrant; Preacher Jacob Christophel, 1782-1868, of the Yellow Creek congregation, who migrated from the Palatinate to America in 1818; Preacher Nobardius Sprohl, 1830-1901, who served in the Howard-Miami congregation, and whose parents brought him from Baden, Germany, to America in 1833; and Deacon David Yontz, 1872-1958, of the Clinton Frame congregation, who was born in Volhynia, then a part of Russia, and whose parents brought him to America in 1874. The number of Mennonites and Amish who came directly from Europe to Indiana is not large, outside of those of Adams County. No Mennonite immigrants at all settled in Michigan except the small Russian group of families at Okemos in Ingham County.

2. Doctrine and Practice

The Anabaptist-Mennonite conception of Christianity and the church differed from that current in Christendom in certain respects. On the so-called major doctrines of the Christian faith: God, Christ, Holy Spirit, Man, Sin, Salvation, the Second Coming of Christ, and the like, Mennonites held the same doctrinal views as prevailed in Protestantism, especially as found in the Reformed faith. But there were certain distinctive emphases which taken together formed a constellation of beliefs which more or less marked off the Anabaptists and their modern descendants from much of Christendom.

(1) The Anabaptists had a strong emphasis on the necessity of *conversion*. It was not enough, they said, to be baptized as an infant, to hold membership in the State Church, and to receive the sacraments. What God demands is holiness of heart and life, an inner "baptism" with the Holy Spirit. In order to be saved a sinner needs to heartily repent and to turn away from sin, and surrender to Christ. No Anabaptist would think of trusting in church membership as such for salvation. Neither did the Anabaptists believe that salvation was mediated by the sacraments. Only faith, they said, could lay hold on Christ for salvation. Conversion must be a reality, and not a theory. This emphasis on contrition, and a continuing brokenness of spirit (called in German *Bussfertigkeit*) characterized the Anabaptists.

(2) The Anabaptists stressed the necessity of not merely passively trusting in Christ, but of also becoming *committed disciples* of Christ. Each believer needs to take up the cross for himself. The Scriptures were given to be obeyed. This is one of the symbolisms of baptism. The disciple signified by being baptized his intention to live a life of holy commitment to Jesus Christ. He is prepared to follow Christ at any cost. Coupled with this earnest ethical endeavor was a simple acceptance of the word of Christ at face value, regardless of how Christendom explained away a given commandment. The oath is a good illustration. No language could be plainer than that of Christ when He forbade any and all oaths on the grounds of the finiteness of humanity. The leading theologians, however, of the Reformation period held that it was only the

abuse of the oath, a carelessness of truth which fortifies one's word by many oaths, which was condemned by our Lord.

It was because of this emphasis on the church's being composed of earnest disciples that the Anabaptists insisted on the practice of church discipline. Every effort must be made to bring each member to full maturity, spiritually and ethically, in Christ.

(3) The Anabaptists held that there were *two kingdoms,* that of God, and that of Satan. These two kingdoms are in conflict and will be so until the return of Christ to raise the dead and judge the world on the Last Day. Therefore believers need to keep themselves separate from the sins of the world. As one martyr wrote to his daughter in 1572: "And read the Holy Scriptures, and when you have attained your years, consider and ponder it well; and pray the Lord for understanding then, and you shall be able to discern good from evil, lies from truth, the way of perdition, and the narrow way that leads unto eternal life. And when you then see pomp, boasting, dancing, lying, cheating, cursing, swearing, quarreling, fighting, and other wickedness, such as drinking to intoxication, . . . think then: 'This is not the right way, these are not the works of Christians, as the Holy Scriptures teach.'"

(4) The Anabaptists stressed a *brotherhood church.* All too frequently it has been the case that in the congregations of Christendom such things as education, wealth, and ordination, tend to stratify the members of the church into various levels of importance and status. In the Anabaptist-Mennonite tradition, the church shall be a brotherhood, with all titles omitted in the life of the church, and the members addressing one another as brother or sister. The church is to be a brotherhood of love. Indeed, this seems to have been precisely the emphasis of the Lord Jesus in John 13 when He taught His disciples that they ought to wash one another's feet. Each member, because he regards his brethren as sons of God, is willing to humble himself before them and render the most lowly service as a token of the Christian love which binds together the members of the body of Christ.

(5) The Christian shall be a *nonresistant follower* of the Lord Jesus Christ. That is, he shall deliberately follow the royal law of love. This doctrine of not resisting an evil man, which is taught in the New Testament by Christ and the apostles, was taken in an absolute way by the Anabaptists. They could not bring themselves to have any part in the taking of human life. They renounced absolutely the use of force and violence in human relations, and were prepared to suffer, if need be, rather than to inflict suffering on others. On this point, as on the oath, the Anabaptists believed that Jesus "fulfilled" the law of the Old Testament by lifting His followers to a higher level than God had required

of His people prior to the coming into the world of the Son of God. The doctrine of nonresistance is perhaps the most distinctive emphasis of the Anabaptists.

(6) The Anabaptists also had a strong emphasis on the church as a *missionary body*. In a day when leading theologians considered that the Great Commission had been fulfilled by the Apostolic Church in the first century, and was no longer binding upon the body of Christ, the Anabaptists quietly insisted that the entire New Testament was binding on every believer, and that Christians ought to go everywhere making disciples for the Lord Jesus Christ. This attitude, which refused to recognize the polity which prevailed at that time in which the ruler of a given territory established the faith for his subjects, compelling them by law to conform, was regarded by the Anabaptists as intolerable. The Anabaptists did not hold that there were no saved persons outside their fellowship. What they denied was that the rank and file of the population were born-again Christians, that the rulers had any right to determine the faith of anyone (for faith is a gift of Christ, and the conscience should not be coerced by any human being), and that any ruler had the right to forbid any believer to witness to his faith to those whom he encountered.

(7) The Anabaptists also appealed to those passages in the New Testament which represent Christians as expecting to *suffer* for their faith in a hostile and sinful world. They therefore often referred to those passages of the New Testament on the necessity of entering into the kingdom of God through much suffering, of bearing the cross, and of being willing to witness to the truth with their blood. The original documents do not betray ordinarily an undue desire for martyrdom, but they do reveal the expectation that being a real child of God will likely excite the opposition and hostility of a cruel world, so that fines, imprisonment, and even death will be all too common in the brotherhood.

It must be admitted that after the first generation of the church in Europe, during which time possibly 5,000 men, women, and children were put to death in the Anabaptist brotherhood from Switzerland and Austria to The Netherlands, the church tended to lose its missionary zeal, and to sink back in quiet discouragement into the point of view that the world simply does not care to hear the witness to Biblical Christianity which the Anabaptists had been attempting to give. After several more centuries of petty persecution, when the Mennonites came to America they no longer had any particular desire to do missionary work among the Indians or with anyone else. They had lost ground spiritually, and had become content to be the "quiet people in the land." This is not to say that there was not any real piety among them. Indeed there were many God-fearing and devout men and women in the church. This means, not only the ministry, but also a large number of the so-called laity. Perhaps the description of church services in the period before the Civil War would give us some idea of the type of piety which prevailed in that time.

If one would have dropped into an Amish Mennonite or Mennonite service of 1860 in Indiana, he would have found a small congregation of worshipers in a plain and simple *meetinghouse*. An aisle in the middle would have separated the men and boys, who sat on one side, from the women and girls, who were seated on the other. The *dress* of all would have been plain and simple, with the older men, especially those who were ordained to the ministry, wearing the plain-collared coat without lapels, and in the case of the Amish their coats and vests would have been fastened with hooks and eyes. The older men would have worn their hair much longer than is now the custom, and cut straight across the back, not "shingled" (as the modern way of graded cutting used to be called). Likewise the women would have worn long and full dresses, simple and plain in form. On the head of each baptized woman and maiden would have been seen the *"cap,"* now known as the prayer veiling, which veil was regarded as exhibiting and symbolizing the truth which Paul sets forth in I Corinthians 11:2-16, on the necessity of women being veiled during the services of the church ("praying and prophesying"). Services were formerly held regularly every two weeks, the intervening Sunday being reserved for quiet rest and for visiting with friends and relatives.

The *language* of the services was Pennsylvania German, or perhaps more accurately Pennsylvania German as modified by the German of the Lutheran Bible and the High German hymnbooks which were used. The Bible which was read in the nineteenth century was generally the Lutheran version, although in earlier centuries both the Mennonites and the Amish preferred the Swiss Froschauer version. The original Mennonite and Amish hymnbook was the *Ausbund,* the earliest known edition of which was printed in Europe in 1564. The Mennonites of the Civil War period had several German hymnbooks to choose from if they wished to replace the old *Ausbund:* (1) the Franconia Conference *Kleine Geistliche Harfe* (Small Spiritual Harp); (2) the Lancaster Conference *Unpartheyisches Gesangbuch* (Undenominational Hymnbook); or the (3) Amish *Unparteiische Liedersammlung* (Undenominational Songbook) or (4) the Ontario Conference *Gemeinschaftliche Liedersammlung* (Common Song Collection). For those who were interested there was also an English hymnbook available, published by the Virginia Mennonites in 1847 under the title, *A Collection of Psalms, Hymns, and Spiritual Songs.* The 1859 edition of this book which had on its backbone, *Mennonite Hymnbook,* was the fourth edition.

The German or "Pennsylvania Dutch" *sermons* were simple in character, usually more or less running comments on a chapter. No written outline or notes were prepared, but the sermon was often well thought out and delivered with much earnestness and feeling. The ability of ministers to preach more or less extemporaneously varied considerably. The usual practice was to have a preacher or two in each congregation as well as one or two deacons, and over several congregations a bishop had the oversight.

The regular worship services were deeply impressive. After the singing of possibly two German hymns one of the ministers would make the "Opening," a sort of preparatory message to get the audience into a reverent and worshipful mood. This was followed by a silent prayer. The deacon would read a chapter from the German Bible, after which another hymn was sung. Then came the main sermon which was followed by the "Testimonies," which were brief statements by the other ordained brethren as they remained seated, that the message was sound and in harmony with the Word of God. The minister who preached then arose and expressed appreciation for the testimonies and the added thoughts which they contained. He then called the congregation to another kneeling prayer. This time he prayed an audible prayer which he always concluded with the Lord's Prayer, the *Unser Vater* as it is called in German. After another hymn the congregation arose for the benediction which one of the ministers pronounced.

On the semiannual *communion Sundays,* when the Lord's Supper was to be observed, the service proceeded as usual until the end of the main sermon. At that point the bishop led in a prayer of gratitude before distributing the bread, and again before sharing the cup with the members. What is known as close communion was observed: the emblems were shared only with the members of the denomination. Ordinary bread was broken by the bishop and a small piece handed to each communicant who ate it at once. Another prayer of thanksgiving for redemption through Christ preceded the serving of the wine. When the wine was to be partaken of, the bishop handed the cup to each member in turn who took a small sip and handed the cup back to the bishop. After all the members had received both the bread and the cup, the washing of the saints' feet was observed. This is based on John 13, where Christ washed the feet of the twelve apostles and told them that if He their Lord and Master had washed their feet, they too should wash one another's feet, for He had given them an example to do as He had done to them. Small tubs of water were brought into the assembly room and pairs of men washed each other's feet, while pairs of women did likewise, until all the members had had their own feet washed and each had washed the feet of another member. After each pair of members had

finished with this sacred rite the two clasped hands and greeted one another with a holy kiss (Romans 16:16) and said in German, "The Lord
bless thee." Following a hymn by the entire congregation—and all sang
in unison prior to the Civil War—the bishop pronounced the benediction,
and all went home. There were no other services of the church before
the Civil War except the regular Sunday morning worship services every
two weeks.

Home life in all groups of Mennonites was always strong. Young
people married, frequently in the early twenties, and families were large.
In the nineteenth century it was not unusual for Mennonites to have ten
or more children. In exceptional cases there were more. P. Y. Lehman,
a Mennonite bishop, had seventeen children. Isaac Smucker, an Amish
Mennonite bishop, had twelve. D. D. Miller, another Amish Mennonite
bishop, had thirteen, but two were lost in infancy. Losing children by
death was also common: many homes lost one or more of their sons or
daughters. Young people were expected to marry within their own faith,
but they were to choose their own mates. Marriage was for life, not only
in word but in deed. Divorce was unknown. In rare circumstances, an
occasional couple ceased living together, but such incidents were regarded
as awful tragedies, never was a divorce secured, and neither party re-
married.

Family worship in the modern sense of reading the Bible to the
family and having family prayers was probably not very common in the
nineteenth-century Mennonite and Amish Mennonite groups, but there
was always prayer before meals, likely inaudible prayer in most families.
These German family prayers were more or less stereotyped in many cases.
In a general way the religious life of the Mennonites and Amish Mennonites was happy and satisfying. Children felt secure in their strong homes.
The father took his responsibility seriously as head of the home, but was
kind and considerate to his wife and children. The parents were deeply
concerned to bring up their children in the nurture and admonition of
the Lord, in accordance with the teaching of the New Testament. Many
Mennonites did not speak freely of their faith, even at home, but the
children sensed from little up how Christ's way of life as revealed in the
Bible was "totalitarian" in its claims, reaching into every area of life, and
how it was expected of each child to learn to work, and to grow up as a
good, upright, honest, and devout man or woman. In other words, there
was little direct nurture, but the indirect nurture was powerful and per-
suasive. Most young people who grew up in Mennonite and Amish Mennonite homes did turn out well.

3. The Older Mennonite Settlements

It has already been mentioned that not all the *Mennonites* who settled in Indiana came from the older settlements in Ohio and Pennsylvania; some were direct immigrants from the Jura Mountains in Switzerland who lived briefly in Wayne County, Ohio, and then migrated to
Adams and Wells counties, Indiana. These sturdy pioneers from the
Swiss mountains, speaking their thick Swiss German, and wearing a
severely plain type of clothing, located near Vera Cruz in Wells County
in 1838, the first settlers being Christian and Peter Baumgartner, brothers. Their aged father, Preacher David Baumgartner, came the next year.
Many of the others who followed them settled in Lick Township, Adams
County, across the line from the Vera Cruz group. By 1849 the so-called
Baumgartner congregation of sixteen families, included such names as
Augsburger, Baumgartner, Bieri, Bixler, Falb, Habegger, Hirschy, Lugin-
bill, Moser, Steiner, etc. In 1852 Mennonite families began to come in
larger numbers directly from Switzerland—one party consisted of eighty—
and settled in Adams County. The new immigrants set up a second
congregation, located at Berne. The first church building was built
1856-58 in Berne, and the congregation grew and prospered. In 1886 the
older Baumgartner congregation merged with the Berne church. The
present membership is about 1,400. This congregation is now affiliated
with what is known as the General Conference Mennonite Church, an
organization of the less strict congregations which use musical instruments in worship and no longer have any religious garb.

In 1838 a second settlement of Mennonites, migrants from farther
east, some from Lancaster County, Pennsylvania, and some from the
Shenandoah Valley, Virginia, was made near *Arcadia* in Hamilton
County, between Kokomo and Indianapolis. For some reason this group
did not prosper. No house of worship was erected until 1881, the membership probably remained less than twenty baptized members, and the
last member died in 1906. Known families include Correll, Gascho,
Hildebrand, and Kauffman.

The most successful settlement of Mennonites in the state is found
in *Elkhart County* to which the Mennonites migrated in 1839 and the
following years, coming from such counties in Eastern Ohio as Medina,
Wayne, Columbiana, and Mahoning. The first settlers were Jacob Brown,
1839; Jacob Coppes, 1844; a father and son—the aged Bishop Martin
Hoover, 85, and his son John Hoover, 1845; as well as another father and
son—John and Joseph Smith: all of whom located in Harrison Township west of Goshen, near the present village of South West. In 1848
twenty-seven more families came from Eastern Ohio to Elkhart County.
Included in this latter group were two preachers, one of them from Eur-

ope, Jacob Wisler and Jacob Christophel, respectively. The first-known service of 1848 was held in a schoolhouse north of the village of South West on Ascension Day. In 1849 the first log meetinghouse was built, located one mile north of South West, on the east side of the road where the old cemetery is now located. This congregation was called Yellow Creek after a stream in the area. For many years Yellow Creek was the religious center of the Mennonites of Northern Indiana, with the exception of the Swiss-speaking group in Adams County. Approximately three to four hundred persons participated in a communion service held at Yellow Creek in 1861. According to the list of early Mennonite settlers in Elkhart County, prepared by Ivan Nunemaker, the following families were located in Elkhart County by 1854: Berkey, Blosser, Brown, Buzzard (Boshart), Christophel, Coppes, Culp, Davidhizar, Freed, Garber, Geisinger, Hartman, Heatwole, Henning, Hershey, Holdeman, Hoover, Kehr, Kilmer, Landis, Lechlitner, Loucks, Moyer, Musser, Nunemaker, Ramer, Reed, Shaum, Smeltzer, Smith, Strohm, Ummel, Walters, Weldy, Wisler, and Yoder. The chief Elkhart County congregations west of Goshen which developed before the Civil War, in addition to Yellow Creek, were Olive, Holdeman, Christophel, and Blosser. East of Goshen there was one early Mennonite church, Clinton Brick, where the settlement was made as early as 1845, but the log house of worship was not erected until 1854. The Lake settlement in Newbury Township, Lagrange County, was begun about 1851, and the first meetinghouse, now called Shore, was built in 1871.

About 1850 Mennonites began to settle in *De Kalb* County, near the villages of Ashley and Hudson, east of Kendallville. As late as 1867 there were but seven members, and services were being held in a schoolhouse. It was not until 1883 that the group ventured to put up a house of worship. And even then this Pleasant Valley congregation, located in Fairfield Township of De Kalb County, never prospered. In 1917 the meetinghouse was sold to another denomination, and by 1920, Mennonite services were discontinued completely.

In 1853 a settlement of *Frisian* Mennonites from the Netherlands was made in Elkhart County, west of New Paris. For many years they worshiped in private homes, in the Whitehead or Neff schoolhouse, or the Christophel Mennonite meetinghouse. These Mennonites had such curious names as Brunsma, DeVries, Duisterhout, Hygema, Krull, Postma, Swart, Sijmensma, Vandeveer, and Visser. From the very first the Yellow Creek Mennonites accepted these brethren as belonging to their fellowship and invited them to join in their communion services. Today no Dutch congregation as such is in existence; these families were simply assimilated into the various Christian congregations of Elkhart County.

About the year 1853 Mennonites from Ohio and Pennsylvania began to locate in *Clay and Owen counties* in Southern Indiana. The first-known settler was Bishop Daniel Funk of Logan County, Ohio, a Pennsylvanian by birth. This Bower congregation, named for Preacher Jacob Bower, erected its first meetinghouse in 1861. By 1864 there was a promising congregation of seventy members, but the people suffered frequently from a malarial fever called ague, and began after a time to move into other communities, either to Northern Indiana or to states farther west. The Bower congregation was also slow to adopt such new agencies as the Sunday school and evangelistic meetings. Only the cemetery remains today, and it is in a state of total neglect. It is located a few miles east of Clay City in Section 13 of Marion Township, Owen County.

The small *Gar Creek* settlement in Allen County, eleven miles east of Fort Wayne, started about 1854, never developed into a congregation, nor did the tiny group of families at *Teegarden* in Marshall County where the Mennonites settled in the latter nineteenth century.

4. The Older Amish Settlements

The *Amish* began to settle in Indiana in 1841. The previous year a deputation of four Amish men, Daniel S. Miller, Preacher Joseph Miller, Nathan Smiley, and Joseph Speicher, visited communities in Iowa and Indiana seeking a new location in which to settle. They were most favorably impressed with *Elkhart County* and the next year a little caravan of Amish consisting of Preacher Joseph and Elizabeth Miller with four children, Deacon Joseph and Barbara Borntreger with five children, Daniel S. and Barbara Miller with five children, and Christian and Elizabeth Borntreger with two daughters, a total of eight adults and sixteen children, left Somerset County, Pennsylvania, for Indiana. They visited friends in Holmes County, Ohio, for one week, spent the last night of the journey on the Michigan-Indiana line south of White Pigeon, and arrived in Goshen June 29, 1841. They settled three miles south of Goshen on the west side of the Elkhart Prairie. There they lived a few months in small huts. Preacher Joseph Miller and Deacon Joseph Borntreger each purchased eighty acres in Clinton Township, Elkhart County, while Daniel S. Miller and Christian Borntreger settled ten miles to the northeast in Newbury Township, *Lagrange County*. Other settlers soon arrived including Preacher Isaac Smucker, Jacob Kauffman, Israel Miller, and Jonas Hostetler. The first Amish service was held in the fall of 1841 in the home of Daniel S. Miller, Lagrange County. The first Amish child to be born and survive was Eli, son of Deacon Joseph Borntreger, 1842. The spring of 1842 Amish services were resumed. On Easter, March 27, 1842, the first service of the year was held in the home of

Preacher Joseph Miller in Clinton Township, Elkhart County. At that point there were about fourteen members in the congregation. From then on services were held regularly every two weeks. Eight additional Amish families arrived from Somerset County, Pennsylvania, in 1842, bearing such names as: Hershberger, Miller, Weirich, Hostetler, and Lehman. The fall of 1842 eight additional Amish families from Holmes County, Ohio, settled in Elkhart County, bearing the names of Miller, Chupp, Yoder, and Schrag (Schrock). Many others followed so that the church grew rapidly.

In the course of time the *unity* of the Amish settlement in Elkhart and Lagrange counties was threatened by slight differences between the attitudes and practices of the Amish from Somerset County, Pennsylvania, and those from Holmes County, Ohio. About 1845 the church divided into two congregations. However, two years later the schism was healed by three Amish leaders from Ohio who served as peacemakers: Moses Miller, Peter Gerber, and Jacob Koblenz. The spring of 1854 the Amish Church divided again, and this time the schism proved to be permanent. The more progressive faction, led by Bishops Isaac Smucker and Jonas D. Troyer, formed what was later known as the Amish Mennonite Church, and established the Maple Grove, Clinton Frame, and Forks (1857) congregations. The Maple Grove meetinghouse was built in 1856, Clinton Frame in 1863, and Forks in 1864. The more conservative body, which insisted on maintaining the older customs, came to be known as the Old Order Amish, and they have thrived and prospered greatly in Elkhart County, and more especially in Lagrange County.

In 1849 Preacher David Baumgartner wrote a letter from near *Berne,* Indiana, to his friends in Switzerland. He reported that at that time there were sixteen Mennonite families living in his area, and added: "There are also an equal number of Amish people near here. . . ." The Old Order Amish are still well represented in Adams County, Indiana.

The more progressive Amish Mennonites established other congregations besides the three already mentioned. Near Amboy, Indiana, the *Howard-Miami* Amish Mennonite congregation developed, although there also the Old Order Amish have maintained their existence until this day. The *Pretty Prairie* settlement of Amish Mennonites in Greenfield Township, Lagrange County, was begun as early as 1864, but had no house of worship until 1872. The small Amish Mennonite settlement which was established near Eagle Lake in *Starke County* (southwest of Plymouth, Indiana) after the Civil War lasted only for a decade or so until the members had moved away. Bishop Jonas D. Troyer lived in this area for a time, and Jonathan P. Smucker, son of the pioneer Bishop Isaac Smucker, was ordained both as a deacon and a preacher while living in Starke County. The Amish Mennonite settlement at Leo in Allen County made in the early 1850's enjoyed a degree of prosperity and is today a flourishing congregation.

It should also be reported that the Old Order Amish have flourished in Indiana. Their congregations now number almost fifty, with over 2,200 in Elkhart, Lagrange, Marshall, and Kosciusko counties in Northern Indiana, 180 in Allen County, 140 in Adams and Jay counties, 90 in Howard and Miami counties, and 400 in Daviess County.

IV. THE CIVIL WAR, 1861-65

Because Mennonites, along with German Baptists (Church of the Brethren), the Society of Friends ("Quakers"), and Brethren in Christ ("River Brethren"), refused on grounds of conscience to take human life, the coming of the Civil War brought a certain amount of social pressure and perhaps misunderstanding upon the so-called peace churches. It is interesting to leaf through *The Times,* Goshen, Indiana, for the early days of the Civil War to watch developments. In May 1861, for example, Goshen citizens subscribed $3,000.00 in one week for the families of Northern volunteers who were serving in the Civil War. Sixteen men each gave $100.00 toward this amount (May 9, 1861, issue). The September 19 issue of 1861 reported that on August 12, 1861, President Abraham Lincoln had designated Thursday, September 26, 1861, as a national day of fasting, humiliation, and prayer. *The Times* for June 26, 1862, reported that as of the eighteenth of June 60,000 Indiana men had volunteered for service in the Union Army. In June 1862, the governors of the Northern states invited President Lincoln to "call upon the several states for such numbers of men as may be required" to win the war *(The Times,* July 10, 1862, page 2). On July 1 President Lincoln responded by calling for an additional 300,000 men. "An order fixing the quotas of the several states will be issued by the War Department tomorrow." The July 17, 1862, *Times* reported that Indiana's quota was 16,000 men. Finally on September 10, 1862, *The Times* gave attention to the question of "those who are conscientiously opposed to bearing arms." It was explained that the quota of soldiers for each township will be fixed by the authorities at Indianapolis. Those who have conscientious objections to war will be excused from military service but compelled to pay a fee of $200.00. The government would then use the money so paid to hire a substitute to fill the place.

How many conscientious objectors registered? *The Times* for September 11, 1862, indicated that for the sixteen townships of Elkhart

County plus the Goshen and Elkhart Corporations 3,483 men had been enrolled of which 235 were "conscientious exempts." The largest concentrations of conscientious objectors were: Harrison, forty-one; Union, forty-one; Clinton, thirty-five; Elkhart, thirty-four; Jackson, twenty-two; Middlebury, fifteen; Concord, fourteen; and Olive, thirteen. Locke, Jefferson, Benton, and York had from nine to two conscientious objectors each, and the Goshen and Elkhart Corporations each had one. Baugo, Washington, Osolo, and Cleveland townships had no conscientious objectors registered in 1862.

The editor of *the Times* pleaded as late as September 24, 1862, "Let Elkhart [County] be saved from the draft." It was his plea that the quotas should be filled by volunteers. The editor was George D. Copeland.

Evidently in the interest of public information, and to promote understanding and good will J. P. Siddall, who was in charge of raising the quotas for the state of Indiana from his Indianapolis office, reported in *The Times* for September 24, 1862, that the draft date had been set for September 15, 1862, but that it could not be carried out as of that date. He also stated that if there were enough volunteers in a given township no draft would be made in that township. He stated that 6,000 additional men were needed in Indiana to prevent a state draft. He said that if by September 6, 1862, the ninety-two counties of Indiana did not produce enough volunteers the draft would go into effect. On October 2, 1862, *The Times* reported further on the draft, stating that it would be made on Monday, October 6, at 10:00 a.m. in the Elkhart County Courthouse, Goshen. The names of all citizens liable for the draft were to be placed into a box, and a blindfolded person was to draw out slips until the quota was met. Persons drafted were to be notified immediately by the marshal as to the time to appear "to take up the line of march to the camp."

On the status of conscientious objectors J. P. Siddall, "General Commissioner," published a statement in *The Times* of October 9, 1862, explaining the procedures to be followed as to conscientious exempts: "Our State Constitution exempts this class of persons from military service, but provides that they shall pay an equivalent. The provision is as follows: 'No person conscientiously opposed to bearing arms shall be compelled to do militia duty; but such persons shall pay an equivalent for exemption.' " Siddall explained that the sum of $200.00 had been fixed by the Secretary of War. He then went on: "Their names cannot be placed in the box among those subject to draft, because they are exempt by an express constitutional provision; their exemption is not dependent on payment of the equivalent, but is complete prior to such payment, leaving the equivalent to be collected subsequently." Siddall reported that at that date there were in the state of Indiana 3,169 conscientious exempts between the ages of eighteen and forty-five. Siddall was very clear to indicate that the state would use the $200.00 fee as "the means by which another is induced to go. . . ." So serious was the national emergency that 40 per cent of the male citizenry between the ages of eighteen and forty-five in Indiana needed to be drafted as soldiers. With sincere moral integrity he commented: "I have tried to do justice to the 3,169 conscientious, without infringing on the rights of the 273,000 citizens of Indiana who are on the militia roll, and who are either in the service or liable at any time to be called on to perform military duty."

The Times for October 9, 1862, published a list of ninety-seven conscientious exempts who were required to pay the $200.00 fee. It should be explained that the leveling of this fee upon the conscientious objectors was parallel to the drafting of other citizens for military service. Thus the ninety-seven conscientious objectors of the 235 in the county were by October of 1862 required to pay the stated fee. It is impossible to ascertain which names were Amish, which were German Baptists, and which were Mennonites. The following conjectures as to Mennonite conscientious objectors are hereby made: in Clinton Township, Abraham Hartzler and Emanuel Hartzler; in Concord Township, Christian Shaum; in Harrison Township, Christian Christophel, Abraham Hoover, David L. Hoover, John S. Wenger, and Peter G. Wenger; in Locke Township, John Rineburg—probably John Ringenberg, the Amish Mennonite minister; in Middlebury Township, John Nuesbaum (Nusbaum); in Olive, David Lechlightner, Benjamin Lehman, and Michael Shank; in Union, Henry Christophel (father-in-law of J. S. Hartzler), John M. Christophel, and Joseph Wenger. By August 1864 the conscientious exempt's fee was $300.00. Later on in the Civil War the fee for conscientious objection was raised to $400.00. Because David Burkholder was not yet a member of the church he had to personally hire a substitute in the fall of 1864, which cost him $600.00. It should also be reported that a number of young men from Mennonite families, perhaps most of whom were not yet members of the church, entered the Union Army when drafted.

Early in 1865 George Funk of the Bower congregation in Clay and Owen counties of Southern Indiana reported to the Herald of Truth that four young men had been drafted the previous fall because they were baptized after the draft. However, these men were permitted to attend the sick in hospitals, "which we believe is not contrary to the dictates of our conscience, and no violation of the Gospel or the principles of our church."

V. Stress and Difficulty, 1865-75

The first twenty years of Mennonitism in Northern Indiana were years of prosperity, peace, and growth. But following the Civil War disharmony arose in the leadership of the Elkhart County church. *Jacob Wisler,* who had been ordained bishop by Abraham Rohrer of Ohio in 1851, following the death of the aged Bishop Martin Hoover in 1850, was a sincere and devoted man of God, but lacked the vision which some of his younger colleagues had, such as Daniel Brenneman. On the other hand, Wisler was criticized by such leaders as Deacon Joseph Holdeman for not being sufficiently firm in his discipline. When Preacher John F. Funk moved to Elkhart County in 1867, he was urged by Bishop John M. Brenneman of Ohio to do all in his power to seek to maintain the unity of the church, which seems to have been severely threatened by that time. Sixteen leaders of the Mennonite Church from other states, and from Canada, came to Elkhart County in October 1867, after Bishop Wisler had desisted from preaching for a number of months, and tried to reconcile the two factions, those of Wisler, and those of Brenneman. In 1868 Bishops Joseph Hagey and Tilman Moyer of Ontario made another effort to achieve full reconciliation. Nevertheless on March 2, 1869, Bishop Wisler and two preachers, Christian Bare and John Weaver, withdrew from the other portion of the church in which John F. Funk and Daniel Brenneman were leaders. This schism was not healed until August 5, 1870, when Bishop John M. Brenneman of Ohio succeeded in reconciling all the parties. The trouble broke out afresh in 1871, however, over the Sunday school, with Funk actively promoting it, and Wisler being cool toward all innovations including not only the Sunday school, but evening meetings, bass singing, and probably "excessive" English preaching. The outcome was that six bishops from out of state came to Indiana in October 1871, and on the seventeenth day of that month drew up their findings which involved stripping Jacob Wisler of his bishop oversight, but allowing him to continue as a minister. The outcome of this tension was finalized on January 6, 1872, when Wisler and his supporters withdrew from the Indiana Mennonite Conference, and established what is now known as the Wisler Mennonite Church. Wisler seems to have taken about one hundred members with him into his new church, leaving an estimated 300 members in the conference.

One would have thought that after this difficulty only peace and harmony would have prevailed in the church. But by the close of 1873 the tension was severe between Funk and his fellow ministers on the one hand, and Preacher *Daniel Brenneman* on the other. Brenneman favored the introduction of evangelistic and revival meetings, sometimes accompanied by rather severe emotional outbursts (people shouting, weeping, praying loudly), and also felt that women should be given greater liberty to give testimonies. In December 1873, John Krupp, of Branch County, Michigan, was silenced for advocating the same things as Daniel Brenneman. On April 25, 1874, the Mennonite ministers of Northern Indiana, consisting of two bishops, John M. Christophel and Jacob A. Beutler; five preachers, Christian Christophel, Henry Shaum, J. M. Culbertson, Martin E. Kreider, and John F. Funk; and five deacons, Jacob H. Wisler, Henry B. Brenneman, Henry Christophel, David Martin, and Joseph Holdeman, met in the Yellow Creek meetinghouse and drew up a document expelling Daniel Brenneman from the Mennonite Church, or at least formally declaring that "he can no longer be held as a brother in the church, having of his own accord left the church." Brenneman took along either immediately or shortly thereafter approximately fifty-four members of the Mennonite Church, and also won for his new group twenty-nine persons "who had been standing aloof for years —too much Mennonites to be Evangelicals and too much Evangelicals to be Mennonites." Needless to say both the Wisler and Brenneman schisms were most regrettable. John F. Funk was a great and good man, an able leader, a preacher gifted far above any of his colleagues in many ways, but he lacked sufficient humility and patience and tact to maintain the confidence of his co-workers. All three groups—the Mennonite Church led by Funk, the Wisler Mennonite Church led by Jacob Wisler, and the Reformed Mennonite Church (now United Missionary Church) led by Daniel Brenneman—suffered by these unfortunate divisions.

VI. The Elkhart Team, Funk and Coffman

God was gracious to the Mennonite Church in Indiana by sending an able young minister from Virginia named John S. Coffman to Elkhart in 1879. Coffman and Funk became an unusually effective team in leading the Mennonites, not only of Indiana, but of North America, to adopt many new methods of Christian work, to deepen the piety and religious life, and to increase their sense of heritage. Funk himself had introduced Sunday schools to the Indiana Mennonite Church, the older congregations adopting them between 1867 and 1880. The Sunday school proved to be one of the greatest blessings that ever came to the Mennonite Church, for it greatly deepened the knowledge of the Bible, and developed teaching ability on the part of many laymen.

Funk had started the monthly *Herald of Truth,* and its German equivalent, the *Herold der Wahrheit,* in the year 1864, while he was still living in Chicago. It was Funk's privilege to be both a Sunday-school pupil and teacher, as well as superintendent, and colleague of D. L. Moody, in Sunday-school work in Chicago. This accounts for the vision which he had of the good which Sunday schools could accomplish for his own denomination.

After Funk moved to Indiana in 1867 he continued his good work of publishing what became the unofficial church organ of the Mennonites of North America, the two Heralds. He also began to publish books, the first of which was John M. Brenneman, *Pride and Humility,* and the same work in German. Funk also issued such books as Brenneman, *Christianity and War,* in both German and English editions; *A Collection of Psalms, Hymns, and Spiritual Songs,* 1868; *Mennonite Family Almanac* from 1870; a new hymnbook called *Die Allgemeine Lieder-Sammlung* (General Hymnbook), 1871. In 1871 Funk issued his largest publishing effort to date, *The Complete Works of Menno Simon,* a large book of about 750 pages; the next year Funk issued Dirk Philips, *Enchiridion oder Handbuechlein* (Handbook of Christian Doctrine). Finally in 1875 Funk incorporated as The Mennonite Publishing Company, for a period of fifty years. Strangely enough Funk outlived his corporation by five years, dying in 1930 in his ninety-fifth year. Funk's largest publishing effort was not *The Complete Works of Menno Simon* in English (1871) or German (1876, 1881) but *The Martyrs Mirror* translated by Joseph F. Sohm (1855-1902), 1886. It is impossible to estimate how great was the influence of John F. Funk in arousing in the Mennonite Church a keener sense of its heritage, and thereby engendering a more dynamic sense of mission.

But the contribution of *John S. Coffman* must also be mentioned. Coffman was a handsome man, smooth-shaved, a former schoolteacher, a man who was deeply interested in the young people of the church, especially in those who were attempting to secure an education, and a man with a genuine concern for the salvation of men. Coffman had the same vision for the renewal of the church which Daniel Brenneman had, but he exercised sufficient patience and tact not to break the unity of the church by a too rapid introduction of such a fine institution as *evangelistic meetings,* then known as "protracted meetings." With fasting and prayer Coffman cried to the Lord to open the way for protracted meetings. From 1881 to 1899, when Coffman passed away at the early age of fifty, he had held a large number of "protracted meetings" in which a vast number of people, largely young people, were gathered into the church. But Coffman's preaching did more than merely win the unsaved. He also helped a large number of people to a deeper life with Christ, and he brought to the young people of the church a new respect for their denomination. Equally important was his contribution as a leading promoter, guiding spirit, and president of the board of the *Elkhart Institute,* which in 1903 became Goshen College.

Funk and Coffman also supported strongly the *mission spirit* which had been so vigorous in Anabaptism, but which had been lost. As early as 1865 Funk published an article by Philip Mosemann of Lancaster County, Pennsylvania, son of Immigrant Bishop Jacob Mosemann of Germany, favoring missions. The *Herald of Truth* in the 1890's also brought occasional reports of such missionaries as Eusebius Hershey (1823-1891), a member of the Evangelical Mennonites (which later became a part of the MBC Church), who went to Africa as a missionary in 1890. Funk also reported in the *Herald of Truth* new items from Missionary Sarah Alice Troyer of China, a Mennonite who served under the China Inland Mission.

As early as 1882 Funk organized the *Mennonite Evangelizing Committee* which functioned for ten years and was then reorganized as the Mennonite Evangelizing Board. About 1890 a number of brethren met in Chicago and organized the Mennonite Benevolent Board, which in 1896 merged with the Evangelizing Board to form the Mennonite Evangelizing and Benevolent Board. Later, in 1899, the Mennonite Board of Charitable Homes was created at Marshallville, Ohio, and the name changed in 1903 to the Mennonite Board of Charitable Homes and Missions. In 1906 the Mennonite Evangelizing and Benevolent Board merged with the Mennonite Board of Charitable Homes and Missions to form the present Mennonite Board of Missions and Charities.

Funk was fairly jubilant on November 6, 1893, when he recorded in his diary: "M. S. Steiner went to Chicago this afternoon to start a mission. He went out now as the first Mennonite missionary of the Old Mennonite Church in America. May God bless him and his work." A little over five years later, on February 12, 1899, Funk commissioned Dr. and Mrs. W. B. Page and J. A. Ressler the first foreign missionaries of the Mennonite Church to India. Little did Funk suppose that by 1960 the General Mission Board would be handling well over $1,000,000.00 a year in its program of missions and eleemosynary work (not to mention the budget of the Eastern—Lancaster Conference—Board, which amounts to over $650,000.00). The Mennonite Board of Missions and Charities is commonly referred to in Mennonite circles as the "General Mission Board," to distinguish it from the various district boards of the denomination, the local one of which is known as the Indiana-Michigan Mennonite Mission Board.

In 1882 Funk persuaded the Indiana-Michigan Conference to give its moral support to the organization of a *"Mennonite Aid Plan,"* a company of individual Mennonites who would organize to reimburse members who suffer losses by fire. As early as the third report members were located not only in Indiana and Michigan but in Ohio, Illinois, Missouri, and at Mountain Lake, Minnesota. Gradually the service of the organization covered Mennonties of many states, and in 1912 the headquarters of the Aid Plan were transferred to Freeman, South Dakota. The membership is now over 4,000 in at least seventeen states, with a total property evaluation of $40,000,000.00.

Funk was also a leader in the transition of the conference from the use of German to the *English language.* He himself was able to preach sermons in good German, but felt equally free to speak in English. This was characteristic of many of the ministers in the conference in the 1880's: they were bilingual.

At the present time the Mennonite ministers west of Goshen meet on the last Saturday of March annually, and the last Saturday in September. The ministers of east of Goshen meet one week later in the spring and the fall. The ministers of Michigan meet annually in August. It is not certain when these *district ministerial meetings* were created. But as early as 1877 Funk referred in his diary to a ministers' meeting held on Saturday, May 5; he simply calls it a "Conference." Later references in his diary to this institution refer to it usually as the Home Conference, evidently meaning "of the Home District." These ministers' meetings are for fellowship, for the discussion of mutual problems, and for the presentation of addresses which will be helpful to the ordained brethren in their work. They are not authoritative bodies.

In 1892 the first *General Sunday School Conference* of the Mennonite Church was held in the Clinton Frame Amish Mennonite meetinghouse east of Goshen. On August 13 of that year J. S. Coffman recorded in his diary that he had met with the committee which was to prepare the program: Jonathan P. Smucker, D. J. Johns, M. S. Steiner, D. D. Miller, A. B. Kolb, and John Zook. "This is a new venture and we are taking the matter very prayerfully that it may be for the prosperity of the church." On the second day of the Sunday School Conference, October 6, 1892, Coffman wrote: "The program was readily carried out all day and the proceedings were very interesting and displayed talent among our young people that was a surprise to many. The good part was that it was practical teaching that will enable the observant Sunday-school worker to go to his work better prepared." The General Sunday School Conferences were discontinued in the course of time but in their place were organized District Sunday School Conferences. In Indiana and Michigan the Sunday School Conference prepared a constitution which was approved by the Mennonite Conference in 1915 and by the Amish Mennonite Conference in 1916, after which it was declared in effect. The purpose of the Indiana-Michigan Sunday School Conference was to "unify and safeguard Sunday-school interests." In 1943 the name was changed to the Indiana-Michigan Christian Workers' Conference. It sponsors an annual meeting and carries on a vast program of Christian education through divisional secretaries in such fields as Young People's Activities, Sacred Music, Summer Bible Schools, Christian Workers' Training, Mission Study, Sunday Schools, Home Interests, Lay Evangelism, etc.

In the diary of John F. Funk for March 2, 1897, he reported the holding of a meeting to adopt measures to aid the suffering and perishing ones in India: "Effected an organization and started to work up the cause." This organization was the *Home and Foreign Relief Commission* which originated under the auspices of the Mennonite Evangelizing and Benevolent Board, which then served as the General Mission Board of the denomination. By the close of 1897 the Home and Foreign Relief Commission had collected more than $20,000.00 for India relief and had sent George Lambert to supervise the distribution of grain. The Commission continued to serve, although with some decline in the course of time, until the year 1906 when it was disbanded. This interest in foreign relief led directly to the sending of the first Mennonite missionaries to India.

Funk and his Prairie Street congregation pioneered in many activities. As early as February 18, 1874, Funk mentioned attending *teachers' meeting* in the home of Henry B. Brenneman. "Had a pleasant evening." It is not clear whether or not this was the first teachers' meeting held in the congregation, but it is certain that Prairie Street led all other congregations in this activity. When the teachers' meeting became a regular institution is not known, but on February 6, 1894, Funk reports that teachers' meeting was held "at our house. Good attendance."

Another activity in which Funk and the Prairie Street congregation pioneered was in the holding of *children's meetings*. Mention is made of these meetings occasionally, such as June 25, 1882; September 14, 1884; December 14, 1884; and March 8, 1885. The country congregations of Elkhart County would likely not have conducted such meetings at that time.

As early as 1878 Funk reports attending a *"Bible Reading"* in the home of Deacon H. B. Brenneman of Elkhart. On October 25, 1883, Funk mentions in his diary that there was "no Bible Class. There seems to be no interest any more. Must try and stir up again." On July 28, 1887, R. J. Heatwole attended the Bible Reading at Prairie Street Mennonite Church and was much impressed. He wrote up his account for the *Herald of Truth* which was published on page 281: "The subject of the lesson was *Sanctification,* and the one proposed for the next meeting was *Redemption.* We felt edified in having been present; each one had sought out some Scripture bearing upon the subject giving light and knowledge upon the same, while some explanations were also made to those present that were younger in experience and understanding. The brotherhood in Elkhart is rather small in number, but they have Sunday school on Sunday morning at 9:15 o'clock, preaching at 10:30, and in the evening at 7:00 o'clock."

The concept of Bible Readings spread to other congregations and in 1889 the Howard-Miami congregation organized one, to meet on Tuesday evenings. Prairie Street was then meeting on Thursday evenings. Preacher Noah Metzler of the Yellow Creek congregation was overjoyed on November 24, 1892, when that congregation voted to approve Bible Readings. Finally the Indiana-Michigan Mennonite Conference in 1897 recommended "that Bible Readings should be maintained in all the churches where they can be held with the counsel of the church and to the edification of the congregation, and that the ministers and the old people should attend and assist in conducting them." But even prior to this the Holdeman congregation (1896), Nappanee congregation (1896), and the Shore congregation (1897) had adopted Bible Readings. In the course of time the name was changed to Young People's Bible Meeting.

The story in connection with Mennonite *prayer meetings* is not a happy one. As early as January 22, 1871, John F. Funk attended a prayer meeting in the home of J. Detweiler of the Caledonia congregation. Funk mentioned in his diary that this was the first time he had ever attended a Mennonite prayer meeting. Unfortunately the prayer meeting movement was led by men such as Daniel Brenneman, who later lost the confidence of many members of the Mennonite Church. The loss of Brenneman and his supporters in 1874 was a real setback to evangelistic meetings, prayer meetings, and the like. Indeed, as early as October 1872, the Indiana Mennonite Conference Minutes recorded: "The subject of Prayer Meetings was then taken up, which was considered a delicate subject to decide upon as we must on the one hand guard against doing anything that would discourage prayer; on the other hand we must take heed that we do not adopt, teach, and follow customs that are not acceptable unto God. It was therefore held by the conference, that according to the teachings of the Gospel of Christ it is not required to make special appointments and come together at regular times for the purpose of holding prayer meetings, and that under existing circumstances it is not edifying or conducive to the peace, unity, and prosperity of the church, and according to the long established practices and customs of the church it can not be tolerated." This action could not have been taken to prevent the Wisler schism, for that had already occurred. Perhaps the most charitable interpretation is that Funk and his fellow ministers were attempting to keep the door open for the return of the Wisler group. The consequence of this unfortunate resolution was a long delay in the establishment of midweek Bible study and prayer meetings. One of the first congregations to have prayer meetings was Fort Wayne, where the mission church was established in 1903 and which started prayer meetings in the "early years." The Olive Church under the leadership of D. A. Yoder established prayer meetings as early as 1912, and Pigeon in 1916. Most of the other country congregations of Northern Indiana established midweek meetings between 1920 and 1950.

The first known *church wedding* in the Indiana-Michigan Mennonite Conference was held at Prairie Street on April 14, 1894, when E. B. Betzner and Jennie Steiner were united in marriage.

Another organization which is now found in every Mennonite congregation is the *women's sewing circle*. The first sewing circle in the Indiana-Michigan Conference was organized at Prairie Street in 1900. Mary Brubaker, a member of the United Brethren Church, spoke to Mrs. McClintic and a few other women about starting a sewing circle in the Prairie Street congregation, and they decided to make the attempt. To their great surprise sixty women attended. They did not have enough chairs; so some of the women had to stand. The meeting was held in the Albert Brubaker home, on the corner of Prairie Street and Park Avenue, where C. P. Martin later lived. After deciding to organize, the women elected their first officers: Mary Brubaker (host to the meeting), president; Mrs. William Coffman, secretary-treasurer. They met one afternoon each month. The materials needed were donated by different persons who felt led to do so. In the second year Mrs. Rutt was elected president, and a cutting committee was appointed: Anna Brubaker, Mrs. McClintic, and Mary Brubaker. Mrs. Daniel Weldy was inspector. Among the women who were members in the early years were Mrs. Herman Yoder, Grandma Kulp, Mrs. Kohl, Phoebe (Funk) Kolb, Martha Funk, Mrs. Dr. Mumaw, Mrs. John Lehman, Mrs. John Martin, Mrs. Jacob Mast, Grandma Coffman, Jennie Betzner, Mrs. Rutt, and many others. Most of the sewing done in the early years was for the Chicago Mission. The meetings were held in different homes and sewing machines were brought in for the day. Mrs. C. W. Leininger writes: "It was a happy day in 1915 when the Administration Building was built [on Prairie Street, Elkhart]. Bro. George [L.] Bender made it possible for us to have a room in this building and we heartily agreed to do sewing for the building, like making bedding and curtains. Also at this time Sister Anna Moyer donated two new Singer sewing machines which were a great help." The sewing circle always had a devotional period.

Other sewing circles were organized in the next few decades, such as Maple Grove, in the early 1900's; Howard-Miami, about 1906; Clinton Frame, 1907; West Market Street, Nappanee, 1908; North Main Street, Nappanee, 1910; Salem, 1910; Fairview, 1914; Middlebury, 1915; Yellow Creek, 1916; Pigeon, 1917; Emma, 1918; Clinton Brick, 1920; Leo, about 1920; etc.

Only congregational sewing circles were in existence prior to 1917, and there was no over-all organization. Mary Burkhard called a meeting on July 25, 1917, and presented the need to organize the work. There was no program, just an open discussion. The challenge was made to support the church work in India. A committee met to plan for the next meeting which was held in November 1917, at which time there was a program, and an organization was effected. The name adopted for the new organization was, "Indiana-Michigan Branch, Women's Work of the Mennonite Church." Later the name was changed to, "Women's Missionary and Sewing Circle Organization of the Mennonite Board of Missions and Charities." In 1954 the present name was adopted, "Women's Missionary and Service Auxiliary." By 1958 the Service Auxiliary consisted of seventy sewing circles with 1,072 active members and 200 associates. The cash receipts for that year amounted to $17,200.34. There were 11,809 garments made, with 2,300 baby garments, 834 Christmas bundles sent, 2,380 pieces of bedding and linen made, etc. The work of the Women's Missionary and Service Auxiliary has become a worldwide project. In addition to the $17,200.34 received in cash, other contributions in kind amounted to $21,275.89. The 1958 report of the WMSA also includes a report of the Girls' Missionary and Service Auxiliary indicating twenty-three auxiliaries, with twelve which failed to report. The Girls' Auxiliary carried on a ministry similar to the adult units: sent a box to Japan, helped equip a house trailer at a mission station, filled and delivered Christmas boxes, caroled, gave a Christmas program at the Froh Brothers' Home for the Aged, sent money to an orphanage in Germany, contributed to a Puerto Rico blanket fund, etc.

In addition to the German *hymnbooks* of the Franconia, Lancaster, and Ontario conferences, as well as the Elkhart hymn collection of 1877, Funk issued in 1890 a fine little work known as *Hymns and Tunes*. The churches which wanted to use a Mennonite hymnbook with English hymns were no longer confined to the Virginia book of 1847, *A Collection of Psalms, Hymns, and Spiritual Songs,* which had gone through many editions. The singing of proper hymns was quite a concern to John F. Funk. On the editorial page of the *Herald of Truth* for 1890, page 136, Funk wrote: "Let us sing what we teach. Many hymns used by our people are not at all in accordance with our principles of faith and, as we believe, with the teachings of the Bible. Many of these hymns are learned from popular Sunday-school hymnbooks, and from the sentiments expressed in the words the young people and even the older ones form ideas that are not in the line of Bible teaching. Let us be careful to select books that do not conflict with the Word of God." Nevertheless, the *Herald of Truth* regularly carried advertisements of the *Gospel Hymns,* numbers one to four, and later one to six. Funk also sold the German equivalent, *Evangeliums-Lieder.*

In 1902 Funk issued the *Church and Sunday School Hymnal,* a book with the words printed with the music, with J. D. Brunk as musical editor. The book contained a German appendix. Funk published the following endorsement of the *Church and Sunday School Hymnal,* which had been copyrighted by J. S. Shoemaker: "Many of our congregations who had used the *Gospel Hymns* have now adopted the new *Church and Sunday School Hymnal* and have no practical use for the *Gospel Hymns* any more. . . ."

In 1927 the Mennonite Publishing House, Scottdale, Pennsylvania, issued a fine new hymnbook entitled, *Church Hymnal, Mennonite,* with J. D. Brunk as musical editor and S. F. Coffman as hymn editor. This book is now used almost universally in the congregations of the Indiana-Michigan Mennonite Conference. The Wisler Mennonites at Yellow Creek still sing from *A Collection of Psalms and Hymns Suited to the Various Occasions of Public Worship and Private Devotion,* first published by Funk, 1880. The Old Order group, however, which separated from the Wisler Mennonites in 1907, still sing from the old Ontario hymnal, *Die Gemeinschaftliche Lieder-Sammlung,* first printed at Berlin (Kitchener), Ontario, in 1836.

It should also be pointed out that down through the decades since the Sunday school was adopted by the Mennonites various hymnbooks were used from outside the denomination. For example, the Olive congregation used the German *Liederbuch für Sonntagsschulen,* St. Charles, Missouri, 1882; *Sacred Songs No. 1,* by Ira B. Sankey, James McGranahan, and Geo. C. Stebbins, Biglow and Main Company, New York and Chicago, 1896; *Songs of Faith and Hope No. 2,* edited by James M. Black, Jennings and Graham, Eaten and Mains, 1909. They also used the Mennonite book, *Hymns and Tunes,* Elkhart, Indiana, 1890.

John F. Funk's Prairie Street congregation also pioneered in the conducting of *singing schools.* As early as 1892 A. B. Kolb conducted a singing school at Prairie Street. Later that same year William P. Coffman conducted a singing school at Howard-Miami, and two years later at Forks. In 1901 J. W. Yoder held singing school classes with the Howard-Miami congregation, on which occasion G. W. North wrote in the *Herald of Truth:* "Bro. Yoder is a very able instructor and we would recommend

him to everyone as a first class teacher." The purpose of these singing
schools was to teach people to read notes and thus to be able to learn
to sing new hymns, and to sing the four parts well. This is especially
important to Mennonites since they sing a cappella.

The Prairie Street congregation was also the first to have *Christmas
programs*. On Sunday, December 28, 1890, Funk reported in his diary
that on Sunday evening the Prairie Street Church had had its Christmas
exercises. The house was full, he wrote, and a very entertaining meeting
was conducted. He stated that many strangers were there, and that all
did their parts well. In 1893 he speaks of giving prizes and candy to the
Sunday-school pupils on New Year's Day. In the course of time this
practice of having Christmas programs for the Sunday school spread to
the other congregations of the conference.

Another organization which was promoted occasionally by Funk for
many years was the *Mennonite General Conference,* the over-all representative body of the Mennonite Church. Although Funk had spoken
favorably of the Mennonite General Conference long before the preliminary meeting of 1897, and the formal organization in 1898, yet the
General Conference was not organized very long until Funk began to
speak critically of it. Nevertheless the General Conference grew and
became one of the most influential organizations of the church. (The
following committees now serve the General Conference: Executive,
Music, Historical and Research, Commission for Christian Education,
Peace Problems, Economic and Social Relations, Church Welfare, Ministerial, Mennonite Mutual Aid, and since·1949, the General Council
which is composed of the Executive Committee, of one member from
each committee of General Conference, of one member from each of the
three boards of the Mennonite Church [Education, Missions, Publica-
tion], one representative from each district conference of the Mennonite
Church, and the past moderator of Mennonite General Conference. This
committee of thirty-four men meets semiannually. The General Conference meets biennially in the odd years.)

Elkhart Institute was established by H. A. Mumaw, a Mennonite
physician of Elkhart, in 1894. A year later he turned the school over to
the Elkhart Institute Association, an incorporation of Mennonite educational leaders. H. S. Bender writes as follows: "After a period of weakness (1895-98), during which the principals (four of them in succession),
much of the small staff, and most of the small student body were non-
Mennonite and the program of the school was poorly defined, N. E. Byers,
B.A., a Mennonite from Sterling, Illinois, became the principal.
Byers reorganized the school, established it on a sound academic basis,
and led its development into a junior college (1903) and finally a senior

college (1908). J. S. Hartzler, a preacher of Topeka, Indiana, was the other strong figure in the school, along with the president of the Board, Preacher-Evangelist J. S. Coffman. Lewis Kulp, treasurer of the Board, early business manager and financial supporter, was a strong asset. C. Henry Smith, who came in as a teacher the same year as Byers (1898), was an important faculty member. Other important teachers were D. S. Gerig (1900-3), E. J. Zook (1901-3), J. W. Yoder (1900-2), and W. K. Jacobs (1899-1903)." After the school moved to Goshen in 1903 the following served as president: N. E. Byers, 1903-13; J. E. Hartzler 1913-18; George J. Lapp, 1918-19; H. F. Reist, 1919-20; I. R. Detweiler, Acting President, 1920-22; and Daniel Kauffman, 1922-23. The Board then closed the college for one year because of an unsatisfactory financial situation and because the school had somewhat lost the confidence of the church. In 1924 the college reopened with S. C. Yoder as president, who served until 1940; Ernest E. Miller, 1940-54; and Paul Mininger, 1954- .

Goshen College has exerted a significant influence for good, not only in the Mennonite Church as a whole, but particularly in Northern Indiana where its spiritual, educational, and cultural influence has lifted the Mennonites to a significantly higher level of life. This is true not only of the many students who have attended Goshen College, and there acquired a real vision of Biblical Christianity, but the influence of the school has also been felt through the programs of the Lecture-Music series, as well as missionary and Bible speakers who serve at the College from time to time. In 1933 the College added to its Bible School what is now known as the Goshen College Biblical Seminary, which institution has made possible the placing of seminary graduates in many of the congregations of Northern Indiana and elsewhere in the states of Indiana and Michigan. The Goshen College School of Nursing was opened in 1951. One of the most significant aspects of the work of Goshen College is the teacher-training work which has fitted many hundreds of fine young people to serve the public and church schools of the nation, as well as abroad.

VII. THE MENNONITE AND AMISH MENNONITE CONFERENCES

The exact date of organization of what is now the *Indiana-Michigan Mennonite Conference* is not known. In fact, for a number of years the conference in Indiana was a sort of extension of the Ohio Conference. As early as 1857 a private letter refers to conference being held in Indiana. John M. Brenneman presided at the 1862 sessions of the Indiana Conference, when John F. Funk visited it for the first time. A private letter of 1863 indicates that Bishop Abraham Rohrer of Ohio was to preside that year. In 1864 John M. Brenneman was again in the chair. All conferences were held at Yellow Creek from the 1850's until 1881. In 1882 the conference began meeting more or less alternately at the Yellow Creek and Holdeman meetinghouses, and after 1891 at Olive, Shore, Nappanee, Bowne, Salem, Clinton Brick, Elkhart, Emma, etc. Any congregation which felt strong enough to serve as host to the conference has been welcome to invite the conference to meet there. "During the first decades of the life of the conference, it was customary for the ordained men to come quietly together with no appointed moderator and no prepared program. The older bishops led in messages of exhortation after the singing of one or more hymns. The entire meeting was conducted in the Pennsylvania German dialect, with the exception of the hymns and Scripture reading, which were in High German. The opening prayer was silent. After the devotional service was over, one or more bishops exhorted the ministers to hold fast to the historic and Biblical principles of the brotherhood. Anyone was then free to make any further remarks or to bring questions before the group for counsel and decision. If the decisions met with too much opposition in the congregations, the ministers did not hesitate to reverse themselves at a later conference. . . .

"Especially in the 1870's the Indiana Mennonite Conference struggled long and hard with the problems occasioned by the transition from the old to new customs relating to new methods of Christian work, the transition from German to English, and the like. . . .

"Gradually the conference began to organize more fully and thus acquire its present form. In the meeting of October 9, 1885, the conference authorized the bishops thereafter to meet on the Thursday afternoon preceding conference to receive in writing all questions to be submitted on the day of conference. Six years later, in 1891, the conference took the new step of choosing a moderator and a secretary as the first item of business for the day. In 1898 it was further decided to 'elect a permanent secretary whose duty it shall be to keep a record of the proceedings of conference in a book for that special purpose. He shall serve for a term of three years.' . . ."—*The Mennonite Encyclopedia*, III, 30 (slightly revised).

In 1905 the Indiana-Michigan Mennonite Conference decided, "That the moderator appoint three brethren, who with the bishops shall constitute a committee to frame a Constitution and By-laws for the Indiana-Michigan Conference, and present the same to our next annual conference for consideration and adoption." The committee which served was David Burkholder, Jacob Christophel, John F. Funk, John Garber, Noah Hoover, and J. P. Miller. The next year the conference approved of the proposed constitution after revising it but submitted it to the individual congregations for ratification. The congregations voted down the document. Consequently in 1907 the conference appointed a committee of three, J. K. Bixler, J. S. Hartzler, and George L. Bender, as a committee to revise the statement and make it acceptable. This was accomplished, and after the congregations had approved it, the 1909 conference declared that the new Constitution, Rules and Discipline was in force.

The Amish Mennonites who originated in 1854 in Indiana were congregationalists in government from the beginning until 1888 when the first *"Annual District Conference for the State of Indiana, of the Amish Mennonite Church,"* met at the Maple Grove Church in Lagrange County. As was the case with the Mennonites, there were no continuing officers between the sessions of the Amish Mennonite Conference at first. In 1904 the A.M. Conference chose a moderator for the next meeting for the first time. The 1904 session of conference appointed a committee, D. J. Johns, A. J. Yontz, and D. D. Miller, to prepare a constitution for the Amish Mennonite Conference. The 1905 minutes read: "The report of committee on Constitution and Discipline of Conference was then read and after some discussion and revision the Constitution was adopted."

Both conferences prospered, so that by 1909 the Mennonite membership was reported as 1,387, and the next June the Amish Mennonite membership totaled 1,587. The first step toward *uniting* the two conferences was taken by the Mennonite Conference in 1911: "Resolved, that we favor the appointment of a joint committee of both conferences to carefully investigate conditions and to work out plans to be submitted to both conferences looking to the unity of the two conferences." The next June the Amish Mennonite Conference responded: "This conference endorses the resolution passed by the Indiana-Michigan Mennonite Conference and favors the appointing of a committee in accordance with said resolution." Those who served from the Mennonite Conference were J. K. Bixler, J. S. Hartzler, David Burkholder, John Garber, and D. A. Yoder; those from the Indiana-Michigan A.M. Conference were Jonathan Kurtz, D. J. Johns, D. D. Miller, A. J. Hostetler, and I. R. Detweiler. In 1914 the Amish Mennonite Conference took action requesting that a joint committee attempt to prepare Rules and Discipline that would be satisfactory to both conferences. This was done, and the Constitution, Rules, and Discipline was submitted to all the congregations of both conferences for their vote. The Amish Mennonite Conference minutes simply report that the constitution was approved, whereas the Mennonite Conference minutes indicate that the vote was 89 per cent in favor of the new document: 1,319 yes; 155 no. The last sessions of the individual conferences were held in 1916, at the end of which the Mennonite secretary wrote: "There was a general rejoicing at the thought that hereafter we would not be known as Spring and Fall Conferences, but that after centuries of separation, we are again made one in Christ Jesus." Conference closed with the singing of the hymn, "Blest Be the Tie That Binds."

After the merger of the two conferences congregational government suffered something of a decline, and the Executive Committee of the new united conference assumed more and more authority as the years passed by. This was particularly true under the moderatorship of J. K. Bixler, 1917-19, 1921-22, and 1929-33. In recent years the Executive Committee has tended to recognize the right of individual congregations to handle their internal affairs for themselves provided the general polity of the church is kept in mind.

VIII. WORLD WAR I

Those who are interested in reading more fully the story of Mennonites during the first World War may consult the book by J. S. Hartzler, *Mennonites in the World War* (Scottdale, Pa.: Mennonite Publishing House, second edition, 1922). Suffice it to say, the system which obtained in Indiana during the Civil War did not apply to Mennonites anywhere in World War I. The Mennonites suffered in some cases because of local hatred against those who were regarded as pro-German, or disloyal to the United States. As a matter of fact the Mennonites of America, both of Swiss and Dutch backgrounds, have the highest regard for and appreciation of their nation and their government. But because of their understanding of the will of Christ for His disciples, they find themselves unable to serve in the military. A note in a local newspaper reported, for example:

"Because Rev. Andrew Hostetter [Hostetler], Pastor of the Mennonite Church at Middlebury, had refused on religious grounds to purchase Liberty Bonds, the Chicago Cream Station at Middlebury, managed by Hostetter's son, is today adorned with signs and yellow paint, reading: 'We love the Kaiser,' 'We are hoarding wheat and flour,' 'I am a slacker.'

"A gang of Middlebury people, incensed by Hostetter's refusal to aid the Liberty Loan, are responsible for the painting.

"The son has been drafted and underwent his physical examination. . . ."

In some cases extreme pressure (even threats) was used against conscientious objectors in an attempt to force them to buy Liberty Bonds.

Those who went to camp were in some cases treated with relative kindness, while in other cases fairly extreme measures were employed in an attempt to coerce the young men into accepting the uniform and military service. The case of John Smeltzer will be given as one of medium severity, neither the most severe, nor the mildest. John Smeltzer the son of

Deacon Samuel and Salome (Burkey) Smeltzer, was born July 2, 1893, in St. Joseph County, Indiana. John united with the Mennonite Church in his youth, at the age of fifteen or sixteen. He was baptized and received into the Holdeman congregation. On July 23, 1918, just twenty-one days after John was twenty-five years of age, he was inducted into the U.S. Army at South Bend, Indiana, and taken to Camp Zachary Taylor, Kentucky. Upon arrival at camp John refused the uniform, and as a conscientious objector refused to obey military orders. Various measures were then employed by officers, guards, and private soldiers in an attempt to break the will of John, "soldier" No. 15,142, and induce him to become a real soldier. A guard, for example, ordered John to run. The guard ran behind him, intending to wear him out, but it so happened that John had greater endurance than did the guard, and after severely panting for a time, the guard finally said: "Let's walk." On another occasion many heavy army blankets were piled upon John after he was put to bed in his clothing, and he sweated until the color of his outer garments stained his underwear.

A certain guard gave John a verbal dressing down, and became so angry that he wept. He declared that if he ever got a chance he would take John out, shoot him, and report that his gun was accidentally discharged.

On one occasion a provost sergeant, accompanied by two soldiers, brought a heavy rope to John, and told him to put the noose around his neck. After putting the rope over some sort of beam overhead, he gave it to the two soldiers and told them not to pull until he gave the order. He then attempted to intimidate John. John stood his ground and waited for the provost sergeant to give the orders to pull, since he had told the soldiers, "Do not pull until I say so, but when I say pull, then pull!" After the provost sergeant saw that John would not be intimidated he came up to him and said: "You're a fool. You would have let them do it."

Perhaps the severest treatment which he received was that he was made to stand on tiptoe during which time ropes were attached to his thumbs and fastened to a point in the building higher than himself. John stood on tiptoe as long as possible but finally had to let down his weight, whereupon he hung by his thumbs in great distress. The outcome of all this effort was that John was given a court-martial, which resulted in his being given a dishonorable discharge on yellow paper, which reads as follows:

DISHONORABLE DISCHARGE FROM THE ARMY OF THE UNITED STATES

To All Whom It May Concern

This is to Certify That *John H. Smeltzer Private, Salvage Division, Sub Depot Q. M. C., U. S. Army,* is hereby *Dishonorably Discharged* from the military service of the *United States* by reason of the sentence of a General Court-Martial *Order No. 36, Hq. Camp Zachary Taylor, Ky., October 11th, 1918.* Said *John H. Smeltzer* was born in *Wakarusa,* in the State of *Indiana.* When enlisted he was *25 1/12* years and by occupation a *Farmer.* He had *Blue* eyes, *Brown* hair, *Light* complexion, and was *Five* feet *Ten* [two] inches in height.

Given under my hand at *Camp Zachary Taylor, Ky.,* this *5th* day of *November,* One thousand nine hundred and *Eighteen.*

[S:] S. J. CAUGER
Major Q. M. C.
Sub Depot Quartermaster
Commanding

On the other side of this discharge is printed:

ENLISTMENT RECORD

Name: *John H. Smeltzer* Grade: *Private* Enlisted *July 23/18* at *South Bend, Ind.* Serving in *First* Enlistment at date of discharge.

Prior Service: _____

_____

_____

Noncommissioned Officer: _____
Marksmanship, gunner qualification or rating:

_____

Horsemanship: _____
Battles, engagements, skirmishes, expeditions: _____

_____

_____

Knowledge of any vocation: *Farming* _____
Wounds received in service: _____
Physical condition when discharged: *Excellent*
Typhoid prophylaxis completed: *No Record*
Paratyphoid prophylaxis completed: *No Record*
Married or single: *Single*
Remarks: *Never Paid*

Conscientious Objector

To be Dishonorably Discharged [from] the Service and forfeit all pay and allowance due or to become [due] and to be confined at hard labor for 5 yrs. at Disciplinary Bks., Ft. Leavenworth, Kans.
Violation of 64th Article of War

> [S.] M. BRUUER
> 2d Lieut. Q. M. C.
> Commanding
> Salvage Div.
> Sub Depot QMC

Typed across the right side of the Enlistment Record is the following note:

> United States Disciplinary Barracks
> Ft. Leavenworth, Kansas
> August 10, 1919

General Prisoner John H. Smeltzer, formerly a private, Salvage Division, Sub Depot Q. M. C., has this date been released from this Barracks, by expiration of sentence . .
Reenlistment not recommended . . . .

> [S.] J. B. ALLISON
> J. B. Allison
> Colonel infantry,
> Asst. Commandant

It should be noted that all of John's maltreatment ceased the moment he was transferred to Ft. Leavenworth. He was no longer a soldier, and was of course a model prisoner. He was detailed to dairy work and milked cows four times daily.

According to *The Mennonite Encyclopedia* 138 Mennonites were court-martialed during the second World War. "Prison sentences ranged all the way from one year or less to life. . . . Sentences from five to thirty years were very common. None of these severe sentences were fully served" (III, page 902).

IX. The Troubled Twenties

The merger of the Mennonite and Amish Mennonite conferences in 1916 appeared to be a splendid victory for the forces of love and good will. The second last sentence of the Mennonite secretary's minutes (J. S. Hartzler) reads as follows: "Warnings were also given that Satan does not favor such a union and that we need to be watchful that this which is the source of our joy does not become a weapon in the adversary's hand to do us injury."

Unfortunately the warnings must not have been taken sufficiently to heart. Naturally, it is unrealistic to attempt to account for anything so complicated as a schism by one or two easy answers. The centralization of power in the Executive Committee, with the consequent diminution of congregational rights, was certainly a major factor in the trouble which came to a head in 1923 and 1924. This trouble seems to have been especially acute in a number of congregations which had formerly been members of the Amish Mennonite Conference, a group which had always tended to stress congregational government even more than the Mennonites.

As early as February 1923, I. R. Detweiler incurred the displeasure of the conference by accepting a temporary pastorate in "another denomination" (Eighth Street Mennonite Church).

At the June 1923 conference it was decided to appoint a committee of eleven persons to enforce more strictly the rules pertaining to dress and life insurance in the conference. This Committee of Eleven, which was to try to "save" the church situation, consisted of D. A. Yoder, D. J. Johns, and J. S. Hartzler from the Executive Committee; D. D. Miller, a bishop not then on the Executive Committee; A. J. Hostetler, a preacher; J. J. Mishler and J. I. Weldy, two deacons; and Clarence Lehman, Ezra Bleile, John Emmert, and Frank Gardner, four laymen. As early as June 25, 1923, Simeon P. Martin withdrew from the Zion congregation at Vestaburg, although it is doubtful whether his withdrawal had any connection with the issues which were then exercising conference. On August 8, 1923, the Executive Committee of conference summoned a number of brethren to appear before the Executive Committee: I. R. Detweiler, R. L. Hartzler, M. D. Lantz, A. S. Landis, W. W. Oesch, and S. S. Yoder. All of the six men appeared except Deacon A. S. Landis. On September 4 the conference Executive Committee decided to silence the ministers who were no longer in sympathy with the discipline of the conference. Consequently on September 8 the following men had their office revoked by the conference Executive Committee: I. R. Detweiler, R. L. Hartzler, E. S. Mullett, W. W. Oesch, and S. S. Yoder. The congregations of these preachers were notified of the action taken.

The next year two more ordained men were lost to the conference: Levi W. Yoder, a minister in the *Nappanee* Amish Mennonite Church, withdrew from the conference and united with the Mennonite Brethren in Christ. Also in May of 1924 Wilbur W. Miller forfeited his ministry by action of the Executive Committee, which action was ratified by the *Forks* congregation.

No one can read the story of this trouble without an aching heart. The ministers who lost their offices and left the church felt that an authoritarian conference was reaching into matters that properly belonged to the congregation. The conference Executive Committee, on the other hand, felt that the church should not allow women to wear hats (rather than bonnets) nor should life insurance be tolerated. The consequence of these two irreconcilable positions was the painful loss of a number of fine men, and a total of some 400 members who withdrew from the College, Nappanee West, Maple Grove, Barker Street, and Middlebury congregations.

By June 1924 it was decided to send a committee of three persons, J. C. Frey of Ohio, D. H. Coffman, and A. S. Miller, to visit the *Maple Grove* congregation at Topeka and attempt to reconcile the two parties there. On the thirtieth of the month the committee of three was locked out of the meetinghouse. The committee interviewed 142 members, seventy-two of whom stood by conference, and seventy of whom withdrew. A few members were not seen. The members who withdrew from conference were later affiliated with the Central Conference of Mennonites. This is true also of many of those who withdrew from other congregations. For example, many of the almost 200 members of the *Goshen College congregation* who withdrew from conference affiliated with the Eighth Street Mennonite Church, although a few members united with the Church of the Brethren and a few scattered elsewhere. The West Market Street, *Nappanee, Amish Mennonite Church* affiliated with the General Conference Mennonites, although about a third of the 150 members withdrew from the congregation and joined the North Main Street congregation which remained in conference. To partially offset this, about twenty-five members withdrew from the North Main Street congregation and united with the West Market Street Church.

It will be remembered that possibly a fourth of the members of the conference withdrew in the "unsettled seventies" following the Civil War. Possibly an eighth of the conference membership withdrew in the "troubled twenties" which followed World War I.

X. PROGRESS AFTER THE STORM

But not everything was bad. After the Civil War the *Sunday school* was introduced into the Mennonite and Amish Mennonite congregations of Northern Indiana, and accomplished untold good. The church was strengthened, the laity became more active, Bible knowledge was enhanced, spiritual life was deepened, and new convictions for the "clean life" (without the use of alcohol and tobacco) were developed. (As recently as the turn of the century a deacon's wife still smoked a clay pipe in the privacy of her home, but this was an exceptional case. A strong conscience against the use of tobacco in any form had come to the church, and various resolutions discouraging its use were adopted from 1884.)

In the latter nineteenth century a second agency for Christian education and nurture made its appearance: the *Bible conference*. For these conferences a congregation would gather at least twice daily for a number of days or a week, and gifted visiting ministers would present lectures on various aspects of Bible doctrine: the doctrine of the church, the ordinances of the church, the Christian life, and the like. These Bible conferences did much to enhance Bible knowledge, and to teach methods of Bible study. It was the testimony of the late J. S. Hartzler (1857-1953) that the Bible conferences were a significant factor in improving the quality of Mennonite sermons in the latter nineteenth and early twentieth centuries. People were no longer satisfied to hear unprepared messages which consisted largely of exhortations; they wanted to be taught God's Word; they hungered for the truth of the Gospel. Frequently the Bible conference speakers used charts to illustrate the truths which they were presenting. They also gave out references which the members avidly accepted and which they read to the audience when their verses were called for by the minister. In some cases the Bible conferences were used to introduce a new system of eschatology to the brotherhood, the premillenarianism of Moody Bible Institute where some of the able young ministers of the church had studied. The Bible conferences molded a whole generation of Mennonites in a simple Bible-centered theology.

The chief new agency for Christian education which came to the church after the first World War was the summer Bible school. The congregation which pioneered in this work was Holdeman. On May 15, 1922, the first known "Vacation Bible School" in the entire Mennonite Church was opened at Holdeman with Edwin L. Weaver serying as superintendent. The school was held for a two-week period. On September 30, 1922, C. W. Leininger of the Indiana-Michigan Christian Workers' Conference (then known as the Sunday School Conference) notified S. S. Yoder, Edwin L. Weaver, and Wilbur W. Miller that they were appointed as a committee to make curriculum, administrative, and teaching suggestions for such schools, including suggestions for a daily program. At the Sunday-school meeting, held at the Holdeman Church on November 30, 1922, Edwin L. Weaver was asked to speak on Vacation Bible Schools. The committee of three met on February 10, 1923, and came to the conclusion that a church-wide committee ought to take up the assignments which the district Sunday-school conference had given it. In June 1923 a "summer Bible school" was held at Holdeman, and the next month another at the Prairie Street Church in Elkhart.

One by one the several congregations of the Indiana-Michigan Mennonite Conference began to hold summer Bible schools, and this has become one of the most effective agencies to reach unchurched children which the church has. In the year 1960 there were eighty-seven summer Bible schools held in the congregations of the conference, with a total enrollment of 10,064. Expenses amounted to $10,231.00. (In the same year the congregations operated ninety Sunday schools, with an enrollment of 14,066, including all ages.)

XI. WORLD WAR II

Taking conscientious objectors to military camps against their wishes and attempting to force them to perform military service when many of them were ready to die rather than to do so was recognized by both the church and the government as not the solution to the problem of conscientious objection as the second World War approached. The consequence was that as a result of representations made to Congressional leaders by representatives of the historic peace churches the Selective Training and Service Act of 1940 provided that persons "who by reason of religious training and belief" were conscientiously opposed to all forms of military service should, if conscripted for service, "be assigned to work of national importance under civilian direction." The historic peace churches, Mennonite, Brethren, and the Society of Friends, created in 1940 the National Service Board for Religious Objectors, which became the agency through which these churches dealt with Selective Service. The final plan which was worked out for the conscientious objectors to render their service to their country in lieu of military service involved the gathering of such conscientious objectors into *Civilian Public Service camps*. The first CPS camp under Mennonite Central Committee ("MCC") direction was opened May 22, 1941, as Camp Number 4, Grottoes, Rockingham County, Virginia. The director was John H. Mosemann, currently (1961) pastor of the College Mennonite Church, Goshen, Indiana. A large number of CPS camps were established across the United States, which cost the Mennonite Central Committee (the all-Mennonite relief agency) over $3,000,000.00 for their operation, 1941-47. Guy F. Hershberger, *The Mennonite Church in the Second World War*, reports: "Apart from the resettlement program [of refugees], the total relief program of the Mennonite Central Committee and the Mennonite Relief Committee during the years 1937 to 1948 represented cash contributions amounting to $3,520,000.00, and gifts-in-kind amounting to $6,100,000.00. The contribution of the (Old) Mennonite Church to the Refugee Settlement Program (1947-48) was approximately $278,000.00 in gifts and $134,000.00 in loans. Of the general relief program, 1937-48 (not including resettlement), its cash contribution was approximately $1,275,000.00. The value of its gifts-in-kind is unknown." Many of the young men who were drafted into CPS would have been very eager to do relief work abroad, but were prevented from doing so by Congressional action.

The draft law of 1948, which was activated in 1950, deferred conscientious objectors, but the new law of 1951 assigned them to civilian work of national importance for two years. The men so assigned receive the classification, I-O, and after they are at work, I-W.

One of the finest forms of service was established in 1951 under the name *Pax*, which is the Latin word for peace. It is the term used to designate the foreign service of I-W men (I-W is the draft classification of conscientious objectors who are serving their two years of "alternative service") who serve without wages in a foreign program administered by the MCC. Pax was first established in 1951 in Germany, and has since been extended to Greece, 1952; to Holland, 1953; to Hungarian refugees in Austria, 1956; to Korea, 1954; to road building in Peru, 1954; and in the Paraguayan Chaco, 1956. Other types of service have been rendered in Jordan, Nepal, Vietnam, and Liberia. In the first eight years over 200 Pax men have served overseas. In 1958 alone the number in service was 110.

Of the 4,665 Mennonites who served in Civilian Public Service in World War II, some 1,500 volunteered for service in mental hospitals "in order to relieve the critical shortage of attendants in these institutions." The Mennonite Central Committee then "joined with the American Friends Service Committee and the Brethren Service Commission in helping to finance the operations" of the *National Mental Health Foundation* which was established in May 1946. In 1950 this foundation was merged with the National Committee for Mental Hygiene and the American Psychiatric Foundation to form the National Association for Mental Health. The National Mental Health Foundation "owned its origin largely to the stimulus provided by CPS men of Mennonite, Brethren, and Quaker connection, who had worked in mental hospitals and as a consequence got a vision of the need for a better type of care for the mentally ill" (*The Mennonite Encyclopedia*, III, page 813).

It is fairly common for conscientious objectors to have to bear the taunt that they did not render significant service in time of national emergency. It is therefore refreshing to read in the *Christian Century*, after citing statistical data of the National Service Board for Religious Objectors, on conscientious objectors in the United States: "So a comparatively small number of conscientious objectors, coming mainly from the historic peace churches, still carry the brunt of personal protest against the insanity and evil of modern warfare. Let those who hold the CO's in derision come forward with their own alternatives to organized extinction. Let them offer their alternatives with devotion which will equal that of the young men who silently and sacrificially bear the burden of conscience for all of us" (*G.H.*, 1-24-1961, pages 95, 96).

XII. THE MODERN MISSIONARY AWAKENING

The Indiana-Michigan Mennonite Mission Board was created in 1911 as the result of Mennonite conference action in 1908 which appointed J. K. Bixler, D. H. Coffman, and G. L. Bender as a committee "to investigate what such boards do and what need they fill." N. E. Byers was designated by conference as the president of the new district mission board, and J. K. Bixler as secretary. Each congregation was invited to appoint a member to the new board, which members met December 1, 1911, and organized as a board, incorporated August 13, 1914.

"The actual situation which gave rise to the discussion of missions in the 1908 conference was the proposal of Goshen College students to establish a *mission station in North Goshen*. It should also be mentioned that the Indiana-Michigan Amish Mennonite Conference of 1912 appointed D. J. Johns and D. D. Miller to work with the Executive Committee of the Mennonite Mission Board in investigating the opening of a mission in North Goshen. Although the North Goshen plan fell through for the time being, yet the plan was used of God to directly bring about the organization of the Mission Board in 1911. The 1912 Mennonite conference appointed J. K. Bixler as bishop of all the small outlying congregations, which congregations were at the same time placed under the care of the new district mission board. For many years the main work of the board was looking after small groups of Mennonite families which settled in various points in Michigan and struggled to establish congregations, as well as to care for old congregations which had dwindled in number so badly as to face extinction. In the former class were such settlements as Midland, Homestead, Vestaburg, Brutus, Sunnyside, Lewiston, and Chief (Michigan), while the weak or dying congregations included such places as Barker Street, Pleasant Valley (De Kalb County), Maple River (Brutus), White Cloud, Imlay City, and Pretty Prairie. In the early years the dominant figure in the work of the board was J. K. Bixler, secretary from 1911 until 1925. Other influential men were N. E. Byers, B. B. King, J. E. Hartzler, E. J. Yoder, C. A. Shank, D. J. Johns, D. A. Yoder, and Homer F. North. J. K. Bixler served as mission bishop or superintendent from 1911 until 1934 except for the years 1925-33 when D. D. Troyer held that position" (*Mennonite Handbook*, pages 51, 52).

As was indicated above, the chief work of the *district mission board* for the first twenty-five years of its existence was caring for weak, scattered, and dying congregations. Beginning about 1935, however, and continuing until the time of this writing, the district mission board and many individual congregations of the Indiana-Michigan Mennonite Church have established numerous mission outposts and daughter congregations as follows: Pleasant View and North Goshen, 1936; Fernland in the Upper Peninsula of Michigan, 1937; Wildwood in the Upper Peninsula, 1939; Calvary at Pinckney, Michigan, 1941; Locust Grove and Naubinway, 1943; Benton, 1944; Cady and Bean Blossom, 1945; Liberty and Seney, 1946; Wawasee, Sunnyside, Moorepark, and Bon Air, 1947; Toto, Rexton, Wayside, Grand Marais, and Cold Springs, 1948; Plato and English Lake, 1949; New Bethel, Plymouth Street Chapel in Goshen, and Roselawn, 1949; Fish Lake, Petoskey, Hudson Lake, Saginaw, and Rainy River, Minnesota, 1950; Osceola, Mt. Pleasant, and Cedar Grove, 1951; Morgantown, Caney Creek, and Talcum (all in Kentucky), Herrick, Battle Creek, and Soo Hill, 1952; Providence and Elmwood, 1953; Fair Haven, South Colon, and Indianapolis, 1954; East Side, Saginaw, and Wellington, 1955; Lake Bethel, California (Michigan), Walnut Hill, and Big Branch (Kentucky), 1956; Clarion and Stutsmanville (Michigan), 1957; Waterford and Smith School (Kentucky), 1959; Santa Fe, South Bend, Kalamazoo, and Tri-Lakes, 1960. This means that some sixty outposts and mission stations were established in the twenty-five-year period from 1935 to 1960.

Of the ninety-four congregations and outposts of the Mennonites in Indiana and Michigan, seventeen were Mennonite congregations prior to 1916, eight were Amish Mennonite, and the remaining sixty-nine have been established since the merger. The General Mission Board slogan, "A mission outpost for every congregation," has surely borne fruit!

XIII. Other Areas of Progress

Around the year 1900 D. J. Johns of the Clinton Frame congregation was active in attempting to organize a Mutual Aid Insurance Company to take care of members of the church who suffered loss by fire. This occasioned an attack on Johns by Preacher P. J. Kaufman, an independent as to church relationships, in his periodical, *The Gospel Teacher*, 1901, entitled "An Open Letter Addressed to Daniel J. Johns, an Amish Mennonite Bishop at Goshen, Indiana." Kaufman addressed thirty questions to Bishop Johns. Number 22 reads: "Tell us, when did God attach a Fire Department to His church, and name it, 'The Mennonite Aid Plan'?" Number 23 reads: "Give Bible proof that a Christian in order to receive help from his brethren, in case his buildings burn, must be a member of your Fire Department." There was sufficient apathy or opposition to the Aid Plan within the Amish Mennonite congregations that it was not organized until 1911. The association began actual business operations on November 1 of that year. At the close of its first year of business there were 133 policies totaling $311,806.00. By 1960 the organization had grown to 3,140 policies totaling $37,101,049.00. The Mennonite Aid Association was not set up as a business venture to make money for stockholders, but is purely a Mutual Aid organization, designed to help members of the church who suffer loss. The aim is not intended to be personal remuneration, but help for those who suffer misfortune. This is intended as a practical application of Galatians 6:2, "Bear ye one another's burdens, and so fulfill the law of Christ."

In 1924 interested scholars at Goshen College created an organization of persons deeply interested in Anabaptist and Mennonite history. The organization has the name, *The Mennonite Historical Society*. The Society began publishing in 1929 a series known as *Studies in Anabaptist and Mennonite History*. H. S. Bender has served as president of the Society and chief editor of its monograph series, now published by Herald Press, Scottdale, Pennsylvania. This organization and this series have done much to awaken in Mennonites a consciousness of their heritage, and to make that heritage known to the world of scholarship.

The ordained men of the Indiana-Michigan Mennonite Conference meet since 1944 in annual *ministers' meetings* for instruction, fellowship, and inspiration. These meetings are held early in December.

In 1947 the Mennonites purchased a sixteen-room house at 412 East Lincoln Avenue, Goshen, Indiana, and made of it a *Mennonite Girls' Center*. It was dedicated December 1, 1947. The Indiana-Michigan Mennonite Mission Board and the Women's Missionary and Service Auxiliary sponsored the work of the Center through a committee of five members. Down through the years the Center served "more than 165 girls from twelve states and various denominations, providing Christian fellowship, conveniences, various activities, and social contacts." Nevertheless more and more girls preferred to find their own housing accommodations, resulting in the closing of the Center in 1960.

In 1949 Mennonites purchased a wooded tract of land containing a small lake which is now known as *Mennonite Youth Village*. It is located north of U.S. Highway 112 in Southern Michigan and has the address, Route 1, White Pigeon, Michigan. The camp is owned by the Mennonite Board of Missions and Charities. It serves the various city and rural mission churches by offering facilities for summer camping. "It is operated with a welfare and missionary emphasis." The director from 1952 has been Mervin Yoder.

5

Goshen College is not the only institution of higher education operated by the Mennonites in the state of Indiana. In 1950 the *Clinton Christian Day School* was established a few miles east of Goshen, and offers grades one through ten. The present principal is Galen Johns. In 1959 Clinton had an enrollment of 165.

In Michigan the outstanding institution since 1946 has been the Michigan Mennonite Bible School, which meets each winter for six weeks. Leaders in the program have included C. C. Culp, Oscar Leinbach, T. E. Schrock, and Galen Johns. The school meets at the Fairview Mennonite meetinghouse. Included in the program is a two-weeks ministers' course.

The first-known *literary society* in Indiana, outside of Elkhart Institute, was established by the young people of the Yellow Creek and Holdeman congregations in 1900, but was disbanded upon order of the young leader, J. K. Bixler. Later most of the congregations saw "literaries" organized, for the most part between 1913 and 1934. In some cases these literaries had a rather light form of entertainment, and were not very effective in the development of talent. In 1924 Huber A. Yoder conceived the idea of a convention for all the literaries of Northern Indiana. The first meeting of this Literary Convention was held at Goshen College August 22, 1924. The first constitution for the organization was adopted in 1936. In 1949 the organization decided to affiliate with the new church-wide Mennonite Youth Fellowship. This was the occasion for the preparation of a new constitution which was adopted in 1950. "Since that time each local unit is generally referred to as 'MYF' rather than as literary. These MYF units follow a much broader program than did the earlier literaries in most cases. The major areas of concern of MYF relate to Faith, Fellowship, and Service" (*Mennonite Handbook*, page 80).

Hope Rescue Mission was opened February 28, 1954, at 530-32 South Michigan Street in South Bend, Indiana, the first rescue mission to be operated by the Mennonite Board of Missions and Charities. Men from congregations of Northern Indiana donated 1,750 man-hours of labor to clean and renovate a tavern and gambling hall, and transform it into a fine rescue mission. The mission "serves two meals daily to transients, distributes clothing daily, and operates a medical clinic, a barber shop, and an employment service," in addition to conducting a public religious service and two classes daily. Tobe E. Schmucker is superintendent.

In 1954 *Bethany Christian High School* was established by the Indiana-Michigan Mennonite Conference, representing the largest undertaking of the conference in its history. This project for ground, buildings, and equipment has cost approximately $240,000.00, of which over $200,000.00 was paid off by 1960. Within six years the enrollment has built up to approximately 255. The superintendent from the beginning has been John S. Steiner, assisted by Principal C. J. Holoway, and a staff of able teachers.

Another fine illustration of a desire to minister to human need is *Mennonite Disaster Service*. *The Mennonite Handbook* of the Indiana-Michigan Mennonite Conference, 1956, contains the following account of the creation of *Mennonite Disaster Service*: "Being keenly aware of the teaching of the Saviour on the crucial importance of love, good will, and works of charity . . . the Mennonite Church believes strongly in rendering every effective service possible to mankind both in times of war and peace—providing such service can be rendered under civilian direction. During the second World War thousands of Mennonite young men served in Civilian Public Service camps, doing work of national importance in lieu of military service. After the war was over the CPS men of various peace churches met together occasionally for fellowship and inspiration. One of these regional reunions comprised the CPS men from Ohio, Indiana, Michigan, and Illinois. Out of this reunion came a committee known as the 'Crusaders for Peace.' Besides its concerns for peace, the group was also interested in organizing some sort of disaster unit, following the example of the 'Mennonite Service Organization' of Hesston, Kansas. The purpose of such a Mennonite Disaster Service was to be prepared to render instant assistance to people suffering from such major catastrophes as tornadoes. The group by 1953 was clear on a number of its plans: (1) Begin such Disaster Service units on the congregational level. (2) Have the local units send representatives to a central organization meeting to create a co-ordinating committee. (3) Keep in touch with the local church conference as well as with the all-Mennonite Relief and Service Organization, the Mennonite Central Committee. By the grace and blessing of God these plans came to good fruition, and the result is a smoothly functioning organization in the states of Indiana and Michigan, the constitution of which is presented herewith. The areas which have been served by the MDS have been warmly grateful for the service rendered 'In the Name of Christ.' " The organization adopted a constitution January 4, 1956. The organization itself was set up in 1955.

In 1956 the *Indiana-Michigan Camp Association, Incorporated*, was created. It owns and operates Camp Amigo which was established in 1957, and which is located about five miles north of Sturgis, Michigan. It is sponsored by the Indiana-Michigan Christian Workers' Conference, but is under the control of a Board of Directors appointed by its shareholders. To this camp go various groups of young people and children, such as children who have memorized several hundred verses of Scripture, and who are given camp experience for a week in recognition of this memory work.

At this writing (1961) the Mennonites of Indiana, Michigan, Ohio, and Illinois are co-operating under the direction of the Mennonite Central Committee in raising money for and planning for the construction of the *Oaklawn Psychiatric Center* at Elkhart, Indiana. This will be a center to contribute toward "the complete rehabilitation of the mentally and emotionally disturbed." It is planned that the first building will include treatment rooms for the use of ten psychiatrists, psychologists, and social workers. It will contain a chapel and chaplain's office, as well as administrative offices and a medical treatment section. The building will also have an activity center with lounge, crafts rooms, and a small auditorium. It is hoped later to build living quarters for thirty patients. It is estimated that the total cost of the first building and equipment will be $600,000.00, of which it is hoped to receive from the Federal government possibly one third. The first Board of Directors consisted of three members of the Mennonite Church, two members of the General Conference Church, one from the Wisler Mennonites, one Conservative Mennonite, one Evangelical Mennonite, one Old Order Amish member, and one member from the Brethren in Christ.

It will be noted that since the Civil War, and especially in the last twenty-five years the *lay activity* of the Mennonite Church has been enormously increased. This applies not only to Sunday schools, summer Bible schools, young people's Bible meetings, committee work, church councils, lay delegates to the conference sessions, etc., but also to the total work of the church through its boards and committees.

One of the areas of concern which faces the leadership of the Indiana-Michigan Conference in recent years is that of deepening the level of *spiritual life* in the rank and file of the brotherhood. It is felt that it is not sufficient to operate an active program of mission work by appointed workers, but rather each member of the body of Christ ought to be prayerfully concerned for the growth of the church numerically and spiritually, and especially for its outreach in the community. Consequently, the Executive Committee of the Indiana-Michigan Mennonite Conference appointed in 1960 a Committee on Spiritual Life and Outreach which is sponsoring self-studies in each of the congregations which desire to co-operate, is proposing series of doctrinal sermons to prepare for conference-wide evangelistic meetings in each of the congregations, and such other steps as the committee may feel led to inaugurate. This program is being planned for 1960 and 1961, and is to culminate in series of evangelistic meetings operated more or less concurrently late in 1961.

Traditionally, Mennonite ministers and deacons were ordained from the laity without any special educational preparation. When a minister was needed in a given church, the congregation voted on the ordination of one. If the vote carried, the members then voted for nominees from the membership roll of the congregation. *Ordination was by lot,* that is, as many books were placed on the pulpit desk as there were nominees for the office, and near the close of the ordination service, after a sermon, and after solemn prayer, each nominee selected a book and sat down again. The presiding bishop then asked each man to present his book for examination. The man in whose book the lot (a slip of paper designating the person as called of God to the office needed) was found was immediately ordained. Some ordinations are still conducted in this way in the congregations of the Indiana-Michigan Conference. But an increasing number of churches since about 1940 have been appointing a pastor committee to try to find a possible person to serve as preacher, which person is then voted on by the congregation.

Prior to the second World War very few congregations gave any regular support to the ministers. The ministers were not thought of as "pastors," but as "preachers." Every member of the church was expected to live a holy life, and to attend the services of the church regularly and faithfully—which a remarkably high percentage did. The preachers called in the homes at times of critical illness and death, but few "pastoral visits" as such were made. This was almost universally true in the nineteenth century. But in recent decades there has been a growing tendency to call *seminary-trained* young men as ministers and pastors, and since the 1940's a growing number of congregations are giving a *monthly love offering* to their pastor. The principle of ministerial support was first recognized in the 1956 *Rules and Discipline* of the conference. A few congregations, generally city churches, are giving full support to their pastors.

XIV. NUMERICAL GROWTH

Not too much is known of accurate membership figures in the early years of the Mennonite life in Indiana and Michigan. When John F. Funk, then an active young man of twenty-seven, first visited the annual sessions of the Indiana Conference in 1862, he estimated the Elkhart County Mennonite membership at 400 to 500. (It may be noted that although Deacon David Good estimated the number who communed at Yellow Creek in 1862 at over 600, the bishop who presided, John M. Brenneman, stated that he supposed "between three and four hundred persons" communed.) In the light of Funk's estimate this figure is certainly more correct. This would mean that about 1860 the membership of the Indiana-Michigan Mennonites was in the neighborhood of 400. The next figures known with any certainty were compiled by John F. Funk in 1890 for the *U.S. Government Census of Religious Bodies.* (1890

H.T., page 345.) See also Funk's Diary for January 5, 1891: "Census reports are coming in very good. Have a large number of the churches already in, and a few coming in almost every day." Funk indicated that as of 1890 there were fourteen Mennonite congregations in Indiana with a total of 700 communicants. These congregations were likely Yellow Creek, Olive, Holdeman, Salem, Elkhart, Nappanee, Clinton Brick, Pleasant Valley, Bower, Shore, Augsburger (Berne), Gar Creek, Lakeville, and possibly Samuel Yoder's Mikesell congregation in St. Joseph County. At the same time Funk indicated that there were five congregations of Mennonites in Michigan with a total of 155 communicants. (He probably meant Caledonia, Bowne, Maple River, Pleasant Hill, and possibly Berne, now Pigeon, at that time a part of the Ontario Conference.) Eighteen of these nineteen congregations were affiliated with the Indiana Mennonite Conference and according to Funk had a total membership of 840.

Funk lists the Amish Mennonite congregations of Indiana as ten in number with a total of 929 communicants. Assuming that Funk did not confuse any Old Order Amish congregations as Amish Mennonites, he must have included congregations such as Clinton Frame, Haw Patch, Forks, Howard-Miami, Nappanee, Pretty Prairie, Yoder (at Berne), Barker Street, Townline, and possibly Leo. According to Funk there were no Amish Mennonite congregations in Michigan in 1890. Adding the 700 Mennonites in Indiana, the 155 Mennonites in Michigan, and the 929 Amish Mennonites in Indiana produces a total of 1,784. If the Berne congregation was counted in, this would make a grand total of approximately 1,800 members, which is probably a rather accurate figure for 1890. This means that the church increased from around 400 members in 1860 to 1,800 members in 1890 after having lost 100 members in the Wisler schism and some fifty members in the Brenneman schism. The 1905 Mennonite statistics show a total for these Mennonite and Amish Mennonite congregations of 2,182. The congregations seemed to prosper in the 1890's, but went through some difficulties in the Elkhart County area in connection with the silencing of both Indiana bishops in 1902. It is possible that the 1900 membership would have been approximately 2,100. By 1920 the united conference had a membership of approximately 3,600; by 1940, approximately 5,500; and by 1960, approximately 9,400.

Surely this growth is a matter of great gratitude. It does not fulfill the prophecy printed by the *New York Tribune* for October 28, 1900: ". . . It is not improbable that the Mennonite Church within the next generation or two will have become either extinct or absorbed into other and more flourishing denominations." A. B. Kolb, editor of the *Herald of Truth* at that time, quoted this judgment and added: "Maybe; by the grace of God, maybe not" (1901 *HT*, pages 13, 14).

Perhaps some readers will be interested in knowing something of world statistics on Mennonites. Only five countries have more than 25,000 baptized members: U.S.A., 160,000; Canada, 53,000; Holland, 39,000; India, 29,000; and the Congo, 26,000; it is estimated that Russia has possibly 40,000 Mennonite "souls," but the organized life of the church there is broken. Four other countries have 5,000 members or more; Germany, 12,000; Mexico, 8,000; Paraguay, 7,000; and Indonesia, 5,000. The estimated number of Mennonites in China is 4,000. Other scattered countries, including Switzerland with 1,900, have a total of 12,000 members, making a grand total for all conferences of Mennonites in the whole world of a little less than 400,000 members.

Chapters one through five of this book relate to that branch of the church known simply as the Mennonite Church. Chapter six discusses briefly eight other Mennonite bodies, and chapter seven, eight other Amish Mennonite bodies. The last chapter of the book is devoted to related and similar groups.

II

The Older Mennonite Congregations

INDIANA

AUGSBURGER MENNONITE CHURCH
Adams County, Indiana

The Swiss Mennonites began to settle in Adams County, Indiana, some thirty miles south of Fort Wayne, in the year 1838. Those who are interested in a full account of this settlement and the development of one of the largest Mennonite congregations in North America, now affiliated with the General Conference Mennonite Church, should consult the excellent monograph by Eva F. Sprunger, *The First Hundred Years, A History of the Mennonite Church in Adams County, Indiana, 1838-1938* (Berne, Indiana, 1938). The Swiss Mennonites who settled in Adams County brought extreme simplicity and plainness with them from the Swiss mountains. The women wore long dresses and aprons made of a somber color, and without any pleats, ruffles, or lace. They wore a neckerchief over the shoulders, and a plain cashmere or silk "cap" (prayer veiling). On communion Sunday the head shawl had to be of a white material. The women wore capes instead of coats. The men were not allowed to wear the mustache, for historically it savored of the military. They were required to comb their hair to conform to the plain customs of the church, a plain-collared coat was required, and even hooks and eyes were worn instead of buttons. The language of these sturdy pioneers was the Swiss dialect of the canton of Bern. Even the church services had to be in this Swiss dialect. Eva Sprunger reports that when it was time to begin the service one minister would turn to the other and say in Swiss, "Es isch ziet a z'fa" (It is time to begin). The second preacher, observing that one of the members was still absent, would comment, "Ya, der Johannes isch no' nid da" (Yes, but John is not yet here). After the main message the other members of the ministry would give their testimony which they called in their Swiss German, "Zuegsamme," which perhaps meant a brief supplement. One deacon used to begin, "I' cha ja und ame' saega zu alles dem es gredt worde isch" (I can say Yea and Amen to all that has been spoken). In the course of time the rigid plainness and even some of the simplicity of the pioneers was lost.

In reaction to the gradual cultural accommodation of the Berne congregation a small group withdrew in 1869, consisting of the families of Preacher Christian Augsburger, George Fox, John Stauffer, and Peter Steiner. Eva F. Sprunger wrote to the present writer in 1955: "The Augsburger congregation did not build a church building. Sometimes they used a school building but mostly they met in the homes, usually a Sunday in the Augsburger home, the next in the Peter Steiner home. Mr. Augsburger did not ordain anyone. This group died in 1902. They sometimes fellowshiped with Rev. Peter Neuenschwander's group who also worshiped in homes. The two ministers sometimes exchanged pulpits. The Neuenschwander group also was very small and died in about 1945." The schism of Peter M. Neuenschwander, who had been ordained preacher in Switzerland at the age of seventeen, occurred in Adams County in 1879. He felt that the 1879 new meetinghouse of the Berne Mennonites was "too stylish." He held separate services with a handful of members for about sixty-five years.

In 1955 the author was in correspondence with Chris Augsburger of Berne, who was a grandson of Preacher Christian Augsburger's brother. He confirmed that the Augsburger group never built a meetinghouse.

The Augsburger congregation was recognized by the (Old) Mennonite Church, of which John F. Funk was the outstanding editor and publisher. In the church calendar for the *Herald of Truth,* June 1871, Funk lists services in the Augsburger Church, Adams County, every three weeks. On April 29 and 30, 1871, Preachers John F. Funk and Daniel Brenneman, and Deacon Henry Brenneman visited the small Augsburger congregation. On that occasion services were conducted in the P. C. Steiner and the Christian Augsburger homes and in a schoolhouse. The formal affiliation of the Augsburger congregation with the Mennonite Church occurred June 11, 1871, when Bishop John M. Brenneman went to Adams County and received ten members, including Preacher Augsburger, into the fellowship of the "Mennonite Church." Some of these members came from the Swiss Mennonites, and some from the Swiss Amish who had also settled in Adams County. There was an additional woman who had already been a member of the (Old) Mennonite Church, which made a total charter membership in 1871 of eleven members. But the congregation never prospered. In about three more decades its life was over. When Augsburger died on January 19, 1903, the funeral service was held three days later in the meetinghouse of the Defenseless Mennonite Church of Adams County by two preachers of the (Old) Mennonite Church, Moses Brenneman and J. M. Shenk, both of Allen County, Ohio. Strangely enough there was some anxiety as to whether Augsburger was really dead and so burial was delayed for two days after the funeral to be certain that he would not revive.

On June 6, 1909, Bishop Moses Brenneman of Ohio returned to Berne, Indiana, and received six new members into the tiny remnant of the Augsburger congregation. But in spite of occasional efforts to keep the (Old) Mennonite congregation alive after the death of its resident preacher the congregation nevertheless died. In the course of time even the occasional visits of (Old) Mennonite preachers finally ceased altogether.

In the year 1955 John C. Augsburger of Berne, a son of the late preacher, reported to the present writer in a letter that he and his sister were the only survivors of Preacher Christian Augsburger's family, which had consisted of nine sons and seven daughters. "My sister and I," he wrote, "are the only survivors of our family and we are here in my home. She is still a Mennonite and there is none of her denomination in this community." She was then eighty-two years of age. This means that over fifty years after the (Old) Mennonite services were discontinued in Adams County, there was still one member left. When asked what churches the last members had joined, when the (Old) Mennonite services were discontinued, J. C. Augsburger replied that of the few that remained, "some joined the Egly [Defenseless] Church and some the Swiss Mennonite Church at Berne. My father and mother, and Mr. and Mrs. Peter C. Steiner, and George Fox, and Christian Neuenschwander stayed with their church as long as they lived."

Arcadia Mennonite Church

Section 13, Jackson Township, Hamilton County, Indiana

The Arcadia Church was located roughly halfway between Kokomo and Indianapolis, about five miles east of U.S. Highway 31. Mennonites began moving into Hamilton County in the year 1838. The early settlers, such as Christian Kauffman, John Correll, and John Stock, came from Lancaster County, Pennsylvania. Other early settlers included Henry Hildebrand of Virginia and Henry Gascho of Lancaster County, Pennsylvania.

In the year 1865 John M. Brenneman, who served as a sort of roving bishop or district superintendent for all the Mennonite congregations of the Midwest, visited Hamilton County and found fourteen Mennonites living there. On that occasion John S. Correll's wife was critically ill. Brenneman reported in the *Herald of Truth* that the Hamilton County Mennonites were "now minded to meet regularly." In October 1865, Brenneman ordained Christian Kauffman to the office of deacon. The next year Kauffman's son John was ordained as a preacher. These are the only two ordained men ever to serve in the Hamilton County church. Brenneman's account of his visit in October 1865 reads as follows: "We

went thither to a small flock consisting of four families. . . . We held
six meetings during which six persons were baptized, the sacrament of the
Lord's Supper administered, and Bro. Christian Kauffman elected to the
office of deacon. There are now fourteen members there." The 1865
Herald of Truth mentions the fact that John L. Rhodes of Virginia was
then living with his uncle, Henry Hildebrand, in Hamilton County. In
1879 Bishop Jacob Hildebrand of Virginia visited Henry Hildebrand of
Hamilton County, who was his brother. He preached in the home of
"Bro. John Kauffman." Preacher John M. Greider of Montgomery
County, Ohio, visited the Arcadia congregation in 1866. When John M.
Brenneman spent six days with the Arcadia congregation in 1866, he
reported that the congregation then numbered seventeen members. This
was probably the high point in the life of the church.

From obituaries published in the *Herald of Truth,* it appears that
the Arcadia Mennonites called ministers of the nearby German Baptists
(now Church of the Brethren) to conduct their funeral services.

On December 31, 1872, Deacon Christian Kauffman and Mary his
wife conveyed one acre of land on the northeast quarter of Section 13
of Jackson Township to Andrew Kauffman, John Kauffman, Anna Kline,
Elizabeth Bird, and the heirs of Jacob Kauffman. The deed was recorded
in February 1880. The land was sold for church and burial purposes.
(Deed Book 29, page 401.)

D. S. Brunk of Elida, Ohio, visited Hamilton County in 1890. "Here
we met Bro. and Sister John S. Kauffman and wife . . . only a few members here." The *Herald of Truth* for 1900 reported that Bro. Andrew
Kauffman of Arcadia, Indiana, who has been in poor health for some
months, is at present confined to his bed. He bequeathed $1,000.00 to
the Mennonite Evangelizing Board. When his son, former Preacher
John S. Kauffman, died in 1906, the *Herald of Truth* reported that he
was "denied the help of church fellowship and privileges most of his life,
as there was no organized congregation at the place where he resided."

In 1957 Bishop A. G. Horner drove to Arcadia to see what he could
learn of the history of the congregation. He was able to find the Kauffman burial lot, adjoining the spot where the meetinghouse of 1881 had
earlier stood, and he also found a couple, Ott and Elizabeth Etchison, in
Arcadia. They were married in the year 1902. Mrs. Etchison well remembers her grandfather, John S. Kauffman. She knew that the Kauffmans were Mennonites, but she was not aware that he had been a
preacher. She recalled that the Kauffmans worshiped with the Methodists
as old people. She said that her forebears lived northeast of Arcadia,
within a mile or two, and some of them were buried in the neglected,
unused Kauffman Cemetery.

In the cemetery of the Arcadia Church of the Brethren, one-half mile east of the village of Arcadia, one finds such names as Boyer, Burkhart, Coffman, Myers, Smeltzer, Snyder, Whisler, and Wissler. It is likely that most of these were members of the Church of the Brethren, however, rather than Mennonites. Actually, there are a considerable number of names which are common to the two denominations.

The puzzling fact in the history of the Arcadia congregation is the building of a meetinghouse in 1881, when the congregation was in a state of extreme weakness. Christian Kauffman, the deacon, had died in 1879, and we do not know when Preacher John S. Kauffman, his son, gave up the ministry. The *Herald of Truth* for 1886 reports the presence of six or seven members in Hamilton County, without a preacher. No wonder the congregation died out!

YELLOW CREEK MENNONITE CHURCH

Section 28, Harrison Township, Elkhart County, Indiana

Mennonites began to settle in Harrison Township some six miles west of Goshen, about 1840. The first-known Mennonite settlers were: Jacob Brown, 1839; Jacob Koppes, 1844; Bishop Martin Hoover, his son John, John Strohm, John Smith, and son Joseph, and Christian Henning, 1845. In 1846 came Thomas Nunemaker, in 1847 Jacob C. Buzzard and wife Elizabeth (Kreider), and Abraham and Martha (Garber) Hoover. In 1848 came Christian Christophel, Preacher Jacob Christophel, Preacher Jacob Wisler, Jacob and Katharine (Reed) Ramer, Frederick and Catherine (Holdeman) Landis, George Holdeman, Valentine and Nancy (Smeltzer) Hartman, Adam and Elizabeth (Ramer) Hartman, and (Preacher) Daniel and Catharine (Swartz) Moyer. One of the finest summaries of the early settlement of the Mennonites in Elkhart County appeared anonymously in the 1874 *Historical Atlas of Elkhart County:*

". . . in the spring of 1848, Christian Christophel, Jacob Christophel, and Jacob Wisler, with their families, joined the little colony; the latter two were ministers of the Gospel and on Ascension Day [June 1] they appointed and held their first meeting, in the old log schoolhouse, on the corner of the farm on which [Preacher] Joseph Rohrer is now living, opposite to the Brethren's meetinghouse, built a few years since. The three ministers were present, the principal discourse being delivered by Jacob Wisler. Bishop Hoover was then eighty-eight years old, and only made a few remarks sitting. No hymn was sung, because no one present was able to lead the singing. The meeting was attended by only sixteen persons. From this time forward, however, regular services were held, every two weeks, sometimes in barns, private dwellings, etc.

"During a summer (1848) twenty-four families more arrived from

Wayne, Medina, and Columbiana counties, Ohio, among whom were the Hartmans, Holdemans, Moyers, Smeltzers, etc.

"In the summer of 1849, a log meetinghouse, twenty-six feet square, was built . . . this building once took fire from the stovepipe, burning four of the ceiling boards, and charring the girder to coals, half the length of the building. An addition of twenty-four feet in length was afterwards made to this house, and in 1861 the old house was moved [to the present location of the Blosser meetinghouse], and the new frame house, still there, forty by sixty, put in its stead.

"In 1850, [Preacher] Benjamin Hershey came from Canada and settled here. He also was a minister, and later, removed to Illinois. Daniel Moyer, being chosen to the ministry, served in that capacity for a number of years. His earthly labors were brought to a sudden close by a collision on the railroad, while on his way to Canada, in December 1864. . . .

"The church now numbers quite a large membership in the county, embracing six distinct congregations, and maintaining services at eleven different places, as follows:

"Yellow Creek Church, in Harrison Township; Holdeman's Church, in Olive Township; Blosser's Church, in Union Township; Christophel's Church, in Jackson Township; Shaum's Church, in Baugo Township; Elkhart Church, in the town of Elkhart; [South] Union meetinghouse, in Locke Township; Jones' schoolhouse, in Harrison Township; Stump's schoolhouse, in Union Township; and Clinton Church, in Clinton Township. The latter also holds regular services in the Union meeting-house, at Forest Grove, in Middlebury Township."

The original 1849 log meetinghouse at Yellow Creek was built in the northwest corner of what is now the East Cemetery, across the road from the Wisler (frame) meetinghouse. The owner of the land on which the meetinghouse was built was himself a Mennonite, Adam Hartman (1811-1894), and he did not get around to giving a deed until March 27, 1854, when he and his wife Elizabeth (Ramer) conveyed one-half acre of land to the *Menonite Church* in Section 27 of Harrison Township. This land was granted for "a graveyard for the use of the public forever, and said house to be used as a meetinghouse forever."

In 1861 the Mennonites purchased the land across the road where the present Wisler frame meetinghouse stands, from Andrew Bigler and his wife Lydia, for $200.00. This involved two acres of land in the north-east corner of Section 28. Bigler and wife conveyed the property to the *Old Menonite Church* on April 16, 1861. The 1861 plot was enlarged by additional purchases for cemetery purposes on August 9, 1884, on May 9, 1902, on January 2, 1912, and on October 10, 1929. . .

The aged Martin Hoover, first Mennonite bishop in Elkhart County, died in 1850. But, as was noted above, Preacher Jacob Christophel and Preacher Jacob Wisler both moved into the settlement in 1848. Three years later, in 1851, Bishop Abraham Rohrer of Medina County, Ohio, who had ordained Martin Hoover bishop before his coming to Elkhart County, ordained Jacob Wisler to the office of bishop. Another early minister in Elkhart County was John Bare, who lived west of Waterford, and who died in 1855. Joseph Rohrer was ordained about 1830 in the Rowland Mennonite Church, Canton, Ohio, and removed to Harrison Township in 1850, settling on the farm now owned by Dr. Maurice L. and Irene Anna Weldy. In the 1850's the Mennonites of Elkhart County were therefore served by the following ministers: Bishop Jacob Wisler, Jacob Christophel, Daniel Moyer, John Bare, Benjamin Hershey, John Snyder, and Joseph Rohrer. In 1864 an additional minister moved into the area, one who was destined to exert a tremendous influence for good, but who also unfortunately was later involved in a schism. His name was Daniel Brenneman, and he moved to Elkhart County from Fairfield County, Ohio, where he had been ordained preacher in 1857. The first period in the life of the Elkhart County church was therefore one of beginnings, 1845-48; the second period was one of growth and prosperity, 1848-66. It was in this second era that the first two Yellow Creek meeting-houses were built, the latter of which is still standing and is being used by the Wisler congregation.

The fall of 1862, John F. Funk, who was then a young businessman in Chicago, visited the Elkhart County Mennonites at the time of the annual conference which convened annually on the second Friday of October. Funk reports that the conference convened at nine o'clock in the morning and extended to one or two o'clock in the afternoon. The attendants at the conference did not bother to serve meals but took some biscuits in their pockets to eat at noon. Funk was particularly impressed with the able leadership of John M. Brenneman of Elida, Ohio, who presided at the 1862 conference. On this occasion forty-six new converts were baptized and received into the church. Funk also commented on the 1861 meetinghouse which was a frame building with "good seats." But he commented that it was already too small for the congregation. Its cost, he says, was $1,300.00. Funk estimated the membership of the district at 400 to 500. Deacon David Good of the Yellow Creek congregation estimated the communicants in 1862 at over 600, a figure which has often been repeated. But Bishop Brenneman himself, who presided, estimated the number who communed as between 300 and 400. Strange as it may seem to modern readers, Funk reports that there were nonmembers, that is, people from the community, who attended the 1862 conference at

Yellow Creek, and he adds: "Even hucksters were present with their wagons loaded with cakes and other refreshments, soft drinks, etc." Then Funk adds with his characteristic vigor: "This was of course in a short time cut out."

In listing the Mennonite preachers of Elkhart County no mention was made of the Frisian congregation in Jackson Township, since that group kept somewhat apart from the rest of the Mennonites of the area because of the language barrier.

The years from 1866 to 1874 might be characterized as troubled years. In this era two schisms occurred to the extreme damage of the Elkhart County congregations. After a number of years of friction and difficulty, occasioned by the desire of leaders such as Funk and Brenneman to introduce more English into the services, to establish Sunday schools, and other progressive activities, together with the extreme resistance to these new activities on the part of Jacob Wisler, the bishop, and of his supporters, the Wisler schism of January 6, 1872, occurred. Wisler took with him Preachers Christian Bare and John Weaver, and Deacons Tobias Ramer and John Troxel. The first three deacons at Yellow Creek, David Good, Benjamin Hoover, and Henry Newcomer, had all died respectively in the years 1864, 1866, and 1867. Wisler took with him approximately a hundred members out of a total of possibly 400 members in Elkhart County.

The most influential leader in the Mennonite Church, not only in Elkhart County but in the denomination as a whole, was John F. Funk, who had located in Elkhart in the year 1867. (See the biographical sketch of Funk in chapter five.) Funk was the strong leader for the thirty or thirty-five years following his coming to Elkhart County. The result of his vision, assisted by Daniel Brenneman, enabled the church to take forward steps. The real tragedy was the loss of approximately one fourth of the members through the schism of Wisler in 1872, and the perhaps still more tragic division of 1874 when Daniel Brenneman, the former staunch colleague of Funk, was driven out of the Mennonite Church because of his favoring a rather emotional type of evangelistic and revival meetings, because of the freedom he gave to women to speak in the testimony meetings of his group, and because of his somewhat defiant attitude toward the other ministers of the conference who did not share his vision. According to the tabulation made by Brenneman's own son, Timothy H. Brenneman, a total of approximately eighty-six persons united with Brenneman's Reformed Mennonite Church in 1874 or shortly thereafter. By an active program of evangelism Brenneman had won a total of approximately 200 persons to his following by the year 1880. If a leader such as John M. Brenneman had lived in Elkhart

County in the post-Civil War period, one must wonder if he might have been able to maintain the unity of the Mennonite Church without losing either Bishop Wisler or Daniel Brenneman. One is compelled to fear that both divisions may in part have been due to the iron will and unbending disposition of John F. Funk, excellent as his contribution to the Mennonite Church otherwise was. Daniel Brenneman's daughter, Phoebe, Mrs. Calvin F. Snyder, reports that her father fainted only one time in his entire life, which was on the occasion when he was told that he had been expelled from the Mennonite Church.

David B. Martin and Tobias Ramer were both deacons at Yellow Creek as early as 1869, and both eventually identified themselves with Wisler's conference. Christian Christophel was ordained preacher in 1872, after the Wisler schism, and served until his death in 1883. Martin E. Kreider was ordained preacher in the Blosser meetinghouse in 1873 and served until his early death four years later. Meanwhile John M. Brenneman of Ohio had come to Elkhart County in October 1872 and ordained two ministers as cobishops: John M. Christophel, 53, of the Yellow Creek congregation, and Jacob A. Beutler, 38, of the Holdeman congregation. Preacher Jacob C. Buzzard was ordained in 1877 but died three years later. Deacon Daniel Hoover was ordained deacon in 1877 and served seven years before his death. Jacob Long was ordained deacon at the Shaum Church, now Olive, in 1882, but frequently alternated Sunday by Sunday between the Shaum and Yellow Creek congregations; he actually handled the finances of the Yellow Creek congregation as well as those of the Shaum Church. Noah Metzler was ordained preacher in the Shaum Church in 1880, but removed to a farm near the village of South West in 1885 and served at Yellow Creek as a preacher until 1903, when he removed to Nappanee. Jonas Loucks was ordained preacher at Holdeman, perhaps for the entire district, in 1886, but did his lifework in the Yellow Creek congregation, where he died in 1938. Noah S. Hoover was ordained deacon about 1887 and served until his death in 1913. He was succeeded in 1914 by Henry B. Weaver, who served for twenty-four years in the Yellow Creek Church (he was later a deacon in the North Goshen congregation). Jacob W. Christophel was ordained preacher in 1893 and bishop in 1918, and served faithfully until his death in 1937. His son, Allen B. Christophel, served as a preacher from 1924 until his untimely death in 1932. Two years before Bishop Christophel's death, in the year 1935, Virgil C. Weaver was ordained minister and served for seven years.

During the years from 1874, after the Brenneman schism, various new activities were introduced by Funk and his fellow ministers in the congregations west of Goshen. Sunday school had actually been begun at

Yellow Creek as early as 1869, but it was not until about 1895 that it became "evergreen" (met all year). As early as 1892 John S. Coffman held evangelistic meetings at Yellow Creek with about twenty-five converts. Twenty-three were baptized with water in the stream known as Yellow Creek on June 4, 1892, by John F. Funk; two were ill and so could not be present. Bible Readings were begun in 1892 in the Yellow Creek congregation, but have been known as young people's Bible meetings, at least from the year 1914. Through the influence of Eva Wenger a sewing circle was started at Yellow Creek in the year 1916. In 1920 the young people organized a literary society called Amaranth. All the literaries of the Mennonite congregations of Indiana and Michigan are now known as Mennonite Youth Fellowships.

After the division of 1872 the so-called Wisler and Funk Mennonite congregations alternated in the use of the Yellow Creek meetinghouse until the year 1912. The new meetinghouse of 1912 is a brick building forty by sixty-six feet in size, with an annex twelve by twenty feet. This building was remodeled and enlarged in the year 1948.

According to certain old records kept by John F. Funk the membership of the Yellow Creek congregation in the 1880's is recorded as eighty. In 1896 Yellow Creek is said to have grown to 129 members. Perhaps due to the difficulties associated with the replacement of John F. Funk as a bishop in the first years of this century, the congregation seems to have dropped somewhat in membership, so that by 1905 there were only 120 members. By 1920 the number had risen to 195, and in 1940 the *Yearbook* gives the figure as 254.

This brings us to the most recent era in the life of the congregation. The last local man to be ordained in the history of the Yellow Creek Church was Abram Hartman, to the office of deacon, in 1938. Brother Hartman has served as a genuine stabilizing influence in the life of the congregation in the last quarter of a century. Since 1940 all the ministers have been brought into the congregation. India Missionary Ralph R. Smucker, a grandson of Amish Mennonite Bishop Jonathan P. Smucker, served as pastor for five years at Yellow Creek, beginning in 1942, and again, 1950-51. Africa Missionary John H. Mosemann then served as interim pastor from 1947 until 1950. In the year 1951 a young graduate of Goshen College Biblical Seminary, Peter B. Wiebe, assumed the leadership of the congregation and proved to be a dynamic pastor and preacher. He was ordained bishop in 1954 and served an additional five years before accepting a call to become pastor of the Hesston, Kansas, Mennonite Church in 1959. In the years 1956-58 Clayton Swartzentruber served as a licensed minister at Yellow Creek. John D. Zehr was installed as assistant pastor at Yellow Creek in the year 1958, and in 1960 was made

6

full pastor, succeeding Peter B. Wiebe; Zehr was ordained as bishop on September 18, 1960, and he and Abram Hartman are therefore the ordained leaders of the Yellow Creek congregation, which has according to the 1960 *Mennonite Yearbook* a total of 355 members.

Beginning in 1958 a number of Yellow Creek families began to meet each Sunday for their services in the chapel auditorium of Bethany Christian High School at Waterford. This move was made by action of the entire Yellow Creek congregation and the transfer to Waterford was a voluntary matter. The congregation was actually organized in the year 1959 with Virgil J. Brenneman, formerly a minister in Iowa City, Iowa, but then a seminary student, as pastor. The formation of this new daughter congregation at Waterford was done to relieve the crowded situation in the Yellow Creek meetinghouse.

HOLDEMAN MENNONITE CHURCH

Section 27, Olive Township, Elkhart County, Indiana

One can do no better than quote from the excellent historical summary made by Lloyd V. Conrad of the Holdeman congregation: "Among the twenty-four families who came to Elkhart County in 1848 were the George Holdeman and the Frederick Landis families who settled in Elkhart Township. Frederick Landis was married to Catherine Holdeman, a sister of George. With them also were Frederick Landis's widowed mother, his brother Jacob and family, and his nephew Joseph Landis. This Joseph Landis later (1870) located in Wakarusa and married Christiana Freed. In the fall of 1849, the George Holdeman family located in Olive Township on a farm which was purchased from the government. About the same time, the widowed mother of George Holdeman, Christiana (Buzzard) Holdeman, with her nephew Christian Shaum, and her younger children, John, Susannah, and Abraham, came from Wayne County, Ohio, and located in Baugo Township. John, having married in 1847, was accompanied by his wife and small daughter. John Davidhizar, a young man of Mennonite parentage from Butler County, Pennsylvania, who purchased land in St. Joseph County, Indiana, in 1848, also came with the widow Christiana Holdeman. Later he married a daughter of Jacob Landis (who had settled in Elkhart Township in 1848) and then united with the church. During the following year (1850) the Samuel and Joseph Holdeman families also made the trek from Wayne County, Ohio, to Elkhart County, Indiana, the latter coming late in the fall. The next spring (1851) Abraham Weldy, whose wife Nancy was a daughter of Margaret (Holdeman) (Yoder) Freed, left Holmes County, Ohio, for Elkhart County, Indiana. Besides his wife and one child, he was accompanied by his father John Weldy and family, and his wife's sister Elizabeth Yoder. In November of this same year Elizabeth Yoder married Henry Smeltzer who had come from Richland County, Ohio, in 1849 with his parents, Michael Smeltzers. During the year 1851 the John Weldy family located in St. Joseph County. In the fall of 1851, the David S. Holdeman and the Jacob Freed families also joined the westward migration of the Mennonites, coming from Wayne County, Ohio, to Elkhart County, Indiana. Jacob Freed had made the trip in the spring with the Weldy families in order to invest in land and then returned to Ohio to bring the entire family to this community. The David Holdeman family returned to Ohio in 1856 and then moved to Kansas in 1873. Others who arrived in these early years included David Lechlitner who came from Richland County, Ohio, before 1851, for in March of that year he was married to Susannah Holdeman; the Peter Loucks family who came in 1851 from Wayne County, Ohio; the Valentine Hartman family who came from Ashland County, Ohio, in 1848; the Adam Hartman family who came from the same county in 1849. The Mark Tintsman family located in Locke Township in 1851. The John Culp family settled in the community in the same year or soon afterward and a number of other families within the next year or two."

It should be explained that there was really only one Elkhart County congregation west of Goshen in the beginning. Yellow Creek was considered more or less the official center, it was the first place where a meetinghouse was built, and all the district conferences were held at Yellow Creek for the first thirty years. The Elkhart County Mennonite ministers, however, not only preached at the services at Yellow Creek, but also supplied the smaller groups of families in the outlying areas which met in private homes or in schoolhouses. In the case of the members who later formed the Holdeman congregation, the place of meeting was the George Holdeman house which was located southwest of the town of Salem (now Wakarusa), and services were held there every four weeks.

In the year 1851 a lease was secured to the plot of ground on the east side of the road directly east of the present meetinghouse, and a log house of worship was erected on this plot in 1851 (Section 26, Olive Township.) This lease does not seem to have been recorded in the Elkhart County courthouse records. The man in whose home the services were held, George Holdeman, 1813-1878, was a brother of Joseph Holdeman, who later served as a deacon in the congregation; George was married to Anna Eicher, 1818-1863. On February 6, 1854, the congregation purchased the lot which had been leased, amounting to 1.1 acres of land, from George and Sophia Beach for $1.00. Of the sixteen members which constituted the unorganized Holdeman Church at that point, fourteen of them belonged to the Holdeman family. Edwin L. Weaver wrote in his *Holdeman Descendants* (Nappanee, Indiana, 1937): "This first building, erected under the leadership of Joseph Holdeman, was a log structure about twenty-four by thirty-four feet in size, east and west in length. The house had two windows at each end and three on each side. The pulpit, which was at the east end, consisted of a plank with legs fastened into it; the seats were benches without backs made from slabs off the side of logs with holes bored into which legs were fastened."

On June 27, 1866, the congregation purchased of Amos and Magdalena Jones one acre and sixteen rods on the west side of the road, the present location of the meetinghouse, for a consideration of $100.00. On this the church built a house of worship in the year 1875. Jacob Link is said to have served as head carpenter. While the 1875 meetinghouse was being built the services of the church were held in the Bunker Hill United Brethren Church in Wakarusa. The new building had an assembly room forty by forty-two feet in size, with two cloakrooms and a hall at the east end of the building. There was a newspaper published in Wakarusa at that time entitled, *The Wakarusa Sun.* The issue of May 13, 1875, page 3, states: "The Menonites are about building a new 'meetinghouse' one mile west of town. The old one has become [bedimmed] with age. . . ."

Deacon Joseph Holdeman kept a record of at least some of the gifts, a total of about $400.60, given by sixty-nine donors, some of whom contributed more than once, making a total of eighty-two gifts, for an average of something over $5.00 per gift. The amounts given ranged from 25¢ to $25.00. The list of donors alphabetized is as follows: Elizabeth Bare, John Bechtel, Elizabeth Beutler, Joseph Blosser, Tobias Blosser, Christian Bowers, John Brown, D. Burkholder, John Buzzard, Henry Christophel, J. M. Christophel, John W. Christophel, Abraham Climenhaga, Abraham Culp, Anthony Culp, George Culp, Jr., Isaac Culp, John Culp, Sr., John Culp, Jr., Jacob Dausman, Enoch Eby, Jacob Eby, Jacob Eyman, Klaas H. Fisher, Margaret Freed, John F. Funk, Christian Henning, a Bro. Hernley, Abraham Herr, A. Holdeman, John Holdeman, Sr., William Holdeman, A. Hoover, Daniel Hoover, Isaac Kilmer, Joseph Kindig, David Kreider, Martin E. Kreider, Rudolph Kagey, Frederick Landis, Jacob Landis, Joseph Landis, Peter Loucks, Daniel Martin, David Metzler, Noah Metzler, Charles Mowrer, Christian Moyer, Jacob Moyer, Tobias Myers, Christian Null, Christian Nusbaum, Peter Nusbaum, Levi Ressler, Daniel Saunders, Benjamin Sease, Samuel Seits, Henry Shaum, Henry Smeltzer, Henry Stauffer, Anna Weldy, Jacob B. Weldy, Jonathan Willard, Christian Witmer, Samuel Witmer, Jacob Wisler, and John Wisler.

In addition to the Yellow Creek ministers who also served in the Holdeman congregation in the first several decades, the following were resident ministers in the congregation. Preacher Jacob Freed served from 1851 until his death in 1868. Deacon John Eyer (Oyer in German) served from possibly about 1855 until he left the church several years later. Deacon Joseph Holdeman served from about 1860 until 1880 when he resigned, but lived until 1894 and was a deacon in the conference for his entire life. Bishop Henry Yother baptized six at the Holdeman meetinghouse on March 18, 1868, and ordained J. A. Beutler as preacher by lot. Beutler was ordained bishop in 1872 and served until his early death in 1886. James Culbertson was ordained preacher in 1871 and resigned in 1879; considerable trouble evolved around him, as will be mentioned later. Daniel Freed served as deacon from 1881, following the resignation of Holdeman, until 1897. Amos Mumaw was ordained preacher, and Abram Culp was ordained deacon in 1886; Culp served until his death in 1910, but Mumaw removed to the state of Ohio in 1898. Jonas Loucks was ordained, evidently for the district, in 1886 but did his lifework in the Yellow Creek congregation. The next year his brother, Jacob O. Loucks, was ordained, but never felt able to take up the ministry. In 1889 Henry Weldy was ordained to the ministry and served for forty-five years, until his death in 1934. Weldy was an active man of positive convictions, of a conservative turn of mind, and had concern for the welfare of the church. He used to go to Teegarden in Marshall County, Indiana, to preach for the few members there. John Hygema was ordained preacher in 1893, but suffered with ill health and died in California in 1908. Samuel Smeltzer was ordained deacon in 1896 and served until 1933.

The Holdeman congregation was under the care of Bishop Jacob Wisler from 1851 until the division of 1872. Jacob Beutler was then the resident bishop of the congregation, although his fellow bishop, John M. Christophel of Yellow Creek, served with him in the district. Henry Shaum served as bishop of the Elkhart County Mennonites west of Goshen from his ordination in 1886 until his death in 1892. In the latter year, prior to his death, Shaum ordained his successor, the well-known John F. Funk, who served for ten years.

The strains and stresses of the Wisler trouble were probably less severe in the Holdeman congregation than at Yellow Creek. But Holdeman had its own troubles in the year 1879 because of the attitudes taken by Preacher James Culbertson and Deacon Joseph Holdeman. John F. Funk reported in his diary that on June 5 he had taken Joseph Summers with him to see Deacon Joseph Holdeman, and took Holdeman along to see James Culbertson, "to try and help them to settle their difficulty—

with little success." On Saturday, June 21, "Bro. James Culbertson, who has been a minister for some years in the church, on account of a misunderstanding between himself and Deacon Joseph Holdeman, withdrew from the membership of the church." Funk then added in his diary, "Holdeman made his confession and did more than the church required, and Culbertson would not be satisfied but said that Holdeman and himself could not be members in the same church, and that he would withdraw."

In an effort to settle the difficulties the ministers of the district met at the Holdeman meetinghouse on Thursday, August 7, 1879. Funk reported that they had "a stormy time." The item which most disturbed the ministers of the Elkhart County Mennonite Church was an action taken by the members of the Holdeman congregation on June 28, 1879, in which they announced that they were as a congregation withdrawing from "all the bishops and ministers until they recall what they have done in the case of Joseph Holdeman . . . and [until they] consider him as no member of the church until he makes peace with Culbertson." In the August 7 meeting the ministers attempted to state tactfully that they felt the congregation was out of order in taking action to withdraw as it did. Further, "in regard to Joseph Holdeman, the bishops acknowledge that they may not have been as careful as they should have been, yet they do not see that they have any right, or that they can reject him and consider him as no brother, because he was given his right as a brother by the counsel of the church, but they are willing to do all they can to bring about a reconciliation between themselves and the church, consistently with the Scriptures: and with this all the ministers agree.

"In regard to James M. Culbertson we hold that because he publicly and voluntarily withdrew from the church, he committed an error, and it will be required of him to acknowledge his fault, and make satisfaction to the church, and agree to accept, and yield obedience to the rules and order of the same."

The ten ordained brethren who signed this statement also appointed Preachers Henry Shaum and Jacob Buzzard as a committee to visit Culbertson and attempt to induce him to yield to the decision of the conference and reconcile himself again with the church. It was not until December 23, 1879, that a full reconciliation was made between the bishops and ministers of the church on the one hand, and the Holdeman congregation on the other. In the end the congregation accepted fully the ordained brethren, but Culbertson refused to be reconciled to the church.

Milo Kauffman, who made a thorough investigation of the history of Sunday schools in Elkhart County for his 1931 M.A. in Religious Education thesis, *The Rise and Development of Sunday Schools in the Mennonite Church in Indiana,* concluded on the basis of his research that the first Sunday school was started in the Holdeman congregation in the year 1872. This conclusion may be correct. However, on May 25, 1942, Peter B. Yoder (1855-1943), father of Bishop D. A. Yoder, told the present writer that his father, Henry B. Yoder, removed from Mahoning County, Ohio, to Wakarusa in 1865. Peter Yoder stated that Sunday school was started at Holdeman in the year 1866. He seemed to imply that Daniel Brenneman may have had a hand in this action, for he added that after Daniel Brenneman left the church the Sunday school was stopped briefly at Holdeman's. John F. Funk always insisted that when he came to Elkhart County in April 1867 there were no Sunday schools among the Mennonites of Elkhart County. It must be remembered, of course, that all the early Sunday schools in that era met only during the summer months.

John F. Funk recorded in his diary for September 19, 1896, that at the Holdeman counsel meeting held on that date the question of a Bible Reading came up. "Almost the entire church is satisfied to have a Bible Reading," but two or three persons who took no part, and who were unable to do so. It is probable that Bible Readings were then begun immediately.

After Funk's bishop oversight was taken from him in 1902 the Mennonites of Northern Indiana were without a bishop until the ordination of David Burkholder in 1904. Out-of-state bishops came to the several congregations with the necessary care in that interval. David Burkholder was the active and senior bishop at the Holdeman Church until 1913, but was assisted by J. K. Bixler from the year 1907. In 1913 D. A. Yoder became associated with J. K. Bixler in the bishop care of the Holdeman Church, and in 1919 J. K. Bixler was relieved, leaving D. A. Yoder as the sole bishop in charge until his resignation in the year 1949. George J. Lapp was then chosen as the bishop of the church, but died in the year 1951. Lee J. Miller of the Shore Church served from 1951 until 1956, since which time J. C. Wenger has had the bishop care of the congregation.

Silas L. Weldy, one of the most dynamic ministers in the Indiana-Michigan Mennonite Conference, was ordained in the year 1908 and served until feeble health and partial blindness incapacitated him in his last years; he died in 1955. Elias J. Christophel moved into the congregation as a deacon, and was accepted by the congregation as a deacon in the year 1934; he died in 1949. The long-time deacon in the church in the twentieth century was Jacob I. Weldy, father of Professor Dwight Weldy of Goshen College, who was ordained in the year 1913 and served until his death in 1953. Simon Gingerich, a graduate of Goshen College Biblical Seminary, was ordained preacher in 1950 and has had the pastoral care of the Holdeman congregation since that date. It was also in the year 1950 that Manford Freed, who had earlier been a deacon in Michigan, was asked by the Holdeman Church to become their deacon, and has served since that time. In 1936 Warren C. Shaum was ordained to the ministry and served until the year 1953 when he moved to the Pleasantview congregation in Manistee, Michigan, to care for that church. With the approval of the congregation J. C. Wenger licensed Clifford E. King to preach in the Holdeman congregation for the school year 1957-58 while he was a student in the Goshen College Biblical Seminary. Since 1958 Kermit H. Derstine has been serving as a licensed minister, also.

The 1875 meetinghouse was enlarged in the year 1913. The work was done between August 3 and December 6, during which time services were held by the Holdeman congregation in the North Union congregation southwest of Wakarusa. In 1915 the basement was prepared for the primary department of the Sunday school. In 1941 a blower was added to the furnace, a water system was installed, rest rooms were placed in the basement, and the sheds for horses and buggies on the north side of the meetinghouse were removed. In 1946 new pulpit furniture was placed in the auditorium, the floor was finished, and the auditorium was papered and painted. In 1949 the last church sheds were removed from the meetinghouse lot. In 1950 a new ceiling was placed in the main auditorium, and a new roof was put on the building. In 1951 the basement was further improved and a new oil furnace installed. In 1960 a simple wooden cross was placed on the wall behind the pulpit.

The young people organized a literary society in 1922, which was reorganized in 1927, and which in recent years has become the Mennonite Youth Fellowship. The first series of evangelistic meetings at Holdeman seemed to have been held by John S. Coffman in the year 1894. One of the most successful series was conducted by J. E. Hartzler of Missouri in the year 1907, when there were forty-six converts. In 1898 Holdeman served as host to the first regular session of Mennonite General Conference. In May 1922 Edwin L. Weaver served as superintendent of the first "Vacation Bible School" in the Holdeman congregation, the first in the Mennonite Church. In 1904 the Sunday School reached its highest attendance level to that time. In the second quarter the average attendance was 142, with D. A. Yoder serving as superintendent (at Yellow Creek Sunday School, by comparison, in 1902 the average attendance was sixty-one). As early as 1888 John S. Coffman had commented in his diary that Holdeman had "the largest congregation of our people in this county."

In the 1880's John F. Funk listed the church membership of the Holdeman congregation as 126; in 1905 it was 140; in 1920, 257; in 1940, 285; and the 1960 *Mennonite Yearbook* gives the Holdeman membership as 237. One of the highest membership figures of the congregation was in 1944 when the membership stood at 314.

CHRISTOPHEL MENNONITE CHURCH

Section 6, Jackson Township, Elkhart County, Indiana

The Christophel Church is named for and centers in Preacher Jacob Christophel, born December 31, 1782, at Rothenbach in the Palatinate. In the year 1818 Jacob Christophel emigrated to America. His grandson, Wesley W. Christophel of Elkhart, still has the passport which his grandfather brought with him to this country. In it Jacob is described as thirty-six years of age, about five feet three inches tall, with blond hair and beard, light gray eyes, and a face marked with smallpox pits.

Jacob Christophel first settled in Westmoreland County, Pennsylvania, in the year 1818, only to move to Allegheny County, Pennsylvania, in 1824. In 1827 Bishop David Funk ordained him as a Mennonite preacher. Jacob became a United States citizen in the year 1831 at Pittsburgh, Pennsylvania. In 1835 he removed to Columbiana County, Ohio, and in 1848 to Jackson Township, Elkhart County, Indiana, a little over two miles east of the village of Foraker. Here he lived, worshiped, and preached until his death which occurred December 3, 1868, at the advanced age of eighty-five years, eleven months, and three days. Jacob was a linen weaver and a farmer, as well as a preacher. The farm where Jacob lived is now occupied by a Wisler Mennonite named Eugene Martin. According to tradition it was about the year 1850 when the Mennonites of Jackson and Union townships, Elkhart County, built a log church building on what is now County Road 142, on Section 6 of Jackson Township. The 1874 *Historical Atlas of Elkhart County* shows the Christophel meetinghouse about one eighth of a mile from the Union Township line, with the label *M. Ch.*, meaning Mennonite Church. Wesley W. Christophel says that the building stood along the south side of County Road 142, and parallel with the road. He well remembers worshiping in the Christophel meetinghouse as a child. The door of the meetinghouse was at the east end of the building. There was a porch at this east end, but there was no roof over it. Wesley remembers three windows on both the north and south sides of the meetinghouse, and two windows on the west end. Wesley was told that the first windowpanes were made of oiled paper. There was no formal pulpit in the meetinghouse, but instead of a pulpit there was a table at the west end which served the same function as a pulpit desk does now.

According to tradition there was no deed given for the meetinghouse, but in this respect tradition is mistaken. On April 22, 1854, Jacob Christophel and Barbara his wife conveyed one-half acre for a public burying ground, "and the Meeting House to be for the use of the Menonite [sic] Church forever." The consideration for this transaction was $5.00.

Various visiting ministers are reported in the *Herald of Truth* as having preached at the Christophel meetinghouse. On Monday, October 18, 1863, Preacher David Sherk of Waterloo, Canada West (Ontario), preached at the Christophel meetinghouse in the forenoon, apparently for the small Frisian group of Mennonites led by R. J. Smid. On Wednesday, October 11, 1865, the famous John M. Brenneman of Elida, Ohio, also preached at the Christophel Church. On November 23, 1878, while John S. Coffman was still living in Virginia, he visited Elkhart County and preached at the Christophel meetinghouse. Bishop Moses Brenneman of Ohio preached at the Christophel meetinghouse on November 18, 1887. Three years earlier, on March 2, 1884, John F. Funk preached at Christophel's where there was a "fair attendance" and "good attention." The *Herald of Truth* for 1871, which gives a list of the various services being held by the Elkhart County Mennonites, indicates that services were held at Christophel's every four weeks on the same Sunday as Elkhart and Shaum (Olive) but not on the same Sunday as Yellow Creek and Holdeman. One of the ministers who is known to have been ordained in the "Christophel District" was Martin E. Kreider; the service took place on June 22, 1873. When John F. Funk listed the memberships of the various Mennonite congregations in Indiana in the 1880's, he put down twenty-five as the number of members at the Christophel Church. Wesley W. Christophel believes that the majority of these were Frisian Mennonites. W. W. Christophel writes: "There are no written records to my knowledge. Jacob Fisher was one of the first trustees for Salem Church when it was built, and I suppose he was the one who closed the affairs of the log church as no one was appointed to trustee until it was sold for $20.00 to a farmer near-by named [Jan] Belt." The Christophel congregation came to an end in 1889 with the building of the Salem meetinghouse which absorbed both the Christophel and Blosser Mennonite congregations and made one new church of them.

OLIVE MENNONITE CHURCH

Section 2, Olive Township, Elkhart County, Indiana

Holdeman was not the only outpost of the Yellow Creek congregation at the middle of the nineteenth century. Another such outpost was located nine tenths of a mile (following the crooked road along the

Baugo Creek) north of the present Olive meetinghouse on the land where Earl Cook's home now stands. This log building stood in Section 35 of Baugo Township, a few miles southwest of Elkhart. In it the Mennonites gathered to hold their services prior to the erection of the first meeting- house on the farm of Jacob and Mary (Troxel) Shaum. Because of the location of the 1862 meetinghouse on the present site, the congregation was usually spoken of as the Shaum Church, although occasionally it was also called the Baugo congregation, because the meetinghouse was very close to the Baugo Creek. The early sources do not agree on the date of the first Olive meetinghouse on the present location. The 1874 Atlas gives no date at all for the building of the Shaum meetinghouse. The 1881 *Elkhart County History* states that the first Olive meetinghouse was built in 1861. Edwin L. Weaver in the *Holdeman Descendants* indicates correctly that the building was erected the fall of 1862. It was thirty- six by sixty feet in size. Various authorities state that the cemetery across the road to the east of the Olive Church was platted in the year 1855. The land for this cemetery was given for the burial of the dead by James C. and Harriet Dodge on April 7, 1860.

The first Mennonite preacher to live in the Olive area was Daniel Moyer who lived southwest of Jamestown until his untimely death in 1864. The second minister to live in the area was the well-known Daniel Brenneman. The other ministers of the Elkhart County Mennonite Church, such as Jacob Wisler, John Snyder from north of Elkhart, and John F. Funk from the town of Elkhart, all preached from time to time to the little flock which worshiped along the Baugo.

Jacob and Mary Shaum, who were Mennonites, did not bother to give a deed for the land on which the 1861-62 meetinghouse stood until November 9, 1872. On that date they conveyed one and one-half acres to the "Old Mennonite Church" for a consideration of $1.00. It was in this meetinghouse of 1862 that the first Mennonite Sunday school of In- diana was established through the influence of John F. Funk in the year 1867. Abraham Holdeman served as the Sunday-school superintendent that first year, and Funk was one of those who attended frequently.

By the year 1888 the Shaum congregation was minded to build a new meetinghouse. A business meeting was called for May 14, 1888. John F. Funk called the meeting to order, and Joseph Holdeman was elected chairman, while John F. Funk was requested to serve as secretary. A resolution was offered and adopted that the meetinghouse should be built on the site of the old meetinghouse, forty by sixty feet in size, fifteen feet to the ceiling, with a stone foundation. The main auditorium was to be forty by forty feet in size, and there were to be two anterooms, sixteen by twenty feet, at the east end. The building was to be of brick veneer construction. There should be folding doors between the main auditorium and the anterooms, and the building was to be roofed with slate. The building committee was to consist of Jacob Berkey, treasurer, Joseph Wenger, and Martin Loucks. The solicitors chosen were Jacob Eby, John Schrock, Thomas Moore, Abraham Weldy, Christian Holdeman, and Samuel Herrington. On June 4, 1888, another meeting was called because there seemed to be some dissatisfaction with the decisions taken at the May 14 meeting. On June 4 Henry Shaum served as chairman and John F. Funk was again secretary. The entire question was reopened, and by a decision of forty-one to eighteen the group confirmed its decision to build a frame building with a brick veneer which would be roofed with slate. It was decided to add doors to the north and south sides of the meetinghouse at each end of an aisle in front of the pulpit. The earlier building committee was reaffirmed, but a new group of solicitors was chosen: David Wisler, Thomas Moore, Christian Holdeman, John Buzzard, John Schrock, Abraham Weldy, Samuel Herrington, Joel Blosser, and Moses Weaver. John Berkey was elected treasurer. It was decided to move the old meetinghouse aside while building the new meetinghouse, and to use the old one for services during the building period. This new 1888 meetinghouse was completed and dedicated on December 25, 1888, with the chief discourse being delivered by John S. Coffman of Elkhart. Coffman wrote this brief account in his diary: "10 a.m. Elizabeth and Daniel and I attended the meeting at Shaum's. It was both a Christmas and dedicatory service. The brethren insisted on me to speak the principle [sic] discourse. Haggai 2:9. The contrast between the two temples of the Jews, the two covenants, and the use we shall make of this house under this new covenant." The cost of this building was $1,800.00. Moses Weaver bought the 1862 building and made it into a dwelling east of Foraker.

The first-known ordination in the Shaum congregation was that of Deacon Henry Christophel in the year 1871; he served until his death ten years later. In 1880 Noah Metzler was ordained preacher, but five years later he removed to a farm near the village of South West and served the Yellow Creek congregation for many years. Deacon Jacob G. Long was ordained in the Shaum congregation in 1882 and served until 1900 when he moved east of Goshen and identified himself with the Clinton Brick congregation. Long also served the Yellow Creek congregation as deacon; this was possible because the churches alternated their services Sunday by Sunday. Jonas Brubaker was ordained deacon in 1886, and served for many years until his death in 1932. The next preacher to be ordained at Olive was Jacob Shank, ordained in 1896, but who died in 1905. The next year, 1906, William H. Hartman was ordained to the ministry, but never felt able to take up the work. In the year 1908 a young minister from the Holdeman congregation, who had been ordained with the understanding that he would go wherever he was needed, D. A. Yoder, was called to shepherd the Olive Church. In the year 1910 he was ordained bishop and is still living at this writing. Preacher Jacob Shank's son, Clarence A., was ordained preacher in 1917, and is also still living. As Deacon Jonas Brubaker became quite aged, Irvin A. Long was chosen to serve as deacon in the Olive Church, which he did from 1927 until about 1931. In the year 1933 two new deacons were ordained, Merrill Weaver who served for sixteen years, and Andrew J. Miller who is active. In the year 1950 the congregation asked Paul Mininger to assume bishop oversight of the church, which he did for a number of years. In 1951 Bishop Mininger ordained Elno W. Steiner as preacher, and J. C. Wenger as bishop. Both of these men are still serving. The congregation received Calvin Pletcher as a retired minister in the year 1960. The congregation also chose Merrill J. Yoder (born 1916) as its first visiting brother; installed July 31, 1960; ordained deacon Sept. 10, 1961.

The 1867 Sunday school was of course held only during the summer months, from spring through late fall. As late as 1894 the *Herald of Truth* reports the closing of the Olive Sunday School for the season on October 21. The average attendance in the Sunday school that year was fifty-five. The school was scheduled to open the first Sunday in April 1895, with Levi Barkey and Henry Long as superintendents, and Anna Holdeman as secretary-treasurer. The first mention in the *Herald of Truth* of the Sunday school's meeting all year round was in 1902: "We have an evergreen school." The average attendance in 1902 had risen to seventy-five. In 1903 Daniel H. Coffman was superintendent, C. N. Holdeman was assistant, Martha Yoder, secretary, Nettie Culp, assistant secretary, H. L. Horning, treasurer, and David Culp, chorister.

Funk's membership figures for the Indiana congregations in the 1880's show that Olive had a membership at that time of fifty. Even as late as 1905 the membership was but fifty-one. Under the ministry of D. A. Yoder, who was joined in 1917 by C. A. Shank, the congregation grew rapidly. In 1920 the membership had risen to 143 and in 1940 to 250. The formation of the Crumstown and Hudson Lake congregations, which now have respectively forty-four and twenty-eight members, may be part of the reason that the 1960 *Mennonite Yearbook* shows an increase of only three members over 1940.

In 1948 the 1888 meetinghouse was raised, and a new brick veneer placed on the building. Extensive alterations were also made in the meetinghouse at that time. (The addition, sixteen by forty feet in size, at the west end of the 1888 meetinghouse was made in the year 1920.) Dedicatory services were held for the remodeled and enlarged Olive meeting-house November 28, 1948, with S. F. Coffman of Vineland, Ontario, bringing the dedicatory address.

BLOSSER MENNONITE CHURCH

Section 16, Union Township, Elkhart County, Indiana

When the new meetinghouse was built at Yellow Creek in 1861, the old log meetinghouse of 1849 was moved to the farm of Enos Blosser in the northwest corner of Section 16 (the southeast corner of County Roads 9 and 46.) No congregation of any size ever developed at the Blosser Church. Occasional notices are found in the *Herald of Truth* down through the years. For example, Bishop Samuel Coffman of Virginia, the father of John S. Coffman, preached in the Blosser meetinghouse October 13, 1867. "A good number" were present. On March 18, 1868, Henry Yother of Illinois preached at the Blosser Church. The calendar of appointments printed in 1871 *Herald of Truth* shows that services were then held at Blosser every four weeks, alternating with the Christophel services which were also held every four weeks. The Blosser services fell on the same Sunday as the Elkhart and Shaum congregations every other service, but never conflicted with the Yellow Creek and Holdeman services. John F. Funk started a Sunday school in the Blosser meetinghouse in the year 1869. In private notes of John F. Funk of the 1880's he lists a membership in the Blosser Church of fifty.

The only two ordinations ever conducted in the Blosser meeting-house for the Mennonites of the Indiana-Michigan Conference were those of Jacob H. Wisler, deacon, 1872, apparently by John M. Brenneman of Ohio; and Martin E. Kreider, preacher, 1873, who died four years later. Deacon Wisler also did not remain permanently with the Blosser congregation, but transferred to the Nappanee Church about 1890, only to again move on to the Prairie Street Church ten years later.

The Blosser Church was always more or less of an outpost of the Yellow Creek Church, and never developed into a permanent congregation as did Olive and Holdeman. For the first thirty years the Blosser meetinghouse stood on the land of Enos Blosser without deed. In the year 1891, however, the Wisler congregation decided to build a new Blosser meetinghouse. The diary of Aaron Reed (1848-1934) reports as of December 6, 1890: "To Yellow Creek. Had collection meeting to build a new church house. Carried." The reference is to the new Blosser meeting-house. On August 13, 1891, Reed reported in his diary that he attended the harvest meeting at the new meetinghouse. It was on this occasion that the Wisler Mennonites deemed it prudent to secure a deed for the church property. Consequently Enos Blosser and Nancy his wife granted a scant acre of ground (150 square rods) "to Rev. Christian Shaum, Rev. John Weaver, and Rev. Christian Bare, members of the First Church of the Menonites." The consideration was $80.00. The date of the transfer was January 19, 1891. (Deed Book 81, page 293.) The Wisler Mennonites renovated the 1891 Blosser meetinghouse in 1947.

In the year 1907 the Wisler Mennonites divided into two groups, commonly known as Wisler and Old Order Mennonites. These two groups then alternated their services as between the Blosser and Yellow Creek meetinghouses. In the year 1959 the two groups amicably agreed that the Wisler group should take the Yellow Creek meetinghouse, while the Old Order group accepted the ownership of the Blosser meetinghouse.

The Mennonites of the Blosser congregation who were living in 1889 transferred to the newly formed Salem congregation when the Salem meetinghouse was built. The last-known reference in the *Herald of Truth* to services of the Indiana-Michigan Conference group in the Blosser meetinghouse is of the year 1889 when Eli Stofer of the Pleasant Valley congregation (in De Kalb County) preached there.

NAPPANEE MENNONITE CHURCH

Section 36, Locke Township, Elkhart County, Indiana

One of the finest summaries of the conditions in the Nappanee area something over a hundred years ago was written by David Burkholder, the first minister and bishop of the Nappanee congregation. Here is his story, in slightly condensed form and corrected spelling.

"Between the years 1854 and 1863 a number of Mennonite families from Mahoning and Columbiana counties, Ohio, where I was born and raised, moved to Elkhart County, Indiana. Most of them settled in Harrison Township along the Yellow Creek, where there was a church started already. Among the members there were the Christophels, Hoovers, Wislers, Weavers, Metzlers, Stauffers, Bixlers, Blossers, and Culps. A cousin of mine, Enos Burkholder, whose parents died near Harrisonburg in the Shenandoah Valley, Virginia, when he was a small child, inherited the snug sum of $4,000.00 when he reached the age of twenty-one. He brought this money with him to Indiana and invested it in a 273-acre tract of land in the Blosser settlement close to where Foraker now is. This cousin experienced various difficulties and finally became mentally ill. So in January 1854 my father and I brought him to Indiana, had a guardian appointed for him, and committed him to a mental hospital. As soon as this was done my father returned home, but I remained in Elkhart County and fired the engine for William Funk's sawmill, six miles south of Elkhart. Sometime in May my father returned to Indiana to buy land. We looked at different farms in Harrison Township, but did not have enough money to buy there. They were asking $1,200.00 to $1,500.00 for an 80-acre farm; so we had to go farther away from the large congregations and the market places. We found in Locke Township a 200-acre plot for $1,000.00, one mile south of what was then called Wisler Town, but which is now known as Locke (two miles north of Nappanee, and one-half mile west). Of course some people laughed at us and said we were foolish to go back there to our home in the marshes and bushes, where there was no railroad and no market place. I was then in my twenty-second year, and when I was ready to return to Ohio I hired two Culp boys to 'deaden' sixty acres for me [deaden seems to mean to kill the trees, probably by girdling them]. I remained six years in Ohio, and in August 1863 I again packed up and moved into my homestead during the Civil War, right after a heavy frost which killed everything. I came by way of the Pennsylvania Railroad to Warsaw, whence I had to haul my goods with teams to the Locke area. John Ringenberg [the Amish Mennonite preacher] and Elias Rupert did the hauling for me. I soon married [September 27, 1863] Mary Bucher who had come from Mahoning County, Ohio, the previous year. We soon put up a log house, and by November 10 we moved into it. The two young men had cleared ten acres for us before we came here, and John Ringenberg had put it out in wheat. But there were fifty more acres of 'deadening' to clear, and it looked dreadful. It was all grown up with briers and bushes, with trees and dead limbs lying around. In the fall of 1864 I was drafted, which was quite a drawback to me. I had not yet given my heart to God, and so had to hire a substitute for $600.00 where I could have got through with a fine of $400.00 [If I had been a member of the church]. I taught school the winter of 1863-64 in the Culp schoolhouse [one and one-half miles northeast of Nappanee]. The hardships which we had to endure here in the backwoods in those times can better be imagined than described. Goshen was our nearest market place and railroad station. Roads were full of corduroy 'bridges' [logs laid crosswise over soft spots] and very muddy part of the year. I helped to open the road which is now called Main Street, Nappanee, half a mile south from the corner to the Kosciusko County line, and also a mile north across the marsh, which was not then yet drained. In the spring there used to be water knee deep in it, and it was all grown up in bushes. In order to build a road through in the first place we had to cut down the bushes through the road limit and throw them on the road bed, then dig a ditch along each side and throw the mud on the brush in order to make it passable for teams to cross as they hauled in dirt. There were only seven men in the district to work; so we had to put in a lot of extra work gratis.

"There were a few deer here in Elkhart County at that time, and lots of wild turkey. We were lucky once in a while to get a good-sized gobbler on our table for a change. I believe there were more foxes in the county at that time than sheep. They would boldly come up to the barnyard in broad daylight and kill and eat sitting hens, together with a nest full of eggs. Raccoons were also plentiful and made havoc in the cornfields. Some places it looked as if hogs had gotten into the cornfield. The hunters did more harm than the coons; they would not hesitate to cut down the most valuable tree in the woods for the sake of catching a coon whose hide was worth perhaps forty or fifty cents. They cut a nice poplar tree down on our farm that was about four feet in diameter, and eighty feet to the first limb. Pheasants were very plentiful too; in the springtime during the sugar season, you could hear them drumming in every direction. Post offices and mail service were very inconvenient at that time. We got our mail from Goshen.

"In 1863 when we came out here there were strong congregations at Yellow Creek and at Holdeman. Members had moved into Elkhart County not only from Mahoning County, Ohio, but from other counties of that state and from other states. In the Holdeman congregation were the Freed, Lechlitner, Weldy, Davidhizar, and Holdeman families. At that time they had a log meetinghouse for a church building, but later [1875] they built a frame meetinghouse which was much larger. At Olive, then called the Shaum Church, there were quite a number of members. At the Blosser Church, about halfway between Nappanee and Yellow Creek, there was a small congregation.

"As stated before, land was high close to these churches and there were more families that were situated like we, who were not blessed so abundantly with earthly goods, and therefore had to go farther back where land was cheaper. There were some brethren in the Yellow Creek district who were quite well to do. For instance, George Culp, Sr., moved out here in 1849 when land was cheap. He was the father of eleven children, ten sons and one daughter, and he had eighty acres of land for each child. John Culp, commonly known as Uncle John, the uncle of John and Anthony Culp of Harrison Township, and of Henry Culp of Union, came to Harrison Township in the early 1850's and settled near to where Foraker now is. In the course of time John became a backslider and a heavy drinker. But finally, God had mercy on him and gave him the victory and delivered him from sin. He lived to be extremely old, and died June 27, 1900, at the advanced age of ninety-five years, seven months, and twenty days. In the last few years he was blind. We visited him not long before he died and found his memory to be strong and clear. Uncle John chewed tobacco for fifty years, but one day

7

as he was sitting in a church service the minister touched on this evil filthy habit and among other things said, 'Let him that is filthy be filthy still.' This made such a forcible impression on his mind that he immediately quit using tobacco.

"When we came to the Locke area in the fall of 1863, a number of Mennonite families had already settled in Locke and Union townships in the vicinity of the Culp schoolhouse northeast of Nappanee. They had preaching services every four weeks by various ministers from the Holdeman and Yellow Creek districts. Among those who preached for the Mennonites of Locke Township were John M. Christophel, Christian Christophel, Martin Kreider, Daniel Brundage, Jacob Wisler, Christian Bare, and later Bishops Jacob Beutler and Henry Shaum. The first Mennonite members in Locke Township were Henry Culp, wife and daughter Lydia; Elias D. Rupert and wife Mary Ann; Christian P. Housour and wife Sarah; Justus Walter and wife Elizabeth; and Daniel Metzler and wife Barbara, a total of eleven. In 1865 my wife and I joined the little flock, making a total of thirteen members. We were all from Mahoning County, Ohio, except C. P. Housour and Daniel Metzler's wife. Daniel Metzler had come to Indiana about 1861, and about a year later was married to Barbara Stahly, daughter of Christian Stahly who owned the eighty acres on the northwest corner of Nappanee, the tract running north and south. He was a shoemaker by trade. His log house stood where Kauffman's store is now located. The Baltimore and Ohio Railroad was built through here in 1875 [the 1881 County History states that it was laid out in 1874]. Justus Walter came here about 1856 and located on eighty acres one mile east and one and one-fourth miles north, on what is now known as the old Walter place. Henry Culp, Sr., came here about 1858 and located on the farm on which the Culp schoolhouse now stands. He was an industrious and hard-working man; he had a shingle machine and was also a farmer. He died in 1875 at the age of forty-seven years. Elias D. Rupert and wife came here about the same time as the Culps and located on an eighty-acre farm on what is now called East Market Street on the south side, opposite the Brethren Church. They moved to Lagrange County soon after we got here. Christian P. Housour and wife lived on what was later known as the Emmert farm on East Market Street.

"About 1867 the small frame schoolhouse was built on North Main Street. We then abandoned the Culp schoolhouse as a place of worship and from that time on we held our services in the Nappanee schoolhouse every four weeks until the year 1878 when a new brick schoolhouse was built. We then bought the old frame schoolhouse and remodeled it somewhat, and put new seats in it. It is now the Hoover barn.

"The preaching thus far had nearly all been in the German language and the attendance was small. About this time the Sunday school was organized. On May 15, 1880, I was ordained to the ministry and the church was considered organized. I had charge of the congregation, and we had preaching every two weeks. From 1863 until 1880 we received six members by baptism, four from other denominations, two moved in from other districts, making a total of twelve. We lost the following: five died, one went to another denomination, and two became backsliders. So the membership about New Year's Day, 1880, was eighteen. A number of families of Old Order Amish later united with our congregation and about 1888 [according to Bishop Jonathan P. Smucker's records, 1889] Preacher Jacob Bleile came over with his family of five members from the West Market Street Amish Mennonite congregation and assisted me in the work. A good many Mennonite families moved in from other districts so that our membership increased quite rapidly. After working with us for about ten years Bro. Bleile objected to a conference decision that was passed in the Nappanee Church on the temperance question, and became dissatisfied and quit preaching about four years before his death, which occurred in 1902. I was then left alone in the ministry again for a year or more. On January [15], 1899, a young brother, Frank Hartman, son of Adam Hartman, about eighteen years of age, was ordained to the ministry by Bishop John F. Funk. He possessed talent along some lines and was an expert in memorizing. He could write down his sermon, read it over several times, and he then had it by heart. But he lacked Mennonite principles and discarded our rules of order. After serving a few years he became dissatisfied with the simple nonresistant Mennonite doctrine, left the church, and united with the Evangelical denomination where he had more liberty, and where he received a salary. That left me alone again in the ministry for several years, until 1903 when Preacher Noah Metzler moved here from the Yellow Creek district. He assisted me in the ministry for about four years until he died in 1907. That fall [August 18, 1907] Ezra Mullet was ordained [by me], who is now a colaborer with me in this congregation. The church was without a deacon most of the time since it was organized until about 1890 when Jacob Wisler, who had been deacon in the Salem congregation, transferred into the Nappanee district and served us for a number of years until he moved to Elkhart [about 1900]. Then [on April 8, 1906, according to the *Herald of Truth* and the *Gospel Witness*] Franklin B. Maust was ordained as a deacon.

"Our records show that there were eighteen members in the congregation on January 1, 1880, and during the next seventeen years our membership increased as follows: received from other denominations, twelve;

moved in from other districts, sixteen; received by baptism, seven; received from the Salem congregation, three. In this same period we lost by death four, and six moved out of the district. This means that in 1893 we had a membership of forty-seven. By the year 1893 the old schoolhouse was too small, and the question of building a new meetinghouse was discussed pro and con. In the spring of 1893 we had a special business meeting at which time we came to the conclusion that we would build. We therefore appointed the following building committee: J. B. Weldy, D. Lehman, N. A. Lehman, Jost Yoder, and Henry Culp. It was their duty to plan the building, find a location, and let out the contract, which they did. The job was given to Coppes Brothers and Zook. The expense of the building proved to be somewhat heavy because only a few of the members were at that time able to give very much. We appealed to other congregations for help and some of them responded quite liberally, not only in Indiana, but also in Ohio and Pennsylvania. Isaac Eby of Lancaster sent us a check of $100.00. Businessmen of Nappanee and elsewhere also donated considerable money, so that the debt was reduced to about five or six hundred dollars on which we paid interest for several years. But in the course of time as the congregation increased numerically, and prospered financially through God's blessings, the debt was finally canceled.

"The members of the church in 1893 were as follows: David Burkholder and wife; Jacob Bleile and wife; Fred, Caroline, and Sophia Bleile; Catharine (Weber) Culp; J. B. Weldy and wife; Nelson Maust and wife; Irene Culp; Jost Yoder and wife; Mary Osborn; Cornelius Mast and wife; Dan Beverstein and wife; Christian Stahly and wife; Jacob Smeltzer and wife; George Culp, Sr.; Alvin and Emma Housour; Benjamin Maust and wife; Sarah Coppes; N. A. Lehman and wife; Yared Defrees; Jacob Wisler and wife; Anna Wisler; "Dutchie" Defries; Klaas Fisher and wife; C. M. Housour and wife; Elizabeth Walter; Joe Hamsher and wife; and Barbara Hoover: a total of forty-seven.

"Sometime after the new meetinghouse was built we had preaching every Sunday and started young people's meeting, and had a series of meetings about every year, which created a greater interest in the church, and was the means of gathering lost souls into the fold of Christ."

Before leaving the account of David Burkholder a number of facts should be mentioned, in order to avoid possible misunderstandings. There are a number of references in the *Herald of Truth* to the Locke congregation. This seems to refer to the Nappanee Church. The town of Locke was laid out in the year 1867, two and a half miles northwest of Nappanee. Nappanee was laid out in 1874, the same year the plans were made for the building of the Baltimore and Ohio Railroad. And even after there was a tiny village at the location of the present Nappanee, the village was still called Locke Station. Nappanee was named after a town in Canada which was spelled Napanee. For many years some people spelled Nappanee, Indiana, with one p and others with two. Mention is made, for example, in the 1872 *Herald of Truth* of four persons who were baptized at Locke and added to the church. This referred to what we now know as the Nappanee congregation. John F. Funk recorded in his diary for September 8, 1889, that Nappanee had services only every four weeks, and added that they ought to have a meeting at least every two weeks!

When the Nappanee congregation was going to build its 1893 meetinghouse Jacob B. Weldy purchased the lot himself, and in turn gave a deed to the trustees on April 27, 1894, for one acre of ground. The price was $575.00. The deed was made out to the trustees of the Old Mennonite *(sic)* Church, David Burkholder, Jacob B. Weldy, and Yost I. Yoder. (Deed Book 90, page 52.)

John F. Funk was much opposed to the dedication of church buildings. He therefore recorded simply in his diary, October 29, 1893, that the new meetinghouse in Nappanee was "opened" this afternoon; J. F. Funk preached. John S. Coffman reported in his diary: "This a.m. at six I started from home in Dinehart's two-seated buggy for Napanee [*sic*] where I arrived at nine in good time for the dedication services for their meetinghouse. Services at nine thirty, standard. A densely crowded house. A good many preachers present. I spoke from the text I often used, Haggai 2:9. The glory of the Christian age. What dedication means. This house will be dedicated if holy people use it. Went over dinner with old Sister Coppes. We started home at three." Coffman returned to Nappanee in 1894 and held a series of meetings. He was disappointed that "only three persons came out to confess Christ at all these meetings."

For many years David Burkholder and Ezra S. Mullett served side by side in the congregation on North Main Street. In 1923 the tragic division occurred in a number of Indiana-Michigan congregations. On this occasion thirty-five members withdrew from the North Main Street Mennonite Church and transferred to the West Market Street Amish Mennonite congregation, while fifty members went over to the North Main Street Mennonite Church from the West Market Street Amish Mennonite congregation.

The North Main Street Mennonite Church has long had the usual activities of the Mennonite congregations of the area. As was indicated above, Sunday school was started in the neighborhood of 1880; Bishop Homer F. North thinks possibly as early as 1878. The *Herald of Truth* in 1895 reported that the church was gaining a little "in strength and numbers." The correspondent added, "They maintain a good Sunday school in their church house. . . . Some of the members are also interested and take an active part in a Union Sunday School a few miles west of town." Young people's Bible meetings were started in the Nappanee congregation about 1908. The sewing circle was organized about two years later. Midweek meetings were started about 1920. H. F. North reports: "We have mostly Bible Study followed with prayer meeting, sometimes teachers' training." A mission outpost was started at Osceola, Indiana, in October 1951. It was organized as a congregation July 29, 1956, with twenty-six charter members.

In the year 1926 Homer F. North, who was formerly a lay leader in the West Market Street Amish Mennonite congregation, was ordained to the ministry. In the interval from the division of 1923 until that date various ministers supplied the pulpit, including D. D. Troyer. During the ministry of Homer F. North the Nappanee congregation prospered in a remarkable way. He was ordained bishop in the year 1954. Franklin B. Maust served as deacon until his death in 1932. Ezra P. Bleile was ordained deacon in 1938 and is still living. Mitchell D. McCloud was ordained to assist Deacon Bleile in 1953 but died six years later. Richard W. Yoder was licensed to assist in the ministry in the year 1956, and two years later he was ordained as a preacher. He was installed as pastor in 1960. He received the Th.B. degree from Goshen College Biblical Seminary in 1956. Clyde L. Hershberger and Alvin R. Miller were ordained as deacons for the congregation in 1960. About the year 1955 a few families withdrew from the congregation and affiliated with the Gospel Light Mission, a small group of people who meet in a hall on South Main Street, Nappanee. The man responsible for the movement was a former Mennonite from Pennsylvania, Gerald C. Derstine.

The Nappanee congregation long remained one of the smallest Mennonite churches of Northern Indiana, for many years held church services only every four weeks, and was rather slow to adopt the Sunday school. In the year 1905 the membership was listed as 100, in 1920 it had risen to 169, and the congregation had slightly passed the 200 mark when Homer F. North was ordained preacher in 1926. By 1940 the membership had risen to 305, and in 1960 to 358.

The 1893 meetinghouse, which had been built at a cost of $2,800.00, was enlarged in the year 1912, and a basement was added. In 1921 a balcony was put into the building. In 1952 the entire building was enlarged and remodeled at a cost of $46,359.49. It is one of the finest Mennonite church buildings in Northern Indiana. New church furniture cost an additional $4,800.60. The seating capacity of the 1952 meetinghouse is 450. The 1952 meetinghouse was dedicated in October 1953. About five years later the congregation built a splendid cabin a short distance southwest of the meetinghouse at a cost of $16,490.97; it was first used in 1958.

CLINTON BRICK MENNONITE CHURCH

Section 10, Clinton Township, Elkhart County, Indiana

We must now leave the churches west of Goshen for the time being, and go east of the city to Section 10, along what is now State Highway 13, four and one-half miles north of the village of Millersburg. The first Mennonites began moving into this area about the year 1845. According to tradition the first log meetinghouse was built in the year 1854. During the early years of the Clinton Brick congregation the pulpit was supplied by the ministers from Yellow Creek, six miles west of Goshen. No deed was given for this land until November 14, 1856, when Joseph and Elizabeth Kauffman and Stephen R. and Martha Smith conveyed to Andrew Kauffman and Henry Hoover, trustees of the Menonite (sic) Church, and to their successors in office, two lots in Section 10, Clinton Township, for a consideration of $11.00. (Deed Book 20, page 507.) In addition to the members who were trustees, it is known that Isaac and Charlotte (Swartz) Hoover moved from Haldimand County, Ontario, to Elkhart County in 1854. The first resident minister was a Mennonite from Switzerland named John Nusbaum, who was ordained preacher in Ashland County, Ohio, in 1827, and who settled in Clinton Township in 1860. He preached until his death in 1876. His son, John Nusbaum, Jr., was ordained deacon at a very early date, prior to the Civil War, and served until his death in 1900.

John M. Brenneman, of Elida, Ohio, spent the night of October 19, 1865, "with Pre. Jacob Wisler [of the Yellow Creek congregation]. On Saturday I went with him to Clinton Township, eight miles east of Goshen, where we held meeting in the afternoon and received a new member into the church by water baptism. On Sunday [October 22, 1865] we had meeting at the same place again, commemorating our Lord's death by the breaking of bread, and ordained to the ministry a brother by the name of William Pletcher." (Pletcher was the grandfather of Curtis Pletcher of Goshen.) The *Herald of Truth* contains many references to another ordained man in the Clinton Brick congregation, Deacon John A. Hoover, son of Preacher Henry Hoover of Pennsylvania, who was serving as deacon at Clinton Brick in 1864, and possibly earlier, and who died in 1907. In the year 1880 the Clinton Brick congregation replaced their log meetinghouse with a new brick structure, in which the opening services were held October 30, 1880. Henry Miller of the Shore congregation opened the meeting, Preacher J. S. Coffman preached on the "Consecration of the heart rather than churches" (Coffman diary), and Preacher J. J. Weaver of the Shore congregation closed the meeting.

In 1875 the ministers were therefore the aged Preacher John Nusbaum, the young Preacher William Pletcher, and the two deacons—John Nusbaum and John A. Hoover. William Pletcher was killed by a tornado in 1877. Another minister in the early life of the congregation was Preacher Henry Martin, who was born in Lancaster County, Pennsylvania, who was ordained a preacher in the Slate Hill meetinghouse of Cumberland County, Pennsylvania, who served as a minister in Wayne County, Ohio, and who moved to Clinton Township, Elkhart County, in 1874, at the age of seventy-two. He was the maternal grandfather of Bishops John and David Garber, and died in 1883. Another early minister in the congregation was Abraham Hoover, whose wife Martha (Garber) was the aunt of Bishops John and David Garber. Hoover was the son of Abraham Hoover and Christena (Martin), both of Lancaster County, but who later lived in Wayne County, Ohio, and who came to Indiana late in life. Abraham Hoover bought land in Middlebury Township in 1847. We know from the *Herald of Truth* that he was a preacher as early as 1868, and in 1866 John Lapp of New York state referred to him as a deacon. Hoover served as a preacher for possibly twenty years, but seems to have been silenced. In his late years he was a member of the Methodist Episcopal Church. In 1884 Preacher Peter Y. Lehman moved into the district, after having served for many years as a minister in the Lakeville congregation in St. Joseph County, Indiana. Preacher John C. Gnagy served as a minister in the Clinton Brick congregation from about 1881 until his death in 1889. Gnagy had earlier been an Amish preacher, and he united with Clinton Brick in 1881. In those days a man was free to move anywhere, and his office was automatically recognized wherever he located.

Deacon John Nusbaum died in 1900, and Deacon John A. Hoover was quite feeble by that time. About 1900 Deacon Jacob G. Long of the Olive congregation moved east of Goshen and served in the Clinton Brick Church until his death in 1903. Jacob C. Hershberger served as deacon from 1901 until 1911 at Clinton Brick, after which he transferred to the Middlebury congregation. Deacon Daniel H. Coffman, brother of John S. Coffman the evangelist, moved into the Clinton Brick area and served as deacon from 1905 until his death in 1941. Meanwhile other preachers had been ordained. David Garber, later a widely known evangelist and bishop, was ordained preacher in 1889, but soon entered the evangelistic field and moved to Ohio in 1894. His older brother, John

Garber, a man of much less ability, was ordained preacher in 1892, and bishop in 1903. Samuel Honderich was ordained preacher in 1902, but five years later he moved to Toronto, Ontario, where he entered mission work, but did his lifework at Filer, Idaho, where he is still living. Preacher John C. Springer of White Cloud, Michigan, moved to Indiana in 1908, but remained only about a year. He died in 1910 of tuberculosis. Finally the long-time preacher of the congregation was ordained: Amos Nusbaum, son of Deacon John Nusbaum, and grandson of Bishop Henry Miller of the Shore Church. Amos Nusbaum was ordained preacher in 1907 and served until his death forty-seven years later. Charles M. Bute, a deacon from Minnesota, served in the Clinton Brick Church from 1928 until 1932. In the year 1936 Samuel S. Miller, son of the well-known bishop, D. D. Miller, was ordained to the ministry. He served at Clinton Brick until 1953, with the exception of two years, 1946-48, when he was a schoolteacher near Walkerton, Indiana. Samuel located with the Hopewell congregation in 1953 where he is now serving as bishop and pastor. Harold Lehman was ordained deacon in 1939 and served for twelve years.

The 1880 brick meetinghouse was enlarged, and a basement was added, in 1919. Ten years later electric lights were added to the building and in 1945 a balcony was built. Tragedy struck December 7, 1945, when the building was burned to the ground. At that time things looked very dark for the congregation. The next year the congregation was left temporarily without a minister, and in 1951 without a deacon. The congregation refused to accept defeat, however, and a new brick meetinghouse was completed in 1947 at a cost of $34,000.00 It was dedicated December 7, 1947. It should be stated that much credit is due O. S. Hostetler, who served as the long-time bishop of the congregation. One more ordination remains to be mentioned, that of John M. Troyer, who was chosen deacon in 1952, and who served seven years before removing to the state of Oklahoma. John J. Yoder, an Ohio minister who came to Goshen to take seminary work, began to serve as a minister in the Clinton Brick congregation in 1955, and became pastor on December 6, 1959. A north wing was added to the building in 1961.

It should also be stressed that the congregation prospered splendidly under the pastoral leadership of A. H. Kauffman. When he came to Clinton Brick in 1947, the membership of the congregation stood at 123. Within five years the congregation voted to ordain him bishop.

The congregation has the usual activities of the Mennonites of Northern Indiana. According to Milo Kauffman, a union Sunday school was started in the Clinton community about 1873. It became a Mennonite Sunday school about seven years later. It was not until the year 1896, however, that it became "evergreen." A young people's Bible meeting was organized March 10, 1896. A sewing circle was organized in the congregation in 1920. Regular midweek meetings began in the congregation about 1945.

The congregation did not grow very much prior to 1940. According to the notations of John F. Funk the membership of the Clinton Brick congregation in the 1880's was seventy-five. In 1905 it was still seventy-five. By 1920 it had risen to ninety-six, by 1940 to 101, and the 1960 *Mennonite Yearbook* gives a membership of 205.

PRAIRIE STREET MENNONITE CHURCH

1316 Prairie Street, Elkhart, Indiana

In the cemetery of the Prairie Street congregation on Hively Avenue, Elkhart, there is a tombstone with this inscription:

John Fretz Funk
Born in Bucks Co., Pa., April 6, 1835
Died in Elkhart, Jan. 8, 1930
Salome Kratz Funk
1839-1917
Bishop Funk was converted in Chicago,
Baptized at Line Lexington, Pa., 1859
Founded "Herald of Truth" and "Herold der Wahrheit"
In Chicago 1864.
First publication of the
Mennonite Church in America.
Married Salome Kratz of Bucks Co., Pa., 1864
Called to Ministry of the Gospel 1865
Moved his Printing Press to Elkhart 1867
Founded Prairie St. Mennonite Church 1871
Ordained bishop 1892
Bro. Funk was widely known as an aggressive
Leader in Sunday School and Church Movement
Psalm 103
Let me die the death of the Righteous. Num. 23:10

Who was this bishop, represented as the founder of the Prairie Street Mennonite Church? He was the great-great-grandson of Henrich Funck of Franconia, which is now in Montgomery County, Pennsylvania. The genealogical line is as follows: Henrich—Abraham—John—Jacob—John F. Funk. John was the son of Jacob Funk (1796-1875) and Susanna Fretz (1802-1890). John was born, as the tombstone reports, on April 6, 1835. In 1854, when nineteen years of age, he began teaching school in Hilltown Township, Bucks County, Pennsylvania. He taught several years during which time he took two summer terms at Freeland Seminary, now Ursinus College, Collegeville, Pennsylvania.

In the spring of 1857 at the age of twenty-two, Funk went to Chicago and entered the employ of his brother-in-law, Jacob Beidler, who was in the lumber business. He remained in Chicago ten years.

During the winter of 1857-58 he attended evangelistic services at the Third Presbyterian Church, and was converted. But he later jokingly told a friend that God had not predestined him to be a Presbyterian. He returned to his parental congregation in Bucks County, the church at Line Lexington, where he was baptized by Bishop Jacob Kulp on February 13, 1859, while in his twenty-fourth year.

Upon returning to Chicago he threw himself into the work of the Lord. The area of his special interest and activity was the Sunday school. Funk had attended a Sunday school in a Baptist Church in Bucks County; and as a boy of nine had memorized over 1,600 Bible verses. In Chicago Funk worked hand in hand with another Sunday-school worker, who later became an international figure, D. L. Moody. In 1861 Funk became superintendent of the Milwaukee Depot Mission Sunday School. At one point he was a pupil in one Sunday school, a teacher in a second, and the superintendent of a third!

As a young man Funk burned with the desire to awaken his denomination from its sleep, and lead it to a more fruitful life and witness. As a symbol of this desire we may mention his 1863 booklet, *War—Its Evils—Our Duty*, published in the very midst of the Civil War years.

In January 1864 two major events occurred in the life of Funk. First, he launched the first church paper in the life of his denomination, the *Herald of Truth*, in two editions, German and English. Secondly, on January 19, 1864, he was united in marriage with Salome Kratz of his native Bucks County. Six children graced this home: Martha, 1864-1930, who never married; Susan Mary, 1866, died at six months, and was buried in the Graceland Cemetery, Chicago; Phoebe, 1867-1918, who married A. B. Kolb; Rebecca, 1870, died at twenty-seven days; Grace Anna, 1874, died in her second month; and John Edwin, 1880, died at thirty-one days.

Funk somehow learned that there was a small congregation of Mennonites in Grundy County, Illinois, which was worshiping in a schoolhouse. It was there that John M. Brenneman, the active bishop who served the entire Midwest as a spiritual father, ordained Funk as a preacher on May 28, 1865. But Funk did not long serve in Grundy County. He had become interested in the Mennonite settlement in Elkhart County, Indiana.

As early as 1862 Funk had attended the annual Indiana Conference. He was deeply impressed with the prosperous condition of the church in this area, and also with the ability of Bishop Brenneman of Allen County, Ohio, who presided. The consequence was that on his thirty-second birthday anniversary, April 6, 1867, John F. and Salome Funk, and their little Martha, located in Elkhart, which was then a town of 3,100. Baby Phoebe entered their home on May 30 of that year. Here Funk lived for the remainder of his long and eventful life. His wife Salome lived with him in holy matrimony for fifty-three years, and died September 5, 1917. As she was slipping away the old patriarch patted her cheek and said, "It's all right, Mother; you are going Home."

Perhaps Funk's biggest disappointment in Elkhart County was the finding of no Sunday schools among the Mennonites. He was instrumental in organizing a number, beginning with the Shaum (now Olive) congregation in 1867. The May *Herald of Truth* for that year pleaded eloquently for the establishment of Sunday schools. Funk also became an author, his most effective book being a polemic entitled, *The Mennonite Church and Her Accusers.* Even more significant was his contribution as a publisher. In this area his two most significant publications were undoubtedly the English edition of the *Martyrs Mirror,* and *The Complete Works of Menno Simon[s].* He was also an important organizer. Two of the organizations which he fathered were the "Mennonite Aid Plan," a church mutual aid fire insurance company which was organized in 1882, and which by 1895 covered ten states and represented property assessed for a total of $1,700,000.00; and secondly Funk organized the "Mennonite Evangelizing Fund," which developed into our General Mission Board, the Mennonite Board of Missions and Charities.

We must now pass by the history of Funk's huge printing business and turn to the life of the Mennonite Church in Elkhart which Funk founded. This congregation is now known as the Prairie Street Mennonite Church. Funk probably saw to it that occasional services were held in private homes in Elkhart almost as soon as he located in the city. For example, in February 1868 Preacher C. D. Beery of Burr Oak, Michigan, preached in Elkhart. On December 4, 1870, regular services were begun in the home of Deacon H. B. Brenneman, brother of the noted Daniel Brenneman. On December 10, 1870, Jesse C. Rush and Eliza Jane his wife conveyed to John F. Funk, H. B. Brenneman, A. K. Funk, and others, as representatives of the "Mennite" Church, Lot number 31 in the Pleasant Point Addition to the town of Elkhart, for a consideration of $350.00. (Deed Book 40, page 434.) The meetinghouse was completed in 1871, in size thirty-six by forty feet, at a cost of $1,200.00

The congregation grew slowly but steadily under the ministry of

John F. Funk. At first the services followed the traditional pattern, every other Sunday. But about two years later, an innovation was made: services were held weekly. But this was nothing compared with the other innovations of the Prairie Street congregation: teachers' meetings, to assist Sunday-school teachers with their preparation, were held in the Prairie Street congregation as early as 1874; children's meetings by 1882; Bible Readings (which later developed into young people's Bible meetings) by 1887. In all these areas Prairie Street was decades ahead of the country Mennonite congregations of the county. Prairie Street was also a pioneer in the organization of a women's sewing circle, 1900.

Mennonites must have felt somewhat unsure of themselves in a city environment. Should the women wear only their prayer veilings in the worship services, or should they keep on their large bonnets? In 1932 Mary E. (Mrs. C. A.) Shantz, mother of Mrs. R. R. Smucker, wrote of the early 1890's at Prairie Street: "When we first moved back here to Indiana every woman in the Elkhart Church kept her bonnet on in church. But we were taught to appear in our coverings, and not with bonnets on; so we, Grandma, Aunt Anna, and I, did so here too, every Sunday. It was not long until gradually one by one left their bonnets in the hall, and appeared in their coverings. Now no one thinks of leaving on her bonnet in church."

By 1890 there were sixty members in the Prairie Street congregation. The more progressive members from the country congregations often visited the Elkhart Church. In 1892, for example, 145 persons communed. On March 16, 1892, a meeting of the congregation was held to consider enlarging the meetinghouse. Funk summarized the meeting in his blunt style in his diary: "Much talk and nothing done." But eight months later, on November 28, 1892, it was decided to add twenty feet to the building. By December 30 the work was almost completed. In fact the first services were held in the meetinghouse on Christmas Day, 1892, according to the diary of John S. Coffman. During the first quarter of 1893 the Sunday school attendance at Prairie Street passed 200.

In 1879 a most effective teammate stepped to Funk's side. It was the devout and able preacher, John S. Coffman of the Shenandoah Valley, Virginia. Coffman was a schoolteacher who had a gracious personality, and who was a man of much prayer. He was disturbed about the lethargy and evangelistic ineffectiveness of the Mennonite Church of that era. As a sample of Coffman's concern one may note his diary entry for January 20, 1888: "My mind has been much taken up with the evangelizing work, and especially have I been considering how we can get our young people at Elkhart to make a start in the Christian life. Over this I have thought and wept and prayed, and I look to God for direction in the matter." It was this spirit of prayer and waiting upon God which made John S. Coffman succeed where Daniel Brenneman had failed. Coffman made no attempt to force open the door for evangelistic meetings, or as they were then called, "protracted meetings." Rather, Coffman fasted and prayed for God Himself to open the door in His own time and way. In 1881 the door unexpectedly opened. The Bowne congregation of Kent County, Michigan, invited Coffman to hold a series of meetings there. J. S. Coffman responded, and the evident blessing of God rested on the meetings. A number of persons were converted. The consequence was that other churches heard of the successful effort, and also called for Coffman to come and hold protracted meetings for them also. Soon converts were being counted by the dozens. Coffman frequently prayed audibly for a whole night. People would awaken at midnight or three o'clock in the morning and hear him earnestly crying to God for the church and for the lost. His lamentable death in 1899, when only fifty years of age, was a great loss not only to the Prairie Street congregation, but also to the entire Mennonite Church. The members of the Elkhart Ministerial Association attended Coffman's funeral as a body.

By 1890 Funk was the most influential man in the Mennonite Church. His *Herald of Truth* was a welcome visitor in a vast number of homes. He was a symbol of all that was good in the "great awakening" which was coming to the Mennonite Church. But it was almost a tragic mistake on June 6, 1892, when the aged bishop, Henry Shaum, ordained Funk as his successor in the Yellow Creek meetinghouse. Funk was ordained to serve the Mennonite congregations west of Goshen. John F. Funk had in his mind the conception of a bishop which had prevailed in Eastern Pennsylvania in his boyhood, and which was not to the liking of the more democratic Hoosier Mennonites. Funk was also disliked by some people for effecting so many changes in the church. Finally, Funk also now gave freer rein to his tendency to push through his program regardless of how his fellow ministers and their congregations felt about it.

Whatever the causes may be, Funk was keenly conscious of strained relations with his fellow ministers of Elkhart County during the 1890's. In 1900 the troubles became acute, especially in the Prairie Street congregation. The fall of 1900 an open break came, and the dissatisfied part of the congregation withdrew, and held separate services in private homes, later in a storeroom, and finally in the building of the Elkhart Institute, which stood diagonally across the street from the Prairie Street church building. Preachers Samuel Yoder and J. S. Hartzler ministered to the new group. Amish Mennonite Bishops D. J. Johns and Jonathan Kurtz looked favorably on the new group and gave them assistance.

Finally, in 1902, a special committee of church leaders took from J. F. Funk his bishop oversight on a temporary basis, this oversight to be restored to him by the favorable vote of the churches. Unfortunately Funk was never reinstated.

After Funk's deposition there was no longer any occasion for a divided congregation, and the two groups reunited. The 1902 *Herald of Truth* reported that the smallpox epidemic which had stopped the Prairie Street church services for several weeks had subsided, and services were resumed on March 10. "More than this, our hearts rejoiced because of a united church, for which we thank and praise God." Three years later, a correspondent wrote in the *Herald of Truth:* "Our church, which for some years had been torn by heartbreaking trials and siftings, is once more a unit, and the brotherhood rejoices to see that once more 'the people have a mind to work' in that sweet harmony and fellowship that characterized our congregation years ago." The bishops who succeeded John F. Funk in the oversight of the Prairie Street congregation were David Burkholder and J. K. Bixler, and finally for many decades D. A. Yoder. The present pastor and bishop, Howard J. Zehr, was preceded by J. D. Graber.

Bishop Funk gathered around himself a number of preachers who preached regularly for longer or shorter periods as his helpers: John S. Coffman, Samuel Yoder, J. S. Lehman, D. H. Bender, M. S. Steiner, George Lambert, and others. The ministers who succeeded Funk in the care of the Prairie Street congregation were J. E. Hartzler, 1910-13; William B. Weaver, 1914-20; J. S. Hartzler, 1923-33; John E. Gingrich, 1933-53; J. B. Shenk, 1953-57; and the present pastor, Howard J. Zehr, 1958-. Deacons who have served were H. B. Brenneman, 1867-87; Daniel H. Coffman, 1893-1904; George L. Bender, 1907-21; Oliver P. Grosh, 1920-ca. 32; and Harold S. Alexander, 1935-53. At the present time the congregation has no ordained deacon, but is served by visiting brothers.

Time does not permit a full report on the many branch Sunday schools and preaching outposts that were established by the Prairie Street congregation. In 1892, for example, they established a Sunday school in the South Side Ward schoolhouse, and soon had over 300 pupils. M. S. Steiner, 1866-1911, was superintendent, and A. B. Kolb served as song leader. Later, A. L. Buzzard and Aaron C. Kolb were sent to the empty Rowe church building, east of Elkhart, to organize a Sunday school; this work was later taken over by the Lutheran Church. Bishop Funk also found a United Brethren church building north of Elkhart where a Sunday school was established in the year 1900, chiefly under the direction of Jacob Burkhard and A. C. Kolb. Attendance reached the figure of 104. Another branch Sunday school was established on Cleveland Avenue which developed ultimately into an Evangelical congregation. In 1920 a Sunday school was started in the Sterling Addition in the east part of Elkhart in the McQuinsten schoolhouse. Harold S. Bender was superintendent. In 1928 another Sunday school was established, in co-operation with the Holdeman and Olive congregations, on the outskirts of Mishawaka. The work on Belmont Avenue was started in 1930 and developed into a flourishing congregation. In 1936 the Pleasant View congregation was founded in Jefferson Township east of Elkhart. In 1950 another work for Christ was begun on Independence Street which developed into the Roselawn congregation.

As a result of J. F. Funk's vision and program, Elkhart, Indiana, became the spiritual center of the Mennonite Church in the latter nineteenth century. Not only was it the mission center of the church, but it was the educational center as well. It was in the old Prairie Street meetinghouse of 1871 that J. A. Ressler and Dr. and Mrs. W. B. Page were commissioned for the India mission field on February 12, 1899. And more than five years earlier, on Monday, November 6, 1893, M. S. Steiner left Elkhart to establish a mission in Chicago. Funk wrote in his diary that Steiner was the first missionary of the (Old) Mennonite Church. He added: "May God bless him and his work." In 1931 Dora Shantz was sent to India as another missionary from this congregation. Other mission workers from the Prairie Street Church were Mrs. Protus Brubaker of Missouri; Melinda King, Fort Wayne; Carol (Miller) Kauffman, Hannibal, Missouri; and Lela Mann, Detroit.

The congregation suffered a blow on February 15, 1931, when fire damaged the 1871 meetinghouse so severely that it had to be rebuilt. Until a new house of worship could be erected, services were held in the Roosevelt school. The new basement church was sufficiently built by July 26, 1931, that basement services could be started. Over two years later, on December 17, 1933, the first services were held in the main auditorium of the new meetinghouse. But it was not until November 3, 1940, that the 1931 house of worship could be dedicated.

In 1905 the membership of the Prairie Street congregation stood at eighty. In 1920 the membership was 207, and in 1940, 351. The 1960 *Mennonite Yearbook* gives the membership of the Prairie Street congregation as 300. The explanation for this apparent drop is the creation of three daughter congregations: Belmont in 1929, with a present membership of 124; Pleasant View in 1936, with a present membership of 156; and Roselawn, established in 1949, and with a present membership of sixty-three.

The congregation enlarged and remodeled extensively its meetinghouse in the years 1959 and 1960, at an approximate cost of $125,000.00.

At the dedication services on Sunday, September 11, 1960, J. C. Wenger preached in the forenoon service, and H. S. Bender brought the dedicatory address in the afternoon service. The Prairie Street congregation now has a splendid house of worship, with excellent facilities for its well-rounded program of Christian education and evangelism.

SALEM MENNONITE CHURCH

Section 14, Union Township, Elkhart County, Indiana

The beginnings of the Salem Church lie in the history of the Christophel and Blosser congregations, which has already been given. There was an additional source for the charter membership of the Salem Church, and that was in the settlement of "Old Frisian" Mennonites from Balk in Friesland, The Netherlands, who migrated to Elkhart County in the years 1853 and 1854. A total of fifty-two souls came over, among which were nineteen members, one bishop, R. J. Smid, 1814-1893, and one preacher, R. J. Sijmensma, 1816-1854. The article on Balk in *The Mennonite Encyclopedia* indicates that a number of Dutch families who were not Mennonites accompanied the Mennonite groups in the 1853-54 emigration to America. Among the names of the Dutch families, including the non-Mennonites, were Belt, Brunsma, DeJong, DeVries, Douma, Duisterhout (now Darkwood), Duker, Hoogeboom, Hygema, Hytema, Krull, Nymyer, Pelsma, Postma, Rystra, Sijmensma, Smid (now Smith), Swart, Tromp, Vandeveer, and Visser (now Fisher).

Preacher Sijmensma, who had been ordained in Friesland in 1842, died in Elkhart County in 1854. But Bishop R. J. Smid, who had been ordained preacher in 1847, and bishop in 1849, served his people for about forty years in America and died April 26, 1893. Both Sijmensma and Smid are buried in the Whitehead Cemetery, across the road from the Maple Grove Church of the Brethren, two miles southwest of New Paris on County Road 46. The Frisian families settled in the west half of Jackson Township and the eastern part of Union Township. At first they seem to have held their worship services every four weeks, and later every two weeks. They conducted these services in the Frisian language. They met in private homes and schoolhouses, and sometimes in the Christophel meetinghouse; it is said that the Frisian Mennonites held meetings for about twenty years in a Rystra home. (The 1874 *Elkhart County Atlas* shows a J. Rystra farm one and one-half miles west of the Whitehead Cemetery and one mile south; this location is also two and one-half miles south of the Christophel meetinghouse.) Early records also mention services held at Jan Belt's. Once again, the 1874 *Atlas* shows that J. Belt lived directly across the road from the Christophel meeting-

8

house. Is it possible that the Frisian families referred to this church
building in terms of their member who lived close to it? It appears that
frequently the Frisian Mennonites held their Dutch services every other
Sunday, and worshiped with the Elkhart County Mennonites at the
Christophel church building on the intervening Sundays. In any case,
the so-called Hollanders were on perfectly cordial terms with the Old
Mennonites. These Frisians held strictly to nonresistance. Indeed it
was the desire to maintain the doctrine of nonresistance, together with an
effort to improve themselves economically, which brought them to
America in the first place. John F. Funk speaks in very respectful terms
of Bishop R. J. Smith. A private diary of January 2, 1887, mentions the
Dutch congregation worshiping in the Christophel meetinghouse. The
same diary for April 5, 1888, records: "Holland meetings started in
Whitehead schoolhouse." The Whitehead schoolhouse was located a
little more than a half mile west of the Whitehead Cemetery and one
mile south. Services were also conducted in the Swoveland schoolhouse,
one-half mile south of the Christophel meetinghouse, and one mile west.

When the Mennonites of Union and Jackson townships decided to
build what is now known as the Salem meetinghouse in the year 1889
they chose a rather central spot in reference to the Yellow Creek, Blosser,
and Christophel meetinghouses, and the Whitehead and Swoveland
schoolhouses. The Salem meetinghouse is four miles from the Whitehead
schoolhouse, three and a half miles from the Christophel meetinghouse,
two miles east of the Blosser meetinghouse, and five miles from the Yellow
Creek meetinghouse. The 1889 *Herald of Truth,* page 216, reports:
"The brethren in the Blosser and Christophel district in Elkhart County,
Indiana, have built a new meetinghouse, which is now about completed
and will be opened for public worship on Sunday, July 28." The meetinghouse was thirty-six by forty-six feet in size. A later issue of the
Herald of Truth reported a large attendance on the day of the formal
opening, including six ministers. The *Herald of Truth* added that the
new meetinghouse "will take the place of Christophel's and Blosser's."
When the congregation began to worship in the Salem meetinghouse it
was made up of approximately half Frisian families, and half "Old Mennonite" (Swiss) families.

The deed for the Salem meetinghouse was given by Henry and
Elizabeth Pletcher, and Samuel and Mary Pletcher, to Samuel Pletcher,
Levi A. Ressler, and Jacob K. Fisher, trustees of the Old Mennonite
Church, on January 8, 1889. The consideration for the acre of ground
was $5.00. (Deed Book 75, page 133.) Hartzler and Kauffman in their
Mennonite Church History of 1905 reported: "For many years they con-
ducted their services in their native dialect, but after the death of the

older members, and especially of their ministers, the remaining ones
united with the Salem congregation, and at present their posterity forms
a large part of that body of worshipers."

The quotation from Hartzler and Kauffman is misleading in one
respect; it would suggest that both the original Frisian Mennonite ministers were dead in 1889. As a matter of fact, Ruurd J. Smid served
actively until shortly before his death. His wife wrote in her diary for
April 16, 1893: "This was the last time Ruurd and I were together in the
meeting." She reported that on April 20 he became ill, and on April 26,
"in the morning at 4:00, he died; he was seventy-nine years, eight months,
and four days of age."

The first brother to be ordained in the Salem congregation after the
building of the new meetinghouse was John H. Bare, father of Serenus,
who was ordained deacon in the year 1894, succeeding Jacob H. Wisler
who had served in the district from 1872 until 1890 when he transferred
to the Nappanee congregation. He became preacher in the year 1905
after which he served an additional twenty-five years. The ordination of
Bare as preacher necessitated the choosing of another deacon for the
congregation; Isaiah Christophel was chosen in 1906 and served until
1912 when he was killed by lightning. That same year Noah Weaver
was ordained as a deacon to succeed Christophel, and served until 1926
when he removed to California.

A new chapter in the life of the church began with the ordination of
an able young man in 1918, Ray F. Yoder. He served as a preacher from
that year until 1937 when he was ordained as a bishop; he is still living.
Deacon Samuel D. Metzler was ordained deacon in 1932 and served until
his death in 1952. Bishop Yoder's brother-in-law and double first cousin,
Francis E. Freed, Sr., was ordained as a preacher in 1939, and is still
serving.

The present new era in the life of the church centers in Harold
D. Myers, ordained deacon in 1945, preacher in 1957, and bishop in 1960.
Dwight Newcomer was ordained deacon in 1958 but resigned that same
year. William McGrath served as a licensed minister in the congregation in 1954, but did not long remain there.

The 1889 meetinghouse was enlarged, and a basement added in 1919.
In 1940 Sunday-school classrooms were also built onto the building.

The Salem congregation has the usual activities of the Northern
Indiana Mennonite congregation. The Sunday school which was started
immediately following the building of the first meetinghouse of 1889,
with J. K. Fisher as Sunday-school superintendent, became "evergreen"
in the year 1908. In that same year, 1908, church and Sunday school
began to be held every Sunday. Young people's Bible meetings began

about the year 1912. The women's sewing circle of the congregation was organized about 1910. Regular midweek meetings began about 1935. Salem led all the congregations of the county, except Prairie Street, in holding evangelistic meetings. John S. Coffman gave the first public invitation in the country churches of Elkhart County at Salem in the year 1890. (Coffman diary, November 25, 1890.)

One of the distinguishing characteristics of the Salem congregation has been the retention of baptism with water in streams, which had been practiced by all the Mennonites of Northern Indiana, as well as the Amish Mennonites, in the late nineteenth and early twentieth centuries.

Perhaps the greatest tragedy in the life of the Salem congregation was the total loss of the Frisian element. Only a generation ago there were a considerable number of Hollanders in the congregation. Today there is not a single one left.

John F. Funk listed the membership of the Salem congregation in the late 1880's as sixty-five. By 1905 the membership had risen to seventy-five. In 1913 it was seventy; in 1920, sixty-two; in 1940, 147; and in 1960, 182. A part of the substantial growth during the 1950's was due to the transfer of a number of families from the Holdeman congregation.

GOSHEN COLLEGE MENNONITE CHURCH

South Main Street, Goshen, Indiana

The College Mennonite church building is located on Section 21 of Elkhart Township, Elkhart County. The occasion for the formation of a Mennonite Church in Goshen is explained in the *Herald of Truth* for September 17, 1903, as follows: Several Mennonite families lately moved to this city, who with those already here urged that church services be held. The group rented the First Christian Church on South Main Street, Goshen. They held their first services there on September 6, 1903, with Preacher J. S. Hartzler in charge. N. E. Byers, President of Goshen College, served as leader of the young people's Bible meeting in the evening. "Services will probably be held at the same place until the chapel room in the College building is completed."

The Goshen congregation, as it was thought of at that time, chose a poor time to be organized as far as the bishop situation in the conference was concerned. Prior to 1902 the Mennonite bishop for the congregations west of Goshen was John F. Funk, while east of Goshen P. Y. Lehman had the bishop oversight. Both of these bishops had been relieved of their oversight in the year 1902, which left only one Mennonite bishop in the entire conference, J. P. Miller of the White Cloud, Michigan, congregation. The congregation petitioned the Indiana-Michigan Mennonite Conference to be organized as a union congregation, composed of both Mennonite and Amish Mennonite members. J. P. Miller, representing the Mennonite conference, met with the group in the home of Preacher J. S. Hartzler in Goshen on Sunday evening, November 8, but evidently was himself not in favor of a union congregation. He declared that he found too much sentiment against the formation of a union congregation. The *Herald of Truth* reported: "A Mennonite congregation was organized at the home of Preacher J. S. Hartzler in Goshen on Sunday evening, November 8, by Bishop J. P. Miller of White Cloud, Michigan, with J. S. Hartzler as minister in charge. The Amish Mennonite members will probably take similar steps in the near future." This was precisely the opposite of what the congregation desired and intended. The November 8 meeting seems to have been the second meeting that Miller held with the congregation. Sunday school was organized, according to the *Herald of Truth,* on November 18, 1903, with N. E. Byers as superintendent, C. K. Hostetler, assistant, Lulu Greenwalt, secretary, A. B. Rupp, treasurer, C. Henry Smith, chorister, and E. J. Zook, superintendent of the intermediate and primary departments. The first meeting of the Sunday school was held November 27. Approximately 100 pupils were enrolled in this newly organized Sunday school.

Meanwhile the congregation continued its efforts to be a union church. A congregational meeting was held March 2, 1904, and a committee of four was chosen, two from each group, to manage the affairs of the church. J. S. Hartzler declared that as far as he was concerned the members of both bodies would have equal rights in the spiritual affairs of the congregation. The congregation then voted unanimously to organize as a union church. At that point the membership stood at fifty-seven.

By February 1904 there were a number of persons who desired to be baptized into the Mennonite Church. David Burkholder was ordained bishop on February 4 of that year by Bishop J. S. Shoemaker of Illinois. The congregation therefore summoned Bishop Burkholder to do the baptizing, which he kindly consented to do. In April of 1904 D. J. Johns similarly took the persons who wished to unite with the Amish Mennonites, to a stream and baptized them. This indicates that there was a rather keen awareness of the slight differences which then existed between the Mennonites and the Amish Mennonites, and perhaps also reveals the earnest desire of the congregation to co-operate with the two conferences involved. According to a note in one of John F. Funk's private notebooks of about the year 1907 there were sixty-three Mennonite members in the College congregation, and forty-five Amish Mennonite members: this information supplied to Bishop Funk by J. S. Hartzler, pastor. Rudy

Senger of the College congregation reported in the 1903 *Herald of Truth* that the young people's Bible meetings were being well attended and that the congregation was served by the ministering brethren J. S. Hartzler and Paul E. Whitmer. Officially, it appears that Hartzler was the pastor, but that he used Professor Whitmer part of the time to preach.

The first time that Bishop J. P. Miller came to interview the prospective Goshen congregation he had brought along D. J. Johns, the well-known Amish Mennonite bishop. But at the official organizational meeting of the *Mennonite* congregation, the fall of 1903, Miller was alone. Because the congregation kept quietly working toward a union church, a meeting of the congregation, representing both groups, Mennonite and Amish Mennonite, met with the Mennonite bishop, David Burkholder, and with the Amish Mennonite bishop, D. J. Johns, on October 26, 1904, and the union congregation was officially organized. This union congregation was jointly under the Mennonite and Amish Mennonite conferences, and was so reported in the *Herald of Truth* (page 380). David Burkholder and D. J. Johns had the joint oversight of the congregation, and the official ministers were J. S. Hartzler and I. W. Royer; it appears that Hartzler was pastor and I. W. Royer was his assistant. The congregation began meeting in the dining hall of what was then the girls' dormitory as soon as that was available. Early in 1904 when the Administration Building was completed, Sunday school and preaching services were held in the Assembly Hall. In the year 1906 A. S. Landis was accepted as a deacon in the congregation; he had moved to Goshen from Sterling, Illinois.

Pastor J. S. Hartzler was also busy with his work in Goshen College and in 1907 the congregation, feeling the need of more pastoral work, designated I. W. Royer to do it. The congregational records indicate that in 1908 the congregation gave $5.00 to the Mennonite Conference for its expenses, and an equal sum to the Amish Mennonite Conference. In 1910 the congregation chose Paul E. Whitmer to be its pastor, and it re-elected him for 1911. In 1912 it was decided that J. S. Hartzler and P. E. Whitmer should be "joint pastors." In 1913, because of the pressure of Professor Whitmer's college work, I. R. Detweiler became joint pastor with J. S. Hartzler. In 1914 I. R. Detweiler was chosen as pastor; in 1916 and 1917 he was re-elected. George J. Lapp served 1918-19, with I. R. Detweiler beginning again as pastor in May 1919. When I. R. Detweiler was elected acting president of Goshen College in 1920, he resigned as pastor of the College congregation. The church requested A. E. Kreider to assume the pastorate, but he declined. During 1920 and 1921 J. S. Hartzler seems to have supplied the pulpit. I. R. Detweiler was again serving as pastor 1922-23, although he had tendered his resignation as early as March 30, 1922. The congregation did not accept his resignation until June 14, 1922, and even thereafter Detweiler seems to have been in charge of supplying the pulpit. The congregation designated a committee, consisting of the brethren, J. S. Hartzler, A. S. Landis, and I. R. Detweiler, to try to find a regular pastor, June 22, 1922. In October of that year the congregation again discussed the resignation of I. R. Detweiler, and requested D. D. Miller, who had served as sole bishop of the congregation from 1917, to make provisions for the supply of the pulpit. Many members followed Detweiler to the Eighth Street Mennonite Church when he became pastor there.

The fall of 1923 was a trying one, both for the College and the College Mennonite Church, as well as for a number of other congregations in Northern Indiana. The Mennonite Board of Education decided to close Goshen College for the academic year, 1923-24, partly because of financial difficulties, and perhaps even more significantly, because the Board had lost confidence in the leadership of the College. The Executive Committee of the Indiana-Michigan Conference (both the Mennonite and the Amish Mennonite conferences had voted in 1916 to merge into a united conference under the name, Indiana-Michigan Mennonite Conference, which held its first meeting in 1917) was also gravely concerned with what it considered to be evidences of serious conformity to the fashions of the world in various places, and with a partial breakdown of the principle of separation from the world in general. The consequence was that a number of ministers were silenced in several congregations of Northern Indiana in 1923 and 1924. The fall of 1923 found the College congregation also in difficulty with the Executive Committee of conference, which difficulty was aggravated by the fact that the congregation had no pastor. It was decided that Bishop S. E. Allgyer of West Liberty, Ohio, should hold a series of meetings January 21 to February 4, 1923, which was done. He held twelve public meetings and visited about thirty homes. The Executive Committee of conference also met with the congregation as early as February 21, 1923, in an attempt to work out the matters of concern. J. S. Hartzler withdrew even from membership in the congregation on May 29, 1923, and transferred to the Prairie Street congregation.

D. D. Miller, bishop of the College Church, made a valiant effort to retain as many members as possible through the times of crisis which were rapidly developing during 1923. At the meeting of February 21, 1923, Bishop Miller explained to the congregation that it was necessary for him to abide by the decisions of conference even though certain actions were adopted by the conference that he did not approve of. At the meeting of February 21, 1923, contrary to the wishes of the members of the congregation who were eager to maintain congregational unity, it was decided to take a private counsel of the Goshen College Church members on this question: "Are you willing to stand by the Indiana-Michigan Conference?" This question had to be answered by yes or no. The late summer of 1923 Bishop Miller requested Preacher A. E. Kreider to supply the pulpit of the pastorless congregation, which he did. During 1923 and 1924 various families from the College congregation began to withdraw and to unite with the Eighth Street Mennonite Church, which was affiliated with the Central Conference of Mennonites. On August 17, 1924, the lay officers of the College Church sent a communication to A. E. Kreider expressing appreciation for the valuable services which he had rendered to the church "for more than a year."

The final straw came August 27, 1924, when the College congregation met to elect Sunday-school officers. It appears that many members of the congregation were by that time somewhat hostile to the conference Executive Committee for its stand on dress regulations, such as objecting to the wearing of hats by women, and other matters. The College Church had always been influenced by the College. Indeed, the leaders of the College tended also to serve as leaders of the congregation. The form of church government had always been strongly congregational. The congregation was therefore distrustful of any effort to reach into the disciplinary affairs of the congregation. On the other hand, the conference Executive Committee was concerned with what appeared to it to be unvarnished worldliness. A showdown appeared imminent. In any case, on August 27, 1924, when the congregation met to elect Sunday-school officers, Bishop D. D. Miller, accompanied by D. D. Troyer, representing the conference, appeared at the meeting. The secretary of the congregation, A. P. Shetler, recorded in his minutes: "Bro. Miller informed those present that it was of no use to reorganize, as such organization would not be recognized by conference or school board." There was a lengthy discussion of two hours.

The outcome of this struggle between the congregation and the conference resulted in the departure of a large number of members during 1923 and 1924. The *Mennonite Yearbook* for 1924 reported the 1923 membership figure, 213. It is reported that of the members of the congregation in 1923, only fifteen remained by the fall of 1924 when the congregation was reorganized. When the congregation was reorganized in September, 1924, Noah Oyer, Dean of the College, was designated as pastor, and D. D. Miller continued to serve as bishop. A. S. Landis, who was quite aged, and who had tried to resign in January, 1921, but had been retained by the congregation, was now no longer active as a deacon and his name does not appear in the 1925 *Mennonite Yearbook*. The reopening of Goshen College in September, 1924, brought to the congregation a substantial number of new teachers and other persons. In connection with the reorganization of the congregation each member who desired to affiliate with the group had to sign this statement: "We the undersigned reaffirm our loyalty to the principles of the Mennonite Church and are willing to work in harmony with the rules and regulations of the Indiana-Michigan Conference and to maintain the vital Christian principles for which the church stands." The result was that sixty-nine members signed, thus becoming the charter members of the reorganized congregation. During the school year of 1924-25 an additional fifty-seven persons united with the congregation, although seven letters were also granted. The consequence was that as of May 20, 1925, the membership of the College congregation stood at 108. This is also the figure which appears in the 1925 *Mennonite Yearbook*. Noah Oyer had seven church letters on hand on May 20 which would have actually brought the membership up to 115, had those members been received as of that date.

The high point in the membership of the College Mennonite Church prior to 1920 was probably 195 in the year 1913. It was in that year that the Eighth Street Mennonite Church (Central Conference Mennonite) was formed. In 1920 the membership stood at 176, and by 1923, when the trouble began, had reached for that time an all-time high of 213. After the reorganization of the congregation the growth was at first slow. By 1930 the membership had reached only 149. Pastor Noah Oyer died in 1931, to the great sorrow of congregation and College. He was succeeded as pastor by C. L. Graber in 1931. By the year 1940 the membership had climbed to 226. In 1942 C. L. Graber resigned, but his resignation did not become effective until S. C. Yoder was secured as his successor in 1943. S. C. Yoder became the first resident bishop of the congregation, relieving D. D. Miller of this responsibility. Under Bishop Yoder's leadership the College congregation prospered and thrived in a remarkable way. By 1950 when he turned over the pastorate to John H. Mosemann, formerly a missionary in Africa and more recently a professor in the Goshen College Biblical Seminary, the membership had risen to 416. Under the leadership of Pastor Mosemann, who was ordained bishop in 1956, the congregation continued its remarkable growth, so that by the beginning of 1961 the membership stood at 661. J. Robert Detweiler of the staff of the radio program, *The Calvary Hour*, and a minister in the Ohio and Eastern Conference, was secured by the congregation as assistant pastor in 1960.

It was not long after the formation of the College congregation until there began to be a concern to build a church building somewhere in the general area of the College in the southern part of the city of Goshen. As early as 1909 a majority of the members of the congregation favored erecting a house of worship. In a congregational meeting in 1916 the chairman of the "directors" (which served in a similar way to what is now known as a Church Council) was instructed to secure an option for a building site for the proposed church building. The matter was still being agitated in 1921 and the congregation seriously considered the purchase of three lots on the southeast corner of South Seventh and Franklin streets; these lots could then have been purchased for $35.00. Perhaps the difficulties of 1923-24 prevented the congregation from going ahead with plans to build. After the reopening of Goshen College in 1924, and the reorganization of the congregation, the group was weak numerically and therefore did little about a separate church building, except to start a building fund. In the middle 1950's the congregation once more took steps to have its own place of worship. The College was also faced with the need of greater chapel facilities. The outcome of this situation was the building of a church-chapel to serve both the congregation and the College, with the church and the Board of Education sharing in the building costs, which amounted to about half a million dollars. Ground was broken in 1957 for the proposed church-chapel. The first significant use of the still unfinished building was the holding of the 1959 sessions of Mennonite General Conference in August 1959. The building was dedicated April 3, 1960. In the forenoon session the dedicatory message was brought by Paul Erb, editor of the Mennonite Church organ, the *Gospel Herald*. In the afternoon President Paul Mininger of the College spoke on, "The Role of the Christian College in the Community," and Pastor John H. Mosemann spoke on, "The Role of the Church in the Community." Greetings were brought from the community by Attorney Charles W. Ainlay; from the churches of the city by Pastor Paul M. Brosy; from the Lilly Endowment, Incorporated, which had given a generous gift for the construction of the church-chapel, by Manning M. Pattillo; from the Indiana-Michigan Conference by the moderator, J. C. Wenger; from the Mennonite Board of Education by Nelson E. Kauffman; and from the student body of the College by Marlin Wenger. President Mininger and Pastor Mosemann united in leading the Litany of Dedication. Various choral groups of the College and congregation furnished special music in the morning, afternoon, and evening sessions.

The College congregation has tended to be a gathering place for ministers of the area who are without charge, or who have moved to Goshen to retire. At the present time (1961) there are twenty ministers in the congregation who have no pastoral responsibility, in addition to the five who have ministerial responsibility in the congregation.

The College Mennonite Church is today by far the largest congregation in the conference. It has tended to set a good pace for the rest of the conference in many respects, including missionary support, an active Sunday-school program, young people's Bible meetings, revival and evangelistic services, sewing circle work, women's missionary society, and the like. It has also been active, in co-operation with the Young People's Christian Association of the College, in establishing mission Sunday schools and outposts in Northern Indiana. Just a few illustrations will be given. Within eight years after the founding of the College congregation an outpost in North Goshen had been established. It was decided on September 5, 1911, that I. R. Detweiler, Rudy Senger, and C. L. Shank were to assume charge of the North Goshen Church. The Amish Mennonite Conference in June 1912 appointed a committee to investigate this mission effort. A year later, in 1913, the Amish Mennonite Conference deemed inadvisable the establishment of work in North Goshen "at present." The effort was evidently given up because of this conference action. The North Goshen congregation was established in 1936 through the efforts of the College Y.P.C.A. and the College congregation, and later the East Goshen congregation was formed as a daughter of North Goshen. In 1943 an outpost was started at Locust Grove, south of Elkhart, which by 1960 had a membership of fifty-four. In 1947 the Sunnyside work was begun in Dunlap, which by 1960 had developed into a congregation of forty-six members. Wawasee Lakeside Chapel was started in 1947. The College congregation and Goshen College have also conjointly brought to the Northern Indiana community excellent speakers representing missionary, relief, educational, and similar concerns. Goshen has become the spiritual center not only for the Mennonites of Indiana and Michigan, but also for the church of the Midwest. A great responsibility rests upon the College and the congregation to maintain a program which is dynamic and spiritual and which will conserve the best in the heritage of Christendom and of Mennonitism, for from this center are going out hundreds of young people to serve as the leaders of many congregations, institutions, and missions throughout the world.

LAKEVILLE MENNONITE CHURCH

Section 5, Union Township, St. Joseph County, Indiana

Mennonites began to move into the vicinity of Lakeville in Union Township, St. Joseph County, as early as 1865. The man who kept aware it would seem, of every last settlement of Mennonites, was Bishop John M. Brenneman of Elida, Ohio. The 1865 *Herald of Truth* contains the following account written by Bishop Brenneman: "On Tuesday the 17th [of October] I went with Preacher Daniel Brundage [of Elkhart County] to the southwest part of St. Joseph County, about twenty-five miles from the Yellow Creek Church. A small number of brothers and sisters are living there who have lately moved to that place. . . . We had meeting here three times on Wednesday and observed also the breaking of bread. On Thursday morning [October 19, 1865] we met again and ordained Bro. Peter [Y.] Lehman to the ministry, and Bro. Michael [Shank] to the office of deacon. . . ." The 1866 *Herald of Truth*, page 42, also makes mention of the small flock of God's children near Walkerton where the new minister is Brother Lehman. (This meant Lakeville.)

Some sort of difficulty seems to have arisen in the congregation by 1867, for on December 1 of that year Preacher John F. Funk of Elkhart and Deacon Joseph Holdeman of the Holdeman Church went to Lakeville and had a meeting on December 2 with the church. Funk reports in his diary that the difficulties were settled satisfactorily. Deacon Michael W. Shank was ordained preacher about the year 1867; it is said that Bishop Tilman Moyer of Ontario performed this ordination.

The 1875 *Atlas of St. Joseph County* shows that M. W. Shank owned 120 acres in the southwest corner of Section 5 of Union Township. The cemetery in which the Mennonites buried was located on the southwest corner of his farm, while the Dice schoolhouse, diagonally across the intersection, was located in Section 7 of Liberty Township. This cemetery is located on the northeast corner of the intersection of Oak and Riley roads, one and one-half miles south and two miles west of the village of Lakeville.

Buried in the cemetery, known as the Dice Cemetery, on the corner of Preacher Shank's farm are the bodies of such persons as Michael Shank (died in 1865), father of Preacher M. W. Shank; John Hoover, who died in 1867, and his wife Susanna, who died in 1865; David J. Hoover, who died in 1890; Michael Shank's wife, Susanna, who died in 1904; George A. Longaker, who died in 1902, and his wife Lydia, who died in 1866; and the children of J. M. and N. Reed.

In November 1870 Daniel Brenneman of Elkhart County visited "the brethren near Lakeville," and held two meetings. He reported that he enjoyed himself exceedingly well with the brethren and sisters. (*Herald of Truth*, 1871, page 9.) In the year 1867 Daniel Brenneman had spoken of the Lakeville neighborhood in connection with "the brethren Lehman and Shank." In 1881 John F. Funk refers to Michael Shank's schoolhouse near Lakeville. In February 1884 P. Y. Lehman sold his farm in Union Township and moved to Clinton Township, Elkhart County, east of Goshen, where he affiliated with the Clinton Brick congregation. In reporting this moving in his diary, Funk adds: "and his wife and daughter were badly hurt by the upsetting of the wagons." (See also the *Herald of Truth* for March 1, 1884.) In the 1880's Funk refers in private notes to the Lakeville congregation in St. Joseph County as being pastored by Michael Shank, and as having twelve members.

When Jacob Wisler led his schism from the Elkhart County Mennonite Church in 1872, Preacher Peter Lehman evidently followed Wisler, for the *Herald of Truth* for July 1881 reports that Preacher Peter Lehman and his wife were received back into the fellowship of the church. This withdrawal of P. Y. Lehman was of course no help to the congregation. Neither was the removal of the other minister, M. W. Shank, to Finney County, Kansas, in the year 1886. When Susanna Hoover, wife of David Hoover of Markham, Ontario, died in 1904 at the age of seventy-six, the *Herald of Truth* reports that she was a faithful Mennonite, and that her body was buried near Lakeville. Services were conducted by the Elkhart County Mennonite preachers, Noah Metzler and J. W. Christophel, also by Jacob Hildebrand, evidently of Virginia. David Hoover was not the only one at Lakeville who came from Markham, Ontario. Preacher Michael Shank was the son of Michael Shank, 1783-1865, and his wife Barbara (Weidman), 1790-1836, of Ontario. Also John Hoover, 1788-1857, the son of Bishop Martin Hoover, *c.* 1760-1850, and his wife Susanna (Kurtz), 1789-1865, were both natives of Markham, Ontario.

The membership of twelve reported by John F. Funk in the 1880's was likely the high point of the tiny congregation at Lakeville, which never had a meetinghouse, but always met in the Dice schoolhouse.

THE MIKESELL MENNONITE CHURCH
Warren Township, St. Joseph County, Indiana

In the *Herald of Truth* this congregation, or rather the schoolhouse in which the members met, is always referred to as the Mixel schoolhouse, but the correct spelling seems to have been Mikesell. According to the 1875 *Atlas of St. Joseph County*, Preacher Samuel Yoder owned a 40-acre farm in Section 24 of Warren Township.

The first mention of Mennonites in the area occurs in the *Herald of Truth* for 1866 where under date of February 20, 1866, Daniel Brenneman reported: "Upon the oft repeated request of Bro. M. Shelly and a number of other friends and acquaintances who removed from Elkhart to St. Joseph County, some six miles [south] west of South Bend, a number of us went to pay them a visit last Saturday (February 17th) and returned yesterday." Daniel Brenneman preached on Saturday night and again on Sunday. "Both meetings were well attended and we received the strictest attention."

The next item in the *Herald of Truth* occurred in the March 1867 *Herald of Truth,* where John M. Brenneman wrote: "On the eighth of January, we went by railroad to Warsaw, and on the ninth, we arrived safe at Bro. Daniel Brenneman's in Elkhart County, Indiana. On the tenth, we went with him eighteen miles to Bro. Samuel Yoder's in St. Joseph County, six miles west of South Bend, where we had meeting on the eleventh, and where Bro. Yoder was chosen to the ministry. May God bless him and give him His Spirit and strength from on high, and fit him for the important work, that he may be wise to win souls to God and a faithful watchman over the little flock entrusted to his care. . . ."

A later reference to the congregation is made in a news item from page 169 of the November 1868 *Herald of Truth,* apparently from the pen of John F. Funk: "Several pleasant and well attended meetings were held in Mixel's [Mikesell's] schoolhouse, about six miles S.W. of South Bend, on Saturday and Sunday the 31st of October and the 1st of November. On Sunday forenoon four precious souls, who had felt the need of a Saviour . . . were baptized. In the afternoon the communion of the Lord's Supper was celebrated. There are only a small number of brethren and sisters in this place. . . ."

After reporting a trip to Chicago on February 4, 1871, John F. Funk added: "The next day we attended a pleasant and interesting meeting at Mixel's schoolhouse (Bro. Samuel Yoder's church). In the evening we had meeting again at the same place and again (though the weather was cold and rather unpleasant) a goodly number were present. On Monday evening we had services again at another schoolhouse, where the house was filled; the audience was remarkably still and attentive during the services." Funk then goes on to relate the death of a child of Samuel Holdeman. *(Herald of Truth,* 1871, page 40.) In the *Herald of Truth* for 1871, page 104, a calendar of Mennonite services indicates that preaching services were held every four weeks in the Mixel schoolhouse, on the same Sunday as Yellow Creek and Holdeman, but not on the same Sunday as at Elkhart, Shaum, and Christophel meetinghouses.

For some reason the congregation in Warren Township, St. Joseph County, never prospered. Tragedy struck on September 20, 1879, when Preacher Yoder's son Alexander was murdered by a neighborhood youth. Alexander was at that time twenty years of age, and the boy who shot him, at the command of his father, was only twelve years of age. Alexander died the next day.

The names of known heads of families in the Mikesell congregation were Henry Baker, Peter Hatler, Samuel Holdeman, and Preacher Samuel Yoder.

In the year 1885 Samuel Yoder and family removed from St. Joseph

County to Elkhart where he remained another forty years until his death at the advanced age of almost ninety years.

Samuel Yoder's meetings were at first held in the Mikesell school-house, two miles northeast of Crumstown, at the corner of Pear and Harrison roads. Sometime later, possibly about 1870, Samuel Yoder purchased an abandoned schoolhouse for the sum of $50.00 and moved it to a lot in Crumstown donated by Christian Holler, and remodeled it. Here he continued to hold church services as long as he lived in the area. The building is still standing, close to the present Crumstown Mennonite Church.

There is no connection between the present Crumstown congregation and the so-called Mikesell Church of the period of Samuel Yoder's ministry. After Samuel Yoder had removed to Elkhart the tiny congregation was so nearly disintegrated that regular services ceased, and the Mennonite witness was ultimately completely abandoned.

SHORE MENNONITE CHURCH

Section 14, Newbury Township, Lagrange County, Indiana

The Shore meetinghouse is located one and one-half miles south of the town of Shipshewana, and one-half mile east, on U.S. Highway 20. The lake near which it is located was one time known as the Hood Lake, but later came to be called Shore Lake. Indeed, a tiny village called Shore, containing a store, post office, sawmill, blacksmith shop, woodworking shop, cane press and cider mill, etc., grew up in the locality of the lake. Dr. Henry Schrock also practiced medicine there. The congregation is referred to in the *Herald of Truth* as the Lake Church in the early years. Later it is referred to as either the Shore or the Shipshewana congregation.

The date of organization of the congregation is not known. Henry A. Miller of Pennsylvania settled in Elkhart County near the town of Waterford in 1844, and in 1851 in Clay Township, Lagrange County. At this point Henry was not yet a Christian. The date of his conversion is not known. It is traditional that the first church services were held in a barn where Elva Nelson now lives, and that John M. Brenneman of Elida, Ohio, preached a sermon there on the subject of faith. At a later date services were held in a schoolhouse on the shore of Hood Lake. The *Herald of Truth* for 1867 refers to services held in a schoolhouse, "near Preacher Henry Miller's," in January. How long before this Miller had been ordained preacher, we do not know. The 1871 *Herald of Truth* shows that services were held every two weeks in the "Lake School House." Henry A. Miller was the first resident preacher of the Shore congregation, and became bishop in 1883. His able colleague was J. J. Weaver, who was serving as a preacher as early as 1868, who traveled far and wide in the interests of the church and evangelism, and who served with great effectiveness until his removal from the ministry in 1896; he then began attending the Forks Amish Mennonite Church, which he ultimately joined, and died in 1920 at the advanced age of ninety years. His body is buried in the Keightley Cemetery northwest of Shipshewana.

Early in 1874 the congregation decided to build a meetinghouse and with that end in view purchased from Jacob Weiler and Harriet his wife, fifty rods of land near the north end of Shore Lake. The consideration was $1.00. (Deed Book 25, page 139.) During that year, 1874, the congregation built its first meetinghouse, thirty by forty feet in size; it stood a little closer to the lake than the present house of worship. The first deacon of the congregation was James J. Mishler, who was ordained in 1883 and served until his death in 1941. Preacher Amos S. Cripe was ordained in 1887 and served until 1938. In the private records of John F. Funk of the 1880's he indicates that the membership of the "Lake" congregation was 124. (At the same time, only one congregation in the conference was stronger, Holdeman with 126 members.) According to tradition a union Sunday school was organized in a schoolhouse of the community in 1887, and in 1890 a Mennonite Sunday school was organized by the Shore congregation. The 1883 *Herald of Truth*, however, reports that Sunday school was reorganized "at the Lake" on May 6, 1883, with J. J. Hostetler as superintendent, and over 100 scholars. This corrects the tradition. In 1890 the congregation adopted *Hymns and Tunes* as its songbook.

In the year 1892 the meetinghouse was moved across the road, remodeled and enlarged by an addition of fourteen feet, and anterooms built on the east side. "Buggy sheds were built along the north fence, and hitching racks along the east fence, and along the west fence south of the church. These were used until about 1941 when the last buggy disappeared among the membership." As Henry A. Miller became older in years, P. Y. Lehman of the Clinton Brick congregation was ordained bishop in 1892 and served about nine years. The congregation then had no Indiana bishop to look after it until 1903, when John Garber of the Clinton Brick congregation was ordained bishop. He served the Shore Church until 1916 when Bishop Jacob P. Miller moved from Kent County, Michigan, to the Shore area; he served until his death in 1927. Seth P. Hershberger, a preacher from Illinois, moved into the community in 1908 and served about eleven years in the Shore ministry.

In the twentieth century five men have been ordained to the ministry in the Shore Church: Josiah J. Miller, 1902, who served until his death in 1958; his son, Percy J. Miller, deacon, 1927, and preacher, 1933; he is still active. Lee J. Miller, great-grandson of Bishop Henry A. Miller, was ordained deacon in 1934 and bishop in 1945. Homer J. Miller, grandson of Preacher Yost C. Miller, was ordained deacon in 1945. These four Millers, all with the middle initial J., served together until the death of Josiah in 1958. The next year, 1959, the congregation chose Arnold C. Roth of Iowa, a student in the Goshen College Biblical Seminary, and ordained him to the ministry.

The first Bible Reading was held in 1897 under the direction of John F. Funk; later these meetings came to be known as young people's Bible meetings.

The 1874 meetinghouse, which was enlarged in 1892, was used until 1929. The last service in the old meetinghouse was held May 12 of that year. Both men and women worked hard at the building of a new meetinghouse in 1929, and enthusiasm ran high. At the time of the dedication the entire cost of $10,944.33 was paid except for $200.00. The 1929 meetinghouse was forty-three by seventy feet in size. The dedicatory services were held August 18, 1929. Yost C. Miller, the senior minister, preached on the Holy Spirit, Romans 8:14, in the morning service. In the afternoon service D. D. Miller preached the dedication sermon on the text, Psalm 8:4. The final message in the evening service was brought by Ray F. Yoder.

The congregation has the usual activities of the Mennonites of Northern Indiana. A sewing circle was organized by the women in 1918, and a junior sewing circle in 1940. The young people started a literary society, now Mennonite Youth Fellowship, in 1923. The Sunday-school library was started in 1936, and church bulletins in 1952.

The first outpost of the congregation was at White Cloud, Michigan, to which the settlers of the Shore Church moved in the years 1897-99. The Emma Church was organized in 1901 as another outpost of the Shore congregation. The Locust Grove congregation near Findley, Michigan, was established in 1940. The Marion Church near Seybert, Indiana, was started in 1941. The work at Smith School, Jetson, Kentucky, was established in 1959, and John Wickey was placed in charge.

The first evangelistic meetings in the congregation were held by John S. Coffman in February 1888. From his diary we learn the names of some of the people whom he visited, as well as the topics on which he preached —Grace; What to Do to Be Saved; Justification; Baptism; Born of the Water and the Spirit; Ordinances; and the final subject, God Perfect in Nature and Revelation—in the Shipshewana Chapel: "The house is large and was filled to crowding."

The membership of the Shore Church in 1905 was 200; in 1913 it

9

was still 200; in 1920, 224; in 1940, 324; and the 1960 *Mennonite Year-book* indicates 369. Emma, its daughter of 1901, has 214 members in 1960; Locust Grove, 168; Marion, ninety-five; and South Colon, forty-seven.

EMMA MENNONITE CHURCH

Section 36, Newbury Township, Lagrange County, Indiana

In the year 1901 the Emma congregation was established as an outpost of the Shore Mennonite Church, with members coming from other congregations such as Forks A.M. Land was bought for $60.00 from Rudy E. Hostetler on April 8, 1901, and the deed made out to the trustees of the Mennonite Church of Emma, Indiana, and their successors. Additional land was bought from the same man on April 29, 1925, and the deed was granted to Moses M. Miller, Elmer C. Greenawalt, and Amos I. Schrock, as trustees of the Emma Mennonite Church, and their successors in office. The meetinghouse was built in the year 1901. This building is still in use except that a basement was added in 1926, at which time the entrance was changed. An annex was built to the rear of the building, and other improvements made, in 1949.

During the first year the services were in charge of the ministry of the Shore congregation. Sunday school and church services were held every other Sunday morning. On the intervening Sundays, Sunday school was held in the evening, but there was no preaching service. The charter membership of the congregation consisted of forty persons. The first Sunday-school superintendent was Oscar S. Hostetler, and John J. Troyer was assistant.

In 1902 the congregation decided to choose a resident minister and deacon. Oscar S. Hostetler was ordained preacher, and in the same service Menno J. Yoder was ordained to the office of deacon. These two men served as teammates in these offices until 1923 when O. S. Hostetler was chosen as bishop, and Menno J. Yoder was ordained preacher. This left no one to serve in the office of deacon; so the next year, 1924, Amos O. Hostetler was ordained as deacon. He served in that office twenty years, and in 1944 was ordained as preacher because the original ministers were growing older in years. The next year, 1945, Ivan M. Miller was ordained to the office of deacon, and in 1953 he became the second bishop of the church. For the third time the congregation then chose a deacon, Orvan Bontrager, in 1954. It is remarkable that of these five men, who have served in the years 1902 to 1961, all are living except Menno J. Yoder who died in 1957. These five men have served in ten offices: four as deacon, three as preacher, and two as bishop. The only man to occupy only one office thus far is Deacon Orvan Bontrager.

The Emma Sunday School was started in the spring of 1902. It has met each Sunday since the beginning. Young people's Bible meetings were begun in the year 1903. The young people's Bible meeting meets every Sunday evening and is occasionally followed by a preaching service. The sewing circle of the congregation was organized in 1918. Midweek meetings were started soon after the year 1930.

By 1905 the membership of the congregation had risen to sixty, but by 1913 was only fifty-three. In 1920 it was seventy-nine, in 1940 it was 194, and the 1960 *Mennonite Yearbook* shows 214 members.

The Hostetler family has played a major role in the life of the Emma Church. O. S. Hostetler, the bishop since 1923, served as pastor almost from the beginning, that is, from 1902. He has also served as bishop of many other congregations and as moderator of the conference; he has been a man of great influence in the Indiana-Michigan Conference. His son, Amos O. Hostetler, has not only served in the ministry since 1924, but was for many years the secretary of Mennonite General Conference, and the long-time secretary of the Indiana-Michigan Sunday School Conference (now the Christian Workers' Conference). The present bishop of the congregation, Ivan M. Miller, is also a quiet man of God who has the heart of a shepherd.

The Emma congregation established an outpost at Plato, east of the town of Lagrange, on U.S. Highway 20. The Shore congregation had established a Sunday school in an abandoned church near Plato in June 1928. It met only during the summer months. "The work was stopped during the second year because of an agreement among the officials of the former church that the building would not dare be used except for funerals. . . ." In 1948 the Emma congregation returned to the Plato community, purchased land, and built a meetinghouse, 1948-49. The Plato outpost was then established as a daughter congregation which has flourished since that time. The 1960 *Mennonite Yearbook* indicates a membership in the Plato congregation of eighty-four members.

Gar Creek Mennonite Church

Section 34, Milan Township, Allen County, Indiana

About the year 1854 Mennonites first began to settle at the tiny village of Gar Creek, about eleven miles east northeast of Fort Wayne, Indiana. Most of the settlers seemed to belong to the Rothgeb and the Bixler families. One of the few persons who is still living, who was baptized into the Gar Creek congregation, is the elder Samuel B. Bixler, born 1867, of the Holdeman congregation. In an interview with him, when he was ninety-three, on April 13, 1960, he reported the names of the people that he knew of who had lived at Gar Creek. Among them were his own parents Abraham and Margaret (Rothgeb) Bixler; his Uncle Hezekiah Rothgeb, 1812-1892, of Rockingham County, Virginia; his three uncles Henry, William, and George Rothgeb; his cousin Jesse Rothgeb; and his cousins Michael and William Bixler; John Federspiel was married to Matilda, sister of Samuel B. Bixler, and his Aunt Phoebe Ann Rothgeb was married to another cousin named Bixler. Polly Bixler, also Samuel B. Bixler's cousin, was married to a man named Cook who was not a Mennonite. Another Mennonite settler was Jacob Bixler, 1815-1886, whose obituary was published in the *Herald of Truth,* as was that of Hezekiah Rothgeb. Samuel B. Bixler lived at Gar Creek, 1874-94. He then lived in Fort Wayne for six years. In the year 1900 he purchased the farm of his maternal grandfather (Rothgeb) and lived on it from 1900 to 1903. Samuel says that the congregation died out because the young people did not unite with the church, and the old people died. Samuel was seventeen years of age when Eli Stofer of the Pleasant Valley Mennonite Church in De Kalb County baptized him. Eli Stofer preached regularly for the Gar Creek congregation. Samuel also remembers when Noah Blosser and John Blosser came from Ohio to minister at Gar Creek. The Fort Wayne ministers, B. B. King and J. I. Byler, also preached at Gar Creek.

The 1885 *Herald of Truth* reports (page 73) that Preachers James Coyle and Eli Stofer of De Kalb County held five meetings at Gar Creek. In 1886 Daniel Shenk of Elida, Ohio, reported in the *Herald of Truth:* "Several members have been living here [at Gar Creek] about thirty years without a preacher, and nearly the whole time without any preaching of our own denomination." The *Herald of Truth* for 1894 reports the death of Levi Rothgeb, 1814-1894, who had been born in Page County, Virginia, and who died in Allen County, Indiana, November 20, 1894, Preacher Eli Stofer officiated at the funeral service.

In the year 1895 the Christian people of the Gar Creek community decided to build a union house of worship. Samuel Bixler says that he and a man named Billy Harper sponsored a supper to raise money for the building of the new church building. The Mennonite representative at the dedication services on July 20 was John S. Coffman of Elkhart.

"At one-thirty I started from Elkhart for Waterloo, Fort Wayne, and Gar Creek. Allen Grower of near Gar Creek met me at Fort Wayne and took me out to Gar Creek. I soon found that the dedication was a United Brethren affair, and we are counted very secondary. I was on the program for this evening when only a few were present. I Peter 4:1, Have the Mind of Christ to Suffer. Great preparations are made to entertain the people with dinner, etc. Too much indeed.

"July 21. Last night Bro. Stofer and I stayed at Eli Rothgebs and had a pleasant visit. This forenoon Preacher Ballenger of the United Brethren Church at Fort Wayne preached the dedicatory service. I followed in an after talk. There was an immense crowd of people here; nearly $100.00 was raised. Took dinner at old Sister Bixlers. Bro. Stofer preached a German sermon at 2, followed by a sermon by Evans, Protestant Methodist. This evening H. D. Meads, United Brethren, preached. I followed again. The house was dedicated as a union house open to all evangelical people. May the Lord save these people from strife, and may this house be the means of much good to Gar Creek."

In 1898, when Amos Mumaw moved from Elkhart County to Wayne County, Ohio, he stopped en route at Gar Creek and preached for "the little brotherhood" there.

In connection with the Mennonite evangelistic effort in Fort Wayne, M. S. Steiner and John Blosser decided to hold services at Gar Creek every two weeks in the evening, following a three o'clock afternoon service in private homes in the city of Fort Wayne. (1903 *H.T.*, page 186.)

The membership in 1900 is reported as twenty. The 1895 church building was remodeled in 1905, and rededication services were held October 22. On that occasion Jonathan Kurtz, George Lambert, and M. S. Steiner were present. Regular services in the "Bethel Chapel" at Gar Creek were discontinued about the year 1910. The Gar Creek church building stands about six miles south of the present Cuba Conservative Mennonite Church. The last member of the Gar Creek Mennonite congregation was Jesse Rothgeb, nephew of Hezekiah Rothgeb; Jesse died in the year 1927. When John I. Byler lived at Fort Wayne, 1907-8, only one Mennonite member was living in the Gar Creek area. "He was deacon, storekeeper, railroad express agent, postmaster, and Sunday-school superintendent." Sunday-school attendance ran from twenty to forty at that time.

About 1921 services were revived in the Gar Creek Bethel Chapel for a time by the workers at the Ft. Wayne Mission. The building, which stood a quarter of a mile west of the village of Gar Creek, and west of and adjacent to the cemetery, was sold about 1940 for $152.00; it was torn down, and the materials used in the construction of a house in Ft. Wayne. The money was turned over to the trustees of the Gar Creek cemetery. The bell and the pulpit were acquired by the Danner Wrecking Company of Ft. Wayne (data from Herbert L. Osborne).

First Mennonite Church

1213 St. Mary's Avenue, Fort Wayne, Indiana

In a sense, the establishment of a Mennonite mission in the city of Fort Wayne was the result of a Gar Creek convert, John D. Federspiel, who lived in Fort Wayne about two decades before the establishment of the mission, but who constantly worked and prayed to the end that a Mennonite witness might eventually be established in that city. He received strong support from Preacher Eli Stofer of De Kalb County, who finally persuaded the Ohio Mennonite Conference in 1902 to begin Christian work in Fort Wayne. Preacher M. S. Steiner was appointed to take up this work, and received the enthusiastic support of Federspiel. The 1903 *Herald of Truth* reported that Preachers M. S. Steiner and John Blosser had decided to hold services in private homes in Fort Wayne every two weeks at three p.m., rather than to rent a hall. That same year, however, this decision was reversed. A Sunday school was opened at 1921 South Hanna Street. The summer of 1903 John F. Bressler was appointed as superintendent of the new Mennonite mission. The *Herald of Truth* reported October 22, 1903, that a mission had been opened at Fort Wayne by J. F. Bressler, formerly of the Home Mission, Chicago. Bressler soon received the assistance of Levi S. Yoder of Nappanee. The spring of 1904 a store building was rented at 2237 Oliver Street, and was used for church and Sunday school purposes. The first converts were baptized in November 1904 by L. J. Lehman (of Cullom, Illinois), namely, Frank J. and Pearl Martin.

A new chapter in the life of the Mennonite mission in Fort Wayne began the fall of 1904 when two young men from West Liberty, Ohio, came to Fort Wayne to support themselves economically, and to work in the mission enterprise. These men were Joseph H. Borntrager and Ben B. King. Although Bressler was ordained on December 4, 1904, he did not long remain at the mission; the *Herald of Truth* for 1905 reported that Bressler was leaving for Nampa, Idaho, and that J. E. Hartzler of Missouri had been appointed to take charge of the mission for a few weeks. B. B. King was ordained preacher on July 16, 1905, by Bishop David Burkholder of Nappanee. With the exception of a year, 1907-8, he was in charge of the Fort Wayne Mission until the year 1930. He was assisted at various times by different workers, who gave excellent support to him. But it must be stated that it was B. B. King more than any other man who made a success as leader of the team in the Fort Wayne Mission.

The *Herald of Truth* reported in 1905, in the issue of July 20, that the Mennonite Evangelizing and Benevolent Board, and the Mennonite Board of Charitable Homes and Missions (which later merged to form the Mennonite Board of Missions and Charities), through a joint committee, had selected and purchased a lot on St. Mary's Avenue for the Fort Wayne Mission Chapel, soon to be built. Until the building of this proposed mission hall the workers lived and held services at 1436 Third Street, and later at 1419 St. Mary's Avenue. The mission hall was a two-story cement block structure with the first floor being used as a worship auditorium, and the second floor as living quarters. During the fall and winter of 1905-6 construction continued as funds were available. This hall stood just south of the present church building. Correspondents in the *Herald of Truth* of January 8, 1906, reported that the building was about to be plastered. On February 26, 1906, it was reported that Sunday school was organized on that day in the new building with sixty-eight pupils enrolled. The mission hall was opened February 19, 1906, but dedicatory services were postponed until September 9, 1906, when it was free of debt. (1906 *H.T.*, page 326.) Walter E. Yoder and Edwin J. Yoder visited the Fort Wayne Mission in 1907 and reported that the membership was then about sixty.

During the year 1907-8, when B. B. King was gone, John I. Byler and John M. Hartzler (father of Professor H. Harold Hartzler) were in charge of the mission.

It has been traditional in America for every established Mennonite congregation to have at least one deacon. Consequently in 1909 Bishop David Burkholder went to Fort Wayne and ordained the first convert, Frank J. Martin, as a deacon.

There was evidently considerable fluctuation in church membership, for in 1910 only twenty-nine members were reported, whereas two years later the membership figure was given as fifty-seven. In 1914 twenty-two were baptized. The present house of worship was built in 1914 at a cost of approximately $5,500.00. One of the most effective lay workers at that time was C. C. Culp. By 1920 the membership had risen to seventy-five. Early in the 1920's the congregation was organized substantially as a self-governing body, but the district conference continued to appoint a local board of control for another quarter century. Perry Heller was ordained in 1924. A branch Sunday school was conducted at 1924 Ellen Street from the years 1924 to 1932. Federspiel, the man who had long prayed for the establishment of a mission in Fort Wayne, spent part of the day, April 9, 1926, trimming shrubbery at the church. That evening he attended prayer meeting, went home, and died on his knees in prayer. The historian of the congregation, Herbert L. Osborne, writes: "As he had brought about the birth of the mission, he also left it—in intercession with his Lord."

After B. B. King left the Fort Wayne Mission for church work in

Ohio in 1930, Deacon Frank J. Martin served as superintendent for four years. From March until November 1934 India Missionary Lloy A. Kniss served as superintendent. Newton S. Weber served as superintendent from 1934 until 1941. By the year 1940 the membership had risen to eighty-four.

A new chapter in the history of the Fort Wayne Mission began in 1941 when Allen B. Ebersole became pastor. He served until 1952 when he transferred to the Canton, Ohio, Mission.

The original mission hall had been converted into a parsonage and was so used until the year 1942 when the present parsonage was purchased, a short distance north of the church building. In 1948 the church building was remodeled by making classrooms and storage space in the basement. That same year the congregation adopted a constitution which provided for a church council. The formation of the church council marked the end of the appointment of a local board for the Fort Wayne Mission Church. Rudy S. Borntrager was ordained preacher in 1951 to assist Pastor Ebersole. The next year he became pastor and served until 1959 when he transferred to the Lima, Ohio, Mennonite Church. The congregation was strengthened in 1953 when twenty-four members from the Anderson congregation north of Fort Wayne transferred their membership to the Mission Church. That same year the congregation became fully independent of the Mission Board.

Down through the years the Fort Wayne Mennonite Mission, which has been listed in the *Mennonite Yearbook* as the First Mennonite Church of Fort Wayne since 1948, has had an unusually active church program, Sunday school, preaching services, young people's Bible meeting, home visitation, cottage meetings, summer Bible school, boys' shop, girls' club, women's sewing circle, weekday Bible classes, radio broadcasts, participation in rescue mission services, etc.

In the year 1959 Rudy Borntrager transferred to the Lima, Ohio, Mennonite Church, and was succeeded in 1960 by John R. Smucker, a graduate of the Goshen College Biblical Seminary. Paul M. Miller had succeeded the long-time bishop of the congregation, D. A. Yoder, in 1959. During 1960 the congregation undertook extensive remodeling work including a new front on the auditorium, new auditorium furniture, carpet in the aisles and under the pews, new doors and trim, two furnace units, new rest rooms at the east end of the basement, soundproof preschool classrooms, fluorescent basement lighting, folding doors and rolling dividers in the basement, folding chairs for classroom use, kitchen cupboards and hot water heater, library shelving, Sunday-school and sewing circle storage space, the rebuilding of the public-address system, and concrete work at the front and rear entrances. The total cost of this remodeling amounted to about $26,000.00. Dedicatory services were held January 1, 1961, with Paul M. Miller preaching the sermon. The 1960 *Mennonite Yearbook* lists the membership of the congregation at 150.

BOWER MENNONITE CHURCH
Section 13, Marion Township, Owen County, Indiana

Mennonites began moving into the Clay and Owen County areas of Southern Indiana soon after the middle of the nineteenth century. Abraham and Jane (Pittman) Funk, he of Virginia, and she of Logan County, Ohio, located there about 1852. About 1854 Daniel and Sarah Jane (Ellis) Funk, who were married in Champaign County, Ohio, in 1846, located there. In 1855 Preacher Joseph Bixler of Fayette County, Pennsylvania, moved into the settlement, was immediately ordained bishop, but after the death of his wife that same year moved to Mahoning County, Ohio. In August 1864 Bishop John M. Brenneman of Elida, Ohio, visited the Bower congregation. He held six meetings and visited many families. He reported in the *Herald of Truth* (page 56) that there were seventy or more members in the congregation, served by four ministers, two of whom were rather young and timid, and two deacons. The preachers were likely Jacob Bower, Michael Mishler, William Silvius, and Elias Mishler. The deacons were probably John Royer and Jacob Kilmer. Brenneman reported that the congregation was not conforming fully to Mennonite practices in dress. He mentions having visited Preacher Jacob Bauer. He also complimented the congregation for its kind attention: "Never did I have more devout and attentive hearers before me than here." Brenneman commented that the Eel River flows through the area, and is said to be well supplied with fish. The 1864 *Herald of Truth* also reports a funeral, at which Michael Mishler preached the German sermon, and "Eli" Mishler, the English sermon.

The congregation purchased land in 1861 and on it built a meetinghouse. The first mention of the Bower meetinghouse appeared in the 1866 *Herald of Truth,* page 7.

In a letter of George Funk, November 1869, mention is made of Bishop Michael Mishler, and Preachers Eli Mishler and David Oberholtzer. The very first bishop, Daniel Funk, had died in 1859. Bishop Joseph Bixler moved away in 1855. Bishop Michael Mishler was serving as the sole minister in the early part of 1872. Preacher Jacob Hoffer was ordained in 1872, and a few weeks later Daniel Royer was ordained also; Royer was ordained to preach English, and was made bishop about 1881. He lived until 1903.

The June 15, 1883, *Herald of Truth* reports that a tornado had demolished the meetinghouse. That same year Bishop George Brenneman of Ohio visited the congregation. Another outstanding visitor in 1883 was John S. Coffman who reported in the *Herald of Truth:* "The church here consists principally of aged members, while the young people are taking but little interest. The members are much less in number than they were some years ago, and it is plainly to be seen that unless greater efforts are made to interest the young people and gain them into membership the church will rapidly decline, and ere long become extinct." In 1884 the congregation is reported as having dwindled to fifteen or twenty members, and was then served by Preachers Daniel Royer and Jacob Hoffer. In 1885 a man named Daniel E. Kinports was ordained to the ministry, and lived until 1912; he was the last preacher in the congregation. The 1890 *Herald of Truth* reports that the membership consisted of fifteen or sixteen members. Writing in the 1890 *Herald of Truth* D. S. Brunk of Elida, Ohio, said: "There is evidently a lack here of that Christian love and devotion, so necessary to the growth and prosperity of the church."

John F. Funk gave communion to the Bower congregation in June 1895, at which time "some fourteen or fifteen" went to communion. "Old Bro. George Funk was there and served as deacon with trembling hands and almost fell while so engaged. Bro. Daniel Funk goes very feebly on crutches" (J. F. Funk diary, June 23, 1895).

About the only references to the Bower congregation or its "Oberholtzer meetinghouse" (so named after Preacher David Oberholtzer) after 1900 were the obituaries of the aged members, who died one by one, bringing certain extinction to the church. In 1921 three members were left: Mary, the second wife of Bishop Daniel Royer, and Joseph Royer and wife.

The cemetery adjoining the meetinghouse lot contains about seventy-five marked graves. A transcript of the tombstones was made by Mrs. William G. (Edith Bauer) Cogswell of Bloomington, Indiana, in May 1951. Among the names on the tombstones are Jacob Bauer, Delp, Eckerle, Freed, Fretz, Funk (including Deacon George), Hochstettler, Hoffer (including Preacher Jacob), Kilmer (including Deacon Jacob), Preacher Daniel E. Kinports, Longenecker, Markley, Nice, Oberholtzer, Rasler, Royer, and Preacher William Silvius.

In 1928 the Indiana-Michigan Mennonite Conference sold the meetinghouse for $115.00. The meetinghouse was then taken away from the site and used as a dwelling house.

In 1955 the present writer located the meetinghouse lot and cemetery. On this occasion he talked to two men, George Miller, who was the grandson of a Bower Mennonite named George Markley, and A. P.

Megenhardt, a Lutheran; both Markley and Megenhardt then being in their eightieth year. Markley remembered "Joe Royer and Dan Kinport." These aged men emphasized that the leadership of the Bower congregation did not favor such progressive institutions as the Sunday school.

To reach the site of the Bower meetinghouse one starts at North Main and Fourth streets in Clay City, drives east on Highway 246 for 4.8 miles (which is 1.5 miles beyond the Clay-Owen County line), then turns north at the Pleasant View Baptist church ground, for one-half mile, then west .4 of a mile, then north 1.1 miles. The cemetery is in an abandoned state, growing up in weeds and brush.

Henry B. and Elizabeth Bixler (sister of Bishop Joseph Bixler) Yoder lived in the Bower community in 1855 when their son Peter B. Yoder (1855-1943), father of D. A. Yoder, was born. D. A. Yoder reports that a number of families moved out of the Owen County congregation because of the ague, an intermittent fever which was accompanied by violent trembling. Jacob and Catherine (Acker) Long were also living in Clay County in 1868 when their son Irvin was born. Both the father, Jacob Long, and the son, Irvin, were later deacons in the Olive congregation.

PLEASANT VALLEY MENNONITE CHURCH

Fairfield Township, De Kalb County, Indiana

One of the finest summaries of the beginnings of the Pleasant Valley Mennonite Church was written by Herbert L. Osborne for the mimeographed booklet, "History of the Mennonite Church in Fort Wayne, Indiana, 1903-1953." Osborne writes: "Christian Newcomer and family moved there in the spring of 1849 from Columbiana County, Ohio. Henry Bechtels, natives of Holmes County, Ohio, moved there in 1850. Abraham Hunsbergers came in 1855. In the fall of 1863, Henry Freed moved here with his bride from Stark County, Ohio. His brother, John, also settled here. In 1864, their father, Peter Freed, a native of Shenandoah County, Virginia, came to live with Henry. James Coyle, the first resident ordained minister, arrived about 1863. Eli Stofer, the next ordained minister, came from Columbiana County, Ohio, in 1864. Daniel Smith, a deacon from [Putnam County,] Ohio, located here in 1874." Anthony Freed settled in Steuben County in 1851.

In November 1867 Preacher Daniel Brenneman of Elkhart County, accompanied by several brethren, including Preacher J. M. Christophel, left on the Michigan Southern and Northern Indiana Air Line Railroad (now New York Central) for Corunna, for the purpose of visiting the Mennonites of De Kalb County. Services were held in a schoolhouse.

On November 22, 1867, Daniel Brenneman's revered brother, Bishop J. M. Brenneman, received two members into the congregation. At that point there were seven members in the church. Brenneman held services in a schoolhouse near the home of Peter Freed. The members lived about nine miles northwest of Waterloo, a station on the "Air Line Railway."

This was not the first information which John M. Brenneman had of Mennonites in De Kalb County, for in May 1864, when he held communion for a family in Allen County named Amstutz, in the company of Bishop Henry Yother, a man named John Bechtel, his wife, and his mother, of De Kalb County, came twenty miles to the Amstutz home in order to receive communion.

In May 1867 Preacher John F. Funk and Bishop Jacob Wisler preached in De Kalb County in a schoolhouse, and also in the Evangelical Church. The next year, on June 28, 1868, George Brenneman, a bishop of Delphos, Ohio, and brother of John M. Brenneman, visited De Kalb County, Indiana, and conducted an ordination by lot for preacher. (In the west of Goshen ministerial meeting, March 31, 1945, Preacher J. S. Hartzler recounted this ordination service. Hartzler said there were sixteen members in the Mennonite congregation in De Kalb County at the time of the ordination. Eli Stofer got all the votes cast, fifteen. The Mennonite leaders in charge of the ordination were embarrassed, not knowing how to ordain by lot when only one person received votes! So they inquired of Stofer as to why he had not voted. He replied that he did not feel led to vote for anyone. They insisted that he ought to vote He said, "Well, if I have to vote, I will vote for Jim Coyle." The ministers then cast lots between the two brethren and—declared J. S. Hartzler —"You might know that God allowed the lot to fall on James Coyle.") Coyle was never able to function very much as a minister. The consequence was that Stofer was in turn ordained preacher in 1871 and served until his death in 1915.

In the 1869 *Herald of Truth* John F. Funk refers to the De Kalb County congregation as "still small." But by 1883 the congregation had gained sufficient strength to build a meetinghouse. The first services were held in the new church building on the third Sunday of September 1883 (September 16). Three years later Preacher Eli Stofer, Preacher Henry Huber, who had moved from Allen County, Ohio, to De Kalb County about 1882, and Deacon Daniel Smith visited the Gar Creek Mennonite Church. John S. Coffman, the evangelist of Elkhart, Indiana, labored with the Pleasant Valley congregation in series of meetings twice in the year 1884, in 1889, and again in 1893. Coffman's diary gives a full account of these meetings. When he arrived at Waterloo on February 2, 1884, he was met at the station by Preacher Henry Huber. Coffman commented:

"The brethren here have built a nice convenient house [of worship] and have it well lighted up at the evening services." Coffman returned for another series of meetings in December 1884. He was met at Corunna by Preacher James Coyle; on this occasion Coffman was accompanied by Deacon Henry Brenneman of Elkhart. In connection with his June meetings of 1893 Coffman wrote in his diary: "May a brighter day dawn in this place, O God." During that series of meetings Coffman held a communion service for the Pleasant Valley congregation; he comments in his diary that this is one of the few times which he had done so. (Ordinarily, Mennonite bishops presided in communion services.) In 1893 the Sunday school which was being held in the Pleasant Valley meeting-house was a union Sunday school. Coffman explained this as, "outsiders helping principally in the work, that is, members of other churches." On April 28, 1893, Coffman "talked with old Brother Peter Freed again, who is now supposed to be ninety-seven years old. The exact record is lost on account of his father burning the record at the time of the 1812 War, so that he would not be known to be old enough for military service. He sees splendidly and hears pretty well. He thinks he is over one hundred." On June 15 Coffman was again at the Pleasant Valley Church: "One more soul confessed Christ. This makes fourteen in all, including the three that made a new start. The work seems revived here, and we must believe it has been in answer to prayer. May God now grant that the work may be permanent and that this may be a beginning of a great work here and many conversions." On July 2, 1893, Coffman was again in De Kalb County and attended the Sunday-school services at nine o'clock, and church services an hour later. Coffman spoke on the subject of baptism, and was followed by Preacher Elson of the Church of the Brethren, because one of the converts, Etta Urie, desired to be baptized and received into the Church of the Brethren, "and yet desires to be along with these young people. Went down to the water at Wertz Mill, where we baptized ten in the water with water, and Elson baptized the one by immersion. The first I ever saw two denominations work together in that way." The next day Coffman added: "I have hopes that the work in De Kalb can now prosper if it is vigorously continued. There were nine new converts baptized, and one that was not satisfied with previous baptism was done again. Two were reclaimed." The *Herald of Truth* contains the obituary of Peter Freed, 1795-1894, who had been born in Virginia, who married Hannah Miller in Columbiana County, Ohio, and who came to De Kalb County in 1864. He was a Mennonite over seventy years.

In 1905 Eli Stofer pleaded through the editor of the *Herald of Truth* for ministerial help. This may or may not have been the reason that

Reuben R. Ebersole located in the area in 1906, where David Burkholder ordained him as preacher. He did not long remain in that area, however, but entered the School of Medicine of Indiana University in 1907, and never returned to the Pleasant Valley Church. In 1906 Preachers Andrew Yontz and Silas Yoder held successful meetings in the Pleasant Valley congregation. There were seven converts, and the meetinghouse was filled to overflowing thirty minutes before starting time in the last service of January 7. In 1905 William H. Bickel wrote in the *Herald of Truth:* "We have reorganized our Sunday school with Bro. W. Bickel as superintendent, and Bro. Brand, assistant. The prospects are encouraging, but we need more outside help. We need a young minister to locate at this place. This field is white to harvest with middle-aged and young whose sympathies are with us, and there seems to be a tendency toward religion among the people in this community. My age and the condition of my health disqualify me from doing much of this important work." R. R. Ebersole reported in the *Herald of Truth* in 1906 that "the evening Bible meeting is progressing nicely, considering that this is a new line of work for this place." In 1906 there were thirty-five members in the congregation. In 1909 the congregation enjoyed a Sunday-school meeting with many attendants from the more heavily populated areas of Northern Indiana. By 1914 the membership had dropped to eleven.

The *Herald of Truth* contains numerous obituaries from this congregation. For example, Anthony and Elizabeth (Benner) Freed were married in Stark County, Ohio, in 1858. (Anthony had settled in Steuben County, Indiana, in 1851.) Eli Stofer preached her funeral sermon in 1905.

On April 20, 1914, a legal agreement was signed by John H. Urey, elder of the Church of the Brethren, and Samuel C. Perkins, trustee, as well as by Eli Stofer, minister in the Mennonite Church, and G. B. Brand, trustee. This agreement permitted the Church of the Brethren to "transfer their Sunday school and church services which they are conducting at the Putt schoolhouse" into the Pleasant Valley Mennonite meetinghouse, "which is one mile south and one-half mile west, and there continue the same, using their literature, lesson helps, etc., as heretofore, and provide fuel for the stoves and lamps, and a janitor to care for the house, for all meetings that may be held in said house, and pay for same, as well as other necessary expenses of the Sunday school. . . ." The agreement permitted the Mennonites to "attend and work in said Sunday school, and after Sunday school may have preaching services or such other Christian meetings, except festivals, as they may desire during the remainder of the day on the second and fourth Sundays of each month, also on the Saturday evening preceding. . . ." "Should anything come up which this agreement does not cover and on which said parties cannot agree same is to be left to a committee of three whose decision is to be final and adhered to by all parties. Said committee to be appointed, one by each party and the third by the two thus appointed." The date of this document was April 20, 1914. (Archives of the Mennonite Church.)

One final effort was made to save the congregation from extinction. Preacher Silas Weldy was asked to come to De Kalb County and preach regularly for the dying Mennonite congregation, which he did for a number of years, beginning about the year 1915. But the effort proved to be in vain, and in 1917 the Mennonites sold their house of worship to the Church of the Brethren, who renamed it the Pleasant Chapel Church of the Brethren. To reach the Pleasant Chapel one may start at North Riley and East Dowling streets, Kendallville, and go east 8.9 miles on Highway 6, and turn north 4.2 miles to the Chapel. The building is located two and one-half miles east of Corunna and 4.2 miles north. The De Kalb Mennonites buried in the Fairfield Center Cemetery, which is reached from the Pleasant Chapel by going south one-half mile, west one and one-half miles, and again south an additional one-half mile. In this cemetery are found such names as Bair, Baughman, Bickel, Bixler, Bower, Brenneman, Carper, Conrad, Freed, Gardner, Hartman, Hening, Martin, Metzger, Miller, Myers, Resler, Rohrer, Shellenberger, Sherrick, Slaubaugh, Smith, Stahl, Weirich, and Wert. Preachers James Coyle, Eli Stofer, and Daniel B. Smith, ordained preacher about 1889, all have tombstones in the Fairfield Center Cemetery. The grave of R. R. Ebersole, who died in 1960, is located in the Violett Cemetery south of Goshen, near Waterford.

TEEGARDEN OUTPOST

Marshall County, Indiana

The first-known mention of Teegarden is in the *Herald of Truth* for 1890, which reports the death of David J. Hoover, 1827-1890, a Mennonite for many years who died on June 11 near Teegarden in Marshall County. John F. Funk recorded in his diary for Friday, September 22, 1893, that he left for Marshall County at five o'clock in the morning. He met Preacher Noah Metzler at Wakarusa and they took dinner in the home of Peter Hartman. The three, Funk, Metzler, and Hartman, then set out for Teegarden and arrived at the home of Jacob Freed. They conducted a church service in a schoolhouse, and stayed in the Freed home that night. Funk mentioned that the distance from Elkhart to Teegarden was forty-one miles. The next day, Saturday, September 23, Funk visited the Josiah Culp home, and in the evening held another service in a schoolhouse. He went home for the night with Frank Leatherman. On

Sunday morning, September 24, services were again held at the schoolhouse. Funk also received into the fellowship of the Mennonite Church Josiah Culp, and baptized his wife and daughter. He took the noon meal in the home of Jacob Lehman. In the evening another service was conducted in the schoolhouse.

The preacher who supplied the pulpit for the few Mennonites living at Teegarden was Henry Weldy of the Holdeman congregation. (His son, Cornelius S. Weldy, remembers the names of Josiah Culp and wife, Andrew Mott and wife, and a Hornsby couple, who were members around the year 1900.) In November 1899 Henry Weldy held a series of meetings at Teegarden, with two converts. This is reported in the *Herald of Truth* of December 1, 1899. Other items from the *Herald of Truth* include the fact that Preacher George Lambert held a series of meetings at Teegarden in January 1905. Also, Henry Weldy spent Easter Sunday, April 15, 1906, at Teegarden, "where our people have for some years maintained a meeting." He reports a good meeting and feels encouraged in the work. Weldy received an additional member into the small number of believers at Teegarden on July 8, 1906.

The minutes of the Indiana-Michigan Mennonite Conference for 1906 report that the committee which had been appointed to sell the Pleasant Hill Mennonite meetinghouse in Branch County, Michigan, paid $100.00 "on the debt of the church at Teegarden, Indiana." The conference advised the committee "not to hold this as a debt against the latter church. Future arrangements for this place [Teegarden] were left to the brotherhood of the Holdeman congregation." The *Herald of Truth* for 1906 reports that Henry Weldy was again at Teegarden on October 28, "where our people have nearly a half-interest in a union meetinghouse." In December 1906 the Holdeman congregation decided to hold services every two weeks, rather than every four weeks as had been the previous practice at Teegarden. But the little flock at Teegarden diminished, rather than grew. Finally, it was decided to abandon the work. C. S. Weldy estimates that services were discontinued in the period, 1910-12. (The article on Teegarden in *The Mennonite Encyclopedia* confuses the Lakeville group with Teegarden.)

SCHOOLHOUSES AND UNION CHURCH BUILDINGS

At various times, especially prior to 1900, the Mennonites of Northern Indiana held preaching services, and sometimes Sunday schools, in a variety of schoolhouses. In Elkhart County, for example, such preaching points and/or Sunday schools were conducted in the following schoolhouses: Center, Culp in Union Township, Jones in Harrison Township ("The Jones Meeting has been kept up to my knowledge for about thirty years"—J. F. Funk diary, August 10, 1891), Metzler, Mitchell in Olive Township, Neff in Jackson Township, Paulus in Concord Township, Swoveland in Jackson Township, and Stump in Union Township. Services were also held in the North and South Union church buildings (both in Locke Township, southwest of Wakarusa), and in the Forest Grove Union church building, southeast of Middlebury, in Middlebury Township. The Madison Union Chapel, four miles west of Wakarusa, was built in 1906; I. W. Royer preached at the forenoon session of the all-day dedicatory services. The Mennonites held services there for thirty years. The following schoolhouses in St. Joseph County were also utilized by Mennonites: Johnson, Madison, and Poplar Grove.

SCATTERED MENNONITE FAMILIES IN INDIANA

No permanent work was established in the community of Maysville, Allen County, Indiana, but various references to the Amstutz families of that community appear in the nineteenth century. A woman named Barbara Schlunegger, who was born in Germany in 1817, and who came to America at the age of four, married Peter Amstutz in 1842. Ten years later they settled in Allen County, Indiana. The husband died in 1882. She died in the year 1904, and burial was held in the family cemetery. Services were held in the Defenseless Mennonite meetinghouse near Leo by Eli Stofer of the Pleasant Valley congregation in De Kalb County. Jacob Amstutz, 1846-1896, was survived by his widow, two sons and six daughters, his mother, three brothers and two sisters, in 1896. His body was also buried in the family cemetery. Services were conducted by J. M. Shenk of Elida, Ohio, and by Eli Stofer of De Kalb County, Indiana. Joseph Amstutz, 1844-1899, also lived in the same community. His wife preceded him in death, but his aged mother survived him. Eli Stofer and Andrew Gerig preached the funeral sermons in English and German respectively.

One of the earliest references to these Mennonite Amstutz families (not Amish Mennonites) appeared in the very first year of the *Herald of Truth*, 1864, which reports an earlier visit of J. M. Brenneman to the Amstutz home in May 1864. Brenneman was met at Fort Wayne and taken to the home where he baptized two Amstutz sons "in the bloom of youth." On that occasion Brenneman gave communion, not only to the Amstutz family, but also to John Bechtel, his wife, and his mother, of De Kalb County. They came twenty miles to commune. Brenneman speaks of the communicants being eleven in number: "Eleven of us were present." In 1866 Brenneman again spent several days in Allen County, fourteen miles north of Fort Wayne, and once more gave communion to the group. He also visited some [Leo] "Omish Brethren and Sisters."

10

The 1867 *Herald of Truth,* page 187, reports that Bishop John M. Brenneman of Elida, Ohio, held communion services in the home of Peter Amstutz of Allen County. Brenneman reported that at the evening service there were "many Omish Brethren" present. More than twenty years later Preacher Daniel Shenk of Elida, Ohio, and others, visited Jacob Amstutz near Maysville, Allen County, Indiana. Preaching services were held at a schoolhouse one-half mile north of the Cuba community, and west of Maysville. Another reference is made by C. P. Steiner of Allen County, Ohio, to this tiny group of six members, who were without a preacher in 1888.

No congregation ever developed at Maysville, and the references after 1900 are to funerals only.

In 1896 Jacob S. Augspurger reported the obituary of Peter Bender, 1805-1896, of Germany, who lived in Butler County, Ohio, prior to 1855, and from 1855 to 1896 in Boone County, Indiana, three and one-half miles west of Zionsville. Bender may have been a Mennonite.

In the 1880's a convert to the Mennonite faith, Andrew Crook of Rosamund in Dubois County, Indiana, wrote many letters to the *Herald of Truth,* soliciting Mennonites to preach in the Roach schoolhouse near his home. One of those who responded was Evangelist J. S. Coffman.

Daniel Brenneman was called to Porter County in 1871 to preach the funeral sermon for the child of John Holdeman, who lived near Valparaiso. Brenneman wrote: "I remained in this neighborhood over Sunday, and met with the people three times for public worship. The congregations, though small, seemed very attentive, and eager to hear the Word, and an earnest desire was manifested that they might frequently be visited by the ministering brethren. There are in this neighborhood no members of our church. There are those, however, whose faith is in unity with ours, and who hold in sentiment to the same nonresistance principles for which we contend. The belief was expressed that if frequently visited, a church might be organized in this place." Brenneman probably meant that there were people with Mennonite and/or Church of the Brethren background in that area, or possibly Reformed Mennonite families.

The *Herald of Truth* for 1895 indicates that a French emigrant named Christian Salzman, 1811-1895, lived successively in Lancaster County, Pennsylvania; Butler County, Ohio; Tippecanoe County, Indiana (1849-93); and finally Pawnee County, Kansas.

The *Herald of Truth* for 1867 reported the death of Gertrude (Kauffman), wife of John Binkley. She was born in Lancaster County, Pennsylvania, in 1778, removed to Wayne County, Indiana, in 1849, bore six sons and two daughters, and died September 14, 1867, at the age of eighty-eight years, nine months, and one day. The obituary reports that she became a Mennonite in her youth and remained one until her death.

The 1868 *Herald of Truth* reports that in August of that year John F. Funk visited David Bowman, ten miles south of Ligonier, Indiana, as well as David and Moses Baer, twenty miles south of Ligonier. Funk held a Sunday morning service with the Baers on August 9, 1868, and a Sunday afternoon service in the Bowman home. The *Herald of Truth* for 1869 also reports the death of Magdalena, wife of David Baer of Whitley County. George Brenneman of Ohio preached the funeral sermon.

TENNESSEE

In the 1890's there was also a Mennonite settlement in Dickson County, in Northern Tennessee, for which the Indiana Mennonite leaders felt responsible. In 1893, for example, John F. Funk visited a Slonaker family there, also the Joseph Lichty and Daniel Grabill families. At the services Funk reported good attendance and attention. He baptized David, John, and Mary Slonaker. In 1896 Funk made another trip to Tennessee and mentions the following Mennonite families who lived near Tennessee City: Bower, Holderman, Kohli, Leidig, Miller, Schrock, Slonaker, and Yoder; and a Brandenburg family at Colesburg. On March 2, 1896, the Dickson County congregation decided to organize, and they met the following day at the home of M. Slonaker and chose Amos I. Yoder as preacher, and David D. Holderman (father of Deo T. Holderman of Goshen) as deacon. "The brethren were examined and ordained in the afternoon." The new congregation also observed communion and feet-washing services. Funk reported, "gladness and great rejoicing." The colony did not last long, however. Preacher A. I. Yoder moved away within a year or two (he did his lifework at West Liberty, Ohio), and the congregation died out.

MICHIGAN

PLEASANT HILL MENNONITE CHURCH

Branch County, Michigan

About the close of the Civil War, 1865, Mennonites began moving into Branch County, Michigan, not far from the village of Burr Oak, which village was located about two miles southwest of the town of Bronson (Bronson is now on U.S. Highway 112). One of the early settlers was C. D. Beery, who had been ordained to the office of deacon in 1852 in Franklin County, Ohio, and who was living in Branch County, Michigan, as early as 1865. Another early settler was Abraham G. Beery and his wife Sarah (Keller). Isaac Good, and Henry and Diana Good (Henry Good and wife came from Virginia) also lived in Branch County, as did Eli and Matilda Blosser. Other early settlers included Abraham Blosser, Abraham S. Friesner, and John Krupp.

One of the earliest references to the "Burr Oak" or the "Michigan Church" is made on Saturday and Sunday, December 2, 3, 1865, by Daniel Brenneman. He wrote in the *Herald of Truth* of his trip to Burr Oak, "where Bro. C. D. Beery (Dea.) was awaiting our arrival, and conveyed us to his house, a distance of about nine miles. In this neighborhood we found seven families of my relatives and acquaintances, who have recently removed from Fairfield and Allen counties, Ohio, among whom are six members of the Mennonite Church." Brenneman held services the next day in a schoolhouse.

In February 1866 Deacon C. D. Beery reported to John F. Funk of Elkhart that there were six members living in that community, and that they had no preacher. "We moved here last summer." He reported that three ministers had so far visited them: George Brenneman of Ohio, John Snyder from Elkhart County, Indiana, and Daniel Brenneman also of Elkhart County. "We have meeting every four weeks." He reported that there was no meetinghouse within eight or ten miles of where he lived. The 1867 *Herald of Truth* (page 152) reported that there were then living twenty-three members of the Mennonite Church in the vicinity. On August 26, 1867, Bishop John M. Brenneman ordained C. D. Beery to the office of preacher. It appears to have been 1866 when Abraham S. Friesner was also ordained to the ministry. John M. Brenneman received six members in November 1867, bringing the total at that point to twenty-eight members. "They are very much in need of a meetinghouse," but felt unable to build one.

In the year 1868 Henry Yother of Reading, Illinois, accompanied by John F. Funk and several other persons, went to Burr Oak and baptized four converts in a schoolhouse, and preached in another schoolhouse that afternoon. On Monday morning, March 23, the little congregation met in the home of Isaac Good, and Abraham Blosser was chosen as deacon and ordained by Henry Yother. The congregation also observed the Lord's Supper.

In the year 1869 the little congregation felt able to undertake the building of a meetinghouse, which was accomplished. The building was not yet finished when the first services were held in it November 14, 1869. On December 22 of that year Bishop Henry Yother ordained C. D. Beery to the office of bishop, and he served faithfully and effectively until his death in 1878.

On January 8, 9, 1870, Preachers John F. Funk and Samuel Yoder attended two pleasant and interesting meetings in the new Pleasant Hill meetinghouse, and one at the Troyer schoolhouse. In 1872 the *Herald of Truth* (page 154) reported that the Sunday school in Branch County then had seventy-five scholars and teachers. Funk's private notes of the 1880's indicate that the church membership then consisted of but eighteen persons.

Preacher A. S. Friesner died of tuberculosis December 31, 1870. On June 17, 1876, his son Harvey was ordained as minister, less than two years before the death of Bishop C. D. Beery. John S. Coffman wrote in the *Herald of Truth* for 1879: "There is an interesting little flock of brothers and sisters at this place. Bro. Harvey Friesner is their minister, and Bro. Daniel Beery their deacon. They have a comfortable and convenient meetinghouse, in which they hold regular services every two weeks. On one occasion John F. Funk and wife visited A. S. Friesner, held a meeting at Hickory Corners, and spent the night in the home of Tobias Kreider."

Somehow the work at Pleasant Hill did not thrive. It is known that Preacher Henry Shaum of Elkhart County was present on May 5, 1885, when the Sunday school was again organized for the summer. In the 1890 *Herald of Truth* Preacher Harvey Friesner reported that Sunday school had been started at Pleasant Hill in 1883; he seemed unaware of the 1872 Sunday school which must have been discontinued.

A new day for the congregation almost dawned with the ordination of John Krupp in 1870. Krupp was a dynamic preacher, but later affiliated with the group which eventually became the United Missionary Church, and unfortunately had his ministry revoked late in the year 1873. It appears that during the following decade the Mennonite group grew weaker and weaker, while the Mennonite Brethren in Christ group grew stronger. In 1897 Preacher Samuel Yoder of Elkhart went to Bronson (.8 of a mile east and 5.4 miles north of the Pleasant Hill meetinghouse) "on the wrong Sunday." Yoder arrived when it was the time for the M.B.C. "quarterly meeting." Nevertheless on Saturday evening the group kindly allowed Yoder to preach, and the next day, Sunday morning and evening, Daniel Brenneman filled the pulpit. It is known that Samuel Yoder again preached at Pleasant Hill May 18, 1904.

It is said that the high point in the membership of the congregation was reached when there were forty members. By the year 1905 the membership had declined to two. Preacher Jacob W. Christophel and Deacon Noah S. Hoover of the Yellow Creek congregation investigated the situation in September of that year. They reported: "The probability is that the [meeting] house will be sold to another denomination." Later that year the *Herald of Truth* reported that the meetinghouse had indeed been sold to the Mennonite Brethren in Christ Church for $650.00. The last members of the church were Deacon Daniel F. Beery and wife; he died March 19, 1911, while his wife Rebecca lived until 1923. The death of the congregation is probably to be attributed to weak leadership, and to the inability of the Indiana-Michigan Conference to absorb the enthusiasm and revivalistic emphasis of Daniel Brenneman and his Pleasant Hill supporters, which included Preacher John Krupp.

CALEDONIA MENNONITE CHURCH

Section 18, Caledonia Township, Kent County, Michigan

The first printed reference to the Caledonia Mennonite Church is found in the 1864 *Herald of Truth* in which Preacher David Sherk of Ontario reported his visit to Kent County in October 1863. He left Berlin (now Kitchener, Ontario) on October 13 and took the train to Grand Rapids, Michigan. He was welcomed by the "only brother in the vicinity," who lived in Kent County, about sixteen miles from Grand Rapids. The brother's name was Johnson, and he and three "sisters" (Mennonites) from "our community" have settled in Kent County. Sherk reported that one sister had lived more than ten years in Kent County as of that date; her husband was dead. Only one Mennonite preacher had visited the Kent County Mennonites from 1853 to 1863, Jacob Hallman, "several years ago." Johnson "grasped us by the hand and with tearful eyes wished us God's blessing and happiness. This brother located in Kent County the spring of 1863." The two widows of the community bore the names Detweiler and Kinzie. They requested that Preacher Sherk serve them communion. When he got to the home of Widow Detweiler two persons requested baptism, and one desired to be reinstated to full membership in the Mennonite Church. At a meeting held in the Johnson home the next day all these requests were fulfilled; also baptism, Lord's Supper, and feet washing were observed "in the presence of a number of attentive hearers and spectators." Another note in the *Herald of Truth* for 1864 (page 49) reported that there were now seven members of the church in Kent County. Elias and Polly (Clemens) Bowman are reported to have moved from Ontario to Kent County in 1863. Polly was a native of Bucks County, Pennsylvania. Another 1863 settler was Amos Clemens, also a native of Bucks County, but who came from Ontario to Michigan; his wife was Mary Wismer. Other early settlers included Abraham and Esther (Blough) Hershberger (she was a native of Somerset County, Pennsylvania); Joseph C. and Anna Bowman of Ontario; and John and Mary Leatherman.

The first ordained men in the congregation were Preacher Abraham

Detweiler and Deacon Martin Good. D. H. Landes of Fairfield County, Ohio, visited Kent County, Michigan, January 22, 1865. He met Deacon Martin Good and Preacher Detweiler. "They are making preparations to build a meetinghouse there." He also reported that "more members are still moving there." Landes said: "We attended one meeting there at Bro. Martin Good's house." In 1865 the aged mother of Preacher Daniel Brundage was living eight miles from Petersburg, Michigan. Daniel Brenneman speaks of visiting in 1865, "the newly organized church in Kent County, Michigan." The 1866 *Herald of Truth* (page 50) speaks of "Martin Good's meetinghouse." The first deed was granted on June 1, 1865, by Martin Good to the West Caledonia Burial Society. (*Liber* 36, page 491.) The second deed was granted October 10, 1867, by Martin Good to David Martin, deacon in the "Old Menonite Church or Society of Caledonia," for a consideration of $1.00, "in trust for church purposes." This plot was located on the southeast corner of Section 18 of Caledonia Township, on the northwest corner of the intersection of what is now Eighty-fourth Street with Kraft Avenue. The "Good" meetinghouse evidently took its name from the member on whose land it was built, Martin Good.

By the year 1867 the Caledonia congregation consisted of over forty members and was served by Preachers Abraham Detweiler and Henry Wismer (ordained by John M. Brenneman April 30 1866), and by Deacon David Martin. In 1867 John M. Brenneman not only met with the congregation in the Caledonia meetinghouse, but also held a meeting in "Bro. Wismer's schoolhouse." At this point the future of the congregation looked bright. But John F. Funk recorded in his diary for 1871 that on March 25 Abraham Detweiler was silenced for improper and disorderly conduct; possibly Funk meant, not immorality but undue exuberance and emotional excesses associated with revivalism: we do not know. We do know that in 1873 Preacher Henry Wismer had united with what is now the United Missionary Church. John Moyer, who was probably born about 1825, was ordained deacon in 1869, and served for some time. Peter D. Steiner was ordained preacher in 1875, but in a few years moved to the state of Ohio. From 1879 until 1886 there was no ordained preacher in the congregation.

In the year 1889 J. S. Hartzler, then an alert young minister of thirty-two, "at the request of Bro. Christian Wenger . . . visited the Caledonia Church in Kent County. This is the largest church visited thus far. They have one minister who preaches German [Jacob Hahn] and two who preach English [C. C. Beery and Christian Wenger]. . . . A cold wave has gone over both these churches [Caledonia and Bowne] from which they are now recovering, and by the earnest work of the ministers and laity the effects will soon disappear." Hartzler reported that the young people were inclined to follow the world's "follies and vanities" and to stand outside the church. The *Herald of Truth* for 1880 had reported that there were living about twelve families in the Caledonia Church. Preacher Beery seems to have been ordained about 1885, Wenger in 1886, and Hahn moved into the community in 1889. All three of these ministers terminated their service with the Caledonia congregation in the year 1897. At that point there was a great upheaval in the life of the Caledonia Church.

The trouble which came to a head in 1897 involved a struggle between Bishop John F. Funk and Preacher Christian G. Wenger. Funk went to Caledonia in June of that year to give communion to the congregation. Funk felt that it was his obligation to uphold the standards of the church, while Wenger was more inclined to allow the congregation to follow its own course in reference to garb and other matters of church discipline. Wenger "raised a big issue" over Funk's alleged requirements for the women to wear bonnets. Funk in turn regarded Wenger and his wife as "stumbling blocks in the church for years." He charged that Wenger avoided teaching Mennonite doctrine. He also claimed that Wenger intimidated the church, "so that neither the members nor his fellow ministers ever dared to say anything to him." The break came at the close of the Sunday-school session on Sunday, June 20, 1897. Wenger asked the Caledonia Mennonite Sunday School to elect another superintendent, saying, "I am separated from this church." Thereupon nearly the whole Sunday school walked out, including the young people. Twenty-one members remained after Wenger and his group withdrew. Perhaps the most acute issue was the wearing of the prayer veiling by the women of the church. Wenger was inclined to regard this item as a cultural matter, while Funk was just as certain that it was a part of the religious practice of the denomination.

The Caledonia congregation never rallied after this blow. Had the members known in 1881 that this trouble was to come, they would no doubt have decided not to build their new meetinghouse, which in January 1881 was "not entirely finished." In 1907 a woman named Salome Good reopened the Caledonia Mennonite Sunday School which had been closed for ten years. The date of opening was May 12, and fifteen were present. On June 2 there were present twenty-five children, plus seven teachers and other adults, making a total attendance of thirty-two. The *Gospel Witness* of 1907 reported (page 233): "The place was once supplied with three ministers and the church filled with people. In 1897 the devil came into the church and after some time there were left only a few old people and one young sister with a family. The church is now in the hands of the heirs but is not for sale. The sister married to one of the heirs has now opened a Sunday school. On May 12 fifteen were present and on June 30th, thirty-five." The 1908 *Herald of Truth* reported: "Here still remains the nucleus of a church, a small membership, mostly old people, and here also are the descendants of members, who from early childhood had the principles and practices of the Mennonite people implanted into their minds and hearts. . . . A young brother ought to locate there and be their preacher! 'Who will go?' " Even as early as 1901 the *Herald of Truth* reported: "This congregation has passed through many severe trials, and only a small number remain." At that point Preacher Isaac Weaver of Bowne was holding services every four weeks. The membership in 1905 was reported in the *Herald of Truth* as down to thirteen. J. P. Miller served communion both in 1905 and 1906. The 1909 sessions of the Indiana-Michigan Mennonite Conference appointed Aldus Brackbill of the Bowne congregation to take charge of the work at Caledonia "for another year." In 1909 the "Holy Corner [Caledonia] Sunday School" was reorganized on April 4. Joseph Mishler of the Bowne congregation then served the tiny group as deacon. It was probably only a few years after this until all services ceased in the Caledonia congregation, and one by one the last old people who were members there passed away.

The following Mennonite names appear in the cemetery of the Caledonia congregation: Beery, Blough, Bowman, Detweiler, Dirstein, Eby, Eyman, Fischer, Good, Hahn, Hershberger, Hilty, Lehman, Martin, Miller, Moyer, Schantz, Schultz, Sherk, Wenger, and Wismer. The 1881 meetinghouse burned to the ground in the year 1923. So all that is left of the onetime Caledonia congregation at Holy Corners is the old Mennonite cemetery. Two Brubaker families moved from Caledonia to Elkhart about the year 1900. The congregation probably never recovered from the shock occasioned by the loss of its two ministers in the early 1870's, Abraham W. Detweiler and Henry Wismer, and by the withdrawal of a third, the able Christian Wenger, in 1897. As early as 1891 the matter of the wearing of the prayer veiling in the Caledonia congregation was discussed in the Indiana Conference, but was evidently handled with such patience and love that both Preacher Wenger and the congregation were satisfied. But it was a different story in June 1897, when John F. Funk, a man of iron will, clashed sharply with Christian Wenger, who was equally firm. Funk reported in his diary for June 19 of that year that he had "another talk with Christ Wenger . . . found him a very scheming and tough man to handle." The fact is that within ten years Funk himself was relieved of his bishop oversight for the very qualities which he found so trying in Christian Wenger.

BOWNE MENNONITE CHURCH

Section 13, Bowne Township, Kent County, Michigan

The first-known Mennonite settlers in Bowne Township moved there in 1865, and came from Somerset County, Pennsylvania: Herman Bentler, Peter Keim, Alexander Stahl, and Emanuel Weaver. About the same time several families moved to Bowne Township from Ontario, including John Smith. The first services were held in a private home across the county line in Ionia County. Here the Mennonites were worshiping in November 1867 when Jacob Hildebrand of Virginia visited them. He speaks of holding services for Preacher Cline, which seems to be a mistake for Keim, and calls the private home a meetinghouse. Hildebrand served communion on November 11, 1867. There were at that time thirty members in the congregation. (Caledonia then had forty members.)

In April 1866, John M. Brenneman of Elida, Ohio, who always seemed to be aware of new Mennonite settlements in need of congregational organization and the ordination of preachers, visited Bowne Township. On April 28, 1866, he ordained Peter Keim as preacher and Herman Bentler as deacon. The 1905 *Herald of Truth* (page 135) declares that these ordinations occurred "at the organization of the church in Bowne." In 1866 the congregation bought an acre of land, east of the present meetinghouse, where the cemetery is now located, for $80.00 of Loren Tyler. On December 5, 1866, Loren B. Tyler and Abigail M., his wife, conveyed the square plot of ground, one acre in extent, to the officers of the Menonist Church and their successors. *(Liber* 64, page 469.) This lot was located along what is now Seventy-sixth Street where it intersects with the Freeport Avenue Road, in the south central portion of Section 13 of Bowne Township. Tyler conveyed an additional one-half acre of land to the officers of the "Old Mennonite Church," on July 10, 1894.

In 1867 John P. Speicher, who had transferred to the Bowne congregation from Caledonia, was ordained preacher, and a little over two years later, the fall of 1869, he was ordained bishop. In 1870 the congregation decided to build a meetinghouse on the first plot of land purchased from Tyler in 1866. A note in the January 1871 *Herald of Truth* reports that services were held at Bowne and that "the house is yet new and not entirely finished." This building was used as a house of worship by the German Baptists every other Sunday until they built their own meetinghouse in 1879. The 1870 meetinghouse was a log structure.

The Bowne congregation has the distinction of being the first church in which John S. Coffman held "protracted meetings," now known as evangelistic services. This was in the year 1881. In that year the congregation had a Sunday school of fifty scholars. (1881 *H.T., p*age 137.)

In the year 1889 Preacher J. S. Hartzler, then a young minister of thirty-two, visited a number of congregations in Michigan. In reference to the Bowne congregation he wrote: "This church is still larger than the Caledonia Church. They have two ministers here [Peter Keim and John P. Speicher] but both preach in German. They greatly need one who can preach in English. A cold wave has gone over both these churches from which they are now recovering."

In 1891 Isaac Weaver was ordained preacher and served until his death in 1917. John F. Funk visited the congregation in 1893 and, surprising as it may seem, on February 26 baptized eleven converts who knelt in a stream through a hole which had been chopped in the ice! Three years later the membership at Bowne was reported as forty, two thirds of whom communed on July 5, 1896, when John F. Funk officiated. By 1899 the congregation numbered sixty-four. That winter the Sunday school became evergreen, as a note in the *Herald of Truth* reported three years later: "Our Sunday school is 'evergreen' and we intend to keep it so." In the year 1900 Joseph W. Mishler was ordained deacon and served until his death in 1928.

In 1901 the Bowne congregation decided no longer to use its old log meetinghouse, but to build a new frame house of worship, the one which is still in use. The 1901 *Herald of Truth* (page 170) reports that the congregation now numbered eighty members, with sixty scholars in its "prosperous Sunday school." B. F. Thut of Ohio held singing schools in the Bowne congregation in 1899 and again in 1900. The *Herald of Truth* for 1902 reported that the congregation had a good new meetinghouse, and that the church appeared to be in good condition. In 1903 B. F. Thut again conducted a singing school. In 1905 Niles M. Slabaugh taught a singing school at Bowne. A number of ministers moved into the congregation and continued their service there. Preacher Aldus Brackbill of Lancaster, Pennsylvania, served from 1907 until 1928. Deacon Eli Zook served from 1911 until 1924. Bishop Jacob P. Miller served from 1911 until 1916. Deacon George Stahl served from 1925 until 1948. T. E. Schrock was ordained preacher for Bowne in 1931, and bishop in 1936. Deacon Eli Zook's son, Daniel E. Zook, was ordained preacher in 1940. Harold M. Christophel was ordained deacon in 1945, and in the year 1958 undertook the pastoral care of the Heath Street Mennonite Mission in Battle Creek, Michigan, which had been started as an outpost of Bowne in 1952.

By 1905 the membership of the Bowne congregation was eighty-two, in 1915 it was 101, in 1920 it was seventy-eight, in 1940 it was 104, and the 1960 *Mennonite Yearbook* shows a membership of ninety-nine.

Mennonites as well as non-Mennonites from the community bury in

the Bowne Mennonite Cemetery. Mennonite names such as the following are found on the tombstones: Beck, Berkey, Blough, Bowman, Boyer,
Burkholder, Davidhizar, Dintaman, Eash, Erb, Harr, Hoffman, Kauffman, Keim, Keller, King, Long, Miller, Mishler, Oesch, Overholt, Rosenberger, Shroyer, Snyder, Speicher, Stahl, Thomas, Troyer, Weaver, Yoder,
and Zook.

MAPLE RIVER MENNONITE CHURCH

Section 21, Maple River Township, Emmet County, Michigan

One of the best summaries of the settlement of the Mennonites in
the Brutus, Michigan, area (north of Petoskey and not far south of the
Straits of Mackinac) is found in the 1929 Minute Book of the Indiana-
Michigan Mennonite Conference: "The first Mennonites to migrate to
this section were the family of Abraham Detweiler, a minister formerly
from Ontario, but later a resident of Kent County, Michigan, and a
minister in the Caledonia Mennonite Church. They came to Brutus in
1879, as did also Jonas Brubachers. Later settlers in this community were
the families of Joseph Detweilers in 1880 from Ontario, Jacob Souders in
1881 from Ontario, John Kilmers in 1882 from Indiana, and Christian
Detweiler from Kent County, Michigan. Still later came Owen Sniders,
Jonathan Gehmans, and Jonas Leinbachs, all from Indiana, Amos Brubachers from Ontario, and the Tyson families: David, Daniel, John, and
Isaac; Abraham and David Boyers, and Benjamin Legrons, all from
Wood County, Ohio, and others. Many of these had grown children and
soon a number of other homes were established."

The congregation built a frame meetinghouse in the year 1883, one
mile west of the village of Brutus. This building is still in use. Preacher
J. J. Weaver of the Shore congregation visited the Maple River congregation, often known as the Detweiler Church, in the year 1884. He reported that the congregation had a "commodious meetinghouse." It was
not long until there was not only a congregation at Brutus, but there
were also Mennonites living at Bliss in Emmet County. (Preachers who
went to Bliss to serve the Mennonites of that area got off the train at
Levering.) The *Herald of Truth* for 1887 reports that in the previous
year Preacher Harvey Friesner of Branch County, Michigan, had
preached for the Mennonites at Bliss.

Although Abraham W. Detweiler did not locate in Emmet County
until 1879, the *Herald of Truth* for 1880 reports that the first Mennonites settled in Emmet County in 1875. The writer went on to say that
land sold from four to eight dollars per acre. The *Herald of Truth* for
1887 reported that there were then sixteen members in Emmet County,
ten of them living "near together."

About the year 1886 Bishop Jacob Wisler of Indiana ordained
Jonathan Gehman of Emmet County to the ministry. The division of
the Maple River congregation, resulting in the formation of a Wisler
congregation, occurred in 1886. In 1887 Bishop Henry Shaum of
Indiana ordained Christian W. Detweiler to the ministry in the Maple
River congregation. In 1890 Preacher J. S. Hartzler, 32, visited the
Mennonites in Emmet County. "The church here is not in a good condition; there are only about thirty or forty members here and [they]
are considerably divided. Love seems to be lost to a very great degree."
Hartzler evidently had in mind the troubled conditions which followed
the Wisler division in 1886. As to the work at Bliss Hartzler added:
"There are only a few members here. They seem to live in peace and
harmony but they have no minister, and seem to be somewhat discour-
aged on that account." Samuel Yoder reported in 1895 that there were
two ministers in the Maple River congregation (Abraham W. and Christian W. Detweiler). He said that the outlook was discouraging, and that
the congregation had no Sunday school. "That charitable spirit and
bond of peace and love is not so manifest as [it] should be."

In the year 1896 Bishop J. F. Funk went to Brutus and adjusted a
difficulty between Preacher Abraham Detweiler and his tenant, a man
named Souder. Funk requested Detweiler to desist from preaching until
a council meeting could be held in the fall. "Let Christ Detweiler conduct the meeting alone." It was probably following this incident that
Abraham W. Detweiler transferred to the Wisler congregation. In any
case in 1897 when Funk went to Brutus for the communion service he
listed the following members as being present and communing: Christian
W. Detweiler and wife, D. B. Shelly and wife, Joseph Detweiler, Sr., and
wife, Abraham Detweiler, Jr., and wife, Jacob Reinhold and wife,
Schwartzentruber and wife, Jacob Souder and wife, Mrs. Peter Schrock,
Mrs. Annie Fetters, Mrs. Hernley, Mrs. Kurtz, John Kurtz, and Amos
Brubaker's wife. This made a total of twenty. Funk regarded the prospects of the church as bright. He wrote in his diary that more members
had gone to communion than at any other previous time. Funk mentions that Sunday school was held in the afternoon on that day (July
4, 1897). In his characteristically vigorous manner Funk had written in
his diary on the previous day: "We established peace . . . and nailed it
down. . . . Anyone who again stirs up strife will have [to] answer for it
before the public meeting." In the year 1898 twenty-two members communed at Maple River. In 1902 John Reinbold was ordained to the
office of deacon, but in 1910 he moved to Alberta. By the year 1912 only
seven members communed. In 1917 Christian W. Detweiler, the preacher, died. In 1919 only three members were left.

The district mission board then took charge of the situation and in 1920 arranged for the ordination of Clyde X. Kauffman of the Clinton Frame congregation as preacher. He located at Brutus the spring of 1921. This event marked the beginning of a new chapter in the life of the congregation. At the end of his first year's service, the membership had built up to twenty-five, and in a few years even that figure was doubled. This was partly due to members transferring from the Wisler congregation to that of Kauffman. In the year 1925 Manford Freed was ordained deacon, but following the death of his wife in 1929 he returned to Indiana. In 1932 Jeremiah B. Eby was ordained to the office of deacon and served about three years. By 1952 Clyde X. Kauffman felt the need of help in the ministry, and the bishop of the congregation, Ray F. Yoder, ordained Earl Hartman of the Olive congregation to the ministry; Hartman located at Brutus in 1954. Perhaps the high point in the life of the church came in 1940 when there were eighty-three members. The 1960 *Yearbook* lists fifty-three. Ray F. Yoder resigned as bishop, because of the state of his health, in 1960. The congregation chose Floyd F. Bontrager as his successor.

It should also be mentioned that scattered Mennonites were living in Petoskey and community in the first decades of the Maple River congregation. John F. Funk in 1896 mentioned a woman Annie Kindig Fetter one mile north of Harbor Springs, and also a Mrs. Kurtz in Petoskey, who were Mennonites; he also speaks of a John Kurtz.

ANTRIM COUNTY, MICHIGAN

As early as 1880 David and Elizabeth (Hoover) Garber, the parents of Preacher C. J. Garber of Alpha, Minnesota, moved from Branch County, Michigan, to Antrim County for the sake of cheaper land, and because it was a good lumbering country. Among the Mennonite families who located in Antrim County in the general area of Mancelona were families by the name of Baumgartner, Cleveland, Dester, Eash, Emmert, Haarer, Hostetler, Kauffman, Kindy, Reed, Schrock, Shelly, Springer, Stutzman, and Troyer: most of whom moved there from Northern Indiana. Included in the group were several daughters of Preacher J. J. Weaver of the Shore congregation, and their families. Weaver himself used to visit the Mancelona settlement, as did Preachers Christian Wenger and Jacob Hahn of Caledonia, John F. Funk and J. S. Hartzler of Elkhart, and Joseph Miller of the Forks congregation. C. J. Garber remembers when John S. Coffman baptized a class of eight in the John Troyer home.

The Mancelona Mennonites always worshiped in homes, meeting regularly every two weeks. C. J. Garber remembers that they enjoyed singing together. D. B. Shelly used to preach to the group, but was never ordained.

The *Herald of Truth* for 1883 reported that there were twenty-two members at Mancelona. The next year the *Herald of Truth* reported that: "It would be very desirable to have an organized church at Mancelona." Adam Schrock was at that time the superintendent of the "Good Sunday School" at Mancelona. In 1884 Bishop Henry A. Miller and J. J. Weaver of the Shore congregation held six meetings with the Mancelona Mennonites, and served them communion.

There were also Mennonites living at Arcona, eight miles west of Mancelona. They organized a Sunday school on February 8, 1885.

The 1886 *Herald of Truth* reported that there were twelve Amish Mennonites and ten Mennonite members living in Antrim County who were "willing to join hand in hand, and be united as one body in the Lord." It was reported that they had maintained a Sunday school without intermission for three years. The 1886 *Herald of Truth* also speaks of meetings in the Mancelona area, and three in the Troyer Amish Mennonite settlement nine miles west. Nine converts resulted from this evangelistic effort. In 1887 Harvey Friesner visited the Antrim County Mennonites and made mention of Isaac Garber, Leonard Garber, Nicholas Blosser, and David Garber. Around the turn of the century most of the Mennonites moved to other communities, but as late as 1908 the *Gospel Herald* spoke of the "little flock" in Antrim County.

In 1908 P. S. Weirich, Jacob Yoder, and D. E. Kauffman were living at Elmira, near Mancelona, in Otsego County, Michigan, close to the Antrim County line. "There has been some talk of starting a Mennonite colony near Elmira." In 1910 a man named Urbane Cotterman was baptized into the Mennonite Church near Mancelona on Christmas Day. In 1918 he moved to Jackson, Minnesota.

When John F. Funk visited Mancelona in 1894, he stopped in the homes of Isaac Garber, Christian Garber, D. B. Shelly at Wetzel, and Samuel Shelly his son; he also mentions a widow named Amstutz. On that occasion sixteen partook of communion. But in 1898 only four members were left.

The *Herald of Truth* for 1881 reports the trip of John S. Coffman to the area. He walked five miles west of Petoskey to the home of John Hernley, formerly of Indiana, who had moved to Michigan in 1880. He then visited Henry Garbers and Jacob Garbers ten miles east of Cross Village. Fourteen miles north of Petoskey he met Abraham and Joseph Detweiler, Jonas Brubaker, and "some other families of the brethren and sisters." Coffman reported that Bro. A. Detweiler (of Brutus) regularly holds services, preaching for them in the German language. A member of the church named Brower was then living in Petoskey with her son Joseph. Coffman reported that services were held at Mancelona in Antrim County, in the home of Brother Jacob Kauffman, and Brother David Garber. Coffman had hopes that a church could soon be established. But his anticipations were never realized. No congregation was organized, and the Mennonite settlement died.

PIGEON MENNONITE CHURCH

Section 2, Windsor Township, Huron County, Michigan

Many years ago Harold S. Bender of Goshen College had an interview with a man who was evidently quite aged, Abram Wambold. He recited to H. S. Bender the story of the movement of Mennonites from the Hay congregation in Ontario to Fairfield, Michigan, about 1878-80. (Samuel Reesor, a deacon, had moved back to Markham, 1872.) In fact, Wambold declared, most of the Hay members moved to Pigeon, Michigan. He reported that the congregation was not very old when the Wambold family moved there. The members at that time were Samuel and Benjamin Reesor, Joseph Smith, Donald Lehman (all from Markham), Samuel Freed from Waterloo, and Abraham Vincent. All these were in the ("thumb of Michigan") area before 1860. Others came later, including: Henry Detweiler, Daniel Steckley, Henry Otterbein, John Moyer from Waterloo, Samuel Grove and Benjamin Lehman from Markham, William Bechtel, Noah Bechtel, and Thomas Clemens. (In many cases Wambold gave only nicknames, such as Sam and Joe).

The settlement which Wambold described seems to apply more particularly to Tuscola County than to Huron County. It is known, however, that William Bechtel was living at Pigeon in the year 1890. Preacher Daniel Lehman, who was ordained in the Hay congregation in 1861, according to L. J. Burkholder, lived at Fairgrove (not Fairfield) for about thirty-five years (*ca.* 1884-1919). Wambold concluded his account to H. S. Bender by remarking that the congregation disintegrated and "closed down" in the 1890's.

The chief problem in the testimony of Wambold is the question as to why he referred to the settlement as Pigeon. Is it possible that Mennonites were living in the general area between Fairgrove and Berne (one mile north of Pigeon), a distance of thirty miles or less? It should be noted that Wambold implied that Samuel Reesor had served for a time with Daniel Lehman in the Mennonite Church in the thumb of Michigan. These families were always affiliated with the Ontario Conference, rather than with Indiana-Michigan.

The first reference in the *Herald of Truth* to the Mennonites of

Huron County occurred in a letter of J. S. Hartzler, then a young minister of thirty-two, who visited William Bechtel and family who lived near Bay Port "in the midst of a congregation of Latter Day Saints." Mrs. Bechtel commented to Hartzler: "Our family worship is all that is left for us whereby to kindle the flame of the love of God. " Is this sentence perhaps a confirmation of the theory that there were originally Mennonite families in Huron County attached to the Tuscola County congregation served by Preacher Daniel Lehman and Deacon Samuel Reesor?

In 1890 there was living at Elkton, a few miles east of Pigeon, a Ramseyer family which had come from Zurich, Ontario. A member of this family, Joseph E. Ramseyer, 1869-1944, experienced the "gift of the Holy Spirit," in 1891, and seven years later became one of the founders of the Missionary Church Association. (See chapter 7.)

In February 1894 Preachers J. J. Weaver of Indiana, Daniel Lehman of Tuscola County, and Samuel S. Bowman of Ontario visited the Huron County Mennonites. There were at that time eleven Mennonite families there; evidently ten of them had moved into the area between 1890 and 1894. The 1894 *Herald of Truth* also reported that Preacher J. J. Weaver held meetings in Antrim, Emmet, Tuscola, and Huron counties, with a total of nineteen converts. Weaver reported that: "Those in Huron County will be under the care of the church in Canada, while those in the north expect to be received by someone from here."

On December 11, 1896, a special conference was held at the Christian Eby meetinghouse, Berlin, Ontario (now First Mennonite Church, Kitchener), "to consider the matter of aiding our brethren at Berne, Huron County, Michigan, in their church work. There are now resident there eleven families, with thirty-eight children, whose ages range from eighteen years down. For the past three years our ministers in Canada have visited them regularly in October and February, one of the bishops holding communion in June." It was decided that a minister should settle there for one year. Samuel S. Bowman was chosen for this assignment. He agreed to do so, provided the Berne congregation was willing to ordain a preacher and a deacon from their own number, that Sunday school and church services should be held every Sunday, and that a meetinghouse should be built. The lot and meetinghouse were to cost $400.00, of which the Berne members would raise $100.00, the Canadian Mennonites would raise $200.00, and the Indiana Mennonites were requested to raise the final $100.00: this to be accomplished by July 1, 1897. All of this was communicated by four Ontario bishops to Bishop John F. Funk of Elkhart, who in turn was to present it to the Indiana Conference.

The outcome of the Ontario Conference session was that Preacher Samuel S. Bowman located at Berne on May 3, 1897. He remained there

11

until the conditions originally stipulated had been realized. The frame for the Berne meetinghouse was raised on Saturday, May 8, 1897. The next day Sunday school was organized with Peter Ropp as superintendent, Joel Reist as assistant, and Elias Wideman as secretary. These services were held at the Joel Reist home on May 9, and one week later at the home of Menno Wideman. Bowman reported in the *Herald of Truth:* "I would advise all brethren who are looking for new homes to visit this part of Michigan before buying elsewhere. The soil is good and there are good railway connections. It is a very good fruit country."

The meetinghouse was formally opened June 20, 1897. Preacher Daniel Lehman of Tuscola County opened the meeting, and two Egly Amish Mennonite preachers were present, one of whom preached in English. Communion services were held in the new meetinghouse in care of Bishop Amos Cressman of Ontario on July 4, 1897. The next day the congregation ordained a preacher, Peter Ropp, and a deacon, Menno Wideman; Amos Cressman officiated.

Preacher Samuel S. Bowman returned to Ontario January 24, 1898. Just before he left, David Garber of Orrville, Ohio, held meetings, December 30, 1897, through January 17, 1898, with a total of thirteen converts. In 1901 Preacher M. S. Steiner delivered five sermons in the month of August. The congregation at that time had "faithful preaching every Sunday." Sunday-school attendance during 1901 averaged about forty.

In 1906 Peter Ropp, the local preacher, and Israel Shantz of Ontario held a series of meetings for two weeks, and a Bible conference, which resulted in seventeen more converts, nine of whom decided to unite with the Mennonite Church. Ropp baptized them February 11, 1906. One of the most successful series of meetings was held by L. J. Burkholder from February 23 to March 8, 1908, with twenty-five converts.

Deacon Menno Wideman served until his death in 1923. Peter Ropp served until 1917, when he transferred to the Bethany congregation. Preacher Alfred Weidman served from 1917 until 1924, when he transferred to the Missionary Church Association.

The congregation was transferred from the Ontario Conference to Indiana-Michigan in the year 1916. In 1926 Samuel J. Miller was ordained to the ministry and served there eighteen years, during which time a new meetinghouse was built. Dedication services were held on December 2, 1934, with Oscar Burkholder preaching the sermon. Deacon Joseph J. Shetler served from 1929 until his death in 1951. In 1933 Sherman Maust was ordained to the ministry to assist Samuel J. Miller, but he removed to California in 1944, leaving the congregation without a minister. This need was met in 1946 when Donald E. King, a graduate of Goshen College Biblical Seminary, was engaged to serve the congregation; he was ordained bishop in 1957. In 1958 the pulpit was supplied by Don D. Reber, the missionary to Japan, while Donald King returned to the Seminary for additional work.

By the close of the first World War the Berne congregation, as it was known prior to the building of the 1934 meetinghouse in the village of Pigeon, had a membership of seventy-nine. In 1920 the membership still stood at the same figure. Under the ministry of S. J. Miller the congregation prospered, so that by 1944 the membership stood at 132. In later years the membership somewhat declined so that the 1960 *Mennonite Yearbook* indicates ninety-six members.

OKEMOS MENNONITE CHURCH

Ingham County, Michigan

In 1880 references to the congregation of Russian Mennonites living in the Okemos area, about seven miles east of Lansing, Michigan, began to appear in the diary of John F. Funk. The congregation at that time numbered twenty-five, with Cornelius Unruh serving as minister. Funk preached for the little group on August 8, 1880, and also baptized John and David Unruh, as well as reinstating Henry Pauls and a daughter of Brother Tjiart. Funk reported that of the twenty-seven members on August 9, 1880, twenty were ready to affiliate with the (Old) Mennonite Church, and to organize a congregation. In his usual vigorous manner, Funk proceeded to organize the church and to give them communion. He required the men to remove their mustaches, while the women needed to adopt the bonnet as their headgear, and "drop the gatherings in their dresses." In November 1882 Funk was at Okemos again, and baptized five converts, as well as reinstating one member. Twenty partook of communion.

In the back of the 1886 notebook Funk recorded the names of the family heads at Okemos as follows: Peter Kerber, August Zilke, Jakob Ratslaff, Cornelius Unruh, Leonard Pauls, John Kliever, Peter Tjiart, Jacob Tjiart, ———— Evert, and Jacob Nickels.

In 1890 the *Herald of Truth* reported that at "Okemos . . . there are about thirty or thirty-five members of Russian Brethren. They had two ministers, one of whom quit preaching on his own accord and the other one was silenced on account of preaching doctrines which the membership considered unscriptural. They have no minister now." That same year Preacher Joseph D. Miller of the Forks Amish Mennonite Church held several meetings there. In 1893 John P. Speicher visited the congregation on July 8: "The number of attendants was not large, but they were very attentive. The members here formerly lived near together but now they are so scattered that it is hard to get them [all together] to the meetings. They have no Sunday school; their children attend other schools, and in this way may be led away from the church of their fathers. . . . This little flock should be visited more frequently."

This remark about there being no Sunday school indicates that the congregation was losing ground, for the 1887 *Herald of Truth* reports that there were nine or ten families at Okemos, most of whom came from Russian Poland during the last ten or twelve years. "They hold Sunday school each week."

The 1897 *Herald of Truth* reported: "There are still in Ingham County a number of families who desire to maintain the principles and doctrines of the church. They have been without a minister and have held no meetings for some time. Arrangements have been made to supply them with preaching at regular intervals and the intervening Sundays they will hold meetings among themselves. Bro. J. F. Funk spent Sunday, November 28, [with] them and held several meetings." Funk's diary indicated that the congregation decided to have preaching every four weeks from this date (November 28, 1897). The group was to meet in a "social meeting" every week on Sunday morning; monthly meetings were to be arranged by Brother John Culp.

The *Herald of Truth* for the late 1890's contains a number of references to John Culp. Funk met him at Big Rapids, Michigan, on December 2, 1897, and they went together to the White Cloud congregation. The next year Funk again met Culp at Cadillac. In 1899 John Culp of Gratiot County, Michigan, attended communion services in the Bowne congregation. There is no evidence, however, that Culp was ordained.

Apparently the fears of Bishop Speicher, that the young people of the Okemos congregation would be lost to the church, were realized. In 1898 four brethren and one sister from Okemos communed at Bowne, when John F. Funk officiated. The last reference to the group is in the diary of Funk for June 5, 1898, when he recorded: "Have some encouragement that the little cluster of members may yet be brought into order as a church." Does this indicate that Funk never was fully satisfied with the way the Russian Mennonites obeyed the disciplinary standards of the conference? We do not know. It is evident, however, that the Okemos, or Haslett Lake, or Lansing congregation (all of which names were applied to it) died out, probably in the early years of this century.

MIDLAND MENNONITE CHURCH

Stewart and Patterson Roads,

Midland Township, Midland County, Michigan

The first Mennonite family to move into Midland Township was that of Jacob Emmert from the Emma congregation, Lagrange County, Indiana, who arrived on Thanksgiving Day, 1910, and settled six miles north of the city of Midland. The spring of 1912 another Emma family arrived, that of Abram D. Miller, who settled five miles north of Midland. In 1913 came the families of Jerry Yoder and Moses Yoder of Middlebury, Indiana; William Haarer of Shipshewana, Indiana; David Schloneger, Reuben Schloneger, and David Sommer of Elkhart, Indiana.

Prior to the coming of William Haarer, who served as a licensed minister from June 1913 until February 1916, the Mennonite families of the Midland community sometimes worshiped with the Old Order Amish who lived in a community twelve miles north of Midland on the Eastman Road. Occasional services were held in 1912 and 1913 by O. S. Hostetler of Topeka, Indiana, by Joseph Mast of Holmes County, Ohio, by J. K. Bixler of Elkhart, Indiana, by Samuel Greaser of Fulton County, Ohio, and by J. S. Hartzler of Elkhart, Indiana. These services were held in private homes and in the Gray, Cassiday, and Thornton schoolhouses.

The congregation was organized in June 1913. When Preacher Eli A. Bontrager of Fairview, Michigan, moved to Midland County in April 1916, the congregation numbered only fourteen members. By the close of 1916 the membership had grown to thirty-four. The families worshiped in an old log dwelling house on the A. D. Miller farm five miles north of Midland. The congregation remodeled the building and used it until the fall of 1917. At this time the congregation was strengthened by a number of families moving from Fulton County, Ohio, to Midland County, Michigan, namely, the families of Albert Wyse, Abram Yoder, Aaron Nafziger, and George Short. Abram B. Millers and Levi Yoders came from Brandon, Colorado. Ora Troyers moved from Oklahoma to Midland. Ezra Yoder and family came from Kansas, and David Kauffmans from Fairview, Michigan. These families located south of Midland, where Preacher Eli Bontrager also settled. The consequence was that the congregation decided to begin holding their services south of Midland.

Albert Wyse donated a plot of ground on the corner of his farm and an old Grange Hall was purchased and moved just north of the present meetinghouse, using five or six teams. This former Grange Hall was lighted, first with kerosene lamps, and later with carbide lights.

The old Grange Hall was used until a new meetinghouse was built, which meetinghouse was dedicated on March 4, 1928.

Floyd F. Bontrager was ordained preacher in 1926 to assist his father, who served until 1939. Floyd was ordained bishop in 1934. Clarence Yoder was ordained preacher in 1936, and J. Otis Yoder in 1938 (served only three years, and then entered educational work; he is now a teacher in Eastern Mennonite College in Virginia). Erie Kindy was ordained in 1952 and served a number of years. Albert Wyse was ordained deacon in 1919, and Melvin Yoder in 1944. Donald E. King has served as bishop of the congregation since 1958. A number of persons from the Midland congregation are now serving as ministers in other communities: Erie Bontrager at Vestaburg, Michigan, Ernest Bontrager in Oregon, Lester Wyse at Hartville, Ohio, and Ora Wyse in the Upper Peninsula of Michigan. The congregation has also sponsored outposts at Bombay, ten miles north of Midland; at Cady, four miles north of Midland, with Oscar Wyse in charge; and at Herrick, thirty miles northwest of Midland, near Clare, where F. F. Bontrager is now serving as pastor. Herrick was organized as an independent congregation on September 11, 1960.

In 1960 the Midland congregation decided to build a new meeting-house. The first service was held in the new building on November 20 of that year. The meetinghouse is forty by seventy feet in size, with an annex twenty by twenty-one feet, and cost approximately $50,000.00. The new house of worship was dedicated on January 29, 1961, with J. C. Wenger bringing the dedicatory address.

The membership of the congregation had grown to fifty in 1920, to 133 in 1940, and the 1960 *Yearbook* shows 138 members.

HOMESTEAD MENNONITE CHURCH
Benzie County, Michigan

In the Indiana-Michigan Mennonite Conference sessions for 1911 mention is made of a petition from the members at Homestead, Michigan, with the conference deciding to request Bishop J. P. Miller to organize a congregation and to supply it with a minister. Bishop Miller seems to have requested Deacon Harvey Sarver of the White Cloud congregation to take charge of the congregation, which he did briefly. The membership of the group was about fifteen, and consisted of families who moved there from Middlebury, Indiana, and from Kenmare, North Dakota. Sarver served for a year, 1912-13, and was succeeded by John M. Yoder who served 1913-14, and then also moved away. The 1913 sessions of the Indiana-Michigan Mennonite Conference received the Homestead congregation as a full member of conference. John M. Yoder was then in charge.

The Homestead congregation participated in union Sunday school and church services, and had no building of its own. In 1916 the conference declared that the congregation was "disorganized." The year 1918 marked the departure of the last Mennonite family from the area.

The late Daniel S. Oyer wrote the following account of the congregation at Homestead: "In the month of April, 1911, three families, namely, Horace M. Zook, wife and four children, John Mecum and wife, and the writer and wife, members of the Middlebury congregation, Middlebury, Indiana, left their homes for a new location near Homestead, Michigan. At the same time Milton Zook (brother to Horace) with his wife and son from Kenmare, North Dakota, joined our group. The Mecum family returned to Middlebury several months later.

"In the autumn of the same year death visited the Milton Zook home, taking a small baby girl whom they had adopted a few months earlier. In the fall of 1911 and continuing through the summer months of the following year, Bishop J. P. Miller from Kent County, Michigan, visited our group several times, organized a congregation, and transferred Harvey Sarver, a deacon from White Cloud, Michigan, to our community to preach for us, as we had no ministers at the time. Brother Sarver remained with us about one year, then returned to his home.

"During the time Brother Miller served as our bishop we had communion once or twice, and two young people were received into church fellowship by water baptism, namely, Ellis Zook and Fern Morningstar. The Morningstar family joined our group in the spring of 1912, coming from Minot, North Dakota, where they had lived for a number of years.

"Early in the fall of 1912 J. K. Bixler, who at that time was superintendent and bishop of the congregations under the Indiana-Michigan Mennonite Mission Board, visited us and took further steps to establish the work. In the month of June, 1913, the mission board moved John M. Yoder, formerly from Missouri, a graduate of Goshen College, to our community with a license to preach. Our group now consisted of five families with a total of fifteen members. Following is a list of them. The names underscored [in italic type] were members.

"*John M. and Nannie Yoder,* and one or two children; *Horace M. and Sally Zook, Walter, Bertha, Ellis,* and Ruth; *Louis and Fannie Morningstar, Fern,* Flossie, William, Titus, Mabel, Esther, Lela, and Ora; *Daniel S. and Frances Oyer* and Lois.

"Since we had no meetinghouse of our own we worshiped in union with other groups. One Quaker family, Methodist, Baptist, Dunkard Brethren [Church of the Brethren], and Mennonites, the latter two predominating in number.

"Prior to Brother Yoder's coming the [Church of the] Brethren from Manistee County supplied the pulpit on alternate Sundays. After Yoder arrived he filled in the vacant Sundays. The Sunday school was 'evergreen' with a Quaker for a superintendent, a Mennonite assistant, a Brethren secretary-treasurer, a Mennonite chorister, and the teachers mostly from the latter two groups.

"We also had services on Sunday evenings, similar to our Y.P.B.M. of today, and sometimes preaching.

"But the work at Homestead was short-lived. In December, 1913, the H. M. Zook family moved to South Boston, Virginia. January, 1914, the writer and family moved to Woodford County, Illinois, and the Milton Zook family to Oregon. After Brother Yoder's school closed the mission board moved him with his family to Vestaburg, Michigan, where a new work had just been launched, and where he was later ordained to the ministry. This left the Morningstar family stranded alone until the fall of 1918 when they moved to Woodford County, Illinois.

"Sometime during the winter of 1912-13 J. W. Christophel of the Yellow Creek congregation conducted a short series of meetings. In the fall of 1913 Brother D. D. Miller . . . conducted similar services. There were several confessions, as I recall, but no accessions to the church. . . .

"I was thrilled a few years ago when one Saturday afternoon my wife and I drove by this little church. The door was open and we went in. Two or three little girls were cleaning up the place for Sunday school the next day. They were children of the children who attended when I worshiped there."

TUSCOLA COUNTY MENNONITE CHURCH

Tuscola County, Michigan

Some information was given on the settlement of Mennonites in Tuscola and Huron counties in the section which gave the history of the Pigeon congregation. One of the first references to the congregation in Tuscola County was made by J. S. Hartzler, then a young minister of thirty-two, in 1889. He reported in the *Herald of Truth:* "From [Mancelona] I went to Unionville, Tuscola County. Bro. Daniel Lehman is their minister here. He labors under great disadvantages. There are only ten or twelve members, and they are scattered a distance of about sixteen miles. They hold their meetings in dwelling houses. Regardless of all these difficulties Bro. Lehman has regular appointments."

In May 1890 John F. Funk of Elkhart traveled to Caro in Tuscola County, and according to his diary, "was met by Bro. Grove . . . stayed with him all night. Met at Caro William Lehman, a son of Pre. Daniel Lehman." The next day, Sunday, May 4, 1890, Funk held a service at

the home of Brother Grove. He reported a small attendance. In the after-
noon he spoke at a schoolhouse. "Small attendance, but good attention."
On Monday Funk took dinner with George Babcock, a son-in-law of
Abram Grove. That evening he preached from Acts 2:42: "Baptism,
Feet Washing, Communion, Secret Societies, Oaths, etc." On Tuesday
Abram Grove, a son of Samuel Grove, took Funk to visit Preacher Daniel
Lehman, where he took dinner. Then he visited Noah Bechtel, where he
remained that night. On Wednesday he visited a widow named Moyer,
in whose home he held a service. "Small attendance." Mrs. Moyer's
maiden name was Bechtel. Funk noted that all of them were "related to
the Stumps." He also met Mrs. Guengerich, whose maiden name also was
Bechtel; she was a sister of Amos Bechtel. "She just came from Canada."
Funk also visited a man named Detweiler, whose wife had been a Wideman. He also met Isaac Culp, a son of Joseph Culp of Isabella County.
"He is a fine boy; works and saves; a brother in the church."

In the *Herald of Truth* for 1890 Funk reported: "There is a small
church there in charge of Bro. Daniel Lehman. They live very scattered.
. . . They have as yet no church house, and their meetings are held in
private houses or schoolhouses. The country is still new, and most of
the brethren have much hard work to do, to clear up their farms. . . ."
Land varied from five to twenty-five dollars per acre in price. "Church
services are held every four weeks, and probably will be held oftener
hereafter, changing to different localities. . . . Samuel Grove with his
family lives near Caro. Preacher Daniel Lehman lives near Fair Grove,
and north of this most of the brethren are located. William Bechtel
with his family, however, lives near Bay Port, some twenty miles farther
north."

In 1894 Preacher J. J. Weaver of the Shore congregation reported in
the *Herald of Truth:* "Bro. Lehman also desires to have it made known
that he wishes to labor under our conference, and desires to be visited."

The exact date when Preacher Daniel Lehman located in Tuscola
County is not known. In the year 1883 Samuel Good of Akron, Tuscola
County, reported in the *Herald of Truth* that Preacher Henry Moyer and
Brother William Kratz of Bucks County, Pennsylvania, had visited the
Mennonites of Tuscola County. "We had a pleasant meeting and Sunday
school, and we hope others of the brethren will visit us." Good also
reported: "There are a number of brethren living here without a shepherd." Various ministers from Indiana visited the Tuscola Mennonites in
the 1890's. Joseph D. Miller, an older brother of Bishop D. D. Miller,
preached for the Tuscola congregation in 1890.

In 1897 Bishop Amos Cressman and Preacher Samuel S. Bowman
held communion services in the home of Noah Bechtel, Tuscola County.

On August 7, 1897, Preacher Bowman and wife of Berne, Michigan, drove from their home to Tuscola County by horse and buggy. Preacher Peter Ropp and Deacon Menno Wideman arrived that evening. The report says that it was thirty-five miles from Berne to Fair Grove. The brethren and sisters of the community were all present. Services were held in the home of Israel Detweiler. As late as 1901 Preacher Samuel Wideman of Ontario visited the Tuscola Mennonites and appealed for continued visits for the remaining Mennonites of that county on the part of the preachers of Indiana.

In the year 1904 Daniel Lehman reported in the *Herald of Truth* that Peter Ropp and Menno Wideman had visited in Tuscola County the previous Sunday. Lehman reported that he had taken the *Herald* almost from the time it began. He also made a plea for Indiana preachers to visit in the community.

It appears that the Tuscola County congregation did not thrive. One of the last members was Preacher Lehman himself who died October 6, 1919, at Fair Grove. Funeral services were held by Peter Ropp of the Berne (now Pigeon) congregation; the services were held in the Fair Grove Presbyterian Church, and Lehman's obituary was published in the *Gospel Herald*. Thus another ill-fated Mennonite congregation died out.

Zion Mennonite Church

Ferris Township, Montcalm County, Michigan

This congregation was formerly known as the Oak Grove Church. The Conference Minute Book of 1929 reports that the first Mennonites who are known to have resided in the Vestaburg, Michigan, community were Mrs. Henry Detweiler and her daughter, Mrs. Frank B. Switzer, "who resided here for years before the organization of the church." Another family, which moved to Alma, Michigan, about twelve miles east, several years before the organization of the church, was the family of Christian Eichelberger. The fall of 1913 four Mennonite families from other parts of Michigan located near Vestaburg: Abram Snyder, David Schloneger, Reuben Schloneger, and David Sommer. The first Mennonite services in the community were held December 1, 2, 1913, in the meetinghouse of the Church of the Brethren, in charge of Jacob K. Bixler of Elkhart. The district mission board then requested John M. Yoder of Homestead, Michigan, to locate at Vestaburg and assume the pastoral oversight of the Mennonite families in the community. On July 26, 1914, the Zion congregation was formally organized, John M. Yoder was ordained to the ministry, and regular services were started. The first communion service was held July 28, 1914. The congregation purchased and remodeled an abandoned schoolhouse and used it as a place of worship until the fall of 1919, when a new meetinghouse was built on a lot which had been donated by Abram Snyder, four miles southwest of Vestaburg. This meetinghouse was dedicated December 7, 1919. On September 23, 1917, Simeon P. Martin was ordained deacon, but he withdrew from the church in 1923. Royal A. Buskirk was ordained preacher on November 27, 1917. John M. Yoder moved to Missouri in 1920. A number of other families began moving away, while others did not continue their membership in the congregation. The consequence was that by 1927 the work was almost dead. Preacher R. A. Buskirk served Zion from 1917 until 1928. The district mission board then secured the services of Erie Bontrager of Midland, Michigan, who moved to Vestaburg the fall of 1928 and was ordained preacher that same year on November 4. By 1940 the membership had risen to nineteen, and the 1960 *Mennonite Yearbook* shows a membership of twenty-five.

WHITE CLOUD MENNONITE CHURCH

Big Prairie Township, Newaygo County, Michigan   .

This congregation was formerly known as the Union congregation. The first Mennonites to settle in the area were Christian Dester and Eli Shultz, both of the Shore congregation in Indiana. Dester and Shultz were in partnership in the operation of a stump-pulling apparatus, and it was this occupation which took them to Newaygo County in 1896. The families of these two men followed them a short time later. Other families came from Shore and settled in the area: Abram Miller, Joseph J. Miller, Joseph Sarver, Isaac Miller, Samuel Jones, Fanny Kauffman, Eli Zook, D. L. Christophel, Harvey A. Miller, John F. Miller, Thomas B. Nelson, T. U. Nelson, Polly Eash, Katie Yoder, Jacob P. Miller, and Alexander Mast. All these families moved to Newaygo County between 1896 and 1901.

In 1897 John F. Funk, accompanied by John Culp, arrived at the settlement near White Cloud, according to Funk's diary. They spent the night in the home of Manasses D. Miller. Funk reported that as of that date (December 4, 1897) nineteen families had bought land in Newaygo County, "and others are coming." Funk reported that eighty acres of land sold for $240.00. Funk evaluated it as "fair land," and added that the climate was healthful, and that there was good water.

The next day, December 5, 1897, which was Sunday, Funk preached for the Old Order Amish at Diamond Loch, at the invitation of Preacher Daniel Miller. Funk reported that there were several families living nine miles from the others. The land in the Amish area was more hilly, and the meetings were held in the home of David Yoder. That evening Funk returned to the home of Miller and held English services. On Monday he drove about twenty-four miles to the home of Samuel S. Miller where he again held services. He received Benjamin Bowman and wife into the church, and baptized M. J. and Phoebe Balyeat.

In the 1898 *Herald of Truth*, correspondence from White Cloud, dated June 19, reports that Sunday school had recently been organized with Christian Dester as superintendent, and with a woman named Miller as secretary-treasurer. The 1899 *Herald of Truth* reported that eleven families were still awaiting the organization of a Mennonite congregation, and more families were coming. Dester's correspondence gives a glowing account of the area.

The June 1, 1899, *Herald of Truth* reported that Bishop P. Y. Lehman and Deacon James J. Mishler, both of Northern Indiana, visited White Cloud and organized a congregation of twenty-seven members. Services began on May 21 that year and were to be held every two weeks. On the fourteenth of May thirty-three members participated in a communion service. The settlement was reported as being four miles east of the village of White Cloud.

The Sunday school of the group was named for the schoolhouse where it was held, the Pleasant Valley Sunday School. In 1900 J. P. Miller was superintendent, H. P. Miller was assistant, Elias Zook was secretary, and Annie and Grace Miller were song leaders. John F. Funk gave communion to thirty-five members at White Cloud on July 1, 1900. On that same day he ordained J. P. Miller as preacher on the basis of the unanimous vote of the congregation. There were at that time, reports the *Herald of Truth*, about forty members, "with prospects for more."

Bishop P. Y. Lehman went to White Cloud on November 20, 1900, preached five sermons, held communion, and ordained Eli Zook to the office of deacon, again on the basis of the unanimous vote of the church. The ordination was held on Saturday afternoon, November 24. In 1902 Eli Zook was serving as superintendent of the "Pleasant Valley Sunday School." In 1903 Jacob P. Miller reported that the Mennonites had earlier been meeting in the Pleasant Valley Schoolhouse, at the west end of the Mennonite settlement. He reported that services were now being held in the Big Prairie Church, which is more centrally located, and can seat almost 200 persons. He reported that they were paying a "reasonable rent." In 1903 Miller reported that the congregation consisted of forty-four members, the next year fifty-one members, and in 1905 sixty-five members with "a few letters not yet presented."

Winifred (Nelson) Beechy, in her thorough history of the congregation reports: "In 1903 began another in-rush of settlers, among which were John C. Springer from Illinois, Daniel Horst, Samuel Madlem, Aaron Smeltzer, Aaron Hartman, Henry Stichter, John Mishler, Henry Rauch, John Rhinesmith, Ephraim Grabill, John R. Lehman, J. J. Eash, David Livingstone, and others from Shore and [from] Elkhart, Indiana. The number grew to nearly ninety, the highest it has been at any time, and represented four states: Indiana, Illinois, Iowa, and Oklahoma." Services were held in the Union Church until the night of June 4, 1911, when the building was struck by lightning and burned.

Preacher J. P. Miller was ordained as bishop on May 5, 1901. He served at White Cloud until 1910, when he moved to Elmira, Michigan, only to return to White Cloud a year later, but after four months he removed to Kent County and served the Bowne congregation until his removal to Indiana. His son-in-law, John C. Springer, served as a preacher at White Cloud, and another son-in-law, Eli Zook, was deacon. The next deacon in the church was Harvey A. Miller, who was ordained in 1912 and served until his death in 1924. The long-time minister of the congregation was T. U. Nelson, who was ordained December 5, 1909, and died in 1950.

The high point in the membership of the church was reached in 1907 when there were nearly ninety members. A decline set in, however, and the membership slowly decreased until the year 1925 when the membership was but twenty-five. This is probably the reason that the congregation was placed under the care of the district mission board in 1918. It was not granted full independence until the year 1947. Harvey Sarver, who was in charge of the Homestead congregation briefly, was ordained deacon in 1910. Ray Bontrager served as a visiting brother (unordained deacon) from about 1947 until 1952.

Following the burning of the Union church building, it was decided to rebuild it as a union building, rather than to erect a separate Mennonite house of worship. This new Union building was used until about 1925 when the Congregational church building at Big Prairie Center was used. This arrangement continued until 1937 when the Mennonites returned to the Union Church on the Big Prairie.

In 1933 Preacher Joseph S. Neuhouser held evangelistic services in the Union Church with sixteen converts, fifteen of whom united with the Mennonite Church. This was a great encouragement to the struggling congregation. Two years later, in 1935, Edward D. Jones of Middlebury, Indiana, was ordained and placed at White Cloud to assist the aged T. U. Nelson in the ministry.

The first summer Bible school was held the summer of 1944 with Ray Bontrager as superintendent.

In December 1947 the White Cloud congregation finally decided to build a meetinghouse of its own. Edward D. Jones donated a plot of land one-half mile south and one-half mile east of White Cloud on the corner of Eighth and Walnut Avenue. The building was first used in August 1949, when William R. Miller of Crumstown, Indiana, held evangelistic services. The meetinghouse was far from complete at that time, but regular services were held from then on. The building is thirty by fifty-two feet in size, with a basement thirty by forty feet, and a balcony thirty by twelve feet. The main auditorium seats 120 persons, and the balcony can accommodate forty-five. Dedication services were held May 18, 1952, with the dedicatory sermon preached by C. C. Culp. Lowell Burkholder was ordained deacon May 18, 1952. Winifred Beechy writes: "The building of the new church has been a venture in co-operation and faith. This experience surely has strengthened each member who has sacrificed to give materials and labor and has bound them together into a more powerful organ in witnessing to the Gospel in their community. The gradual growth in the last twenty years has been noted and there is every reason to believe, with the growing group of young people and the increased activity of the older ones, that this congregation should continue to grow and make a real contribution to this community and Christendom as a whole." There was severe fire damage to the building on December 25, 1956, and the ensuing repairs and remodeling cost $10,577.70. Remodeling included adding rest rooms, insulation, ceiling in basement, oil heating, etc. The 1960 membership is fifty-three.

SCATTERED MEMBERS IN MICHIGAN

It is impossible to make a complete list of all the members who lived in various counties in Michigan in the nineteenth century. Mention must be made of several, however. In 1869 Preacher Abraham Detweiler of Caledonia visited the brethren and sisters in Mecosta County, eighty miles north of Caledonia. He held two meetings in a schoolhouse. The next year he returned, taking along Preacher Henry Wismer, and again conducted services in a schoolhouse and in a private home. John Gingerich lived twenty miles from Big Rapids. Other Mennonite names in the community were Jacob Gingerich and Peter Gingerich. C. D. Beery and others took the train to Big Rapids in 1872, walked twenty miles to the home of John Gingerich, and held services in the homes of Jacob Gingerich and Peter Gingerich. This settlement was known as Wheatland in Mecosta County.

Three children of Moses and Mary Hiestand, formerly of Doylestown, Pennsylvania, died in 1871: Willie, Clara, and Clemmie. The Hiestand family lived at Athens in Calhoun County, Michigan. Joseph K. Overholt, 1804-1887, died January 24, 1887, and his body was taken to

Medina County, Ohio, for burial. Overholt had been born in Northampton County, Pennsylvania; his wife had died four years earlier.

In 1909 John Culp and J. F. Nafziger were living at Elwell in Gratiot County, Michigan. In that year Preacher Aldus Brackbill held services in a schoolhouse on July 4.

A small group of members was living in Fulton, Kalamazoo County, in 1879. Among the known families were those of Christian Berger, Jacob Kindig, and Jacob Krupp. The towns which were mentioned in connection with visits to Mennonites included Wakeshma, Mendon, and Fulton. Mention is made of these Mennonite families as early as 1879. In 1886 Henry A. Miller went to Kalamazoo County to give communion to the members there. In that same year H. A. Miller, J. J. Weaver, and Samuel Yoder were at Mendon on June 6 to give communion. There were at that time seven members of the church there. Christian Berger, 1823-1899, was a German immigrant who had earlier lived in Lancaster County, Pennsylvania, and then Wayne and Williams counties, Ohio. He settled in Kalamazoo County in 1866. Berger wrote to the *Herald of Truth* in 1869: "There are here four of us, members of our church, and we have not had any preaching for quite a while. We would like to have some visitor to visit us." In the 1871 *Herald of Truth* Jacob Kindig reported his hope that English preachers would visit them. He said that two German-speaking Mennonite preachers from Kent County, Michigan, had been there. Isaac Gable, 1844-1897, from Wayne County, Ohio, and his wife Sarah Leatherman of Medina County, Ohio, settled in Kalamazoo County in 1879.

In 1908 P. S. Weirich, Jacob Yoder, and D. E. Kauffman were living at Elmira, in Otsego County, near the Antrim County line. The *Herald of Truth* reported: "There has been some talk of starting a Mennonite colony near Elmira." Urbane Cotterman was baptized into the Mennonite Church on Christmas Day, 1910, near Mancelona in Antrim County. Eight years later he removed to Jackson, Minnesota. The late Eli A. Bontrager reported in a private letter of 1955 that the settlement at Elmira never amounted to much. He stated that one of the Fairview families, that of Jacob Yoder, had moved there. "I went there a few times, and Sunday school was started, but it did not last long." The Yoder family removed to near St. Johns, Michigan, and made their church home with the Bethel congregation. "So that ended Elmira."

Isaac and Mary Rosenberger of Elbridge in Oceana County reported in the 1889 *Herald of Truth* that they were the only Mennonites in that area. In 1893 Funk visited "Sister Rosenberger."

On January 27, 1891, Levi Clemens, 64 died in Allegan County. Preacher Christian Wenger of Caledonia participated in the funeral services. Other settlers there included Joel and Melinda Clemens and John and Martha Clemens.

In 1894 David B. Hershey was living at Yale in Sanilac County.

About 1908 Eli Bontrager heard that there was a Mennonite family living close to Lewiston in Montmorency County. He therefore went twenty miles northwest of Fairview and found a Martin family who invited him to remain for dinner. Bontrager went to see a neighbor of Martin who was a drunkard. He persuaded the man to come to the evening services and when Bontrager gave an invitation for sinners to accept Christ on the third evening the drunkard responded. A total of five persons were converted. They were all baptized and were considered members of the Fairview congregation. They had their own Sunday school for a time, however. As late as 1918 the *Gospel Herald* reported that Sunday-school services were being held at Lewiston, but no preaching services.

In 1880 John L. Hernley (1831-1893) and wife moved to Petoskey. He had been born in Lancaster County, Pennsylvania. He was killed in Petoskey by a falling tree in 1893, and his body was buried in the Greenwood Cemetery.

Only God knows how many people were lost to the Mennonite Church through the settling of families in communities where there were no Mennonite congregations. In many cases the parents considered themselves members of the church as long as they lived, but the children frequently married into the families of the community, and either united with other denominations, or with none at all.

III

The Older Amish Mennonite Congregations

MAPLE GROVE CONGREGATION
(Formerly Haw Patch)

Section 36, Eden Township, Lagrange County, Indiana

By 1854 it was clear to Bishop Isaac Smucker and to Bishop Jonas D. Troyer, whom Smucker had just ordained to that office, as well as to a considerable number of Amish families, that it was not necessary to maintain unchanged the "Old Order" of the Amish Mennonite faith. Consequently a number of "Amish Mennonite" congregations were organized, which to some extent at once were recognized as no longer in full fellowship with what came to be known as the Old Order Amish Church. The Haw Patch, now Maple Grove, Amish Mennonite congregation was organized by Bishop Isaac Smucker in May 1854, with eighteen charter members. The organizational meeting was held in the home of Jonathan E. Yoder, two miles west of Topeka, and one and one-fourth miles south, just inside Noble County. In the year 1856 the Haw Patch Amish Mennonite congregation erected its first house of worship in Section 36 of Eden Township, Lagrange County, along the Noble County line. This building was of frame construction, thirty by fifty feet in size. It was built on the north side of the east-west county line road, facing south. The building had two entrances, one for men and one for women. These doors were on opposite sides of the pulpit, facing the audience room. The first services were held in this Amish Mennonite meetinghouse on September 18, 1856. This was the first Amish Mennonite meetinghouse built in Indiana.

Isaac Smucker has the distinction of being the first Amish bishop to settle in Indiana. He was born in Lancaster County, Pennsylvania, September 29, 1810, the grandson of Swiss immigrant John Smucker and his wife, Barbara Stoltzfus of Zweibrücken, Germany. Isaac's wife was Sarah Troyer of Holmes County whom he married in 1832. They first settled in Wayne County, Ohio, but in 1838 removed to Knox County, Ohio, where he was ordained as an Amish preacher that fall. In November 1841 he and his family removed to Elkhart County, Indiana, where he was ordained bishop two years later. In March 1851 he removed to McLean County, Illinois, only to return to Indiana in August of 1852, when he settled near Haw Patch, now known as Topeka. There he lived the remainder of his life. He died November 16, 1893, and was buried in the Maple Grove Amish Mennonite Cemetery in Lagrange County, on the Noble County line, one-fifth mile east of Indiana Highway 5. Typical names on the tombstones of this Amish Mennonite cemetery are: Blough, Bohn, Boller, Byler, Christner, Chupp, Emmert, Gnagy, Greenawalt, Hartzler, Hooley, Kauffman, Kemp, King, Kurtz, Lantz, Miller, Morrell, Mullet, Plank, Schrock, Slagel, Smucker, Stoltzfus, Stutzman, Wenger, Yoder, Yontz, and Zook.

Many of the Amish Mennonite settlers of the Haw Patch community were originally from Fairfield County, Ohio, but some had also come from Mifflin County, Pennsylvania, and others were from Wayne County, Ohio. Perhaps the most common names in the congregation were Byler, Hartzler, Hooley, Kurtz, Plank, and Yoder. The Maple Grove congregation has raised a fund for the perpetual care of the cemetery where many of their ancestors were buried in Fairfield County, Ohio. At first three trustees from the Maple Grove congregation held $200.00 in trust for the care of the cemetery, but about 1950 this trust fund was turned over to the township trustees where the cemetery is located. It contains about one hundred graves.

It was not many years until Bishop Isaac Smucker had three preachers and one deacon to assist in the work of the Haw Patch congregation. In 1852 Joseph Yoder, great-uncle of Edwin J. Yoder, was ordained as preacher. Joseph served until 1869, then moved to the Barker Street community. In 1876 he helped found the Townline congregation which in recent decades has become affiliated with the Conservative Mennonite Church. Joseph Yoder attended the Amish General Conference sessions nine times between 1864 and 1876. In 1857 George Z. Boller became the deacon of the Haw Patch congregation and served twenty-six years until his death in 1883. He attended the Amish General Conference sessions six times from 1864 to 1874. He was also the first superintendent of the Haw Patch Amish Mennonite Sunday School. In 1858 Preacher David F. Hertzler (pronounced Hartzler) from Fairfield County, Ohio, moved to the Ligonier area and preached for the Haw Patch congregation until his death in 1889. Hertzler attended the Amish General Conference sessions seven times between 1863 and 1873. The fourth man who served with Isaac Smucker in the first decades of the life of the congregation was Joseph Kauffman, who attended the Amish General Conference four times from 1862 to 1867; the year of his ordination is not known. His obituary in the *Herald of Truth* reports simply that he served "for many years in the Amish Mennonite Church." He was sixty-three years of age when he died of tuberculosis on March 12, 1868. The next year the church decided to ordain another preacher. Gideon Plank was ordained

September 5, 1869, but in a few months he moved to Missouri where he died of smallpox the next year. So in 1870 the church tried another ordination: this time David Morrell was chosen. He was ordained October 30, 1870, and served almost thirty-four years until his death in 1904. Morrell was always relieved when he was through preaching a sermon. "Well," he used to say, "that's now over for another month."

A fine chapter in the life of the church began in 1881. In that year Preacher David F. Hertzler was sixty-five years of age, and the church decided to add another man to the ministry. This time the congregation chose an able young schoolteacher named Jonas S. Hartzler, who was then twenty-three years of age. Jonas D. Troyer, bishop of the Clinton Frame and Forks congregations, performed the ordination ceremony, which was held April 18, 1881. Hartzler served effectively for fourteen years before removing to Elkhart and throwing his energies into the Elkhart Institute. In 1882 the congregation added another young man to the ministry, Jonathan Kurtz, twenty-four years of age. Kurtz was ordained as the second bishop of the congregation by Bishop Jonathan P. Smucker, assisted by his father, the aged Isaac Smucker, on April 7, 1888. This completed the ordinations performed in the nineteenth century.

The original frame meetinghouse of 1856 was used until 1879. The old building was moved a mile north of Topeka where it was used for a time as a literary hall, only to find its way eventually into Topeka where it is now used as a storage building by the T. O. Nelson garage. In 1879 the congregation built a new brick meetinghouse, forty by fifty feet, facing south, on the site of the first building. The cost was $2,000.00. The first services in the new building were held on January 11, 1880, but the formal opening services were not held until two weeks later. John F. Funk, outstanding Mennonite leader of Elkhart, held English services Sunday afternoon and evening on January 25, and the next day, Monday forenoon, German services were held. This building was raised four feet in 1915 and a basement placed under it.

The first Amish Mennonite Sunday school in Northern Indiana was organized at Haw Patch the spring of 1868, by Deacon George Z. Boller, then a man of about thirty-nine. The school was of course German at first. In fact, Sunday schools were usually started in the 1870's to teach the children the German language. The German Primer and the German Testament were therefore the main textbooks of these early Sunday schools.

Perhaps this is the point to report the fate of the 1879 brick meetinghouse. The fall of 1923 the Mennonite Board of Education closed Goshen College for one year. In this era of the life of the church there was considerable unrest in the Indiana-Michigan Mennonite Conference.

The Amish Mennonites and the Mennonites had agreed in 1916 to merge the two conferences. The unrest seemed especially acute in the Amish Mennonite congregations, which had had a stronger emphasis on congregational government, and a correspondingly less emphasis on the authority of conference. A number of Amish Mennonite congregations experienced schisms in this era. The Maple Grove congregation was one of them. A portion of the congregation withdrew from the conference in 1924. This portion also took charge of the brick meetinghouse of 1879 and claimed possession. The remaining portion of the congregation quietly withdrew and built a new meetinghouse at the south end of Topeka in the northeast quarter of the same section of Eden Township in which the 1879 building is located. The 1924 meetinghouse was thirty-six by fifty-two feet in size. (The other group abandoned the 1879 meetinghouse in 1926, built a new church building that year and in 1930 merged with the Central Conference Congregation.)

By 1903 Preacher David Morrell was a man of seventy-five and J. S. Hartzler was devoting his energies to Elkhart Institute. Consequently the Maple Grove congregation decided to ordain a new preacher. Andrew Yontz, the older brother of Deacon David Yontz of the Clinton Frame congregation, was ordained as preacher at Maple Grove on September 7, 1903. He served twelve years until he united with the church of his second wife, the Church of the Brethren. Irvin R. Detweiler was ordained preacher at Maple Grove on January 1, 1905, but he soon entered Goshen College for more education, continued elsewhere in his graduate training, and finally entered the educational field. He never returned as a resident minister at Maple Grove. Raymond L. Hartzler, then in his twenty-third year, was ordained as preacher at Maple Grove on April 2, 1916, and served seven years before transferring to the Central Conference of Mennonites.

From the death of Deacon Boller in 1883 the congregation did not have an ordained deacon for thirty years. The congregation employed the services of lay deacons, known in the Indiana-Michigan area as visiting brethren. On April 27, 1913, Bishop Kurtz ordained Melvin D. Lantz and John Emmert to the office of deacon. Emmert served two years and then resigned, while Lantz united with the Central Conference of Mennonites after serving eleven years. Visiting brethren again served for ten years, 1924-34.

The first two eras in the life of the church were the bishop administrations of Isaac Smucker and Jonathan Kurtz. The third era really began with the erection of the new meetinghouse in 1924, and the ordination of Edwin J. Yoder on November 1, 1925. Jonathan Kurtz performed the ordination ceremony. On May 20, 1934, Bishop D. D. Miller of the

Forks congregation ordained Noah J. Schrock, 43, to the office of deacon. The next year, on November 3, 1935, Bishop Miller ordained Preacher E. J. Yoder to the office of bishop. Bishop Isaac Smucker served thirty-nine years, and Jonathan Kurtz forty-eight years, and Edwin J. Yoder has served as minister since 1925. Only one other person served as long in the ministry at Maple Grove: David Morrell labored for thirty-five years. In 1950 the congregation chose as preacher C. Norman Kraus of Virginia, a 1952 graduate of the Goshen College Biblical Seminary. He served until 1958 when he entered graduate training in Duke University, Durham, North Carolina. In 1953 E. J. Yoder licensed Ellis Croyle of Johnstown, Pennsylvania, a student in Goshen College Biblical Seminary, to assist in the ministry of the Word. On October 17, 1954, Bishop Yoder ordained Ellis Croyle to the ministry: he graduated from the seminary in 1955.

Maple Grove has services three times per week as is the custom in the congregations of the Indiana-Michigan Mennonite Conference: Sunday school and preaching services each Sunday morning, on Sunday evenings young people's Bible meetings and occasional preaching services, and midweek Bible study and prayer meetings each Wednesday night. The congregation has strongly supported the Wawasee Lakeside Chapel, Syracuse, Indiana, both in personnel to carry on the work, and in finances.

The membership of the Maple Grove congregation was reported in 1905 as 174, and in the 1923 *Mennonite Yearbook* as 195. The 1960 *Yearbook* lists 199 members. The formation of a General Conference Mennonite Church in Topeka at the turn of this century, and the schism of 1924, have contributed to the slow growth.

The congregation published a *Centennial Memorial* historical booklet in 1954. Patricia Emmert and Lyle Schrock have each written manuscript histories of the church, and Edwin J. Yoder furnished much information in personal interviews and in correspondence.

CLINTON FRAME CONGREGATION

Section 16, Clinton Township, Elkhart County, Indiana

One of the chief leaders in the formation of the Amish Mennonite movement of 1854 was Jonas D. Troyer, 1811-1897. Troyer had removed from Ohio to Indiana as an ordained minister in 1854 and was very shortly ordained as bishop by Isaac Smucker. One of the marked innovations which Troyer made was performing baptism in streams, rather than in private homes as had been the practice of the Amish. Troyer also maintained a milder discipline in the Clinton congregation than did the more conservative group, which is now known as the Old Order Amish. The ministers who followed Troyer in the schism of 1854 were Christian S. Plank, who had been ordained in Ohio before coming to Indiana in 1851; Christian Miller, an uncle of Mrs. O. S. Hostetler, who had been ordained about 1852; and John Smiley, an orphan of Irish extraction who brought his bride to Elkhart County in 1846 where he was ordained in 1849. Smiley served in Indiana only until 1866, however, for in that year he removed to Wayne County, Ohio. Troyer is reported as having been a very gifted speaker, and was a man of firm will, as his attitudes at the Amish General Conference revealed. Troyer served in the Clinton congregation as bishop, and later when the Forks congregation was organized, he also served as bishop there until his removal to western Marshall County where he ministered to the little congregation in Starke County for a number of years. His address in 1872 was Eagle Lake, Indiana. Later Troyer returned to the Forks area again.

We do not know how many members followed Troyer and his fellow ministers out of what is now known as the Old Order Amish Church in 1854. The Amish historian, John (Hans) Bontreger, calls the division *eine bedenkliche, bedauerliche, und vollkommene Spaltung* (a noteworthy, lamentable, and complete division). Children were torn from parents, says Bontreger; brothers and sisters were separated from each other. This division was initiated, he says, in 1854 and was completed in 1857. (Bontreger seems to allude to the formation of the Forks congregation in 1857.) For a number of years Troyer and his new Clinton Amish Mennonite congregation continued to worship in private homes. The preface to the 1881 *History of Elkhart County* was written in January 1881; so the writing of the book should perhaps be dated in the latter 1870's, 1880 at the latest. This volume reports: "Twenty-three years ago [about 1857] the religious sect known as the Amish worshiped in private dwellings, but shortly thereafter [possibly 1863] became enabled to build a house of worship. The first ministers were John Smiley, Chris. Plank, and J. Troyer" (page 694).

There has been much speculation about the date of the first Clinton Amish Mennonite meetinghouse. Perhaps the best source of information is the Recorder of Deeds for Elkhart County. The original Clinton Frame meetinghouse was built just a little north of the present building, in the southeast quarter of Section 16 of Elkhart County. Deed Book 31, page 557, has the record of the deed in question. On August 10, 1863, Michael Stutzman and his wife Elizabeth conveyed an acre of ground to the church trustees, John Smiley, Emanuel Hostetler, and Samuel Stutzman, "for the purpose of erecting a Meeting-House on for said church." Smiley, as we have seen, was one of the ministers. Emanuel Hostetler had also been ordained by this time, for in 1862 he attended the Amish General Conference as a preacher. It appears definite that the meeting-house was built in 1863. This would confirm the record of the 1881 county history. This same source reports that "this church [building] was rebuilt four years ago [likely 1876]." Quite surprising is the report that the membership at the time of writing (about 1880) was about 200.

But the really surprising fact is the name given to the congregation in the deed. It is called the *Waldentz Church* and it is also significant that the little flock in Starke County over which Troyer was later bishop, also had the name *Waldenzer Church*. Since the people who are respon-sible for this strange name are now dead, we are left to our own resources to account for the phenomenon. The name *Waldenser* is the German name for the Waldenses, a pre-Reformation evangelical body of Chris-tians in Europe, who held views similar to those of the Mennonites in some respects. Indeed the most influential book in Mennonite history, T. J. van Braght's *Martyrs Mirror of* 1660, which was available in Ger-man translation in the nineteenth century, teaches that the early Ana-baptists sprang from the Waldenses. It appears that although contem-porary circumstances had made Troyer's movement appear to be some-what of a declension from historic Amish principles, he wanted everyone to know that his church stood in the true succession! His members were actually one in faith with the original Waldenses! (Further research has destroyed the myth that the Anabaptists of Switzerland sprang from the Waldenses.) Evidently this theory of the Waldensian origin of the Ana-baptists excited some interest among the Amish Mennonites of Northern Indiana in the days of Jonas D. Troyer. On February 15, 1879, Preacher Christian Warey of the Pretty Prairie congregation near Lima (now Howe) wrote to Noah Troyer, a preacher in Washington County, Iowa: "I would like to see friend Abner Yoder. If you see him I wish you would ask him what the meaning of the word *Waldenser* is, and what for a church the Waldenser Church was. I am anxious to know."

After the formation of the Forks Amish Mennonite congregation in 1857 the same ministers served the Clinton and Forks congregations for a time. Eventually, however, each ordained man became somewhat more attached to the one church or the other. Plank, Miller, and Hostetler seemed to become attached to the Forks congregation in the course of time. The Elkhart County *History* of 1881 reports that the ministers in the (Clinton Frame) congregation were Benjamin Schrock and Eli Miller. Benjamin Schrock was an Amish Mennonite preacher, originally of Holmes County, Ohio, who had lived from about 1850 to 1863 in Miami County, Indiana, who had lived a few miles north of Goshen from 1863 to 1872, and who had lived in Clinton Township from 1872. Eli S. Miller, another leader from Holmes County, was ordained as an Amish deacon in Ohio in 1849, and as a *Völliger Armendiener* (bishop-deacon) in 1860. In 1870 he removed to Indiana and located near the Eight-Square School, which is 3.4 miles north of Clinton Frame, after which he served in the Clinton Frame congregation. The 1882 *History of Lagrange and Noble Counties* lists the following as serving in the Forks congregation in 1881: Jonas Troyer, the bishop, Emanuel Hostetler, Seth Troyer (son of the bishop), Christian S. Plank, and Christian Miller.

A bright new chapter began in the Clinton Frame Church in 1882 when an able schoolteacher named Daniel J. Johns was ordained to the ministry. His lifetime almost spanned the first century of the history of the congregation. Alert and flexible mentally, with a deep desire for the welfare and witness of the church, Johns was a progressive leader in the best sense of the word. Bishop Joseph Stuckey of Illinois, commonly called Father Stuckey because of the high veneration in which he was held, was on a trip to Indiana in 1882 and was in charge of the ordination of "Daniel Tschantz" as he called him. Johns was the father of the well-known Mennonite leaders, Ira S. Johns of Indiana, and O. N. Johns of Ohio. On November 13, 1887, Bishops Benjamin Schrock of Clinton Frame and J. P. Smucker of the Nappanee West Market Street Amish Mennonite Church ordained D. J. Johns to the office of bishop. The very next year, 1888, a new meetinghouse was built by the Clinton Frame congregation, the building which is still in use.

Clinton Frame was not one of the earliest churches to have Sunday schools; none was started until 1876. The records of the Sunday school are not perfect in some of the early decades of the movement. From 1882 to 1890 the average attendance was 145.

Within five years after the ordination of D. J. Johns as bishop, the church divided over the question, How strict should the discipline of the church be? About fifty members withdrew during the summer of 1892 and organized the Silver Street Church which built a new house of worship a mile north of the Clinton Frame meetinghouse on the Silver Street Road. The new church favored open communion, and a more lenient attitude on various changes including those of dress. Daniel J. Johns had earlier tolerated the wearing of hats (rather than bonnets) by the women, but had felt forced to become more strict through pressure put on him by other Amish Mennonite leaders such as Jonathan Kurtz. Benjamin Schrock, 73, the older bishop, withdrew with those who formed the Silver Street congregation. These members called in Bishop Joseph Stuckey of Illinois to assist them. He hesitated at first, but finally came, bringing along Peter Schantz, a preacher. These Illinois leaders held meetings in the Union Chapel, a short distance southwest of the Clinton Frame meetinghouse, where the Union Cemetery is now located, and there were twenty-two accessions, making a total of seventy-two members in the new congregation. D. J. Johns loaned the Clinton Frame congregation $1,000.00 to reimburse those who withdrew from the congregation for their share in the Clinton Frame meetinghouse. Before this there were, however, some unhappy events, such as one group changing the locks on the church door. The membership of the Clinton Frame congregation before the schism took place was 162. The loss of fifty members brought the membership of the Clinton Frame congregation down to 112.

In 1888, as was noted above, the year following the ordination of D. J. Johns as bishop, the Clinton Frame congregation decided to erect a new meetinghouse. The new house of worship was thirty-six by sixty-six feet in size. A basement was put under the building in 1913, electric lights were installed in 1916 (displacing the old kerosene lights), a balcony was added in 1935, and Sunday-school rooms were constructed in the basement in 1950.

Following the division of 1892 the congregation decided to ordain a young minister. Daniel D. Troyer was chosen by lot. (His grandfather Levi Troyer was a brother of J. D. Troyer, the aged bishop.) Troyer was ordained by J. P. Smucker of the Nappanee Amish Mennonite Church on September 25, 1892. A communion service was held the same day. "D. D.," as he was familiarly known in later years, was but twenty-two years of age at his ordination, and still unmarried.

There was only one ordained deacon in the Clinton Amish Mennonite congregation in the nineteenth century. His name was Daniel Schrock. Deacon Joseph Holdeman of the Holdeman congregation referred to Schrock as "a deacon in the Omish Church." His son David Schrock (1851-1920) served for a time as a visiting brother. Schrock seems to have served for a period of about twelve years. For many years prior to 1909 the congregation then had a number of visiting brothers who served for elected terms as lay deacons. D. J. Johns strongly advocated the ordination of deacons; so D. D. Miller was ordained at Forks in 1890, and Ira S. Johns at Clinton Frame in 1909. Johns served as deacon until April 27, 1924, when he was ordained preacher to serve wherever he would be sent. In the final analysis, however, the Clinton congregation retained him in his home congregation. On January 8, 1925, D. A. Yoder ordained David Yontz as deacon to serve in place of Ira Johns. Yontz served until his death in 1958.

D. J. Johns lived until 1942, but D. D. Troyer, who had been ordained bishop November 7, 1920, for the work of the district mission board, was given the bishop oversight of the congregation a number of years prior to the death of D. J. Johns. He served as bishop for eleven years, after which the Clinton Frame congregation called E. J. Yoder to serve as its bishop. Many ordinations took place during the leadership of E. J. Yoder. On August 27, 1944, he ordained Verle O. Hoffman as preacher. On January 25, 1948, he ordained Galen Johns as preacher, because more ministers were needed after the daughter congregation in Benton, Indiana, was established. On January 23, 1949, he ordained Vernon E. Bontreger as deacon. After Galen Johns was placed in charge of the Benton congregation, E. J. Yoder ordained Deacon Vernon Bontreger as preacher on October 22, 1950. On December 30, 1951, he ordained Norman Kauffman to the office of deacon and on July 13, 1958, he ordained Vernon Bontreger bishop, making a total of six ordinations in six years, in addition to the ordinations performed for mission stations. In 1951 Hoffman was placed in charge of the new Roselawn congregation in Elkhart.

The Clinton Frame congregation has a strong concern to promote the cause of missions and evangelism. An example of this is the establishment of the daughter Benton congregation. In 1944 the trustees of the Clinton Frame congregation purchased what had originally been a Lutheran church building in Benton from the legal owners at that point, the Mennonite Brethren in Christ Church. Mennonite services were begun on July 9, 1944, both Sunday school and church services, with the Clinton Frame ministry supplying the pulpit. In 1946 Hoffman was assigned to supply the pulpit at Benton, but in 1948 the Benton congregation was formally organized with E. J. Yoder as bishop, Galen Johns as pastor, and Amos Yontz as visiting brother. E. J. Yoder ordained Yontz as deacon January 30, 1949.

Another evidence of the missionary spirit of the Clinton Frame congregation is the opening of work in Knott County, Kentucky. The mission committee of the congregation conducted investigations which led to the beginning of the Knott County witness in May 1952. The first thing the workers did was conduct a summer Bible school. Samuel Hostetler, Jr., was placed in charge of the new outpost, and served until 1956; he was ordained preacher on March 1, 1953. His successor was John F. Mishler, who was licensed to preach on December 23, 1956, and who has been in charge ever since that date. The name of the Knott County congregation is the Talcum Mennonite Church, Talcum, Kentucky. Services were also held 1956-57 at Big Branch, Bareville, Kentucky.

In 1905 the Clinton Frame congregation had 185 members, a fine growth from its low point of 112 after the schism in 1892. By 1930 the membership was 178, a slight decline from 1905; but in 1960, even after the formation of the daughter congregation at Benton, the number had nevertheless risen to 234. Many members left the Old Order Amish to join Clinton Frame. The future of the congregation appears bright.

Ira S. Johns and Delton S. Schrock have each written histories of the Clinton Frame congregation, and Raymond Mark Yoder published a substantial book in 1944, entitled *Clinton Frame Sketches*.

FORKS CONGREGATION

Section 19, Newbury Township, Lagrange County, Indiana

The Forks Amish Mennonite congregation was a part of the movement led by Jonas D. Troyer, the bishop who relaxed the standards of the Amish Church, introduced baptism in streams, and whose members began to build meetinghouses in the Civil War era. The practice of baptizing in streams is said to have been found in Holmes County, Ohio, a number of years before it reached Indiana. The Amish historian, Hans E. Bontreger, dates the Indiana schism of the Amish Mennonites from the Old Order Amish as 1854 and remarks that it was completed by 1857, which year is the traditional date for the first service of the Forks Amish Mennonite group. The first service is said to have been held in the home of Joseph Hershberger, one mile north of the present Forks meetinghouse, and one and one-fourth miles east. For the first six or seven years the little flock followed the traditional Amish custom of worshiping in private homes. But in the spring of 1864 the Forks congregation purchased an acre of land on which to build a house of worship. The Lagrange County Deed Books contain the record of the transfer of this acre of ground from John Leib and Elizabeth his wife to Tobias Kauffman, Christian Hostetler, and John Schrock, trustees of the "Ommon Minenit Church," an early example of phonetic spelling. The date of the transfer was May 4, 1864, and the purchase price was $50.00, likely an evidence that the grantor was not a member of the church although we cannot be certain. (Deed Book 17, page 223.) Since this land was located in the forks of the Little Elkhart River and the Emma Creek, it got the name Forks Church. An 1864 map of Lagrange County, hanging in the Lagrange County Courthouse, shows the *Amish Church* where the present meetinghouse stands. The 1882 Lagrange County history claims it was built in 1863 and cost "some $600."

The first members of the ministry at Forks were the same men who served the Clinton Amish Mennonite congregation: Bishop J. D. Troyer, and Preachers Christian S. Plank, Christian Miller, and John Smiley. Sometime in the 1860's, possibly about 1868, Troyer removed to the vicinity of Eagle Lake (Eagle Lake is in Starke County, but Troyer seems to have lived across the line in Marshall County) where he served a small Amish Mennonite congregation for possibly a decade before returning to his Forks and Clinton congregations. Smiley did not long remain with the Forks congregation also, for he returned to Ohio. Plank and Miller served several decades each, however, dying in 1887 and 1891 respectively. By 1862 either the Forks or Clinton congregation had ordained Emanuel Hostetler to the ministry: he served about twenty years before he was silenced for becoming involved in strife with a neighbor. Hostetler located in McPherson County, Kansas, in 1892. Another early minister was Joseph J. Bontrager. The traditional date of his ordination is 1867, but he seems to have been ordained earlier, for in 1864 he attended the Amish General Conference as an ordained man. He served a dozen years, only to withdraw from the Forks congregation in 1876 and become one of the founders of the Townline congregation which many decades later became associated with the Conservative Mennonite Conference. In the year 1883 Bontrager moved to Kansas. By 1881 Seth Troyer, formerly a Starke County Amish Mennonite preacher, and son of Bishop J. D. Troyer, was also serving as a preacher at Forks. Seth Troyer moved around a great deal, and never rendered a very effective service to the congregation. In the year 1887 a brother named Edward Gegax received a vote for preacher, and was ordained by lot. Within a few years he left the congregation and eventually became affiliated with the Seventh-day Adventist Church. As a whole the Forks congregation had considerable difficulty in finding stable and permanent pastors who were willing to render a lifetime of service in the ministry: Christian Plank and Christian Miller were exceptions of course. Mention must also be made of the bishop-deacon Eli S. Miller, who moved into Northern Indiana from Holmes County, Ohio, in 1870. He rendered service both to the Forks and Clinton congregations. Although he was originally a deacon, yet he was empowered to do all the work of a bishop as the occasion arose. He performed both marriages and baptisms at Forks.

We have already seen the large contribution which D. J. Johns rendered in the Clinton congregation. His counterpart in the Forks Church was D. D. Miller. Johns ordained "D. D." as deacon on October 18, 1890; as preacher on October 20, 1891; and as bishop on Good Friday, April 13, 1906. From 1890 until 1944, when his health began to fail in his eightieth year, D. D. Miller was the dynamic leader of the Forks congregation, and a strong influence for all that was good in the entire Mennonite brotherhood in the United States and Canada. He furnished the strong and able leadership which the congregation so badly needed and craved. His older brother, Joseph D. Miller, had been ordained as preacher in 1886, but died of pneumonia at the age of forty-one in 1901. Two of D. D. Miller's sons also served in the Forks ministry: Ernest E. Miller, missionary to India, and later president of Goshen College, was a minister in the congregation from 1937 until 1947. Wilbur Miller, now in public school administration in Columbus, Ohio, was ordained as a minister in the Forks congregation in 1921 and served several years. Three other men also served for rather short periods at Forks. In 1896 the church chose Andrew J. Hostetler as deacon, and two years later he became a preacher, only to transfer to the new Middlebury congregation in 1903. In 1904 the Forks Church chose Samuel E. Weaver as preacher, only to see him resign after a dozen years of effective service, in 1916. Simon S. Yoder was ordained as deacon in 1903, but in a few years transferred to the new Middlebury congregation. There have really been three pairs of men who served for longer periods in the life of the Forks Church: Christian Plank and Christian Miller from 1857 until their deaths in 1887 and 1891; D. D. Miller and J. Y. Hooley, who were ordained bishop and deacon respectively on Good Friday, 1906, and who died in 1955 and 1947; and Earley C. Bontrager and Malvin P. Miller, who will soon have served a total of fifty years as preacher and deacon. Bontrager was ordained preacher at Forks on May 8, 1932, and as bishop on March 25, 1945; and Miller was ordained deacon on March 29, 1942. A third member was added to the Forks ministry on July 12, 1953, when E. C. Bontrager ordained Donald E. Yoder, 24, to the ministry. The next June Donald received his Bachelor of Theology degree from the Goshen College Biblical Seminary. The future of the congregation is bright, as an able team of leaders labor together for the building of Christ's kingdom.

The 1864 building was used until 1893 when it was displaced by a larger frame meetinghouse, forty by seventy feet; the 1864 building was then moved to the farm nearby where Bishop D. D. Miller later lived. Dedicatory services were held November 12, 1893, by D. J. Johns and J. P. Smucker. The 1893 building was remodeled in 1915, only to be struck by lightning and burned to the ground on September 18, 1927. A basement had been put under it in 1915, and a light plant installed. A new meetinghouse was at once built in 1927, with the first service held on January 15, 1928. This building caught fire on April 24, 1949, probably from an overheated furnace, and again burned to the ground. Once again the congregation built a new house of worship. The dedication of the 1949 meetinghouse was held on January 22, 1950. The meetinghouses of 1927 and 1949 were built on the same foundation as the 1893 building, forty by seventy feet, except that the 1949 building has a vestibule added onto the building at the south end. After the 1927 fire the stones of the foundation wall had to be repointed, but in 1949 very little had to be done to the wall. In 1954 the congregation built a church cabin for the use of the sewing circle and for the meetings of the Mennonite Youth Fellowship.

The first Amish Mennonite Sunday school in Northern Indiana was that of the Haw Patch congregation which was started in 1868. Howard-Miami followed in 1869, and Forks in 1871. G. W. North, who had attended the Forks school, believed erroneously that Forks was the first Amish Mennonite Sunday school in the area. He wrote an article for the *Gospel Herald* in 1910, reporting on the Forks Sunday School, stating that Preacher Christian Plank, "our aged brother," had opened the school in the Pashan schoolhouse in June 1871. The older people were somewhat uneasy about this new institution at that time, and some of them stood aloof, but the young people strongly supported Plank's Sunday School. North reported: "As Bro. Plank was full of the Spirit, and his heart was filled with the love of God, he still kept on inviting the older ones to come and help him in the good cause of the Sunday school." The school studied both the German and English Testaments, and sang from the English Mennonite hymnbook, and the German *Allgemeine Liedersammlung*. (The English Mennonite hymnbook had the title, *A Collection of Psalms, Hymns, and Spiritual Songs,* and was published by the Virginia Mennonites at Mountain Valley, Virginia, in 1847 and enjoyed ten reprints. The German *Liedersammlung* was a new work, compiled by a committee consisting of Deacon Henry B. Brenneman of the Elkhart congregation, Preacher John M. Christophel of the Yellow Creek congregation, and Deacon George Z. Boller of the Haw Patch Amish Mennonite congregation, and was published by John F. Funk and Brother in 1871.) In the fall of 1871 the Plank Sunday School was closed for the winter, only to be reopened the spring of 1872. This time the response was so large that other quarters had to be found, and the Forks congregation gave its permission for the Sunday school to use its meetinghouse. In 1886 the Sunday school became "evergreen," that is, it began to meet all year round.

Under the influence of such leaders as D. D. Miller, a strong missionary spirit developed in the Forks congregation. One of the visible outcomes was the going of Ernest E. Miller to India as a missionary. His older brother, Orie O. Miller, was for a whole generation the executive secretary of the Mennonite Central Committee, Akron, Pennsylvania. The first missionaries of the Mennonite Church to India were Dr. and Mrs. W. B. Page of the Forks congregation. They were followed by the S. J. Hostetlers, who have more recently served in Ghana, but who went to India in 1927. Hostetler's brother Wilbur and wife were also missionaries in India. Oscar S. Hostetler from Forks became the first minister and bishop in the Emma Mennonite congregation. Amsa H. Kauffman and wife served among the Spanish Americans in Texas from 1937 to 1948, after which he became the pastor and bishop of the Clinton Brick congregation. Victor Miller and family went to the Upper Peninsula of Michigan as missionaries in 1951. Edward D. Jones was ordained in 1935 and placed as pastor at White Cloud, Michigan. S. J. Miller, who is currently serving as bishop in the Leo congregation, came from the Forks Church, and so did Orvin H. Hooley, bishop of the Locust Grove congregation in Southern Michigan.

The Forks congregation also established a number of outposts and mission Sunday schools. The most successful attempt was the daughter congregation in Middlebury which is now much larger than the mother church. For some time the congregation had a Sunday school in the Wilson schoolhouse on Highway 13 north of Middlebury. Another Sunday school was conducted near White Pigeon, and still another at Fawn River, Michigan. In 1956 another Sunday school was established, this time at California, Michigan. Deacon Malvin P. Miller of the Forks congregation was active in the work at California, and in February 1960 removed to the area; his address is Ray, Indiana.

The Amish Mennonite congregations of Northern Indiana, which withdrew from the Old Order Amish, had no conference organization until the year 1888 when the Indiana Amish Mennonite Conference was formed. In 1916 the Indiana-Michigan Amish Mennonite Conference and the Indiana-Michigan Mennonite Conference agreed to merge. The united conference has met annually since 1917. Forks is a member of this conference.

When Hartzler and Kauffman published their *Mennonite Church History* in 1905, they reported that the membership of the Forks congregation was 204. When S. E. Weaver wrote the section on the Amish and Mennonite churches for the *History of Northeast Indiana* in 1920, he reported that the largest of the Amish Mennonite congregations was Forks with over 300 members. But the *Mennonite Yearbook*, ten years later, gives the membership for 1930 as 273, and the 1960 *Yearbook* gives the figure as 225. Part of the reason for this decline seems to be economic. Many Forks Mennonite families are leaving the farm in favor of town and city residence, and the farms are being eagerly purchased by the Old Order Amish of the community. It is hoped that the numerical decline of the congregation can be reversed.

Histories of the Forks congregation have been written by Alberta (Augsburger) Hartzler and by Floyd L. Rheinheimer, M.D. Mabel (Frey) Bontrager wrote a biographical sketch of Christian Miller.

PRETTY PRAIRIE CONGREGATION

Section 22, Greenfield Township, Lagrange County, Indiana

Amish Mennonites began to move into the vicinity of what became the Pretty Prairie congregation as early as 1864. For example, Christian K. Mast of Lancaster County, Pennsylvania, went with his parents to Holmes County as a boy, and in 1864 he located at Pretty Prairie. In 1866 Preacher Daniel Brenneman of Elkhart County visited the Amish Mennonites at this place. After visiting the congregation at Haw Patch, in November 1866, Brenneman reported: "Taking leave of the brethren here, on the morning of the 24th, we proceeded on our journey with the brethren who had come from near Burr Oak, Michigan, to meet us and attend the meetings, and came to Pretty Prairie where we attended a meeting in the afternoon. There is here a congregation of our Omish brethren, and also several members of our own church." In August 1867 Bishop John M. Brenneman of Ohio, accompanied by his brother George, preached at four o'clock in the afternoon in the home of Eli Kime. After the meeting they went to Brother (Christian) Nofsingers, "an Omish minister." In 1868 Preacher Daniel Brenneman of Elkhart visited Pretty Prairie. He again stopped first at Haw Patch in Lagrange County, then Bishop Isaac Smucker and wife accompanied Brenneman to Pretty Prairie. He preached both at the Methodist Church in the community and at a schoolhouse. The brethren Nofsinger and Warey, who were evidently both ministers by this time, accompanied him to Branch County, Michigan. Brenneman reported in the *Herald of Truth* that the Pretty Prairie brethren were "about to build a meetinghouse." He said that they expected to complete it yet that fall. But the meetinghouse was not built until 1872.

To reach the site of the Pretty Prairie meetinghouse, which has been enlarged, and is used to store farm machinery, one proceeds east from the traffic light in Howe, on Highway 120 for 3.9 miles, and then north 1.5 miles. This meetinghouse stands on the east side of the road, four tenths of a mile south of the new Indiana Turnpike. It is located on the farm of Simon Bontrager, who is now a member of the Marion Mennonite Church.

Ministers who served at Pretty Prairie were Christian Nofsinger, 1819-1892, who had been ordained preacher in Wayne County, Ohio, about 1844, and who was the great-grandfather of Mrs. Paul Lauver, missionary to Puerto Rico; Christian Warey, 1832-1914, who moved to Johnson County, Iowa, in 1884; Jonas C. Yoder, 1833-1914, of Logan County, Ohio, who had been ordained preacher about 1863, and bishop a year or two later, and who returned to Logan County, Ohio, after serving briefly at Pretty Prairie; and Jonathan B. Hartzler, 1850-1950, who was ordained preacher at Pretty Prairie May 18, 1879, but who served there less than a decade, after which he removed to Logan County, Ohio, where he did his lifework. The highest membership attained by the Pretty Prairie congregation was about forty. Mrs. Simon Bontrager recalls the names of family heads as follows: Joseph Bontrager, Jacob Hooley, Daniel Mast, Isaac Mast, Christian Nofsinger, Christian Plank, Isaac Plank, Jacob Plank, Christian Stukey, and Eli Yoder, father of Professor Walter E. Yoder of Goshen College.

The Amish Mennonite Conference in 1894 appointed Joseph D. Miller, older brother of Bishop D. D. Miller, "to see that the Pretty Prairie congregation has regular services." From time to time the conference appointed other ministers to care for the congregation. At the 1909 session of the Indiana-Michigan Amish Mennonite Conference, S. S. Yoder and J. Y. Hooley were retained "to look after the work at Pretty Prairie, holding services there at least every two months." But later in the same session of conference the members of Pretty Prairie were advised "to move to where there is an organized congregation, [since] we believe that they would do so if the services were discontinued, and since there is no hope of building up a congregation, be it, Resolved, that we advise Bro. [Joseph] Bontrager [father of Simon Bontrager of the Marion congregation] to sell his property and locate in a community where there is a church, and that it is the sense of this conference that services there be discontinued after this next conference year." The next year, 1910, conference gave over to the members residing at Pretty Prairie the responsibility for providing for services there. The last note in the conference minutes relating to the Pretty Prairie building was in 1916 when conference authorized the district mission board to sell the building and turn over the proceeds to the General Mission Board.

The cemetery of the Pretty Prairie Amish Mennonite congregation is located on the west side of the road almost one mile north of the meetinghouse. At the Pretty Prairie Methodist Cemetery northeast of the Amish Mennonite meetinghouse are found such names as Bixler, Keim, Kenaga, Mast, Plank, Stukey, and Yoder.

It is not entirely clear why the Pretty Prairie Amish Mennonite Church died. Perhaps the most likely theory is that there was less than perfect unity among the ministry. The only preacher who remained there his entire lifetime was the first man, Christian Nofsinger. After the Mennonite services were discontinued at Pretty Prairie the Church of the Brethren attempted to maintain services for a time, but they too ceased.

WEST MARKET STREET AMISH MENNONITE CHURCH

Section 36, Nappanee, Locke Township, Elkhart County, Indiana

About the year 1928 E. S. Mullett, pastor of the First Mennonite Church, West Market Street, Nappanee, Indiana, conducted historical investigations as to that congregation, which were published as an article in the *Mennonite Yearbook* of the General Conference Mennonite Church, 1929. Mullett reported that the first ministers for the Amish of the Nappanee area were John Ringenberg and Tobias Hochstetler. He gives the date 1853 as the year of their ordination. It was not long until the two ministers separated. Hochstetler and his followers formed what is now known as the Old Order Amish, while Ringenberg and wife, together with five or six other families, organized what came to be known as the Amish Mennonite Church.

Bishop David Burkholder of the Nappanee Mennonite congregation wrote the story of his early life, and a brief history of the Nappanee Mennonite congregation, in an unpublished paper which is now in the Mennonite Historical Library of Goshen College. In the course of his reminiscences, Burkholder wrote: "It would not be out of place to state here that our Amish Mennonite brethren held meetings there too, in the same [Culp] schoolhouse on the intervening Sundays. Their ministers were John Ringenberg, Samuel Yoder, and Samuel Hochstetler, and later on Jonathan Smucker." It is the judgment of the present writer that the division at Nappanee between the Old Order Amish and the Amish Mennonites likely occurred in 1854, the same year as in the Howard-Miami, Maple Grove, and Clinton Frame congregations. However, Abraham E. Weaver in his *Standard History of Elkhart County, Indiana,* 1916, reports that the West Market Street Amish Mennonite Church was "organized in 1857, with Samuel Yoder as bishop and John Ringenberg as minister. John Yoder and Samuel Hochstetler also had charge of the society until it was disbanded in 1871." It is possible that the latter two ministers, John Yoder and Samuel Hochstetler, served only briefly, as there seems to be no other mention of them anywhere in any source so far located. However, the *Herald of Truth* for 1867 reports that Samuel Yoder and John Ringenberg preached several funerals in Union Township in the year 1867. They also drove their team to Howard and Miami counties to the home of Absalom Miller who served as a deacon in the Howard-Miami congregation. They held meetings in the homes of Benjamin Shrock and Daniel Miller, both of whom served as ministers in that congregation. They also held communion services in the Absalom Miller home. "A considerable number of persons were present at these meetings, and a goodly number also partook of the sacred emblems of the bread and wine." The last mention of Samuel Yoder in the *Herald of Truth* seems to be in 1868 when he and John Ringenberg again conducted a funeral service. Yoder's birth and death dates, and place of burial, could not be discovered.

Mullett reports that the Amish Mennonite services in the Nappanee area were first held in various schoolhouses, then in the Culp schoolhouse, and from 1867 until 1878 they worshiped in a new schoolhouse on Main Street, Nappanee. The historian of the congregation, Elva (Schrock) Roth, reports that when this schoolhouse was built in Nappanee the congregation gave $250.00 toward the expense of building it, with the proviso that the congregation could worship in the building.

In 1878 the congregation built a meetinghouse, thirty-four by forty feet in size, which is incorporated in the present building. It was heated by two stoves and lighted by oil lamps. No deed was given for the land; it appears that John and Lydia Ann Ailer allowed the Amish Mennonites to use a half-acre plot of their land for their meetinghouse. This half-acre was at that time west of the town of Nappanee, but is now located on West Market Street (U.S. Highway 6). No deed was given for this half-acre until December 30, 1905, when Samuel Guiss, who then owned the Ailer land, granted a quit claim deed to the trustees of the Amish Mennonite Church, Daniel M. Mast, John H. Walters, and Henry J. Ringenberg, for a consideration of $200.00. (Deed Book 113, page 221.)

When Ringenberg died in 1871 the congregational organization seems to have collapsed. The congregation was revived by the strong Amish Mennonite minister, Jonathan P. Smucker, who moved from Starke County Indiana, to Nappanee in 1875. The charter members of the reorganized congregation at that time were Jonathan P. Smucker and wife, Henry Stahly, Sr., and wife, Christ Stahly and wife, Levi Hershberger and wife, John Johnson and wife, Ulery Miller and wife, and Magdalena (Mrs. Andrew) Bleile. Jonathan P. Smucker was ordained bishop two years later and served until his second marriage in 1895 when he moved east of Goshen. Mrs. Roth reports that a number of the members had been Amish Mennonites in Europe, but that German Lutherans and others united with the group, partly because the German language was used in the services. The congregation itself has no written records before the year 1888.

Worship services in the J. P. Smucker era and beyond were conducted every other Sunday, on the alternate Sundays from the services of the Mennonite congregation on North Main Street. Milo Kauffman reports that the West Market Street Sunday School was organized in 1869. It seems to have become evergreen about twenty years later. John F. Funk preached in the West Market Street Amish Mennonite meetinghouse on

July 15, 1888, and reported that they had "a very good house." He also reported that "they have a good Sunday school also." The earliest record of a mission offering was of the year 1897. The next year Bible Readings, now known as young people's Bible meetings, were inaugurated. The annual allowance for the janitor for the year 1894 was $13.00. In 1902 the total church expenses for the year were $50.24. Visiting ministers were paid $1.00 for preaching, unless they came from a distance when the allowance was $1.50. In the year 1885 J. P. Smucker ordained a minister of forty-four to assist him, Jacob Bleile. Bleile served only until 1889, however, when he became unhappy about the mild discipline of Bishop Smucker and transferred his membership to the North Main Street Mennonite congregation where he served for ten additional years. (Bleile opposed "protracted" meetings, now known as evangelistic meetings; he did not favor the use of the songbook, *Gospel Hymns;* he was not in favor of prayer meetings; and he felt that Bishop Smucker should not allow the young women to wear the form of dress known as the basque, a tight form-fitting garment.)

Prior to the withdrawal of Jacob Bleile, Bishop Smucker added another man to the ministry in 1888 when he ordained Deacon J. H. McGowen as preacher. And in 1900 Smucker ordained Eli A. Bontrager as an additional preacher. Bontrager served only three years, however, until he removed to Oscoda County, Michigan.

On April 4, 1885, on the day when Jacob Bleile was ordained preacher, James Henry McGowen was ordained to the office of deacon. Three years later McGowen became a minister, and served almost forty years in the congregation; he died April 2, 1927. In the year 1911 Bishop Jonathan Kurtz of Topeka ordained Levi W. Yoder to the ministry and Simon J. Smucker as deacon. These men each served about twelve years. Smucker moved to Texas, and Levi W. Yoder joined the MBC Church.

The sewing circle of the West Market Street congregation began to meet informally in 1907, and was organized formally two years later. In 1910 the meetinghouse was remodeled, the building was turned, an addition was built to the front end, a basement was placed under the entire building, the lawn was leveled and seeded, and a circle of trees planted around the meetinghouse.

In common with a number of other Amish Mennonite congregations the West Market Street Church had visiting brothers who served as lay deacons prior to 1911. Included in this list were Henry Culp, Peter Stahly, Dan Mast, and Henry Ringenberg. Soon after the 1911 ordinations of Yoder and Smucker the congregation began to meet each Sunday for Sunday school and church services. A literary society was organized for the young people about the year 1913.

The next major event in the life of the congregation came the fall of 1923 when there was a division in a number of Amish Mennonite congregations in Northern Indiana. Both of the Nappanee congregations were reorganized at this time. From the West Market Street Church fifteen members united with other denominations, and fifty members transferred to the North Main Street Mennonite Church in order to remain in the Indiana-Michigan Mennonite Conference. On the other hand, thirty-five members withdrew from the North Main Street congregation and affiliated with the West Market Street Church, and fifty-six members from other congregations of the Indiana-Michigan Conference united with the West Market Street congregation. In the spring of 1924 an additional twenty-five members affiliated with the West Market Street Church. Among those who came over from the North Main Street Mennonite Church to the West Market Street congregation was Ezra S. Mullett, formerly the pastor at North Main Street, who then served twenty years as pastor of what is now the First Mennonite Church of Nappanee, West Market Street. The further history of the First Mennonite Church is given in chapter seven under the General Conference Mennonite Church.

MIDDLEBURY MENNONITE CHURCH

Lawrence Street, Middlebury, Indiana

The year 1902 found a number of Mennonites and Amish Mennonites residing in the village of Middlebury in Elkhart County, who desired to form a congregation in that town. They contacted the members of a number of neighboring congregations and received "but little encouragement, and active opposition." However, it was not long until the group decided to meet for the study of the Sunday-school lesson in the various homes of the church members living in Middlebury. Soon the group became too large for the average home. Chairs were then rented from A. Haines and Son, Morticians, and the meetings were held in the home of Benjamin A. Bontrager. Dr. W. B. Page, former missionary to India, was elected moderator of the group and a business committee was selected, P. B. Thut, B. A. Bontrager, and Henry Karch. This committee was also made responsible to secure a minister to hold services as soon as a suitable meeting place could be arranged. The place of meeting known as the Prescott Hall became available the spring of 1903 and on May 10 of that year the congregation, as yet unorganized, agreed to pay $40.00 rent per year for the use of this place of meeting. D. D. Miller, preacher of the Forks congregation, preached the first sermon. In the fall of 1903 the Prescott Hall was purchased for $500.00, but with the understanding that it had to be moved off the lot on which it was located.

The first series of meetings was held December 1-9, 1903, by A. H. Leaman of Chicago, with ten confessions of faith.

The congregation was organized June 30, 1904, with D. J. Johns of the Clinton Frame congregation as bishop, and Andrew J. Hostetler, formerly a minister in the Forks congregation, as preacher. The congregation elected visiting brothers until 1911. The first communion service was held November 13, 1904. Deacon Simon S. Yoder of the Forks congregation assisted D. J. Johns in that service. The congregation was able to lease the ground on which the Prescott Hall stood for $20.00 per year until 1911 when three lots were purchased and the present house of worship, a brick structure, was built. About the year 1905 Deacon Simon S. Yoder transferred his membership from the Forks congregation to Middlebury, and in 1907 he was ordained preacher. Andrew J. Hostetler and Simon S. Yoder then served the congregation as ministers for many years. In 1911 Jacob C. Hershberger, deacon in the Clinton Brick congregation, transferred his membership to Middlebury.

At its organization in 1904 the congregation numbered about thirty-five members. By 1920 the total had risen to 228. In November 1923 the membership stood at 209. At this point a lamentable division occurred, when Preacher Simon S. Yoder and about ninety-eight other members withdrew from the Indiana-Michigan Conference and organized the Warren Street congregation, Middlebury, which is now affiliated with the General Conference Mennonite Church. This left, in 1923, only 110 members in the Lawrence Street congregation. In 1924 Earl Miller was ordained to the office of deacon, and is still living. After the death of Andrew J. Hostetler in 1925 the congregation was served by ministers of neighboring congregations until 1936 when Wilbur Yoder was ordained to the ministry; he served until the year 1961. He was ordained bishop August 30, 1959, although Paul M. Miller of the East Goshen congregation served as the senior bishop until 1961. D. J. Johns served as bishop at Middlebury 1903-11, when D. D. Miller assumed the bishop oversight. When D. D. Miller became too feeble to continue with his work, Paul Mininger was chosen by the congregation as bishop in 1945. In 1951 Paul Mininger resigned and Earley C. Bontrager became bishop. He was succeeded in 1956 by Paul M. Miller.

In 1911, when the brick meetinghouse was built at a cost of $6,000.00, the membership stood at 126 on the day of dedication (August 20). The 1940 *Mennonite Yearbook* lists the Middlebury membership as 262. The 1960 *Mennonite Yearbook* gives the Middlebury membership as 433. (Middlebury is one of the congregations which have been partly built up by Old Order Amish members who united with the Mennonites.) The 1911 meetinghouse was enlarged in 1950-51.

Wilbur Yoder has been the pastor since 1936, but after serving ten years was assisted for a number of years by Harold A. Yoder, who was ordained in 1946, and served at Middlebury until 1959. Harold is now preaching at Kalamazoo.

In 1947 the Middlebury congregation established a mission outpost at Moorepark, north of Three Rivers, Michigan.

HOWARD-MIAMI AMISH MENNONITE CHURCH

Section 31, Harrison Township, Miami County, Indiana

The first Amish Mennonite settlers came to Howard and Miami counties in the year 1848, mostly from Holmes and Tuscarawas counties, Ohio. The known settlers of 1848 included the families of Abraham Hostetler, Peter Stineman, and Jacob Schrock. In the following years the Amish settlers included Lewis Hensler, Christian Hershberger, Emanuel Hostetler, Zachariah Hostetler, Joseph Kennedy, Moses Mast, Absalom Miller, the elder Benjamin Schrock, the younger Benjamin Schrock (the two Schrocks were not closely related), Christian Smucker, John Smucker, Nobert Sproal, Joseph Troyer, and John Zook.

Anson G. Horner, the present bishop of the Howard-Miami congregation, reports that four Schrock brothers and their half sister, Barbara, moved from Holmes County, Ohio, to Miami County, Indiana, in the early years of the Amish settlement. The Schrock brothers, Jacob (grandfather of Preacher Niles M. Slabaugh) and Benjamin (great-grandfather of Joseph Troyer), settled in Miami County. Joseph (grandfather of A. G. Horner) and David Schrock settled in the hills north of Peru, near where the Schrock Cemetery is located, in Section 8, Erie Township, Miami County. The half sister of these four Schrock brothers was Barbara (grandmother of Susie Miller Horner). Three of these Schrock brothers were married to four Hostetler sisters, who were members of another large pioneer Amish family. A. G. Horner reports that approximately half the present members of the Howard-Miami congregation are descendants of these two pioneer families, Schrock and Hostetler.

According to the Smucker family genealogy written by Mrs. George Hoover (Wakarusa, Indiana, 1957), the first Amish ministers were ordained the spring of 1851. These men were the elder Benjamin Schrock (1819-1895) and John ("Hans") Smucker (1816-1872).

Parallel with the unrest and divisions which occurred in the Amish Mennonite congregations farther north in Indiana, was the trouble which came to the Howard-Miami Amish congregation in 1854. It should be reported that various dates have been suggested for the time of this division, but the present writer is convinced that the year 1854, as given by Preacher Niles M. Slabaugh in the conference minute book of 1929, is correct: Slabaugh got his information from his mother, Lydia (Schrock) Slabaugh, who was living at the time of the division. Preacher Benjamin Schrock was the leader of the progressive (less strict) Amish Mennonite group, which included the following family heads: Abraham Hostetler, Zachariah Hostetler, Joseph Kennedy, Absalom Miller, the younger Benjamin Schrock, Jacob Schrock, Nobert Sproal, Andrew Troyer, Jacob Troyer, Joseph Troyer, John Yoder, and John Zook. Preacher John ("Hans") Smucker was the leader of the stricter Old Order Amish group, which included the following family heads: Christian Eash, Christian Hershberger, Emanuel Hostetler, Moses Mast, David Miller, Christian Smucker, Peter Stineman, and Samuel Weaver. Possibly eight or nine years after the division of 1854 Preacher Benjamin Schrock removed to an area north of Goshen in Elkhart County, which left the Amish Mennonites of the Howard-Miami area without a preacher. The Old Order Amish congregation was in a flourishing condition, while the services of the Amish Mennonites were actually discontinued. It appeared for a time as if the Amish Mennonite congregation might actually die out. The person who saved the situation was Mary (Hostetler) Schrock, wife of the younger Benjamin Schrock. She invited the young folks of the congregation to her home one Sunday. The group sang hymns together and had a very enjoyable time. They decided to meet again in two weeks and every two weeks thereafter. The older folks in turn also became interested and began to attend these "singings." One of the lay members of the congregation named Absalom Miller, or someone else, would also read a chapter from the Bible on these occasions.

One of the next persons to be ordained was a man named Joseph Kennedy. Some of his descendants insist that he was a deacon, while other historians are equally sure that he was a preacher. Everyone agrees that Kennedy became unhappy and left the Amish Mennonite Church, and united with the German Baptists (who are now known as the Church of the Brethren). John S. Coffman recorded in his diary for 1888 that on August 5 he visited Joseph Kennedy. "He was once a minister among the Amish brethren but has been off the church for years, yet he claims to be living a Christian life. But he confessed that he is not living as he should. It is hard to understand such as he."

The next deacon was a man named Absalom Miller, who was likely ordained in the early 1860's. He served until the year 1898. In the year 1866 there was some sort of difficulty in the Howard-Miami Amish Mennonite congregation, and Bishop Isaac Smucker of Haw Patch (Topeka) came to Howard-Miami, accompanied by J. K. Yoder of Wayne County, Ohio, to settle the difficulty. The *Herald of Truth* for 1866 reports that on August 19 Bishop Smucker and J. K. Yoder held a meeting at Widow Jacob Schrag's (Schrock). Next day they held another meeting at the home of Brother Lewis Hensler. On August 21 they conducted a communion service and ordained Nobert Sproal to the office of preacher. The next year (1867) Daniel C. Miller was ordained as preacher and possibly six years later was ordained as the first Amish Mennonite bishop in the Howard-Miami congregation. In 1869 the younger Benjamin Schrock, husband of the woman who started the Amish Mennonite singings, was also ordained as preacher: he served only nine years, however, for he died at an early age, in 1878. His son Ezra, who was born in 1878, died in Goshen on July 17, 1961.

The year 1869 also witnessed the organization of the first Sunday school for the group. It was held in the Hostetler schoolhouse, one-fourth mile south of the present meetinghouse.

The first Amish Mennonite meetinghouse, a frame building, was built in the year 1871 on the same lot where the meetinghouse now stands. It was used for seventeen years, when it was sold to the German Baptists and moved two miles west to the Absalom Miller farm, only to be moved later to Copper Creek, where it continued to be used as a German Baptist house of worship.

Three more men were ordained in the era 1879-99. In 1879 Emanuel A. Mast was ordained preacher. In 1891 the correspondent for the *Herald of Truth* reported that upwards of eighty-five communed on June 7, 1891, and after the foot-washing service, E. A. Mast was ordained bishop by an almost unanimous vote. He served until his death in 1932. In 1889 Joseph S. Horner, father of the present bishop, A. G. Horner, was ordained preacher and served until his death in 1945 except for the years, 1903-10, when he lived near Chief, Michigan, and served the Pleasantview Amish Mennonite congregation. After the death of Deacon Absalom Miller in 1898, Noah W. King was ordained as deacon and served until his death in 1935. Local historians insist that he was ordained in 1898, but Bishop J. P. Smucker reports ordaining him deacon on May 21, 1899.

In the middle 1880's severe tension developed in the Howard-Miami congregation over the question as to whether the men should be required to continue wearing hooks and eyes on their vests. The Amish custom of wearing hooks and eyes on both coats and vests had been given up at an earlier date as far as the coat was concerned, but it was the sincere conviction of a number of members of the congregation that such a visible symbol of nonconformity to the world as hooks and eyes on the vest needed to be retained. Other members of the church were equally certain that just as these items had been discarded for the coat, so could they be discarded for the vest. The consequence was that considerable tension existed in the congregation, and it seemed best not to hold communion services. Finally a number of brethren, with Gary W. North, father of Bishop Homer F. North of the Nappanee congregation, taking the initiative, wrote to Preacher John S. Coffman of Elkhart, urging him to come to Howard-Miami and help the church through the crisis. J. S. Coffman spent a week with the congregation, preaching earnest messages to the church, and spending one whole night in prayer. At the end of the meetings Bishop Daniel C. Miller of the Howard-Miami congregation announced that from now on the wearing of the hooks and eyes on the vest would be an optional matter; the brethren were free to wear either buttons or hooks and eyes. J. S. Coffman, with his keen sense of humor, suggested that it would also be satisfactory to pin the vest shut! In the *Herald of Truth* for 1887 J. S. Coffman wrote: "The last place I visited was the church in Howard and Miami Counties, Indiana, near Plevna Post Office. There is a considerable membership here of Amish brethren in the care of Daniel C. Miller. His helpers are Nobert Sproll [*sic*] and Emanuel Mast. There are only two families here holding to the Mennonite Church in the care of the Indiana Conference. . . ." Coffman then continued in relation to the Howard-Miami congregation: "There has not been so much of spirituality manifested here (though much of the form of Christianity has been taught) as would be best for the prosperity of the church. Yet there are many precious, earnest souls here, apparently full of the love of God. There has not been that harmony between the older members and some of the younger ones that should exist. . . ." The Howard-Miami Amish Mennonite Sunday School in 1887 had 135 scholars.

When the old 1871 meetinghouse was moved away in 1888, the congregation immediately built a new frame meetinghouse which was completed by late summer of that year. Special services were held the weekend of August 3-5, with J. S. Coffman of Elkhart again preaching. Coffman's report of these meetings in his diary reads as follows:

"August 3, 1888. This a.m. I left Elkhart going to Marion to North Grove in Howard or Miami County. Frank Maust met me and took me to his house. There was a large attendance [in the meetinghouse] as we met for the first time in their new house. It is thirty-six by fifty [feet] with small anterooms in front on the east side of the center aisle. It is a nicely arranged house. The house was filled. [Preached on] John 3:1-14, faith and regeneration.

"August 4. Stayed with Bishop Daniel Miller. This a.m. we went to Eli Millers to look after the accusations that had been made against him. We hope to get the matter all settled so that talk will cease, and all will be peace again. This p.m. funeral of Grandfather Troyer at the Evangelical Church. Full house this eve. Acts 2:9, repentance.

"August 5. . . . Today the house was crowded. The services were made to correspond in a measure to the occasion. The prayer of Solomon was read, I Kings 8; Haggai 2:9 as a text. The attention and order were excellent. Took dinner with Bro. M. Hensler. Afternoon visited at old Bro. Hensler, Eli Miller, and Jacob J. Hostetler. Crowded house this eve. and many outside. Matthew 28:19, baptism."

The *Herald of Truth* for 1891, in correspondence of 1890, reports: "There are here [Howard-Miami] about seventy families of Amish brethren, and though the church, on account of certain difficulties, had for some time been somewhat on the decline, it seems at present to be reviving." It is known that D. J. Johns and J. P. Smucker, two Amish bishops from Elkhart County, Indiana, were at Howard-Miami in 1890 to settle a difficulty. The notebooks of J. P. Smucker reveal that he frequently went to the Howard-Miami congregation in the 1890's to hold the communion services: 1892, 1893, 1894, 1895, 1896, 1898, and 1899. In 1894 D. J. Johns and J. S. Hartzler held meetings in the Howard-Miami congregation which resulted in a great revival and the reception of twenty-one members by baptism and one member reclaimed. In 1896 David Garber, a young minister from the Clinton Brick Mennonite congregation, held meetings which resulted in sixteen converts. In 1898 a total of 106 persons communed on November 13, and the next spring 120 communed on May 21.

One of the unusual families of the Howard-Miami congregation was that of a man named John Troyer. He was first married to a woman named Catherine Schrock who bore him twelve children. Following her death he married her cousin Caroline (Schrock) Kendall, widow of Simon Kendall, who already had two children, Simon and Emma. (Emma became the mother of A. G. Horner.) John and Caroline in turn had seventeen additional children. The *Mennonite Church History of Howard and Miami Counties* says with commendable modesty: "At one time his family was the largest around here." The youngest of these thirty-one children was the well-known George L. Troyer, M.D., long-time missionary to India, and more recently serving in Puerto Rico.

During the year 1904 the Howard-Miami congregation ordained two additional ministers. On June 10 Nathaniel O. Troyer, son of John Troyer above, was ordained to the ministry. He lived briefly at Fairview, Michigan, in that year, and later enrolled at Manchester College, where he married a young woman who was a member of the German Baptists, and he united with her church, in which denomination he served. He died in 1943 and his body was buried in the Mast Cemetery, Liberty

Township, Howard County. The second ordination of 1904 was that of Niles M. Slabaugh who was ordained November 6 and who served until his death in 1961.

In connection with the communion service which was held on May 14, 1893, John S. Coffman wrote in his diary: "Bro. [Jonathan P.] Smucker and I [were] with our young ministering brother, Joseph Horner. This a.m. we attended the Sunday school which was fairly interesting, but might be much improved. This is the communion day here. This a.m. they had a well-attended meeting. I spoke on the communion, its meaning, etc. I Cor. 10:16, 17. They dismissed and took dinner. Then Bro. Smucker spoke on the sufferings of Christ, and officiated in the communion. Over 100 communed. Dinner at Moses Henslers. A crowded house, densely, this eve. Mark 8:34, the cross. Bro. Smucker spoke first. Four more converts.

"[May 15.] Last night Bro. Smucker started home. [Son] William and I stayed at Noah Kings. This a.m. we visited at Preacher Andrew Troyers (Evangelical). We then went to Bro. Steinmans and from there to church. The house was again crowded and we had riveted attention. Matthew 16:26, worth of the soul. After the service when we gave invitation for sinners to confess Christ, thirteen came forward, which makes twenty-four in these three invitations. May God pardon their sins, bless, and save them."

Five years earlier, on November 12, 1888, Coffman wrote in his diary concerning the services at the Howard-Miami congregation: "At ten o'clock there was meeting at the Amish Church for communion services. They hold these services somewhat different from what we do. In the forenoon they read some Scriptures and I spoke from John 1:29, Behold the Lamb of God. A recess was then taken and a lunch eaten, after which they reassembled and Daniel Miller preached on the sufferings of Christ, after which the communion was served very much as the Old Mennonites do, only they use the Prayer Book in their prayers."

In the 1906 *Herald of Truth* the diligent Howard-Miami congregational correspondent, G. W. North, reported that the meetinghouse was being remodeled, and an addition, twenty-two by thirty-six feet, was being built. In correspondence of October 3, 1906, he reported that 143 had communed on September 30, and added: "Our new meetinghouse is almost completed, all except the benches, and the lights are not yet in the house." On March 14, 1907, the *Herald of Truth* reported that the enlarged meetinghouse was now fully completed, and the building had been raised three feet, and a heater placed in the basement. The congregation then had a "good lighting plant." The meetinghouse had a capacity of 600 persons. G. W. North also gave the following membership report for the year 1906: At the beginning of the year the membership stood at 210. Thirty-five persons were received as members during the year. One was lost by death, ten by letter, and two by excommunication, leaving a final membership figure of 232.

Space forbids the reporting of the many series of meetings which have been held in the Howard-Miami congregation. In December 1904 Daniel Kauffman and M. S. Steiner held a Bible conference in the Howard-Miami congregation which resulted in fifty-one confessions. During the year 1906 Noah Metzler of Elkhart County held meetings at Howard-Miami which resulted in thirty more converts. S. G. Shetler of Johnstown, Pennsylvania, held meetings in November 1907, with twenty converts, and two additional persons were received by letter. The church grew rapidly for a number of years, with the result that in the year 1914 it was deemed advisable to enlarge the meetinghouse. On this occasion a basement was put under the entire building and a balcony was added to the main auditorium.

About the year 1906 or 1907 Mrs. Noah King of the Howard-Miami congregation visited a Mennonite mission in Chicago. The workers there told her of their need of clothing and of how they lacked time and material to make the clothing. Mrs. King thereupon initiated the formation of a sewing circle in the congregation. This first sewing circle was not a group activity, however, but was a project in which fifteen or eighteen interested women individually sewed in various homes at the rate of $1.00 per day, and thereby the group raised a total of $46.00 which was donated to the Mennonite Gospel Mission in Chicago. In December 1911 a sewing circle of the more conventional type was organized, and it was decided to meet once a month to sew for the Gospel Mission in Chicago. Beginning in the year 1915 the meetings were held in the basement of the meetinghouse.

In the year 1913 the young people of the congregation, as a direct result of the influence of Goshen College, organized a Young People's Christian Association. Prior to this time the activities of the young people had not been well developed or supervised, and some of the parties which were held were not of much benefit to the young people, and sometimes activities were engaged in which were questioned or criticized by the older members of the church. The first president of the Y.P.C.A. was George L. Troyer who later became a medical missionary to India and Puerto Rico. About a decade later the Y.P.C.A. became the "Young People's Literary Association," and in the 1950's, the Mennonite Youth Fellowship ("MYF").

By the time of the first World War the Howard-Miami congregation was strong numerically. This was a fulfillment of the hope expressed by

M. S. Steiner in the 1889 *Herald of Truth:* "This is a place where I hope to see one of our larger churches some day. They have a membership of about 125 at present, and a prosperous Sunday school." The *Mennonite Church History of Howard and Miami Counties,* the introduction of which is dated December 11, 1916, states, in reference to the membership of the congregation: "Since the first annual Bible conference additions to the membership have been made yearly. At one time the membership was nearly three hundred, but since 1913, a good number have moved away. The membership at present numbers two hundred forty-nine." The 1905 *Mennonite Church History* of Hartzler and Kauffman gives the membership of the Howard-Miami congregation as 180. The 1923 *Mennonite Yearbook* gives the membership as 171. The 1940 *Mennonite Yearbook* lists the membership as 328, which is approximately the size of the congregation twenty years later. It should, however, be mentioned that the Howard-Miami congregation now has a daughter church, Bon Air, in the city of Kokomo with a membership of fifty-five, and another, Sante Fe, south of Peru.

The three ordained brethren who have served in the congregation with Preacher Niles M. Slabaugh since the 1930's are Deacon John W. Horner, ordained 1933; Anson G. Horner, his brother, ordained preacher 1935, and bishop 1937; and Deacon Paul J. Myers, ordained deacon 1936. Only one ordination has been conducted since 1936, that of Emanuel J. Hochstedler, 1947. It should also be mentioned that the settlements at Fairview and Pleasantview, Michigan, were made at least in part by members from the Howard-Miami congregation.

In the spring of 1889 the congregation began to hold what were then called Bible Readings largely through the efforts of G. W. North and Abner Miller. In these Bible Readings chapters or parts of chapters in the Bible were "studied, explained, and discussed." Eventually this organization evolved into the modern young people's Bible meeting. Written records of the Howard-Miami young people's Bible meetings begin as of December 11, 1904.

The last enlargement and remodeling of the meetinghouse was accomplished in the year 1956.

It will soon be a hundred years since Bishop Samuel Yoder and Preacher John Ringenberg of the West Market Street, Nappanee, Amish Mennonite Church drove their buggy to the Howard-Miami Amish Mennonite Church, held services in the homes of the younger Benjamin Schrock and Daniel Miller, and gave communion in the home of Absalom Miller when "a goodly number partook of the sacred emblems of the bread and wine." In these ninety-four years the tiny congregation has grown to a membership of considerable size, the services have changed from German to English, the young people now have splendid Christian organizations, and the members as a whole are vitally interested in the program of Jesus Christ around the world.

SANTA FE MENNONITE CHURCH

In the year 1960 the congregation purchased an abandoned Methodist church at Sante Fe, about four miles south of Peru, renovated it, and established a daughter congregation there. Services began October 9, 1960. No ordination has been effected at this writing; the pulpit is supplied. A number of the younger families from Howard-Miami form the nucleus of the church, which by God's grace shall witness in that community. The attendance averages from seventy-five to one hundred.

THE PERU AMISH MENNONITE SETTLEMENT

When Niles M. Slabaugh wrote his brief history of the congregation for the conference minute book of 1929, he stated: "Several families also moved northeast of Peru but failed to organize a church there, so they united with other denominations." It will be recalled that Joseph Schrock, the great-grandfather of A. G. Horner, and David Schrock, his brother, were among those who settled in the Peru area of Miami County. The Amish and Mennonite families of the area never had a minister to serve them, which is perhaps the reason why no congregation developed. The 1870 *Herald of Truth* reports that Preacher Daniel Brenneman of Elkhart County went to Miami County and held a meeting in the village of Chili in Richland Township, at the invitation of Martin Kling who was formerly of Lancaster County, Pennsylvania. Daniel Brenneman reported that an attentive audience was present. The next day Brenneman conducted a service in the home of Henry Bally, nephew of Preacher Yost Bally of Illinois. That evening he held another meeting in a schoolhouse, which was well attended. He conducted the services chiefly in German. He reported that "many Pennsylvania Germans" were in the community. On Sunday he had three appointments in the vicinity of the village of Lincoln.

Later that same year John Richer reported the death of Widow Mary Ulrich, nee Richer, who died July 27, 1870, at the age of ninety-three years. She had emigrated from the canton of Basel, Switzerland, to Wayne County, Ohio, in 1840, and had settled in the Peru, Indiana, area in 1848. She was the mother of eight children, and had lived as a widow for fifty-four years. She was a member of the "Omish Mennonite Church."

The 1872 *Herald of Truth* reports the death of Christiana Hochstetler, wife of William Hochstetler; she was fifty-nine years of age. Her body was buried in "Jos. Schrock's burying ground."

In 1875 Daniel A. and Mary I. Richer of near Peru lost a son Noah at the age of eight months and twenty-five days.

The other occasions in which Peru is mentioned in the correspondence in the *Herald of Truth* seem to refer to the Howard-Miami congregation. For example, in February 1874 J. P. Smucker, later a bishop in the Nappanee Amish Mennonite Church, went with Preacher Jonas Troyer of Starke County, Indiana, "to visit the church" at Peru, Indiana. Smucker seems to have had in mind the Howard-Miami Church. He makes mention of another visit in January 1875, and again in October 1887, as well as on other occasions.

On the other hand, the *Herald of Truth* as late as 1894 mentions the death of John Richer, 1815-1893, who had been born in the canton of Bern, Switzerland, who came to America in 1840 and settled in Wayne County, Ohio. In 1843 Richer was married to Magdalena Nafziger. In 1848 John and Magdalena Richer settled in Miami County, Indiana, and reared their family near the town of Peru.

LEO AMISH MENNONITE CHURCH

Section 22, Cedar Creek Township, Allen County, Indiana

The Leo congregation is the only one in the Indiana-Michigan Conference which was made up almost exclusively of European immigrants. The early settlers were Alsatian Amish who bore such names as Gerig, Graber, Hostetler, Klopfenstein, Ledermann, Liechty, Miller, Neuhouser, Richard, Schlatter, Stalter, Stoll, Stuckey, and Witmer. Among the Alsatian Amish who migrated to Ohio soon after the middle of the nineteenth century were Daniel Graber and his nine children. Some of the Grabers settled in Allen County, Indiana, in November 1852. In April 1853 a party of fifty-two European Amish made the trip in eleven teams from Stark County, Ohio, to Allen County, Indiana. Among the ministers in the Amish congregation in the first decade or so were three Graber brothers: Peter, 1811-1896, who became an Amish bishop in the Leo area; John, 1816-1877, who became a preacher and later removed to Daviess County, Indiana; and Jacob, 1821-1904, who served first as a deacon, and then a bishop-deacon (Völliger-Armendiener), who also removed to Daviess County. (The brothers John and Jacob were not able to agree with the rather severe discipline of Peter, the bishop.) John was the first of the three to attend the Amish General Conference, 1862; Jacob followed, 1864; and Peter, 1867. Both Bishop Joseph Gerig (1824-1892) and his brother, Preacher Andreas, attended the Amish General Conference in 1864, as did David H. Hostetler. John Klopfenstein attended in 1865.

There was considerable disagreement among the Amish of Allen County as to disciplinary standards, and forms of piety and doctrine. The final result was a three-way division over the years. One portion, under the leadership of Peter Graber, remained Old Order Amish. Another group, under the leadership of Joseph Gerig, united with the Defenseless Mennonites, now Evangelical Mennonites. The third group is the one which concerns us here, namely, the Leo Amish Mennonite congregation, which dates from about 1861.

There is a difference of opinion among the oldest members of the Leo congregation as to a man named Christian Ramseyer. Everyone agrees that he had something to do with the life of the Leo Amish Mennonite congregation prior to the year 1875. One theory is that he was instrumental in the organization of the congregation in the year 1861. According to other persons, Ramseyer actually was imported as a minister (he died in 1875). However, it must be recorded that some of the oldest members of the community deny that there was ever a resident minister named Christian Ramseyer in the congregation.

The first certain resident minister was Christian Lugbill of France who was ordained as a preacher in 1875. The next year he attended the Amish General Conference. He served until his death in 1880. Sometime during his ministry Peter Witmer (1848-1924) was ordained as deacon and served for a number of years. Following the death of Christian Lugbill, his son John C. Lugbill (his name is so spelled on his tombstone in the Yaggy Cemetery, although the people pronounced it, Lugibill) was ordained as a preacher to succeed his father. He served almost a quarter century as a preacher.

In the year that Christian Lugbill was ordained preacher, 1875, the congregation also started to hold Sunday school on the alternate Sundays when there were no preaching services. All services were conducted in private homes until the year 1887.

Elias Yoder was ordained preacher about the year 1880 and served for a little over twenty-five years.

On March 22, 1889, two years after the traditional date for the building of the first meetinghouse, Peter Witmer and his wife Elizabeth conveyed an acre of land in Section 27 of Cedar Creek Township for a consideration of $85.00 to the "St. Joseph Menonite Church." Six years later, on March 11, 1895, Witmer and his wife (who now signed her name Lizzie) granted an additional acre to the same church for a consideration of $80.00. There was evidently something wrong with the surveys of these plots of land, for it became necessary on February 18,

14

1902, for the later owners of that tract of land, John Conrad and Mary his wife, to convey a new deed to Christian S. Neuhouser, Christian D. Schlatter, and Joseph Yoder, trustees of the *St. Joseph Menonite Church.* "This deed is made to correct two deeds made by Peter Witmer and Elizabeth Witmer his wife, to the said grantees, one dated March 22nd, 1889, and recorded in Deed Record 112, page 350, and one dated March 11th, 1895, and recorded in Deed Record 154, page 197, of the Deed Records of said County and State aforesaid." Conrad signed in German script, Johan Conrad. This plot of land is located something over a mile southeast of the present church, on the east side of the St. Joseph River. The 1887 meetinghouse was used until the year 1917.

Christian S. Liechty was ordained deacon about 1893 and served for twenty years, until the year 1913 when he removed to North Dakota.

The Leo congregation united with the Indiana-Michigan Amish Mennonite Conference in 1905, and Jonathan Kurtz was soon given the bishop oversight of the congregation upon the retirement of Elias Yoder as bishop. From 1906 until 1910 the congregation had no resident minister.

In 1907 the Leo congregation began to hold Bible Readings, which gradually evolved into what we now know as young people's Bible meetings. Church and Sunday school have been held weekly since 1912.

In the year 1910 Andrew S. Miller was ordained to the ministry and rendered thirty-five years of faithful service. In the year 1913 John C. Lugbill, who had earlier been a preacher, was ordained by lot for the office of deacon and served until his death in 1926. In 1921 Joseph S. Neuhouser was ordained as a minister to assist Andrew S. Miller. In the year 1933 the congregation established an outpost known as Anderson, and Neuhouser soon threw his active energies into this project, and was eventually released from further ministerial responsibility at Leo. In the year 1926 Simon H. Beck was ordained as deacon, to succeed John C. Lugbill, and served until his death in 1944.

A new chapter in the life of the church began with the year 1944 when Samuel J. Miller, a minister from Pigeon, Michigan, was invited to move into the Leo congregation and serve as pastor. Oscar S. Hostetler had succeeded Jonathan Kurtz as bishop of the congregation in 1926, and served until the year 1950, when he secured the permission of the congregation to ordain S. J. Miller as bishop. Miller is still serving. Ben Graber was ordained deacon in 1946 and served for twelve years.

In the year 1959 the Leo congregation gave a call to Virgil Vogt, a student in the Goshen College Biblical Seminary, to become their minister, and he accepted the call. S. J. Miller ordained him at Leo on October 4, 1959. H. S. Bender preached the ordination sermon.

The 1887 meetinghouse was used until the year 1917 when the congregation purchased the St. John's Reformed church building in the village of Leo and sold the 1887 building to Henry Sauder, bishop in the Apostolic Christian Church. Later the ownership of the 1887 building passed to Sauder's son, Joel Sauder, who was also a bishop in the Apostolic Christian Church. Joel Sauder, in turn, sold it to Joseph Sevits, a brother in the Amish Church, who cut the building into two parts, and used one half to build a small house, and the other half for a barn for his horse and buggy. In 1958 the property was sold to Waldermar Heller, the athletic coach in the Leo High School.

The literary of the Leo congregation was organized in the year 1924, but along with the other literaries of the district is now known as Mennonite Youth Fellowship.

In the year 1905 the membership of the congregation was listed as seventy-five. For a number of years after that it was sixty-four, but rose to eighty in 1913, to ninety-two in 1917, to 101 in 1919, to 138 in 1925, to 185 in 1930, to 227 in 1945, and the 1960 *Mennonite Yearbook* lists the membership as 305.

The congregation has established two mission outposts. About 1944 a Christian witness was inaugurated at Lost Creek, Hicksville, Ohio, which developed into a congregation in 1947, and is now affiliated with the Ohio and Eastern Conference.

The second mission outpost of the congregation is known as Fair Haven and was established, to do Christian work among the colored folks of Fort Wayne, in the year 1954.

YODER AMISH MENNONITE CHURCH

French Township, Adams County, Indiana

One of the small schismatic groups in Adams County, Indiana, was an Amish Mennonite congregation, somewhat parallel to Howard-Miami, Maple Grove, Forks, and Clinton Frame. This small group built a meetinghouse in French Township in the year 1870. This building is no longer standing. In 1886 the Yoder congregation purchased the former meetinghouse of the Baumgartner congregation.

One of the earliest references to the Yoder congregation occurs in the 1871 *Herald of Truth*. In April of that year John F. Funk, Daniel Brenneman, and his brother Deacon Henry B. Brenneman, held services in the "Mennonite meetinghouse" in the vicinity of the Christian Augsberger Mennonite group. The Elkhart visitors reported an overflow crowd. Henry Brenneman added that he was not able to understand them very well, evidently because they spoke Swiss. In the year 1872 an

Iowa minister visited Adams County and on January 30 held services in the Mennonite meetinghouse. In 1888 C. P. Steiner of Allen County, Ohio, reported the presence of a small Amish congregation in Adams County, which owned a meetinghouse. He said that they met biweekly. "Two young ministers have charge of this flock." It is not known who one of the two ministers was. The name of one was Daniel Yoder, who was then thirty-five years of age. In 1892 Preacher Daniel Yoder attended the sessions of the Indiana-Michigan Amish Mennonite Conference. Indeed, in the year 1900 his tiny congregation served as host to the Indiana-Michigan Amish Mennonite Conference, using the facilities of the Egly (Defenseless) Mennonite congregation.

The little congregation never prospered. In 1907 Preacher Daniel Yoder moved to Leo, where his brother, Elias Yoder, had served as bishop. Daniel's own children united with the Missionary Church Association. Both Reuben R. Ebersole and Frances Zook (later Mrs. D. S. Oyer) taught school in Adams County. D. S. Oyer reports that Preacher Daniel Yoder sometimes went to church barefooted. He also reported that Yoder had but little influence in the community.

In the year 1908 the congregation was rapidly approaching its death. At that point the bishops of the Amish Mennonite Conference and Daniel Yoder of Leo were delegated to look after the congregation in Adams County. We know that Preacher A. J. Yontz of the Maple Grove congregation preached there in 1908. But by the year 1909 only two aged women were left. By the year 1910 all regular services had undoubtedly ceased. We do not know how long the two aged women lived.

THE STARKE COUNTY AMISH MENNONITE CHURCH

Section 13, Washington Township, Starke County, Indiana

Soon after the Civil War a number of Amish Mennonite families, and a few Mennonite families, began moving into the area about eight miles east of Knox, Indiana, and ten miles southwest of Plymouth. The leader of the Amish Mennonite settlers was Bishop Jonas D. Troyer, founder of the Clinton Frame Amish Mennonite Church. Besides the families of Jonas D. and Elizabeth Troyer, the following Amish Mennonite families are known to have lived in the area: Christian Berkey, a Hershberger family, Joseph and Rebecca Kauffman, Jonathan P. and Salome Smucker, Amos and Magdalena Troyer, Seth and Elizabeth Troyer, Valentine and Fannie Troyer, Adam Yoder, Andrew Yoder, and David and Magdalena Yoder. A number of these settlers died and were buried in a small Amish Mennonite cemetery in Section 19 of West Township, Marshall County, less than half a mile east of the Amish Mennonite meetinghouse which the settlers erected. Among those who died were Christian Berkey, 59, in 1870; Andrew Yoder, 29, and Magdalena Hershberger, 35, in 1871; and Peter Stutzman, 48, in 1874. The funeral of Christian Berkey who died November 25, 1870, was held two days later, with burial in the "New Omish Mennonite Grave-yard."

During the 1870's a number of letters and news items pertaining to the Amish Mennonites in Starke County appeared in the *Herald of Truth*. For example, Daniel Brenneman, minister from Elkhart County, reported that in November 1870, "in compliance with the request of Daniel Stauffer and wife, of Starke County, Indiana, who had been sick a great deal during the past summer, I left home on Thursday the 3rd of November to visit them. . . . We arrived at the residence of Jonas Troyer (Omish Mennonite minister), where we made a short visit and the same evening went to D. Stauffer's and found them still in delicate health. . . . We conversed with them freely and found them willing and desirous to submit to the yoke and cross of the Saviour. We held two meetings in their house, and one in a neighboring schoolhouse. . . .

"We had very attentive audiences and the Lord seemed to be near on those occasions . . . and to confirm their faith and love by their works they earnestly desired to be baptized and received into the church. . . . There are no members of our church in this neighborhood, save Bro. and Sister Stauffer, and it is their utmost wish to be visited by the brethren. Ministers especially should visit them. Land in this neighborhood is yet cheap, and those of small means might do well by going there. Our Omish Mennonite brethren have been moving there for the last few years, and seem to be well satisfied with the place. They have their meetings regularly. Jonas Troyer is their minister."

A little later, in 1871, Daniel W. and Elizabeth Stauffer, writing from Grovertown in Starke County, reported: "The brethren Samuel Yoder and Michael Shank visited us on Saturday before New Year, and that evening we had meeting at our schoolhouse, and on New Year's evening we had meeting at the schoolhouse two miles north of us."

The 1872 *Herald of Truth* contains the following letter from Preacher M. W. Shank, grandfather of Preacher Clarence A. Shank of the Olive congregation: "On the 17th and 18th of February, the brethren, Samuel Yoder, David Hoover, and myself, had the pleasure of attending three meetings with the Amish brethren in Starke County. On Saturday we had meeting in a schoolhouse near Pre. D. Stouffer's; Sunday morning in Schneider's schoolhouse, and in the evening at the same place. These meetings were well attended, with orderly and attentive audiences. We were received in a very friendly manner, and we felt ourselves at home with our Amish brethren. The following day we returned home."

The assessor of Starke County, Jesse E. Clabaugh, located the following deed for the Amish Mennonite church property: "Joseph D. Kauffman and Rebecca Kauffman, Elkhart County, Indiana, To Valentine Troyer, Adam Yoder, and Abram Hershberger, trustees of the Waldenzer Church, for the use and purposes of said church in the counties of Starke and Marshall.

"Commencing at the southeast corner . . . of the southeast $\frac{1}{4}$ of Section 13 . . . containing $\frac{1}{2}$ acre." The deed is dated October 18, 1871, and was recorded January 20, 1872, in Deed Record M, page 228. The site of this meetinghouse lot was two miles east and five miles south of the town of Grovertown on the Lincoln Highway. If one starts at the north edge of the town of Knox on U.S. 35, and drives east on Division Road for eight miles to the Starke-Marshall County line, the meetinghouse stood on the northwest corner of that intersection. This point is one mile north of Indiana Highway 8.

By the year 1878 the death of the Starke County Amish Mennonite congregation was sufficiently certain that the trustees of the "Waldenzer" Church sold the lot and meetinghouse to the Board of Trustees of the United Brethren in Christ Church. The deed is dated October 19, 1878, and was recorded the same day in Deed Record S, page 332. About 1890 the meetinghouse burned down. Today there is nothing evident of the earlier house of worship in the southeast corner of Section 13 of Washington Township in Starke County. The meetinghouse stood on the same section as the body of water known as Eagle Lake, but there seems to be no evidence that the congregation was ever given any name at all.

In March 1873 Jonathan P. Smucker moved to the little Amish settlement near Eagle Lake, and that spring he was ordained to the office of deacon. At the funeral of Noah Hochstetler who died March 3, 1875, on his thirty-seventh birthday anniversary, the services were conducted by Bishop Jonas D. Troyer, Jonathan P. Smucker, and Seth Troyer. Seth Troyer was a son of J. D. Troyer, and was ordained, probably by his father, as a preacher. The date of his ordination is unknown. In the fall of 1873 Deacon J. P. Smucker was ordained as a preacher.

In June 1875 Preachers J. J. Weaver and Christian S. Plank visited Starke County and on the following Sunday "attended the Sabbath school at the Amish and Mennonite Church, where there was also meeting."

John F. Funk recorded in his diary that on Saturday, November 27, 1875, he "went to W. Overholts in Marshall County, a distance of forty miles from Yellow Creek—a long weary ride. . . . On Sunday went to Starke [County] where I spoke in the Omish meetinghouse in English, and at a schoolhouse near Overholts. Good attendance at both places."

Frank E. Kleinke, Marshall County surveyor, reports that no deed was ever given for the cemetery of the "Waldenzer Church in Section 19 in West Township." He adds: "It is our opinion that when the cemetery was in use a member of the church group allowed the parcel of ground to be used without a deed."

In 1869 a Mennonite family from Elkhart County, William H. and Christina (Sanders) Stauffer, settled in Starke County in the general area of Knox. There William Stauffer died. In 1879 the widow and her daughter Mary (who was born in 1869, and who was later married to Amos Shaum of the Olive congregation) returned to Elkhart County.

The oddest thing about the congregation in Starke County was its use of the term Waldenzer, which is obviously a German pronunciation for Waldenser, which means Waldenses or Waldensian. Evidently Bishop Jonas Troyer, who also got the name "Waldentz" into the deed for the Clinton Frame congregation, believed that the Amish Mennonites stood in the true succession of the Waldenses who were erroneously regarded by T. J. van Braght, author of the *Martyrs Mirror,* as the spiritual forebears of the Anabaptists. Either Troyer or others must have been promoting the use of the name Waldenses among the Amish Mennonites of Northern Indiana, for in 1879 Preacher Christian Warey requested Noah Troyer of Iowa to ask Abner Yoder, "what the meaning of the word Waldenser is, and what for a church the Waldenser Church was." It is likely that the services of the Starke County Amish Mennonites had collapsed by the time they sold the meetinghouse. In any case the congregation had come to its death by about the year 1880.

Barker Street Mennonite Congregation

Section 18, Mottville Township, St. Joseph County, Michigan

As early as the year 1863 Joseph and Rachel (Yoder) Hooley of Mahoning County, Ohio, located in St. Joseph County, Michigan. The *Herald of Truth* for 1868 (page 79) reports that Preacher Joseph Kauffman died March 12, 1868, at his residence near the Indiana-Michigan State Line of consumption, at the age of sixty-three years, seven months, and thirteen days. "The deceased was a preacher of the Gospel for many years in the Omish Mennonite Church, and was beloved by all. Funeral discourses [were preached] by David Hertzler . . . and by Joseph Yoder. . . ." The cemetery of the congregation, which was located in the southeast corner of Section 19 of Mottville Township, at the intersection of Thomas Street and the Indiana-Michigan State Line, contains the graves of Joseph Yoder, 1864; Jonathan King, 1865; Joseph Hooley and Mattie Hartzler, 1868; Susan Troyer, 1877; Jeptha Plank, 1878; Sarah Kauffman, 1879; Esaias Hostetler, 1882; and a number of others.

Another early preacher in the Barker Street congregation was Joseph Yoder. (See his biography in Chapter 5.) The congregation is sometimes referred to as the Joseph Yoder Church in the *Herald of Truth.* Josiah J. Miller, preacher in the Shore congregation, reported that the Amish Mennonite ministers of the Townline congregation, John M. Hostetler and Jonathan (Joni) Troyer, also used to preach at Barker Street.

The congregation was composed of both Mennonites and Amish Mennonites. The early ministers who served the congregation seemed to have been members of the Amish Mennonite Church. As early as 1868 Bishop Jonas D. Troyer married Christian Yoder of Logan County, Ohio, and Rebecca King of Mottville, St. Joseph County, Michigan, in the home of Jonas C. Yoder. (*H.T.*, page 46.) In 1891 the *Herald of Truth* reported: "Although this little community of believers is partly of old Mennonite and partly of Amish Mennonite extraction, the members work together harmoniously for the cause of Christ . . . the church is still without a minister . . . the Sunday school numbers about 40 scholars." In 1892 Preacher Harvey Friesner of the Pleasant Hill congregation in Branch County, Michigan, located with the Barker Street congregation.

The summer of 1893 the Barker Street congregation decided to build a meetinghouse. Prior to this time services were held in private homes and schoolhouses. On March 23, 1893, George W. Huff and Louisa L., his wife, conveyed a plot of land to "The Mennonite and Amish Mennonite Society," which deed is recorded in *Liber* 93, page 61 (kindly reported by Janet C. Hovens of the St. Joseph County Abstract Office, Centerville, Michigan). A meetinghouse was built on this plot, supposedly in the year 1893, although the 1894 *Herald of Truth* still reports services in a schoolhouse, conducted by J. S. Hartzler and John Blosser in November 1893, and by Noah Metzler and David Garber in January 1894.

To reach the site of the Barker Street meetinghouse one goes north from Goshen on State Road 15, crosses the state line into Michigan, whereupon the highway becomes M 103, proceeds four tenths of a mile into the state of Michigan, turns east on the Barker Street Road, and goes east 1.2 miles to the intersection of Barker Street and Thomas Street. The meetinghouse stood on the northeast corner of this intersection. The cemetery is located one-half mile south of the meetinghouse lot on the northwest corner of Thomas Street and the State Line Road. The land for the cemetery was conveyed to the township of Mottville by Anna Yoder on December 27, 1879. (*Liber* 73, page 488.)

By 1908 services were being held monthly; among the speakers of that year were Amos S. Cripe, who preached in German on April 19, 1908, Yost Miller, who also preached in German on June 14, and John F. Funk, who preached on July 12.

The *Herald of Truth* for 1894 reports that Sunday school was reorganized on Easter Sunday, April 25. The Sunday-school officers, all of whom were young people, were the same as for the previous year: George M. Miller, superintendent; S. E. Lantz, assistant; Anna Garber, secretary; Levi Schrock, treasurer. In 1908 the Sunday-school attendance averaged forty pupils.

In the year 1914 W. W. Oesch, who was then living in the community, was ordained preacher. As of about the year 1910 Goshen College students, especially William B. Weaver, were preaching at Barker Street and trying to keep the congregation alive. In 1912 Goshen College sent out what Walter E. Yoder thinks was its first Gospel team. Five men were on the team: Preacher A. W. Geigley, Aaron Eby, Orie O. Miller, William B. Weaver, and Walter E. Yoder, song leader. They held revival meetings at Barker Street, and about forty people were converted, about twelve of whom united with the Barker Street Church. Geigley did the preaching. The ordination of W. W. Oesch also seemed to give good promise for the future. All went fairly well until the year 1923 when tension developed in a number of congregations of the United (Mennonite and Amish Mennonite) Conference. Sensing that trouble lay ahead the Barker Street congregation met on August 5, 1923, and passed a resolution to the effect that if any attempt was made to dismiss any member, or unfrock a minister, without the voice of the congregation, the church would automatically sever its connection with the conference. Unfortunately, W. W. Oesch was one of the preachers whose ministry was revoked that fall. On November 18, 1923, the Barker Street congregation unanimously, except for Preacher Harvey Friesner, voted to declare themselves no longer members of the Indiana-Michigan Conference. The entire group, with the exception of Preacher Harvey Friesner, remained loyal to W. W. Oesch, and consisted of about six families, each of which had from three to eight children. In the village of Mottville, about two miles from the Barker Street meetinghouse, were two rather inactive churches. W. W. Oesch and the Barker Street congregation decided to go to Mottville and worship in an ex-Methodist church building. They made a small payment to the Methodist board for this privilege. Meanwhile the Barker Street meetinghouse was sold at auction, with the building being bought by Cline Brothers, and the lot being purchased by John Juday. In 1959 Ira E. Reed and Edith G. his wife held title to this plot. John Juday was one of the group which worshiped with Preacher Oesch at Mottville. Oesch continued with the services in Mottville, "on a community basis," for about ten years. In his congregation were Mennonites, members of the Church of the Brethren, and Methodists. Oesch withdrew from the congregation about 1935 and the work continued as a community project about five more years. One of the ministers who preached there occasionally was a man by the name of George Bostwick. Eventually the Mennonite aspect of the program was totally lost.

In the 1880's J. F. Funk's records show that there were about fifteen members. In the year 1905 the congregation had twenty-five members; in 1915, forty; and in 1920, thirty-one. The 1940 *Yearbook* makes, of course, no reference to the former Barker Street congregation.

One of the well-known laymen of the Mennonite Church, Simon P. Yoder, 1847-1926, poet, and author of *Poetical Meditations and Thoughtful Paragraphs,* 1916, was the son of Jacob Yoder and his wife Anna (Hertzler) Yoder, originally of Juniata County, Pennsylvania, who settled at Barker Street, in 1863, coming directly from Mahoning County, Ohio. S. P. Yoder, who lived at Denbigh, Virginia, and his wife Mary (Metzler) Yoder were the parents of Alice (Mrs. Joseph E.) Brunk of Goshen, Indiana.

TENNESSEE

The Amish Mennonites established a tiny colony in Coffee County, in north central Tennessee, near the town of Tullahoma, in the 1880's which proved to be short-lived. D. D. Troyer, later a bishop in the Clinton Frame congregation east of Goshen, moved to Tullahoma, at the age of fifteen, with his parents, Noah L. and Mary (Schrock) Troyer. Bishop Jonas D. Troyer, an uncle of Noah, also moved to Tullahoma in 1885, where his wife, Elizabeth (Mishler) Troyer, died on July 17, 1885, at the age of seventy-seven. Some of Bishop Troyer's children were also living in Coffee County in 1885. But the settlement did not prove to be permanent; the members moved out with the same ease that they moved in. D. D. Troyer, for example, returned to Northern Indiana after only four years in Tennessee. Eventually, the members were all gone.

FAIRVIEW AMISH MENNONITE CHURCH

Section 15, Comins Township, Oscoda County, Michigan

In the year 1900 the first Amish Mennonites settled west of what is now the village of Fairview, Michigan. Among the families who came to Oscoda County in the first years were John Stutesmans, Noah Yoders, Levi Kauffmans, and Jeff Millers. The first settlers came from the Howard-Miami congregation in Indiana. There was no minister in the group to conduct services, but beginning in 1902 a Methodist minister named White from Alpena organized a Union Sunday School in the Gusler log schoolhouse one mile west of Fairview, which the Amish Mennonites supported. The superintendent of the Union Sunday School was himself an Amish Mennonite named Ellsworth A. Troyer, Christ Yoder was assistant superintendent, and Lillie Yoder was secretary-treasurer. There were three classes in the Union Sunday School.

During the summer of 1903 Preacher Eli A. Bontrager of the West Market Street Amish Mennonite Church, Nappanee, Indiana, purchased a 160-acre farm in Oscoda County and that fall moved onto it. On New Year's Day, 1904, the Amish Mennonite congregation, which was not yet organized, decided to build a meetinghouse on a corner lot which was donated by E. A. Bontrager. This meetinghouse, thirty by thirty-six feet in size, stood on the lot where the P. J. Miller and Sons feed store is now located, some sixty rods south of the present meetinghouse. This meeting-house was dedicated May 22, 1904. The congregation itself was organized with thirty-five charter members, three months earlier, on February 2, 1904, by D. J. Johns, who authorized E. A. Bontrager to do the work of a bishop in his absence. Preacher Isaac A. Miller and family from the state of Illinois located in the Fairview community on December 24, 1903. However, Miller was in poor health and died on April 19 of the next year. The early settlers came not only from the Howard-Miami congregation, but from Illinois, Iowa, Ohio, and various other areas. The thirty-five charter members consisted largely of the families of E. A. Bontrager, Daniel Hershberger, Silas Hershberger, Levi Kauffman, A. A. Miller, Jeff Miller, Christian Troyer, E. A. Troyer, and Noah Yoder.

The congregation did not long suffer from a lack of ministers. Preacher Nathaniel Troyer of Kokomo was there briefly in the year 1904 —his first year as a preacher. In 1906 Menno Esch, the long-time leader of the congregation, was ordained preacher, and in 1909 he was ordained as bishop: both ordinations being performed by D. J. Johns, the bishop of the congregation. About the year 1906 Preacher Noah Z. Yoder, originally of Juniata County, Pennsylvania, removed from Concord, Tennessee, to Fairview and served until his death in 1918.

The first Sunday-school meeting, an inspirational conference for the enhancement of Sunday-school work, was held at Fairview in 1909. About 1912 the sewing circle of the congregation was organized. Deacon Menno Steiner was ordained in 1908 and served until his death in 1931.

A trial came to the Fairview congregation the night of April 4, 1918. The congregation had grown rapidly, so that by 1906 an addition of twenty feet had been made to the west end of the meetinghouse. On the night of April 4, 1918, four men who disliked the Mennonites because of their position of nonresistance, poured oil on the meetinghouse, and a fifth man set fire to the building and burned it down. The congregation immediately made plans to build a new house of worship, but attempts were then made by certain persons in the community to prevent the building of another Mennonite meetinghouse. The Mennonites consulted the authorities of the county and were told that they had the right to build and no one could forbid them. "Go ahead." The congregation proceeded to follow these instructions and immediately built a meetinghouse forty by fifty-six feet in size.

The congregation was initially extremely poor. The soil was poor and the early settlers had a severe struggle to get sufficient money for food, clothing, and shelter. It is said that one family ate nothing but potatoes for two weeks, and was out of salt part of the time. Some of the members walked as much as eight miles to the Sunday services; others came in wagons, some in buggies, one family with an ox team, and a few in automobiles. Among the first families to buy automobiles (Fords) were E. A. Troyer and J. P. Handrich, uncle of Bishop Harvey Handrich. The poverty of the members was gradually overcome, and various progressive steps were taken in the life of the church. In 1915 the congregation established a Sunday-school library. In 1920 the primary department of the Sunday school was created.

The congregation ordained Moses S. Steiner to the ministry in 1920, and he is still serving. Deacon Otis J. Bontrager was ordained in 1932, and is also still active. Harvey Handrich was ordained as preacher in 1946, and as bishop in 1952, and is now the active leader of the congregation. Floyd M. Yoder, assistant pastor, was ordained in the year 1952.

Largely as a result of the mission interests of Eli A. Bontrager a large number of mission outposts were created by the Fairview congregation and existed for longer or shorter periods of time. Services were held at McKinley under shade trees, not in any building; at Curran schoolhouse; a church was built at Sunnyside, only to be sold after the death of the congregation; services were held in a Congregational church building at Lewiston, and later in three private homes; services were also conducted in the Kittle and Eldorado schoolhouses. Services were established in a town hall at Mancelona in 1948, and in 1955 the Wellington Mission was established in a schoolhouse in Lachine, later in the town hall, and still later in a new Mennonite meetinghouse. On the other hand, some dissatisfied members withdrew in 1924 and formed the Comins congregation of the General Conference Mennonite Church.

Various ministers were ordained to serve the Fairview outposts and other mission stations down through the history of the congregation. In 1909 Levi A. Kauffman was ordained for Sunnyside; in 1947 Bruce Handrich for Germfask; in 1948 Willard Handrich for Grand Marais; in 1950 Willard Bontrager for Mancelona; in 1952 Lloyd Miller for Curtis; in 1956 Harold Sharp for Wellington. Emerson Yordy was licensed in 1958 for the Maple Grove congregation, and was ordained the next year.

The 1918 meetinghouse was enlarged in 1938-39 to forty by eighty feet in size by adding twenty-four feet to the west end. In 1947 an addition was made to the east end. In the year 1960 the congregation decided to build an entirely new meetinghouse. This building was built of block, with brick veneer, seventy by one hundred and twenty-eight feet in size, and the main auditorium seats 585, and the balcony 200. By using donated labor, by purchasing lumber at the government timber sales, and by buying all other materials at cost from dealers who were members of the congregation, the total cost of this excellent structure was kept to the remarkably low figure of $60,000.00.

The membership of the congregation has grown splendidly. In the *Herald of Truth* for 1904 it was reported that as of May 23 there were forty-six members in the congregation, church and Sunday-school services were being held every Sunday morning, and Bible Readings (now young people's Bible meetings) every Sunday evening. On June 19, 1904, it was reported that the membership had risen to fifty-one members, and the Sunday school was "evergreen" (that is, it was held all year round). The attendance at Sunday school was eighty-five. At this point in the life of the church the Fairview Old Order Amish congregation had seventy-three members, while the Mennonite congregation had only fifty-three. (*H.T.*, October 13, 1904.) In 1905 the membership was reported as ninety-two (December 18, 1905). By 1910 the membership had risen to 214, after which it declined to 182 in 1920. In 1930 the membership had again risen to 248, in 1940 to 301, in 1950 to 363, and the 1960 *Mennonite Yearbook* gives the present membership as 376.

Menno Esch, who has done more than any other person, by the grace of God, to take a struggling congregation in an adverse economic situation, and to build it up into a strong and prosperous congregation, reports that from 1909 until 1954 the congregation had received 429 members by baptism, 178 by letter, and 214 from the Amish. In that same period there were lost by death seventy-four members, by letter 279, and lost as members of the church 144. The oldest person baptized was William Newton, who was nearly ninety-two years of age, and the youngest ever baptized in the congregation was about nine years of age. The largest class was baptized on May 4, 1952, when forty-nine young people were received; the bishops Menno Esch and Harvey Handrich both baptized at the same time on this occasion.

Among the influential leaders of the Mennonite Church who made significant contributions to the Fairview congregation should be mentioned D. J. Johns, who served as the bishop at Fairview prior to the ordination of Menno Esch in 1909; S. E. Allgyer, who was active in holding Bible conferences at Fairview; S. G. Shetler, who served in two-week

Bible schools in the congregations; and C. C. Culp, who served as a Bible conference instructor in connection with the Bible school.

In 1909 Mabel Pletcher wrote: "By looking at the results that have come from the faithful efforts made by all the leaders of the church, and especially those who had the burdens of the early inconveniences, we can see that God's never-failing blessings have been poured out on this church during shadows and sunshine, joys and sorrows, trials and encouragements, and to God we express our feeble thanks."

SUNNYSIDE AMISH MENNONITE CHURCH

Montmorency County, Michigan

The *Gospel Witness* of 1907 reported on page 168 that the Fairview congregation had established "a new preaching point," Sunnyside. Some of the attendants were evidently Amish Mennonites who had moved into the Sunnyside area, five miles north of Comins, which was the location of the Sunnyside Church. Sunnyside was ten miles north of Fairview. When Preacher Eli A. Bontrager was ninety-three years of age he wrote the following description of the work at Sunnyside: This Sunnyside was ten miles north of Fairview, and a few families moved into that area. Those were the horse and buggy days, and some folks did not even have buggies! The Fairview congregation built a meetinghouse at Sunnyside, thirty by thirty-six feet in size. It was dedicated June 6, 1909. The ministers from the Fairview congregation organized a Sunday school and preached at Sunnyside. In fact, Levi A. Kauffman was ordained to the ministry to serve the group at Sunnyside, but was not yet married. His wife, whom he married later, came from North Dakota, and in the course of time he left Sunnyside and returned to North Dakota. "At that time the preachers could move just like anybody else." The district mission board then asked Simon W. Sommer to locate at Sunnyside and serve as pastor there. He served (a few years), after which all the members left except three. Preacher S. W. Sommer and family then removed to Imlay City, Michigan. The district mission board then sold the Sunnyside meetinghouse to the county for a township hall. In the course of time, however, the township hall was razed. "So that ended Sunnyside," remarked E. A. Bontrager.

Simon W. Sommer reports that he lived at Sunnyside from June 1915 to September 1919. The total life of the Sunnyside Church was therefore from about 1907, when the outpost began, until the closing of the work when S. W. Sommer left, September 1919. The *Gospel Herald* contains numerous references to the Sunnyside work.

PLEASANTVIEW AMISH MENNONITE CHURCH

Brown Township, Manistee County, Michigan

In the year 1903 William Lantz of Indiana heard of the fine climate of Manistee County, Michigan. For the sake of his wife's health he removed to that area. His report of the favorable climate, cheap land, and good fruit led others to move into the same community. The fall of 1903 further impetus was given to Mennonite settlers locating in Manistee County when Preacher J. S. Horner and family of the Howard-Miami congregation in Indiana settled in Manistee County. On September 9, 1904, Bishop E. A. Mast of the Howard-Miami congregation organized the following members into a congregation, now known as Pleasantview: Preacher Joseph Horner and wife, Samuel Schrock and wife, Altine Shrock and wife, David Sommers and wife, Louis Zook and wife, Israel Harris and wife, Joseph Shrock, and William Lantz. It was not long until Benjamin Klingelsmith and wife, Mrs. Ezra Schrock, Noah Schrock and wife, and Mrs. Valentine Graf moved into the community.

The first services were held in an old log cabin. But in 1906 the present meetinghouse was built on a two-acre lot, which now includes a cemetery, one and one-fourth miles south, and one mile east, of the village of Chief, Michigan. The church is fifteen miles northeast of the town of Manistee. The Pleasantview meetinghouse is twenty-four by thirty-two feet in size, with an anteroom of eight by twelve feet. The meetinghouse was built about a half mile west of the log building which was used prior to 1906.

The *Herald of Truth* for the year 1906 reports the organization of the Sunday school for that year with Ira C. Yoder, superintendent; Henry Schrock, secretary; and Frank Schrock, treasurer. "Sunday school and preaching were held every Sunday." By 1907 the congregation was able to report forty-one members as of April 16. It should also be mentioned that the new meetinghouse was formally opened for public worship, Sunday, May 6, 1906, with Jonathan Kurtz and A. J. Yontz of the Maple Grove, Indiana, congregation present for the occasion.

Not many years after the formal organization of the congregation E. A. Mast requested to be relieved of the bishop oversight, and Menno Esch of the Fairview congregation was placed in charge. Late in the year 1910 Preacher J. S. Horner and family returned to the Howard-Miami congregation. In the year 1913 J. K. Bixler was appointed bishop of the mission congregations of the newly organized district mission board. Finally only one family was left in the congregation, and it was decided to sell the meetinghouse to the Church of the Brethren. However, the property was again acquired by the Mennonites.

In the year 1917 the district mission board arranged for the ordination of Claude C. Culp of the Yellow Creek congregation. Before he could be sent to the church, however, he was drafted and placed in Camp Taylor, Kentucky, and later imprisoned at Fort Leavenworth, Kansas as a conscientious objector. It was therefore May 15, 1919, before C. C. Culp was able to locate with the Pleasantview congregation. There were at that time seven members in the church. He served from 1919 until his death in 1953. He was ordained as a bishop in 1947. During the years 1944 to 1950 Lester A. Wyse assisted C. C. Culp in the ministry. Wyse then moved to Hartville, Ohio. Since the death of C. C. Culp, Warren C. Shaum, formerly a minister in the Holdeman congregation in Indiana, has had charge of the congregation. In the years 1957-58 Ervin Miller, formerly of the Locust Grove, Michigan, congregation, served as a licensed minister to assist Warren C. Shaum. Following the death of Claude C. Culp, T. E. Schrock, Ivan Weaver, and Etril J. Leinbach have successively had the bishop oversight of the congregation. The 1923 *Mennonite Yearbook* indicates that the Pleasantview congregation then had twelve members; the 1940 *Yearbook* shows twenty-three members; and the 1960 *Yearbook* indicates thirty-three members.

IV

The Younger Churches

Established after the merger of 1916

HOPEWELL MENNONITE CHURCH

Section 7, Pleasant Township, Porter County, Indiana

Amish Mennonites from Hopedale, Illinois, began to settle in the vicinity of Kouts, Indiana, in 1916. Among the first families were those of John Reinhardt and Lee Sutter. In 1917 came the William Martin family of Hopedale, and in 1918, Andrew Gingerich and family of Nebraska; Andrew Gut and family of Cowden, Illinois; Dean Birky of Beemer, Nebraska; William Birky and family, and Lewis Birky, of Hopedale, Illinois.

In April 1918 Bishop J. C. Birky of Hopedale, Illinois, organized the Sunday school at Kouts and helped the group choose the name Hopewell. The Hopewell congregation was at first affiliated with the Western District Amish Mennonite Conference. There were eighteen charter members in the congregation. A preacher from Illinois supplied the pulpit monthly. The Sunday-school enrollment was about forty-six.

In September 1918 the congregation was transferred to the Indiana-Michigan Mennonite Conference, with J. K. Bixler serving as bishop. Services were held in the Cook schoolhouse south of Kouts. The first superintendents were William Martin and Dean Birky.

On February 4, 1919, the Indiana-Michigan Mennonite Mission Board purchased a plot of land south of Kouts, about one mile south of the present church building. A meetinghouse was built that summer. Other Mennonite settlers moved into the Kouts community in 1919. The first baptismal service was held in May 1919, when six boys united with the church. Dedication services were held for the new house of worship September 28, 1919, with J. K. Bixler preaching the sermon. The first meetinghouse was thirty-six by fifty feet in size, and was built by Jacob Hershberger of Goshen, assisted by his son Lloyd, and members of the Hopewell congregation.

The first ordained ministers were James Bucher, 1920, and J. Z. Birky, ordained deacon 1923. The congregation was recognized as independent of the mission board, and a full member of conference in 1925. In the spring of 1920 Bishop J. D. Birky of Beemer, Nebraska, moved

15

into the community and assumed the bishop oversight of the congregation. Preacher James Bucher removed to Daviess County, Indiana, in October 1923. In July 1926 Bishop J. D. Birky died. On July 15, 1928, Dean Birky was ordained to the ministry; he served until 1942. Paul Erb, then a professor in Goshen College, served as a supply minister from 1942 until 1944 when Millard Lind was ordained to serve as resident pastor. Lind served until 1947 when he accepted a call to serve as an editor at the Mennonite Publishing House. Chester Osborne succeeded Millard Lind as pastor; he served 1947-1952. The next year Samuel S. Miller, formerly a minister in the Clinton Brick congregation, located at Kouts and became pastor of the congregation. Paul Mininger ordained him bishop in 1955, and he has served in that office since that date.

The Hopewell congregation has the usual organizations of the Mennonites of Northern Indiana. A literary society was organized in 1924, and is now known as the Mennonite Youth Fellowship. A sewing circle was organized in 1929, and a junior sewing circle in 1947. The congregation set up a church council in 1942, and in 1953 the men's brotherhood was organized. In 1949 the congregation established a mission outpost known as English Lake. In 1950 the Hopewell congregation decided that it was time to build a new house of worship. Lewis Birky donated the land on which the present church building stands. Construction work was started in April 1951, and the building was completed the fall of 1952, with dedicatory services held October 26, 1952. Paul Mininger preached the dedication sermon. As of 1959 the congregation consisted of ninety families, with a baptized membership of 267, and a Sunday-school enrollment of 350. The Hopewell congregation has been one of the most successful colonization efforts in Indiana and Michigan.

A member of the congregation writes: "The first settlers came to the community to farm. For the most part the members are still on farms but have increased their interest in raising livestock and dairying. The factories and stores in Valparaiso employ a few, and some own and operate different types of stores and shops. Edd Bechler and Omar Martin have machine stores. Ora Gut has a welding shop in which he remakes and repairs machinery, and Leonard Good has a food processing and freezing plant. Others find jobs in carpentry, auctioneering, and trucking farm products to the Chicago markets."

BURR OAK MENNONITE CHURCH

Section 6, Newton Township, Jasper County, Indiana

In April 1919 Bishop J. K. Bixler of Elkhart, who was always active in supplying scattered Mennonite families with church services, and organizing congregations, learned that a number of Mennonite families were living in Jasper and Newton counties, Indiana. He learned of the name of Menno Chupp and invited the Chupps to participate in a communion service which was to be held that spring at Kouts. Four Mennonite families who were living in the area, those of Menno Chupp, Abner Miller, Adam Miller, and Menno Miller, took communion in the Hopewell services the following week. In May of that year Bishop Bixler visited the Mennonite families in Jasper County and held meetings in a schoolhouse near the town of Surrey. Subsequently a congregation of eight members was organized. That fall Preacher Silas Weldy held a Bible conference and three conversions took place. The first communion service was held December 19, 1919, in a vacant dwelling house near Surrey. The first members to unite with the church were John Leichty and wife, and the first person to be baptized was Eli Chupp. D. D. Miller was appointed to serve as bishop of the new congregation. A Union Sunday School was organized at Parr in October 1920, but did not prove to be very much of a success as far as the community was concerned.

The year 1925 marked a number of forward steps in the life of the tiny congregation. A Catholic named James Love donated a plot of ground of one-half acre, on which the Mennonites built a house of worship twenty-four by thirty-eight feet in size. The total cost of the structure, which was completed in September 1925, was about $1,300.00. Most of the labor was either donated or given at a very low rate. The next step was to secure a minister. Floyd W. Weaver and family of the Yellow Creek congregation were invited to move to Jasper County, which they did in August 1925, and on October 4 of that year the congregation held dedicatory services for the new meetinghouse. D. A. Yoder preached the dedicatory sermon, and in the afternoon of the same day D. D. Troyer ordained Floyd W. Weaver to the office of preacher. In 1932 Henry J. Stoll was chosen as deacon of the congregation. F. W. Weaver served until ill health compelled him to resign in 1945, when he with his family removed to Goshen, Indiana. In 1951 Henry J. Stoll was ordained as preacher. Summer Bible school has been held since 1948.

In 1952 the Burr Oak congregation made extensive renovations in the meetinghouse, placing a basement under the entire building, and adding a new entrance to the front of the building. Later new furniture was placed in the main auditorium. In 1957 Elmer Kauffman was chosen as the first visiting brother of the congregation, to serve a two-year term.

The Burr Oak congregation, so named for the trees which stand on the church lot, is located in a community which is strongly agricultural in character. Many young people who leave the community to attend college never return. A number of other members have discontinued their connections with the church. The consequence is that in 1940 the membership stood at sixty-seven, while the 1960 *Yearbook* reports only fifty-two members.

BEREA MENNONITE CHURCH

Section 31, Van Buren Township, Daviess County, Indiana

The history of this congregation will be given in some detail to indicate how the Indiana Mennonites have tended to receive the more progressive-minded members of the Old Order Amish Church.

In December 1920 Bishop J. K. Bixler of Elkhart, Indiana, received a letter from Michael Wagler of Daviess County who had just moved there from Oregon. He reported that there were five families, former Old Order Amish, who had withdrawn from that group and were conducting a Sunday school among themselves. On December 20, 1920, Silas L. Weldy and J. K. Bixler went to Loogootee where they were met by Michael Wagler, Ephraim Graber, and William Graber. At the home of Ephraim Graber they met Victor Knepp. On Tuesday, December 21, the ministers visited in the homes of Victor Knepp and Isaac Yoder. The next day they visited John Stoll. That evening the first Mennonite service was held at the United Brethren church building, which is now owned by the Berea congregation. Further services were held on December 23. That same day the ministers, accompanied by Victor Knepp and Jacob Graber, went to see Peter Wagler, bishop of the Old Order Amish congregation. No final steps were taken at that point.

On January 24, 1921, Ministers J. K. Bixler, D. D. Troyer, and Jonathan Kurtz left for Daviess County. On January 25 the three Mennonite bishops met with the former Old Order Amish members in the home of Ephraim Graber. That same day the three Mennonite bishops went to the home of Bishop Peter Wagler where they interviewed the local Amish ministers as well as two Amish bishops from Arthur, Illinois, Plank and Mast. A number of Amish brethren (unordained) were also present. The Amish ministry pleaded with the Mennonite leaders to make efforts to get the former Amish members to return to the Amish Church. The Mennonite leaders finally assured the Amish bishops that they would move slowly and cautiously, giving the Amish families who desired to become Mennonites a period of two weeks in which to reflect upon the matter. Nevertheless, the Mennonite leaders met with the Amish applicants for Mennonite membership, and instructed them in the principles of the Mennonite faith.

The outcome of the work done to this point was the formation and signing of a petition from the persons in Daviess County who desired to organize a Mennonite congregation. On February 25, 1921, J. K. Bixler and Amos Weldy, a layman from the Holdeman congregation, went to Daviess County and held a number of services in the United Brethren church building. On Sunday afternoon, February 27, 1921, the Mennonite leaders organized the Berea Mennonite congregation. They received Michael Wagler and wife by letter and the former Amish members by confession of faith. Lewis Swartzendruber was baptized. Bishop Bixler also gave an invitation for any additional persons who wished to unite with the church, and William and Emanuel Graber, and Henry, Mary, and Peter Swartz responded and were also baptized. The first communion service was held on March 1, 1921. In 1921 Amos Weldy decided to remove to Daviess County and identify himself with the Berea congregation. The group began to hold Sunday school in a schoolhouse, following which they rented the United Brethren church building until 1925, in which year it was purchased by the district mission board for $700.00. In the fall of 1921 Bishops Bixler, Johns, and Troyer ordained Amos Weldy to the office of deacon, and in 1923 James Bucher of the Hopewell congregation moved to Daviess County and served as preacher until 1932 when he left the district. Edd P. Shrock was ordained preacher in 1933, and bishop in 1942. For many years Shrock and Weldy were the two ordained brethren of the congregation. In 1946 Tobias Slabaugh was ordained preacher, and in 1959 as bishop. Paul F. Weldy succeeded his father as deacon in 1947. David J. Graber was ordained to the ministry in 1953.

The original United Brethren church building was improved in 1937 by the addition of a basement, and by adding anterooms. In 1950 an addition of twenty feet was made to the main auditorium, making it sixty feet in length. New entrances were also constructed on the northwest and northeast corners of the building, and rest rooms added.

The congregation established a mission outpost at Morgantown, Kentucky, in 1951, and another in nearby Washington in 1953, which is called Providence.

By 1940 the membership at Berea had grown from an initial seventeen members to seventy-six. The 1960 *Yearbook* shows 255 members.

PROVIDENCE MENNONITE CHURCH

511 Northwest 16th Street, Washington, Daviess County, Indiana

The Providence outpost was established by the Berea congregation in the year 1953. Tobias Slabaugh of Route 2, Montgomery, Indiana, serves as pastor. Sunday school is held each Sunday at 9:30, followed by a worship service at 10:30. Sunday evening services are conducted at 7:00

p.m. The Providence group was organized as a dependent congregation, a daughter of the Berea congregation, on March 5, 1961, with a charter membership of thirty-nine.

BELMONT MENNONITE CHURCH

Sterling Addition, City of Elkhart

Concord Township, Elkhart County, Indiana

The Belmont Church originated as an outpost of the Prairie Street congregation in 1929, when a Sunday school was started, and church services were conducted by such ministers of the Prairie Street congregation as Christian Reiff (who served at Belmont, 1929-45) and A. L. Buzzard, who began serving in 1929, who is still living, but who has been in retirement since 1949. LeRoy L. Hostetler served as a minister in the congregation from 1940 until 1950, when he was replaced by S. J. Hostetler. S. J. Hostetler was ordained bishop in 1952, but went to Ghana as a missionary in 1957. Hostetler's successor was Neil Beachy, who had been ordained preacher in the Owl Creek congregation, Ohio, in 1953, but who was in 1957 a student in Goshen College Biblical Seminary. Beachy is still serving at Belmont.

The original church building was built on the present location from materials secured by the dismantling of the Evangelical church building which formerly stood at the small cemetery a short distance north of the new Harrison Township public school building (about a half mile north of the Yellow Creek church building). The Mennonites purchased the Evangelical church building, tore it down, and rebuilt it as the Belmont meetinghouse. In 1953 the basement was enlarged and a new front entrance constructed. In 1956-57 the Belmont church building was enlarged and thoroughly renovated at a cost of $35,000.00. Dedicatory services were held April 14, 1957.

Prior to 1949 the Belmont congregation was reckoned a part of the Prairie Street Church, but at the June conference of 1949 was recognized as an independent congregation and a full member of conference. The 1950 *Mennonite Yearbook* showed a membership of sixty-four at Belmont. Ten years later there are 138 members. Prior to the ordination of S. J. Hostetler as bishop in 1952, D. A. Yoder, who was bishop at Prairie Street, had the oversight of the Belmont Church. Since 1957, when the Hostetlers went to Ghana to do missionary work, Nelson E. Kauffman has served as bishop at Belmont.

NORTH GOSHEN MENNONITE CHURCH

North Eighth and Summit Streets

Goshen, Elkhart Township, Elkhart County, Indiana

There is no connection between the mission Sunday school conducted by T. K. Hershey the latter part of the first decade of the century in North Goshen, and the present North Goshen Mennonite Church. The North Goshen Church is the result of a mission Sunday school which was organized in East Goshen the summer of 1930 by the students of Goshen College. In 1935, after having met in the East Goshen schoolhouse for five years, the work was transferred to a private house which was rented at 414 North Eighth Street. The summer of 1936 the abandoned church building of the Beulah Baptist congregation of near Wayland, Iowa, was purchased, dismantled, and hauled to Goshen. It was rebuilt at the northwest corner of North Eighth and Summit streets at a cost of about $3,000.00. The building committee consisted of C. J. Gunden, J. E. Brunk, and J. M. Long. The college students gave programs in the various Mennonite churches of Northern Indiana and raised funds toward the cost of the project. Paul Mininger, a young teacher in Goshen College, was given charge of the work the fall of 1937. He was ordained as preacher in 1938, and as bishop in 1943. In 1943 another instructor at Goshen College, J. C. Wenger, was ordained deacon, and the next year as preacher. He served the Olive congregation as nonresident pastor, 1949-50, and in 1951 transferred his membership to Olive. Deacon Henry B. Weaver, formerly of the Yellow Creek congregation, was installed as deacon, succeeding J. C. Wenger, in December 1944.

The North Goshen congregation started with a burst of activity the fall of 1937 when C. Warren Long held evangelistic meetings, and there were forty-eight converts, most of whom united with the new North Goshen congregation. The group began worshiping in the new meetinghouse near the end of 1936, but dedicatory services were not held until May 30, 1937. The congregation grew rapidly. In 1943 a weekly church bulletin was inaugurated.

By 1945 it was necessary to enlarge the meetinghouse, and the dedicatory services were held February 10, 1946. Two years later Russell Krabill was called to North Goshen to assist the two college teachers, Mininger and Wenger. Krabill had been serving in the Locust Grove congregation south of Elkhart. By 1952 it was again necessary to enlarge the meetinghouse, which was dedicated April 5, 1953. Vernon U. Miller was ordained deacon that same year. Pastor Krabill was ordained bishop in 1955, and received half support until 1959, since which time he has been on full support. In 1940 the membership stood at fifty-eight. In 1950 it was 305. In the meantime, in 1942, the East Goshen Church was established as a daughter congregation. In 1956 a second outpost was built, namely, Walnut Hill. In 1960 the congregation bought the house and lot adjoining the church property on the west, with the intention of removing the house and enlarging the present meetinghouse. The present membership (1960 *Yearbook*) is 343.

PLEASANT VIEW MENNONITE CHURCH

Section 21, Jefferson Township, Elkhart County, Indiana

The Pleasant View Church is the result of mission outreach on the part of the Prairie Street Mennonite Church, Elkhart. In the summer and fall of 1935 the church appointed committees to conduct investigation in communities which gave good promise of responding to a new evangelistic effort. As a result of the surveys which were made it was decided to open work in an abandoned United Brethren church building in Jefferson Township. No services had been held there, except for funerals, since about 1920. No charge was made for the use of the building beyond its upkeep and insurance. The Prairie Street Church appointed Charles Cocanower, Lester Mann, Paul Wittrig, and Lawrence Yoder to raise the necessary funds for repairing the dilapidated church building. The materials cost about $100.00, and the work was done by volunteer help. The first service was held April 1, 1936, with J. S. Hartzler in charge, and with John E. Gingrich preaching the sermon. The enrollment for the first year was fifty-six, with an average attendance of forty-five. The Prairie Street Church appointed four couples to carry on the work at Pleasant View: the families of Lester Mann, Lawrence Yoder, Paul Wittrig, and Cleo Mann. Florence Blocher was in charge of the primary department.

The congregation prospered and by 1942 felt ready to organize and to request independence. Consequently Lester L. Mann was ordained preacher, Cleo A. Mann was chosen visiting brother, and the Prairie Street Church granted the request of Pleasant View for independence. The charter members numbered fifty-one. In 1948 it was decided to remodel the church building and add a basement. Dedicatory services were held April 4, 1948. In 1949 Cleo A. Mann, who had served in relief work in Belgium, 1945-48, was ordained deacon. In 1955 the congregation constructed a service center and MYF hall.

Pleasant View in turn also desired to have an outpost and in 1950 established one, now known as *Rainy River* at International Falls, Minnesota. The families of Irvin Grabill and Lawrence Yoder moved there, and were followed later by Homer Cender. The new meetinghouse at Rainy River was dedicated August 12, 1951. In 1953 Cleo A. Mann was licensed to serve as pastor of First Mennonite Church, Indianapolis. In 1956 Lester Mann moved to International Falls and assumed the pastoral care of the Rainy River Church, succeeding J. Alton Horst. Mann's successor as pastor at Pleasant View was John S. Steiner, who is the superintendent of Bethany Christian High School. The next year, 1957, J. C. Wenger ordained John S. Steiner as bishop. He also ordained M. John Kauffman as deacon in 1956, succeeding Cleo A. Mann. On January 22, 1961, John S. Steiner licensed Daniel Zehr, a Goshen College Biblical Seminary student, to the ministry.

The Pleasant View congregation prospered and by 1950 had a membership of 122. By 1960 the Pleasant View congregation numbered 156. The congregation then faced the alternatives of enlarging the church building or establishing a daughter congregation. The latter alternative was accepted and twenty-six adults with their twenty-seven children established the *Tri-Lakes congregation* two and one-half miles west of Mottville, Michigan, worshiping initially in an abandoned schoolhouse. By 1961 the attendance at Tri-Lakes was approaching 100.

EAST GOSHEN MENNONITE CHURCH

2600 East Lincoln Avenue, Goshen, Indiana

The present East Goshen Mennonite Church is largely the result of evangelistic work carried on in the east portion of Goshen, Indiana, by Goshen College students. When the congregation organized, a number of Mennonites living in East Goshen, but who were members at North Goshen, transferred to the new work in East Goshen. Among the college students who carried special responsibility for the work in East Goshen mention should be made of Ford Berg, who later served as manager of the Weaver Book Store, Lancaster, Pennsylvania. The services were first held in a small building, sixteen by twenty-four feet in size. Later a basement church was built "on the hill" south of the present house of worship. Among the supporters of the work financially special mention should be made of the late Chris Schrock of the Clinton Frame congregation. Paul M. Miller was ordained as the first resident pastor of the church in 1947, and the congregation was organized on December 6 of that year. A meetinghouse was then built which was dedicated in October 1948. The congregation was also given its independence in 1948. Miller was ordained bishop in 1951, and three years later Ray Keim was added to the ministry. Professor Howard H. Charles of the Goshen College Biblical Seminary holds his membership in the congregation, but carries no pastoral responsibility. By 1950 the membership of the congregation had climbed to 122. In 1957 the congregation began to enlarge its meeting-house and the present lovely brick structure was dedicated October 17, 1958. By 1960 the *Mennonite Yearbook* reported a membership of 215.

THE LIGHTHOUSE

Goshen, Indiana

After the dedication of the new meetinghouse in 1948, there were members in East Goshen, particularly Amos Bauman, who felt that some sort of witness ought to be maintained in the original area of the East Goshen Mennonite Church. Consequently about 1950 Bauman inaugurated a work among the young people "on the hill." He placed a light on top of a building, and called it *The Lighthouse*. Whenever he turned on that light, the young people of the community were thereby notified to come to the building for a meeting. In 1954 a splendid new concrete-block Lighthouse building was constructed, which has been serving as a Sunday school, crafts, hobbies, and recreation center. Students of Goshen College are rendering a valuable service to the young people of the under-privileged of the East Goshen community in this 1954 Lighthouse build-ing. Since 1960 an effort has been made to have converts consider the Lighthouse their church. Four families are now (1961) affiliated, with eight members. Sunday morning attendance averages thirty-five to forty.

LOCUST GROVE MENNONITE CHURCH

Section 13, Baugo Township, Elkhart County, Indiana

The Locust Grove congregation is another outgrowth of the mission-ary and evangelistic program of the students of Goshen College. The Christian witness of the Goshen College Y.P.C.A. was begun in the Locust Grove area in the year 1943, and Sunday school and preaching services were held in a private home until the year 1950. The first resident min-ister was Russell Krabill who was ordained August 5, 1945, and served at Locust Grove until 1948 when he transferred to the North Goshen congregation. Bishop Paul Mininger then ordained Ralph Stahly as preacher at Locust Grove (1948), and in 1954 ordained him to the office of bishop. During most of the history of the congregation Ralph Stahly has therefore been the bishop-pastor. He was assisted, 1956-60, by Aden Horst whose residence is located on a lot adjoining the church property on the east.

In 1950 the Locust Grove meetinghouse was built on the north side of County Road 20, the Mishawaka Road, in Section 13 of Baugo Town-ship. The congregation thrived, especially in the early years, so that by 1950 the membership had risen to forty-seven. The 1960 *Yearbook* indicates a current membership of fifty-four. Goshen College students have been assisting in the work throughout the history of the Locust Grove congregation.

BENTON MENNONITE CHURCH

Section 6, Benton Township, Elkhart County, Indiana

The present Benton congregation is worshiping in a meetinghouse which was originally built by the Lutherans in 1853. (1881 *Elkhart County History*, page 661.) In the course of time the property was acquired by the Mennonite Brethren in Christ, now the United Missionary Church. Mennonites from the Clinton Frame congregation opened work in the Benton church building July 9, 1944, with Sunday school and church services. For almost two years the pulpit was supplied by one of the ministers from the Clinton Frame congregation, but the spring of 1946 Verle O. Hoffman was assigned the pastoral care of the Benton congregation. The trustees of the Clinton Frame congregation purchased the church building in 1944 for $650.00. The Benton congregation became independent September 5, 1948, with the following officers: Edwin J. Yoder, bishop; Galen Johns, preacher; Amos D. Yontz, visiting brother (ordained deacon in 1949).

The Benton congregation thrived from the very beginning and by the year 1950 had a membership of sixty-three, largely from Clinton Frame. The parsonage was purchased in the year 1948. In 1951 the congregation remodeled the church building, and made it a truly attractive house of worship.

During the year 1957-58 Galen Johns accepted the invitation to serve as pastor of the Mennonite Church in Saginaw, during which time Preacher Menno Erb served as pastor of the Benton congregation. Erb was killed in an automobile accident in 1960. In 1960 there was also a complete turnover in the ministry. Galen Johns was succeeded by Irvin Nussbaum, who is still serving as pastor at this writing. Deacon Amos D. Yontz also terminated his service in 1960.

The Benton congregation has the same concern to establish outposts and daughter congregations as does its own mother, Clinton Frame. In 1953 the Benton Church established a Sunday school and preaching point at Kendallville, which has since developed into the Elmwood congregation. The 1960 *Yearbook* indicates that the total membership at Benton and Kendallville is 149.

SUNNYSIDE MENNONITE CHURCH

Section 22, Concord Township, Elkhart County, Indiana

The Sunnyside congregation, located in Dunlap, southeast of Elkhart, was also the result of outreach work conducted by the Goshen College Y.P.C.A. At the suggestion of Paul Mininger a group of students under the leadership of Richard Showalter conducted a survey in 1946. Of the families contacted in the Sunnyside area, thirty-six indicated an attitude of interest. These families had a total of eighty-one children. In 1947, through the generosity of the Mennonite Board of Missions and Charities, a concrete-block meetinghouse, twenty-six by forty-six feet in size, was built at a cost of $5,237.04. Of this money, the Mission Board loaned $4,000.00 without interest. The first services were held in the new building on September 14, 1947, but dedication services were not conducted until May 2, 1948. Six children were baptized on January 11, 1948, representing the first converts. The college students have been active throughout the entire history of the Sunnyside congregation, both in Sunday-school teaching and in club work for boys and girls. The first communion service was held February 13, 1949, in charge of Bishop S. C. Yoder.

Among the many students who were active in the leadership work at Sunnyside mention should be made of Richard Showalter, Ralph Buckwalter, Roy Bucher, Chester Raber (licensed as a minister 1952-53), and Preacher John Lederach, 1954-57. The congregation prospered, and in 1956 it was decided to build a new house of worship, close to the older building. The new church building has a full basement and is twenty-eight by fifty-six feet in size. A breezeway connects the new building to the old one. This new house of worship was dedicated April 21, 1957. S. J. Hostetler served as bishop from 1955 until 1957 when he went to Ghana as a missionary. He was succeeded as bishop by Nelson E. Kauffman, 1957. The present pastor, D. Richard Miller, assumed his duties in 1958. The 1960 *Mennonite Yearbook* indicates that the present membership is forty-six.

ROSELAWN MENNONITE CHURCH

1521 Independence Street, Elkhart, Indiana

The Prairie Street Mennonite Church conducted surveys in the northeast sector of Elkhart in the years 1947 and 1949, particularly in the Hastings Park Addition. The outcome of these surveys was the decision to erect a church building and to begin work in the community. Ground was broken for the prospective house of worship in October 1949, with J. S. Hartzler, veteran minister, then ninety-two years of age, leading in prayer, prior to the beginning of work. By April 1950 the building was sufficiently completed that it was possible to hold services in the basement. It was not until February 11, 1951, however, that services were held in the main auditorium. Benches were installed in October 1951, and the dedication service was held on October 14 of that year, with D. A. Yoder preaching the dedicatory sermon. The building cost $17,926.10.

During the first year, 1950, Darrel D. Otto, a minister attending the Goshen College Biblical Seminary, served as pastor. Francis Troyer was the superintendent of the Sunday school.

The financial aspect of the program received a boost in 1949 when donors indicated that $1,925.00 of money which had been given toward the construction of a Mennonite hospital in Elkhart, should be given to the Roselawn church building fund when the Mennonite hospital did not materialize.

The Prairie Street Mennonite congregation designated five families to carry on the work at Roselawn: those of Charles Cocanower, Jr., Ernest Chupp, Walter Hooley, Francis Troyer, and Lester Ebersole. The original Sunday-school enrollment in 1950 was sixty.

When Darrel Otto indicated late in 1950 that he was not able to continue as pastor at Roselawn, the congregation approached Verle O. Hoffman of the Clinton Frame congregation and invited him to serve as temporary pastor. He preached his first sermon at Roselawn, January 28, 1951, and on June 17 was installed as pastor. He has served since 1951 in that capacity. In 1952 he located in a house across the street from the church, namely, at 1522 Independence Street. In 1954 the Roselawn congregation built a church cabin at a cost of $8,140.78. The 1960 *Mennonite Yearbook* indicates a membership at Roselawn of sixty-three. At this writing it is still officially under the care of the Prairie Street Mennonite Church.

WALNUT HILL MENNONITE CHURCH

911 North Sixth Street, Goshen, Indiana

As early as 1950 workers from the North Goshen Mennonite Church held Sunday-school services in private homes in the area north of Middlebury Street in Goshen. After some time this work was discontinued and an effort was made to bring interested persons to the North Goshen Church.

In October 1955 Goshen College students conducted a survey in the Walnut Hill area of North Goshen and found a total of fifty homes in the area without any church or Sunday-school connections. It was decided by

the North Goshen Church that Marvin J. Miller should serve as superintendent of the proposed work, and Orrin Yoder as assistant. The first
Sunday school was held in the Marvin Miller home, 806 North Sixth
Street, on May 20, 1956. Interest in the project continued to grow and
it was decided that a brickcrete house of worship, twenty-eight by thirty-
four feet in size, with a basement, should be built. The ground-breaking
ceremony was held on October 16, 1956, at the intersection of North
Sixth Street and Wilden Avenue. The building cost $6,500.00. The build-
ing was sufficiently completed by August of 1957 to begin using it for
services. Bible school was held August 12-23, 1957, and the first evangelistic meetings, August 23-25, in charge of Vernon E. Bontreger. The
first teachers consisted of Hazel Garber, Dale Stutzman, Elaine Yoder, and
Orrin Yoder. A half-hour worship service following the Sunday school
was started in November of 1957. Boys' and girls' clubs, each meeting
twice a month, were inaugurated in October of 1958.

The group decided in 1959 to seek to establish a resident membership at Walnut Hill, the first six members to be the couples: Marvin
Miller and wife, Dale Stutzman and wife, and Orrin Yoder and wife. The
group does not welcome Mennonites from other congregations to transfer
their membership to this small congregation, for this would crowd out
the local residents.

On January 31, 1960, Russell Krabill licensed Marvin J. Miller to
the ministry to serve the Walnut Hill congregation.

Dedication services for the new Walnut Hill building were finally
held May 25, 1958.

By 1961 the enrollment was standing at forty, with eight Mennonite
couples carrying the bulk of the responsibility in the congregation,
assisted by a number of students from Goshen College. As of this date
two converts from the community have united with the congregation.

PLYMOUTH STREET CHAPEL

Goshen, Indiana

In 1949 the Goshen College Y.P.C.A. opened a Sunday school in a
restaurant in the southeast sector of the city of Goshen, largely as the
result of the vision of David A. Shank (who in 1961 is a missionary in
Belgium). The workers have since become active in church work elsewhere. Included in the list were Virgil J. Brenneman, Charles Burkholder, Ruth Carper, David Hostetler, David Hurst, Paul King, LaVina
Kramer, Edgar Metzler, James Miller, Glenn Musselman, Chester Raber,
Nelson P. Springer, Betty Weber, Peter B. Wiebe, Rosanna Yoder, and
Ruth Zook. The second winter the attendance reached forty-five. After

the restaurant was no longer available, the Leander Garber residence was used. But that residence also proved too small.

The workers recall with special gratitude the bright conversion of one woman who passed away six months later. By 1952 it was obvious that if the work was to go on, a house of worship would need to be built. This the College Mennonite Church declined to do. (There were already three Mennonite congregations in the city.) So with sad hearts the students closed down the Sunday school. Professor John W. Miller made a final but vain effort to revive the Plymouth Street Chapel witness. Some of the Plymouth Street Chapel attendants found their way to the Mennonite churches of the area. And as late as 1961 Virgil J. Brenneman, pastor of the Waterford Mennonite Church south of Goshen, was maintaining active contact with some persons who had once attended the Plymouth Street Chapel.

WATERFORD MENNONITE CHURCH

2904 South Main Street, Goshen, Indiana

In the year 1958 the Yellow Creek congregation was outgrowing its house of worship so severely that they had to either enlarge their meetinghouse or establish a daughter congregation. After much careful consideration it was decided to do the latter. Consequently on October 5, 1958, the first meeting of the daughter congregation was held in the Bethany Christian High School auditorium. The attendance that day was seventy-seven and the offering amounted to over $100.00. The following three Sundays had an average attendance of 112, with the offerings averaging $150.00.

The initial organization of the group was as follows: Peter B. Wiebe, pastor (who continued his regular pastorate at Yellow Creek); Lester Culp, Sunday-school superintendent; Allen Schrock, treasurer; Warren Myers, song leader; and Clarence Yoder, trustee. The member at large of the church council was Franklin Newcomer. The congregation grew rapidly, partly by Mennonites from other congregations transferring to this new live organization. The congregation was formally organized in the fall of 1959 with seventy-nine charter members, and was recognized by the conference executive committee as an independent congregation on August 28, 1959. Virgil J. Brenneman, formerly pastor of the Iowa City Mennonite Church, assumed the pastorate the fall of 1959, and a few months later S. C. Yoder was elected to serve as bishop of the church.

By early 1961 the average attendance of the Sunday school was 200, and the membership of the congregation stood at 114.

CRUMSTOWN MENNONITE CHURCH

Warren Township, St. Joseph County, Indiana

Mention was made in chapter two of the work of the small congregation which met in a schoolhouse in Crumstown which Samuel Yoder purchased and moved onto a lot donated by Christian Holler. Yoder abandoned the work in 1885 and a number of religious bodies, such as Wesleyan Methodists, Methodists, and Presbyterians, attempted to carry on religious work from time to time in this old schoolhouse at Crumstown, but nothing permanent developed.

In the year 1933 a mission committee from the Olive congregation, consisting of Samuel E. Weaver, Oscar Weaver, E. F. Martin, and Clarence A. Shank, found that the southeast corner of Warren Township in the neighborhood of Crumstown was a promising place to open a Christian outpost. They found that no church services were being held within seven miles of the old schoolhouse in Crumstown where Samuel Yoder had held his services after he quit worshiping at the Mikesell schoolhouse two miles northeast of Crumstown. (The Olive committee knew nothing of the work of Samuel Yoder when they chose to begin services at Crumstown.)

The first service conducted by the Olive Church at Crumstown was held on May 7, 1933. The first workers were the families of Oscar Weaver and Charles Weldy. Sunday school was held on Sunday afternoons for some time, after which it was moved to Sunday forenoons. Every two weeks Sunday evening services were also held. Additional workers who served at Crumstown were the families of Edward F. Martin, Preacher Clarence A. Shank, Samuel E. Weaver, H. B. Fink, Mrs. Lavon Weldy, Alta Housour, Mrs. John Hunsberger, Henry Hunsberger, Martha Hunsberger, Elno and Mabel Steiner, Robert Martin, Esther Yoder and Emma Yoder.

The spring of 1947 the Olive congregation turned the Crumstown work over to the Indiana-Michigan Mennonite Mission Board. The board assumed the responsibility as of May 3, 1947. Before long the district mission board decided to build a new house of worship at Crumstown and to place a resident minister there. The new minister, William R. Miller of the Clinton Frame congregation, was ordained at Clinton Frame for Crumstown on August 1, 1948, by Bishop E. J. Yoder. The new Crumstown house of worship was dedicated August 15, 1948. As the Crumstown congregation became more firmly established, the workers from the Olive Church gradually withdrew, with the exception of Henry Hunsberger who still continues his twenty-five-mile drive to Crumstown each Sunday morning. The first resident Sunday-school superintendent was Willis Hughes, who was also licensed as a minister in 1954, but who later transferred to the Roselawn congregation, Elkhart. In 1960 Calvin Kauffman was licensed to assist his father-in-law, William R. Miller, at Crumstown. In 1960 the membership at Crumstown was, according to the *Yearbook,* forty-four.

Osceola Mennonite Church

Penn Township, St. Joseph County, Indiana

The Osceola Mennonite Church was established by the North Main Street Mennonite Church of Nappanee as the result of a survey in the Osceola community conducted on May 6, 1951, by a group of young people and G. Maurice Long. The group contacted 132 homes and learned that there were 163 children in the community, and that twenty-five homes favored the establishment of a church in the area. When this report was brought to the committee of the Nappanee congregation, it was decided to make plans to attempt to hold a summer Bible school. This plan could not be carried out, for no suitable place of meeting was available. Finally two men from the community, Raymond Loy and Donald Sharp, offered their homes as possible places for Sunday-school services. It was decided to accept this invitation, and the first Sunday-school services were held in the Loy home, October 7, 1951. Sunday school was conducted each Sunday at 2:30 p.m. for the first six months. Services were first held on Sunday forenoon, May 18, 1952. After the Sunday school became too large to meet in the Loy home, two of the classes were sent to the Sharp home for the class period.

On December 10, 1951, the proposal to purchase the basement home of Vern Helenbolt was brought before the mission committee of the Nappanee congregation, and it was decided to make the purchase. The basement was repaired, a ceiling was put up, and the first service held in the new "church building" on March 9, 1952. The staff of workers which started in the new building were: G. Maurice Long, superintendent; Velorus Hoover, intermediate teacher; Jane Strauss, junior teacher; Treva (Yoder) Martin, primary teacher; and Miriam Hochstetler, nursery teacher. The first preaching service was held March 23, 1952, with Homer F. North of the Nappanee congregation preaching the sermon. The first summer Bible school was held in 1952, with G. Maurice Long as superintendent. The first convert, Judith Williams, was baptized June 28, 1952, by J. C. Wenger, at the request of Bishop R. F. Yoder. Sunday-school enrollment for the first year was fifty-four, with an average attendance of twenty-nine. Regular preaching services began March 15, 1953.

On September 27, 1953, G. Maurice Long was licensed as a minister

16

for one year. On December 3, 1954, he was ordained to the ministry and continues to serve as the first and only pastor of the Osceola congregation. Regular Sunday evening services were started September 11, 1955. On July 29, 1956, Homer F. North organized the Osceola congregation with a charter membership of twenty-six. The 1960 *Yearbook* indicates twenty-eight members.

As early as 1956 the mission committee of the Nappanee congregation and the trustees of the Osceola Church were meeting to make plans for the building of a house of worship. It took a number of years for these plans to materialize, but ultimately a lovely meetinghouse was erected, and was dedicated September 13, 1959, with J. C. Wenger preaching the dedicatory sermon.

ANDERSON MENNONITE CHURCH
Section 26, Eel River Township, Allen County, Indiana

The Anderson congregation was established through a mission Sunday school conducted by Henry Easterday and Lee Sailors of the Fort Wayne congregation, but under the sponsorship of the Leo Church, in May 1933. The work prospered under the spiritual leadership of Preacher Joseph S. Neuhouser of the Leo congregation who soon identified himself with the Anderson work. Neuhouser was officially a minister in the Leo Church until 1941, and from 1942 until the present has been the pastor of the Anderson Church. The group at Anderson was recognized as an independent congregation in 1940. Neuhouser was ordained bishop in 1956.

For many years the Anderson congregation worshiped in a schoolhouse, but more recently in an abandoned Baptist church building across the road. These buildings are both located on the Carroll Road, ten miles northwest of Ft. Wayne. In 1957 a new frame building was dedicated.

Under the leadership of J. S. Neuhouser the congregation prospered, and many people were won for Christ and the church. By 1940 the congregation had reached a total of sixty-seven members. In 1949 Anderson in turn sponsored a mission outpost, New Bethel, near Ossian, Indiana, fifteen miles south of Fort Wayne. The Anderson Church was somewhat weakened in 1953 when twenty-four members transferred to the Fort Wayne congregation. The 1960 *Mennonite Yearbook* reports a membership at Anderson of thirty-seven. Oney Hathaway became pastor, 1961.

FAIR HAVEN MENNONITE CHURCH
3101 West Taylor, Fort Wayne, Indiana

The Leo congregation began holding Bible school in the western part of Fort Wayne in 1951. They made the acquaintance of a Mrs. Roy

Scott who was favorably impressed by Mennonite doctrine, life, and piety. Roy Scott had been serving for many years as the founder and pastor of the Fair Haven Mission, but the Scotts were minded to move to the West. Mrs. Scott began to feel that perhaps the Mennonites ought to take over the mission which they had been operating. The Scotts were similar to the Nazarenes in faith, but did not belong to any denomination. They practiced baptism by immersion, opposed the cutting of women's hair, did not believe in worldly amusements, and insisted on simple clothing. They also stressed the holiness interpretation of sanctification. They did not hold to nonresistance.

The outcome of the contact between the Scotts and the Leo Mennonites was that in 1953 the group from Leo held Bible school in the Fair Haven mission building, and enjoyed good success. The Scotts meanwhile decided to move to Idaho, and in 1954 sold the lot and building to the Leo congregation.

The first Mennonite Sunday-school service was held in the Fair Haven Mission July 18, 1954. The attendance was thirty, with half of the people coming from the community. Over the years this number has built up substantially; as early as 1957 the attendance was approaching fifty. The first Mennonite preacher to serve at the Fair Haven Mission was S. J. Miller, bishop of the Leo congregation. Martin Brandenberger served as a licensed minister from November 27, 1955, until he was ordained February 1, 1959. Since 1960 he has been assisted by Arthur Cash, a colored minister who was received into the Indiana-Michigan Conference in June 1960. The Fair Haven congregation serves a colored community. It is sometimes written, Fairhaven.

The first baptismal service was held November 7, 1954, and communion and feet-washing services on November 21, 1954: S. J. Miller was in charge of both services, assisted by Deacon Ben Graber of the Leo Church. One of the members at Fair Haven, Dorothy Phinezy, writes: "Since 1953, when the Mennonites first made themselves known to Westside Fort Wayne, up to the present time services have been held and attended faithfully and regularly. Those in attendance have seen the blessings of God manifested in many ways. And although there have developed no Menno Simons or Conrad Grebels, there have come forth some sincere souls who are serving the Lord 'in word and in deed' at the Fair Haven Mennonite Mission in Fort Wayne, Indiana."

There is at this writing no organized membership at Fair Haven, but the members there are counted in the total for the Leo congregation.

MARION MENNONITE CHURCH

Section 29, Van Buren Township, Lagrange County, Indiana

The Marion Mennonite church building is located five miles west of Howe on Indiana Road 120. The building was originally owned by the Marion Methodist Protestant Church, which was organized in 1851 with thirty members, and the building was erected in 1889 at a cost of approximately $2,000.00. (*The Sturgis,* Michigan, *Daily Journal,* May 29, 1953.)

It was the Shore congregation which started a mission outpost in the abandoned Marion Methodist church building in 1954. The Sunday school was organized December 10 of that year under the direction of the Indiana-Michigan Mennonite Mission Board. There were eighteen charter members of the congregation in 1945. Willard Sommers served as pastor from the beginning. In 1950 the Marion congregation was given the status of an independent church by the district mission board and the church conference. Willard Sommers was ordained to the office of bishop in 1956, and carried the pastoral and bishop oversight until 1960.

In 1950 Paul W. Haarer was ordained preacher and served six years in the Marion congregation. Deacon John J. Mishler was ordained in 1954. In the year 1958 Paul Lauver, who had been a missionary in Puerto Rico, but who is currently taking an extended furlough because of the poor health of his mother-in-law, began serving as preacher in the Marion congregation and at this writing carries the pastoral oversight.

In 1950 the membership of the congregation was forty-five. The 1960 *Yearbook* lists ninety-five members.

PLATO MENNONITE CHURCH

Sections 23, 24, Bloomfield Township, Lagrange County, Indiana

In 1949 the Emma congregation began work at the tiny village of Plato, four miles east of the town of Lagrange on U.S. Highway 20. The group built a new frame meetinghouse, thirty-four by fifty feet in size, which was ready for use by the summer of 1949, and which was dedicated on November 29 of that year. Ministers from the Emma Church supplied the Plato pulpit until August 1950, when Willis C. Troyer was ordained at Emma to serve at Plato. He moved into the Plato community in December of that year. In 1954 John Ray Miller was ordained to the office of deacon. Dean M. Brubaker, who practices dentistry in Shipshewana, was licensed as a minister in the Plato congregation, September 4, 1960. The congregation has grown well, and the 1960 *Yearbook* indicates a present membership of eighty-four.

Lake Bethel Mennonite Church

Section 2, Milford Township, Lagrange County, Indiana

In 1956 the Plato congregation established an outpost at Lake Bethel, 8½ miles east of Lagrange, and 2½ miles south. The next year Ivan Miller, bishop of the Emma and Plato congregations, licensed Titus Morningstar as minister. He served as a licensed minister for two years, and was ordained preacher December 13, 1959, at Plato for Lake Bethel. Services are held in a Church of God building. The 1961 *Mennonite Yearbook* shows a membership at Lake Bethel of twenty-three.

Bean Blossom Mennonite Church

Jackson Township, Brown County, Indiana

The Mennonites began work in Bean Blossom by holding summer Bible school in 1942, 1943, and 1944. More permanent work was established the spring of 1945 when O. S. Hostetler, bishop of the Shore congregation, ordained Charles Haarer to the ministry on April 15, to be placed at Bean Blossom to carry on the work there. Sunday school and church services were initiated, the meetings being held in an abandoned Presbyterian church building which had been erected about 1852. The work prospered from the beginning, and in 1951 the Mt. Pleasant outpost was established at Mahalasville, eighteen miles from Bean Blossom. In 1953 the Bean Blossom Mennonite church building was remodeled and was moved back from the road an additional forty feet.

In addition to the services of Sunday morning and Sunday evening, summer Bible school has been an effective means of reaching the unchurched of the community, and Youth Fellowship meetings are held every other Friday evening, and women's Bible study on the alternating Friday evenings.

The 1960 *Yearbook* shows forty-eight members at Bean Blossom.

Fish Lake Mennonite Church

Section 17, Lincoln Township, La Porte County, Indiana

The first contact of the Mennonites with the Fish Lake community was in 1948 when some members of the Crumstown Mennonite Church became interested in the community. Preacher Samuel S. Miller's wife made a number of trips, hauling Fish Lake children to the Crumstown Mennonite Summer Bible School. In 1949 workers from Crumstown conducted a summer Bible school in the community at Fish Lake, which is located about halfway between North Liberty and La Porte, Indiana, on

State Road 4. The 1949 summer Bible school was held in a conservation club house.

Verl Lehman of the Yellow Creek congregation heard of the Fish Lake community, and urged the leaders of his congregation to take an interest in it. The result was that the Missions Committee of the Yellow Creek congregation, accompanied by Verl Lehman and others, made a religious survey of the Fish Lake community. The outcome of this survey was a summer Bible school in July 1950. Following the summer Bible school, regular Sunday-school services were inaugurated, with fifty-three present the first Sunday.

In October 1950 construction was started on a basement church at Fish Lake, which was completed in 1951. Dedication services were not held, however, until July 20, 1952. Verl Lehman served as leader of the work from the beginning, and as licensed minister from 1952 to 1955 when John Martin, a Goshen College Biblical Seminary student, was licensed for one year. On December 4, 1955, the Fish Lake congregation was organized as a congregation, but dependent upon the Yellow Creek sponsoring church. Late in 1955 the congregation also started work on the completion of the church building. On September 9, 1956, dedicatory services were held for the completed Fish Lake Mennonite church building with J. C. Wenger preaching the dedicatory sermon. In the same service Peter B. Wiebe ordained James L. Christophel to the ministry. James is a graduate of Goshen College Biblical Seminary. The total cost of the Fish Lake project was a little over $20,000.00.

The congregation has grown slowly but steadily from the beginning and the 1960 *Yearbook* shows nineteen members. Verl Lehman was installed as visiting brother on January 8, 1961, by J. D. Zehr.

HUDSON LAKE MENNONITE CHURCH

Section 28, Hudson Township, La Porte County, Indiana

The Hudson Lake Mennonite Church is the outgrowth of work which started in 1950 in Hudson Lake, sponsored initially by the Olive congregation with some help from the Holdeman Church. William Miller, pastor of the Crumstown Mennonite Church, was active in helping to start the 1950 summer Bible school. Following the summer Bible school the Christian workers who had conducted the summer Bible school went right on with Sunday school at Hudson Lake. At that time there was no other church work being carried on in the village. C. A. Shank of the Olive congregation, who was always deeply interested in missions, graciously supplied the pulpit in the early years of the work at Hudson Lake, and has continued with his enthusiastic contribution since the beginning.

For the first several years the Hudson Lake Mennonite Sunday-school services were conducted in a community building, but in 1952 the Olive Church decided to build a basement church. As the basement church was being built, sentiment developed in the Olive congregation to go on up with the superstructure including the roof, so that at least a "shell" could be completed. While the shell was being built, sentiment developed toward proceeding with the actual completion of the building. This was done by the spring of 1953. Dedication services were held April 19 of that year. The total cost of lot, church building, and equipment was nearly $25,000.00.

Meanwhile the Olive congregation was active in seeking to locate a pastor. The committee appointed for the purpose found Daniel H. Stoltzfus, who was that year a graduate from Goshen College Biblical Seminary. Stoltzfus accepted the invitation to assume the pastorate of the Hudson Lake congregation, and was ordained by J. C. Wenger on May 31, 1953, with J. D. Graber, Executive Secretary of the Mennonite Board of Missions and Charities, preaching the ordination sermon.

The Olive congregation also decided to set apart three volunteer families to move to the Hudson Lake community and assist in the work there. The three families who volunteered were those of Raymond Davidhizar, Raymond Hartman, and Paul Shaum. The congregation voted by ballot their approval for these three families to locate at Hudson Lake. They have been of real assistance in the work.

Daniel Stoltzfus and family have been located on the field since 1953 and have done good work in evangelism and Christian nurture. The 1960 *Mennonite Yearbook* shows a membership at Hudson Lake of twenty-eight.

BON AIR MENNONITE CHURCH

2443 Apperson Way North, Kokomo, Howard County, Indiana

The Bon Air Mennonite Church is the result of a survey conducted by the Howard-Miami congregation in 1945. The congregation was able to purchase a suitable building, twenty-eight by fifty feet in size, at 2443 North Kennedy Street, which has since been renamed Apperson Way North. The purchase was made in May 1945. Services were begun in this former residence (originally it was a church building) on October 21, 1945, with only one person present from the community, an eleven-year-old boy, Russell Gillem. Clayton Sommers served as the first superintendent and lay leader, 1945-49. In the year 1949 the Howard-Miami Church designated Preacher Emanuel Hochstedler as the minister in charge of the Bon Air work. He served until 1954, when he returned to the Howard-Miami congregation as assistant pastor. Clayton Sommers was then or-

dained on January 31, 1954, to assume the pastorate of the Bon Air congregation. He is still in charge and has been assisted by Lester Sutter, a
licensed minister, 1957-59, and by another seminary student, Walter
Smeltzer.

Summer Bible school is held annually. There have been some successful evangelistic efforts, especially the series of meetings conducted by
J. S. Neuhouser of the Anderson congregation in 1947. Classrooms were
built in the years 1953 and 1954. The 1960 *Yearbook* shows a membership of fifty-five, most of whom transferred there from the Howard-Miami
congregation. The Bon Air Church is, however, successfully evangelizing
this previously unchurched community, and adults have been uniting
with the church during the last number of years. The congregation has
voted to ordain Clayton Sommers as bishop which was done May 14, 1961.

TIPPECANOE MENNONITE CHURCH

North Webster, Kosciusko County, Indiana

About the year 1929 the Indiana-Michigan Mennonite Mission Board
inaugurated a Christian witness in the vicinity of North Webster, Indiana. An unused church building was leased from the Methodist Church
for ninety-nine years. C. L. Ressler, originally a Wisler Mennonite
preacher, was placed at North Webster and given charge of the mission
station. He proved to be an unusually successful personal evangelist. On
January 11, 1931, D. D. Troyer, superintendent of the churches under the
care of the district mission board, and Edwin J. Yoder, president of the
board, organized the Tippecanoe Mennonite Church, with a charter
membership of twenty-two. E. J. Yoder states that he had never seen
such a promising beginning of a mission church. But the church was soon
killed by the troubles that enveloped C. L. Ressler. He began to fail
financially, and was guilty of such questionable behavior that on September 18, 1931, the conference executive committee relieved him of his ministry. By 1933 the congregation had disbanded, the members moved elsewhere and united with other churches, and Ressler moved to the state of
New York. It is said that no members lost out spiritually; each one united
with one denomination or another. But the Mennonite witness at North
Webster was dead.

WAWASEE LAKESIDE CHAPEL

Section 24, Turkey Creek Township, Kosciusko County, Indiana

The Wawasee Lakeside Chapel is located along the west side of
Indiana Highway 13 Alternate, east of Lake Wawasee, and north of the
village of Wawasee. Work was started by the Goshen College Young

People's Christian Association in the Wawasee area in 1947. For a number of years all services were held in a country club building. But in 1955, with the special help of the "Big Brother," the Maple Grove congregation, a new house of worship was built on the site described above, which is still in use. Dedication services were held July 17, 1955. Herbert L. Yoder, a former student at Goshen College Seminary, was licensed in 1953, and ordained two years later. He served until 1961 when he was succeeded by Jason Martin. Martin is at this writing still a student in Goshen College Biblical Seminary. His ordination was planned for April 23, 1961. The 1961 *Yearbook* indicates thirty-two members at Wawasee.

TOTO MENNONITE GOSPEL MISSION

Section 36, Jackson Township, Starke County, Indiana

The Toto congregation is the result of a survey conducted by the Salem congregation at the request of the Indiana-Michigan Mennonite Mission Board in 1946. The village of Toto, six miles southwest of the county seat of Knox, seemed to be a spiritually needy community. The Salem members were urged to open up a teaching program on "right and wrong" by a Catholic of the community, Arthur McKane.

The first summer Bible school was conducted by the Salem congregation in Gleaners Hall the summer of 1947, with Bishop Ray F. Yoder in charge. After the summer Bible school was over it was decided to hold open-air services for the children on the Gleaners Hall lot, since the hall was no longer available. In 1947 a suitable plot of ground was purchased, and the next year a basement church building, thirty-two by fifty, plus an entrance, was built. The 1948 summer Bible school was held in this new basement church building. Sunday school was organized on June 20 of that year. Of a class of thirteen boys, eight to fifteen years of age, only three had ever been in Sunday school before. The basement church building was dedicated August 29, 1948. The first baptismal service, "with water in water," was held in the Grover Short Gravel Pit on September 18, 1949. Three girls were in the baptismal class.

In 1950 three Salem families, those of Harold D. Myers, Melvin Birkey, and Jency L. Hershberger, moved into the community. Harold D. Myers served as superintendent of the work. Evening services were inaugurated in 1951. The next year, on January 27, 1952, Ray F. Yoder ordained Jency L. Hershberger as the first resident pastor of the congregation. J. C. Wenger preached the ordination sermon. In the course of time the Salem congregation felt able to complete the meetinghouse, and the new completed structure was dedicated on March 23, 1952, with S. C. Yoder preaching the dedicatory message.

Toto is passing through the usual difficulties of evangelistic work in a needy community. The Lord has richly blessed the work, however, and the 1960 *Yearbook* shows a membership of thirty-six.

ENGLISH LAKE MENNONITE CHURCH

Section 1, Railroad Township, Starke County, Indiana

In the year 1948 a number of members from the Hopewell congregation at Kouts, Indiana, drove fifteen miles southeast to the village of English Lake and conducted a ten-mile survey of that community. The immediate area around English Lake had been without any organized church work for twelve years. Of the ninety-two families contacted in the area, a number were interested in seeing Christian work started. The outcome of this survey was that a summer Bible school was held in an old brick schoolhouse in 1949. The response from the community was good, and at the final program a woman from the community pleaded eloquently that a Sunday school be started. Emanuel S. and Elsie Birky agreed to do so. The next Sunday nine children and four adults from the community appeared for Sunday school in the old schoolhouse. Birky served as superintendent of the Sunday school from 1949 until 1954 when he was licensed as a preacher. The next year Bishop S. C. Yoder ordained him to the ministry.

The first evangelistic meetings were held in 1954 by S. S. Miller, the result of which was that thirteen persons united with the church. Paul Mininger, who was then bishop of the Hopewell congregation, baptized these converts on August 8 of that year. The first communion services were held two weeks later.

In 1956 the Hopewell congregation bought the schoolhouse and lot for $2,000.00, and on it the next year erected a new brick house of worship, thirty-two by fifty-two feet in size, with a seating capacity of 120. The cost of the building was $22,000.00 The first services were held in the new house of worship April 5, 1958, with the dedication services in charge of Paul Mininger on April 20, 1958. By 1960 twenty-six converts from the community had been baptized and received into the Mennonite Church, and three were then under instruction preparatory to baptism. Some of the converts have since died. English Lake has been more successful than most mission churches in winning adults and receiving them into the fellowship of the church. The 1960 *Yearbook* shows a membership at English Lake of twenty-six.

NEW BETHEL MENNONITE CHURCH

Section 8, Jefferson Township, Wells County, Indiana

In 1949 the Anderson congregation located a needy community in Jefferson Township, Wells County, south of Fort Wayne, and found an abandoned United Brethren church building. They held tent meetings on the grounds of this church building, and eventually purchased the lot and the building which had been erected, 1871-72. The tent meetings were held in September 1949, and the first service in the former United Brethren church building was conducted December 4, 1949.

By 1952 the work looked sufficiently promising to ordain a minister for the New Bethel outpost of the Anderson congregation. Orvil J. Crossgrove, son-in-law of J. S. Neuhouser, pastor of the Anderson congregation, was ordained preacher on July 15, 1952, by Ray F. Yoder, who then had the bishop oversight of the Anderson congregation. The work has shown steady growth, and the 1960 *Yearbook* indicates a membership at New Bethel of twenty-three.

MT. PLEASANT MENNONITE CHURCH

Section 25, Washington Township, Morgan County, Indiana

The Mt. Pleasant congregation is an outpost of the Bean Blossom Mennonite Church. Members from Bean Blossom conducted a summer Bible school in the Mahalasville area, north northeast of Bloomington, as early as 1945. In 1947 a summer Bible school was held in the Methodist Church of Mahalasville. Regular services were started in Mahalasville in 1951 but were later transferred to a schoolhouse six miles northwest of the town when the church was no longer available. The first services were held in the present church building, the former schoolhouse, on Easter of 1953.

The work was greatly strengthened in 1954 when Oscar Schrock and family moved to Mahalasville to take over the pastorate of the Mt. Pleasant group. Three other families also moved into the area: those of Elvin Yoder of the Berea congregation, and Levi Weirich and Richard Nusbaum of the Middlebury congregation. The first baptismal services were held September 12, 1954, when Edd P. Shrock baptized three converts. Two more were baptized on December 12, 1954.

In 1958, with the help of its "Big Brother," the Leo congregation, the house of worship of Mt. Pleasant was enlarged. The 1960 *Mennonite Yearbook* shows a membership at Mt. Pleasant of eleven.

In 1959 Oscar Schrock accepted the call of the Oak Terrace Mennonite Church, Blountstown, Florida, to become pastor. Since that time Charles Haarer is supplying the pulpit at Mt. Pleasant.

FIRST MENNONITE CHURCH

2311 Kessler Boulevard, North Drive,

Indianapolis, Marion County, Indiana

In 1951 three young Mennonite couples were in Indianapolis as students. Two of them have since become physicians, Floyd Rheinheimer and Paul Hooley, and the third, David Lehman, is now a dental surgeon. These three couples, Floyd and Irene Rheinheimer, Paul and Almeda Hooley, and David and Doris Lehman, began to hold prayer meetings just among themselves. They took up the study of the book, *Separated unto God,* by J. C. Wenger. Six months later Mennonite young men who were given a I-W classification as conscientious objectors began coming to Indianapolis to give their two years of service to their nation, "in the name of Christ." The three Mennonite student couples held religious meetings with these I-W men in the Seville Hotel.

In 1953 the Mennonite Relief and Service Committee purchased a large home at 1820 North Illinois Street in Indianapolis to serve as a Mennonite Service Center. The midweek services of the group were then held at the Service Center. For six months John and Violet Kauffman were in charge of the Service Center. After that David and Doris Lehman took charge until the fall of 1953 when Cleo A. Mann was licensed as a minister for Indianapolis, and Cleo and Nellie Mann became joint directors along with David and Doris Lehman.

While the John Kauffmans were still in Indianapolis, Sunday school was started at the Center, with the first service being held February 8, 1953. Marvin J. Miller served as superintendent, and the first lesson was taught by Floyd Rheinheimer. In a short time more suitable quarters were found for the Mennonite services at the Chapel of the Volunteers of America, a short distance south of the Center. This chapel was used until 1957 when it was possible to move into the basement of the new Mennonite house of worship. Prior to the coming of Cleo Mann visiting ministers were sent to Indianapolis by the area I-W pastor, Verle Hoffman. At his suggestion a church council was set up for the Mennonites of Indianapolis, 1953. The members chosen were Eugene Bontrager, Leon Farmwald, Paul Hooley, John Kauffman, David Lehman, Marvin J. Miller, Floyd Rheinheimer, and Dale Wise.

Arrangements were made in 1953 to hold a summer Bible school, but at the last moment the owner refused permission to place the tent on his property. The first summer Bible schools were therefore held in 1954 in two areas, one at the Service Center, and one in the Kessler area, in which area the church building was later built. A survey revealed that the Kessler area was densely populated. Within a one-half mile radius there are 1,053 homes, and within three fourths of a mile radius, 2,266 homes. In 1956 Cleo A. Mann reported that 1,200 homes had been built in Eagledale within the past fifteen months, a distance from the church lot of only one and one-tenth miles.

The response of the Kessler community residents to the summer Bible schools of the Mennonites was favorable. The average attendance in 1954 was thirty-nine; in 1955 it was ninety-two; in 1956 it was ninety-five; and in 1957 it was 117. At the final program in 1957 the total attendance reached 200. A total of 180 families sent children to the summer Bible schools held in the Kessler area between 1954 and 1957.

On August 8, 1956, ground was broken on the lot where the church is now located, which lot had been purchased by the Indiana-Michigan Mennonite Mission Board. Deacon Paul J. Myers of the Howard-Miami congregation was appointed to be in charge of building operations. Everything moved along well, and by March 3, 1957, it was possible to begin holding services in the basement of the new church building. Formal dedication services were held May 26, 1957. On this impressive occasion Cleo A. Mann, pastor, served as chairman, and Clyde Landis was music director. Anson G. Horner, bishop of the congregation, conducted the devotional service. Dr. David G. Lehman presented historical high lights. Glen E. Yoder, who was then treasurer of the Indiana-Michigan Mission Board, spoke on the topic, "Laborers Together." The dedicatory address was presented by Ralph Stahly who was then president of the district mission board. The pastor presided in the dedication service. In 1958 a house immediately south of the church building became available for a Mennonite Center.

As was stated earlier, Cleo A. and Nellie (Miller) Mann located in Indianapolis in 1953, where he was licensed to preach on October 11. He was ordained preacher May 6, 1956. He had served as director of relief in Belgium, for the Mennonite Relief and Service Committee, from 1945 until 1948.

The fall of 1960 Pastor Mann reported that there were then ninety-one members of the Mennonite Church in Indianapolis, thirty-five of whom were members of the congregation, of which number twenty-four were resident at Indianapolis. There were also at that time eleven men and six women who were members of the General Conference Mennonite Church, living in Indianapolis. There has been active fellowship between the two groups of Mennonites.

In 1956, Russell Krabill of the North Goshen congregation was appointed bishop of the congregation in Indianapolis. The future of the First Mennonite Church, Indianapolis, appears to be bright.

ELMWOOD MENNONITE CHURCH

South Town Street, Kendallville,

Wayne Township, Noble County, Indiana

Sentiment arose in the Benton congregation, which itself was only seven years old, in 1951 to conduct a summer Bible school which might develop into a more permanent work. The final result was the selection of the south part of the city of Kendallville, where a survey was made in 1951. The first Mennonite summer Bible school was held in Kendallville June 16-27, 1952. The response of the community was sufficiently favorable that the Benton Church decided to launch a building program. A lot was purchased and building operations began in April 1953, in care of Lewis Miller who is now pastor of the congregation. The first church service was held on a Sunday morning, July 26, 1953, although the building was not completed until several months later. Lewis Miller was ordained preacher September 20, 1953, by Edwin J. Yoder at Benton, and designated as in charge of the work at Kendallville. The church building was dedicated Sunday, November 15, 1953. Galen Johns, pastor of the Benton congregation, delivered the dedicatory address. The first Sunday evening services were held on December 20, 1953. A sewing circle was organized in 1954. The Mennonite Youth Fellowship has regular meetings the third Sunday of each month, and the fourth Thursday. During the first four years of summer Bible school the averages were respectively sixty-two, seventy-six, seventy-eight, and eighty-eight. The congregation was formally organized October 4, 1959, with thirty-six charter members; the present (1961) membership is thirty-two.

SOUTH BEND MENNONITE CHURCH

South Bend, Indiana

Long before the establishment of the Hope Rescue Mission in 1954, isolated Mennonite families were living in the city of South Bend. Various persons, including Christian students from Goshen College, were long interested in establishing a Mennonite congregation in the city of South Bend. In 1957 the Mennonite families living in that city appealed to both the general and district mission boards of the Mennonite Church for assistance, but received none. In 1959 the South Bend Mennonite families began meeting in private homes for regular fellowship and prayer. In January 1960 these families decided to begin holding regular Sunday school and church services in the chapel of the Hope Rescue Mission.

By November of 1959 four Mennonite families were committed to the plan to establish a Mennonite church in the city, and from four to six other families were interested. The area in which the group is hoping to establish a church building is in the southeast section of the city. In September 1960 the hopes and prayers of the Mennonite families of South Bend were answered with the availability of Carl J. Rudy, who came to Goshen College Biblical Seminary to continue his studies. Rudy was willing to assume the pastorate of the South Bend group while studying in the Goshen Seminary. Consequently on November 6, 1960, installation services were held in the chapel of the Hope Rescue Mission. Howard J. Zehr, pastor of the Prairie Street Mennonite Church, preached the sermon, and Simon Gingerich, president of the Indiana-Michigan Mennonite Mission Board, installed Carl Rudy as pastor of the group. November 20, 1960, was another big day in the life of the church when fifteen members were received by letter and one by baptism. The average attendance at this writing is thirty-five to fifty per Sunday. No house of worship has as yet been built. Howard J. Zehr is bishop.

BETHANY MENNONITE CHURCH

Imlay Township, Lapeer County, Michigan

The beginning of the Bethany congregation near Imlay City, Michigan, occurred in 1917 when a few Mennonite families from Pigeon, Michigan, settled in Lapeer County. They organized a Sunday school the next spring, on March 20, 1918. Services were at first held in a schoolhouse. The congregation was formally organized by Bishop J. K. Bixler on June 29, 1918. The group was fortunate to be able to purchase an abandoned Baptist church building for $1.00. They moved it three fourths of a mile to the present location where one and three-fourths acres of ground was donated to the congregation for church and burial purposes. The *Gospel Herald* of July 1918 indicates that the congregation was busy repairing the church building. The renovated house of worship was dedicated September 22, 1918, at which time the membership stood at twenty-eight.

The first minister of the congregation was Peter Ropp who was one of those who moved there in 1917. In 1926 he was ordained to the office of bishop. Simon W. Sommer served as a minister at Bethany from 1919 to 1928. Paul A. Wittrig, formerly of the Prairie Street, Elkhart, congregation, was ordained preacher in 1938 and served at Bethany until 1959 with the exception of the period, 1945-46, when he was business manager of Hesston College. He moved to Colorado in 1959. Wayne J. Wenger was ordained at Bethany in 1946 and served there until 1952. The present pastor of the Bethany congregation is Samuel Hostetler, of the Clinton Frame congregation who has been serving at Bethany since 1960.

A number of years ago the present writer visited Isaac Kennel, son-in-law of Bishop Peter Ropp, at Albany, Oregon. He reported that it cost the Bethany congregation $1,200.00 to move the former Baptist church building three fourths of a mile, to replaster it, to install a new floor, to get the basement ready for the building, and to put on a new roof. He reported that it took five days to move the building and that during the moving a severe windstorm blew the church building off the cribbing. He said that after about four years' use of the church building, the congregation lowered the ceiling about four feet, which greatly helped the acoustics.

The congregation seems to have grown well until about 1926, which is likely the time when the high membership of fifty-four was reached. Certain internal difficulties then developed within the congregation, various members moved away, and the membership level never rose as high again. The 1960 *Mennonite Yearbook* indicates that the present Bethany membership stands at twenty-three.

BETHEL MENNONITE CHURCH

Washington Township, Gratiot County, Michigan

In the year 1919 a number of Mennonites from Illinois, who were looking for cheaper land, investigated the area near Ashley, Michigan. The crops in Gratiot County were especially good that year. In fact, the first Mennonite family, that of Samuel Slagell, had removed from Fisher, Illinois, to Ashley, Michigan, in 1918. In the spring of 1919 Elmer Slagell moved to a farm a mile east of the Samuel Slagell farm. In 1919 Ray Bontragers moved to Ashley from Midland, Michigan, to a farm south of the Daggett School. His brothers, Ottis and Erie Bontrager, moved from Midland, Michigan, to the Ashley community in 1919 also, as did Joel Bachman from Wayland, Iowa, and Daniel S. Oyer from Eureka, Illinois. On the last Sunday of December 1919, Sunday school was organized in the home of Samuel Slagell. Later it was decided to meet in the Daggett schoolhouse, one and one-half miles west and two miles south of Ashley. The first meeting in the schoolhouse was held January 4, 1920.

In 1920 seven additional families moved into the community, those of John J. Smith, Roanoke, Illinois; George H. Summer, Flanagan, Illinois; Frank Sharick, Metamora, Illinois; Reuben Leidig, Fisher, Illinois; Jacob Yoder, Brutus, Michigan; and John Neuhauser, Imlay City, Michigan.

Included in the 1920 settlers was Preacher George H. Summer, who immediately exercised his office at Ashley. The congregation was formally organized July 6, 1920, by the bishops D. J. Johns and J. K. Bixler. A young people's Bible meeting was organized about the same time. During the winter of 1920-21 the congregation secured the privilege of meeting in the Washington Center Evangelical Church, two miles west of the Daggett schoolhouse, but the third Sunday in April 1921, services were resumed in the Daggett School.

After a number of meetings it was decided, in January 1922, to build a house of worship. The location of the church was to be three miles west of the Daggett schoolhouse. Most of the lumber was donated by the members of the congregation. Work on the timber began January 16, 1922. The foreman of the work was J. E. Bachman. Practically all of the labor was donated by the members of the church. After the building was complete, dedicatory services were held October 8, 1922, in charge of Bishop D. D. Miller. The cost of the building was approximately $3,950.00.

On May 28, 1923, D. S. Oyer was ordained as the first deacon of the congregation. George H. Summer served as pastor until his death in 1937, whereupon Deacon Oyer took charge of the congregation until J. Kore Zook located there in 1937. Zook remained until 1954, but was assisted by Eli Bontrager, 1938-42. In the year 1942 D. S. Oyer was ordained bishop, and served until his death twelve years later. After J. Kore Zook moved away, Preacher John M. Landis served as minister 1954-58. He was succeeded by Herman Weaver in 1958, a graduate of the Goshen College Biblical Seminary. Weaver was in charge for two years.

By 1930 the congregation had a membership of 108, by 1940 of 130, and the 1961 *Yearbook* shows a membership at Bethel of 127.

One of the unusual families of the congregation was that of John P. Oyer, 1858-1957, and his wife Mary (Smith) Oyer, 1861-1955, who were married January 15, 1880, which marriage lasted until her death seventy-five years, four months, and thirteen days later. They were the parents of Bishop D. S. Oyer and of Dean Noah Oyer.

DETROIT MENNONITE CHURCH

15800 Curtis Avenue, Detroit 35, Michigan

The beginnings of the Mennonite Church in Detroit go back to the time in 1926 when Bishop Peter Ropp of the Bethany congregation at Imlay City located temporarily in Detroit, largely to secure employment. He was interested in organizing a Mennonite congregation in the city if

17

possible, and requested the district mission board to try to find someone
to do so. Ropp himself evidently did not long remain in Detroit. In 1927
Clarence C. King, who was licensed rather than ordained, and who had
been working at the Canton, Ohio, Mission, located at Detroit and served
for three years. He was succeeded by Frank B. Raber in 1930, who was
ordained preacher in 1933, and who served until 1950. Deacon David E.
Plank located at Detroit in 1940 and served until his age compelled his
retirement in 1959. Frank Raber was succeeded by J. Frederick Erb in
1950; Erb was ordained bishop in 1953, and served until the close of
1955. He was succeeded by a layman, Kermit H. Derstine. C. Nevin
Miller was the pastor from 1956 until 1959. Since 1960 the minister is
Henry Wyse, formerly a bishop in the Central congregation, Archbold,
Ohio.

The first church building, twenty-eight by forty-two feet in size, was
built in 1927, and dedicated on October 30 of that year. It was enlarged
in 1935 to twenty-eight by sixty feet. It serves the congregation ade-
quately.

The parsonage was rented until the year 1938, in which year it was
purchased by the General Mission Board, which had taken over the
direction of the work in the year 1930.

Among the workers who contributed substantially to the progress
of the Lord's cause on Curtis Avenue special mention should be made
of Anna Smucker, now Mrs. William Ropp; Lela Mann, who is now
serving at Goshen College; and Maryann Hoffman.

City mission work involves many difficulties and obstacles. In the
early years of the work these were overcome in a remarkable way. By
1930 the membership stood at twenty-eight; in 1940 at sixty-seven; in
1950 it had dropped back to fifty-three; and the 1960 *Yearbook* shows
that the membership had dwindled to thirty-five. It is hoped that with the
enthusiasm of the present pastor and his staff of workers, the trend can
be reversed and the congregation again built up.

CALVARY MENNONITE CHURCH

104 Putnam Street, Pinckney,

Putnam Township, Livingston County, Michigan

Impetus for a Mennonite Church in Pinckney, eighteen miles northwest of Ann Arbor, Michigan, came from a Mennonite woman, Mrs.
James Shirey, who was living in Pinckney and maintained her membership with the Mennonite congregation near Continental, Ohio. A small
group of former members of the Congregational Church had withdrawn
from their denomination and erected a basement church in Pinckney in

1929, in size thirty-three by thirty-five feet. The work carried on in this basement church more or less disintegrated, and in 1941 the owners deeded the property over to the Indiana-Michigan Mennonite Mission Board. The district mission board then arranged for the ordination of Ezra Beachy of the Fort Wayne congregation, and he was installed as pastor of the new congregation of ten members on October 5, 1941. The installation service and the organization of the congregation took place at the same meeting. In 1944 the congregation installed a furnace in the building which would be adequate for the entire building after the superstructure was erected. In 1948 the congregation decided to build the superstructure, somewhat larger than the original basement church. The basement was therefore enlarged from a length of thirty-five feet to fifty, and the new church, approximately thirty-two by fifty feet in size, was completed. Building on the superstructure began August 16, and twelve days later (on August 28) the building was under roof. One hundred and forty-two persons donated over 3,000 hours of labor, some of them driving as much as 200 miles. This made a great impression upon the people of the community. This 1948 building was not dedicated until May 29, 1949.

The 1948 summer Bible school had an enrollment of 115, and gave good promise for the future of the work. However, Pinckney is located in an area which is better designed for recreation than for either farming or industry. The village itself is small, and it is located in the heart of a lake area, with fifty lakes located within a radius of fifteen miles. By 1950 the membership had climbed to thirty-six, but the 1960 *Yearbook* indicates that the figure had dwindled to twenty-eight. Ezra Beachy was ordained bishop in 1952. He and his family removed to Goshen, Indiana, in 1957, but he remained responsible for the pulpit at Calvary for two more years. In 1959 the present minister, Melvin Stauffer, was licensed to serve the Calvary congregation. He was ordained in 1961.

LOCUST GROVE MENNONITE CHURCH

Section 13, Burr Oak Township, St. Joseph County, Michigan

Locust Grove originated as an outpost of the Shore congregation, established about the year 1940. In 1941 Leonard Haarer of the Shore congregation was ordained to the ministry and placed in charge of the work at Locust Grove. A new meetinghouse was built in 1941. Haarer served until about 1950 when he transferred to Altoona, Pennsylvania, then to Ontario, and later united with the United Missionary Church. Orvin H. Hooley was ordained preacher in 1945, and bishop in 1957.

The Locust Grove congregation was organized November 18, 1945, with a charter membership of sixty-one. By the year 1950 the congregation had grown sufficiently that it was necessary to enlarge the meetinghouse. LeRoy Rhinesmith was ordained deacon in 1952.

In 1954 the Locust Grove congregation established a daughter church, South Colon, which somewhat reduced the crowded conditions in the house of worship. This explains the fact that although the membership was 150 in 1950, the 1960 *Yearbook* shows an advance of only eighteen members, to 168.

In 1960 the congregation decided to build a new house of worship, however. It is to be fifty-two by ninety feet, plus an annex of twenty-four by thirty-two feet, the entire structure being of brick veneer. The Locust Grove congregation has enjoyed a remarkable growth.

MOOREPARK MENNONITE CHURCH

Section 19, Park Township, St. Joseph County, Michigan

In the spring of 1947, the Mennonites of the Middlebury congregation went north twenty-six miles to the village of Moorepark, which is located five miles north of Three Rivers, and opened a Sunday school. On the first day six persons turned out for the meeting. The next Sunday there were twelve present, and the following Sunday fifteen. Ira Miller and Charles Weldy had gone around in the community inviting people out to the Sunday school. During the first year services were conducted by Wilbur Yoder, and sometimes by the seminary student, John David Zehr, who is now pastor of the Yellow Creek congregation. On July 4, 1948, Etril J. Leinbach was ordained minister to serve the group which was meeting in a former Reformed Church house of worship which had been built in 1876 and which had been standing idle for some time prior to 1947.

The Moorepark congregation has felt free to inaugurate activities which some of the older congregations were a bit more slow to start. For example, in 1949 a mother-daughter banquet was held, which developed into an annual institution. About two years later a sewing circle was organized with about fifteen or eighteen women in attendance, some of whom do not attend the church services at all.

Moorepark became an independent congregation in October 1955, with a charter membership of forty-nine. Leinbach was ordained bishop May 6, 1956.

Naturally growth was slow at the beginning. By 1950 the membership consisted of but nine persons. But in the decade following, the church grew rapidly so that the 1960 *Yearbook* shows a membership of seventy-four.

South Colon Mennonite Church

Section 25, Colon Township, St. Joseph County, Michigan

South Colon began as an outpost of the young Locust Grove congregation in the year 1954. Sunday school was started in that year on October 24, young people's Bible meetings in 1955, and midweek meetings in 1956.

William Wickey was ordained as the first preacher of the group in 1956, prior to which time the pulpit had been supplied by Locust Grove. Harold Mast was ordained deacon in 1957, and preacher in 1960. The 1960 *Yearbook* shows that this active little group already had forty-seven members. Services are held in what had been the St. Paul Reformed church building, which had stood idle for more than twenty years. About the beginning of 1961 the congregation purchased the school building across the road from the church. It is hoped to use it for regular services, but to rent the church building for summer Bible school and "other special meetings."

Cady Mennonite Mission

Midland, Michigan

In the early 1940's the Mennonites of the Midland congregation started a Sunday school in the Cady schoolhouse several miles north of the Midland County courthouse, one mile west of the Eastman Road, on what is now the U.S. Highway 10 bypass. One of the leaders in the establishment of this mission outpost was Oscar Wyse. In the course of time preaching services were held about twice a month. At this writing no congregation has as yet developed.

Herrick Mennonite Church

Section 6, Wise Township, Isabella County, Michigan

The village of Herrick is located on U.S. Highway 10, about three miles east of the city of Clare, which has a population of 3,000, and about forty rods south of the highway. Herrick was originally called Lansingville. Methodists began work in this village in the 1880's, and in 1890 erected a brick house of worship which was dedicated November 9, 1890. The church building, about thirty by forty-six feet in size, stands on a church lot, one-half acre in extent. The building seats over one hundred persons.

In the year 1952 the Mennonites of the Midland congregation learned that the abandoned church building at Herrick was to be sold.

They secured permission to hold summer Bible school in the building in 1952, which proved to be a success, the average attendance being forty-two. Regular Sunday morning and Sunday evening services were begun July 13, 1952, by Floyd F. Bontrager, bishop of the Midland congregation, who has served as pastor at Herrick since that date. On September 19, 1952, the Midland congregation was able to purchase the house of worship for approximately $2,000.00. The Herrick Mennonite congregation was organized September 11, 1960, with eleven charter members. By the spring of 1961 there were fifteen members. On November 20 of that year the new Herrick congregation began to sponsor the international *Mennonite Hour* broadcast over station WCRM, Clare, Michigan.

One of the interesting events in the life of the new church was the home-coming November 5, 1960, when sixty-two persons signed the guest book. The sermon on this occasion was delivered by a former Methodist pastor, George P. Stanford. The congregation is currently making plans to add an educational wing to the house of worship.

LIBERTY MENNONITE CHURCH

Liberty Township, Jackson County, Michigan

The Liberty Mennonite church building is located near Clark Lake, eleven miles south of the city of Jackson, Michigan, on U.S. Highway 127. The building was formerly a Methodist house of worship which had been built in 1867, which has a seating capacity of about 150, and which was closed in 1936.

In the year 1946 the Indiana-Michigan Mennonite Mission Board opened work at Liberty. The first and only pastor was Oscar Leinbach who was ordained preacher January 5, 1947. The congregation was organized in March 1950, with thirteen charter members, largely Mennonites from Daviess County, Indiana. The 1960 *Yearbook* indicates that the congregation had grown to a membership of twenty-three.

COLD SPRINGS MENNONITE CHURCH

Cold Springs Township, Kalkaska County, Michigan

The Cold Springs mission outpost was established by the Fairview congregation in the year 1948, in the general area of Mancelona (which is in the adjoining Antrim County, but this 1948 missionary endeavor has no connection with the nineteenth-century Mennonite settlements at Mancelona). The next year Willard L. Bontrager was ordained to the ministry at Fairview for Cold Springs, the exact date being February 29,

1949. The tiny group has grown steadily so that the 1960 *Mennonite Yearbook* reports a membership at Cold Springs of twenty-two.

PETOSKEY MENNONITE CHURCH

Bear Creek Township, Emmet County, Michigan

The Mennonite congregation in the city of Petoskey resulted from the purchase of an abandoned church building in that city by the Clinton Frame congregation, which in turn conveyed the ownership of the building to the Indiana-Michigan Mennonite Mission Board. The mission board then arranged for the ordination of Ivan K. Weaver to take charge of the prospective mission station in Petoskey; this ordination was performed by his father-in-law, D. A. Yoder, on November 20, 1949, at Weaver's home congregation, Yellow Creek. Weaver located at Petoskey the next June. The work at Petoskey prospered under the leadership of Weaver, and in 1955 George S. Eby was ordained to serve as deacon of the young congregation. In 1957 the Petoskey congregation established a mission outpost, Clarion, Boyne Falls, Michigan. No congregation has as yet developed.

In the year 1958 George S. Eby removed to California, and the next year Ivan K. Weaver accepted a pastorate at Elida, Ohio. His successor was Homer E. Yutzy who had been in charge of the mission station at Gay in Sherman Township, in the northernmost county of Michigan, Keweenaw, which projects from the Upper Peninsula of Michigan into Lake Superior. (The outpost at Gay was started by Ora Wyse of Naubinway, Michigan, who held summer Bible school there from 1950 through 1953. Wyse also initiated preaching services the last Thursday evening of each month, in the year 1951. Yutzy lived at Gay from 1954 until 1959, but accepted the appointment to Petoskey in the latter year, by which time it was considered unlikely that a congregation would develop at Gay.)

The 1960 *Yearbook* shows a membership at Petoskey of forty-seven.

STUTSMANVILLE MENNONITE CHURCH

Section 14, Friendship Township, Emmet County, Michigan

Stutsmanville was established as an outpost of the Petoskey congregation in 1957, but under the direction and ownership of the Indiana-Michigan Mennonite Mission Board. The building at Stutsmanville was actually constructed of the materials of a former house of worship in a village twelve miles north of Stutsmanville. The Christians of Stutsmanville tore down the former church building, and used all the materials, even the nails which the women straightened, and built it as a community church. Later the Methodists acquired the ownership of the

Stutsmanville church building, and sold it to the Mennonites in April 1958. No regular services had been held from 1947 until July of 1957, when the Petoskey Mennonites began their work. The first thing done, under the direction of Willis E. Miller, was to make a survey of the community. The result was the conducting of a summer Bible school, followed by Sunday school, and preaching services later. In the course of several years the average attendance was thirty-five from the community, including a number of adults. There are about forty homes within a two-mile radius of the church. Large numbers of the people of the community do not attend worship services anywhere. The nearest church building from Stutsmanville is five and one-half miles away. Willis E. Miller and family moved to the Stutsmanville community in June 1958. He was licensed to the ministry by Ivan K. Weaver on January 25, 1959. Unfortunately his health broke down with Hodgkin's disease, and Willis passed on to be with the Lord December 22, 1960. At this writing Mrs. Miller is continuing her residence and witness in the community. There is as yet no organized congregation at Stutsmanville.

SAGINAW MENNONITE CHURCH

1119 North Ninth Street, Saginaw, Michigan

The beginnings of the work in Saginaw, a city of over 100,000 population, go back to 1949 when Mennonites began holding services in the northern part of the city. The first summer Bible school was conducted in that year in a tent at Sixth and Norman streets. The attendance from the community was excellent, 250. Even more encouraging was the fact that twenty young people accepted Christ. The result of this was the purchase of a house at 1130 North Eighth Street, the building which is currently used as a parsonage. A number of persons remained with the work during that fall and winter, such as Elsie (Selzer) Miller of Canton, Kansas, Elizabeth Yoder of Ohio, and Melvin Leidig of Midland, Michigan. The workers carried on such activities as weekly Bible classes, clubs for boys and girls, and craft work. Through these means they became acquainted with the community. These activities were attended by grade-school children as well as high-school young people.

The year 1951 proved to be a glorious year for the Mennonite witness in Saginaw. The first baptismal services were conducted in March of that year, when six persons were received into the church. A lot was purchased, the site of the present house of worship. In July, J. D. Graber, who had bishop oversight of the congregation, received twenty members into the church. Dedicatory services for the new house of worship were conducted in November 1951.

The witness was not confined to the Ninth Street area, but summer Bible schools were also held in four other locations: the Seventeenth Street area, East Side, Warren Avenue, and Carrollton (a small rural village near Saginaw).

Present activities include the following: women's sewing circle and prayer meeting which meets weekly, junior and senior MYF, camping, a chorus, and a youth conference. Other young people from Youngstown, Ohio; Cleveland, Ohio; Chicago, Illinois; and St. Anne, Illinois, attend the youth conferences conducted at Saginaw.

The 1960 *Mennonite Yearbook* shows a membership at Saginaw of fifty-eight. Truly the Mennonite Church is grateful for the response of the colored people in Saginaw.

LeRoy Bechler was ordained minister at Pigeon, Michigan, December 2, 1951, by J. D. Graber at the request of the Mennonite Board of Missions and Charities, to serve the Saginaw congregation. He served at Saginaw until 1961 with the exception of the year 1957-58 when he was a university student; during that year Galen Johns of the Benton congregation served as acting pastor at Saginaw. Early in 1961 Marvin Sweigart of Mt. Pleasant, Iowa, became the second pastor of the Ninth Street Mennonite Church, Saginaw. He was licensed to preach by Nelson E. Kauffman on February 19, 1961.

EAST SIDE MENNONITE CHURCH
2202 Janes Street, Saginaw, Michigan

Summer Bible school was held in the East Side of Saginaw in June 1951, with LeRoy Bechler serving as superintendent. Regular services were started February 13, 1955. The services were held in the parsonage, 1803 North Twenty-third Street, from 1955 to 1957. In April 1957 the group began to use the new church building which was built, beginning November 10, 1956 (dedicated May 11, 1958), at 2709 North Washington Street. The building was thirty-six by sixty-two feet in size. By the time of the dedication, the attendance was averaging seventy-five to eighty. In 1959 the city of Saginaw decided to clear the area where the East Side people lived and where the church building was located. This was a great blow to the workers, and to the colored folks who had to move. Melvin Leidig had been licensed as pastor by J. D. Graber of the General Mission Board on December 15, 1955. On October 5, 1960, he moved to the new parsonage at 2126 Janes Street. At present the congregation is assuming the major share of the building costs for a new structure with a sanctuary, thirty-two by forty-eight, and an educational wing, twenty-eight by fifty-two. Ground was broken at 2202 Janes Street on September

4, 1960. It is the hope of the congregation to be able to dedicate the new house of worship before the close of 1961. The estimated cost is $35,000.00, but by donating much labor the group is hoping to lop $15,000.00 off this estimate.

HEATH STREET MENNONITE CHURCH

Battle Creek, Michigan

The Mennonite witness in Battle Creek began in the year 1952 with the establishment of a mission outpost as a daughter of the Bowne congregation. Services were first held in the home of M. C. Brothers. After some time the Indiana-Michigan Mennonite Mission Board was given the oversight of the Heath Street Church. Daniel Zook had pastoral oversight at first. Dedication services for the new church building were held on July 24, 1955, on which date Bishop T. E. Schrock also licensed John M. Snyder as minister. Snyder served until 1958 when he was replaced by Deacon Harold M. Christophel, who is still in charge of the work. The membership at Heath Street is now twenty-one, and the average attendance is about forty.

WELLINGTON MENNONITE MISSION

Lachine, Alpena County, Michigan

The Wellington mission outpost of the Fairview congregation was established in the year 1955. The next year, on September 16, 1956, Harold Sharp was ordained preacher in the Fairview meetinghouse to serve the Wellington outpost. He is still in charge of the work. Wellington is located three miles west of Long Rapids, Michigan. The 1960 *Yearbook* shows a membership at Wellington of twenty-two.

CALIFORNIA MENNONITE CHURCH

Branch County, Michigan

California, located about twelve miles northeast of Angola, Indiana, is a daughter of the Forks congregation. It was established in 1956 in a building which had formerly been a Methodist church, but which was then in the possession of a local farmer. It is of stucco construction, twenty-eight by forty feet in size. After conducting the work for some three years the Forks congregation voted on November 22, 1959, to release Deacon Malvin P. Miller to locate at California as the pastor of the new outpost. He moved to the area in February 1960. The dedicatory services were held for the new Mennonite church building on March 13, 1960, with Donald E. Yoder, pastor of the Forks congregation, delivering the dedicatory address. Bishop E. C. Bontrager installed Malvin P. Miller as pastor of the new California Church. By the close of 1960 six local residents, had united with the new congregation.

KALAMAZOO MENNONITE CHURCH

Kalamazoo, Michigan

On January 3, 1960, Mennonite services were begun in Kalamazoo, with E. J. Leinbach of the Moorepark congregation bringing the message. A number of young men who had done their alternative service (rather than two years of military training) in Kalamazoo form the nucleus of the group. Included in the group are also some schoolteachers and nurses, and other people, including students from the university. Services are being held in the Milwood School, Cork Street and Lover's Lane. During 1960 the average attendance was about twenty, but by the spring of 1961 the attendance doubled. From June 1960 Harold Yoder of the Middlebury congregation has been supplying the pulpit. Sunday school and worship services are held each Lord's day. Kalamazoo is under the wing of the Moorepark congregation. It is hoped soon to build a structure that can be used as a house of worship. The future looks bright.

FERNLAND MENNONITE CHURCH

Germfask, Germfask Township, Schoolcraft County, Michigan

Fernland is the first of a remarkable chain of congregations in the Upper Peninsula of Michigan which the Mennonites of Indiana and Michigan established during the great missionary awakening, 1935- . The work in the Upper Peninsula is the result of the vision of C. A. Shank of the Olive Church, who was also vice-president of the district mission board. He visited the Upper Peninsula in the interest of his health. In 1934 he and Edwin J. Yoder, president of the district mission board, surveyed the area in the interest of establishing summer Bible schools. The consequence was that Yoder and Shank held summer Bible schools at Germfask in 1935 and 1936. The area appeared to be promising for the establishment of a mission church.

In 1937 the board placed Chester Osborne at Germfask as the first Mennonite preacher in the Upper Peninsula. He served there, 1937-1947, then moved to Kouts, Indiana, later to Kansas. His successor was Bruce Handrich, ordained preacher in 1948. Handrich wrote thus in the *Gospel Evangel*, March-April, 1960: "Germfask is a small community of perhaps six square miles in area, sparsely populated, with little industry, and limited means of livelihood. In spite of its limitations, it is a splendid place to live and call home. It is one of the few places in the United States where one can still drive thirty miles without finding the beauties of nature cluttered with houses; where deer, bears, and coyotes can be found fresh in nature's own glorious wonderland. We are glad and count it a privilege to be able to serve our God in His vineyard here at Germfask." The Germfask congregation conducts two services each Sunday, a prayer service in one of the homes every two weeks, with a youth night monthly and another night devoted to a hymn-sing each month. The women's sewing circle meets the first Thursday of each month. The congregation also conducts a service at the Lakefield Rest Home each month. Handrich reported that there were twenty-one active members in 1960, ranging in age from sixteen to sixty.

A splendid review of the first eighteen years of Mennonite witnessing in the Upper Peninsula was published in the *Gospel Herald* (XLVIII, 45, November 8, 1955, 1070-72) under the title, "Visit Upper Michigan," by Freda (Kurtz) Kauffman. Of the ten congregations established to date in the Upper Peninsula, nine are still under the care of the district mission board, and one (Wildwood) has achieved independence. The Upper Peninsula has been divided into two bishop districts which are served by Clarence Troyer and Norman P. Weaver, Weaver in the west half.

MAPLE GROVE MENNONITE CHURCH

Gulliver, Mueller Township, Schoolcraft County, Michigan

The mission outpost, Maple Grove, was established in the year 1942. The next year Norman P. Weaver was ordained to the ministry and placed in charge of the work. Weaver was ordained bishop in 1953. Services were held in a schoolhouse until 1947 when the present building was erected, and dedicated the next year. Weaver licensed Emerson Yordy to the ministry in 1958, and ordained him preacher a year later. But the spring of 1960 Yordy removed to the state of Oregon. The 1960 *Mennonite Yearbook* indicates a membership at Maple Grove of twenty-nine.

SENEY MENNONITE CHURCH

Seney, Section 33, Seney Township, Schoolcraft County, Michigan

The Seney congregation dates back to 1946 when Mennonites established work there. The first resident minister was Victor V. Miller, ordained in 1951, grandson of Preacher Joseph D. Miller of the Forks congregation. The 1960 *Yearbook* indicates seven members at Seney. The meetinghouse was built in 1951-52.

CEDAR GROVE MENNONITE CHURCH

Manistique, Section 28, Manistique Township,

Schoolcraft County, Michigan

The mission outpost now known as Cedar Grove was established in the year 1951. The next year Leonard E. Schmucker, a graduate of Goshen College Biblical Seminary, was ordained preacher, and a basement church was erected. Several years later the superstructure was added to the basement building. The 1960 *Mennonite Yearbook* indicates that the Cedar Grove membership totaled eighteen.

WILDWOOD MENNONITE CHURCH

Curtis, Section 14, Portage Township, Mackinac County, Michigan

Wildwood is one of the older congregations in the Upper Peninsula, having been established in 1939. The next year Clarence Troyer was ordained preacher at Naubinway and placed in charge of the Wildwood outpost. He was ordained bishop in 1948 to succeed T. E. Schrock. Troyer now has the bishop oversight of the congregations in the eastern portion of the Upper Peninsula. Because of the heavy load which this entails, Lloyd R. Miller was ordained preacher in 1952 to assist Clarence Troyer. The congregation worships in a former schoolhouse. In 1955 the congregation became independent of the district mission board and was recognized as a full member of the Indiana-Michigan Conference. The 1960 *Yearbook* indicates a membership at Wildwood of thirty-two.

NAUBINWAY MENNONITE CHURCH

Naubinway, Section 28, Garfield Township, Mackinac County, Michigan

The Mennonite witness at Naubinway was started in 1943. Two years later Ora C. Wyse was ordained as preacher and put in charge of this mission station. The Mennonites purchased a church building from the Presbyterians which had been erected in 1868. The date of purchase was 1947, and as soon as the Mennonites owned the building they remodeled it. The work at Naubinway has prospered, so that the 1960 *Yearbook* reports a membership figure of twenty-two.

REXTON MENNONITE CHURCH

Section 36, Hudson Township, Mackinac County, Michigan

Rexton is located on Michigan Highway 48. The Mennonite witness at this place was started in 1948. The next year Joseph J. Swartz, Jr., was ordained to the ministry and placed in charge of the Rexton station. The work prospered through the years so that the 1960 *Yearbook* shows twenty-five members at Rexton. The group worships in the former Methodist church building of Lakefield, Michigan; this building was purchased and removed about forty miles to Rexton.

WAYSIDE MENNONITE CHURCH

Brimley, Section 14, Superior Township, Chippewa County, Michigan

The Wayside church building is located on Michigan Highway 28 near Brimley, five miles from U.S. Highway 2, and about fifteen miles west of Sault Sainte Marie. The work began at Wayside when the Lester Gage family removed from near Curtis to Brimley in 1947. This caused Clarence Troyer to have an interest in establishing work at Wayside. A summer Bible school was held in 1948 with an average attendance of forty-eight. That same year the Lee Kauffman family from Fairview moved to Brimley. The first Sunday school was held in their home late in 1948 and has continued since that time. The meetinghouse was built in 1950. The membership of the church, according to the 1960 *Yearbook,* is twenty-six.

GRAND MARAIS MENNONITE CHURCH

Grand Marais, Section 6, Burt Township, Alger County, Michigan

Mennonites held summer Bible school in Grand Marais in 1945 and 1946. Local Christians promised to conduct their own Bible school in 1947. In 1948 Bruce Handrich conducted another summer Bible school at Grand Marais, following which he organized a Sunday school. For a time it was necessary for him to haul two dozen chairs forty miles from Germfask, where he was stationed as pastor, to Grand Marais each week. Later the district mission board authorized the purchase of three dozen chairs to be used in the town hall, where all services were held until 1953. In 1948 Willard D. Handrich was ordained to the ministry and placed in charge of the new station at Grand Marais. The house of worship was built in 1953-54, and dedicated on October 10, 1954. The attendance at the Grand Marais services is good. The 1960 *Yearbook* shows a resident membership at Grand Marais of five.

SOO HILL MENNONITE CHURCH

Escanaba, Wells Township, Delta County, Michigan

The Mennonites held summer Bible school in the Danforth schoolhouse in 1950, in charge of Bruce Handrich. The first worship services were held in the same schoolhouse in 1952. The next year Paul H. Horst of the Clinton Frame congregation was ordained to the ministry and placed in charge of the new Soo Hill mission station. A basement church was built in 1953, and the superstructure added three years later. By 1960 the *Yearbook* reported a membership at Soo Hill of thirteen.

SALEM MENNONITE CHURCH

Waldron, Hillsdale County, Michigan

In the year 1953 the ministers of the Lockport Mennonite Church of Ohio were asked to supply the pulpit for an Evangelical United Brethren Church near Waldron, Michigan. The building had been erected by the Evangelical Church in 1887. The Mennonites acquired the ownership of the building and modernized it. Both Sunday school and preaching services were inaugurated in 1953. In 1955 Earl Stuckey was ordained to the ministry in the Lockport congregation, and immediately took a deep interest in the Salem congregation. The renovated house of worship was rededicated May 29, 1960, with J. C. Wenger of Goshen, Indiana, bringing the dedicatory message. By December 1960 five Mennonite families from Ohio had settled in the vicinity of the Salem Church, and seven families from the area were also members. The total membership at the close of 1960 was forty-six, and the average attendance in the Sunday morning services was seventy-eight. Earl Stuckey was preaching three Sundays out of four at the Salem Church, and the fourth Sunday at Lockport, on which occasion a Lockport minister supplied the pulpit at Salem. The Salem congregation is affiliated with the Ohio and Eastern Mennonite Conference.

FIRST MENNONITE CHURCH

New Bremen, Lewis County, New York

In the 1890 *Herald of Truth* M. S. Steiner wrote an account of a visit which he made among the Amish Mennonites at Castorland, New York. Steiner reported that in 1831 an Amish member named Joseph Kieffer of Lothringen, Germany, settled in New York state. Two years later four more families followed, including a preacher. In 1835 Bishop Oesch of Ontario organized what came to be known later as the "Yorker" Amish Church. The first preacher for the Amish Mennonites in Lewis County was Joseph Fahrney. Other Amish immigrants followed.

In 1850 the Christian Apostolic schism occurred, in which all the ministers except Michael Zehr left the Amish Mennonite Church, and only a few families remained with Zehr. However, by 1890 the Zehr group had grown to thirty-two families with about 125 members. These Amish Mennonites were served by Bishops Jacob Roggie and Peter Lehman; by Preachers John Moser, Joseph Yousey, and Christian Roggie; and by Deacon John Nafziger. M. S. Steiner mentioned that other common names in the Amish Mennonite settlement were Hershey, Kennel, Steiner, and Zehr. He added that as to manner of services the Amish Mennonites of Lewis County resembled the Old Order Amish, but in dress and doctrine were like the Eastern Amish Mennonite Conference. Steiner reported that in 1880 Bishop Samuel Yoder of Mifflin County, Pennsylvania, and Bishop John Mast of Berks County, Pennsylvania, had visited the Castorland settlement. In 1888 Bishop John K. Yoder of Wayne County, Ohio, had done so also. Steiner commented that this was "the only Amish Church in the state of New York." (Steiner's misspelled names were corrected by a paper written by Virginia Yancey.)

Virginia Yancey added that the ancestors of the Lewis County Amish Mennonites came from the French province of Lorraine, and settled at Croghan, located in the northeastern part of the state of New York, in the western foothills of the Adirondack Mountains. The settlement is near the center of Lewis County. In the first ten years only twenty families arrived. She said that when Bishop Roggie died in 1894 there were thirty families in the church. All meetings were held in private homes until 1912, at which time the first meetinghouse was built near Croghan, now known as the Conservative Amish Mennonite Church. All services were conducted in German until 1918.

In the year 1941 sixty-eight members withdrew from the Conservative Amish Mennonite Church and formed a new congregation which is now known as the First Mennonite Church, New Bremen, and which is affiliated with the Indiana-Michigan Mennonite Conference. The reason for this affiliation is that two bishops from the conference, S. C. Yoder and D. A. Yoder, were of much assistance to the church in organizing them and providing them with pastoral and bishop oversight.

The meetinghouse was built in 1941, and the next year J. Lawrence Burkholder was ordained to serve as pastor of the congregation. He remained until 1944, when he left for relief work in India and China. He is now a professor in Harvard Divinity School. In 1945 Gordon Schrag of Ontario assumed the pastoral care of the "Croghan" congregation and remained until 1956. The pulpit was then supplied by ministers such as Andrew Gingerich and Donald Jantzi until October 27, 1957, when Jantzi was installed as pastor. The congregation was received as a member of the Indiana-Michigan Mennonite Conference on June 3, 1959. One year later Donald Jantzi was received as a member of conference. The 1960 *Yearbook* shows a membership at New Bremen of 206.

The congregation plans for Jantzi's ordination as bishop the fall of 1961.

The Older Mennonite Ministers

C. D. Beery   D. H. and Ida Bender   Jacob A. Beutler

J. K. Bixler   Daniel Brenneman   David Burkholder   A. L. Buzzard

D. H. Coffman   John S. Coffman

R. R. Ebersole   Harvey Friesner   Amos and Sarah Cripe

John F. Funk   E. S. Hallman   N. S. Hoover   John Hygema

Jonas Loucks   Frank Maust   Jacob P. Miller   Yost C. Miller

T. U. Nelson   Peter Ropp   Henry and Lizzie Weaver

Henry Weldy   D. A. and Frances Yoder   Samuel and Elizabeth Yoder

The Older Amish Mennonite Ministers

J. D. Birky   Eli A. Bontrager   Menno and Nettie Esch

John L. Emmert   Edward Gegax   J. Y. and Gertrude Hooley

J. S. Hartzler   Ira S. Johns

D. J. Johns   J. S. Horner   Jonathan and Elizabeth Kurtz

C. S. and Mary Liechty　　　J. H. McGowen　　　D. D. Miller

Eli S. Miller　　　Joseph D. Miller Family　　　E. S. and Anna Mullett

Dr. W. B. Page Family　　　Isaac Smucker　　　J. P. Smucker

George H. Summer　　　D. D. Troyer　　　Samuel and Laura Weaver

Ministers Ordained Since the Merger of 1916

Ezra Beachy

Harold S. Bender

Emanuel S. Birky

Ezra P. Bleile

Rudy Borntrager

Earley C. Bontrager

Vernon E. Bontreger

Aldus Brackbill

Arthur R. Cash

Howard H. Charles

Allen Christophel

J. W. Christophel

Orvil J. Crossgrove

C. C. Culp

Robert Detweiler   Allen B. Ebersole   George Eby   J. Frederick Erb

Manford Freed   John E. Gingrich   Benjamin Graber   C. L. Graber

Leonard Haarer   Bruce Handrich   Willard Handrich   Abram Hartman

Earl Hartman   Levi C. Hartzler   P. A. Heller   Jency L. Hershberger

J. C. and Martha Hershberger   Emanuel J. Hochstedler   Verle Hoffman

Orvin H. Hooley   A. G. Horner Family   John W. Horner

Aden Horst   Paul H. Horst   Amos and Oscar S. Hostetler

LeRoy L. Hostetler   S. J. Hostetler   Galen I. Johns   Edward D. Jones

A. H. Kauffman   L. A. and Ida Kauffman   Nelson E. Kauffman

Norman D. Kauffman   Ray Keim   Donald King Family

Russell Krabill   George J. Lapp   John Lederach   Etril J. Leinbach

Oscar Leinbach   G. Maurice Long   Irvin Long   Lester Mann

Cleo A. Mann and Wife   Sherman Maust   Mitchell D. McCloud

Samuel Metzler   Andrew J. Miller   C. Nevin Miller   Ernest E. Miller

Homer J. Miller   Ivan Miller   John Ray Miller   Malvin P. Miller

Paul M. Miller   Percy and Josiah Miller   S. J. Miller

S. S. Miller

Vernon U. Miller

William R. Miller

Paul Mininger

John H. Mosemann

Harold D. Myers

Paul J. Myers

Homer F. North

Chester C. Osborne

D. S. Oyer

Noah Oyer

Chester A. Raber

Frank B. Raber

Arnold Roth

Leonard E. Schmucker

Gordon Schrag

| Edd P. Shrock | Oscar Schrock | T. E. Schrock | Clarence A. Shank |

| Niles Slabaugh | Tobias Slaubaugh | John R. Smucker | R. R. Smucker |

| Willard Sommers | Ralph Stahly | Elno Steiner | John S. Steiner |

| Menno Steiner | Henry J. Stoll | Joe J. Swartz | Clarence Troyer |

John M. Troyer   Willis C. Troyer   Isaac and Anna Weaver

Paul F. Weldy   Wayne and Mae Wenger   John C. Wenger

Peter B. Wiebe   Lester A. Wyse   Clarence and Delilah Yoder

E. J. Yoder   Harold A. Yoder   Melvin A. Yoder   Ray F. Yoder

S. C. Yoder   Amos D. Yontz   David Yontz   Howard J. Zehr

Mennonite Meetinghouses in Indiana and Michigan

Bean Blossom

Bon Air

Berea

Brimley

Bethel

Calvary

Caney Creek

East Goshen

Clinton Brick

Elmwood

Clinton Frame

Emma

Fairview (original)

Detroit

Fairview (old)

Fairview (new)

Herrick

First Mennonite, Indianapolis

Holdeman

Forks

Hopewell

Goshen College

Grand Marais

Howard-Miami

Hudson Lake

Maple Grove, Ind. (new)

Leo

Maple River

Liberty

Marion

Maple Grove, Mich.

Maple Grove, Ind. (old)

Midland (old)

Midland (new)

Naubinway

Moorepark

New Bethel

North Goshen

Mt. Pleasant

Olive

Nappanee

Osceola

Pigeon

Pretty Prairie

Plato

Roselawn

Pleasant View, Ind.

Salem

Pleasantview, Mich.

Shore

Prairie Street

Soo Hill

Sunnyside

Toto

Talcum

Yellow Creek

Conservative Mennonite Church Buildings

Bethel

Griner

Cuba

Pleasant Grove

Riverview

Townline

Wisler Meetinghouses   *Other Meetinghouses*

Blosser

Fairhaven (Burkholder Amish Mennonite)

County Line

Union (Brethren in Christ)

Yellow Creek

Goshen College Biblical Seminary

KENTUCKY MISSION STATIONS

The Clinton Frame Mennonite Church, Goshen, Indiana, has opened two mission stations in Kentucky. In 1952 the Ball Creek or Talcum mission station was established at Talcum in Knott County, Kentucky. Samuel Hostetler was ordained preacher the next year and placed at Talcum, 1953-56. He was succeeded by John F. Mishler, first as a licensed minister, 1956-59, and ordained in 1959. Talcum now has a membership of seventeen. In 1956 a second station was started, Big Branch, Bearville, Kentucky, but it lasted for only one year and was closed.

The Indiana-Michigan Mennonite Mission Board opened work at Caney Creek, Breathitt County, about fifteen miles south of Jackson, in 1952. Wayne J. Wenger has been the minister in charge from the beginning. There are five members. Wenger served until 1961.

The Berea Church in Daviess County, Indiana, conducted a summer Bible school at the Leonard Oak School, near Morgantown, Butler County, about 100 miles southwest of Louisville, in 1951. The average attendance was about sixty-seven. Following the 1952 summer Bible school at Morgantown a group drove down from the Berea community, 135 miles north of Morgantown, and conducted Sunday school and preaching services. In 1955 Cledus Slaubaugh was ordained for Morgantown, and located there in 1956. The work is now under the direction of the district mission board. There are eight members at Morgantown.

The Shore Church, Shipshewana, Indiana, opened a mission station at the Smith School, Jetson, Butler County, Kentucky, in 1956. John J. Wickey was ordained for this outpost in 1959. There are six members (1961 *Mennonite Yearbook*).

OAK TERRACE MENNONITE CHURCH

Blountstown, Florida

About 1956 four families from the Hopewell congregation, Kouts, Indiana, moved to the Blountstown area in Florida, which is located in Calhoun County in the long strip of land which projects westward along the Gulf of Mexico south of Alabama. One of the families later returned to Indiana. These Indiana families joined families from many other areas who had settled in this region of Florida. At the request of the Hopewell members Samuel S. Miller licensed Wilmer Good in 1956 to serve as minister for the group. The next year he was replaced by Joseph M. Eash, who served about a year. The Indiana-Michigan Mennonite Mission Board then placed on the field J. Kore Zook, who served from

18

1958 to 1959. In 1959 Oscar Schrock was given the pastoral charge of the congregation. The 1960 *Yearbook* shows thirty members in the Oak Terrace congregation.

Supplement to Chapter V, continued from page 350

MELVIN STAUFFER, 1931-   Preacher   Calvary
    Born at New Haven, Indiana, on May 11, 1931. Married Marjorie Stauffer of Grabill, Indiana, September 16, 1950. Three children. Licensed as a minister at the Calvary Church, Pinckney, Michigan, August 9, 1959. Ordained preacher by Etril Leinbach on September 10, 1961, if plans carried. Gives full time to his pastorate.

WILLARD SWARTLEY, 1936-   Preacher   Locust Grove, Indiana
    Born in Bucks County, Pennsylvania, August 6, 1936. Married Mary Louise Lapp of Montgomery County, Pennsylvania, August 16, 1958. One child. Received B.A. degree from Eastern Mennonite College in 1959. Student, Goshen College Biblical Seminary. If plans carry, is to be ordained preacher by Ralph Stahly in the Locust Grove Congregation, near Elkhart, Indiana, on September 17, 1961.

HENRY WYSE, 1894-   Bishop   Detroit
    Born at Archbold, Ohio, April 3, 1894. Married Lydia Frey of Wauseon, Ohio, April 15, 1915. Eight children. Ordained deacon October 24, 1933; preacher on November 6, 1938; and bishop on September 10, 1950. Served in the Central Church near Archbold. Began to supply pulpit at Detroit irregularly from June 1959. Assumed pastorate there on January 1, 1960. Moved to Detroit, February 1960. United with Conference, 1961.

MERRILL J. YODER, 1916-   Deacon   Olive
    Born Elkhart County, January 4, 1916, a nephew of D. A. Yoder. Married Fay Wenger of Elkhart County, on September 5, 1937. Three children living; one deceased. Also reared a foster daughter. Installed as visiting brother at Olive, July 31, 1960. Ordained deacon September 10, 1961, by J. C. Wenger, if plans carried.

V

Biographical Sketches of the Ordained Men

MENNONITE AND AMISH MENNONITE CONFERENCES

HAROLD S. ALEXANDER, 1897-   Deacon   Prairie Street

Born at Bremen, Indiana, March 23, 1897. Married Susie Ellen Mishler of La-grange County, Indiana, July 28, 1918. Four children; adopted a fifth. He has been employed in a band instrument factory, as well as in a bakery. Ordained deacon in the Prairie Street congregation, Elkhart, by lot, March 24, 1935, by D. A. Yoder. Served until his resignation in 1953.

CHRISTIAN AUGSBURGER, 1821-1903   Preacher   Adams County

Born in Liberty Township, Tioga County, Pennsylvania, in 1821. Married Barbara Leighty on December 1, 1859. Nine sons and seven daughters. Ordained preacher about 1866. A man of deep piety. Died near Berne, Adams County, Indiana, January 19, 1903. Funeral service in the Defenseless Mennonite church building by Bishops Moses Brenneman and J. M. Shenk. Following the funeral there was some anxiety as to whether he was really dead, and burial was deferred for two additional days.

CHRISTIAN BARE, 1816-1904   Preacher   Yellow Creek

Born in Rockingham County, Virginia, May 6, 1816. His parents later settled in Columbiana County, Ohio. Married Esther Shank (1815-1906) on October 16, 1837. Seven children. Ordained preacher in the Riley Creek meetinghouse, Allen County, Ohio, in 1856. Removed to Indiana in 1857 and served in the Elkhart County churches. In the division of 1872 he followed Jacob Wisler. Died in Elkhart County, Indiana, September 24, 1904, at the advanced age of 88. Burial in East Cemetery, Yellow Creek. J. F. Funk gave him a warm testimony when he died.

JOHN BARE, 1810-1855   Preacher   Holdeman

Born in Virginia, December 2, 1810, son of John Bare, 1774-1845, who was later one of the first deacons in Columbiana County, Ohio. Preacher John Bare was the older brother of Preacher Christian Bare. Married Anna Blosser (daughter of Preacher John Blosser, 1780-1864, of Virginia and later of Ohio). Seven children. Lived west of Waterford, Indiana, and was a farmer. Died January 14, 1855.

JOHN H. BARE, 1869-1930   Deacon, Preacher   Salem

Born in Union Township, Elkhart County, Indiana, May 12, 1869, son of Noah and Hannah (Nold) Bare. Married Lovina Rohrer (1873-1945) on January 31, 1891. Two children: Nettie and Serenus. United with the Salem congregation May 12, 1894. Ordained deacon, by lot, December 9, 1894. Ordained preacher at Salem, also by lot, November 26, 1905, by David Burkholder. Farmer. Died May 12, 1930. Burial in Yellow Creek Cemetery.

EZRA BEACHY, 1901-   Preacher, Bishop   Pinckney

Born at Arthur, Illinois, July 29, 1901. Married Bertha Nohejl of Chicago on January 12, 1935. Five children. Ordained preacher at what is now the First Mennonite Church, Fort Wayne, Indiana, October 5, 1941, by D. D. Troyer. Ordained bishop at Pinckney, September 7, 1952, by T. E. Schrock. Received Th.B. degree from Goshen College Biblical Seminary in 1934. Resides in Goshen since 1957.

NEIL BEACHY, 1922-   Preacher   Belmont
    Born at Plain City, Ohio, April 2, 1922. Married Emma Kramer on April 26, 1942.
Four children. Ordained preacher in the Owl Creek meetinghouse, Beaver, Ohio, June
28, 1953. Received into Indiana-Michigan Conference in June 1958.

LEROY BECHLER, 1925-   Preacher   Ninth Street Mennonite, Saginaw
    Born at Pigeon, Michigan, December 4, 1925. Married Irene Springer of Fisher,
Illinois, August 24, 1950. Three children. Ordained preacher at Pigeon, Michigan,
December 2, 1951, by J. D. Graber. Received B.R.E. degree from Hesston College in
?950. Removed to California in 1961.

SIMON H. BECK, 1883-1944   Deacon   Leo
    Born in Fulton County, Ohio, February 11, 1883. Married Caroline Yoder of Allen
County, Indiana, February 19, 1903. Four children. Ordained deacon at Leo, Indiana,
by lot, October 3, 1926, by Oscar S. Hostetler. Died November 28, 1944. Burial in
Leo Cemetery.

CHRISTIAN C. BEERY, 1831-1900   Preacher   Caledonia
    Born in Virginia, August 8, 1831. Ordained preacher in Fairfield County, Ohio,
June 8, 1865. (Henry B. Brenneman was ordained deacon the same day.) Henry's
brother, George Brenneman, bishop of Putnam County, Ohio, performed the ordinations. In 1885 Christian Beery moved from Medina County, Ohio, to Kent County,
Michigan, where he served the remainder of his life, except for a few months in Dickson County, Tennessee, in 1897. Died in Kent County, Michigan, June 29, 1900. Burial
in Caledonia Cemetery.

CHRISTIAN D. BEERY, 1815-1878   Deacon, Preacher, Bishop   Pleasant Hill
    Born in Rockingham County, Virginia, June 20, 1815. As a boy he removed with
his parents to Fairfield County, Ohio. Married Nancy Blosser (1818-1878) when she was
sixteen years of age. They united with the church a few years later. In 1838 they removed to Hocking County, Ohio, and in 1852 to Franklin County, Ohio, where he was
ordained deacon. In 1855 they settled in Allen County, Ohio, and in August 1865
they removed to Branch County, Michigan. Ordained preacher, August 26, 1867, by
John M. Brenneman. Ordained bishop in the Pleasant Hill congregation, December
22, 1869, apparently by Henry Yother. In 1873 he removed to Jewell County, Kansas,
but returned to Branch County the next year. Died March 15, 1878, forty hours after
the death of his wife. The Herald of Truth reports: "He served the church faithfully,
and in the discharge of duties devolving upon him as bishop, he was a man of great
usefulness, and will be greatly missed, not only at home, in his own church, but also
in the surrounding churches." The funeral sermons for Christian and Nancy were
preached by J. J. Weaver, J. F. Funk, and Peter Long, a Brethren minister. He was
an uncle of J. M. Brenneman, Daniel Brenneman, and their brothers.

DANIEL F. BEERY, 1842-1911   Deacon   Pleasant Hill
    Born in Hocking County, Ohio, April 27, 1842. He was a brother of Preacher
Harvey Friesner's wife, Catherine. As a boy he removed with his parents to Franklin
County, Ohio, and later to Allen County, Ohio. Married Rebecca Brenneman on
December 22, 1864. Twelve children. Soon after marriage they located in Branch
County, Michigan, where in 1865 he joined the Mennonite Church. He was later or-
dained deacon, and served until the dissolution of the congregation. Died in Branch
County, Michigan, March 19, 1911, six years after the Pleasant Hill meetinghouse had
been sold to the Mennonite Brethren in Christ Church.

DANIEL H. BENDER, 1866-1945   Preacher, Bishop   Prairie Street
    Born at Grantsville, Maryland, January 8, 1866. Married (1) Ida E. Miller (1876-
1902) of Tub (Springs), Pennsylvania, July 19, 1896. Three children. Married (2) Sallie

L. Miller of Springs, Pennsylvania, April 1, 1906. Two children. Married (3) Anna M. Kreider of Hesston, Kansas, March 27, 1929. Two children. Ordained preacher in what is now the Allegheny Conference in November 1887. Preached in the Prairie Street congregation 1904-6, during which time he was editor of the **Herald of Truth.** He later removed to Hesston where he served as president of Hesston College and Bible School, 1909-30. Ordained bishop in 1912. Died January 21, 1945.

GEORGE L. BENDER, 1867-1921   Deacon   Prairie Street

Born at Grantsville, Maryland, February 2, 1867. Married Elsie Kolb of Breslau, Ontario, October 24, 1896. Eight children. Ordained deacon in the Prairie Street congregation, July 28, 1907, by David Burkholder. Served as treasurer of the Mennonite Evangelizing Board of America, 1893-94; of the Mennonite Evangelizing and Benevolent Board, 1898-1905; of the Mennonite Board of Charitable Homes, 1899-1903; of the Mennonite Board of Charitable Homes and Missions, 1903-5; and of the Mennonite Board of Missions and Charities, 1906-20. Died January 17, 1921. Burial in Prairie Street Church Cemetery.

HAROLD S. BENDER, 1897-   Preacher   (Goshen College)

Born at Elkhart, Indiana, July 19, 1897, son of Deacon George L. Bender. Secured the M.A. degree at Princeton University, the Th.M. degree from Princeton Theological Seminary, and the Doctor of Theology degree at the University of Heidelberg, Germany. Married Elizabeth Horsch of Scottdale, Pennsylvania (daughter of John Horsch, historian), May 9, 1923. Two daughters. Served as instructor at Hesston College, 1918-20, and at Goshen College since 1924. He was dean of the college, 1931-44, and of the Goshen College Biblical Seminary since 1944. He has been president of the Mennonite Historical Society since its founding in 1927, editor of **The Mennonite Quarterly Review** since 1927, chairman of the Historical and Research Committee of Mennonite General Conference since 1947, member of the Mennonite Central Committee since 1930, and president of the Mennonite World Conference since 1952. He is the author of a number of books, and is the editor of the series, **Studies in Anabaptist and Mennonite History,** and of **The Mennonite Encyclopedia.** Ordained preacher in the Goshen College congregation, June 18, 1944, by D. A. Yoder, at the request of the Mennonite Board of Education, which request was endorsed by the Indiana-Michigan Conference.

URIE A. BENDER, 1925-   Preacher   (Mission Board)

Born at Baden, Ontario, January 2, 1925. Married Dorothy Marie Kipfer on June 1, 1946. Three daughters, but one deceased. Ordained preacher at Baden, February 26, 1950, by Moses H. Roth. Served as editor of the **Youth's Christian Companion,** 1955-61. Secretary for Literature Evangelism, Mennonite Board of Missions and Charities, 1960- . Member of conference, 1960- .

HERMAN BENTLER, 1821-1905   Deacon   Bowne

Born in Saxony, Germany, December 5, 1821. Came to America at twenty-two years of age. Married (1) Lydia Croft of Berlin, Ontario, in 1847; she died in 1850. Married (2) Catharine Schmitt (1832-1898) (daughter of Preacher George R. Schmitt of Waterloo, County, Ontario) in 1853. Two children to the first marriage and nine to the second. Located in Kent County, Michigan, in 1866, where he was ordained deacon on April 28, 1866, by John M. Brenneman. Served as deacon about thirty-nine years. Died April 9, 1905. Burial in Bowne Cemetery. Funeral sermons by Christian G. Wenger and Isaac Weaver.

JACOB A. BEUTLER, 1833-1886   Preacher, Bishop   Holdeman

Born near Richland, Ohio, in December 1833, son of John Beutler of Pabsbach, Germany, and nephew of Preacher Peter Beutler of Ashland County, Ohio. Came to Indiana in his youth. United with the Mennonite Church in 1852. Married (1)

Caroline Boyer (1837-1874) on December 13, 1860. Six children. Married (2) Mary Ressler (1843-1935) on April 16, 1876. Three children. Ordained preacher at the Holdeman Church, March 19, 1868, by Henry Yother. Ordained bishop at Yellow Creek, October 18, 1872, by John M. Brenneman. (John M. Christophel was ordained bishop the same day.) Bishops Beutler and Christophel served the Mennonite congregations west of Goshen (Yellow Creek, Holdeman, Olive, Nappanee, Christophel, Blosser, and Prairie Street). In that period the Mennonites also held services at the South Union Church, west of Nappanee; and at the Oak Grove meetinghouse, which is now the property of the United Missionary Church. Beutler died November 3, 1886. Burial in East Cemetery, Olive. I. B. Witmer said that he was a good preacher.

RALPH O. BIRKEY, 1917-   Preacher   Wayside

Born at Dewey, Illinois, May 27, 1917. Married Mary Schrock of Goshen, Indiana, May 25, 1945. Four children. Ordained preacher in the Bowne congregation, April 9, 1950, by T. E. Schrock, for district mission board service. Served in the Wayside congregation of the Upper Peninsula of Michigan since April 1950.

DEAN BIRKY, 1894-   Preacher   Hopewell

Born January 24, 1894, son of Bishop Jacob D. Birky. Married Hazel Fleener on December 5, 1917. Five children. Ordained preacher at the Hopewell Church, July 15, 1928, by D. D. Miller. Served until 1942.

EMANUEL S. BIRKY, 1900-   Preacher   English Lake

Born at Beemer, Nebraska, April 24, 1900. Married Elsie G. Good on December 15, 1921. Three children. Ordained preacher in the Hopewell congregation, for the English Lake mission outpost, October 2, 1955.

JACOB D. BIRKY, 1855-1926   Preacher, Bishop   Hopewell

Born at Morton, Illinois, July 25, 1855, son of Christian Birky of Germany and Catherine Mosemann of France. Married Emma Martin of Hopedale, Illinois, September 25, 1884. Eleven children. Ordained preacher, by lot, in 1895, by Joseph Schlegel of Milford, Nebraska. Ordained bishop in 1902 by the same bishop. Moved to the Hopewell congregation in 1920. He was a brother of Bishop John C. Birky of Hopedale, Illinois. Died July 12, 1926.

JACOB Z. BIRKY, 1880-   Deacon   Hopewell

Born July 17, 1880, son of Bishop John C. Birky of Hopedale, Illinois. Married Emma Oswald of Beemer, Nebraska, January 20, 1907. Seven children. Ordained deacon at the Hopewell Church, February 11, 1923, by D. J. Johns. Released from the office of deacon at his own request. Left the Mennonite Church about 1938 and united with the Calvary Baptist Church, Valparaiso, Indiana. Still living (1961).

JACOB K. BIXLER, 1877-1939   Preacher, Bishop   Holdeman, Prairie Street

Born at Winesburg, Holmes County, Ohio, September 5, 1877, son of John and Barbara (Huber) Bixler. At the age of five he moved to Indiana with his parents. Graduated from Wakarusa High School in 1898. Baptized at the Holdeman Church in 1895 by John F. Funk. Married Susie J. Bailey of Cullom, Illinois, December 22, 1904. One daughter. Jacob taught school 1899-1903. Ordained preacher in the Holdeman congregation, by lot, April 23, 1904, by Bishop David Burkholder. Ordained bishop at Yellow Creek, November 3, 1907, by Bishop Burkholder. Removed to Elkhart in 1914 and served as secretary of the district mission board, 1914-25. He was the bishop-superintendent of the mission congregations for many years. Died December 20, 1939. Burial in Prairie Street Church Cemetery.

JOSEPH S. BIXLER, 1813-1895   Deacon, Preacher, Bishop   Bower
Born in Fayette County, Pennsylvania, April 28, 1813. Joined the Mennonite Church in his early years. Married (1) Catharine Hunsicker on June 6, 1837; she died in 1855. Nine children. Married (2) Susanna Miller in 1857; she died in 1862. Married (3) Widow Mary (Mellinger) Yoder in 1863; she died in 1882. Ordained deacon in 1840. Removed to Mercer County, Pennsylvania, in 1848. Ordained preacher there, by lot, in 1848, by Bishop Rudolph Blosser of Mahoning County, Ohio, brother of Preacher John Bare's wife, Anna Blosser. In 1855 Joseph Bixler located in the vicinity of the Bower Mennonite Church, Owen County, Indiana, where he was almost immediately ordained bishop. The fall of 1855, upon the death of his wife, he returned to Mercer County, Pennsylvania. In 1865 he and his third wife removed to Mahoning County, Ohio, where he died March 10, 1895.

EZRA P. BLEILE, 1874-   Deacon   Nappanee (North)
Born at Nappanee, Indiana, March 15, 1874. Baptized at the West Market Street Amish Mennonite Church, December 19, 1891, by J. P. Smucker. Married (1) Sarah Ann Metzler of Wakarusa (daughter of Preacher Noah Metzler) on November 17, 1898. Nine children. Married (2) Widow Sadie Sherman in 1949. Ordained deacon at the Nappanee Mennonite Church, May 29, 1938, by D. A. Yoder.

JACOB BLEILE, 1841-1902   Preacher   Nappanee A.M.
Born in Wittenberg, Germany, April 22, 1841, uncle of Deacon Ezra P. Bleile. Married Rosanna Brier of Steinberg, Germany, May 19, 1868. Six children. Emigrated to America about 1877, a member of the Lutheran Church. United with the West Market Street Amish Mennonite congregation, where he was ordained preacher on April 4, 1885, by J. P. Smucker. Because of a conflict with Bishop Smucker, whom he considered too mild in his disciplinary work, he transferred his membership to the North Main Street Mennonite Church in Nappanee, where he served until about 1899. Died September 7, 1902. Burial in Union Center Cemetery.

ABRAHAM BLOSSER   Deacon   Pleasant Hill
Henry Yother of Reading, Illinois, went to the Pleasant Hill congregation in Branch County, Michigan, in 1868. The congregation there chose Abraham Blosser as deacon and he was ordained March 22, 1868, likely by lot. It is not known whether he is identical with Abraham M. Blosser who in 1907 left Texas and lived briefly in Kansas, and who visited Elkhart in that same year. Birth and death dates lost.

GEORGE Z. BOLLER, 1828-1883   Deacon   Maple Grove
Born in December 1828. Ordained deacon in 1857. A man of considerable ability. Served on the committee which prepared the German hymmbook **Die Allgemeine Lieder-Sammlung, 1871.** Died in Noble County, Indiana, May 30, 1883. Burial in Maple Grove Cemetery. Isaac Smucker preached in German and J. S. Coffman in English at his funeral.

EARLEY C. BONTRAGER, 1888-   Preacher, Bishop   Forks
Born in Lagrange County, Indiana, June 29, 1888. Married Delcie Mishler, (who had been born in Howard County, Indiana) on January 28, 1912. Four children. Farmer. Ordained preacher at the Forks Church, by lot, May 8, 1932, by D. J. Johns. Ordained bishop at the same place, by vote of the congregation, March 25, 1945, by Oscar S. Hostetler.

ELI A. BONTRAGER, 1861-1956   Preacher   Fairview, Midland, Bethel
Born at Shipshewana, Indiana, December 16, 1861. Married Katie J. Johns (sister of Bishop D. J. Johns) on May 3, 1885. Nine children. Worked in a furniture factory; later was a farmer. Ordained preacher at the West Market Street Amish Mennonite

Church, Nappanee, Indiana, September 23, 1900, by J. P. Smucker. In 1903 he moved from Nappanee to Fairview, Michigan, where he served until 1916, when he moved to Midland, Michigan. From 1938 to 1942 he served as preacher in the Bethel congregation, Ashley, Michigan. The last fourteen years of his life he again lived at Fairview. Died January 19, 1956, at 94.

ERIE E. BONTRAGER, 1896-   Preacher   Zion

Born at Middlebury, Indiana, April 19, 1896, one of the preacher sons of Eli A. Bontrager. Married Dorothea Liechty of Leo, Indiana, November 25, 1920. Seven children. Ordained preacher at Vestaburg, Michigan, November 4, 1928, by his uncle, D. J. Johns, at the request of the district mission board. Erie has been a farmer and a public school teacher.

FLOYD F. BONTRAGER, 1899-   Preacher, Bishop   Midland

Born at Nappanee, Indiana, November 30, 1899, another preacher son of Eli A. Bontrager. Married (1) Laura Emmert (sister of Deacon John L. Emmert) of Lagrange County, Indiana. One child. Married (2) Alma Schantz of Waterloo County, Ontario, December 4, 1928. Three children. Floyd has been a farmer and a mail carrier. Ordained preacher at Midland, by lot, September 5, 1926, by O. S. Hostetler. Ordained bishop, by lot, July 22, 1934, with O. S. Hostetler again performing the ceremony. In recent years he took charge of the mission outpost of the Midland congregation, called Herrick, which was granted its independence at the 1960 session of the Indiana-Michigan Conference.

JOSEPH J. BONTRAGER, 1830-1921   Preacher   Forks

Born in Somerset County, Pennsylvania, September 28, 1830. Married (1) Elizabeth Hershberger on March 21, 1852. Married (2) Barbara Moyer on January 29, 1882. Six children to the second marriage. Ordained preacher in the Forks congregation, by lot, June 2, 1867. In 1876 he withdrew from the Forks congregation and helped to found the Townline congregation which is now a part of the Conservative Mennonite Church. He felt that the Forks Church was losing plainness of apparel and the German language. In 1883 he moved to Kansas, but died November 13, 1921, in the state of Montana. At his death he was in the Old Order Amish Church.

ORVAN L. BONTRAGER, 1910-   Deacon   Locust Grove, Michigan

Born in Lagrange County, Indiana, May 11, 1910. Married Grace Mishler, of the same county, January 17, 1928. Five children. Ordained deacon in the Emma congregation, May 2, 1954, by Bishop O. S. Hostetler. Farmer.

OTIS J. BONTRAGER, 1894-   Deacon   Fairview

Born in Lagrange County, Indiana, June 13, 1894, son of E. A. Bontrager. Married Nora Miller of Kent County, Michigan, April 27, 1918. Five children. Ordained deacon in the Fairview congregation, February 28, 1932, by Menno Esch. Rural mail carrier.

WILLARD L. BONTRAGER, 1923-   Preacher   Cold Springs

Born at Fairview, Michigan, October 1, 1923, son of Otis J. Bontrager. Married Millie Gascho of Mio, Michigan, April 17, 1948. Four children. Carpenter. Ordained preacher in the Fairview congregation, to serve in the Cold Springs congregation, May 29, 1949, by Harvey Handrich.

RUDY S. BORNTRAGER, 1910-   Preacher   Fort Wayne

Born at Bucklin, Kansas, September 2, 1910. Married Clara Mast of Midland, Michigan, June 27, 1937. Seven children. Ordained preacher at Fort Wayne, Indiana, by congregational vote, September 30, 1951, by Bishop D. A. Yoder. Served the First Mennonite Church of Fort Wayne until 1959, when he substituted for Darwin O'Connell, who was on leave of absence from the Lima, Ohio, Mennonite Church.

VERNON E. BONTREGER, 1925-   Deacon, Preacher, Bishop   Clinton Frame

Born at Elkhart, Indiana, February 15, 1925. Married Miriam Louise Hoover of Goshen, Indiana, June 1, 1945. Six sons. Ordained deacon at Clinton Frame, January 23, 1949; preacher in the same congregation, October 22, 1950; and bishop in the same congregation, July 13, 1958; all ordinations performed by E. J. Yoder.

JACOB B. BOWER, 1803-1867   Preacher, Bishop   Bower

Born in Douglas Township, Montgomery County, Pennsylvania, February 3, 1803, great-great-grandson of immigrant Hans Bauer, 1670-1748/49 of Berks County, Pennsylvania. Moved to Westmoreland County, Pennsylvania, in 1816, locating near Alverton. Married (1) Anne Gardner, who died in 1835. Six children. Married (2) Catherine Durstine (1806-1879) of Westmoreland County, Pennsylvania, who bore him six more children. He was chosen by lot to preach, evidently while living in Westmoreland County. In 1853 he moved to Stark County, Ohio, and in 1857 to Marion Township, Owen County, Indiana, on the Clay County line, where he bought 120 acres for $2,200.00 in 1858. He donated the land for the church and cemetery of the congregation, which was named Bower in his memory. After he moved to Indiana he was ordained to the office of bishop. His ministry in the Bower congregation was short, for he died September 26, 1867, and is buried in the cemetery of the congregation.

ALDUS BRACKBILL, 1863-1941   Deacon, Preacher   Lancaster, Bowne

Born near Strasburg, Pennsylvania, January 28, 1863. Married Elizabeth A. Bender of Lancaster County, Pennsylvania, December 12, 1889. One son, Maurice T., was a teacher at Eastern Mennonite College. His trade was a punch and die builder. Ordained deacon at the East Chestnut Street Mennonite Church, Lancaster, Pennsylvania, December 11, 1904. In December 1907 he moved to Clarksville, Michigan, where he was immediately ordained preacher in the Bowne congregation, December 29, 1907, by J. K. Bixler. Died March 28, 1941. Burial in Weaver Cemetery, Harrisonburg, Virginia.

MARTIN L. BRANDENBERGER, 1922-   Preacher   Fair Haven

Born at New Haven, Indiana, September 24, 1922. Married Loraine A. Nofziger of Archbold, Ohio, March 19, 1947. Five children. Ordained preacher at the Leo Mennonite Church, February 1, 1959, for service in the Fair Haven congregation, 3101 West Taylor Street, Fort Wayne, Indiana. This church ministers to the colored people in a section which lies in the southwestern part of the city. Martin had served as a licensed minister for three years, from November 27, 1955, until his ordination as preacher.

DANIEL BRENNEMAN, 1834-1919   Preacher   Yellow Creek

Born near Bremen, Fairfield County, Ohio, June 8, 1834, great-grandson of immigrant Melchior Brenneman who migrated from Switzerland to Lancaster County, Pennsylvania, about 1714. Daniel's grandfather Abraham moved to Virginia and died there in 1815. Daniel's father Henry, 1791-1866, moved to Ohio. Daniel was brightly converted in 1856 at the age of twenty-two. Married (1) Susanna Keagy (1839-1908) of Augusta County, Virginia, March 22, 1857; she died in 1908. Ten children. Married (2) Ardella Mae Troyer (1879-   ) on April 28, 1910. Ordained preacher in Fairfield County, Ohio, by lot, in 1857. He was a man of marked ability as a preacher, both in German and in English. About April 1, 1864, he moved to Elkhart County, Indiana, and soon settled in Baugo Township near Jamestown. In a short time there was considerable tension between Bishop Jacob Wisler, the first active bishop in Northern Indiana, and Brenneman. Daniel had no scruples against English preaching, evening meetings, and singing bass, and when prayer meetings began to appear in the Mennonite Church, Daniel favored them also. John F. Funk and Daniel Brenneman were strong teammates for many years. In 1872, for example, he and Funk held the first evangelistic meetings in the Mennonite Church at Masontown, Pennsylvania. When a revival broke out in Ontario, Brenneman went to observe it firsthand. He was convinced that the movement was of God. He therefore defended revivalism and participated in the meetings with enthusiasm. The tension between the conference and John Krupp of Branch County, Michigan, who had accompanied Brenneman to Ontario in 1873, became so great that Krupp was finally excommunicated for his attitude of insubordination. This happened near the end of the year 1873. Brenneman was deeply hurt that his friend and colleague should be thus expelled. Brenneman also took a tolerant attitude toward the practice of baptism by immersion (although he himself was never immersed) and he had no objection to allowing women full freedom to testify of what Christ had done for them in the meetings of the church. The attitude of Brenneman was sufficiently divergent from that of the other ordained men of the Indiana Mennonite Conference that at a special ministers' meeting on April 25, 1874, he was declared as no longer being in fellowship. When notified of this action, Daniel fainted—the only time in his life that he did so. Immediately or soon thereafter a total of eighty-six men and women, whose names have been preserved, withdrew from the parent body to follow Brenneman into the newly organized Reformed Mennonite Church. He had been a strong and good leader in the Mennonite Church, the same body in which his able brothers, John M. and George, were serving as bishops, and in his newly organized Reformed Mennonite Church he also served effectively as a good and strong leader. Died September 10, 1919, after being sick only a day or so. Burial in Oak Ridge Cemetery, Goshen. His group later adopted the name, United Missionary Church, and their congregation on Eighth Street in Goshen is in his honor named the Brenneman Memorial Church.

HENRY B. BRENNEMAN, 1831-1887   Deacon   Prairie Street

Born near Bremen, Fairfield County, Ohio, August 12, 1831, "Brother Henry" was a brother of Daniel Brenneman and the even more famous Bishop John M. Brenneman. Married Matilda Blosser (1856-1895), but they never had any children. Ordained deacon in Fairfield County, Ohio, June 8, 1865. The fall of 1867 he moved to Elkhart, Indiana, where he worked for John F. Funk in the Mennonite Publishing Company. Died at Elkhart on September 28, 1887. Burial in East Cemetery, Olive Church.

VIRGIL J. BRENNEMAN, 1921-   Preacher   Waterford

Born in Johnson County, Iowa, November 27, 1921. Received Th.B. degree from Goshen College Biblical Seminary in 1952. Did relief work in Holland, Germany, and France, 1946-48. Married Helen Good of Bladensburg, Maryland, November 3, 1947. Four children. Ordained preacher at Iowa City, Iowa, June 15, 1952, by D. J. Fisher. Served here until 1959. Pastor at Waterford, 1959- . Currently (1961) a part-time student, Goshen Seminary.

JOHN F. BRESSLER, 1881-1949   Preacher   Fort Wayne

Born in Juniata County, Pennsylvania, July 31, 1881. In the early years of the Mennonite mission in Fort Wayne, Indiana, he was an energetic worker. Ordained preacher at Fort Wayne, December 4, 1904, by David Burkholder of Nappanee. Married Anastracia Watson, of Fort Wayne, on January 29, 1905. The ceremony was performed by J. N. Kaufman of Rockton, Pennsylvania, later a missionary to India. In July 1905, B. B. King replaced Bressler as superintendent of the Fort Wayne Mission, and the Bresslers went to Idaho and later to Oregon. In 1908 they opened the First Mennonite Mission in Portland, only to return to Pennsylvania in 1909. Died in Lebanon County, Pennsylvania, August 10, 1949.

JONAS A. BRUBAKER, 1850-1932   Deacon   Olive

Born in Juniata County, Pennsylvania, November 4, 1850. Came to Elkhart County, Indiana, in October 1872, where he married Sarah Yoder on November 6, 1873. Four children. He and his wife lived one mile east and three-fourth mile north of the Olive Church. In 1879 he was converted and joined the Mennonite Church. Ordained deacon at Olive, April 24, 1886, by Bishop Henry Miller of the Shore Church, who officiated because of the illness of Bishop J. A. Beutler. Died in Elkhart County, Indiana, December 26, 1932. Burial in Olive Cemetery. His sister Anna was the mother of Dr. William B. Page, who with J. A. Ressler went to India as the first missionaries of the Mennonite Church.

DANIEL BRUNDAGE, 1812-1895   Preacher, Bishop   Holdeman

Born in the Markham District, York County, Ontario, near Toronto, Canada, February 16, 1812. Married (1) Mollie Gayman, of Canada, in 1836. She is said to have taught him to read after his ordination, which took place in the year 1845 at the Schmitt Church, Vaughan Township, York County, Ontario. Four children. Married (2) Mary Beutler (1831-1896) (sister of Bishop J. A. Beutler) on January 2, 1877. No children to the second wife. By trade he was a millwright. His first wife was a sister to Bishop Christian Gayman of Ontario. He seems to have had financial difficulties in Ontario which put his ministry under a cloud. He moved to Indiana in 1858, where he was able to regain financial security and where his ministry was recognized. He moved to Morgan County, Missouri, in 1869, where he was ordained bishop on May 28, 1870. In 1873 he moved to McPherson County, Kansas, only to return to Indiana in 1890. Died December 14, 1895. Burial in East Cemetery, Olive. John F. Funk and D. H. Bender preached his funeral sermons. There is a tradition that in his early years in Indiana he preached from a table (not a pulpit), and in clean working clothes.

JAMES BUCHER, 1887-   Preacher   Hopewell, Berea

Born at Nappanee, Indiana, December 31, 1887. United with the Holdeman Mennonite Church on September 20, 1914. Married Fannie Mills of Goshen, Indiana, March 20, 1909. Three children. Transferred to the Hopewell congregation at Kouts, Indiana, March 4, 1920, on which date he was ordained preacher by J. K. Bixler. Served at Hopewell, 1920-23; at Berea, 1923-32; and in the Pacific Coast Conference, 1932- .

IRVIN E. BURKHART, 1896-   Preacher   Goshen College

Born in Drayton, Ontario, August 8, 1896. Married Gladys Viola Loucks of Scottdale, Pennsylvania, August 16, 1927. Three children. Ordained preacher at Floradale, Ontario, June 11, 1922, by Bishop Abraham Gingrich, at the request of the Ontario rural mission board and approved by vote of the congregation. Served as pastor at Clarence Center, New York, the summers of 1922, 1923, and 1924. Served as minister in charge of the Hesston, Kansas, congregation, 1929-34, and as a minister in the Goshen College congregation from 1935. He has an A.B. degree from Goshen College, 1926; an M.A. degree from the University of Pittsburgh, 1929; and a Th.M. degree from Southern Baptist Theological Seminary, 1929. For a generation he served as field secretary of Goshen College.

DAVID BURKHOLDER, 1835-1923   Preacher, Bishop   Nappanee

Born in Beaver Township, Mahoning County, Ohio, September 21, 1835. His father Abraham was the son of Preacher David Burkholder of Virginia and the grandson of Peter Burkholder. (Abraham Burkholder married Barbara Shank, daughter of Preacher John Shank, who moved from Virginia to Mahoning County, Ohio, late in life.) David accompanied his father to Indiana on a business trip in January 1854 and remained for the winter, working as fireman in William Funk's sawmill, about six miles south of Elkhart. In May 1855 David's father returned to Indiana to buy a farm. The farms of Harrison Township, where many Mennonites were already living, were too expensive; so he finally purchased a farm one mile south of Wislertown, which is now known as Locke. The land was not yet cleared. In August 1863 David Burkholder returned to Indiana to live. He had employed two Culp brothers to "deaden" sixty acres of land. By the time he arrived they had cleared ten acres for him, and John Ringenberg, the Amish Mennonite preacher of West Market Street, Nappanee, had sown wheat on these ten acres. Married Mary Bucher (1838-1926) of Beaver Township, Mahoning County, Ohio, September 27, 1863. They were the parents of a daughter, Susanna, who married Nelson B. Maust. The Mausts in turn had a son Henry who made a painting of his grandfather, Bishop David Burkholder, which painting is reproduced in this book. When the draft was first set up in Indiana, "conscientious exempts" were required to pay a fee of $200.00. By the year 1864 this figure had risen to $400.00, but since David Burkholder was not yet a member of the church when he was drafted in the fall of 1864, it was necessary for him to hire a substitute to serve in his stead as a soldier. The hiring of this substitute cost him $600.00. In 1865 David and Mary Burkholder were baptized and united with the Yellow Creek Mennonite Church. He was ordained preacher in the Blosser meetinghouse, May 15, 1880, by J. M. Christophel, to serve "in the Blosser district." Following the close of John F. Funk's service as bishop in the Elkhart County congregations, J. S. Shoemaker ordained David Burkholder as his successor on February 4, 1904, in the Holdeman meetinghouse. He served faithfully in this office until the year 1918, when he asked to be relieved because of his age. He died January 8, 1923, at the advanced age of 87 years. E. S. Mullett and Daniel Kauffman preached his funeral sermons at Nappanee two days later. Burial in South Cemetery, Yellow Creek. I. B. Witmer said that he was not a fluent speaker, but a man of tact and good judgment.

LOWELL H. BURKHOLDER, 1912-   Deacon   White Cloud

Born at Cullom, Illinois, September 15, 1912. Married Helen Yoder of Elkhart, Indiana, March 4, 1934. Ten children (nine living). Ordained deacon at White Cloud, May 18, 1952, by C. C. Culp.

NEIL C. BUSKIRK, 1920-   Deacon   Zion

Born at Vestaburg, Michigan, June 10, 1920, son of Preacher Royal A. Buskirk. Married Ethel Dintaman of Ithaca, Michigan, April 21, 1945. Two children. Ordained deacon at the Zion Church, Vestaburg, Michigan, May 26, 1946, by Edwin J. Yoder, at the request of the district mission board. Farmer.

ROYAL A. BUSKIRK, 1888-   Preacher   Zion

Born at Stanton, Montcalm County, Michigan, December 23, 1888. Married Sarah Martin of May City, Iowa, April 21, 1918. Seven children. United with the Bowne congregation in August 1913 and was baptized by Jacob P. Miller. Ordained preacher in the Oak Grove schoolhouse, near McBrides, Michigan, by congregational vote, November 27, 1917, by J. K. Bixler. Served the Zion congregation from 1917 to 1928. Farmer. Resides at Brutus, Michigan.

CHARLES M. BUTE, 1874-1959   Deacon   Clinton Brick

Born at Cullom, Livingston County, Illinois, September 1, 1874. Married Valeria A. Leatherman of Elkhart County, Indiana, January 1, 1897. Ten children. Ordained deacon at the Alpha Mennonite Church, Alpha, Minnesota, by lot, May 21, 1919, by J. M. Kreider. Served the Alpha congregation, 1919-28; the Clinton Brick congregation, 1928-32; and returned to the Alpha congregation and served there from 1932 until his death, which occurred June 5, 1959.

ALPHA L. BUZZARD, 1871-   Preacher   Belmont

Born at Goshen, Indiana, January 9, 1871, the seventh of the eleven children of Preacher Jacob C. Buzzard. Married Cora B. Shoemaker (daughter of Bishop J. S.

Shoemaker of Freeport, Illinois) on November 16, 1899. Seven children. Ordained preacher at Freeport, Illinois, September 2, 1906, by J. S. Shoemaker. Served the Union congregation at Washington, Illinois, from 1906 until 1929, and the Belmont congregation from 1931. Secretary of the Illinois Conference from 1916 to 1929.

JACOB C. BUZZARD, 1838-1880   Deacon (?), Preacher   Yellow Creek

Born in Elkhart County, Indiana, in November 1838. Married Elizabeth Kreider of Medina County, Ohio, November 21, 1867. Eleven children. The diaries of John F. Funk indicate that a Brother Buzzard was chosen as deacon in the Yellow Creek congregation, but because of dissatisfaction on the part of the congregation with the methods employed by the bishop, he was again released. Ordained preacher January 1, 1877. He had a very active ministry. He and Michael W. Shank, for example, made an extended trip to Canada in November 1879. John F. Funk characterizes him as "a good, zealous, and earnest teacher." A schoolteacher and farmer. Died June 11, 1880, of tuberculosis. Burial in East Cemetery, Yellow Creek. The Buzzard family came originally from Northampton County, Pennsylvania, and the German spelling of the name had been Boshart.

JOHN I. BYLER, 1881-   Preacher, Bishop   Gar Creek, Fort Wayne, Middlebury

Born in Pennsylvania, June 17, 1881. Married Amanda E. Troyer of Holmes County, Ohio, August 12, 1908. Ten children. Examined by the Mennonite Board of Missions and Charities and appointed as a full-time mission worker at Fort Wayne, Indiana, authorized to preach, and perform the duties of a mission worker. His first charge was Gar Creek, eleven miles east of Fort Wayne, and he also helped in the work of the Fort Wayne Mission. Ordained preacher in Ohio, February 15, 1917. He had been given charge of the Youngstown, Ohio, Mission in 1908. He also served at the Toronto Mission for five years, after which he returned to Youngstown, Ohio, for three more years. In 1917 he transferred to the Church of the Brethren, and on February 9, 1919, was ordained as an elder (bishop) in the Church of the Brethren. After his retirement, following thirty years of service in the Church of the Brethren, he was appointed as a worker under the Illinois Conference, and served at Sheffield. In 1953 he transferred to the Indiana Conference, and united with the Middlebury congregation.

ARTHUR R. CASH, 1922-   Deacon, Preacher   Fair Haven

Born at Pittsburg, Texas, November 26, 1922. Married Nancy F. Johnson of Rusk, Texas, January 2, 1942. Three daughters. Ordained deacon in the state of Washington in 1946, and preacher at Atlanta, Georgia, in 1958. United with the Mennonite Church, and was received as a minister at the June 1, 1960, session of the Indiana-Michigan Mennonite Conference. He has the distinction of being the first colored minister in the conference history.

HOWARD H. CHARLES, 1915-   Preacher   (East Goshen)

Born at Lititz, Pennsylvania, July 19, 1915. Married Miriam Stalter of Elida, Ohio, July 19, 1947. Two sons. Ordained preacher at the Lititz Mennonite Church, by lot, July 15, 1943, by Amos S. Horst. Served the Lititz congregation, 1943-47. He has a Th.B. degree from Goshen College Biblical Seminary, 1940; a B.D. degree from Union Theological Seminary, Richmond, Virginia, 1944; a Th.M. degree from Princeton Seminary, 1948; and a Ph.D. degree from the University of Edinburgh, 1958. He is Professor of New Testament in the Seminary at Goshen College. He worships with the East Goshen congregation.

ALLEN B. CHRISTOPHEL, 1892-1932   Preacher   Yellow Creek

Born near Wakarusa, Indiana, July 31, 1892, son of Bishop Jacob W. Christophel. Never married. Ordained preacher in the Yellow Creek congregation, March 30, 1924, by D. A. Yoder. At the time of the first World War he was imprisoned at Fort Leavenworth, Kansas, as a conscientious objector. Died July 20, 1932. Burial at Yellow Creek. He was a gifted minister and leader, and his sudden death from a heart attack was a severe blow to the congregation.

CHRISTIAN CHRISTOPHEL, 1820-1883   Preacher   Yellow Creek

Born in Westmoreland County, Pennsylvania, February 16, 1820, son of immigrant Jacob Christophel. Removed with his parents to Mahoning County, Ohio, in 1835. Married Anna Hoover (1823-1888) (sister of Mary Hoover who in turn became the wife of Bishop Jacob Wisler) on April 17, 1845. (Anna was born in Franklin County, Pennsylvania.) Six children. Christian came with his parents to Elkhart County, Indiana, in 1848. Ordained preacher at Yellow Creek, March 25, 1872, some two months after the Wisler division. Died October 12, 1883. Burial in East Cemetery, Yellow Creek.

ELIAS J. CHRISTOPHEL, 1868-1949   Deacon   Holdeman

Born in Union Township, Elkhart County, Indiana, June 8, 1868, son of the immigrant Jacob Christophel who came to America in 1840 (not the preacher). Married Martha Hartman of Livingston County, Illinois, December 20, 1893. Four children. Ordained deacon at Cullom, Illinois, June 12, 1909, by J. S. Shoemaker. Transferred to the Holdeman congregation as a member, May 17, 1931, and was accepted as a deacon in that congregation on April 24, 1934. Because of his age he resigned as deacon on April 13, 1948. Died July 5, 1949.

HAROLD M. CHRISTOPHEL, 1912-   Deacon   Bowne, Battle Creek

Born in Elkhart County, Indiana, June 11, 1912. Married Ruth Kauffman of Ionia County, Michigan, October 7, 1934. Seven children. Ordained deacon at the Bowne Mennonite Church, by lot, October 7, 1945, by T. E. Schrock. He is a nephew of Bishop Jacob W. Christophel and his maternal grandfather was Preacher Jonas Loucks. In recent years he has had charge of the outpost of the Bowne congregation in Battle Creek, Michigan.

HENRY CHRISTOPHEL, 1826-1881   Deacon   Olive

Born in Briffling, near Regensburg, Bavaria, Germany, July 24, 1826, brother of Bishop John M. Christophel. He was the fifth child of immigrant Christian Christophel, a brother of Preacher Jacob Christophel. He came to America in 1843, and to Elkhart County, Indiana, in 1848. His wife was Elizabeth Walter (1836-1918) (daughter of Justus and Elizabeth Walter). Six children. Ordained deacon in the Olive congregation, December 23, 1871, by C. D. Beery of Branch County, Michigan, (Henry Shaum was ordained preacher in the same service.) He appointed his oldest son Isaac as the "father" to his brothers and sisters, while on his deathbed. On the morning of his death he called in his children and his wife and gave them his dying admonition and blessing, one by one, and prayed with them. Died September 4, 1881, at the early age of 56. Burial in East Cemetery, Olive. The sermons were preached by Henry Shaum and J. S. Coffman.

ISAIAH CHRISTOPHEL, 1852-1912   Deacon   Salem

Born February 24, 1852, the first cousin of Bishop Jacob W. Christophel. Married Barbara Wenger on January 6, 1878. Four children. Ordained deacon at Salem, September 2, 1906, by David Burkholder. He was killed by lightning August 28, 1912, at the age of 60.

JACOB CHRISTOPHEL, 1782-1868   Preacher   Yellow Creek

Born at Rothenbach in the Palatinate, Germany, about twenty miles from Worms, late in December 1782. He was the son of Matthias Christophel, and his mother was a Decker. He came to America the summer of 1818, when thirty-six years of age. His passport indicates that he was five feet three inches in height, with blond hair, blond beard, and light gray eyes. His face was marked by smallpox pits. He lived in Westmoreland County, Pennsylvania, 1818-24. In 1824 he removed to Allegheny County, Pennsylvania, and in 1827 he was ordained preacher in Westmoreland County, Pennsylvania. On May 2, 1813, while still in Europe, he married Gertrude Berg, who died in 1816, leaving him with a daughter. His second marriage was to Susan Neff on July 29, 1817; she died in 1830 after bearing six children. His third wife was Barbara Bare (1801-1874) (daughter of Deacon John Bare, formerly of Rockingham County, Virginia, but who located in Beaver Township, Columbiana County, Ohio). (Barbara was also the sister of Preachers John and Christian Bare.) In April 1835 Jacob and family settled in Mahoning County, Ohio, and the spring of 1848 they removed to Elkhart County, Indiana. They arrived June 5, 1848. He bought a farm three miles west of New Paris with fifteen acres of cleared land, a log cabin, and a barn. He was a farmer and linen weaver. His third wife was the mother of seven children. Jacob became a United States citizen on February 25, 1831, at Pittsburgh, Pennsylvania. His grandson, Wesley W. Christophel, 1878-   , has worked out a complete genealogical record of all the Christophel immigrants and their descendants. The last three years of his life Preacher Jacob was severely afflicted with palsy. He died on December 3, 1868, at the advanced age of eighty-five years, eleven months, and three days. His funeral sermons were preached by J. J. Weaver of the Shore congregation and by Bishop John M. Brenneman of Elida, Ohio. Burial in East Cemetery, Yellow Creek. Soon after 1850 a log church was built on his farm east of Foraker; the deed is dated April 22, 1854. The church was called the Christophel Church.

JACOB W. CHRISTOPHEL, 1856-1937   Preacher, Bishop   Yellow Creek

Born near Wakarusa, Indiana, July 23, 1856, son of John Christophel and his wife Elizabeth Reed, and grandson of Preacher Jacob Christophel. Married Anna Hoover (1859-1936) (daughter of Deacon Daniel Hoover, and niece of Mary Hoover Wisler, wife of Bishop Jacob Wisler) on January 18, 1885. Three children, including Preacher Allen Christophel. Ordained preacher at Yellow Creek, July 23, 1893, by J. F. Funk and John M. Shenk. Ordained bishop at Yellow Creek, April 28, 1918, by J. K. Bixler and D. J. Johns. Died January 11, 1937.

JAMES L. CHRISTOPHEL, 1932-   Preacher   Fish Lake

Born in Elkhart County, Indiana, August 21, 1932, great-great-grandson of immigrant Jacob Christophel. Licensed to preach at the Mennonite Home Mission, Chicago, in September 1955, by C. Warren Long. Ordained preacher at the Fish Lake Mennonite Church, September 9, 1956, by Peter B. Wiebe. Married Mary Martin of Goshen, Indiana, June 19, 1954. Three children. Received the Th.B. degree from Goshen College Biblical Seminary in 1955.

JOHN M. CHRISTOPHEL, 1819-1886   Preacher, Bishop   Yellow Creek

Born near Regensburg, Bavaria, Germany, February 2, 1819, brother of Deacon Henry, and son of Christian Christophel, who in turn was a brother of Preacher Jacob Christophel. He came to America with his father in 1840. Married Harriet Reed (1824-1896) of Rockingham County, Virginia, January 1, 1847; she was then living in Columbiana County, Ohio. John and Harriet settled in Mahoning County, Ohio, until the year 1850, when they came to Elkhart County, Indiana. Nine children. A preacher was ordained at Yellow Creek on May 31, 1862, if previous plans carried. This is likely the ordination date of John M. Christophel. Ordained bishop October 18, 1872, along with Jacob A. Beutler, by John M. Brenneman of Ohio. Served as a preacher for twenty-six years and a bishop for thirteen years. He became inactive as a bishop in 1884. Died May 31, 1886. Burial at Yellow Creek.

DANIEL H. COFFMAN, 1859-1941   Deacon   Prairie Street, Olive, Clinton Brick

Born at Dale Enterprise, Virginia, April 4, 1859, son of Bishop Samuel Coffman of Virginia. Married Sarah R. Guyer of Rockingham County, Virginia, February 11, 1883. Eleven children. Ordained deacon in the Prairie Street congregation, by lot, March 9, 1893, by John F. Funk. Served in that congregation until 1899, when he transferred to the Olive Church where he remained until 1904. In the latter year he removed to the Clinton Brick congregation where he served for thirty-seven years. In his early years at Clinton Brick he worked with Deacon Jacob Hershberger, but soon after the organization of the church in Middlebury, Hershberger transferred to that congregation, after which Daniel was left as the sole deacon at Clinton Brick. Daniel was an energetic man, a brother of the great evangelist, John S. Coffman. He succeeded in getting the Clinton Brick congregation to have young people's meeting every Sunday evening. He also promoted the use of Sunday-school and church periodicals and urged the need of a church library, which led to the establishment of one at Clinton Brick. Died August 29, 1941. Burial in Clinton Brick Cemetery.

JOHN S. COFFMAN, 1848-1899   Preacher   Prairie Street

Born in Rockingham County, Virginia, October 16, 1848, son of Bishop Samuel Coffman. He was brightly converted in the year 1861 and was baptized in a stream, as was the custom in the Mennonite Church of that period, and received into the fellowship of the Mennonite Church in Virginia on July 4, 1861. He fled north during the Civil War to escape military service. Ordained preacher in the Bank meetinghouse in Virginia, by lot, July 18, 1875. He became perhaps the most effective preacher in the Mennonite Church. Married Elizabeth J. Heatwole of Rockingham County, Virginia, November 11, 1869. Seven children, including Bishop S. F. Coffman. Served in the Virginia Mennonite Church until 1879, when he moved to Elkhart County, Indiana, to become assistant editor of the **Herald of Truth,** and later a writer of Sunday-school materials. The **Herald of Truth** reported editorially on August 1, 1899, on the occasion of his death, "as a fluent speaker he had few equals, and his earnest, eloquent appeals to the unsaved to forsake sin and turn to God were richly blessed." Coffman was a man of fasting and prayer, most earnest and devoted to Christ. He began his evangelistic career, a rare and somewhat misunderstood calling at that time, by holding a series of meetings in the Bowne congregation, Kent County, Michigan, in June 1881. There were nine converts. In December of that year he held another series of meetings at Masontown, Pennsylvania, with twelve converts. In 1882 there were fifteen converts at Cullom, Illinois. Through the years he continued to hold evangelistic services in many areas throughout the Mennonite Church. In 1891, for example, he labored for six weeks in Ontario and won about one hundred and forty converts. He sometimes prayed for an entire night during his evangelistic activity. Perhaps the greatest project of his life was the establishment of Elkhart Institute, which in 1903 became Goshen College. He had a profound appreciation for the Gospel of Christ. In one of his letters he wrote, "Oh, how different are our lives when stepping out of the bondage of fear into the rest and freedom of faith! This is a precious truth that so many fail to see; or shall I say, that only few see. Yes, it is the latter. I find that only here and there one can understand me when I speak of these things."

In a letter written to his young friend and fellow minister, A. D. Wenger, while in the Orient, Coffman wrote: "Yes, I feel that I am living for the church which maintains the doctrine of Him whose feet pressed the valleys and hills of Palestine, who wept over Jerusalem, who lived in the spirit of sacrifice which would make this world glorious, who died for the sins of the world, who is waiting in glory for the time when He shall come to take us to Himself. I am glad that the church has wakened up to the necessity of establishing her institutions and doing vigorous evangelistic and mission work. I think I have lived for this. . . Your journey is a great one indeed. God be your strength. He will be with you to the ends of the earth. No, I shall never look on the Holy Sepulchre, Mount Calvary, Cedron, Gethsemane, Olivet, but I expect to see Him who made these places sacred. Beholding Him I shall be satisfied, when I awake in His likeness." In the year 1899, when Coffman was but fifty years of age, his health collapsed. M. S. Steiner, his biographer, writes: "On Saturday eve, July 22, 1899, at five o'clock, when the sun was sinking in the west and leaving a glimmering light, and the whistles of the factories announced the end of toil for the day and week, and the shadows of the evening gathered in from the east, the spirit of J. S. Coffman took its flight, to be with God who gave it." His body lies buried alongside that of his devoted wife in the cemetery of the Prairie Street Mennonite Church on Hively Avenue, Elkhart, Indiana.

JAMES COYLE, 1826-1906   Preacher   Pleasant Valley

Born in Westmoreland County, Pennsylvania, September 28, 1826. Married Malinda Freed of Stark County, Ohio, February 10, 1848. Three sons and three daughters. Removed to De Kalb County, Indiana, in 1864. Ordained preacher in the Pleasant Valley congregation of De Kalb County, June 28, 1868, apparently by George Brenneman of Putnam County, Ohio. Those who knew him felt that he had an honest and sincere and good heart, but he was not at all gifted as a speaker. J. S. Hartzler reported that he was ordained by lot when fifteen of the sixteen members of the congregation had voted for Eli Stofer. In October 1905 he was rendered almost helpless by a stroke. Died June 24, 1906, at the age of 79. Buried in Fairfield Center Cemetery. John F. Funk and Eli Stofer preached his funeral sermons.

AMOS S. CRIPE, 1856-1938   Preacher   Shore

Born in the year 1856. Married (1) Rebecca Nusbaum (1855-1923). Married (2) Noah Grabill's widow, Sarah Weaver Grabill (1862-1945). Ordained preacher in the Shore congregation, November 13, 1887, by Henry A. Miller. Amos preached long sermons, up to ninety minutes in length, and sometimes prayed as long as twenty minutes. He was a very devout man and one of the last ministers in the Indiana-Michigan Conference to wear a beard. Died June 20, 1938. Burial in Miller Cemetery, one mile east of the Shore Church.

ORVIL J. CROSSGROVE, 1919-   Preacher   New Bethel

Born in Fulton County, Ohio, March 16, 1919. Married Mary Luella Neuhouser of Leo, Indiana (daughter of J. S. Neuhouser), on June 1, 1941. Six children. Ordained preacher in the New Bethel congregation, Ossian, Indiana, by lot, July 15, 1952, by Ray F. Yoder.

ELLIS B. CROYLE, 1930-   Preacher   Maple Grove

Born at Thomas Mills, Somerset County, Pennsylvania, August 1, 1930. Married Ruth Charlotte Hertzler (daughter of Silas Hertzler of Goshen College), on September 12, 1953. Three children. Received the B.D. degree from Goshen College Biblical Seminary in 1955. Ordained preacher in the Maple Grove congregation, Topeka, Indiana, October 17, 1954, by E. J. Yoder. Prior to that time he had served as a licensed minister; the date of his license, granted by E. J. Yoder at Topeka, was October 4, 1953.

JAMES M. CULBERTSON, c.1835-c.1908   Preacher   Holdeman

The exact date of Culbertson's birth is not known, but his first wife was Anna Hartman (1839-1889) (daughter of Preacher John Hartman of Ashland County, Ohio). (Her body is buried in the Olive Cemetery.) Ordained preacher in the Holdeman congregation, by lot (eight nominees), November 2, 1871, by C. D. Beery of Branch County, Michigan. He seems to have remained active as a Mennonite preacher until 1880 or 1881. He apparently was for a time affiliated with the Reformed Mennonite

Church of Daniel Brenneman; however, at a certain point he absconded, taking with him another man's wife. He seems initially to have located in Ohio, but in 1893 John S. Coffman found him cutting meat in the village of Shipshewana. His second wife was Mamie Fought of Lagrange County, Indiana, with whom he had one son. He became separated from his second wife. His relations with his family seem to have been strained. His great-nephew, T. R. Culbertson, believes that he died about the year 1908 and that his body was buried in an abandoned cemetery near Ansonia, Darke County, Ohio.

ABRAHAM CULP, 1838-1910　　　　　　Deacon　　　　　　Holdeman

Born in Mahoning County, Ohio, September 30, 1838. Came with his parents to Indiana in 1852. United with the Mennonite Church in 1867. Married Anna Blosser on November 11, 1866. Five children. Ordained deacon at Holdeman on April 4, 1886, by J. A. Beutler. (Amos Mumaw was ordained preacher the same day.) He was a quiet, unassuming man. Died near Wakarusa on November 4, 1910. His funeral sermons were preached by Henry Weldy and J. F. Funk.

CLAUDE C. CULP, 1893-1953　　　　Preacher, Bishop　　　　Pleasantview

Born in Harrison Township, Elkhart County, Indiana, May 22, 1893. Married Emma Habig of Garrett, Indiana, March 12, 1919. Two daughters. Ordained preacher in the Yellow Creek congregation, December 23, 1917, by J. K. Bixler, at the request of the district mission board. Ordained bishop at White Cloud, Michigan, August 31, 1947, by T. E. Schrock. Farmer. Held many series of evangelistic meetings and Bible conferences. Died May 18, 1953.

ABRAHAM W. DETWEILER, 1828-1912　　Preacher　　Caledonia, Maple River

Ordained preacher in the North Woolwich congregation of Ontario. His wife was Barbara Koch. Moved to Kent County, Michigan, in 1864, and attended the Caledonia congregation. He seems to have been temporarily silenced around the year 1872 for "disorderly conduct," which probably meant that he was too revivalistic. In 1879, his ministry having been restored, he located with the Maple River congregation at Brutus, Michigan. John F. Funk seems to have again temporarily silenced him in 1896. Died in 1912.

CHRISTIAN W. DETWEILER, 1845-1917　　　　Preacher　　　　Maple River

Born December 31, 1845. Married Susanna Johnson on October 3, 1865. Eight children. Ordained preacher in the Maple River congregation, by lot (three nominees), summer of 1888, by Henry Shaum. Died April 1, 1917.

IRVIN R. DETWEILER, 1873-1946　　　　Preacher　　　　Maple Grove

Born at Souderton, Pennsylvania, August 24, 1873. Grew up in Sterling, Illinois. Married (1) Bertha Zook on June 4, 1902. One adopted son and two children of their own. Married (2) Esther Mishler on August 23, 1937. Irvin and Bertha served as missionaries to India, 1902-4. Ordained preacher at Maple Grove, January 1, 1905, by Jonathan Kurtz. Received the B.A. degree from Goshen College in 1911, and the B.D. degree from Garrett Biblical Institute in 1923. He was an instructor in Goshen College, 1912-16, and dean of the Bible School, 1916-19. He was acting president of Goshen College, 1919-22. About 1923 he transferred his membership to the Central Conference of Mennonites, after which he served as pastor of the Eighth Street Mennonite Church, Goshen, Indiana, 1923-31. He taught at Bluffton College, 1930-36. He was also pastor at the Normal, Illinois, Mennonite Church, 1936-41. In his last years he served as a Bible teacher in the Goshen High School. Died of a heart attack February 22, 1946. Burial in Elkhart Prairie (formerly Alwine) Cemetery southeast of Goshen.

J. ROBERT DETWEILER, 1929-   Preacher   College Mennonite

Born at Norristown, Pennsylvania, November 29, 1929, son of the (late) Calvary Hour radio preacher, William G. Detweiler, and his wife Anna (Landes). Received the B.A. degree from Eastern Mennonite College, 1951; the B.D. from Faith Theological Seminary, 1954; and was studying for the Th.M. when his father's sudden death removed him and his twin brother Bill from the classroom. Licensed as a preacher to serve the Martins congregation in Ohio, August 21, 1955, by O. N. Johns. Ordained preacher at Wooster, Ohio, July 28, 1957, by O. N. Johns and Reuben Hofstetter. Married Marjorie Ellen Springer of Hopedale, Illinois, June 7, 1959. Installed as associate pastor of the College Mennonite Church, September 25, 1960, by John H. Mosemann and S. C. Yoder.

ALLEN B. EBERSOLE, 1906-   Preacher (Bishop)   Fort Wayne

Born at Roseland, Nebraska, January 18, 1906. Married Nellie Mae Miller of Lagrange County, Indiana, May 14, 1933. Two daughters and son (deceased). Ordained preacher in the Prairie Street congregation, January 5, 1941, by D. A. Yoder and E. J. Yoder, at the request of the district mission board. Served as pastor at Fort Wayne until 1952, when he transferred to the Mennonite mission, Canton, Ohio. Ordained bishop at Canton on September 27, 1953. Currently serving as head of the Adriel School, a Mennonite institution for retarded children, West Liberty, Ohio.

REUBEN R. EBERSOLE, 1878-1960   Preacher   Pleasant Valley

Born at Sterling, Illinois, February 28. 1878, brother of Mayor Frank S. Ebersole of Goshen. Graduated from the Junior College department of Goshen College in 1905. Taught school in Adams and De Kalb counties, Indiana. Ordained preacher in De Kalb County, by unanimous vote of the congregation, May 8, 1906, by David Burkholder. After a time he decided to prepare himself to be a medical missionary. He went to the Medical School of Indiana University, 1907-09. The fall of 1909, he did not return to school, broke an engagement to be married, and disappeared. In the course of time he turned up in the city of Chicago, where he worked most of his life as a postal clerk. He was found dead on April 25, 1960, and it is believed that he had passed away the previous night. Burial in Violett Cemetery, south of Goshen. Reuben published articles in the Gospel Witness for 1905, pages 174, 182.

GEORGE S. EBY, 1926-   Deacon   Petoskey

Born at Brutus, Michigan, May 7, 1926, son of Jeremiah B. Eby. Married Naomi B. Babcock of Midland, Michigan, July 2, 1947. Three children. Ordained deacon at Petoskey on May 15, 1955. Removed to California in October 1958.

JEREMIAH B. EBY, 1891-   Deacon   Maple River

Born August 2, 1891. Married Mary Shaum on September 19, 1915. Eight children, including Deacon George E. Eby. Ordained deacon at Maple River, September 4, 1932, and served there three years.

JOHN L. EMMERT, 1884-1932   Deacon   Maple Grove

Born at Topeka, Indiana, July 27, 1884. Married Grace Plank of Garden City, Missouri, March 17, 1907. Seven children. Ordained deacon April 4, 1913, by D. J. Johns. Served two years. He was the father-in-law of David Esch, and brother of Mrs. Myron (Bertha) Short.

J. FREDERICK ERB, 1922-   Preacher, Bishop   Detroit

Born at Waterloo, Ontario, January 24, 1922. Married Fern Troyer of Elkhart, Indiana, June 6, 1950. Three children. Received B.R.E. degree from Goshen College Biblical Seminary in 1950. Ordained preacher in the Erb Street Mennonite meetinghouse, Waterloo, Ontario, August 13, 1950, by J. B. Martin. United with the Indiana-Michigan Conference in 1952. Ordained bishop at the Detroit Mennonite Church, September 13, 1953, by Ezra Beachy. Served as pastor of the Detroit congregation, 1950-55, then removed to Sterling, Illinois. Minister, Science Ridge congregation, 1956- .

MENNO C. ERB, 1916-1960   Preacher   Benton

Born at O'Neill, Nebraska, May 5, 1916. Married Lois Eichelberger of Beemer, Nebraska, May 21, 1937. Six children. Ordained preacher at the Lake Region Church, Detroit Lakes, Minnesota, August 8, 1954, by Elmer Hershberger. Served as pastor at Benton, 1957-58, while Galen Johns was serving as acting pastor at Saginaw, Michigan. Killed in an automobile accident June 19, 1960. Burial in Yellow Creek Mennonite Cemetery.

PAUL ERB, 1894-   Preacher   Hopewell

Born at Newton, Kansas, April 26, 1894. Married Alta Mae Eby, who had been born at Downingtown, Pennsylvania, Two children: Winifred and Delbert. (Delbert is now a missionary in Argentina.) Ordained preacher at the Pennsylvania Church, Kansas, May 18, 1919, by T. M. Erb and D. H. Bender. Served the Pennsylvania congregation, 1919-41; the Hopewell Church, Kouts, Indiana, 1943-45; and since 1945 has been editor of the organ of the Mennonite Church, the **Gospel Herald**. Longtime teacher in Hesston and Goshen colleges. Currently (1961) executive secretary of Mennonite General Conference.

MENNO ESCH, 1879-   Preacher, Bishop   Fairview

Born at Wellman, Iowa, July 14, 1879, brother of the late C. D. Esch, M.D., missionary to India. Married Nettie Yoder of Plevna, Indiana, March 25, 1906. Nine children. Ordained preacher at Fairview, December 3, 1906, by congregational vote, by D. J. Johns. Ordained bishop, by lot, April 8, 1909, again by D. J. Johns. Farmer. Served as a member of the Mennonite Board of Education, 1928-42. He proved himself a real leader of his people, especially in the area of the economic development of the community, during the difficult years of the first generation in Oscoda County.

JOHN EYER (OYER), 1800-1864   Deacon   Holdeman

According to tradition there was a deacon John Oyer in the Holdeman congregation in the pre-Civil war period. He is said to have left the Mennonite Church and united with the Evangelical Church. We might conjecture that this happened about the same time as Joseph Rohrer made the same step. John Eyer is buried in the East Olive Cemetery, with a Bible or open book above his name, similar to that on the tombstones of various other ordained men. The stone reads simply: John Eyer. died June 23, 1864, aged 63 Ys. 7 Ms. 7 Ds. Residents of the community report that the name was pronounced Eyer in English, and Oyer in German. His ordination date is lost.

JOHN FAST, SR.   Preacher

The diary of John F. Funk in the 1880's contains a number of references to a Preacher John Fast. He seems to have lived in Goshen. The clearest reference to him is in the **Herald of Truth** for 1882 (page 153): John Fast, formerly of Russia and later of Nebraska, preached at Elkhart and at the Jones schoolhouse. Funk's diary for November 25, 1883, indicates that he took a Brother Harms to Goshen and visited John Fast, Sr., John Fast, Jr., and Daniel Brenneman. How long Fast remained in Elkhart County is not known.

DANIEL FREED, 1830-1897   Deacon   Holdeman

Born in Columbiana County, Ohio, February 11, 1830, maternal grandfather of Bishop Ray F. Yoder. Married Annie Nusbaum in 1852. They first settled in Kosciusko County, Indiana, and two years later in Elkhart County. Daniel joined the Mennonite Church in 1849. Ordained deacon June 18, 1881, by Jacob A. Beutler. Served faithfully for sixteen years. Died November 29, 1897. The funeral was held in the North Union Church.

FRANCIS E. FREED, Sr., 1893-   Preacher   Salem
     Born in Elkhart County, Indiana, January 5, 1893. Married Laura E. Smeltzer of St. Joseph County, Indiana, February 5, 1914. Two children: a daughter who died at six, and a son. They also reared a niece, Lillian Smeltzer. Ordained preacher in the Salem congregation, by lot, April 9, 1939, by J. K. Bixler. Deacon Daniel Freed was the grandfather of Preacher Francis Freed and his half brother, Deacon Manford Freed. Deacon Daniel Freed was in turn the son of Preacher Joseph Freed. Francis is also the son-in-law of Deacon Samuel Smeltzer.

JACOB FREED, 1796-1868   Preacher   Holdeman
     Born in Rockingham County, Virginia, June 11, 1796, son of Jacob and Mary (Beitler) Freed. His parents came from Bucks County, Pennsylvania, to that state. About 1819 Jacob went to Holmes County, Ohio. He had been brought up in Fayette County, Pennsylvania, to which his parents moved in 1803. Married (1) Anna Freed on March 15, 1821; she died in 1834. Two sons. Married (2) Widow Margaret (Holdeman) Yoder (1810-1887) (widow of Samuel Yoder) on November 10, 1836. Four children. Ordained preacher in Holmes County, Ohio, about 1837. Moved to Wayne County, Ohio, in 1844. In 1851 he and Margaret with their family settled in Elkhart County, Indiana. They made the journey in a train of eighteen persons, and were twelve days on the way. They located in Locke Township, Elkhart County, where Jacob bought two hundred and forty acres for $1,900.00. This farm was located one and one-half miles south of Wakarusa. Died April 1, 1868. Burial in East Cemetery at Olive. Margaret had a son Samuel to her first husband who became a preacher in St. Joseph County, Indiana; Samuel Yoder.

MANFORD A. FREED, 1900-   Deacon   Maple River, Holdeman
     Born in Locke Township, Elkhart County, Indiana, July 23, 1900, son of Joseph and Sarah (Davidhizar) Freed. Joined the Holdeman Mennonite Church on November 2, 1919. Married (1) Emma Sarah Smeltzer (1898-1929) (daughter of Deacon Samuel Smeltzer) on July 24, 1921. Two daughters. Married (2) Bertha Hartman (1902-   ) on June 3, 1933. Two sons. Ordained deacon in the Maple River congregation, Brutus, Michigan, November 22, 1925, by O. S. Hostetler. Following the death of his first wife he returned to Indiana. He was chosen to serve as deacon in the Holdeman congregation on May 10, 1950, and was installed on May 14, 1950. Manford is the grandson of Deacon Daniel Freed, the half brother of Francis Freed, and the cousin and brother-in-law of Bishop Ray F. Yoder.

ABRAHAM S. FRIESNER, 1826-1870   Preacher   Pleasant Hill
     Born, evidently in the state of Ohio, in January 1826. He began to farm in the woods six miles south of Elida, Ohio. He also taught school in Allen County, Ohio. His son Harvey, who later became a preacher, was one of his pupils. Abraham had twelve children. Ordained to the ministry in the Pleasant Hill congregation about the year 1866. Died of tuberculosis December 31, 1870, at the age of 44.

HARVEY FRIESNER, 1849-1925   Preacher   Pleasant Hill, Barker Street
     Born in Fairfield County, Ohio, August 12, 1849. Moved to Branch County, Michigan, with his parents when he was sixteen. Married Catherine Beery (1846-1906) (daughter of Abraham Beery) on December 26, 1867. Eight children, six of whom grew to maturity. Ordained preacher at Pleasant Hill on June 17, 1876, by C. D. Beery, the resident bishop of the congregation. Served the Pleasant Hill congregation, 1876-92, when he moved into the area of the Barker Street congregation. He then

served the latter church as a minister until his death, which occurred February 26, 1925. In 1887 he was severely in debt and the churches of the conference attempted to come to his aid. One of the unusual things about him is that he was not able to preach in German, a very exceptional circumstance for a Mennonite preacher in his day.

DANIEL FUNK, 1781-1859   Preacher, Bishop   Bower

Born in Pennsylvania in 1781. The dates and places of his ordination as preacher and bishop are not known. He was the father of Deacon George Funk, 1812-1896. Daniel died in 1859 and was buried in the Funk Cemetery near the Bower Mennonite Church.

GEORGE FUNK, 1812-1896   Deacon   Bower

Born in Rockingham County, Virginia, April 15, 1812. Removed to Logan County, Ohio, early in life. Married (1) Catherine Bowman of Canal Winchester, Ohio. Married (2) Barbara Grove (1825-1895) of Virginia in 1867. Ordained to the office of deacon February 4, 1872. There were five brethren in the lot. George was a third cousin of John F. Funk of Elkhart, Indiana, and the grandson of Bishop Henry Funk of the state of Virginia. Henry in turn was the grandson of immigrant "Henrich" Funck of Franconia, Pennsylvania. George was severely injured the summer of 1882 when two horses got into a fight, threw him to the ground, and broke his hip. Died March 31, 1896, at the age of 83. John S. Coffman and the resident minister in the congregation, Daniel Kinports, preached his funeral sermons.

JOHN F. FUNK, 1835-1930   Preacher, Bishop   Prairie Street

The Funk line of John F. Funk is as follows: Henrich—Abraham—John—Jacob—John F. Funk. He was born in Hilltown Township, Bucks County, Pennsylvania, April 6, 1835. In 1854, at the age of nineteen, he began to teach school. He took educational training in Freeland Seminary, now Ursinus College, in summer courses. On April 11, 1857, he entered the lumber business in Chicago with his brother-in-law, Jacob Beidler. During his first winter in Chicago, 1857-58, he was converted in evangelistic meetings in the Third Presbyterian Church; however, he deferred baptism until February 13, 1859, when he was able to appear in his home congregation, Line Lexington, Pennsylvania. Bishop Jacob Kulp baptized him. Returning to Chicago Funk threw himself into Sunday-school work in that city. One of his co-workers was D. L. Moody who later became famous as an evangelist. In 1863 Funk wrote a booklet, **War—Its Evils—Our Duty,** which brought him considerable recognition in the Mennonite Church. He also began to plan in 1863 for the establishment of the first permanent church periodical in the Mennonite Church, the **Herald of Truth,** and its German twin, **Herold der Wahrheit.** These periodicals made their appearance for the first time in January 1864. He married Salome Kratz (1839-1917) (daughter of Jacob and Mary [Meyers] Kratz) on January 19, 1864. Six children graced their home: Martha, who never married and who died in 1930, a few months after her father; Susan Mary, who died at six months and was buried in Chicago; Phoebe, who married A. B. Kolb; Rebecca, who died at the age of twenty-seven days; Grace Anna, who was one month and twenty-six days of age when she died; and John Edwin, who died at the age of thirty-one days.

When his last child, John Edwin, died (July 13, 1880), Funk wrote in his diary: "[At] ten-twenty-five in the forenoon he calmly expired, and the light of our home went out to shine more brightly in the glories of the better and more enduring home above. But sad the thought, the child of many prayers, the light and joy of the household, the hope of our family name, all faded, lost, crushed out by the hand of death. O Father, help us bear this severe affliction with meekness and full resignation to Thy will."

Funk learned that there was a small Mennonite congregation in Grundy County, Illinois, which worshiped in a schoolhouse near the town of Gardner. He began to worship with this congregation occasionally and on May 28, 1865, was ordained preacher in that congregation by John M. Brenneman of Allen County, Ohio. On April 6, 1867, Funk and family located in Elkhart, Indiana, which was then a town with a population of 3,100.

When Funk came to Elkhart County, he found not a single Sunday school. (The late Peter B. Yoder, 1855-1943, reported to the writer that in 1866 a Sunday school had been started in the Holdeman congregation; his parents, Henry B. Yoder, 1829-99 and Elizabeth Bixler, 1833-89, had located in Elkhart County in 1865.) It was Funk who inaugurated the Sunday-school movement in the Elkhart County Mennonite settlement. He was also the founder of the Mennonite Aid Plan, which was a system of fire insurance for the members of the Mennonite Church, and other branches of the denomination. He was also the founder of the Mennonite Evangelizing Committee, which eventually developed into the Mennonite Board of Missions and Charities. His Mennonite Publishing Company was active not only in the publication of periodicals, and later of Sunday-school quarterlies and supplies, but also in the publication of such great Mennonite classics as **The Martyrs Mirror** and **The Complete Works of Menno Simons**, in English. He had these large works translated and published them. Funk became the most influential man in the Mennonite Church in his generation. He exerted great influence far and wide through the books which came from his presses and through the periodicals which he issued, especially his **Herald of Truth** and its German counterpart, which entered large numbers of Mennonite homes all over the denomination. When the Russian Mennonites came to America in the 1870's, Funk devoted a vast amount of time and energy to help them find homes in the prairie states.

He was ordained bishop in the Yellow Creek meetinghouse, June 6, 1892, by Henry Shaum. There were five brethren in the lot. Funk immediately entered upon a most vigorous ten-year chapter in which he sought to build up the Mennonite congregations of Indiana, Michigan, and the Midwest in general. He promoted all the progressive movements of that period with great vigor. Perhaps he manifested too much vigor, or at least may not have been sufficiently considerate of his brethren who may not always have had as great vision as he. In any case he gradually lost the confidence of many of his fellow ministers which resulted in a division in the Prairie Street congregation and finally brought about the suspension of his bishop oversight, January 31, 1902, through the work of a special committee which had been appointed to settle the problems of the church in Elkhart County. Fortunately Funk outlived this shadow on his life and in his great age was once more held in high esteem in the Mennonite Church. He died January 8, 1930, at the age of ninety-four years, nine months, and two days, and was buried in the cemetery of the Prairie Street Mennonite Church on Hively Avenue, Elkhart. The congregation erected a suitable tombstone at his grave commemorating his great services to his brotherhood.

N. E. Byers, who was principal of Elkhart Institute and president of Goshen College, and who was well acquainted with Funk, says that there were three major facets to his personality: in the home he was a polished gentleman; in his plant he was a vigorous businessman; and in the pulpit he was a pious and good preacher.

DAVID GARBER, 1862-1934   Preacher (Bishop)   Clinton Brick

Born at Goshen, Indiana, February 14, 1862. Married Malissa Ellen Plank of Wayne County, Ohio, March 21, 1893. Six children, including Bishop John F. Garber of Burton, Ohio. Ordained preacher in the Clinton Brick congregation, by lot, September 8, 1889, by Henry Shaum. Served at Clinton Brick until 1900, when he transferred to Nampa, Idaho, where he remained three years. Served at La Junta, Colorado, 1906-10. Ordained bishop in 1907, while at La Junta. Served at South Boston, Virginia, 1930-34. He was a brother of Bishop John Garber of the Clinton Brick congregation. Died June 21, 1934. Burial in the cemetery of the Springdale Mennonite Church, Waynesboro, Virginia.

JOHN GARBER, 1860-1944   Preacher, Bishop   Clinton Brick

John was the older brother of David Garber. Ordained preacher at the Clinton Brick Church, November 27, 1892, by John F. Funk. Three brethren were in the lot. He preached in the English language. Ordained bishop at Clinton Brick. November 2, 1903, by J. P. Miller. He had bishop oversight of the Mennonite congregations east of Goshen, which in his day meant Clinton Brick, Shore, and Emma. Died February 20, 1944. Burial in Forest Grove Cemetery.

EDWARD GEGAX, 1857-1947   Preacher   Forks

Born at Detroit, Michigan, in 1857. Married (1) Lizzie Miller about the year 1883. Eleven children, five of whom grew to maturity. (One of them is the veterinarian, Dr. C. L. Gegax of Millersburg.) Married (2) Salome (Smeltzer) Locker on March 5, 1921. Ordained preacher in the Forks congregation, by lot, April 24, 1887, by J. P. Smucker. He published an article in the **Herald of Truth** in 1889 (page 99) entitled "The Word Try." About the year 1890 he withdrew from the Mennonite Church and united with another denomination. On this occasion he was immersed through the ice. Later he transferred to the Seventh-day Adventist denomination, in which faith he died in 1947.

DANIEL GEISINGER, 1827-1898   (Holdeman)

Born in Medina County, Ohio, in 1827. Married (1) —— Blough. Seven children. Married (2) Mrs. Angeline Swartz in 1868, the same year in which he came to Goshen. Removed to Wakarusa in 1873 where he was a blacksmith and a local preacher in the United Brethren Church. Served in this capacity about twenty years. He became an invalid in 1896. Received into the Mennonite Church on February 9, 1897, by John F. Funk. He was probably considered a member of the Holdeman congregation. Died August 20, 1898, without having actually served as a preacher in the Mennonite Church.

SIMON G. GINGERICH, 1923-   Preacher   Holdeman

Born at Versailles, Missouri, son of Preacher Amos Gingerich, now of Parnell, Iowa. Married Dorothy Luella Horst on December 8, 1945. No children. Received Th.B. degree from Goshen College Biblical Seminary, 1950. Ordained preacher at Holdeman, November 12, 1950, by George J. Lapp, who was then the resident bishop of the congregation. Following the death of Brother Lapp he was made minister in charge, February 12, 1951.

JOHN E. GINGRICH, 1900-   Preacher (Bishop)   Prairie Street

Born in Preston, Ontario, October 7, 1900. Married Mary Weaver of Wakarusa, Indiana, September 14, 1927. Two children, one of whom died when small. Ordained preacher at the Prairie Street Mennonite Church, December 10, 1933, by D. A. Yoder. He was a member of the Indiana-Michigan Conference for almost twenty years. In June 1953 he got his conference letter for transfer to what is now the Allegheny Conference, for he had accepted the pastorate of the Mennonite Church in Johnstown, Pennsylvania. Ordained bishop at Johnstown, August 7, 1955; served until 1961.

JOHN C. GNAGY, 1817-1889   Preacher   Clinton Brick

Born in Somerset County, Pennsylvania, April 27, 1817. Married (1) Magdalena Lehman (1818-1878). Nine children. Married (2) Elizabeth Troyer on December 28, 1879. Ordained as an Amish preacher in Somerset County, Pennsylvania, about 1837. Moved to Lawrence County, Ohio, in 1852, where he preached thirteen years. He became involved with his Amish brethren because he would not shun his Amish father, who was a preacher and who had united with what is now the Church of the Brethren. In 1864 he settled in Elkhart County, Indiana. Considerable difficulty arose about him in 1879 and a committee of Amish leaders from Daviess County, Indiana, attempted to settle it. On Ascension Day, May 6, 1880, he was put under the ban. In

1881 he applied to the Mennonite Church for admission and was received. He served as a Mennonite preacher at Clinton Brick for eight years. Died March 27, 1889, at the age of 71. Burial in Miller Cemetery, near the Eight-Square schoolhouse. Services were held at Forest Grove by P. Y. Lehman, J. J. Weaver, and Levi Weaver. Many references are made to this man with the erroneous spelling Kenagy.

DAVID GOOD, 1804-1864   Deacon   Yellow Creek
    Born in Lancaster County, Pennsylvania, in March 1804. Removed to Ontario about the year 1828. Married Susanna Bauman (1799-1884) in 1831. Ordained deacon by the year 1842. Removed from Canada to Elkhart County, Indiana, in 1857, where he continued to serve as a deacon. He corresponded with John F. Funk when the latter still lived in Chicago. Died March 16, 1864, just a few days before his sixtieth birthday. Burial at Yellow Creek.

MARTIN B. GOOD, 1836-1878   Deacon   Caledonia
    The records also refer to this man by the German name Guth. He was serving as a deacon in the Caledonia congregation as early as the year 1864.

BEN GRABER, 1895-   Deacon   Leo
    Born in Daviess County, Indiana, May 20, 1895. Married Anna Liechty of Allen County, Indiana, March 17, 1918. Eight children. Ordained deacon in the Leo congregation, September 29, 1946, by O. S. Hostetler. Served until 1958. Farmer. Ben's grandfather, Preacher John Graber of the Amish Church, moved from Leo to Daviess County in 1874. His father, John J. Graber, was also an Amish preacher in Daviess County.

CHRISTIAN L. GRABER, 1895-   Preacher   Goshen College
    Born at Noble, Iowa, December 20, 1895, son of Preacher Daniel Graber. Married Mina Amanda Roth of Wayland, Iowa, May 11, 1920. Six children. Ordained preacher in the Sugar Creek congregation, Wayland, Iowa, by congregational vote, October 15, 1922, by Bishop D. H. Bender. Served at Wayland, 1922-23, when he transferred to Goshen College to serve as business manager of the institution. He has been a long-time member of the Peace Problems Committee of Mennonite General Conference, has been active in Mennonite Mutual Aid organizations, and has served widely in the relief program of the Mennonite Church. He is the older brother of Bishop J. D. Graber.

DAVID J. GRABER, 1910-   Preacher   Berea
    Born at Mylo, North Dakota, October 4, 1910. Married Edith Slaubaugh of Daviess County, Indiana, in 1932. Nine children. Ordained preacher in the Berea congregation of Daviess County, by lot, April 23, 1953, by Edd P. Shrock.

JOSEPH DANIEL GRABER, 1900-   Preacher, Bishop   Prairie Street
    Born at Noble, Iowa, October 18, 1900. Married Minnie Ruth Swartzendruber of Eagle Grove, Iowa, June 28, 1925. Two children. Ordained preacher in the Sugar Creek congregation, Wayland, Iowa, July 12, 1925, by Bishop Simon Gingerich, at the request of the General Mission Board. The Grabers served as missionaries in India. He was pastor of the Shantipur congregation, 1928-32; of the Sunderganj congregation, 1934-36; and of the Maradeo congregation, 1936-42. Ordained bishop at Dhamtari, India, by lot, December 30, 1939, by P. A. Friesen. The actual ordination ceremony was performed in the village of Maradeo, four miles from Dhamtari, in the annual church conference which was held along the river. Accepted appointment as the executive secretary of the Mennonite Board of Missions and Charities and was received into the Indiana-Michigan Conference in June 1951. Served as bishop of the Prairie Street congregation, 1955-58.

OLIVER P. GROSH, 1867-1947   Deacon   Prairie Street

Born in Elkhart County, Indiana, December 6, 1867. Married Emma Garber of Elkhart County, Indiana, October 18, 1890. Five children. Ordained deacon at the Prairie Street Mennonite Church, Elkhart, by lot, October 17, 1920, by Jonathan Kurtz. Served about twelve years as deacon. Died April 28, 1947. Burial in the cemetery of the Prairie Street congregation on Hively Avenue.

CHARLES C. HAARER, 1916-   Preacher   Bean Blossom

Born at Shipshewana, Indiana, June 9, 1916. Married Gladys Witmer of Grabill, Indiana, September 4, 1938. Seven children. Ordained preacher at the Shore Mennonite Church, April 15, 1945, by O. S. Hostetler, at the request of the district mission board. He began his ministry at Bean Blossom on May 1, 1945, and has continued to serve there.

LEONARD A. HAARER, 1918-   Preacher   Locust Grove

Born at Goshen, Indiana, February 9, 1918. Married Lois Mishler of Lagrange, Indiana, June 29, 1941. One child. Ordained preacher at the Shore Mennonite Church, by lot, July 13, 1941, by O. S. Hostetler. Served as minister in the Locust Grove congregation, 1941-42. He is now a minister in the United Missionary Church.

PAUL W. HAARER, 1927-   Preacher   Marion

Born at Shipshewana, Indiana, October 3, 1927. Married Shirley Mishler of Shipshewana, June 3, 1951. Two children. Ordained preacher at the Shore Mennonite Church, by congregational vote, November 12, 1950, by Lee Miller. Served as minister in the Marion congregation from 1950 until December 1956. He holds the Th.B. degree from Goshen College Biblical Seminary and the B.A. degree from Goshen College. Served as secretary of the Indiana-Michigan Christian Workers' Conference, 1952-55.

JACOB HAHN, 1839-1926   Preacher   Caledonia

Born in Kaiserslautern, Germany, April 1, 1839. Came to America at the age of thirteen and lived at Clarence Center, New York. Ordained deacon at Clarence Center in 1864, and preacher in 1866. Served as preacher in the Caledonia congregation, Michigan, 1889-97. In the latter year he moved to Denbigh, Virginia. He was the father of Mrs. Mahlon Lapp, the missionary to India. Died August 2, 1926. Jacob was twice ordained as a single man. His first ordination preceded his marriage to Anna Eyman of Elkhart, Indiana, whom he married March 19, 1867. Following her death he was ordained preacher. He then married Anna Moyer of Jordan, Ontario. He preached German until his removal to Virginia.

ELI S. HALLMAN, 1866-1955   Preacher (Bishop)   Goshen College

Born near Plattsville, Ontario, February 26, 1866, son of Abraham Clemmer Hallman and Mary (Schmitt) Hallman. Married Melinda Bowman Clemens on August 9, 1893. Five children. Ordained to the ministry at the First Mennonite Church, Kitchener, Ontario, by lot, June 17, 1897. The bishops who officiated were Elias Weber, Amos Cressman, and Daniel Wismer. Ordained bishop at the same church, November 24, 1907, at the request of the Alberta-Saskatchewan Conference to serve in that district. The bishops who officiated were Jonas Snider and Elias Weber. Served in many different areas including Goshen, Indiana, 1913-15, in which period he was field secretary for Goshen College. He writes: "Over the weekend I usually filled appointments in nearby churches; occasionally in adjoining states." He officiated at numerous communion and baptismal services, held evangelistic meetings, and assisted at Bible conferences. A man of influence for good in the entire Mennonite Church. Wrote the music to the hymn, "O Everlasting Light."

BRUCE E. HANDRICH, 1924-   Preacher   Fernland

Born at Fairview, Michigan, February 19, 1924. Married Savilla Irene Troyer of Mio, Michigan, March 31, 1946. Seven children. Ordained preacher at Germfask, November 9, 1947, by T. E. Schrock. He served there since that date.

HARVEY HANDRICH, 1901-   Preacher, Bishop   Fairview

Born at Dover, Iowa, March 17, 1901. Married Ruby Miller of Lake Charles, Louisiana, April 16, 1926. Six children. Ordained preacher in the Fairview congregation, by lot, August 4, 1946, by Menno Esch. Ordained bishop August 17, 1952, also by Menno Esch. Farmer.

WILLARD D. HANDRICH, 1916-   Preacher   Grand Marais

Born at Fairview, Michigan, December 25, 1916. Married Mary Lehman (who had been born at Kenmare, North Dakota) on December 31, 1941. Five children. Ordained preacher in the Fairview congregation, October 3, 1948, at the request of the district mission board. Bishops Menno Esch and T. E. Schrock officiated. Served at Grand Marais since his ordination.

ABRAM HARTMAN, 1890-   Deacon   Yellow Creek

Born in Elkhart County, Indiana, near Wakarusa, July 9, 1890, brother of Preacher William H. Hartman of the Olive congregation, and nephew of Preacher Henry Weldy. Married Ada Mae Hoover of Elkhart County, January 1, 1916. Six children. Ordained deacon in the Yellow Creek congregation, by congregational vote, May 22, 1938, by Ray F. Yoder. Served faithfully and effectively since that time. Brother Hartman writes: "I have a special concern for our young people that they may be indoctrinated, and definite convictions developed in them to live true to the principles taught by our Saviour, that the 'faith of our fathers' might be preserved in its entirety." Abram's mother was a great-granddaughter of Bishop Abraham Weldy of Westmoreland County, Pennsylvania, and Tuscarawas, Ohio.

EARL W. HARTMAN, 1914-   Preacher   Maple River

Born in Elkhart County, Indiana, June 25, 1914, son of Preacher William H. Hartman and nephew of Deacon Abram Hartman. Married Irene Shriner on October 1, 1936. Two sons. Ordained preacher in the Maple River congregation, Brutus, Michigan, with congregational approval, October 19, 1952, by Ray F. Yoder. Continued to live in Elkhart County until 1954, when he removed to his assigned field. He was formally installed as pastor of the congregation October 14, 1955. In 1958 he became a member of the Michigan Mennonite Bible School Board.

FRANK HARTMAN, 1881-1945   Preacher   Nappanee

Born February 1, 1881. Married Anna Weldy on February 24, 1903. Five children. Ordained preacher at the North Main Street Mennonite Church, Nappanee, by vote of the congregation, January 15, 1899 (he was the sole nominee). Frank is one of the youngest persons ever to be ordained in the conference since he was a few weeks short of eighteen years of age. In the year 1902 he withdrew from the Mennonite Church and united with the Evangelical Church. He later became identified with the Presbyterian Church and held pastorates in Indiana, Wisconsin, Illinois, Ohio, Kentucky, and Tennessee. He visited Palestine in 1908. Died April 25, 1945. Burial in the cemetery of the Yellow Creek (Brick) Church.

WILLIAM H. HARTMAN, 1875-1939   Preacher   Olive

Born in Elkhart County, Indiana, March 12, 1875, son of Peter S. and Anna (Weldy) Hartman of Ashland County, Ohio. Married Mary Ann Everest (1875-1961) on February 26, 1898. Seven children, the youngest of whom is Preacher Earl Hartman. He united with the Holdeman congregation at the age of sixteen and later transferred to the Olive congregation. Ordained preacher in the Olive congregation, by lot, July 15, 1906, by David Burkholder. William never felt able to take up the work of the ministry. He was a farmer. Died September 18, 1939. Burial in Olive Cemetery.

JOHN E. HARTZLER, 1879-   Preacher (Bishop)   Prairie Street, Goshen College
Born at Ligonier, Indiana, February 2, 1879. Married (1) Mamie Yoder of West Liberty, Ohio, October 5, 1910. Two children. Ordained preacher at Garden City, Missouri, by congregational vote, September 4, 1904, by Andrew Shenk. Served the Bethel congregation at Garden City, 1904-10. In the latter year he transferred to Elkhart, Indiana, and was pastor of the Prairie Street congregation, 1910-14. Served as president of Goshen College, 1913-18. He then became president of the Witmarsum Theological Seminary, 1918-27. In 1927 he accepted the presidency of Bethel College, Newton, Kansas, and served one year. In 1928 he began a twenty-year term of service as a professor in Hartford Theological Seminary. He holds the B.A. degree from Goshen College, the A.M. degree from the University of Chicago, the B.D. degree from Union Theological Seminary, the LL.B. from Hamilton College of Law, and the Ph.D. from Hartford Seminary Foundation. Served as minister at New Stark, Ohio, 1921-37. Ordained as elder (bishop) in the Central Conference of Mennonites in June 1944. Married (2) Mrs. Myra H. Weaver, R.N., of New Holland, Pennsylvania, August 8, 1957. Prominent citizen of Goshen and popular lecturer. Author of numerous books.

JOHN M. HARTZLER, 1871-1925   Preacher   Fort Wayne
Born at Allensville, Pennsylvania, September 21, 1871. Married Anna King on August 22, 1906. Six children. Studied at Goshen College, 1907. He had been ordained preacher at Surrey, North Dakota, about 1905. He succeeded B. B. King as superintendent of the Fort Wayne Mission about March 1907 and served until June 1908. He had also assisted in the mission before B. B. King was superintendent. He returned to West Liberty, Ohio, in June 1908, only to go back to Surrey, North Dakota, in August 1908. In October 1909, he moved to Long Green, Maryland, where he served until April 1916. He then moved to Belleville, Pennsylvania, where he died March 27, 1925. He was a schoolteacher about thirty-five years. He is the father of H. Harold Hartzler, who served many years on the faculty of Goshen College.

JONAS S. HARTZLER, 1857-1953   Preacher
Maple Grove, Prairie Street, Goshen College
Born near Topeka, Indiana, August 8, 1857. Married (1) Fannie E. Stutzman of Wakarusa, Indiana, January 5, 1880. One son: Vernon (1881-1908). Married (2) Catherine (Christophel) Bauer on July 14, 1930. Ordained preacher in the Maple Grove congregation, Topeka, Indiana, by majority vote of the congregation, April 18, 1881, by Jonas D. Troyer. Served the Maple Grove congregation, 1881-95; Prairie Street congregation, 1895-1903; Goshen College, 1903-23; Prairie Street again, 1923-53. Longtime secretary of the Indiana-Michigan Conference. Served on the committee to unite the Mennonite and Amish Mennonite conferences. Teacher in the Elkhart Institute, 1895-1903. Teacher in Goshen College, 1903-15. Secretary of Mennonite General Conference, 1898-1924. Secretary of Indiana-Michigan A.M. Conference, 1888-96. Secretary of the Indiana-Michigan Mennonite Conference, 1916-23. Member of the Mennonite Board of Education, 1895-1917; treasurer, 1907-17. A man of influence in the community, in the church, and in the conference. Hartzler wrote: "I wrote all of **Missions in the Orient.** Bro. Shoemaker looked after its publication. I wrote **Mennonites in the World War,** also a booklet, **Nonresistance in Practice;** the latter would possibly never have been written had Major Kellogg not written a book entitled, **The Conscientious Objector.** The last chapter in the booklet corrects some of his mistakes. I also wrote a small part of Bro. Kauffman's **Mennonite Church History.**"

J. S. Hartzler died April 1, 1953, at the age of 95. He remained remarkably alert and active until near the close of his life.

JONATHAN B. HARTZLER, 1850-1950   Preacher   Pretty Prairie

Born near Lancaster, Fairfield County, Ohio. His wife was Esther Hooley. Ordained preacher at Pretty Prairie on May 18, 1879. Removed to Logan County, Ohio, in 1885 where he did his lifework. Reached the extreme age of one hundred years. Died November 25, 1950. Jonathan Hartzler was the father of eleven children, including Simon C. Hartzler of the Holdeman congregation, and Bishop Enos F. Hartzler of the Ohio and Eastern Mennonite Conference.

LEVI C. HARTZLER, 1909-   Deacon   Goshen College

Born at Bellefontaine, Ohio, March 20, 1909. Married Irene Mayercik of Chicago on September 23, 1939. A daughter and a son graced their home. Ordained deacon at the Goshen College Mennonite Church, by congregational vote, June 27, 1943, by S. C. Yoder. Levi did relief work in Spain, and was a long-time employee of the Mennonite Board of Missions and Charities. He is currently a high-school teacher in Elkhart, Indiana. He holds the B.A. degree from Goshen College, 1935, and the M.A. degree from Northwestern University, 1940.

RAYMOND L. HARTZLER, 1893-   Preacher   Maple Grove

Born at Topeka, Indiana, November 28, 1893. Married Nora E. Burkholder of Smithville, Ohio, February 12, 1919. Four children. Ordained preacher in the Maple Grove congregation, Topeka, Indiana, by congregational vote, April 2, 1916, by Jonathan Kurtz. Served in the Maple Grove congregation, 1916-28. He then transferred to the Mennonite Church at Carlock, Illinois. He has been secretary of the Central Conference of Mennonites, 1929-38, and editor of the **Christian Evangel** from 1938. He is a nephew of J. S. Hartzler. Raymond accepted Christ on New Year's Day, 1906, during meetings which I. W. Royer was conducting in the Maple Grove Church. He was baptized by Jonathan Kurtz on April 1, 1906. He secured the B.A. degree from Goshen College in 1918. He writes: "I shall always cherish (Old) Mennonite background and training and particularly the spirit of my Alma Mater as expressed in her motto, 'Culture for Service.' What better motto could any church college espouse?"

See also HERTZLER

PERRY A. HELLER, 1883-1949   Preacher   Fort Wayne

Converted at Fort Wayne in the year 1917. Ordained preacher in the Fort Wayne congregation, March 7, 1924, by J. K. Bixler. Removed to Los Angeles, California, in 1930. Returned in later years to Indiana and became a member of the Leo congregation. Died March 4, 1949, at the age of 65.

CLYDE L. HERSHBERGER, 1912-   Deacon   Nappanee

Born eleven miles north of Kokomo, Indiana, July 6, 1912. Married Maxine Weldy of Wakarusa, Indiana, August 19, 1936. Six children. Ordained deacon at the North Main Street Mennonite Church, Nappanee, May 8, 1960, by lot, by Homer F. North. (Alvin R. Miller was ordained the same day.)

JACOB C. HERSHBERGER, 1858-1920   Deacon   Clinton Brick, Middlebury

Born in Howard County, Indiana, January 26, 1858. Married Martha Nusbaum on August 15, 1880. Eight children, including Lloyd I. Hershberger of the Holdeman congregation. Ordained deacon at Clinton Brick, in May 1895, by P. Y. Lehman. Transferred from the Clinton Brick Mennonite Church to the Middlebury Amish Mennonite Church on November 11, 1911. Died December 20, 1920.

JENCY L. HERSHBERGER, 1918-   Preacher   Toto

Born at Goshen, Indiana, February 23, 1918. Married (1) Lovina Garber (1918-1959) on November 27, 1939. Eight children. Ordained preacher in the Toto Mennonite Gospel Mission, by lot, January 27, 1952, by Ray F. Yoder. Salesman. Married (2) Ethel Fern Davidhizar of New Paris, Indiana, June 8, 1960.

SETH P. HERSHBERGER, 1860-1941   Preacher   Shore

Born in Holmes County, Ohio, January 21, 1860. Married Susanna Miller on January 29, 1895. Three children, including Anna Miller of the North Goshen congregation. Ordained preacher in Moultrie County, Illinois, November 9, 1896, by John Smith. Located later in Northern Indiana and served for a time in the Shore congregation. As a young man, before marriage, he lost a hand in a corn husking machine. Died in September 1941. Burial in Shore Cemetery.

TOBIAS HERSHBERGER, 1843-1918   Deacon   Caledonia

Born in Somerset County, Pennsylvania, March 22, 1843. Moved with his parents to Kent County, Michigan, in 1865. His wife was Leah Gingerich. Two sons. Ordained deacon on September 30, 1883. Moved to Knox County, Tennessee, and in 1900 to Oklahoma, where he died May 4, 1918.

BENJAMIN HERSHEY, 1814-1888   Preacher (Bishop)   Yellow Creek

Born in "Upper Canada" (Ontario), January 5, 1814. Married (1) Magdalena Dausman on May 25, 1835. Married (2) Widow Barbara Potter in 1873. Removed to Pennsylvania about 1838 and remained there two years, after which he returned to Ontario. Ordained preacher about the year 1843 in Welland County. Removed to Northern Indiana in 1850, and in 1860 to Sterling, Whiteside County, Illinois. Ordained bishop at Sterling in 1870. In the same year he removed to Shelby County, Missouri, where he remained until his death on January 3, 1888.

DAVID F. HERTZLER, 1816-1889   Preacher   Maple Grove

Born in Mifflin County, Pennsylvania, August 4, 1816. Married Barbara Yoder (1822-1884) on December 2, 1841. Eleven children. The first six children were born in Pennsylvania and Ohio, but the latter five, beginning with Nancy in 1855, were born at Ligonier, Indiana. His addresses in Ohio had been Lancaster and Huntsville. Served as a preacher at Maple Grove from the middle 1850's until his death, which occurred January 14, 1889. Pennsylvania Germans pronounce Hertzler as Hartzler, which is the spelling often used with his name.

EMANUEL J. HOCHSTEDLER, 1909-   Preacher   Howard-Miami

Born near Kokomo, Indiana, April 16, 1909. Married Mattie Schlabach of Fairview, Michigan, August 13, 1928. Ten children. Ordained preacher in the Howard-Miami Mennonite congregation, by lot, December 21, 1947, by A. G. Horner and T. E. Schrock. Much interested in mission work. Served as a worker in the Bean Blossom congregation from October 1946 to July 1947. His grandfather, Noah Hochstedler, was a bishop in the Old Order Amish Church in Howard County. Emanuel is a successful farmer.

SAMUEL HOCHSTETLER   Preacher   West Market Street A.M. Church

Abraham E. Weaver, in his **Standard History of Elkhart County, Indiana,** Vol. 1, 1916, page 385, lists Samuel Hochstetler as a minister in the West Market Street Amish Mennonite Church, evidently around the year 1870. Bishop David Burkholder of the North Main Street Mennonite Church in Nappanee also referred to this same man and said that he was a minister. His grave could not be located nor could any other references to him be found.

JACOB HOFFER, 1827-1906   Preacher   Bower

Born in November 1827. His wife's first name was Susanna. Ordained preacher from a group of four nominees, by lot, May 19, 1872, to preach German, to assist feeble old Bishop Michael Mishler. Served until his death on November 17, 1906, at the age of seventy-nine years and four days. Burial in the cemetery of the Bower Church lot.

VERLE O. HOFFMAN, 1920-   Preacher   Clinton Frame, Benton, Roselawn

Ordained preacher in the Clinton Frame congregation, by lot, August 27, 1944, by Edwin J. Yoder. Supplied the pulpit of the new Benton congregation, 1946-48. Accepted a call to become pastor of the Roselawn congregation in 1951, where he continues to serve. Was in CPS at the time of his ordination. Married Berdine Elizabeth Byler of Goshen, Indiana, June 4, 1944. Five children.

JOSEPH HOLDEMAN, 1823-1894   Deacon   Holdeman

Born in Bucks County, Pennsylvania, May 11, 1823, son of Christian and Christiana (Buzzard) Holdeman. Moved to Wayne County, Ohio, with his parents at the age of two. Married Anna Nusbaum (1830-1907) of Ashland County, Ohio, September 24, 1846. Fifteen children. Settled in Elkhart County, Indiana, one and one-fourth miles west of the village of Salem, which was later renamed Wakarusa, in October 1850. Received into the Mennonite Church in 1851. A successful schoolteacher. Edwin L. Weaver, author of a book, **Holdeman Descendants,** 1937, writes: "There are perhaps few, if any, Mennonite families that have produced more teachers than have the Holdemans of Elkhart County. For example, all the sons and daughters of Catherine (Holdeman) Landis, sister of Joseph Holdeman, were teachers; and Joseph Landis, nephew of Joseph Holdeman, moved to Valparaiso, Indiana, about 1875, and put all his eight sons and daughters through Valparaiso University. . . . A daughter of Joseph Holdeman attended Valparaiso and some of his grandsons attended colleges, and I do not suppose they received much opposition from their grandfather." Ordained deacon sometime in the 1860's. Served as an early Sunday-school superintendent at Holdeman 1872. First secretary of the Mennonite Aid Plan. Prospered financially. Was conservative, fearless, outspoken. Lloyd V. Conrad, the historian of the Holdeman congregation, reports that Joseph Holdeman resigned his local responsibilities as deacon about the year 1880. He continued to serve as a member of conference, however, until his death at Wakarusa on August 19, 1894. Burial in Olive Cemetery.

SAMUEL HONDERICH, 1878-   Preacher   Clinton Brick

Born at Goshen, Indiana, June 22, 1878. Married (1) Olivia Winifred Good of Freeport, Illinois, December 25, 1902. Three children. Ordained preacher at Clinton Brick by lot (five nominees), October 17, 1902, by John Nice of Illinois, in the period when both bishops, John F. Funk and P. Y. Lehman, were inactive. Served at Clinton Brick, 1902-7, when he transferred to the Toronto Mission, where he remained four years. Served in the Cullom, Illinois, congregation, 1911-13. Since 1913 he has labored at Filer, Idaho. Married (2) Anna M. Kauffman of Nampa, Idaho, September 30, 1952.

JOSEPH Y. HOOLEY, 1861-1947   Deacon   Forks

Born in Mahoning County, Ohio, June 30, 1861, son of Jacob Hooley of Mifflin County, Pennsylvania, who later migrated to St. Joseph County, Michigan, and worshiped in the Barker Street congregation. Married Gertrude Yoder of Lagrange County, Indiana, March 1, 1884. Eight children. Ordained deacon on April 13, 1906 (Good Friday), by D. J. Johns. (In the same service D. D. Miller was ordained bishop). Served faithfully until his death on July 29, 1947. Burial in Bontrager Cemetery, Lagrange County.

ORVIN H. HOOLEY, 1910-   Preacher, Bishop   Locust Grove

Born at Shipshewana, Lagrange County, Indiana, March 12, 1910. Married Vera Pauline Miller of Lagrange County, May 24, 1936. Four children. Ordained preacher at the Locust Grove Mennonite Church, Burr Oak, Michigan, November 18, 1945, by Lee J. Miller, upon recommendation of the ministry of the Shore congregation of which the Locust Grove Church was a mission outpost. Ordained bishop at Locust Grove, April 28, 1957. Farmer and auctioneer.

ABRAHAM HOOVER, Jr., 1822-1896   Preacher   Clinton Brick

Born in York County, Pennsylvania, March 9, 1822, son of Abraham and Christina (Martin) Hoover of Lancaster County, who later removed to Wayne County, Ohio. (Abraham, Sr., also settled in Indiana as an old man.) Married (1) Martha Garber (1827-1879) (daughter of Jacob and Esther [Rush] Garber) on October 2, 1845. Ten children. Married (2) Mary (Greiner) Frederick on November 9, 1884. The date and place of his ordination are not known, but he is referred to as a preacher in Clinton Township as early as February 1868. The book, **Pictorial and Biographical Memoirs of Elkhart and St. Joseph Counties Indiana** (Chicago, 1893), speaks of him as though he were still a minister, but he did not serve until his death. His obituary in the **Herald of Truth** speaks of him as having been a minister "at one time" in the Mennonite Church. Died April 19, 1896. His son David, who was born in 1863, was a Methodist preacher in Wichita, Kansas. Abraham Hoover, Jr., bought land in Middlebury Township, Elkhart County, in 1847. He retired to Millersburg in 1889.

BENJAMIN HOOVER (or Huber), 1778-1866   Deacon   Yellow Creek

Born in November 1778. Removed from "Canada West" (Ontario) to Elkhart County, Indiana. He is listed as a deacon in the Ontario Conference as early as 1825. In 1866 Preacher John Lapp of the state of New York visited "the aged brother and deacon, Benjamin Huber, two miles from Goshen." Huber was at that time eighty-seven years of age. Died December 19, 1866, at the advanced age of eighty-eight years, one month, and three days.

DANIEL HOOVER, 1821-1884   Deacon   Yellow Creek

Born in Franklin County, Pennsylvania, September 14, 1821, son of David (1781-1834) and Esther (Lehman) Hoover (1787-1850). Removed with his parents to Columbiana County, Ohio, in 1826. Settled in Harrison Township, Elkhart County, Indiana, in 1855. Married (1) Rebecca Shank (1830-1867) in September 1851. Seven children. Married (2) Nancy Myers (1845-1922) on June 18, 1874. Four children. United with the Mennonite Church in 1852, the year following his first marriage. Ordained deacon at Yellow Creek, January 1, 1877. (Jacob C. Buzzard was ordained preacher in the same service.) Among the children of Deacon Daniel Hoover should be mentioned Attorney David M. Hoover (1877-1956), who served as mayor of the city of Elkhart, as judge, and as a leader in the Republican party. He served as the GOP chairman of the third Indiana district. Deacon Daniel Hoover's sister Mary (1809-1860) was the wife of Bishop Jacob Wisler. Hoover, however, remained with the Indiana-Michigan Conference. Died February 9, 1884, in Harrison Township, of "lung fever" (pneumonia). Burial in East Cemetery of the Yellow Creek (frame) Mennonite Church.

JOHN A. HOOVER, 1825-1907   Deacon   Clinton Brick

Born in York County, Pennsylvania, March 2, 1825, grandson of Preacher Henry Hoover. As a boy he removed with his parents to Wayne County, Ohio. Married Susanna H. Eschliman (1826-1907) on February 17, 1848. Removed to Clinton Township, Elkhart County, Indiana, in 1852. The date of his ordination as deacon is lost, but he was serving as early as 1864. The **Herald of Truth** contains numerous references to visits which John F. Funk and others made to Deacon Hoover of Clinton. His wife's funeral sermons were preached by Wisler ministers, Bishop John Martin and Preacher Martin Ramer. John died in Clinton Township, October 2, 1907, at the age of 82. John F. Funk and A. S. Cripe preached his funeral sermons.

MARTIN HOOVER, c.1760-1850   Bishop   Yellow Creek

Born in Europe probably late in the year 1760. Came to Philadelphia with his father Ludwig in 1764 and settled in Lancaster County, Pennsylvania. Martin and two of his brothers migrated to Markham, Ontario, in 1804. He seems to have been ordained in Franklin County, Pennsylvania, for he often preached with "Old Peter Lehman" in Franklin County. He served as a preacher at Markham from 1804 until his removal to Medina County, Ohio, in 1837. The spring of 1845 he removed from Medina County, Ohio, to Elkhart County, Indiana, with his son, John Hoover (1788-1867). They arrived in Harrison Township in June 1845. He is described as a very old man with a long white beard and long white hair. He was a tall man. His son John settled on the farm which is now owned by Dr. M. L. Weldy, just east of the village of South West. He lived in Elkhart County a little over five years and served the church to the best of his ability, although quite feeble from his extreme age. He died October 15, 1850, and was buried in the church lot of the Yellow Creek congregation, at the east end of the lot, where a tiny cemetery was just beginning. Later the lot was devoted entirely to burial purposes and a new meetinghouse was erected on the other side of the road, namely, the present Yellow Creek frame meetinghouse. Martin's wife was Elizabeth Stauffer. They had five children: John, who married Susannah Kurtz (1785-1865); Abraham, who died young in Canada; Susannah, who married Abraham Nighswander of Washington County, Maryland; Esther, who married John Ramer of Markham; and Polly, who married Christian Barkey of Markham. Bishop Martin Hoover's son John in turn was the father of Martin Hoover (1813-1896), the Brethren in Christ preacher. Preacher Martin Hoover of the Brethren in Christ Church was in turn the father of Frances ("Fanny") Hoover, the wife of Preacher Michael M. Shirk (1832-1912), also of the Brethren in Christ Church.

NOAH S. HOOVER, 1855-1913   Deacon   Yellow Creek

Born in Mahoning County, Ohio, February 15, 1855, son of Deacon Daniel Hoover (1821-1884). Married Sarah A. Kreider (1853-1932) of Medina County, Ohio (sister of Drs. Martin K. and William B. Kreider of Goshen, Indiana, and daughter of Jacob Kreider and Anna Overholt), on March 19, 1882. Three children, the youngest of whom, Ada, married Abram Hartman, deacon in the Yellow Creek congregation. Came to Elkhart County in 1855 with his parents. United with the Mennonite Church in 1883. Both Noah and his wife, Sarah, taught school. Ordained deacon at Yellow Creek, November 12, 1898, by John F. Funk. Died April 22, 1913, at the early age of 58. Burial in Yellow Creek Cemetery.

ANSON G. HORNER, 1895-   Preacher, Bishop   Howard-Miami

Born in Howard County, Indiana, May 8, 1895, son of Preacher J. S. Horner. Married Susie Miller of Howard County, Indiana, April 20, 1918, Five children, of whom the oldest and the youngest are deceased. Ordained preacher in the Howard-Miami congregation, January 27, 1935, by J. K. Bixler, and bishop in the same church, September 26, 1937, also by J. K. Bixler. Schoolteacher and farmer. Was converted in Manistee County, Michigan, in 1909, during meetings conducted by J. E. Hartzler. Served on the executive committee of the Indiana-Michigan Conference, and was moderator, 1950-52. Graduated from the Normal School of Ball State Teachers' College, Muncie, Indiana, 1924. The Horner family came from Holmes County to Indiana about the year 1849. Anson's mother was Emma Kendall, the daughter of Simon and Caroline Kendall. The Kendalls came from Holmes County, Ohio, to Indiana about 1850.

JOHN W. HORNER, 1893-   Deacon   Howard-Miami

Born in Howard County, Indiana, July 13, 1893, son of J. S. Horner. Married Verda Schrock of Howard County, September 1, 1917. Nine children. Ordained deacon in the Howard-Miami congregation, by lot, April 23, 1933, with J. K. Bixler officiating. Schoolteacher and farmer. Converted in Manistee County, Michigan, in October 1907, during meetings conducted by J. E. Hartzler.

JOSEPH S. HORNER, 1864-1945   Preacher   Pleasantview, Howard-Miami

Born northwest of Peru, Indiana, November 2, 1864. Married Emma Kendall (daughter of Simon and Caroline Kendall) on December 29, 1889. Daniel Miller performed the ceremony. Eight children, including Deacon John and Bishop Anson. Ordained preacher December 15, 1889, by D. J. Johns of Elkhart County. As a young man he had joined the United Brethren Church, but became convinced through Bible study that the Mennonite Church was closer to God's Word. Served in the Howard-Miami congregation until 1903, when he removed to Manistee County, Michigan. Returned to the Howard-Miami congregation in 1910 and served until his death January 18, 1945. His last sermon was preached on February 6, 1944, on the subject, "The Power of God." Burial in Mast Cemetery in Liberty Township, Howard County.

ADEN H. HORST, 1920-   Preacher   Locust Grove

Born at Maugansville, Maryland, September 20, 1920, grandson of Deacon Daniel Horst. Married Mary Edith Troyer of Darlow, Kansas, June 6, 1950. Five children. Has a B.A. degree from Goshen College. Ordained preacher at the Locust Grove Mennonite Church, south of Elkhart, Indiana, by congregational vote, February 5, 1955, by Ralph Stahly.

PAUL H. HORST, 1917-   Preacher   Soo Hill

Born at New Holland, Lancaster County, Pennsylvania, February 3, 1917. Married Pauline Johns on February 12, 1938. Four children. Ordained preacher in the Clinton Frame congregation, March 1, 1953, for service in the Upper Peninsula of Michigan. Has served pastor of the Soo Hill congregation, Escanaba, Michigan, since that date.

AMOS O. HOSTETLER, 1901-   Deacon, Preacher   Emma

Born at Topeka, Lagrange County, Indiana, April 1, 1901, son of Bishop O. S. Hostetler. Married Thersa Viola Hooley of Shipshewana, Lagrange County, March 8, 1924. Eight children. Ordained deacon in the Emma congregation, by lot, June 29, 1924, with D. J. Johns officiating. Ordained preacher in the Emma congregation, by congregational vote, September 3, 1944, by O. S. Hostetler. Has served as a member of the Mennonite Board of Education, and for many years as secretary of Mennonite General Conference. Schoolteacher and farmer.

ANDREW J. HOSTETLER, 1858-1925   Deacon, Preacher   Forks, Middlebury

Born in Holmes County, Ohio, in August 1858, uncle of Bishop O. S. Hostetler. Came to Indiana with his parents at the age of six. Lived near the village of Emma until 1890. Married (1) Anna A. Schrock (who died February 20, 1891) on July 30, 1885. Two children. Married (2) Rebecca Hostetler on December 27, 1891. Two children. Ordained deacon in the Forks congregation, by lot (four nominees), October 25, 1896, by J. P. Smucker. Ordained preacher in the same congregation, by lot (five nominees), August 11, 1901, by D. J. Johns. Served the Forks congregation until 1903, when he transferred to the new Middlebury congregation. Died November 24, 1925, in Middlebury.

EMANUEL HOSTETLER, 1817-1897   Preacher   Forks

Born in Somerset County, Pennsylvania, August 5, 1817. Lived for a time in Canada. Came to Lagrange County, Indiana, in 1842. Married Fannie Stutzman (1828-1909) on April 24, 1847, "in his own log cabin in the woods of Indiana." Ten children, including Lydia whose second husband was John C. Miller, and who in turn was the maternal grandfather of Glen E. Yoder of Shipshewana. Ordained preacher by 1862 according to the minutes of the Amish General Conference. Served the Forks congregation for almost two decades. The Hostetler family genealogy sometimes refers to him as a bishop, probably in error. His ministry was revoked because of strife with a neighbor. Removed to McPherson County, Kansas, in 1892. Died at Monitor, McPherson County, Kansas, July 20, 1897. Burial in Union Cemetery.

See also HOCHSTEDLER

LEROY L. HOSTETLER, 1904-   Preacher   Belmont

Born at Elkhart, Indiana, July 7, 1904. Married Louella Eash of Jet, Oklahoma, May 31, 1928. Four children. Ordained preacher in the Prairie Street congregation, Elkhart, by lot, September 29, 1940, by D. A. Yoder. Served the Belmont congregation as preacher from the time of his ordination until September 9, 1951, when he withdrew his membership from the Mennonite Church.

OSCAR S. HOSTETLER, 1874-   Preacher, Bishop   Emma

Born in Lagrange County, Indiana, September 20, 1874, son of Samuel J. and Katie (Mehl) Hostetler, who were members of the Forks Amish Mennonite congregation. Married Fannie Yoder of Lagrange County, (who had been born north of the village of Shipshewana) on December 17, 1893. Seven children, including Preacher Amos O. Hostetler. Ordained preacher in the Emma Mennonite congregation by lot, October 16, 1902, by John Nice of Illinois, during the time when Northern Indiana was left without an active Mennonite bishop. Ordained bishop in the Emma congregation, by congregational vote, May 13, 1923, by D. J. Johns. Farmer. Was an active bishop, serving the Emma, Shore, and Clinton Brick congregations, as well as many more distant churches, such as assisting Jonathan Kurtz in the Maple Grove congregation, serving as bishop in the Berea congregation, at Midland, Michigan, at Anderson, and at Locust Grove, Michigan. He conducted many ordinations. Served as moderator of the Indiana-Michigan Conference, 1933-40. A conservative, courageous, and well-balanced leader. Lived on the farm on which he was born for seventy-four years, after which he retired to a new home in the village of Emma, across the street from the meetinghouse of the congregation which he has served almost sixty years.

S. JAY HOSTETLER, 1901-   Preacher, Bishop   Belmont

Born at Shipshewana, Indiana, March 7, 1901. Married Ida Miller of Lagrange, Indiana, August 22, 1924. Three children. Schoolteacher. Missionary to India. Ordained preacher at Cullom, Illinois, September 25, 1927, by J. A. Heiser, at the request of the General Mission Board. Ordained bishop at Belmont, July 20, 1952, by D. A. Yoder. Served the Cullom congregation, 1926-28; Central Province, India, 1928-40; Bihar, India, 1940-49; Belmont congregation, Elkhart, Indiana, 1950-57; Ghana and Nigeria, 1957-   .

SAMUEL HOSTETLER, Jr., 1922-   Preacher   Knott County, Kentucky; Bethany

Born at Goshen, Indiana, February 24, 1922. Married Dorothy Livengood of Goshen, Indiana, September 18, 1943. Six children. Ordained preacher in the Clinton Frame congregation, for the pastorate of the mission station in Talcum, Kentucky, March 1, 1953. Stayed there three years. Removed from Goshen to Imlay City, Michigan, in 1960, to become pastor of the Bethany congregation. Installed there September 4, 1960.

HENRY HUBER, 1849-1923   Preacher   Pleasant Valley

Born in Fairfield County, Ohio, March 10, 1849. Moved to Putnam County about 1852; later to Allen County, Ohio. Married Elizabeth Myers (1851-1923) on June 30, 1870. Ordained preacher in the Pike-Salem congregation, Allen County, Ohio, about 1880. Moved to De Kalb County about 1882. Within a few years he united with the Church of the Brethren and moved to Jefferson County, Tennessee. About 1900 he removed to Elkhart County, Indiana, where he died November 3, 1923. Burial in South Cemetery, Yellow Creek (brick) Church.

PAUL A. HUNSBERGER, 1919-   Preacher   Tri-Lakes
    Born at Kitchener, Ontario, January 19, 1919. Married Edna Martin on August 3, 1946. Four children. Ordained preacher at the St. Jacobs Mennonite Church, St. Jacobs, Ontario, March 18, 1951, by J. B. Martin. Served as pastor at Monetville, Ontario. Entered Goshen College in September 1959. Chosen pastor at Tri-Lakes, April 1961.

JOHN HYGEMA, 1864-1908   Preacher   Holdeman
    Born in Elkhart County, Indiana, October 4, 1864, son of Romka and Yetska Hygema, immigrants from Friesland, The Netherlands, 1853. Married Lydia Ann Yoder (1859-1932) (daughter of Jacob Yoder) on November 1, 1885. Five children. Ordained preacher at Holdeman, by lot (two nominees), August 27, 1893, by J. F. Funk. Was briefly inactive because of a financial failure in 1897. Suffered with poor health the last five years of his life. Removed to California for his health in November 1907. Preacher John F. Bressler cared for him for a time. Died at Corning, California, June 21, 1908, at the early age of 43. His body was returned to Indiana and interred in the East Cemetery at the Olive Church. J. K. Bixler preached the funeral sermon on June 28, 1908. Preacher I. B. Witmer (1865-1958) of the Ohio and Eastern Conference, who lived in Indiana as a youth, said that John Hygema was a good preacher and that he quoted vast amounts of Scripture by memory.

DONALD D. JANTZI, 1918-   Preacher, Bishop   New Bremen
    Born at Pigeon, Michigan, July 27, 1918. Married Doris Schaeffer of West Carthage, New York, October 19, 1943. Six children. Ordained preacher at Lowville, New York, September 7, 1952, by Emanuel B. Peachey of Belleville, Pennsylvania. In 1957 he accepted a call from the First Mennonite Church, New Bremen, New York, to serve as its pastor, and was installed by S. C. Yoder on October 27, 1957. He was received as a member of Conference in June 1960. Bishop, Fall 1961.

DANIEL J. JOHNS, 1850-1942   Preacher, Bishop   Clinton Frame
    Born in Somerset County, Pennsylvania, September 8, 1850. Came with his parents to Elkhart County, Indiana, in 1865. Married Nancy Yoder (1849-1930) of Wayne County, Ohio, May 6, 1875. Eli Miller officiated. Six children, including Preacher Ira of the Indiana-Michigan Conference, and Bishop Otis of the Ohio and Eastern Conference. Was converted about the year 1876 and united with the Clinton Frame Amish Mennonite Church. Ordained preacher there, by a strong congregational vote, May 28, 1882. Joseph Stuckey of Illinois officiated. Ordained bishop at Clinton Frame, November 13, 1887, by Bishops Benjamin Schrock, the resident bishop of the congregation, and J. P. Smucker, assisted by the aged Isaac Smucker of Topeka. He wore a beard because of the strong feeling on the subject on the part of the founder of the Amish Mennonite Church in Indiana, Jonas D. Troyer. (Isaac Smucker was a cofounder of the group.) He was a successful schoolteacher, a good preacher, an able organizer, and a church statesman in the best sense of the word. Served on the publishing committee of Mennonite Publication Board from the beginning until 1941. Was moderator of Mennonite General Conference in 1907. Reached the ripe old age of ninety-one years, eight months, and fourteen days. Died May 22, 1942. Burial in Clinton Union Cemetery. D. J. Johns was one of the ablest bishops in the Indiana-Michigan Amish Mennonite Conference, a man of strong influence from east to west, and a good church leader. He held many Bible conferences, and served on numerous committees which adjusted church difficulties in various areas of his brotherhood.

GALEN I. JOHNS, 1920-   Preacher   Clinton Frame, Benton
    Born at Goshen, Indiana, February 26, 1920, youngest son of Preacher Ira S. Johns. Married Edith Hoover of Goshen, Indiana, May 16, 1943. Five children. Ordained preacher at Clinton Frame, by lot, January 25, 1948, by E. J. Yoder. Served there

briefly, but the same year was installed as pastor of the Benton congregation, where he served until 1960. He is again a member of the Clinton Frame congregation.

IRA S. JOHNS, 1879-1956   Deacon, Preacher   Clinton Frame

Born at Goshen, Indiana, July 10, 1879, second child of Bishop D. J. Johns. Married Elizabeth Rickert of Columbiana, Ohio, August 17, 1901. Eight children. Ordained deacon at Clinton Frame, by lot, July 18, 1909, by Jonathan Kurtz. Ordained preacher at Clinton Frame, April 27, 1924, by D. A. Yoder, at the request of the district mission board. He was ordained preacher with the understanding that he would be available to be sent wherever he would be needed, but the Clinton Frame congregation subsequently requested that he remain there and serve them as a minister. He was a strong conference man, much concerned for the welfare of the church, and deeply burdened that the church should not drift into worldliness. Served as secretary of the conference for twenty-nine years. Was converted in the first series of meetings which D. D. Miller conducted. Died June 27, 1956. Burial in Clinton Community Cemetery. His wife was born January 26, 1877, and died August 7, 1960, at the advanced age of 83.

EDWARD D. JONES, 1906-   Preacher   White Cloud

Born at Mylo, North Dakota, April 23, 1906. Married Cleo Berniece Nusbaum of Middlebury, Indiana, August 22, 1935. Six children. Ordained preacher at Middlebury, Indiana, April 21, 1935, by D. D. Miller, at the request of the district mission board. Has served the White Cloud congregation since that date.

AMSA H. KAUFFMAN, 1894-   Preacher, Bishop   Clinton Brick

Born at Goshen, Indiana, January 31, 1894. Married Nona M. Miller of Shipshewana, Indiana, September 2, 1928. Three daughters. Ordained preacher at Normanna, Texas, January 1, 1939, by Bishop E. S. Hallman, at the request of the General Mission Board. He had been given charge of the Mexican work in South Texas on June 26, 1937, and his ordination was performed to enhance the effectiveness of his service in that area. When the Clinton Brick Church was left without a pastor, he was recalled in 1947 and installed as pastor of the Clinton Brick congregation. Here he was called to the office of bishop and ordained by O. S. Hostetler on December 21, 1952. Received the B.A. degree from Goshen College, 1928. Under his quiet and effective leadership the Clinton Brick congregation reached its highest membership in history.

CHRISTIAN KAUFFMAN, 1800-1879   Deacon   Arcadia

Born in June 1800. One of the fourteen members of the Mennonite Church in Hamilton County, Indiana, at the time of his ordination. Ordained deacon in October 1865 by John M. Brenneman of Allen County, Ohio. Died March 12, 1879, at the age of 78. Burial in the cemetery of the Arcadia Church of the Brethren, one-half mile east of the village of Arcadia.

CLYDE X. KAUFFMAN, 1890-   Preacher   Maple River

Born in Elkhart County, Indiana, May 13, 1890. Married Rosetta Tyson of Wakarusa, Indiana, March 18, 1915. No children. Ordained preacher in the Clinton Frame congregation, November 7, 1920, by D. J. Johns, at the request of the district mission board, for service in the Maple River congregation, Brutus, Michigan. His work was richly blessed of God and the Maple River congregation was revived and grew rapidly. He has invested his life in the building of the church in Emmet County, Michigan.

JOHN S. KAUFFMAN, 1828-1906   Preacher   Arcadia

Born August 4, 1828, son of Deacon Christian Kauffman. Ordained preacher in October 1866 by John M. Brenneman of Ohio, when there were seventeen members of the Mennonite Church located in Hamilton County, Indiana. He probably served a number of years, but eventually relinquished his ministry; so the little flock was left without a shepherd. Died August 8, 1906, at the age of 78. Burial in the cemetery of the Church of the Brethren east of Arcadia.

JOSEPH KAUFFMAN, 1804-1868   Preacher   Maple Grove, Barker Street

Born in July 1804. According to the **Mast Family History,** page 215, Joseph Kauffman's wife was Nancy Smucker (1807-1896) (sister of Bishop Isaac Smucker). Five sons and one daughter. In 1868 he was living near the Indiana-Michigan state line, and probably preached for the small Barker Street congregation. Earlier he was affiliated with the Maple Grove congregation. The date of his ordination is not known, but he preached "for many years in the Omish Mennonite Church." He died in March 1868. The **Herald of Truth** gives the date as March 12, while the **Mast History** indicates the date, March 17.

LEVI A. KAUFFMAN, 1881-1955   Preacher   Fairview

Born at West Liberty, Ohio, November 12, 1881. Married Nettie Mae Sharp of Gunn City, Missouri, October 7, 1907. Sixteen children. Ordained preacher April 8, 1909. (In the same service Menno Esch was ordained to the office of bishop.) He did not serve very long at Fairview, but located in the state of Montana, where he served as pastor of the Glendive congregation in Dawson County. Died October 2, 1955.

M. JOHN KAUFFMAN, 1915-   Deacon   Pleasant View

Born at Shelbyville, Illinois, April 18, 1915. Married Katie (sister of Preacher Ray Keim) of Peru, Indiana, November 8, 1936. Three daughters. Ordained deacon in the Pleasant View congregation, August 5, 1956, by J. C. Wenger.

MOSES KAUFFMAN, 1805-1872   Preacher   Clinton Frame

Mayor Frank S. Ebersole of Goshen was married to Labona Berkey, daughter of John C. and Fannie (Kauffman) Berkey. Mrs. Berkey, in turn, was the daughter of Preacher Moses Kauffman (1805-1872). The Berkey family reports that Moses Kauffman was at first an Old Order Amish preacher, but that he later became Amish Mennonite. This report is confirmed in the small German history of the Amish Mennonites in Indiana written by Hans E. Borntreger in 1907. He says on page 18: "About the year 1872 Preacher Moses Kauffman left the Clinton [Amish] Church and united with the church of J. [D.] Troyer. Soon afterwards he died, however." According to the **Herald of Truth** for 1873, page 14, Preacher Moses Kauffman, who had served in the ministry "for a considerable time," died in Middlebury Township, Elkhart County, December 8, 1872.

NELSON E. KAUFFMAN, 1904-   Preacher, Bishop   Belmont

Born at Garden City, Missouri, October 5, 1904. Married Christmas Carol (Miller) Hostetler of Elkhart, Indiana, June 10, 1929. Four children. Ordained preacher at Hannibal, Missouri, July 26, 1934, by J. M. Kreider of Palmyra, Missouri. Ordained bishop at Hannibal, September 22, 1940, again by J. M. Kreider. Transferred to the Indiana-Michigan Conference in June 1958. Has the bishop oversight of the Belmont and Sunnyside congregations of Elkhart, Indiana. Has received Th.B. degrees, from Hesston College and Bible School, 1931, and Goshen College Biblical Seminary, 1943.

NORMAN D. KAUFFMAN, 1923-   Deacon   Clinton Frame

Born at Creston, Montana, July 19, 1923, grandson of Preacher D. D. Kauffman. Married Margaret Stutzman of Goshen, Indiana, June 16, 1950. Four children. Ordained deacon at Clinton Frame, by lot, December 30, 1951, by Edwin J. Yoder. Received an A.B. degree in Bible from Eastern Mennonite College, 1950. Had received the Associate in Arts degree from Hesston College and Bible School, 1948.

Received a B.S. in Elementary Education from Goshen College, 1957. He is a school-teacher and has served as principal of the Clinton Christian Day School.

PETER KEIM, 1836-1904   Preacher   Bowne
Born in Somerset County, Pennsylvania, June 9, 1836. Married Sarah Yoder on February 17, 1856. Six children. Moved to Kent County, Michigan, in January 1866. Three months later, on April 28, 1866, he was ordained preacher by J. M. Brenneman. (In the same service Herman Bentler was ordained deacon.) Served for almost forty years as a faithful minister of the Gospel. Died in Kent County, Michigan, November 28, 1904, at the age of 68. Burial in Bowne Mennonite Cemetery.

RAY KEIM, 1926-   Preacher   East Goshen
Born in Howard County, Indiana, February 16, 1926. Married Clara Elizabeth Bontrager of Howard County, June 7, 1952. Three children. Ordained preacher in the East Goshen Mennonite congregation, by congregational vote, March 28, 1954, by Paul M. Miller. Served for several years as secretary of the Indiana-Michigan Mennonite Mission Board. Has taken considerable work in the Goshen College Biblical Seminary. He writes: "I wish to be an evangelistic pastor, feeding the flock of God as Christ Himself did. . . . I wish to see the Mennonite Church grow into a strong, soul-winning church. The heart of the Anabaptist vision has a message for our day."

JOSEPH KENNEDY, 1826-1906   Deacon, Preacher   Howard-Miami
Joseph Kennedy may have been the very first deacon to serve in the Howard-Miami congregation; however, his granddaughter insists that he was a preacher. Her claim is substantiated by the diary of John S. Coffman who recorded on March 27, 1887: "Home with Joseph Kennedy who was once a minister here [Howard-Miami] but is not in any church now." His wife was Anna ("Nancy") (1825-1898), whom he married on January 15, 1850. Seven children. She died as a member of the Howard-Miami Amish Mennonite Church, and E. A. Mast and J. S. Horner preached at her funeral services. Joseph Kennedy died in 1906. His funeral was held in the meeting-house of the Church of the Brethren in Plevna, Indiana. The minister of that congregation, Amos Kendall, preached his funeral sermon.

JACOB KILMER, 1819-1909   Deacon   Bower
Born in 1819. His wife was Elizabeth Moyer (1826-1909). The date of his ordination is lost. John F. Funk refers to him as a deacon in 1893, when he was already seventy-four years of age. In 1905 he wrote to Funk, reporting that he was then in his eighty-seventh year, very feeble, hard of hearing, and his eyesight was failing. He reported that he did not get away from home any more. He sent $2.00 to renew his subscription to the **Herald of Truth** to the end of 1906. He died in 1909 and was buried in the cemetery of the Bower Mennonite Church, Owen County.

ERIE KINDY, 1920-   Preacher   Midland
Born at Midland, Michigan, March 11, 1920. Married Beatrice Mast of Fairview, Michigan, May 3, 1942. Five children. Ordained preacher at the Midland Mennonite Church, by lot, October 26, 1952, by Floyd F. Bontrager. Served in the Midland congregation, 1952-58.

BEN B. KING, 1881-   Preacher (Bishop)   Fort Wayne
Born at West Liberty, Ohio, November 24, 1881. Married Melinda M. Mann of Elkhart, Indiana, May 26, 1908. Four daughters. Ordained preacher in the Fort Wayne Mennonite Mission, July 16, 1905, by David Burkholder. Served as superintendent and pastor of the Fort Wayne Mission, 1904-30, then transferred to the Pike congregation, Elida, Ohio, where he served from 1932 to 1942 and where he was ordained bishop by vote of the church, November 20, 1932, with J. M. Shenk officiating. In 1942 he

transferred to Sheldon, Wisconsin, where he served for five years. He is now living retired in Scottdale, Pennsylvania. B. B. King was a successful city mission worker and evangelist in the Mennonite Church. He held two hundred and fifty series of evangelistic meetings in many different Mennonite congregations. His sister Siddie was the wife of Dean Noah Oyer of Goshen College.

DONALD E. KING, 1917-   Preacher, Bishop   Pigeon

Born at Newton, Kansas, February 19, 1917. Married Thelma Ruth Yoder of Hubbard, Oregon, May 4, 1941. Four children. Ordained preacher at the Crystal Springs, Kansas, Mennonite Church, by congregational vote, November 25, 1942, by Bishops H. A. Diener and Milo Kauffman. Served the Crystal Springs congregation, 1942-46. He also took work in the Goshen College Biblical Seminary from which he received the Th.B. degree in 1946 and the B.D. degree in 1959. Since 1946 he has been pastor of the Pigeon Mennonite Church. At the request of the congregation he was ordained bishop there, July 7, 1957, by J. D. Graber. He is a nephew of B. B. King and a son of L. O. King. Allen H. and Paul Erb are his uncles.

NOAH W. KING, 1858-1935   Deacon   Howard-Miami

Born in Holmes County, Ohio, December 19, 1858. Married Elizabeth Miller of Miami County, Indiana, March 26, 1886. Seven children. Taught school. Ordained deacon May 21, 1899, by J. P. Smucker. Like a number of other ordained men in the Indiana-Michigan Amish Mennonite Conference he wore a regular lapel coat for many years. Died January 18, 1935. Burial in Schrock Cemetery. Noah was the grandfather of Paul King of the Howard-Miami congregation.

DANIEL E. KINPORTS, 1830-1912   Preacher   Bower

Born in Lebanon County, Pennsylvania, November 18, 1830. Was living in Wabash County, Illinois, in 1880, and in Patricksburg, Indiana, in 1882. United with the Mennonite Church when about forty years of age. Ordained preacher in the Bower congregation about 1885. Married Anna Orth on November 30, 1854. John S. Coffman, the Mennonite evangelist, visited Kinports in 1887. He used language remarkably sharp for John S. Coffman in his diary: "Today I listened to the conversation of Bro. Kinports which was an animated effusion of words with some scarcity of thought from a fertile, yet uncultured mind that had been imposed upon by the ignorance of forty years ago, which instead of implanting intelligent reasoning power, filled it with belief in witchcraft and other kindred superstitions." Coffman may have been a bit severe in his judgment, but Kinports was undoubtedly not a very effective pastor. Died January 21, 1912, at the age of 81, and was buried in the cemetery adjoining the Bower meetinghouse.

RUSSELL R. KRABILL, 1917-   Preacher, Bishop   Locust Grove, North Goshen

Born at Brighton, Iowa, July 5, 1917. Married Martha Elizabeth Hiestand of Bainbridge, Pennsylvania, August 30, 1947. Two children. Ordained preacher in the Locust Grove congregation, near Elkhart, Indiana, by congregational vote, August 5, 1945, by Paul Mininger. Ordained bishop in the North Goshen congregation, again by congregational vote, September 11, 1955, by Paul Mininger. Had transferred from the Locust Grove to the North Goshen congregation in February 1948. Received the Th.B. degree from Goshen College Biblical Seminary in 1946. Has served on the executive committee of the Indiana-Michigan Conference for a number of years, and is currently the assistant moderator of conference.

C. NORMAN KRAUS, 1924-   Preacher   Maple Grove

Born at Denbigh, Virginia, February 20, 1924. Married Ruth Elizabeth Smith of Lima, Ohio, May 16, 1945. Five children. Ordained preacher in the Maple Grove congregation, by congregational vote, July 30, 1950, by Edwin J. Yoder. Has a B.A. from Goshen College, 1946; a B.D. from Goshen College Biblical Seminary, 1951; a

Th.M., from Princeton Theological Seminary, 1954; and in 1961 received the Ph.D. degree from Duke University. Teaches Bible in Goshen College.

AMOS E. KREIDER, 1889-   Preacher   Maple Grove

Born at Sterling, Illinois, October 19, 1889. Married Stella R. Shoemaker (daughter of Bishop J. S. Shoemaker) on September 5, 1917. Two sons. Studied in the Goshen Academy, 1908-10; in Goshen College, 1911-15, where he received the A.B. degree; in Garrett Biblical Institute, 1915-17, where he received the B.D. degree; and at Northwestern University, 1916-17. During his senior year at Goshen College he worshiped with the Maple Grove congregation at Topeka, and was there chosen by congregational vote and ordained preacher May 5, 1915, by Jonathan Kurtz. He served the summer of 1915 at Maple Grove but never returned thereafter. He was a teacher at Goshen College, 1917-18; associate pastor at Sterling, Illinois, 1918-21; and dean of the Bible School, Goshen College, 1921-23. He then transferred to the General Conference Mennonite Church and served as Professor of New Testament at Witmarsum Theological Seminary, 1923-31. After that he was pastor of the First Mennonite Church, Bluffton, Ohio, 1931-35; and finally served as professor of Bible at Bethel College from 1935. He is currently living at Goshen, Indiana, and serving as a lecturer at Mennonite Biblical Seminary, Elkhart, Indiana.

J. ROBERT KREIDER, 1919-   Preacher   (Goshen College)

Born at Wadsworth, Ohio, December 30, 1919. Married Virginia Stalter of Livingston County, Illinois, June 10, 1941. Five children. Ordained preacher at the Bethel Church near Wadsworth, Ohio, by congregational vote, June 13, 1943, by A. J. Steiner and O. N. Johns. Served as pastor until the year 1956 when he moved to Goshen to become Director of Development for Goshen College. Has also served as treasurer of Mennonite General Conference since 1953.

MARTIN E. KREIDER, 1838-1877   Preacher   Blosser

Came from Medina County, Ohio, in the year 1866. Married Catharine Musser (1840-1900) in 1865. (Following his death she married Joseph Brenneman of Elida, Ohio, in 1880.) Ordained preacher in the "Christophel district," June 22, 1873. Preacher Allen Christophel, who wrote a careful history of the Yellow Creek congregation, lists Martin Kreider as a preacher in the Blosser congregation. John F. Funk wrote that he "was an earnest, zealous preacher and often caused offense by his boldness and plain appeals." This may be a somewhat biased judgment, for the opinion of Kreider's contemporaries was that he was a very zealous worker and a very earnest preacher. He died of typhoid fever, November 2, 1877, a few weeks before his thirty-ninth birthday anniversary.

JOHN KRUPP, 1840-1911   Preacher   Pleasant Hill

A colleague and friend of Daniel Brenneman. Ordained preacher in the Pleasant Hill congregation near Burr Oak, Branch County, Michigan, June 12, 1879. Was silenced late in 1873 for unbalanced "holiness" leanings. Daniel Brenneman was much displeased by this action of the church leaders. Krupp did his lifework in the Mennonite Brethren in Christ Church, now known as the United Missionary Church.

JONATHAN KURTZ, 1848-1930   Preacher, Bishop   Maple Grove

Born in Fairfield County, Ohio (the community from which many of the members of the Maple Grove, Indiana, congregation originally came), July 8, 1848. As a young man he also settled near Ligonier, Indiana. Married Elizabeth Byler (1852-1932) (daughter of Jonathan and Catherine [Kauffman] Byler) on March 19, 1878. Five children. Ordained preacher June 18, 1882. Ordained bishop April 8, 1888, by Bishops J. P. Smucker and Isaac Smucker. He was a good and strong leader. His daughter, Alta Kurtz Christophel, published a booklet: **Ascending and Descending**

Genealogy of the Children of Joseph Kurtz and Lydia Zook. Jonathan Kurtz was one of the finest leaders in the Indiana-Michigan Amish Mennonite Conference. He, D. J. Johns, and D. D. Miller were the three men who most often served as moderator of that conference. Died July 10, 1930, at the age of eighty-two years and two days. Burial in Maple Grove Cemetery, Topeka, Indiana.

GEORGE LAMBERT, 1853-1928   Preacher   Prairie Street

Born in Northampton County, Pennsylvania, May 11, 1853. Married Amanda Gehman (daughter of William Gehman, minister in the Evangelical Mennonite Church) on August 10, 1872. Eight children. Entered the ministry in 1878 and was ordained in 1879. Served the church in Kent County, Michigan, for two years, after which he was called to Elkhart County, Indiana, where he served in Wakarusa until 1897. Withdrew from the Mennonite Brethren in Christ Church in 1896. Was a member of the Mennonite Church, 1902-11. Made a trip around the world and wrote a book about his experiences in 1896 entitled, **Around the Globe and Through Bible Lands.** Served as a relief commissioner for the Mennonite organization, the Home and Foreign Relief Commission, which was organized in 1897. As a result of his experiences in India in relief work he published another book in 1898 entitled, **India, the Horror Stricken Empire.** In 1912 he brought suit against the three bishops, David Burkholder, J. K. Bixler, and D. A. Yoder, for $10,000.00, but two years later withdrew the suit. Returned to the Mennonite Brethren in Christ Church after leaving the Mennonite Church, but did not remain in that fellowship. Joined later the Evangelical Association. Died July 3, 1928.

AMOS S. LANDIS, 1851-1926   Deacon   Goshen College

Born in Lancaster County, Pennsylvania, August 2, 1851. Married Sabina Rutt Ebersole (who also had been born in Lancaster County) on December 11, 1874. Eleven children, including Alice, the wife of Professor John S. Umble of Goshen College. Ordained deacon at Sterling, Illinois, in 1891, by Emanuel Hartman. A farmer and stonecutter. Moved to Oregon in 1894, to Missouri in 1900, to Sterling, Illinois, in 1901, and to Northern Indiana in 1906. Lived on the Fish Lake Road one mile east of Goshen from 1906 until about 1915, after which he resided on South Eighth Street, Goshen, until his death which occurred January 1, 1926.

JOHN M. LANDIS, 1914-   Preacher   Bethel

Born at Newton, Kansas, October 19, 1914. Married Violet Minner of Havre, Montana, August 20, 1939. Two daughters. Was a member of the Evangelical Church, in which fellowship he was ordained deacon at Wichita, Kansas, in 1941. Ordained elder at Abilene, Kansas, August 11, 1946. In both cases he was chosen by the vote of the congregation. Transferred his membership from the E.U.B. Church to the Mennonite Church and was installed in the Bethel congregation as preacher by D. S. Oyer on April 7, 1954. Has the B.A. degree from the John Fletcher College, 1938, and the B.D. degree from the Evangelical Theological Seminary, 1944. His grandfather, George Landis, was a Mennonite minister; and his father, M. D. Landis, taught at Hesston College and later served as a pastor in the Evangelical United Brethren Church.

MELVIN D. LANTZ, 1867-1957   Deacon   Maple Grove

Married (1) Tillie Hartzler (1868-1891) on October 12, 1890. Married (2) Kate E. Yoder of Wayne County, Ohio. Ordained deacon in the Maple Grove congregation, April 27, 1913. (John L. Emmert was ordained deacon in the same service.) Served as deacon until the division in the congregation in 1924.

GEORGE J. LAPP, 1879-1951   Preacher, Bishop   Holdeman

Born in Juniata, Nebraska, May 26, 1879. Married (1) Esther Ebersole of Cullom, Illinois, June 25, 1905. Three daughters. Married (2) Fannie Hershey of Manheim,

Pennsylvania, April 14, 1920. Ordained preacher at the Mennonite Mission, 145 West Eighteenth Street, Chicago, March 27, 1904, by J. S. Shoemaker, for service in India, in which land he invested his life for Christ. Ordained bishop, in India, March 2, 1928, by P. A. Friesen and C. D. Esch. Labored in India from 1905 to 1945, except for a period in which he served as pastor of the Goshen College congregation, 1918-19, while on furlough. Secured a B.A. degree from Goshen College, 1913, and the M.R.E. degree from Bethany Biblical Seminary, Chicago, 1930. Served as president of Goshen College for the academic year, 1918-19. Goshen College Biblical Seminary conferred on him the B.D. degree in 1947. During his retirement at Goshen, he was called by the Holdeman congregation to assume the bishop oversight of that church in 1949, which he did. On November 12, 1950, he ordained Simon G. Gingerich as preacher in the Holdeman congregation. No one anticipated the sudden death of Brother Lapp less than three months later. He passed away January 25, 1951, of a heart attack. Burial in Elkhart Prairie (formerly Alwine) Cemetery southeast of Goshen.

JOHN M. LEDERACH, 1932-   Preacher (Bishop)   Sunnyside
Born at Trooper, Montgomery County, Pennsylvania, March 9, 1932. Married Naomi J. Kauffman (daughter of Bishop A. H. Kauffman) on May 16, 1954. Three children. Licensed to preach in the Sunnyside congregation March 7, 1954, by S. J. Hostetler. Ordained preacher there, August, 7, 1955. Removed to Oregon in October 1957. Ordained bishop there, September 11, 1960.

DANIEL LEHMAN, 1834-1919   Preacher   Tuscola County
Born in Oxford County, Ontario, in 1834. Ordained preacher in the Hay congregation, Ontario, September 22, 1861. Removed to Tuscola County, Michigan, about the year 1884. Three sons and one daughter survived him. Died at Fairgrove, Michigan, October 6, 1919. Funeral services were conducted by Peter Ropp in the Fairgrove Presbyterian Church.

DAVID Y. LEHMAN, 1842-1928   Deacon
Born near North Lima, Ohio. United with the Mennonite Church when a youth. Married (1) Anna Kilmer of Wakarusa, Indiana, in 1865. L. J. Burkholder, in his **Ontario Mennonite History,** page 299, reports that he was ordained as deacon in Indiana in 1866 or 1867. There seems to be no reference in Indiana to this man. Removed to Ontario in 1882, and two years later united with the Stauffer branch of the church there. Married (2) Catherine Krupp, widow of Joseph Krupp. United with the Reformed Mennonites in 1890, and in 1891 removed to Iowa. Died at Shelby, Michigan, in 1928.

HAROLD R. LEHMAN, 1906-   Deacon   Clinton Brick
Born January 20, 1906. Ordained deacon in the Clinton Brick congregation, October 22, 1939, by O. S. Hostetler. Served until January 1951.

JOSEPH S. LEHMAN, 1847-1936   Preacher   Prairie Street
Born in Lancaster County, Pennsylvania, in 1847, son of Joseph Lehman (1812-1899) of Franklin County, Pennsylvania. As a young man he removed to Freeport, Illinois. Ordained preacher in the Freeport congregation in 1886. Six years later John F. Funk called him to Elkhart, where he became the business manager of the Mennonite Publishing Company. Returned to Lancaster, Pennsylvania, in 1904, where he spent the remainder of his life. He was not a minister the last several decades of his career. Died in 1936. Both J. S. Hartzler and N. E. Byers, men who were close to the situation in Elkhart around the turn of the century, reported that J. S. Lehman aggravated the difficulties of John F. Funk in that era. He seemed to excite hostility between Funk and his other ministers as well as with the Elkhart Institute.

LEWIS J. LEHMAN, 1871-1950   Preacher

Born at Cullom, Livingston County, Illinois, August 1, 1871, son of the second wife of Preacher Samuel Yoder of Elkhart. He was married twice. Four children to the first wife and three to the second wife. His second companion was Lydia C. Huber whom he married February 9, 1905. Ordained preacher at Cullom, Illinois, January 22, 1899, by Bishop Nice. Removed to Elkhart, Indiana, about the year 1907. Joined the Mennonite Brethren in Christ Church in 1912. Died September 5, 1950.

MARTIN CLIFFORD LEHMAN, 1883-   Preacher

Born at Dalton, Ohio, March 16, 1883. Married Lydia Liechty of Sterling, Ohio, August 16, 1905. Three children. Received the B.A. degree from Goshen College, 1914, and the M.A. degree in 1915. Later secured the Ph.D. degree from Yale University. Served as a missionary to India for twenty-four years. Ordained preacher February 5, 1911, the same day as C. D. Esch. Was head of the Mennonite High School at Dhamtari, C.P., India, 1906-24. Served as a minister in the Indiana-Michigan Conference, after returning from India, until December 1945.

PETER Y. LEHMAN, 1836-1925   Preacher, Bishop   Lakeville, Clinton Brick

Born in Mahoning County, Ohio, October 2, 1836. Located in Elkhart County, Indiana, at the age of twenty-one. Married Lydia Ann Good (1844-1920) on November 23, 1862. Seventeen children, including Isaac, the father of R. C. Lehman, long-time editor of the Goshen News. Peter and Lydia Ann united with the Mennonite Church in 1863, the year following their marriage, a rather typical practice in that period. Ordained preacher in the small Mennonite congregation near Lakeville, Indiana, October 19, 1865, by John M. Brenneman of Elida, Ohio. (Michael W. Shank was ordained deacon in the same service.) In the Funk-Wisler division of 1872 he followed Wisler, but was reunited with the Indiana conference group on June 12, 1881, when he was received back into church fellowship in the Blosser meetinghouse. Moved east of Goshen in 1884 and affiliated with the Clinton Brick congregation. Preached both at Clinton Brick and at Shore. Ordained bishop at Clinton Brick, by lot, April 30, 1892, possibly by Bishop Henry A. Miller of Shore. In the year 1901 severe tension developed between Bishop P. Y. Lehman and Deacon Jacob C. Hershberger, each of the ordained brethren having a following in the congregation. The conference exerted strenuous efforts to restore peace, and appointed a special committee to make recommendations to the congregation: Bishops Daniel Kauffman of Pennsylvania, John Nice of Illinois, and Moses Brenneman of Ohio. Bishop Lehman refused to yield to the decisions of the committee. The outcome of this situation was that Lehman withdrew from the conference. In the year 1905 he affiliated himself with the Wisler Mennonite Church as a layman. D. D. Miller reported that later P. Y. Lehman returned to the Indiana-Michigan Conference as a layman, and united with the Goshen College congregation. Died March 31, 1925, at the advanced age of eighty-eight years, five months, and twenty-nine days. J. S. Hartzler and J. F. Funk preached his funeral sermons. Burial in South Cemetery at the Yellow Creek (brick) Church.

ETRIL J. LEINBACH, 1910-   Preacher, Bishop   Moorepark

Born in Elkhart County, Indiana, February 8, 1910. Married Wilma P. Pletcher on October 7, 1933. Three sons. Ordained preacher in the Middlebury congregation, by congregational vote, July 4, 1948, by Paul Mininger, for service in the Moorepark outpost of the Middlebury congregation. Ordained bishop at Moorepark, May 6, 1956, by E. C. Bontrager and Lee J. Miller. He is actively associated with the work of the district mission board.

OSCAR L. LEINBACH, 1914-   Preacher   Liberty

Born in Elkhart County, Indiana, January 28, 1914. Married Laurene Bontrager on December 4, 1938. Five children. Ordained preacher in the Yellow Creek congregation, January 5, 1947, by Ray F. Yoder, at the request of the district mission board. Has served the Liberty congregation as preacher from its beginning. He writes: "I had a conviction from my youth that I should become a minister of the Gospel. It was brought to pass when the mission board asked for my ordination and gave me a charge."

CHRISTIAN S. LIECHTY, 1861-1944   Deacon   Leo

Born January 31, 1861. Married Mary Witmer of Leo, Indiana, October 13, 1887. Eleven children. Ordained deacon, by lot, probably in the early 1890's. Served at Leo from the time of his ordination until 1913, probably about twenty years. Farmer. Moved to North Dakota in 1913. Died January 1, 1944. Burial in Community Cemetery at Pettisville, Ohio. His oldest daughter is Malinda Liechty, R.N., of Wauseon, Ohio.

MILLARD C. LIND, 1918-   Preacher   Hopewell

Born at Bakersfield, California, October 10, 1918, son of Bishop N. A. Lind. Married Miriam Esther Sieber of Filer, Idaho, April 17, 1943. Five sons and one daughter. Ordained preacher in the Hopewell congregation, Kouts, Indiana, by congregational vote, May 28, 1944, by D. A. Yoder. Served in the Hopewell congregation, 1944-47, when he transferred to Mennonite Publishing House as writer of **Herald Adult Bible Studies.** Transferred to Goshen College Biblical Seminary as Professor of Old Testament in 1960. Has a B.A. degree from Goshen College, 1942; a Th.B. from Goshen College Biblical Seminary, 1944; a B.D. from the same institution, 1947; and a Th.M. from Pittsburgh-Xenia Theological Seminary, 1955. Is currently a candidate for the doctorate.

G. MAURICE LONG, 1903-   Preacher   Osceola

Born at Nappanee, Indiana, September 1, 1903. Married Mabel Bechtel of Nappanee, December 21, 1924. Three children. Ordained preacher at Osceola, by congregational vote, December 5, 1954, by Homer F. North. He had been licensed on September 27, 1953, to serve as a minister at Osceola. He is a brother of Bishop C. Warren Long of Illinois, a nephew of Deacon Irvin Long, and a grandson of Deacon Jacob Long.

IRVIN A. LONG, 1868-1937   Deacon   Olive

Born in Clay County, Indiana, March 10, 1868. Married Priscilla Holdeman (1869-1946) (daughter of Abraham and Mary [Kilmer] Holdeman) on August 14, 1892. Seven children. Joined Olive Church, April 25, 1903, and was baptized by J. S. Shoemaker of Illinois, in the period when Indiana had no Mennonite bishop. Lived in Baugo Township, Elkhart County, until he retired from farming, then lived near the Olive Church. Ordained deacon at Olive, by lot, February 6, 1927, by D. A. Yoder. Served until about 1931. Died September 9, 1937. Burial in Olive Cemetery.

JACOB G. LONG, 1836-1903   Deacon   Olive

Born in Wadsworth Township, Medina County, Ohio, April 17, 1836, son of John (1784-1862) and Elizabeth (Geissinger) Long (1796-1881). Married Catharine Acker (1839-1906) (born in Bucks County, Pennsylvania) at Wadsworth, Ohio, August 18, 1859. Eight children. Ordained deacon at Olive, in "Shaum's district," May 13, 1882. Lived about halfway between the Olive and Yellow Creek meetinghouses, and frequently alternated back and forth between the two churches. The archives of the Mennonite Church contain his deacon's book which is labeled, "Shaum's and Yellow Creek Churches by Jacob Long, Deacon." Both the 1882 and 1885 files of the **Herald of Truth** contain articles by Jacob. Moved east of Goshen into the Clinton area in 1900 and served the Clinton Brick congregation until his death, December 15, 1903. His obituary in the **Herald of Truth** speaks of him as "highly esteemed and respected."

Burial in East Cemetery, Olive Church. Jacob had removed from Clay County to St. Joseph County, Indiana, in 1867, and settled in Elkhart County the next year.

JACOB O. LOUCKS, 1831-1893   Preacher   Holdeman

Born in Holmes County, Ohio, September 9, 1831, son of Peter (1805-1895) and Anna (Berkey) Loucks. (Peter had been born in Westmoreland County, Pennsylvania.) Removed with his parents to Elkhart County, Indiana, in 1851 and settled in Locke Township. Married Catharine Freed (1837-1907) (daughter of Jacob Freed of Virginia). Eight children. Ordained preacher at Holdeman on October 20, 1887, by Henry Shaum. Never felt able to assume the work of the ministry. Died October 23, 1893, of typhoid fever. Burial in Olive Cemetery.

JONAS LOUCKS, 1853-1938   Preacher   Holdeman, Yellow Creek

Born in Harrison Township, Elkhart County, Indiana, January 3, 1853, younger brother of Jacob Loucks. Married (1) Anna Ramer (1854-1900) (daughter of Deacon Tobias and Esther [Hoover] Ramer) on July 30, 1876. Five children. Married (2) Susannah Ramer (1866-1907) (younger sister of his first wife) on January 3, 1901. One daughter. Married (3) Irena Belle Culp (1874-1959) on September 6, 1911. No children. Ordained preacher at Holdeman, October 12, 1886, by Bishop Michael Horst of Ohio. (Henry Shaum was ordained bishop in the same service.) The ordinations of Jonas Loucks and Henry Shaum in the Holdeman congregation may have been performed there because Holdeman was at that time the largest congregation west of Goshen, but Jonas served his entire ministry in the Yellow Creek congregation. He was much concerned for the welfare of the church, officiated at many funerals, and was a great lover of his brotherhood. Died August 20, 1938. Burial in Yellow Creek Cemetery.

CHRISTIAN LUGBILL, 1825-1880   Preacher   Leo

Christian Lugbill is reported to have been ordained preacher at the Leo Amish Mennonite Church in 1875. Served only five years. Died August 30, 1880. He and his wife, Catharine Lugbill (1831-1881), are buried in the Yaggy Cemetery in Allen County.

JOHN C. LUGBILL, 1857-1926   Preacher, Deacon   Leo

Son of Preacher Christian Lugbill. Ordained preacher in the Leo congregation in 1880. Wrote letters to the **Herald of Truth** in the years 1888 and 1890, signing them J. C. Lugbill. The name is apparently pronounced with a slight syllable following the **g** so that others who wrote his name for the **Herald of Truth** often spelled it Lugibill. He was active until the 1890's, when his ministry seems to have terminated. Oddly enough he was chosen deacon by the Leo congregation and ordained as deacon May 25, 1913. Died January 10, 1926. Burial in Schlatter Cemetery.

CLEO A. MANN, 1900-   Deacon, Preacher   Pleasant View, Indianapolis

Born at Elkhart, Indiana, May 11, 1900. Married Nellie Marie Miller of Elkhart, Indiana, August 28, 1924. Two children, the younger of whom, David, is a bishop at Albany, Oregon. Ordained deacon at Pleasant View, December 18, 1949, by D. A. Yoder. His family had been one of the four commissioned by the Prairie Street congregation to open the Pleasant View Sunday School in 1936. Served as superintendent until 1945. Served as director of Belgium relief work, under Mennonite Relief Committee, from October 1945 to November 1948. Licensed to preach at Indianapolis, October 11, 1953, by D. A. Yoder. Ordained preacher at the First Mennonite Church of Indianapolis on May 6, 1956.

LESTER L. MANN, 1909-   Preacher   Pleasant View

Born at Goshen, Indiana, June 27, 1909. Married (1) Sarah Leona Miller of Sugarcreek, Ohio. Four sons. Married (2) Elsie Maud Hooley of Tuleta, Texas, August

22, 1943. No children. Ordained preacher in the Pleasant View congregation, by lot, September 27, 1942, by D. A. Yoder. Lester's first wife died five days after his ordination. Transferred to the North Central Conference to serve the Rainy River congregation, and secured his conference letter in June 1956.

DAVID B. MARTIN, 1829-1902   Deacon   Caledonia, Yellow Creek

Born in Waterloo County, Ontario, February 13, 1829. The **Herald of Truth** mentions a Deacon D. Martin at Caledonia in 1867. Deacon David Martin appears in the history of the Yellow Creek Church as early as 1869. This was likely the same man. He may have been married three times. His first wife was Elizabeth Eyman, (1839-1884). Four children. The records of David Burkholder mention the death of Susanna, wife of Deacon David Martin, near Wakarusa, September 10, 1888. Again David Burkholder records the death of Kate, wife of Deacon David Martin, on May 19, 1905. In his late years he transferred to the Wisler Mennonites. Attended the Indiana-Michigan Mennonite Conference sessions as late as 1892. Died June 19, 1902, of apoplexy. His funeral sermons were preached by Jonas Loucks of the Indiana-Michigan Conference, and by Christian Shaum and John W. Martin, who were Wisler Mennonites.

FRANK J. MARTIN, 1879-1944   Deacon   Fort Wayne

Born near Maysville, Indiana, July 1, 1879. Married Pearl Mertz (died 1940) on February 22, 1902. Five children. He was converted to Christ in the Fort Wayne Mennonite Mission. He and his wife Pearl were baptized in November 1904 by L. J. Lehman. He is the only deacon which the Mennonite Church at Fort Wayne ever had. He was ordained July 8, 1909, by David Burkholder. Because of his health he asked to be released from active obligations in October 1942. He had served as superintendent of the Fort Wayne Mennonite Mission, 1930-34. He is described as "an ardent and faithful worker in the church and Sunday school" (Herbert Osborne). Died January 3, 1944. **Burial at Leo, Indiana.**

HENRY MARTIN, 1801-1883   Preacher   Clinton Brick

Born in Lancaster County, Pennsylvania, December 2, 1801. His line of descent was Pioneer Henry Martin—Bishop Henry Martin of the Lancaster Conference—David Martin of Cumberland County, Pennsylvania—Preacher Henry Martin. Ordained preacher in the Slate Hill congregation, Cumberland County, Pennsylvania, 1818, and served in Wayne County, Ohio, prior to the Civil War. David Sherk of Ontario, for example, fellowshiped with him in 1863 in Ohio. John F. Funk mentions visiting him in May 1867 at Orrville. Removed to Clinton Township, Elkhart County, Indiana, in 1874, when he was seventy-two years of age. Died nine years later, November 1, 1883, at the age of 81. Burial in Clinton Brick Cemetery. His tombstone reads, "Rev. Henry Martin." He was the maternal grandfather of Bishops John Garber and David Garber.

JASON S. MARTIN, 1927-   Preacher   Wawasee

Born near Wakarusa, Indiana, January 23, 1927, son of Bishop Joseph E. Martin of the Wisler Mennonite Church. Married Mary F. Baer, R.N. (daughter of Preacher Isaac M. Baer, now of Washington, D.C.), on December 25, 1956. Three children. Ordained at the Wawasee Lakeside Chapel (to succeed Herbert L. Yoder, who resigned to take further schoolwork as a schoolteacher) on April 23, 1961. He is a student in Goshen College Biblical Seminary.

SIMEON P. MARTIN, 1890-1955   Deacon   Zion

Born at May City, Iowa, in 1890. Married Ruby Andrews (1896-1955). Ordained deacon in the Zion congregation at Vestaburg, Michigan, by lot, September 23, 1917, by J. K. Bixler. Served as deacon about six years. Left the church in 1923. Died in 1955.

EMANUEL A. MAST, 1856-1932   Preacher, Bishop   Howard-Miami

Born in Somerset County, Pennsylvania, September 16, 1856. Married (1) Elizabeth Mast on October 14, 1877. Two foster children. Married (2) Clara (Troyer) Schrock (widow of Christian Schrock) on December 17, 1891. Five children. Farmer. Converted at the age of twenty. Ordained preacher in the Howard-Miami congregation 1881. Ordained bishop in the same church on June 7, 1891. (1891 **H.T.**, 185; 1892 **H.T.**, 9.) His second ordination was performed by Jonas C. Yoder, formerly of the Pretty Prairie congregation, but then of Logan County, Ohio. "Man" died July 26, 1932, of cancer of the stomach. Burial in Mast Cemetery, Liberty Township, Howard County.

HAROLD L. MAST, 1935-   Deacon, Preacher   South Colon

Born in Elkhart County, Indiana, May 4, 1935. (His father had come from Holmes County, Ohio, to Elkhart County at the age of twenty-one. Married Mildred Boyer of Middlebury in 1932.) Married Edna Marie Yoder on August 24, 1956. One son. Ordained deacon in the South Colon congregation, May 19, 1957. Ordained preacher October 23, 1960, by T. E. Schrock.

FRANKLIN B. MAUST, 1861-1932   Deacon   Nappanee (North)

Born at Meyersdale, Pennsylvania, January 11, 1861, first cousin of O. S. Hostetler's father. Came to Elkhart County, Indiana, at the age of twenty-one. Farmer. Married (1) Catharine Mishler of Howard County (where he lived a few years) on May 20, 1882. Eight children. They resided in Arkansas a few years, then settled at Nappanee. Catharine died December 31, 1912. Married (2) Minnie Dennison on February 19, 1914. Ordained deacon, by lot (to take the place of Deacon Jacob H. Wisler who had moved to Elkhart), April 8, 1906, by David Burkholder. Died June 23, 1932, after twenty-six years of faithful service. He was the son of Ben Maust (1835-1911), who came from Somerset County, Pennsylvania.

SHERMAN MAUST, 1902-   Preacher (Bishop)   Pigeon

Born at Meyersdale, Pennsylvania, August 7, 1902. Married Laura Mae Kipfer of Zurich, Ontario, November 27, 1924. Four children. Ordained preacher at Berne, Michigan, September 17, 1933, by Menno Esch. Moved to California in the year 1945 and was ordained bishop in the Upland congregation, April 29, 1947, by J. P. Bontrager.

MITCHELL D. McCLOUD, 1908-1959   Deacon   Nappanee (North)

Born at Nappanee, Indiana, August 23, 1908. Married Beulah Chupp of White Cloud, Michigan, September 8, 1928. No children. Ordained deacon in the Nappanee congregation, by lot, September 11, 1953, by Ray F. Yoder. Served the Nappanee Church faithfully from 1953 until his early death July 10, 1959. Will long be remembered for the unusual amount of Scripture which he committed to memory, and which he was requested to give publicly in various churches. Worked as a maintenance man in a factory. Burial in Union Center Cemetery.

JAMES HENRY McGOWEN, 1851-1927   Deacon, Preacher   Nappanee (West)

Born in Morrow County, Ohio, March 11, 1851. Came to Indiana with his parents in 1856. Married Elizabeth Weber (1852-1924) on February 25, 1875. Four children. Ordained deacon at the West Market Street Amish Mennonite Church, April 4, 1885. (Jacob Bleile was ordained preacher in the same service.) Ordained preacher in the same congregation, July 22, 1888, by J. P. Smucker. An able and fluent preacher. The older people remember his long white beard. Died April 2, 1927. He has been described as the "John Funk type," that is, serious, sober, and "to the point" in his preaching.

NOAH METZLER, 1854-1907   Preacher   Olive, Yellow Creek, Nappanee

Born in Mahoning County, Ohio, April 26, 1854. Married Nancy Hartman on December 24, 1874. Seven children. Converted to Christ in 1875. A sincere Christian, a man of deep spirituality, an able preacher, and a good evangelist. A very serious man. O. S. Hostetler says he cannot recall that he ever saw him smile. Ordained preacher in the Shaum (Olive) congregation, Saturday, June 5, 1880, by Bishop Jacob A. Beutler. There were three brethren in the lot: Noah Metzler, Jacob Welty, and John Martin. Served five years at Olive, then moved to a farm in Harrison Township, near the Yellow Creek meetinghouse, and began to preach at Yellow Creek. Moved to Nappanee in 1903 and assisted in the work there until his death. Preached at Yellow Creek on June 2, 1907; text, Genesis 3:6, 7. During his message he grew weak, looked at his wife, and reported that he would need to speak more slowly. In a short while he sat down. Jonas Loucks then took over the discourse. Noah made his way to an anteroom, followed by his wife and others. He soon lost the power of speech, and was carried to the home of Nancy Hoover nearby. His last words to the congregation were to the effect that they should meet him in heaven. Died at two o'clock that day, aged fifty-three years, one month, and six days. Burial in Union Center Cemetery. In 1896 he served for a time at the Mennonite Mission at 168 West Eighteenth Street, Chicago.

SAMUEL B. METZLER, 1878-1952   Deacon   Salem

Born in Mahoning County, Ohio, January 4, 1878, son of Samuel and Veronica Metzler. Married (1) Nora Reed on January 20, 1905. (She died in 1907.) One daughter. Married (2) Phoebe Christophel (1880-1952) on September 19, 1908. Three sons. Ordained deacon in the Salem congregation, May 15, 1932, by Jacob K. Bixler. Served almost twenty years. Died February 28, 1952. Burial at Yellow Creek.

ABSALOM MILLER, 1827-1898   Deacon   Howard-Miami

Born in Holmes County, Ohio, February 19, 1827. Removed to Howard County, Indiana, in 1850. Married Barbara Shrock in December 1850. Eight children. Carpenter. Also operated an eight-horsepower threshing machine. Helped to establish the first steam sawmill in Miami County. Ordained in the early years of the Civil War, possibly around 1862. Died March 11, 1898. Burial in Shrock Cemetery, Liberty Township, Howard County.

ALVIN R. MILLER, 1917-   Deacon   Nappanee

Born at Mt. Ayr, Indiana, October 15, 1917. Married Nora Nissley of Hutchinson, Kansas, November 2, 1937. Ordained deacon at Nappanee, by lot, May 8, 1960, by Homer F. North.

ANDREW J. MILLER, 1895-   Deacon   Olive

Born at Troy, Ohio, March 29, 1895. Married Mary Yoder of Arthur, Illinois, January 15, 1922. Three children. Ordained deacon (along with M. C. Weaver), at the Olive Church by lot, November 5, 1933, by D. A. Yoder. He is the grandson of Old Order Amish Bishop Moses Borkholder of Nappanee, Indiana.

ANDREW S. MILLER, 1876-1945   Preacher   Leo

Born in Lagrange County, Indiana, December 31, 1876, son of Daniel C. and Nancy (Plank) Miller. United with the Shore Mennonite Church as a young man. Married Emma Stuckey (daughter of Joseph and Fannie [Schlatter] Stuckey) October 29, 1903. Three children, the oldest being a foster child. Moved from the Shore congregation to the Leo congregation about 1905 and was chiefly instrumental in arranging for that congregation to unite with the Indiana-Michigan A.M. Conference. Ordained preacher at Leo, by majority vote of the congregation, May 28, 1910, by D. J. Johns and Jonathan Kurtz. Died March 7, 1945. Burial at Leo.

21

C. NEVIN MILLER, 1927-   Preacher   Detroit

Born in Lancaster County, Pennsylvania, February 25, 1927. Married Evelyn Marie Shoemaker on October 18, 1947. Three sons. Ordained preacher at Good's Church, February 6, 1947, by Noah W. Risser. Served as pastor at Detroit, June 24, 1956, to June 24, 1959. Returned to Pennsylvania.

CHRISTIAN C. MILLER, 1818-1891   Preacher   Forks

Born in Somerset County, Pennsylvania, June 5, 1818. Married (1) Lydia Hochstetler (1822-1849) of Somerset County, Pennsylvania. Three children. Moved to Lagrange County, Indiana in 1844. Married (2) Barbara Mast (1816-1872). Three children. Married (3) Fannie (Miller) Kauffman (1839-1905) (daughter of Solomon and Rachel Miller). Three children. Ordained preacher about the year 1852. Served in the ministry about thirty-eight years. Died July 25, 1891. His funeral was held in the Townline meetinghouse, with Jonas D. Troyer, 80, Christian Nofsinger, 72, of the Pretty Prairie congregation, and D. J. Johns, 39, all speaking. Burial at Townline. In 1887 he made an extended trip of seven weeks to Somerset County, Pennsylvania, and Holmes and Wayne counties, Ohio. He was an uncle of Mrs. O. S. Hostetler.

D. RICHARD MILLER, 1932-   Preacher   Sunnyside

Born at Smithville, Ohio, October 22, 1932. Married Marilyn Swinehart of Orrville, Ohio, August 27, 1955. Two children. Has Th.B. degree from Goshen College Biblical Seminary. Assistant pastor, Hannibal, Missouri, 1955-56; pastor, Pleasant Hill, Illinois, 1956-58; pastor, Sunnyside congregation, Elkhart, Indiana, 1958- .

DANIEL C. MILLER, 1824-1902   Preacher, Bishop   Howard-Miami

Born in Tuscarawas County, Ohio, December 13, 1824. Married Magdalena Fry in 1854. Five children. Removed from Ohio to Howard County, Indiana, in 1856. Ordained minister about the time of the Civil War; his obituary gives the year as 1867. Ordained bishop about 1873. His obituary in the **Herald of Truth** indicates that he was a man who was much concerned for peace. Died April 7, 1902, at the age of 77. Burial in Mast Cemetery, Liberty Township, Howard County, Indiana. He was the grandfather of Ammon J. Mast of Goshen.

DANIEL D. MILLER, 1864-1955   Deacon, Preacher, Bishop   Forks

Born in Lagrange County, Indiana, November 10, 1864, son of Daniel P. and Anna (Hershberger) Miller. Married Jeanette Hostetler on May 26, 1889. Thirteen children, the first two of whom died in infancy. Schoolteacher and farmer; and all his children taught school for greater or lesser periods of time. He himself taught twenty years. Ordained deacon at the Forks Church, by lot, October 18, 1890, by D. J. Johns. Ordained preacher at Forks, by congregational vote, October 20, 1891, by D. J. Johns. Ordained bishop, by congregational vote, April 13, 1906, again by D. J. Johns. (J. Y. Hooley was ordained deacon in the same service.) He was one of the ablest bishops in the Amish Mennonite Church. He, Jonathan Kurtz, and D. J. Johns constituted the three most effective leaders in that conference. He became ill in 1944, but partly recovered in 1945. The last few years of his life he was in fragile health. Died January 19, 1955, at 90 years of age. Burial in Forest Grove Cemetery. He wrote articles on the veil and on life insurance in the **Bible Doctrine** of 1914. He was moderator of Mennonite General Conference in 1913, and a member for many years of each of the three boards of the church: the Mennonite Board of Education, the Mennonite Board of Missions and Charities, and the Mennonite Publication Board. Served as moderator of the Indiana-Michigan Amish Mennonite Conference five times, was moderator at the time of the merger, and served as the first moderator of the united conference, 1916-17. Served as president of the Mennonite Board of Missions and Charities from 1920 through 1935, and as treasurer from 1936 to 1938. He was a firm disciplinarian, and a progressive leader in all good things. A few years after his death his son Ernest published a biographical sketch of him entitled, **Daniel D. Miller, a Biographical Sketch.** . . .

EARL MILLER, 1880-   Deacon   Middlebury

Born in Lagrange County, Indiana, October 16, 1880. Married (1) Mattie Troyer of Lagrange County, Indiana, January 17, 1904. Two foster children. Married (2) Phoebe A. Smucker of Logan County, Ohio, June 15, 1941. Ordained deacon in the Middlebury congregation, by congregational vote, November 16, 1924, by D. D. Miller. Served as treasurer of the Indiana-Michigan Mennonite Conference for many years. Farmer and carpenter.

ELI S. MILLER, 1821-1917   Deacon, Bishop   Clinton Frame

Born in Holmes County, Ohio, September 11, 1821. Married Mary (Maria) Kauffman (1823-1900) in 1843. Fifteen children. Ordained deacon in Ohio in the year 1849. Ordained bishop **(Voelliger Armendiener,** which really means a confirmed or bishop-deacon) in Ohio in 1860. Removed to Elkhart County, Indiana, the summer of 1870 and located near the Eighth-Square schoolhouse. Served as a leader in the Elkhart County Amish Mennonite Church for forty-seven years. Performed weddings gave communion, and in various ways functioned as a bishop. Learned the Sermon on the Mount by heart after he was ninety years of age.

About 1883 he went to Logan and Champaign counties, Ohio, and organized a group of Amish Mennonites who were locally out of fellowship for allowing a member to have an organ in his home, and for the use of the English language in Sunday school. This congregation therefore got the name, the Indiana (or "Miller") Amish Mennonite Church. He ordained Samuel H. Detweiler as bishop, and John H. Kauffman as minister, and the congregation was accepted as a member of the Indiana Amish Mennonite Conference. The congregation was eventually largely absorbed by the Bethel Mennonite Church in the village of West Liberty, Ohio. Died March 1, 1917, at the age of 95. D. J. Johns and D. D. Miller preached his funeral sermons. Burial in Miller Cemetery, east of the Shore Church. Eli wore a beard, but not a plain (clerical) coat.

ERNEST E. MILLER, 1893-   Preacher   Forks

Born in Lagrange County, Indiana, September 16, 1893, son of Bishop D. D. Miller. Married Ruth Blosser of Ada, Ohio, June 20, 1918. Two children, the younger of whom is D. G. Miller, M.D., of Middlebury, Indiana. The older child, Thelma, is the wife of India missionary Weyburn W. Groff. Secured the B.A. degree from Goshen College, 1917; the M.A. degree from New York University, 1929; and the Ph.D., also from New York University, 1939. Served as a missionary to India, 1929-37; and president of Goshen College, 1940-54. He is currently Professor of Education in Goshen College. Ordained preacher at the Forks Church, December 9, 1917, by J. S. Shoemaker, who was then secretary of the Mennonite Board of Missions and Charities, the organization under which Ernest was to serve in India. Served as a preacher, following his return from his India service, in the Forks congregation, 1937-47. Was received as a member and preacher in the Goshen College Mennonite Church, March 16, 1947. Holds the title, President Emeritus of Goshen College.

HARVEY A. MILLER, 1863-1924   Deacon   White Cloud

Born in Elkhart County, Indiana, October 15, 1863. Married Sarah J. Nelson on November 21, 1886. Two children. Baptized in the Shore Mennonite Church in 1894. Removed five years later to the area of the White Cloud Mennonite congregation. Ordained deacon September 28, 1912, by J. P. Miller. Served for almost twelve years. Died August 21, 1924. Burial at White Cloud, Michigan.

HENRY MILLER, 1800-1870

According to L. J. Burkholder, Henry Miller, whose wife was Lydia Null, was ordained as preacher in the Rainham congregation, Ontario. When it was found that he was unable to preach, he was charged with performing the work of a deacon. "He later moved to Indiana." There seems to be no record of any service on his part as a deacon in Indiana, however.

HENRY A. MILLER, 1820-1893   Preacher, Bishop   Shore

Born in Somerset County, Pennsylvania, April 17, 1820, son of Jacob and Katie Miller. Married Martha Thomas (1820-1902) (who united with the Mennonite Church in 1849) in 1840. Four children, three of whom grew to maturity. Lived four years in Cambria County, Pennsylvania. Removed to a farm near Waterford, Elkhart County, Indiana, in 1844. Settled in Clay Township, Lagrange County, Indiana, in 1852, where he finally united with the Mennonite Church. Ordained preacher in what is now known as the Shore congregation (at that time the church worshiped in the Lake schoolhouse) about the year 1865. In 1865 he reported a funeral to the **Herald of Truth,** which could indicate that he was then a minister. In January 1866, John Lapp of New York state speaks of "Brother Henry Miller, minister." Ordained bishop in an afternoon service in the Clinton Brick meetinghouse, June 18, 1883, apparently by Bishop George Brenneman, assisted by J. A. Beutler and John Gnagy. He was in the lot on this occasion with the well-known preacher, J. J. Weaver. This was one day after James J. Mishler was ordained deacon in the "Lake Shore" congregation. Served as a faithful and beloved shepherd until his death November 30, 1893. Burial in Miller Cemetery one mile east of the Shore meetinghouse. Henry was the great-grandfather of Lee J. Miller, the present bishop of the Shore Church.

HOMER J. MILLER, 1898-   Deacon   Shore

Born in Elkhart County, Indiana, July 31, 1898. Married Lizzie Troyer of Lagrange County, Indiana, September 1, 1917. Four children. Ordained deacon in the Shore congregation, by congregational vote, April 29, 1945, by Lee J. Miller and O. S. Hostetler. Has served faithfully and effectively.

ISAAC A. MILLER, 1839-1904   Preacher   Fairview

Born near Johnstown, Pennsylvania, May 4, 1839. Married (1) Catherine Yoder on March 25, 1860. Eleven children. (She died in 1886.) Married (2) Magdalena Miller on January 4, 1888. Served as a minister in several states, and in December 1903 moved to Oscoda County, Michigan, and affiliated himself with the Fairview congregation. His address in Illinois had been Chesterville. He preferred to preach in German, but was able to preach in English also. Served only four months at Fairview. Died in a chair April 19, 1904. Eli A. Bontrager preached a funeral sermon on that occasion in a Fairview schoolhouse.

IVAN M. MILLER, 1906-   Deacon, Bishop   Emma

Born in Lagrange County, Indiana, December 6, 1906. Married Erma Miller, also of Lagrange County, February 8, 1930. Seven children. Ordained deacon in the Emma congregation, by congregational vote, April 1, 1945, by O. S. Hostetler. Ordained bishop in the same congregation, October 11, 1953, again by O. S. Hostetler, and again by the vote of the church.

JACOB P. MILLER, 1850-1927   Preacher, Bishop   White Cloud, Bowne, Shore

Born near Johnstown, Pennsylvania, December 16, 1850. He was a brother of D. D. Miller's father Daniel. Removed to Lagrange County, Indiana, in 1856. He was originally an Amish Mennonite, but transferred his membership to the Shore Mennonite Church. Married (1) Fannie Hostetler, 1903. Married (2) Mary Kime on July 1, 1911. Moved to White Cloud, Michigan, in 1900, where he was ordained preacher July 1,

1900, by John F. Funk. Ordained bishop there on May 5, 1901, by P. Y. Lehman. Removed to the Bowne congregation in Kent County, Michigan, in July 1911. Served there until March 1916, when he moved back to Indiana to the Shore congregation. Here he served until his death. Prior to his locating at Shore, the Clinton Brick and Shore congregations had been in one bishop district, but from his time on, John Garber served as bishop at Clinton Brick and Jacob P. Miller at Shore. Died August 13, 1927, near Shipshewana. Burial at Shore.

JOHN RAY MILLER, 1927-   Deacon   Plato, Pleasantview

Born September 20, 1927. Married Darlene Elizabeth Miller of Johnson County, Iowa, July 26, 1947. Two sons. Ordained deacon at Plato, by congregational vote, March 14, 1954, by O. S. Hostetler. He was converted while in the army. "Through God's leading I was discharged." In 1961 transferred to the Pleasantview Congregation where he served as a minister.

JOSEPH D. MILLER, 1858-1901   Preacher   Forks

Born in Elkhart County, Indiana, September 20, 1858, an older brother of D. D. Miller. United with the Amish Mennonite Church in 1878, when twenty years of age. Married Catharine (Katy) Johns (first cousin of D. J. Johns). Seven children. Ordained preacher, by lot (four nominees),June 19, 1886, by J. P. Smucker. In January 1901, he contracted pleurisy and pneumonia. He was conscious until the last moments before his death. He called in each one of his children and gave them farewell. After the family thought he was dead, he lifted his hands heavenward and smiled. His death occurred January 14, 1901. Burial in Bontrager Cemetery in Lagrange County. Jonathan Kurtz and D. J. Johns preached his funeral sermons. He was familiarly known as "Joely."

JOSIAH J. MILLER, 1870-1958   Preacher   Shore

Born near Shipshewana, Indiana, October 19, 1870. Married (1) Magdalena Yoder of near Shipshewana, January 13, 1895. Seven children. Married (2) Annie (Nelson) Weaver on December 10, 1910. One daughter. Married (3) Lizzie (Eash) Hostetler on June 29, 1940. Ordained preacher at the Shore Mennonite Church, by congregational vote, October 15, 1902, by John Nice of Morrison, Illinois, in the period when Indiana had no Mennonite bishop. He was an earnest and faithful Mennonite preacher, with a deep concern for the welfare of the church. Died April 24, 1958, in his eighty-eighth year. Burial in Shore Cemetery.

LEE J. MILLER, 1907-   Deacon, Bishop   Shore

Born near Shipshewana, Indiana, October 21, 1907, great-grandson of Henry A. Miller. Married Ruth Troyer of Lagrange, Indiana, April 22, 1928. Nine children. Ordained deacon, by lot, March 25, 1934, by O. S. Hostetler. Ordained bishop at the Shore Church January 28, 1945, again by O. S. Hostetler. Has served as bishop at Shore since his ordination, and at Locust Grove until the ordination of Orvin H. Hooley.

LEWIS B. MILLER, 1929-   Preacher   Elmwood

Born at Goshen, Indiana, July 12, 1929, son of Preacher Ira S. Miller of the Old Order Amish Church. Married Lois Mary Hartman of Goshen, November 23, 1950. Four children, two of whom survive. Ordained preacher at the Benton Mennonite Church, by congregational vote, September 20, 1953, by Edwin J. Yoder, for service in the outpost of the Benton congregation, Elmwood at Kendallville. He has four uncles who are also in the ministry, two of them Amish, and two Conservative Mennonite.

LLOYD R. MILLER, 1920-   Preacher   Wildwood

Born at Fairview, Oscoda County, Michigan, August 25, 1920. Married Clara Terwillegar of Newaygo County Michigan, June 30, 1943. Six children. Ordained preacher at Fairview, February 10, 1952, by Menno Esch, at the request of the district mission board. Has served as minister at Wildwood from that date. Poultry farmer.

MALVIN P. MILLER, 1899-   Deacon   Forks, California
    Born at Sugarcreek, Ohio, March 3, 1899. Married Anna Mae Yoder of Middlebury, Indiana, December 25, 1922. Five children. Ordained deacon at the Forks Church, by congregational vote, March 29, 1942, by D. D. Miller. Served as deacon at Forks until February 1960, when he removed to Reading, Michigan, and was installed as pastor of the mission outpost of the Forks Church, "California," in Michigan. He had driven to California by car for some time before he moved to Michigan.

PAUL M. MILLER, 1914-   Preacher, Bishop   East Goshen
    Born at Bainbridge, Pennsylvania, April 2, 1914. Married Bertha Mumma of Landisville, Pennsylvania, May 14, 1938. Four children. Ordained preacher at the East Goshen Mennonite Church, by congregational vote, March 9, 1947, by Paul Mininger. Ordained bishop at East Goshen, November 18, 1951, by Paul Mininger. Holds the Th.B. degree from Goshen College Biblical Seminary, 1950; and the B.D., 1952. Received the Th.M. degree from Southern Baptist Theological Seminary, 1955, and the Doctor of Theology in 1961. He is Professor of Practical Theology and Director of Practical Work in the Goshen College Biblical Seminary. Has served as bishop of the Bethel congregation, Ashley, Michigan, from 1954; of Middlebury, from 1957; and of Fort Wayne, from 1959. He became chairman of the Commission for Christian Education in 1957. He is the author of the book, **Group Dynamics in Evangelism.**

PERCY J. MILLER, 1897-   Deacon, Preacher   Shore
    Born near Shipshewana, Indiana, September 17, 1897, son of Preacher Josiah J. Miller, and named Percival. This name, however, has been shortened to Percy. Married Artie Yoder of Lagrange, Indiana, February 1, 1920. Three children. Ordained deacon at the Shore Mennonite Church, by lot, January 16, 1927, by O. S. Hostetler. Ordained preacher at Shore, again by lot, December 3, 1933, by O. S. Hostetler. Served for many years as secretary of the Indiana-Michigan Mennonite Mission Board. He has the kind of pastoral heart which builds churches.

SAMUEL J. MILLER, 1893-   Preacher, Bishop   Pigeon, Leo
    Born in Lagrange County, Indiana, July 10, 1893. Married Sarah Schlatter of Allen County, Indiana, June 22, 1916. Five children. Ordained preacher at the Pigeon Mennonite Church, by congregational vote, April 4, 1926, by D. A. Yoder. Ordained bishop at the Leo Mennonite Church, by approval of the congregation, January 15, 1950, by O. S. Hostetler. Served at Pigeon, 1926-44, and from 1944 at Leo. Since 1929 he has frequently been engaged in evangelistic work from coast to coast in the United States and Canada. He held meetings in over 120 congregations with 1,277 responses to the invitation of the Gospel (figures of 1945).

SAMUEL S. MILLER, 1908-   Preacher, Bishop   Clinton Brick, Hopewell
    Born at Middlebury, Indiana, February 21, 1908, son of Bishop D. D. Miller. Married Ellen Gardner of Middlebury, Indiana, December 24, 1932. Four children. Schoolteacher. Ordained preacher at the Clinton Brick Mennonite Church, by congregational vote, January 5, 1936, by D. A. Yoder. Served at Clinton Brick from 1936 to 1946. Was called to the Hopewell congregation, Kouts, Indiana, in the year 1953, where he was installed as pastor on August 16, and where he was ordained as bishop, by congregational vote, May 8, 1955, by Paul Mininger.

VERNON U. MILLER, 1917-   Deacon   North Goshen
    Born in Lagrange County, Indiana, February 13, 1917. Married Bertha M. Stauffer of Elkhart County, Indiana, January 1, 1946. Four children. Ordained deacon at North Goshen, by lot, July 19, 1953, by Paul Mininger. Has served effectively in the office of deacon since the time of his ordination. Farmer.

VICTOR V. MILLER, 1920-   Preacher   Seney
Born at Middlebury, Indiana, March 29, 1920, grandson of Preacher Joseph D. Miller. Married Eva Mae Mishler of Shipshewana, Indiana, June 23, 1946. Six children. Ordained preacher at the Forks Mennonite Church, Middlebury, Indiana, July 22, 1951, by E. C. Bontrager, at the request of the district mission board. Has served as pastor of the Seney Mennonite Church since that date. Electrician.

W. WILBUR MILLER, 1889-   Preacher   Forks
Born near Middlebury, Indiana, May 28, 1899. Married Mary G. Warye of Ohio, May 6, 1923. Three daughters. Ordained preacher at the Forks Mennonite Church, by congregational vote, June 5, 1921, by D. D. Miller. Served about three years. Is now a school administrator in Columbus, Ohio. His name was originally Wilbur W., not W. Wilbur.

WILLIAM R. MILLER, 1908-   Preacher   Crumstown
Born in Newton County, Indiana, May 30, 1908. Married Esther N. Miller of St. Joseph County, Michigan, July 4, 1932. Six children. Ordained preacher at the Clinton Frame Church, August 1, 1948, by D. A. Yoder, to serve at Crumstown, Indiana, under the direction of the Indiana-Michigan Mennonite Mission Board.

YOST C. MILLER, 1855-1943   Preacher   Shore
Born in Newbury Township, Lagrange County, Indiana, April 28, 1855. Married Lydia Mishler (1854-1901) on December 2, 1873. Seven sons and two daughters. Ordained preacher at Shore, December 4, 1892, by P. Y. Lehman. Served for fifty years in the ministry of the Shore congregation. Died March 17, 1943. Burial in Yoder Cemetery, Lagrange County.

PAUL E. MININGER, 1908-   Preacher, Bishop   North Goshen
Born at Marshallville, Ohio, January 24, 1908, son of the well-known preacher, J. D. Mininger (1879-1941). Married Mary Ellen Erb of Wellman, Iowa, June 25, 1933. Three children. Ordained preacher in the Goshen College congregation, by congregational vote, February 13, 1938, by D. D. Miller, for the North Goshen outpost of the College Church. Ordained bishop at North Goshen, by congregational vote, October 17, 1943, by D. D. Miller. Has a B.A. degree from Goshen College, 1934; a B.D. from Kansas City Baptist Seminary, 1934; an M.R.E. from Eastern Baptist Seminary, 1936; and the Ph.D. degree from the University of Pennsylvania, 1949. He has been president of Goshen College since 1954. Has performed many ordination ceremonies. Taught in the public schools of Missouri, 1926-27; and of Kansas, 1930-31; was superintendent of the Norristown, Pennsylvania, Mennonite Mission, 1935-36; began to teach in Goshen College, 1937; was moderator of the Indiana-Michigan Conference, 1945-48; was moderator of the Mennonite General Conference, 1953; and was for many years a member of the Mennonite Commission for Christian Education, and chairman of the Curriculum Committee.

ELIAS MISHLER, 1830-1871   Preacher   Bower
Born in December 1830. Lived at Hausertown, Owen County, Indiana. Was a preacher by the year 1864, possibly earlier. Died January 6, 1871, at the early age of forty years and nine days. His wife and three children survived. He was frequently referred to as Eli, although his correct name was Elias.

JAMES J. MISHLER, 1855-1941   Deacon   Shore
Born in Somerset County, Pennsylvania, November 21, 1855. Married (1) Lydia Yoder (1858-1896) (daughter of Jacob and Barbara [Miller] Yoder on March 2, 1879). Eight children. Married (2) Amanda Miller on February 28, 1899. Three children. Married (3) Elva Nelson on March 6, 1927. One daughter. Moved to Lagrange County, Indiana, in 1878. Ordained deacon at Shore, by lot (four nominees), June 17, 1883.

The others in the lot were Amos Cripe (later a preacher), George Mishler, and David Speicher. Jacob Miller was excused as a nominee. George Brenneman, the Mennonite bishop from Putnam County, Ohio, seems to have officiated. Served a total of forty-eight years as a deacon in the Shore congregation. Died October 5, 1941.

JOHN F. MISHLER, 1931- Preacher Talcum, Kentucky

Born in Lagrange County, Indiana. February 1, 1931. Married Dema Chupp of Arthur, Illinois, February 5, 1949. Three daughters. Licensed for Clinton Frame's Kentucky outpost, Talcum, in 1956, 1957, and 1958. Ordained at Clinton Frame (for Talcum), December 27, 1959, by E. J. Yoder.

JOHN J. MISHLER, 1906- Deacon Marion

Born at White Cloud, Michigan, November 29, 1906. Married Ruth E. Dintaman, on February 19, 1932. Four children. Ordained deacon at the Marion Mennonite Church, January 31, 1954, by Lee J. Miller.

JOSEPH W. MISHLER, 1851-1928 Deacon Bowne, Caledonia

Ordained at the Bowne Mennonite Church, November 20, 1900, by P. Y. Lehman. Died November 2, 1928. Burial in Bowne Cemetery. In 1909 he was serving the Caledonia congregation in Kent County, Michigan, as a deacon.

MICHAEL MISHLER, 1811-1890 Preacher, Bishop Bower

The date of his ordination is not known. The very first year of the **Herald of Truth,** 1864, speaks of him as a preacher; he may have been ordained a number of years before 1864. The fore part of 1872 he is spoken of as an "old bishop," and was then alone in the ministry in the Bower congregation. He was not well the last eleven years of his life. He moved to Cherokee County, in southeast Kansas, where he died October 4, 1890.

SAMUEL MISHLER, 1826-1896 Preacher Bower

Born in Pennsylvania, March 17, 1826, son of Abraham and Anna Mishler. Removed to Holmes County, Ohio, in his boyhood days. Married Catharine Miller (daughter of Abraham and Barbara Miller) in 1848. (She was born, 1829.) Eleven children. Ordained to the ministry in Owen County, Indiana, in 1874. Removed to McLean County, Illinois, October 1, 1877. Transferred his membership to the Central Conference of Mennonites. Died April 10, 1896, and his beloved wife died September 19, 1908. Both buried in the East White Oak Union Cemetery. (WBW, page 205).

TITUS LEE MORNINGSTAR, 1908- Preacher Lake Bethel

Born at Kenmare, North Dakota, January 19, 1908. Married Charlotte Miller of Lagrange, Indiana, March 6, 1938. No children. Licensed 1957-59 to serve the mission outpost of the Plato Church, Lake Bethel. Ordained for Lake Bethel at Plato, December 13, 1959, by Ivan Miller.

DAVID MORRELL, 1828-1904 Preacher Maple Grove

Born in Mifflin County, Pennsylvania, October 10, 1828. Removed with his parents to Fairfield County, Ohio, at the age of six. Married Lydia Stutzman (1828-1894) of Holmes County, Ohio, April 13, 1852. Ten children, six of whom survived him. Moved to Noble County, Indiana, in 1853. Moved to Missouri in 1881, where he remained until 1894, when his companion died. Ordained preacher in the Maple Grove congregation, Topeka, Indiana, October 30, 1870. Died August 9, 1904, at the age of 75. Burial in Maple Grove Cemetery, near Topeka.

JOHN H. MOSEMANN, 1907- Preacher, Bishop Goshen College

Born at Lancaster, Pennsylvania, August 6, 1907, son of Bishop John H. Mosemann. Married Ruth L. Histand of Doylestown, Pennsylvania, November 20, 1932.

One daughter. Ordained preacher at the Mellinger Mennonite Church by Noah H. Mack, April 19, 1933, when under appointment as a missionary to Tanganyika, Africa, where he served, 1934-39, under the Eastern Mennonite Board of Missions and Charities. Was director of the first Mennonite CPS Camp No. 4, Grottoes, Virginia, 1941. Served on the faculty of Goshen College Biblical Seminary as Professor of Missions beginning in 1946. Was received into the Indiana-Michigan Mennonite Conference in June 1948. Became pastor of the College Mennonite Church where he was ordained bishop September 9, 1956, by S. C. Yoder. Has served continuously as president of the Mennonite Board of Missions and Charities since 1948.

DANIEL MOYER, 1812-1864   Preacher   Olive

Born in Bucks County, Pennsylvania, in January 1812, son of Samuel Moyer, 1770-1851, of Bucks County, Pennsylvania, later of Butler County, Pennsylvania. (His father moved to Butler County, near Harmony, in 1818.) Married Catharine Swartz (1803-1884) of Bucks County, Pennsylvania. Five sons, four of whom were still living when their mother died in 1884. In 1848 Daniel was living with his family in Ashland County, Ohio. In 1848 they removed to Elkhart County, Indiana, settling near Jamestown. It is not entirely certain whether he was ordained preacher in Ashland County, Ohio, or Elkhart County, Indiana. J. B. Moyer, the schoolteacher, investigated the subject and concluded that he had been ordained at Yellow Creek about 1850. There seems to be no firm evidence on the subject. He served faithfully until his death in a train wreck at Osseo, near Hillsdale, Michigan, when a train stove fell upon him in the wreck, December 21, 1864. His body was brought back to Indiana, and his funeral was held at "the new meetinghouse on the Baugo," December 25, 1864. Bishop Jacob Wisler and Preacher Daniel Brundage preached German sermons, while Daniel Brenneman delivered an English discourse. Burial in East Cemetery at Olive. His age was fifty-two years, ten months, and twenty-eight days. His funeral procession consisted of 170 teams and was about one mile in length. His grandson is William Moyer, born 1868, who lives near Jamestown. William has his grandfather's copy of Funk's **Ein Spiegel der Taufe.**

JOHN MOYER   Deacon   Caledonia

The birth and death dates of this deacon are unknown. He lived in Gaines Township, Kent County, Michigan, and in the year 1869 is referred to in the **Herald of Truth** as a deacon. We can form a rough conception of the period in which he lived by the birth and death dates of his wife. She was born in 1829 and died in 1869. Samuel Sherk and Henry Wismer preached her funeral sermons. If John Moyer lived a normal life span, he was probably born in the period, 1825-30, and perhaps died in the period, 1895-1900.

EZRA S. MULLETT, 1882-   Preacher   Nappanee (North)

Born in Marshall County, Indiana, near Bremen, October 17, 1882. Married (1) Annetta Metzler of Nappanee, Indiana, April 12, 1906. (She died May 15, 1908.) No children. Married (2) Anna E. Christophel of Elkhart County, Indiana, May 2, 1916. Three children. A very active member of the North Main Street Mennonite Church of Nappanee. First he was a Sunday-school chorister, then superintendent of Sunday school, and while superintendent was on August 18, 1907, ordained as a preacher. There were three brethren in the lot: A. N. Culp, Deacon Frank Maust, and E. S. Mullett. He was too modest to select one of the three books, but waited until the other two had each taken a book, and the lot was found in the remaining book which he accepted. He writes: "I can truly testify that God has richly blessed my life, and in spite of my unworthiness He has richly rewarded me and 'brought me into a large place.'" Bishop David Burkholder performed the ordination. Ezra served in the North Main Street congregation from August 1907 to August 1923. He then transferred to the West Market Street congregation, formerly Amish Mennonite, which was in 1923 re-

314 THE MENNONITES IN INDIANA AND MICHIGAN

organized, and which united with the General Conference Mennonite Church in 1926 and became the First Mennonite Church of Nappanee.

The parents of E. S. Mullett were members of the Amish Church and did not transfer to the Mennonite Church until he was nearly grown. He accepted Christ during revival meetings held at the North Main Street Mennonite Church, conducted by J. S. Shoemaker of Illinois, in or about the year 1900. In 1908, after his ordination, he felt the need of more training; so he entered Goshen College and graduated from the academy the spring of 1912. In 1922 he took Normal work during the summer term. He taught school in Elkhart County from 1922 to 1928. During the early part of his ministry Bishop Burkholder carried the major responsibility of the pastorate and Mullett devoted himself more particularly to Sunday-school work and young people's activities. He was especially active in the Sunday evening young people's Bible meetings. He reports that he feels greatly indebted to Goshen College as a whole, and especially to such men as N. E. Byers and Paul E. Whitmer.

AMOS MUMAW, 1852-1906   Preacher   Holdeman

Born near Winesburg, Holmes County, Ohio, June 27, 1852. Married Catharine Shaum on August 24, 1876. Eleven children, the youngest of whom is President John R. Mumaw of Eastern Mennonite College. Moved to Wayne County, Ohio, in 1881, to Allen County, Ohio, in 1882, and to Elkhart County, Indiana, in 1883. Ordained preacher at Holdeman, April 4, 1886, by Jacob A. Beutler. (Abraham Culp was ordained deacon in the same service.) Served twelve years in the ministry in the Holdeman congregation, whereupon he returned to Ohio and lived in Wayne County for the remainder of his short life. Died May 15, 1906, at the age of 53 years, following a gall-bladder operation. He was the brother of Dr. H. A. Mumaw, founder of Elkhart Institute, which in 1903 became Goshen College. His obituary in the **Herald of Truth** reports that he was "firm and consistent." He was the son of George Mumaw, 1820-1903, of Westmoreland County, Pennsylvania; his mother was Lydia Fisher.

HAROLD D. MYERS, 1914-   Deacon, Preacher, Bishop   Salem, Toto

Born in St. Joseph County, Indiana, May 21, 1914. Married Rozetta N. Flora of Carroll County, Indiana, January 2, 1938. Four children. Farmer. Ordained deacon in the Salem Mennonite congregation, by congregational vote, May 27, 1945, by Ray F. Yoder. Ordained preacher at Salem, by lot, December 1, 1957, by Ray F. Yoder. Lived in Starke County, Indiana, 1950-1952, and served the Toto congregation before the ordination of Jency L. Hershberger. Ordained bishop at Salem, September 18, 1960, by Ray F. Yoder.

PAUL J. MYERS, 1898-   Deacon   Howard-Miami

Born in Jay Township, Miami County, Indiana, January 13, 1898. Married Lona L. Shrock of Liberty Township, Howard County, February 2, 1918. Three children. Ordained deacon in the Howard-Miami congregation, by lot, April 5, 1936, by J. K. Bixler. Farmer and carpenter. Was converted during meetings held in the Howard-Miami congregation by C. Z. Yoder and Daniel Kauffman. Was baptized by Bishop E. S. Hallman, who happened to be visiting the Howard-Miami congregation at the time of his baptism. Has been active in the pastoral ministry to young men in I-W service (the draft classification held by conscientious objectors while they are rendering their two years of service to the nation in lieu of military service).

THOMAS U. NELSON, 1870-1950   Preacher   White Cloud

Born at Shipshewana, Indiana, June 14, 1870. Married (1) Susan Bontrager of Goshen, Indiana, July 2, 1892. (She died November 26, 1892.) No children. (Susan was a member of the Elkhart County Normal in 1889.) Married (2) Elizabeth Miller of Shipshewana, Indiana, November 4, 1899. Nine children, including Winifred, wife of Atlee Beechy, Dean of Students, Goshen College. Ordained preacher at White Cloud, Michigan, December 5, 1909, by Jacob P. Miller. Served faithfully for almost forty-one years. Died July 22, 1950. Was a teacher, a farmer, and a U.S. postal clerk for twenty-six years. Was a nephew of Jacob P. Miller, the bishop who ordained him. Was also a cousin of Bishop D. D. Miller, and of Preacher Josiah J. Miller. His great-uncle, Joseph Nelson, was a Methodist lay preacher, who on Christmas Day, 1837, held the first religious services in Newbury Township, Lagrange County, three quarters of a mile north of the Townline Conservative Mennonite meetinghouse. Was converted at the Shore Church during the evangelistic meetings held by J. S. Coffman, in 1893. Daniel Kauffman of Scottdale, Pennsylvania, was a church leader who meant a great deal to Brother Nelson. "He inspired a confidence greater than any other minister with which I had contact."

JOSEPH S. NEUHOUSER, 1896-　　　　Preacher, Bishop　　　　Anderson
Born in Allen County, Indiana, August 25, 1896. Married Hattie Kathyrn Tonkel on May 13, 1914. Six children. Accepted Christ at Leo during evangelistic meetings conducted by S. E. Allgyer. Ordained preacher in the Leo Mennonite congregation, by lot, June 26, 1921, by Jonathan Kurtz. Served in the Leo congregation, 1921-41. Since 1942 he has been pastor of the Anderson Mennonite Church. Ordained bishop at Anderson, March 25, 1956, by T. E. Schrock. Has been remarkably successful in winning unchurched people for Christ and receiving them into the Anderson congregation.

DWIGHT NEWCOMER, 1916-　　　　Deacon　　　　Salem
Born August 24, 1916. Ordained deacon at Salem, July 28, 1958. Resigned November 16, 1958, after serving less than four months.

HENRY NEWCOMER, 1813-1867　　　　Deacon　　　　Yellow Creek
Born in March 1813. A man named Henry Newcomer married Catherine Stauffer in Columbiana County, Ohio, May 12, 1834; this was likely the Yellow Creek deacon. The 1868 **Herald of Truth,** page 15, reports that he served as deacon a number of years. He came to Elkhart County, Indiana, from Ashland County, Ohio, Died November 27, 1867, at the early age of 54. Burial at Yellow Creek. The **Herald of Truth** reports that two deacons were to be ordained the spring of 1864; Henry Newcomer may have been one of the two chosen.

CHRISTIAN VALENTINE NOFSINGER, 1819-1892　　Preacher　　Pretty Prairie
Born in Condoman, Weisenburgh, France, June 24, 1819. Came to America with his parents in 1831 and settled in Wayne County, Ohio. Married Elizabeth Plank (1823-1912) in 1840. Six children, one of whom died as a youth. (His daughter Mattie was the mother of Mrs. Rollin Swihart of Howe, Indiana, who in turn is the mother-in-law of Preacher Paul Lauver, missionary to Puerto Rico.) Ordained preacher in Ohio, evidently in Wayne County, about 1844. Was living at Pretty Prairie by 1868, and perhaps earlier. Served faithfully in the Pretty Prairie congregation for many years. The **Herald of Truth** for 1892 (page 73) reports that "our aged ministering brother" arrived in the Smithville, Wayne County, Ohio, community in September of 1891 "to visit once more his relatives and old acquaintances. . . ." He fell sick while on this visit and was put to bed in the home of his nephew, J. S. Yoder, "where his aged sister" lived. Returned to Indiana following his recovery, but died March 21, 1892, at the age of seventy-two years and nine months. Burial in the cemetery of the Pretty Prairie Methodist Church northeast of the Pretty Prairie Mennonite meetinghouse. He chose D. J. Johns to preach his funeral sermon on the text, II Timothy 4:7, 8.

HOMER F. NORTH, 1890-　　　　Preacher, Bishop　　　　Nappanee (North)
Born in Howard County, Indiana, November 24, 1890, son of Gary W. North, one of the most active correspondents which the **Herald of Truth** ever had. Married Bertha Bechtel of Nappanee, Indiana, September 14, 1916. Two children, the son being Preacher Wayne North of Vineland, Ontario. Ordained preacher at the North

Main Street Church, Nappanee, by congregational vote August 1, 1926, by D. A. Yoder. August 1, 1961, therefore marked the completion of a thirty-five year pastorate in the North Main Street congregation. Has served as a member of the Mennonite Board of Missions and Charities as well as of the Mennonite Publication Board; also of the district mission board. Ordained bishop in the North Main Street Mennonite meetinghouse, January 31, 1954, by Ray F. Yoder. Was a member of the West Market Street Amish Mennonite congregation prior to its reorganization in 1923, when he transferred his membership to the North Main Street Mennonite congregation. Was secretary of the Indiana-Michigan Mennonite Mission Board from 1934 to 1943. Studied at Goshen College for one year. Was converted to Christ at the age of thirteen through the ministry of Daniel Kauffman of Scottdale, Pennsylvania, "whose staunch and steadfast Christian character, and kind and encouraging words have been a great help especially in my early ministry." Possesses those qualities which make for a successful pastorate, especially the tender heart of a shepherd.

AMOS NUSBAUM, 1868-1954   Preacher   Clinton Brick

Born in Elkhart County, Indiana, July 27, 1868. Married Anna Sunthimer (1868-1956) on July 7, 1889. Three children, all of whom united with the Clinton Brick congregation. Ordained preacher in the Clinton Brick congregation, January 27, 1907, by John Garber. (He succeeded Samuel Honderich who was about to move away.) Was the grandson of Bishop Henry A. Miller and of Preacher John Nusbaum. Was also the son of Daniel Nusbaum and Charity Miller; Charity, in turn, married Daniel's half brother, Deacon John Nusbaum, who therefore became Amos's stepfather. Died March 12, 1954, after serving in the ministry for forty-seven years. Burial at Forest Grove.

See also NUSSBAUM

JOHN NUSBAUM, Sr., 1800-1876   Preacher   Clinton Brick

Born December 27, 1800, in the canton of Bern. Came with his parents from Switzerland to America to escape military service about 1818. Settled in Ashland County, Ohio. Married (1) Elizabeth Pletcher, who died in 1847, and was buried in Ohio. Six sons and two daughters. Married (2) Mary Pletcher (1828-1869) (sister of his first wife) in 1849. Three sons and four daughters, making a total of fifteen children. Ordained preacher in Ashland County, Ohio, in 1827. Moved to Indiana in 1860, arriving September 4. (The first Mennonite settlers had located in Clinton Township about 1845.) Is described as short and heavy-set, with a white beard. Died April 7, 1876, at the age of seventy-five years, three months, and ten days. J. J. Weaver and Martin E. Kreider preached his funeral sermons. Burial at Clinton Brick.

JOHN NUSBAUM, Jr., 1832-1900   Deacon   Clinton Brick

Born in Ashland County, Ohio, December 17, 1832, son of Preacher John Nusbaum, Sr. Moved, as a boy, with his father to Richland County, Ohio. Married (1) Elizabeth Freed (1833-1873) of Richland County, Ohio (daughter of Preacher Joseph Freed), on November 25, 1852. Ten children. Came to Indiana in 1860. Married (2) Charity (Miller) Nusbaum (1845-1933) (daughter of Bishop Henry Miller, and widow of his half brother, Daniel) in June 1873. Five children. Settled in Elkhart County in 1860, in Lagrange County in 1864, and returned to Elkhart County in 1873. The **Herald of Truth** reports in his obituary that he had been ordained "about twenty years ago." This would mean about 1880. It is possible, however, that he had been ordained soon after he came to Indiana. Died November 28, 1900, in his home southeast of Middlebury. The **Herald of Truth** obituary (1901 **H.T.**, 14) reports that in his entire life he had affiliated with but two organizations: his home and his church, a typical Mennonite record, especially in that period.

IRVIN A. NUSSBAUM, 1925-   Preacher   Benton
    Born in Wayne County, Ohio, April 11, 1925. Married Arlene Steiner of Wayne County, Ohio, June 26, 1948. Six children. Ordained preacher at Walker, Missouri, for the little congregation of Mennonites who settled there, on March 21, 1954. Served several years before locating in Indiana. Installed as pastor of the Benton congregation, September 4, 1960, by Edwin J. Yoder.

DAVID OBERHOLTZER   Preacher   Bower
    Neither the birth nor death dates of Preacher David Oberholtzer could be found. His name, in conformity with Pennsylvania German pronunciation, is sometimes spelled Overholtzer in the **Herald of Truth**. He is referred to as a preacher in the year 1869, when Elias Mishler and D. Overholtzer preached at a funeral in the Bower meetinghouse on February 15 of that year. Again in 1870 Elias Mishler and David Oberholtzer preached at the funeral of John Rohrer, 1804-1870. The same two ministers preached at the funeral of William Markley, also in 1870. Finally Preacher Elias Mishler himself died, and it fell to David Oberholtzer to preach the funeral sermon of his co-worker in January 1871. Oberholtzer must have been a man of some prominence, for in 1902 the **Herald of Truth** reports a burial in the "Mennonite graveyard at the Oberholtzer meetinghouse." By 1872, however, Oberholtzer must have either died or moved away, for he was no longer serving as a preacher in the Bower congregation.

WILLIAM W. OESCH, 1884-   Preacher   Barker Street
    Born near Garden City, Missouri, July 16, 1884. Married Elva Alice Garber (niece of Bishops John and David Garber) from near Petoskey, Michigan, August 10, 1910. Four children. Converted at the age of sixteen under the ministry of C. Z. Yoder. Ordained preacher in the Barker Street meetinghouse, October 18, 1914, by J. K. Bixler, at the request of the Indiana-Michigan Mennonite Mission Board. Served at Barker Street about ten years. On or about September 8, 1923, his relation with the Indiana-Michigan Mennonite Conference was terminated. He and the congregation then united with the **Central Conference of Mennonites**, with the exception of Preacher Harvey Friesner who remained with the Indiana-Michigan Mennonite Conference. Received the B.A. degree from Goshen College in 1910. Was a high-school teacher and farmer when he was ordained. At the present time his membership is with the Eighth Street Mennonite Church. He reports that Daniel Kauffman, who had earlier resided at Versailles, Missouri, preached frequently for the congregation in Cass County, Missouri, where he (Oesch) worshiped in his younger years. "I always had high regard for him as an effective preacher, which regard I still hold. . . ."

CHESTER C. OSBORNE, 1913-   Preacher   Fernland, Hopewell
    Born in Miami County, Indiana, June 26, 1913 (through the error of a physician it is recorded as June 27, he reports). Married Eva Lucille Troyer of Miami County, December 24, 1936. Four children. Ordained preacher in the Howard-Miami congregation, June 27, 1937, by J. K. Bixler, at the request of the mission board. He was immediately placed in the Fernland congregation, Germfask, Michigan, where he served for many years. He served at Kouts, Indiana, 1947-1952. He got his conference letter in June 1955 for transfer to the South Central Mennonite Conference. His wife is the niece of Preacher G. D. Troyer, M.D., and of Preacher J. S. Horner, and cousin of Bishop A. G. Horner and of Deacon John W. Horner. She is also the granddaughter of Preacher Amos Kendall of the Church of the Brethren, and niece of Preachers Fred Kendall, Sherman Kendall, and Nathaniel Troyer: all of the Church of the Brethren. The Osborne family is of Quaker extraction.

DANIEL S. OYER, 1882-1954   Deacon, Bishop   Bethel
    Born at Gridley, Illinois, December 5, 1882. Married (1) Frances R. Zook, who had been born near Mattawana, Pennsylvania, on August 5, 1909. One daughter. Married

(2) Phoebe A. Zook of Allensville, Pennsylvania, August 18, 1929. One son: Preacher John Paul Oyer. Ordained deacon in the Bethel Mennonite congregation near Ashley, Michigan, by lot (four nominees), May 28, 1923, by J. K. Bixler. Ordained bishop, by lot, October 4, 1942, by D. D. Troyer. He had charge of the Detroit congregation from 1943, as well as his home church, Bethel. Died September 15, 1954.

NOAH OYER, 1891-1931   Preacher   Goshen College

Born at Metamora, Woodford County, Illinois, April 11, 1891. Married Siddie B. King of West Liberty, Ohio, August 9, 1916. Three children: Verna, and Professors Mary and John of the Goshen College faculty. Ordained preacher at Hesston, Kansas, by congregational vote, September 30, 1923, by D. H. Bender. Served the Hesston congregation, 1923-24; and the Goshen College Mennonite Church, 1924 until his death. Was a member of the Mennonite Board of Education for many years, and chairman of the General Sunday School Committee of the Mennonite Church. Held the B.A. degree from Hesston College and Bible School, 1919, and the Th.B. degree from Princeton Theological Seminary, 1922. Was a brother to D. S. Oyer, the Michigan bishop; and also a brother to Deacon Ed H. Oyer of the Illinois Conference. Was dean of Hesston College and Bible School, and later dean of Goshen College and head of the Bible Department. Also served as pastor of the Goshen College Mennonite Church. Died unexpectedly of typhoid fever, February 25, 1931, in his fortieth year. Burial in Prairie Street Cemetery on Hively Avenue, Elkhart.

CHRISTIAN S. PLANK, 1819-1887   Preacher   Clinton Frame, Forks

Born in Wayne County, Ohio, April 6, 1819. Married Elizabeth Schrock (1823-1877) on October 1, 1840. Six children. Moved to Indiana in 1851. Ordained preacher before leaving Ohio. Served in the Amish Mennonite congregations of Clinton Frame and Forks, 1851-87, when he died. Attended services at Forks as usual December 30, 1886, and led in singing. After a while he got up and went out. He was found in a sled, moaning with pain. Died January 1, 1887, near Middlebury, Indiana. D. J. Johns and a preacher named John Feldhouse preached his funeral sermons at the Forks meetinghouse. Burial in Pashan Cemetery. In 1877 Christian Plank and J. J. Weaver of the Shore congregation visited the congregations in Kent County, Michigan.

DAVID E. PLANK, 1884-   Deacon   Detroit

Born at Danvers, Illinois, July 28, 1884. Accepted Christ in 1895 and was baptized by John S. Coffman at Macclenny, Florida, in January 1895. Married (1) Fannie Florence Zook of Garden City, Missouri, March 21, 1912. Three children. Ordained deacon in the Roanoke, Illinois, congregation, by lot, August 10, 1924, by C. F. Derstine. Served the Roanoke congregation, 1924-35; and the Detroit, Michigan, congregation, 1940-59, when he removed to West Liberty, Ohio. Married (2) Alta King on November 26, 1959. Wrote the booklet, **The Temperate Life.**

GIDEON PLANK,——d. 1870   Preacher   Maple Grove

Ordained preacher in the Maple Grove congregation at Topeka, September 5, 1869. In a few months he moved to Missouri and shortly thereafter died of smallpox in the year 1870. He therefore never served for any substantial period in the Indiana-Michigan Amish Mennonite brotherhood.

CALVIN PLETCHER, 1883-   Preacher   Olive

Born in Harrison Township, Elkhart County, Indiana, July 6, 1883. Married (1) Myrtle Shank, June 20, 1909. Seven children. Married (2) Grace McDowell, February 10, 1932. Three children. Ordained deacon in the Goshen Dunkard Brethren meetinghouse in 1933, and preacher a year or two later. Served only briefly. Later, a licensed minister in the Mennonite Brethren in Christ Church. United with the Olive Mennonite Church as a retired minister on May 8, 1960.

HENRY P. PLETCHER, 1836-1919   Deacon, Preacher   Christophel, Yellow Creek

Born in Wood County, Ohio, February 23, 1836. His wife was Elizabeth Risser, and they had twelve children. Ordained deacon in Wood County, June 9, 1866, by George Brenneman. Sometime later he was ordained preacher. Served the Mennonite congregation in Bloom Township, Wood County, which is now extinct. Moved to Indiana in 1882. He is said to have preached at the Christophel log meetinghouse, and sometimes at Yellow Creek. Was a strong supporter of the Sunday school, and a violent opponent of the use of tobacco. Donated the land for the Salem meetinghouse in 1889. Died in July 1919. Burial at Yellow Creek. John F. Funk visited him in 1879 in Wood County and "found him a warm and devoted brother." John F. Funk and John S. Coffman anointed his sick wife October 5, 1884. Unfortunately he does not seem to have served very long as a minister. He was unable to get along with his fellow ministers and was silenced. He continued his connection with the Mennonite Church, however, for some time thereafter. His son Daniel, who is now approaching 90, attends the Pleasant View Mennonite Church, North of Goshen.

WILLIAM PLETCHER, 1816-1877   Preacher   Clinton Brick

Born August 2, 1816, grandson of Samuel Pletcher of Wiesloch, Baden, Germany, who emigrated to America about 1750. Married Anna Eichelberger (1817-1893) in Wood County, Ohio, July 3, 1842. Eleven children. The son William was the father of Curtis, Lendon, etc. The son Abraham was the father of William, and the grandfather of William E. Pletcher, Principal of the Parkside School, Goshen, Indiana, 1929-51. Ordained preacher at the Clinton Brick Church, October 22, 1865, by John M. Brenneman of Ohio. Served faithfully almost twelve years, until he was killed by a tornado which also destroyed his barn, July 2, 1877. Lived on Highway 4 east of Goshen, at the intersection of Highway 13 with 4 at the "Y." Burial at Clinton Brick.

CHESTER A. RABER, 1929-   Preacher

Born at Goshen, Indiana, July 21, 1929, son of Preacher Frank B. Raber. Licensed June 10, 1954, while at Goshen College as religious counselor, by S. Jay Hostetler, to serve the Sunnyside congregation. Married Geraldine Landis (daughter of Preacher Abram K. Landis of Souderton, Pennsylvania) on October 13, 1951. Two children. Ordained preacher in the Goshen College congregation, December 7, 1958, to serve without immediate congregational assignment. Was at that time a student in Southern Baptist Theological Seminary, and was working as a counselor in a mental hospital. B.D. degree from Goshen, 1953.

FRANK B. RABER, 1898-   Preacher   Detroit

Born at Holden, Missouri, December 26, 1898, son of Preacher Dan B. Raber. Married Clara S. Jennings (daughter of Bishop William Jennings of Concord, Tennessee) on May 4, 1926. Three children. Ordained preacher at the Detroit Mennonite Church on Easter, April 16, 1933, by D. D. Troyer, at the request of the General Mission Board. Served as a member of the Mennonite Board of Missions and Charities for many years. B.A. degree from Goshen College, 1929. Preacher at the Detroit Mennonite Church almost twenty years. Got his conference letter in June 1952. Now resides at Sarasota, Florida.

TOBIAS RAMER, 1824-1887   Deacon   Yellow Creek

Born in Pennsylvania, possibly Lancaster County, in February 1824. Married Esther Hoover (granddaughter of Bishop Martin Hoover, c.1760-1850). (She died in 1906.) Five children, including Bishop Martin Ramer of the Wisler Mennonite brotherhood. The daughters Annie and Susan were respectively the first and second wives of Preacher Jonas Loucks. The date of his ordination is lost, but it is known that he was serving as a deacon as early as 1869. He followed Bishop Jacob Wisler in the division of 1872. Died October 21, 1887, three miles southwest of Wakarusa. Burial at Yellow Creek.

DON D. REBER, 1925-   Preacher   Pigeon

Born in Seward County, Nebraska, November 12, 1925. Married Barbara Kathryn Bender on June 16, 1946. Four daughters. Ordained preacher at the East Fairview Mennonite Church, Milford, Nebraska, June 29, 1952, by S. C. Yoder, at the request of the General Mission Board. Serves as a missionary in Japan. On his furlough, 1958-59, he served as acting pastor of the Pigeon congregation while Donald E. King took a sabbatical leave to study in the Goshen College Biblical Seminary.

CHRISTIAN REIFF, 1867-1945   Preacher   Elkhart

Born in Maugansville, Maryland, August 20, 1867. Married Annie Erb of Lancaster County, Pennsylvania, September 24, 1889. Eight children, including Vernon E., treasurer of Mennonite Board of Missions and Charities, 1921-34. Was a brother-in-law of Bishop T. M. Erb. Ordained preacher at the Pennsylvania Mennonite Church, Newton, Kansas, September 24, 1907, by T. M. Erb. (He was chosen by the Mission Board.) Served at Newkirk, Oklahoma, 1907-12; at Yoder and Newton, Kansas, 1912-24; and at Elkhart, Indiana, 1924-45. His son Vernon describes him as "very zealous," and "believed in being born again, and depended much on the leading of the Holy Spirit in his ministry." Died October 15, 1945. Burial in the cemetery of the Prairie Street Mennonite Church, where he had served.

JOHN N. REINBOLD, 1849-1918   Deacon   Maple River

Born January 26, 1849. Ordained deacon, by lot, the afternoon of June 27, 1898, by John F. Funk. He is said to have moved to Alberta, Canada, in 1910. Died in December 1918.

CHRISTIAN L. RESSLER, 1879-1958   Preacher   Tippecanoe

Born in Union Township, Elkhart County, Indiana, February 23, 1879. Married Anna Zimmerman of Elkhart County, Indiana, in 1901. Eight children. He was the son of Deacon Levi A. Ressler, and nephew of Bishop J. A. Ressler. (Levi and J. A. were in turn the sons of Martin B. Ressler, 1816-1895, of Strasburg Township, Lancaster County, Pennsylvania. Martin in turn was the son of Jacob Resler and his wife Susanna Boehm.) Ordained preacher in the Yellow Creek (frame) Mennonite meetinghouse, June 21, 1907, by Wisler Mennonite Bishops Henry Hursh and Isaac Good. (His father was ordained deacon in the same service.) There were five in the lot for preacher. Served in many different states: Yellow Creek, Indiana, 1907-17; Allemands, Louisiana, 1917-22; Podres, Louisiana, 1922-23; Tuleta, Texas, 1923-26; Clarence, New York, 1926-29; Tippecanoe congregation, North Webster, Indiana, 1929-31; Lewis County, New York, 1933-43; Gladys, Virginia, 1944-58. Died May 25, 1958, at the age of 79. He was a member of the Indiana-Michigan Conference only for the period while he was at North Webster, Indiana. He was a member of the Conservative Mennonite Church at his death. Funeral at the Pleasant View Mennonite Church, North Lawrence, Ohio.

LeROY RHINESMITH, 1912-   Deacon   Locust Grove

Born in Noble County, Indiana, April 25, 1912. Married Laura M. Mishler of Lagrange County, Indiana, July 28, 1934. Five children. Ordained deacon in the Locust Grove congregation, by lot, January 27, 1952, by Lee J. Miller. Farmer. Some years ago Brother Rhinesmith wrote: "I came into the Mennonite Church twenty-five years ago from another denomination, and gladly conformed to the teaching of the Mennonite Church, even though it meant many changes, giving up many practices."

JOHN RINGENBERG, 1827-1871   Preacher   Nappanee (West)

Born in Germany. Brought to America by his mother when he was less than a year old. Nothing is known of his European ancestry. His granddaughter, Elva May (Schrock) Roth of Morton, Illinois, writes: "I do not know the date of his ordination; it may have been 1854. We do know that a group of Amish Mennonites, most of them being settlers direct from Germany, were meeting for worship as early as 1852—at least they met whenever a minister from Ohio or Pennsylvania visited and preached for them. . . . The farm on which he lived and worked is the first farm north of Nappanee on the west side of the road. Of course, Nappanee wasn't yet built—the town was Locke. . . . I think my grandfather must have been a man of some ability." E. S. Mullett made an investigation of the history of the West Market Street Amish Mennonite Church, and published his findings in the **Mennonite Year Book and Almanac**, 1923. John Ringenberg married Barbara Stahly, who died February 13, 1869, from a fall suffered while pregnant. He and another Amish Mennonite preacher gave communion in the homes of Benjamin Schrock and Daniel Miller of the Howard-Miami congregation in June 1867. On June 27, 1871, Ringenberg died of rheumatism and dropsy. He left six orphans. Burial in Union Cemetery.

JOSEPH ROHRER, 1801-1884   Preacher   Yellow Creek

Born near Mountville, West Hempfield Township, Lancaster County, Pennsylvania, in October 1801, first cousin of Bishop Abraham Rohrer, 1788-1878, of Medina County, Ohio. Married Mary Forey (1799-1885) in 1828. Eight children. Removed from Lancaster County, Pennsylvania, to Stark County, Ohio, in 1830, and settled about two miles east of Canton, where they lived for twenty years. Ordained preacher at the Rowland Mennonite Church (now the First Mennonite Church, Canton) about 1830. Removed in 1850 to Harrison Township, Elkhart County, Indiana, six miles southwest of Goshen, on the present "Maurana" farm of Dr. M. L. Weldy. The first Mennonite settlers of Elkhart County worshiped in a log meetinghouse on his farm for a time. Rohrer was a very earnest preacher who stressed the "strait and narrow way." He became somewhat exuberant in preaching, which displeased Bishop Jacob Wisler who felt that Rohrer had too much of a "Methodist spirit." He finally insulted Rohrer, and either expelled him, or succeeded in getting him to leave. Rohrer then united with the Evangelical Church. He was the son of David Rohrer, who in turn was the son of emigrant John Rohrer, 1700-1772. Died June 5, 1884, at the age of 82. Burial in the cemetery of the Evangelical Church, a short distance north of the new Harrison Township School.

PETER ROPP, 1864-1944   Preacher, Bishop   Berne (Pigeon), Bethany

Born in Perth County, Ontario, November 23, 1864. Grew to manhood in Canada. Married Katherine Gascho of Zurich, Ontario, December 23, 1885. Eleven children. Moved to Huron County, Michigan, near Pigeon, in 1888, and helped to organize the Berne congregation. Ordained preacher there, by lot, July 5, 1897, with Amos Cressman of Ontario officiating. Removed to Imlay City in 1917, and in June 1918, with the assistance of the Indiana-Michigan Mennonite Mission Board, organized the Bethany congregation. He purchased an abandoned church from the Baptists for $1.00, and donated the land for the meetinghouse and the cemetery. It did cost $1,200.00, however to move the building three fourths of a mile, plaster it, put in new flooring, and add a basement and a new roof. Ordained bishop at Imlay City, June 5, 1926, by D. J. Johns. Removed to Detroit, in 1926, where he founded the Mennonite congregation. Served as a bishop until January 1938, and continued his work as a preacher until his death, which occurred February 7, 1944, in his eightieth year. He preached German in his earlier years as a minister, but changed over to English.

ARNOLD C. ROTH, 1932-   Preacher   Shore

Born at Wayland, Iowa, February 23, 1932. Married Lucille M. Schultz of Chicago on December 17, 1955. Three children. Ordained preacher at Shore, August 2, 1959, by Lee J. Miller. Is continuing with his studies in Goshen College Biblical Seminary. Served effectively as a Pax man in Germany and Greece, 1951-54.

DANIEL ROYER, 1829-1893   Preacher, Bishop   Bower

Born in October 1829, grandson of Bishop Daniel Funk. Married —— Overholt, who came from Deep Run, Pennsylvania. Ordained preacher, by lot, June 9, 1872, to preach English, and to assist the old bishop, Michael Mishler, and the newly ordained preacher, Jacob Hoffer. Ordained bishop some years later, and was serving as bishop in 1882. He and his wife visited the church in Bucks County, Pennsylvania, in 1887. In the 1880's he often attended the sessions of the Indiana Mennonite Conference. Died April 2, 1893, near Clay City, Clay County, Indiana, after "failing for some time." Services were conducted two days later by Daniel Kinports, the resident minister of the Bower congregation.

ISAIAH W. ROYER, 1873-   Preacher   Goshen College

Born at Orrville, Ohio, May 2, 1873, son of Urias C. and Elizabeth (Schrock) Royer. Married Christina Neuhauser of Knoxville, Tennessee, October 16, 1906. Three daughters, one of whom is Professor Mary Royer of Goshen College. Studied at Ada, Ohio, Normal, 1893-97; Elkhart Institute, 1898-1901; Goshen College, 1905-8; Bethany Bible School, Chicago, 1907, 1909-12. Worker at the Mennonite Home Mission, Chicago, 1902-4. Ordained preacher at 145 West Eighteenth Street, Chicago, March 27, 1904, by J. S. Shoemaker. Served as associate pastor of the Goshen College congregation, 1904-10. Did his lifework as pastor of the Mennonite Church at Orrville, Ohio. He is now retired and lives in California.

JOHN ROYER, 1804-1870   Deacon   Bower

Born in July 1804. Served for some time as a deacon in the Bower Mennonite Church, Owen County, Indiana. Died April 16, 1870, in Clay County, Indiana, and was buried in Funk's Burying Ground.

CARL J. RUDY, 1927-   Preacher   South Bend

Born at Breslau, Ontario, December 14, 1927. Ordained preacher in the Cressman congregation, Breslau, while he was a student at Eastern Mennonite College (B.R.E. degree, 1954), April 5, 1953, by Moses H. Roth and Oscar Burkholder. Married Ruth Mohler of Pennsylvania, July 23, 1955. Two children. Came to Goshen College Biblical Seminary the fall of 1960 as a part-time student. Installed as pastor of the new South Bend Mennonite Church, November 6, 1960, by Simon G. Gingerich, president of the Indiana-Michigan Mennonite Mission Board.

HARVEY W. SARVER, 1885-   Deacon   White Cloud

Born in Indiana, May 18, 1885. He and his wife Nellie (born 1900) had one son, Lawrence. Ordained deacon at White Cloud, by lot, May 24, 1910, by J. P. Miller, and served several years. Also labored briefly in Benzie County, Michigan, at the request of the district mission board. Later he left the church and the community and is currently residing at Orleans, Michigan.

LEONARD E. SCHMUCKER, 1923-   Preacher   Cedar Grove

Married Lucille Faye Sommers (daughter of Deacon John E. Sommers of Louisville, Ohio) on February 20, 1945. Four children. Ordained preacher in the Locust Grove, Indiana, congregation, November 30, 1952, by Paul Mininger, at the request of the district mission board. Served at Cedar Grove from December 1952. Has a B.A. degree from Goshen College, 1950; and a Th.B., 1951. Is interested in prison evangelism, and makes regular contacts at the Manistique jail. He writes: "Brother C. F. Derstine influenced my life toward full-time Christian work in Youth Institute, Sebring, Ohio."

GORDON SCHRAG, 1906-   Preacher   New Bremen

Born in Huron County, Ontario, February 28, 1906. Married Laura Sherk (1914-) on June 16, 1937. Four children. Ordained preacher at the Zurich, Ontario, Mennonite Church, August 22, 1937, by Moses H. Roth, at the request of the Ontario Mennonite Mission Board. Served at Glasgow, Ontario, 1937-42; at Alma, Ontario, 1942-45; at the First Mennonite Church, New Bremen, New York, 1945-56. Has never served a pastorate in the Indiana-Michigan Mennonite Conference, but the New Bremen congregation was received into the Indiana-Michigan Conference in June 1959.

BENJAMIN SCHROCK, 1819-1895 Preacher, Bishop Howard-Miami, Clinton Frame

Born in Holmes County, Ohio, February 22, 1819, son of John Schrock, who in turn was the son of an emigrant from Zweibrücken, Germany. Married Mary Stutzman (1821-1901) (daughter of Jonas and Magdalena [Garber] Stutzman of Holmes County, Ohio) on November 9, 1842. Twelve children. Moved to Miami County, Indiana, about 1850. Became an Amish Mennonite in Ohio about 1842. Ordained preacher at the Howard-Miami Amish Church in 1852, and became a bishop about 1854. In the division of 1854, whether before or after his ordination we do not know, he went with the progressives which are now the Howard-Miami congregation. Moved to Northern Indiana about 1863, and to Clinton Township in 1872. Located in Middlebury Township, Elkhart County, in 1878. Was affiliated in Elkhart County with the Clinton Frame congregation. In the division of 1892 he withdrew with the minority which formed the Silver Street Mennonite Church, which is now affiliated with the General Conference Mennonite Church. Died in 1895. Burial at Forest Grove.

BENJAMIN SCHROCK, 1829-1878   Preacher   Howard-Miami

Born in Holmes County, Ohio, May 5, 1829, father of Ezra Schrock of Goshen, Indiana, and grandfather of Glen Troyer of Kokomo, Indiana. (This preacher was no close relative of Bishop Benjamin Schrock, 1819-1895.) Married Mary Hostetler. Ten children. A schoolteacher. Ordained preacher about 1869. Church services were at first held in a schoolhouse in his era. He favored and succeeded in having a meetinghouse built. His son Ezra insists (erroneously) that his father "started the church" in the Howard-Miami Amish Mennonite settlement. Died April 19, 1878.

DANIEL D. SCHROCK, 1830-1917   Deacon   Clinton Frame

Born in Holmes County, Ohio, September 6, 1830, son of Daniel and Margaret (Bontrager) Schrock. Removed to Indiana with his parents. Married Susanna Schrock (1826-1905) (daughter of Jacob and Phoebe [Maurer] Schrock) on March 19, 1850. Seven children, including Nancy, the mother of Curtis Pletcher. His son David (1851-1920) was a visiting brother in the Clinton Frame congregation. Daniel was a farmer and also operated a sawmill; he was often called "Sawmill Dan." Ordained deacon in the Clinton Frame congregation, the first deacon of that church, about 1870, and served for twelve years. Died in 1917. Burial in Clinton Brick Cemetery.

NOAH J. SCHROCK, 1890-   Deacon   Maple Grove

Born in Kansas, October 3, 1890. Married Jennie Hooley (1896-1956) on March 1, 1917. Three children. Ordained deacon, by vote of the church, May 20, 1934, by D. D. Miller. Was a member of conference until June 1959, when he got his conference letter, and moved to Hammett, Idaho.

OSCAR T. SCHROCK, 1926-   Preacher   Mt. Pleasant, Oak Terrace

Born near Goshen, Indiana, December 7, 1926, son of Bishop T. E. Schrock. Married Glennys Showalter of near Waynesboro, Virginia, June 20, 1950. Three children. Licensed to preach at Mahalasville, Indiana, March 14, 1954, by Edd P. Shrock. Ordained preacher at the Mt. Pleasant Mennonite Church, Martinsville, Indiana, April 3, 1955, by his father, T. E. Schrock, at the request of the district mission board. Served the Mt. Pleasant congregation until July 1959. Removed to Blountstown,

Florida, where he assumed the pastorate of the Oak Terrace Mennonite Church in August 1959. Carpenter by trade.

TOBIAS E. SCHROCK, 1897-   Preacher, Bishop   Bowne

Born near Shipshewana, Indiana, September 2, 1897. Married Martha E. Miller of Middlebury, Indiana, April 3, 1919. Six children, including Preachers Orie and Oscar; his daughter Mae is married to Preacher Wayne J. Wenger; and Mary is the wife of Preacher Ralph Birkey. Farmer. Ordained preacher at the Bowne Mennonite Church, March 29, 1931, by D. A. Yoder. Ordained bishop at the Bowne Mennonite Church, May 10, 1936, again by D. A. Yoder. He is one of the active leaders in the Indiana-Michigan Conference, a positive force for conservatism, and the senior member of the executive committee on which committee he has served for more than twenty years. He is deeply devoted to the Mennonite Church and her principles, and is active in seeking to indoctrinate the present generation for Christ. He writes: "I am deeply concerned that the church prayerfully seek to remain in the center of God's will, whatever the cost."

CLARENCE A. SHANK, 1885-   Preacher   Olive

Born in Elkhart County, Indiana, February 26, 1885, son of Preacher Jacob Shank of the Olive congregation, and grandson of Preacher Michael W. Shank of the Lakeville congregation, which is now extinct. Married Maggie E. Everest of Harrison Township, Elkhart County (sister of Preacher William H. Hartman's wife), on March 16, 1907. Four children, three of whom are living. Ordained preacher at the Olive Church, by lot, May 5, 1917, by D. J. Johns. Served at Olive since that date. Studied in the academy of Elkhart Institute, 1900-01. A strong promoter of missions, he helped establish the Crumstown Mission Sunday School, which has since developed into a congregation; also Hudson Lake Sunday School, which is a congregation now also. He also brought to the attention of the district mission board the spiritual needs in the Upper Peninsula of Michigan which led to the establishment of a chain of congregations in that area. He has been richly blessed of the Lord in the field of personal evangelism.

JACOB SHANK, 1856-1905   Preacher   Olive

Born in Olive Township, Elkhart County, Indiana, February 19, 1856. Married Margaret Hunsberger, also of Olive Township, on February 3, 1884. One son: Preacher Clarence. United with the Mennonite Church the spring of 1896, and was baptized as a member of the Prairie Street congregation, Elkhart. The district system more or less prevailed in those days and Jacob received one or more votes at Olive in April 1896, when a preacher was to be ordained. The lot was cast April 16, 1896, evidently by John F. Funk, and Jacob Shank was chosen. He had been in the church about two months at this time. Three brethren had received votes, but Henry Long had been excused. Served from the date of his ordination, April 16, 1896, until his early death, November 27, 1905. Burial in South Cemetery at the Olive Church. Studied at Elkhart Institute, 1899-1900. Served as the first elected treasurer of Mennonite General Conference. In March 1903 he held a series of meetings for the Blanchard congregation in Putnam County, Ohio, with nine confessions. I. B. Witmer said that he was a friendly person and a rapid speaker.

MICHAEL W. SHANK, 1833-1905   Deacon, Preacher   Lakeville

Born at Markham, Ontario, October 15, 1833, son of Michael Shank, 1783-1865, and Barbara (Weidmann) Shank, 1790-1836, of Markham, Ontario. About 1832 this family removed from Ontario to Putnam County, Ohio. In 1862 the elder Michael Shank with his family removed to St. Joseph County, Indiana, taking along his preacher son, Michael W. Shank. The elder Michael Shank, who died in 1865, is buried diagonally across from the Dice schoolhouse one and one-half miles south of

Lakeville and two miles west. In the year 1849 the Michael Shanks, father and son, located in Elkhart County, Indiana, where they lived until 1862, when they moved to Lakeville. A small group of Mennonites met for worship in the Dice schoolhouse diagonally across the intersection from the Dice Cemetery. Here J. M. Brenneman of Ohio ordained the younger Michael Shank, 1833-1905, as deacon on October 19, 1865. (P. Y. Lehman was ordained preacher in the same service.) In 1867 Tillman Moyer of Ontario appeared at the little congregation and ordained Michael W. Shank as preacher. Michael had letters in the **Herald of Truth** in 1869, 1871, and 1877. On June 17, 1854, Michael Shank married Nancy Ramer (1838-1896) of Richland County, Ohio. Eleven children, including Preacher Jacob Shank, 1856-1905. In 1886 Michael W. Shank removed to Finney County, Kansas, and in 1904 to La Junta, Colorado. There he died the next year, February 13, 1905, of apoplexy. Burial in Garden City, Kansas.

HAROLD SHARP, 1915-   Preacher   Wellington

Born at Fairview, Michigan, June 20, 1915. Married Anna Troyer on June 2, 1940. Seven children. Ordained preacher at Fairview, by lot, September 16, 1956, by Harvey Handrich, to serve the Wellington Mennonite Mission, Lachine, Michigan.

HENRY SHAUM, 1826-1892   Preacher, Bishop   Olive

Born in Northampton County, Pennsylvania, February 3, 1826, son of Bishop John Shaum, 1797-1882, and his wife Sarah (Buzzard) Shaum (daughter of George and Rachel Buzzard). (Henry was the grandson of immigrant Johannes Shaum, who died in 1812.) John and Sarah Shaum removed to Wayne County, Ohio, in 1829. Henry Shaum married Elizabeth Holdeman (1830-1895) on March 25, 1847. They lived in Seneca County, Ohio, 1847-53, and then settled in Elkhart County, Indiana. Twelve children. Henry united with the Mennonite Church in 1866. Ordained preacher at the Shaum (Olive) Church by lot, December 23, 1871, by C. D. Beery. In the year 1886 the congregations west of Goshen decided to ordain a bishop, and votes were taken at the Yellow Creek, Holdeman, and Shaum congregations. The ordination service was held in the largest congregation at that time, Holdeman, on October 12, 1886, and Henry Shaum was ordained bishop by lot. He was able to preach in both German and English. J. F. Funk held him in high esteem. Henry's brother Jacob gave the land on which the Olive meetinghouse stands. His brother Christian was a Wisler Mennonite bishop. Henry died October 2, 1892, at the age of 66. Burial in East Cemetery at the Olive Church.

WARREN C. SHAUM, 1891-   Preacher   Holdeman, Pleasantview

Born at Wakarusa, Indiana, August 7, 1891. Married Amy Valeria Good on December 14, 1916. Three daughters. Was a member of the Yellow Creek congregation, 1917-25. He then returned to the Holdeman Church with which he had united May 13, 1911. Ordained preacher at Holdeman, by lot, June 28, 1936, by D. A. Yoder. Served until 1951. In 1953 he accepted a call to serve as minister in the Pleasantview congregation near Brethren, Michigan.

JACOB B. SHENK, Jr., 1927-   Preacher   Prairie Street

Born at Nampa, Idaho, February 26, 1927, grandson of Bishop John M. Shenk of Elida, Ohio. A.A., Hesston College, 1948; B.A., Goshen College, 1951; Th.B., Goshen College Biblical Seminary, 1952. Married Beatrice Ann Frey of Archbold, Ohio (daughter of Preacher P. L. Frey), on August 16, 1952. Three children. Ordained preacher in the Prairie Street congregation, by congregational vote, June 7, 1953, by D. A. Yoder. Served at the Prairie Street Church, 1953-57. He had also been a licensed minister in the North Goshen congregation, 1952-53. Is currently serving as registrar of Goshen College, director of admissions, and assistant to the president.

JOSEPH J. SHETLER, 1871-1951   Deacon   Pigeon
    Born in Johnson County, Iowa, April 21, 1871. Married Anna Hochstetler, also of Johnson County, Iowa, August 13, 1893. Ten children. Ordained deacon by lot, at the Pigeon, Michigan, Mennonite Church, September 22, 1929, by Menno Esch. Died September 30, 1951.

EDD P. SHROCK, 1899-   Preacher, Bishop   Berea
    Born in Lagrange County, Indiana, August 14, 1899. Married Fanny Yoder of Reno County, Kansas, July 10, 1919. Nine children. Ordained preacher in the Shore congregation, October 8, 1933, by O. S. Hostetler, at the request of the district mission board. Served the Berea congregation from that date. Ordained bishop in the Berea Mennonite congregation, by the voice of the congregation, October 11, 1942, again by O. S. Hostetler. Retired and was released from his congregational responsibilities at the Berea Church in 1960.

RUURD JACOBS SIJMENSMA, 1816-1854   Preacher   Frisian Congregation
    Born in The Netherlands, probably at Balk in Friesland, September 10, 1816. His wife Elizabeth lived from 1810 to 1893. Ordained preacher in the Balk congregation, July 10, 1842, by Meine Obes Smid. Emigrated with the Frisian group to America in 1853 and located west of New Paris, Indiana. Served in America only a little over a year. Died November 1, 1854. Burial in Whitehead Cemetery on County Road 46 southwest of New Paris, across the road from the Maple Grove Church of the Brethren meetinghouse.

WILLIAM SILVIUS, 1813-1865   Preacher   Bower
    Born July 9, 1813. Ordained preacher in the Bower congregation; the date has been lost. Died in Owen County, September 13, 1865. The funeral was held in the Bower meetinghouse, with burial in the Funk Cemetery. The next year George Funk of the Bower congregation, in writing to his third cousin, John F. Funk, speaks of "Maria Silvius, widow of Preacher William Silvius."

NILES M. SLABAUGH, 1876-1961   Preacher   Howard-Miami
    Born in Harrison Township, Miami County, Indiana, February 17, 1876, nephew of Preacher Nobert Sproal and of Preacher Benjamin Shrock, 1843-1878. Married Sadie J. Hoffman of Clarksville, Kent County, Michigan, March 29, 1906. Five children. Ordained preacher in the Howard-Miami congregation, by lot, November 6, 1904, by Jonathan Kurtz. Served the Howard-Miami congregation from that date. Accepted Christ when seventeen years of age under the ministry of J. S. Coffman in the first revival meetings held in the Howard-Miami congregation. Niles writes: "Leaders who meant much to me were M. S. Steiner, J. S. Coffman, Daniel Kauffman, D. J. Johns, and Eli Frey." Community feeling ran high against him during the first World War because of his outspoken position for nonresistance. Died May 14, 1961. Burial in Shrock Cemetery.

CLEDUS SLAUBAUGH, 1908-   Preacher   Morgantown
    Born at Mylo, North Dakota, August 30, 1908, great-grandson of Amish preacher, John C. Schlabach. Married Beatrice Regina Norris of Indianapolis, March 8, 1941. Three children. Ordained preacher at the Berea Church, Daviess County, September 28, 1955, by Edd P. Shrock. Serves as pastor of the mission outpost at Morgantown, Butler County, Kentucky.

TOBIAS J. SLAUBAUGH, 1915-   Preacher, Bishop   Berea
    Born at Mylo, North Dakota, January 5, 1915, great-grandson of Preacher John C. Schlabach of Marshall County, Indiana, an Old Order Amish preacher. Married Ada Mae Graber of Mylo, North Dakota, November 25, 1937. Four daughters. Or-

dained preacher in the Berea Mennonite congregation, Montgomery, Indiana, by vote, July 28, 1946, by Edd P. Shrock. Ordained bishop in the same congregation, August 30, 1959, by Edd P. Shrock. Deep well driller. He writes: "The spiritual leadership of Bishop Eli G. Hochstetler, Mylo, North Dakota, has had a great influence on my life."

SAMUEL SMELTZER, 1857-1933   Deacon   Holdeman

Born in Elkhart County, Indiana, February 2, 1857, son of Henry Smeltzer, 1825-1895, and Elizabeth (Yoder) Smeltzer. (Henry was born in Lancaster County, Pennsylvania; removed to Richland County, Ohio, in 1826, and to Elkhart County, Indiana, in 1849). Married Salome Burkey (1866-1955) (daughter of John and Sarah [Bixler] Burkey) on September 5, 1886. Eleven children. Conforming to the practice of that day they deferred baptism and church membership until after they were married. United with the Holdeman congregation in 1887. Farmer in St. Joseph County. Ordained deacon at Holdeman, April 16, 1898, by John F. Funk. Served faithfully for over thirty-five years. Died June 25, 1933, at the age of 76. Burial in South Cemetery, Olive Church.

RUURD J. SMID, 1814-1893   Preacher, Bishop   Frisian Congregation

Born at Balk in Friesland, The Netherlands, son of Preacher Johannes Smid, who had been ordained in 1796. Married Margaret J. Sijmensma (1820-1911) (sister of Preacher R. J. Sijmensma) on May 13, 1840. Seven children. Baptized and received into the Mennonite Church (Old Frisians) at Balk, Holland, January 22, 1843. Ordained preacher, September 12, 1847, by Haite Haantjes. Ordained bishop, 1849. Left Friesland on April 9, 1853, in a party of seventeen Mennonite souls, including Preacher R. J. Sijmensma. These Frisian Mennonites, who called themselves **Mennisten** rather than the more common Dutch appellation, **Doopsgezinden,** established a settlement in Jackson and Union townships, Elkhart County, Indiana, in 1853. Others joined the settlement later. They worshiped in dwellings and in the Whitehead schoolhouse, and used the Frisian language. Smid is described as possessing a mild and loving nature. He always worked for the unity of the brotherhood. He was exceptionally modest. John F. Funk wrote: Smid "is a bishop and a man of considerable talent." He was well read. He knew Mennonite history well. He remained a trusted adviser of his people all his days. He died of apoplexy in his eightieth year, on April 26, 1893, in Jackson Township, Elkhart County. Noah Metzler preached in English at his funeral, and John F. Funk in German. Burial in the Whitehead Cemetery, across the road from the Maple Grove Church of the Brethren meetinghouse. His tombstone reads: "Ruurd J. Smith, Died April 26, 1893, aged seventy-nine years, eight months, and fourteen days. EMIGRATED FROM THE NETHERLANDS IN COMPANY WITH R. J. SYMENSMA, WITH THE FIRST COLONY OF HOLLAND MENNONITES WHO SETTLED NEAR NEW PARIS, ELKHART COUNTY, INDIANA, IN 1853."

JOHN SMILEY, 1822-1879   Preacher   Clinton Frame

Born in Somerset County, Pennsylvania, October 2, 1822, son of an Irish orphan, Nathan Smiley, 1797-1872, who was reared by an Amish Mennonite family. Removed with his parents to Elkhart County, Indiana, in 1842. Was baptized in Mifflin County, Pennsylvania, in 1845, and united with the Amish Mennonite Church. Ordained preacher in 1849. Served the Clinton Frame congregation from the time of its withdrawal from the Old Order Amish in 1854 until the year 1866, when he removed to Wayne County, Ohio. Married Mary Conrad (1825-1912) from Wayne County, Ohio, January 15, 1846. Eight children, one of whom, Lydia (1846-1922), married Preacher C. Z. Yoder, 1845-1939, of the Oak Grove Amish Mennonite Church, Smithville, Ohio. Died September 16, 1879, of heart failure, at the early age of 56.

DANIEL B. SMITH, 1846-1895   Deacon, Preacher   Pleasant Valley
    Born in Hancock County, Ohio, in June 1846. Married Susanna Myers on April 22, 1866. (She died in 1914.) Twelve children. United with the Mennonite Church in Putnam County, Ohio, where he was ordained to the office of deacon. Removed to De Kalb County, Indiana, in 1874. Chosen preacher by the unanimous vote of the Pleasant Valley congregation, November 7, 1891, and ordained by Henry Shaum. Served less than four years as a preacher. Died September 11, 1895, in his fiftieth year. Burial in the Fairfield Center Cemetery, De Kalb County.

CHRISTIAN SMUCKER, 1805-1887   Preacher   Howard-Miami
    Moved to the Howard-Miami congregation as an aged minister about the time of the Civil War. He never preached. He did conduct devotional services. Buried in Shrock Cemetery.

ISAAC SMUCKER (Schmucker), 1810-1893 Preacher, Bishop Clinton, Maple Grove
    Born in Lancaster County, Pennsylvania, September 29, 1810. Married Sarah Troyer (1811-1886) (daughter of John and Magdalena [Miller] Troyer) of Holmes County, Ohio, on June 10, 1832. Six sons and six daughters. Settled in Wayne County, Ohio, and then in Knox County, near Martinsburg, about twelve miles from Mt. Vernon. Ordained as an Amish preacher in Knox County in 1838, in the fall of the year. Removed with his family to Clinton Township, Elkhart County, Indiana, in November 1841. By Easter Sunday, 1842, there were fourteen members in the Amish congregation of Clinton Township, and Isaac assisted Preacher Joseph Miller in organizing a congregation in Miller's home. Isaac "opened the meeting and exhorted to prayer." Preacher Joseph Miller preached the sermon. In 1843 Isaac was ordained to the office of bishop. He lived in McLean County, Illinois, from March 1851 until August 1852, when he returned to "Haw Patch" (Topeka). The traditional date for the organization of the Maple Grove congregation at "Haw Patch" is 1854. This date appears on the church building which was erected in 1879 in section 36 of Eden Township, along the Noble County line, six tenths of a mile south and three tenths of a mile west of the present Maple Grove meetinghouse. The stone in this 1879 meetinghouse reads: "Organized 1854; Built 1879; Rebuilt 1915." It appears entirely probable that Smucker held meetings with his Progressive Amish Mennonite followers as soon as he returned from McLean County, Illinois, in 1852. But the actual division from the Old Order Amish did not occur until the year 1854. The stone is therefore correct. Smucker spent the remainder of his life, from 1852 until 1893, at Topeka. The church was regularly called "Haw Patch" until about 1890. The first observed occurrence of the name Maple Grove in the **Herald of Truth** was in 1891. Smucker retained much of the outward appearance of an Old Order Amish member, but in his inner attitude he was quite flexible and progressive. He was somewhat inactive the last ten years of his life because of his advanced age. However, he did retain remarkably good health until nearly the end. He attended a funeral, for example, one week before his death. He died November 16, 1893, while seated on a chair. His age was eighty-three years, one month, and eighteen days. Jonathan Kurtz preached in English at his funeral, and J. S. Hartzler in German. Buried in the Maple Grove Amish Mennonite Cemetery, one and a half miles west of the old 1879 brick meetinghouse, or one fifth of a mile west of Highway 5 on the Lagrange-Noble County line. Bishop Isaac Schmucker Anglicized his name as Smoker, but his son, J. P. Smucker, adopted the form which the family still uses, Smucker. He thought that a preacher should not be a "smoker." However, Isaac's half brother, Jacob, also took the name Smoker, and his family still retains that spelling. Jacob Smoker, 1866-1957, was the founder of Smoker Lumber Company, New Paris, Indiana.

JOHN R. SMUCKER, 1932-   Preacher   Fort Wayne
    Born at Smithville, Ohio, July 28, 1932. Married Donna Gerber of Sugarcreek, Ohio, July 21, 1956. One daughter. Licensed December 9, 1958, by M. L. Troyer,

Elida, Ohio, of the Ohio Mennonite Mission Board, for service at the Hi-Way Chapel (East Greenville), Route 1, North Lawrence, Ohio. Received the B.D. degree from Goshen College Biblical Seminary, 1960. Ordained preacher at the First Mennonite Church, Fort Wayne, Indiana, by congregational vote, April 10, by Paul M. Miller.

JONATHAN P. SMUCKER, 1834-1903 Preacher, Bishop, Eagle Lake Nappanee (West)

Born in Wayne County, Ohio, May 8, 1834, son of Bishop Isaac Smucker, grandson of Christian Smucker, 1775-1857, and great-grandson of immigrant John Smucker, 1740-1809, the son of Christian Smucker of Montbeliard, France.

Jonathan came to Indiana with his parents in November 1841. As a young man he united with the Amish Mennonite Church. Married (1) Salome Peight (1837-1893) on December 4, 1856. Eleven children. In March 1873 Jonathan Smucker and family removed to Starke County, Indiana, and settled near Eagle Lake. The Amish Mennonites of that community worshiped for a while in a schoolhouse, and then built a meetinghouse. Jonathan was ordained deacon the spring of 1873. That same fall Jonas D. Troyer, who also lived in the community, ordained Smucker to the office of preacher. Two years later, in 1875, J. P. Smucker returned to Marshall County, and located west of Nappanee. There he revived and reorganized the old Nappanee Amish Mennonite congregation. In this congregation he was ordained bishop the spring of 1878, by Bishops Joseph Stuckey and Isaac Smucker, his father, according to his records. He was a very active man, for his ministry extended from eastern Pennsylvania to Oregon. He was a strong advocate of church unity, and gave loyal support to the conference work of the Amish Mennonite brotherhood. He was an active servant of the Mennonite Evangelizing Committee from 1888. Married (2) Mary ("Polly") E. (Stutzman) Kauffman of Goshen, Indiana, on February 17, 1895. He moved east of Goshen the spring of 1895. Died November 23, 1903, in his seventieth year. Burial in Union Center Cemetery, northeast of Nappanee. Funeral services were held by James Henry McGowan, D. J. Johns, Jonathan Kurtz, and D. D. Troyer. He served the church at Long Green, Maryland, as bishop in the 1890's.

RALPH R. SMUCKER, 1894- Preacher North Goshen, Yellow Creek

Born at Aurora, Nebraska, November 27, 1894, son of Bishop J. P. Smucker's son John. Married (1) Alma A. Albrecht of Tiskilwa, Illinois, November 27, 1915. Three sons, of whom one is deceased. Ordained preacher in the Willow Springs Mennonite congregation, Tiskilwa, Illinois, by congregational vote at the suggestion of the General Mission Board, December 21, 1919, by Bishops C. A. Hartzler and J. S. Shoemaker. Served as a missionary in India, 1922-37; as acting pastor in the North Goshen congregation, 1940-41; and at Yellow Creek, 1942-52, with the exception of a short term in India, 1947-50. Married (2) Fannie Bell Shantz on December 12, 1950.

SIMON J. SMUCKER Deacon Nappanee (West)

Ordained deacon, June 16, 1911, by Jonathan Kurtz. (Levi W. Yoder was ordained preacher in the same service.) Served until about 1923, when he moved to Texas.

JOHN SNYDER, 1807-1886 Preacher Olive

Born in Pennsylvania, April 25, 1807, the brother of Bishop Jacob Snyder of Huntingdon County, Pennsylvania, who died in 1865. Ordained preacher about 1845, prior to his removal to Elkhart County, Indiana, which occurred in 1856. He lived on the Adamsville Road about one and one-half miles north of the town of Elkhart. He used to drive two ponies in an uncovered buggy to the Shaum Church and pick up John F. Funk on the way. He preached many funerals in the period of the Civil War, in Elkhart County, Indiana. He left Indiana in 1872 and settled in Jewell County, Kansas. He died in that county on January 27, 1886. He was survived by his wife, the former Phoebe Albaugh (1810-1893) of Huntingdon County, Pennsylvania, with whom he lived in matrimony fifty-five years. They had eight children. His last words were: "I'm going home to my Jesus." John F. Funk described him as "a good-hearted old-fashioned Mennonite from Snyder County, Pennsylvania."

SIMON W. SOMMER, 1882- Preacher Sunnyside, Imlay City
Born in Wayne County, Ohio, February 22, 1882. Was a student at Goshen College, 1913-15. Married Sarah Lehman on October 19, 1905. Ten children. Ordained preacher at the Sunnyside Mennonite Church, five miles north of Comins, Michigan, in Montmorency County, July 25, 1915, by J. K. Bixler. (This church was ten miles north of the Fairview Amish Mennonite Church.) Served the Sunnyside congregation from June 1915 to September 1919. Moved to Imlay City and served the Bethany congregation, 1919-28, whereupon he removed to Holmes County, Ohio.

CLAYTON SOMMERS, 1912- Preacher, Bishop Bon Air
Born in Howard County, Indiana, October 22, 1912, brother of Bishop Willard Sommers and brother-in-law of Dr. G. D. Troyer. Married Ruth Arlene Hershberger of Miami County, Indiana, September 29, 1935. Three children. Ordained preacher in the Howard-Miami congregation, by congregational vote, January 31, 1954, by A. G. Horner. Served the Bon Air congregation from that date. Was on the executive committee of the Christian Workers' Conference, 1956-58. He writes: "I believe in the future of the Mennonite Church. . . . Change is inevitable . . . and will be Spirit-directed as men will yield themselves to our Lord." His ordination as bishop was planned for May 14, 1961.

WILLARD SOMMERS, 1903- Preacher, Bishop Marion
Born in Howard County, Indiana, June 18, 1903. Married Norma Miller of Howard County, Indiana, December 27, 1924. Four daughters. Ordained preacher in the Howard-Miami congregation, November 26, 1944, by A. G. Horner, at the request of the district mission board. Served in the Marion congregation since December 1944. Ordained bishop at Marion, by congregational vote, August 26, 1956, by Lee J. Miller. Studied seven months at the Indiana Business College, Kokomo, Indiana. Farmer.

JOHN P. SPEICHER, 1833-1894 Preacher, Bishop Bowne
Born in Somerset County, Pennsylvania, July 9, 1833. United with the Mennonite Church in 1853. Married Magdalena Hershberger (1840-1909) on May 23, 1858. One son and one daughter survived him. Ordained preacher at the Bowne Mennonite Church, May 25, 1867. Ordained bishop the fall of 1869. Served until within three months of his death, when ill health forced him to become inactive. Died in Kent County, Michigan, June 26, 1894, at the age of 60. Burial at Bowne.

JOHN C. SPRINGER, 1871-1910 Preacher White Cloud, Clinton Brick
Removed from Illinois to Michigan, and from Michigan to Indiana in 1908. Married Nancy J. Miller (1873-1958) (daughter of Bishop J. P. Miller). Ordained preacher in the White Cloud congregation, Newaygo County, Michigan, by lot, November 27, 1904, by J. P. Miller. Served there from 1904 until 1908, when he came to Northern Indiana and began to serve in the Clinton Brick congregation. Served only about one year because of ill health. Removed to Upland, California, in June 1909. Died of tuberculosis, October 12, 1910, at the early age of 39. Burial at Clinton Brick.

NOBERT SPROAL, 1830-1901 Preacher Howard-Miami
Born in Baden, Germany, November 7, 1830: Nobertus Sprohl. Anglicized his name as Sproal. Emigrated with his parents to America the spring of 1833, and to Howard County, Indiana, in 1848. Married Catharine Schrock. Seven children. Ordained preacher at a meeting in the home of Lewis Hensler, August 21, 1866, by Isaac Smucker of Haw Patch and John K. Yoder of Wayne County, Ohio, to serve the Howard-Miami congregation. "Nobe" preached faithfully for over thirty-four years. He preached in German. He was a faithful shepherd in pastoral visitation. The **Herald**

of Truth obituary reports: "He was often looked upon as a preacher out of date, for the reason that he would not try to change after every fashion of the world." Died near Plevna in Howard County, January 17, 1901, at the age of 70. Burial in Shrock Cemetery, Liberty Township, Howard County, Indiana. C. K. Yoder of Logan County, Ohio, preached in German at his funeral, and J. S. Horner in English.

GEORGE STAHL, 1871-1948   Deacon   Bowne

Born in Somerset County, Pennsylvania, June 29, 1871. Ordained deacon at Bowne, July 8, 1925, by D. A. Yoder. Served for twenty-two years. Died January 3, 1948, at the age of 76. Burial at Bowne. His wife Lydia lived from 1878 to 1917.

RALPH STAHLY, 1908-   Preacher, Bishop   Locust Grove

Born at Nappanee, Indiana, September 2, 1908, great-grandson of Bishop J. P. Smucker through his father's mother, and grandson of Preacher J. H. McGowen, his maternal grandfather. Married Sevilla Miller of Howard County, Indiana, May 15, 1932. Two adopted children. Ordained preacher at Locust Grove, February 8, 1948, by Paul Mininger. Ordained bishop in the same congregation March 7, 1954, again by Paul Mininger. Is active in the Indiana-Michigan Mennonite Mission Board, having served for a number of years as president, and is currently field worker. His great-grandfather, Henry Stahly, 1810-1894, was a native of Kaiserslautern, Germany.

ELNO W. STEINER, 1924-   Preacher   Olive

Born in Wayne County, Ohio, November 28, 1924. Married Mabel Smeltzer on June 14, 1947. Four children; one of the four is deceased. Ordained preacher at Olive, upon recommendation of a pastoral committee, which was approved by the congregation, May 6, 1951, by Paul Mininger. Completed the Th.B. degree in the Goshen College Biblical Seminary, 1951. Is an effective pastor. (His great-grandfather, Christian Steiner, was ordained minister in 1856 and bishop in 1871, in Wayne County, Ohio.) Works part time in a factory. He reports that he is "thankful for the amazing growth in evangelism and missions, stewardship, voluntary service, MYF, etc." He is also "concerned about lukewarmness and worldliness" in the Mennonite Church.

JOHN S. STEINER, 1912-   Preacher, Bishop   Pleasant View

Born at North Lima, Ohio, July 24, 1912, son of Bishop A. J. Steiner, and nephew of Preacher M. S. Steiner. Married Mildred Metzler of Columbiana, Ohio, June 6, 1936. Five children. Ordained preacher at Hesston, Kansas, April 16, 1950, by Allen Erb. Ordained bishop in the Pleasant View congregation north of Goshen, by congregational vote, March 31, 1957, by J. C. Wenger. Served the Shallow Water Gospel Church, 1950-52; and since 1955, the Pleasant View congregation. Has been a member of the Mennonite Board of Education. Has the B.S. degree from Youngstown College and the M.Ed. degree from Pittsburgh University. Has taught at Hesston College, 1947-50; has been superintendent of the Berean Academy in Kansas, 1952-54; and since 1954 has been superintendent of Bethany Christian High School, Goshen, Indiana.

MENNO STEINER, 1872-1931   Deacon   Fairview

Born at Morrison, Illinois, February 16, 1872. Married Margaret Gsell in 1897. Eleven children. Ordained deacon in the Fairview congregation, January 19, 1908, by D. J. Johns. Served until his death, November 12, 1931, at Fairview. Burial at Fairview.

MENNO S. STEINER, 1866-1911   Preacher   Prairie Street

Born near Beaverdam, Ohio, April 30, 1866, older brother of Bishop A. J. Steiner of North Lima, Ohio. Married Clara Eby of Putnam County, Ohio, in April 1894. Ordained preacher in the Prairie Street congregation, by the unanimous vote of the church, March 9, 1893. Eight months later, on November 6, 1893, he left for Chicago "to start a mission." John F. Funk describes him as the "first missionary of the Old

Mennonite Church in America." Removed to Canton, Ohio, in 1894, to work in the mission there, and settled in Allen County, Ohio, in 1895. Died March 12, 1911, at the early age of forty-five. Burial in Zion Cemetery west of Bluffton, Ohio.

MOSES S. STEINER, 1880-   Preacher   Fairview

Born in Ustick Township, Whiteside County, Illinois (Morrison area), October 24, 1880, brother of Deacon Menno Steiner of Fairview. Never married. Ordained preacher in the Fairview congregation, July 11, 1920, by Menno Esch. Is still serving faithfully in that congregation.

PETER D. STEINER, 1841-1917   Preacher   Caledonia

Born in Wayne County, Ohio, December 15, 1841. Married Anna Leatherman (1842-1882) in Medina County, Ohio, January 8, 1870. Nine children. Ordained preacher at Caledonia, by lot, December 3 or 4, 1875, by Bishops J. A. Beutler and Henry Shaum. (Caledonia had been without a preacher for some time prior to this date). Later removed to Ohio, and died at Bluffton, of apoplexy, April 18, 1917, at the age of 75. T. K. Hershey and John Blosser preached his funeral sermons.

ELI STOFER, 1836-1915   Preacher   Pleasant Valley

Born April 26, 1836. Married Elizabeth Weaver (1836-1914) on January 27, 1856. Three sons and four daughters. Came to Fairfield Township, De Kalb County, Indiana, probably from Stark County, Ohio, in 1864. Ordained preacher in the Pleasant Valley congregation, De Kalb County, in 1871. He made a valiant effort to build up the Pleasant Valley congregation and keep it from dying out. He also preached in the congregations of Elkhart County, Indiana. Died September 26, 1915, in De Kalb County, in his eightieth year. Burial in Fairfield Center Cemetery.

HENRY J. STOLL, 1899-   Deacon, Preacher   Burr Oak

Born at Montgomery, Indiana, October 2, 1899. Married Goldie Miller of Fair Oaks, Indiana, October 18, 1924. Two sons. Ordained deacon in the Burr Oak congregation, by lot, November 6, 1932, by O. S. Hostetler. Ordained preacher in the same congregation, by the vote of the church, September 23, 1951. Has labored faithfully to try to build up the small congregation near Rensselaer.

DANIEL H. STOLTZFUS, 1924-   Preacher   Hudson Lake

Born at Martinsburg, Pennsylvania, October 20, 1924. Married Rosalie Ellen Garber of Jackson, Minnesota, June 9, 1949. Six children. Received Th.B. degree from Goshen College Biblical Seminary, 1953. Ordained preacher in the Hudson Lake meetinghouse, an outpost of the Olive congregation, by vote of the Olive Church, May 31, 1953, by J. C. Wenger. Has served from that date as the pastor of the Hudson Lake congregation. Served a three-year term under the Mennonite Central Committee in Hong Kong and Formosa, July 1949 to July 1952. At the end of this term of service he visited the MCC work in Osaka, Japan, and the new Mennonite missions in Hokkaido. He pays warm tribute to Preacher Paul Roth of Masontown, Pennsylvania, who led him to a life of concern for the church and dedication to the Lord.

GEORGE H. SUMMER, 1871-1937   Preacher, Bishop   Bethel

Born in Woodford County, Illinois, July 11, 1871. Married Minnie Schertz of Metamora, Illinois, January 11, 1890. Six children. Ordained preacher in the Waldo congregation, Flanagan, Illinois, June 3, 1906, by John Smith. Ordained bishop in the Waldo congregation, June 6, 1908, by John C. Birky. Served as a bishop only six years, but continued as a minister. Removed from Illinois to Ashley, Michigan, in March 1920. Died May 12, 1937. Burial in Gratiot County, Michigan.

JOSEPH J. SWARTZ, Jr., 1917-   Preacher   Wildwood

Born in Turner, Michigan, June 18, 1917. Married Naomi Byler of Pigeon, Michigan, June 22, 1941. Five children. Ordained preacher at the Wildwood Church,

July 10, 1949, by T. E. Schrock. Served since that date as pastor of the Rexton Mennonite Church in Hudson Township, Mackinac County, Michigan.

JOHN TROXEL, 1826-1907   Deacon   Holdeman

Born in Wayne County, Ohio, December 30, 1826, son of Preacher Peter and Anna (Clingaman) Troxel. Married (1) Elizabeth Meyers niece of Bishop Jacob Wisler in 1851. Six children. Married (2) Elizabeth Keller (1841-1900) in 1866. Eight children. Two of his daughters, Mary Etta of the first wife, and Saloma of the second wife, married Wenger brothers, Eli (grandfather of Russell Wenger of the Yellow Creek congregation and Clifford Wenger of the Olive congregation) and Michael Wenger. John was serving as a deacon as early as 1867; he may have been ordained as deacon as early as 1864. He identified himself with the Wisler branch of the church after the division of 1872. Died March 7, 1907. Burial in East Cemetery, Olive.

CLARENCE TROYER, 1907-   Preacher, Bishop   Wildwood

Born in Clay Township, Lagrange County, Indiana February 5, 1907. Married Wavia Irene Troyer of Lagrange County, November 29, 1928. Eight children. Ordained preacher in the Shore congregation, April 14, 1950, by D. A. Yoder, at the request of the district mission board. Served the Wildwood congregation in the Upper Peninsula of Michigan from 1940. Ordained bishop at Naubinway, August 22, 1948, by T. E. Schrock. Farmer. He is an example of the consecrated mission workers who are making considerable sacrifices in order to live and serve on the mission field in the hope that Christ through them will build His church.

DANIEL D. TROYER, 1870-1953   Preacher, Bishop   Clinton Frame

Born near Knox, and Eagle Lake, Indiana, January 12, 1870. Removed to Scott, Lagrange County, at the age of seven. At fifteen he went with his parents to Tullahoma, Coffee County, Tennessee. The Troyers lived in Tennessee only four years; so at nineteen Daniel returned to Elkhart County and lived near Goshen. United with the Clinton Frame Amish Mennonite Church in 1890. Ordained preacher at Clinton Frame, by lot (two nominees), September 23, 1892, by J. P. Smucker. Married (1) Mary E. Pletcher of Wood County, Ohio, January 8, 1893. Four children. Ordained bishop November 9, 1920, at the request of the district mission board and the executive committee of the Indiana-Michigan Conference, and with the approval of the congregation. D. J. Johns officiated at Clinton Frame. Married (2) Ada (Stutzman) Lehman, widow of Henry Lehman. When the North Main Street Mennonite Church in Nappanee was left without a pastor in 1923, D. D. Troyer supplied the pulpit for almost two years. Served as bishop of the Bethel congregation, Ashley, Michigan, 1923-41. Served as vice-president of the Mennonite Publication Board, 1908-42. Farmer. He wrote: "Brother D. J. Johns has been a real help to me in the beginning of my ministry." Served on the executive committee of the Indian-Michigan Mennonite Conference, 1925-39. Died July 18, 1953, in his eighty-third year. Burial in Clinton Union Cemetery.

JOHN M. TROYER, 1912-   Deacon   Clinton Brick

Born at Bucklin, Kansas, December 30, 1912, son of Bishop Moses J. Troyer and brother of Preacher Tobe M. Troyer. Married Katie Yoder of Wolford, North Dakota, June 4, 1939. Six children. Ordained deacon in the Clinton Brick congregation, by congregational vote, December 21, 1952, by O. S. Hostetler. Served at Clinton Brick, 1952-59, when he removed to Adair, Oklahoma; he got his conference letter in June 1959. In Oklahoma he serves as pastor of the Zion congregation near Pryor.

JONAS D. TROYER, 1811-1897   Preacher, Bishop   Clinton Frame, "Eagle Lake"

Born in Holmes County, Ohio, February 11, 1811. In 1841 he was living in Logan County, Ohio. When he came to Indiana in 1854, he was already a preacher. The place of his ordination is not known. Immediately after arriving in Indiana, in 1854, Isaac Smucker ordained him to the office of bishop. He served in the Clinton Frame congregation for about ten years, and then moved to a farm in the general area of Eagle Lake, Starke County, Indiana. He may have lived on the Marshall County side of the line; at least this was the case in 1869. It is not definitely known how long he remained in the Eagle Lake area, but he served the small Amish Mennonite congregation near Eagle Lake for a number of years. In 1885 he decided to move to Tennessee, where his wife, Elizabeth Mishler (1807-1885), died. She was survived by seven children. He did not long remain in Tennessee, but returned to Elkhart County, where he continued to serve in the Amish Mennonite congregations as needed. He attained a great age, and was blind for possibly ten years near the end of his life. However, a cataract operation restored his sight so that he could again see prior to his death. He devoted much time to the memorization of Scripture, and was able to quote extensively by memory. He performed several weddings after he was blind. In 1894 he visited the Howard-Miami Amish Mennonites, preached at the meetinghouse on May 6, and fell from a porch, breaking his right leg below the knee. The Clinton Frame and Forks congregations gave him financial support as an old man. He lived for a time with the John C. Birkey family, also with "Felty" Schrock. He is listed in the 1881 **Elkhart County History** as a bishop in the Forks congregation. He died October 7, 1897. Buried in the Miller Cemetery, northwest of the Eight-Square schoolhouse, and strangely the tombstone reads Jonathan Troyer, by mistake. He was commonly called "Yohn" (German abbreviation for Jonas), and someone must have thought that "Yohn" stood for Jonathan. J. D. Troyer always preached in German. He was, along with Isaac Smucker, the founder of the Amish Mennonite Church (in distinction from the Old Order Amish) in Northern Indiana. He introduced the practice of baptizing in the stream (by pouring, not immersion). He also had no objection to his congregations' erecting meetinghouses. His discipline was much milder than that of the Old Order Amish. On one point, however, he resembled the Amish; he felt strongly that at least the ministers ought to wear beards. An Old Order Amish writer describes him as "a very gifted preacher."

NATHANIEL O. TROYER, 1883-1943   Preacher   Howard-Miami

Born at Kokomo, Indiana, July 9, 1883, the older brother of George D. Troyer, M.D., Mennonite missionary to India and Puerto Rico. Ordained preacher in the Howard-Miami congregation, June 10, 1904, while yet a single man. Lived briefly at Fairview, Michigan, that same year. Attended Manchester College, an institution of the Church of the Brethren, and married a Church of the Brethren young woman, Pearl Shively, on April 18, 1906. He united with her church. Four children. Nathaniel was a twin brother of **Emanuel Troyer,** and Emanuel in turn was the father of Florence Troyer, the second wife of Bishop Norman Weaver of the Upper Peninsula of Michigan. Nathaniel died at Fisher, Illinois, May 6, 1943. Burial in Mast Cemetery, Liberty Township, Howard County, Indiana.

SETH TROYER, 1835-1910   Preacher   Eagle Lake, Forks

Born October 4, 1835, son of Bishop Jonas D. Troyer. Married Elizabeth ("Betsy") Kanagy on March 27, 1856. Six children. Was evidently ordained preacher at the "Eagle Lake" Amish Mennonite Church, Starke County, Indiana, probably by his father, J. D. Troyer. By the year 1881 he was serving as a preacher in the Forks congregation. He seems not to have been very active as a preacher, for Sadie Robinson of Goshen, whose mother was married to Seth's brother James Troyer, knew nothing of Seth's being a preacher. Perhaps he did not preach at all in his later years. O. S. Hostetler reports that Seth Troyer "moved around a great deal." The **Herald of Truth** indicates that Seth Troyer of Indiana preached twice at Big Prairie, Michigan, on April 23, 1905. He died May 5, 1910, at the age of 74. Burial in Forest Grove Cemetery.

WILLIS C. TROYER, 1913-   Preacher   Plato

Born in Lagrange County, Indiana, April 29, 1913. Married Vera Ellen Miller of Bloomfield, Montana, April 21, 1935. Eight children. Ordained preacher in the Emma congregation, by lot, August 6, 1950, by O. S. Hostetler, to serve in the Plato congregation, where he has labored since that date. Farmer.

CORNELIUS UNRUH   Preacher   Okemos

In the 1880's there was a small group of Russian Mennonites living at Okemos, Ingham County, Michigan, near Lansing. A brother named Cornelius Unruh served as their minister for a time. Birth and death dates are not available.

VIRGIL V. VOGT, 1934-   Preacher   Leo

Born in Darjeeling, India, June 4, 1934, son of Missionary Milton C. Vogt. Married Joan Miller of Harrisonville, Missouri, August 14, 1953. Received the B.A. degree from Goshen College in 1954, after which he took the B.D. course in the Biblical Seminary, beginning in 1957. Ordained preacher at Leo, October 4, 1959, by S. J. Miller.

CHRISTIAN WAREY, 1832-1914   Preacher, Bishop   Pretty Prairie

Born in Ohio, probably in Holmes County, August 5, 1832. Married Mary Troyer (1833-1940) on October 14, 1855. Three children. The date of his ordination as preacher is unknown, but he was serving by the year 1871. A note in the **Herald of Truth** for 1868 would hint that he may have already been a preacher at that time. Served the Pretty Prairie congregation in Lagrange County, Indiana. Removed to Johnson County, Iowa, in 1884, where he was ordained bishop, at Kalona, October 18, 1885, by J. P. Smucker and Joseph C. Buerckey. His wife Mary was a sister of Noah Troyer, the so-called "sleeping preacher," a man who preached while in a hypnotic trance. Died September 30, 1914. Burial in East Union Amish Mennonite Cemetery, Kalona, Iowa.

FLOYD W. WEAVER, 1896-   Preacher   Burr Oak

Born in Elkhart County, Indiana, May 1, 1896, nephew of Deacon H. B. Weaver, and brother-in-law of Bishop John Gingrich. Married Hazel Lehman of Elkhart County, February 19, 1920. Five children. Ordained preacher in the Burr Oak congregation, October 4, 1925, by D. D. Troyer, at the request of the district mission board. Served there twenty years, after which he removed to Goshen, Indiana, and no longer carried pastoral responsibility. Electrician. He writes: "Uncle H. B. Weaver was a help in leading me to Christ. J. S. Hartzler has been a spiritual father to me for years."

HENRY B. WEAVER, 1883-   Deacon   Yellow Creek, North Goshen

Born in Elkhart County, Indiana June 25, 1883. Married Lizzie Markley of Medina County, Ohio, November 22, 1903. Seven children, including Miriam Beachy, missionary to India. Ordained deacon in the Yellow Creek congregation, by lot, January 11, 1914, by David Burkholder. Served the Yellow Creek congregation from 1914 to 1931, and the North Goshen congregation from 1944 to date. He was treasurer of the Indiana-Michigan Mennonite Conference, 1919-30. Deacon Jonas Brubaker and wife of the Olive congregation visited in the Henry B. Weaver home and were instrumental in the conversion of the Weavers. He reports that D. J. Johns and J. S. Shoemaker were among those who meant much to him spiritually.

HERMAN WEAVER, 1932-   Preacher   Bethel

Born at Rensselaer, Indiana, April 8, 1932, son of Preacher Floyd W. Weaver. Graduated from Goshen College, and then took the Bachelor of Divinity course in the Goshen College Biblical Seminary, receiving his degree in 1957. Married Grace Mininger (daughter of President Paul Mininger of Goshen College) on May 8,

1954. Two children. Ordained in the Bethel Mennonite congregation, Ashley, Michigan, August 17, 1958, by Paul M. Miller.

ISAAC WEAVER, 1847-1917   Preacher   Bowne

Born in Cambria County, Pennsylvania, January 8, 1847. Married Anna Speicher (sister of Bishop J. P. Speicher) October 16, 1867. Eight children. Removed from Pennsylvania to Bowne, Michigan, October 20, 1873. Ordained preacher in the Bowne Mennonite congregation, May 10, 1891, by J. P. Speicher. Served twenty-six years in the ministry. Died December 27, 1917, at the age of 70. Burial in Bowne Mennonite Cemetery.

IVAN K. WEAVER, 1915-   Preacher, Bishop   Petoskey

Born in Elkhart County, Indiana, September 20, 1915.. Married A. Lois Yoder (daughter of Bishop D. A. Yoder of Elkhart County) on June 20, 1939. Six children. Ordained preacher in the Yellow Creek congregation, November 20, 1949, by D. A. Yoder, at the request of the district mission board. Served the Petoskey congregation from 1950 until 1959, when he removed to Elida, Ohio. Ordained bishop at Petoskey, August 17, 1951, by R. F. Yoder. Served as a member of the Ministerial Committee, Constitution Revision Committee, and Michigan Mennonite Bible School Board.

JOHN JACOB WEAVER, 1830-1920   Preacher   Lakeville, Shore

Born in Stark County Ohio, April 17, 1830. Married (1) Elizabeth Nusbaum (1834-1902) of Ashland County, Ohio, November 4, 1852. Nine children: the first four were born in Richland County, Ohio, 1853-57; the next three in St. Joseph County, Indiana, 1859-64; and the last two in Lagrange County, Indiana, 1867-70. Married (2) Anna (Bontrager) Miller (daughter of Christian and Elizabeth [Baumgartner] Bontrager) on August 11, 1904. Removed from Crestline, Ohio, to Indiana in 1858. From 1858 until about 1865, during which time he lived in St. Joseph County, Indiana, he likely worshiped with the small group of believers near Lakeville, Indiana. While in this fellowship he was evidently ordained preacher, although there is no evidence for the actual date of his ordination. About 1865 he removed to Lagrange County, where his post-office address was at first Scott. It is definitely known that he was a preacher by 1868. He was an able man, tall, well-built, smooth-shaved, and an effective preacher. He made many preaching trips to other areas, especially to Northern Michigan, during his active years. The news items and conference reports in the Herald of Truth indicate that he was active until the year 1896. One of the practices of J. J. Weaver was to "powwow," that is, to engage in secret incantations and prayers for the healing of various ailments. It was possibly this practice which led to undue intimacy with one of his patients. After 1896 he no longer appears as a preacher in the Mennonite Church. In the course of time he united with the Forks Amish Mennonite congregation as a layman. He died July 5, 1920, at the age of 90, fifteen days after a happy visit with John F. Funk. In his latter years he was almost blind. Burial in Keightley Cemetery, one-half mile west of Shipshewana, and one and one-half miles north.

JOHN WEAVER, 1821-1907   Preacher   Yellow Creek

Born in Lancaster County, Pennsylvania, September 2, 1821. United with the Mennonite Church in 1843, was instructed in the faith, and baptized by Bishop Jacob Zimmerman. Married (1) Mary (Maria) Zimmerman on December 5, 1823. (She died Jaunary 21, 1879.) Twelve children. Married (2) Elizabeth Lehman (1839-1907) on October 16, 1888. Ordained preacher, June 3, 1856, by Bishop Henry Shenk, Lancaster County, Pennsylvania. Removed to Elkhart County, Indiana, the spring of 1868, where he served as a preacher in the Yellow Creek district. In the division of 1872 he remained loyal to Bishop Jacob Wisler. Died on his eighty-sixth birthday anniversary, September 2, 1907. Burial in East Cemetery at the Yellow Creek (frame) meetinghouse. (Weaver is Weber in German.)

MERRILL C. WEAVER, 1900-   Deacon   Olive

Born in Olive Township, Elkhart County, Indiana, January 10, 1900. Married Clara Mae Fink of Harrison Township, Elkhart County, June 3, 1922. One son. Ordained deacon in the Olive Mennonite congregation, by lot, November 5, 1933, by D. A. Yoder. Served faithfully and effectively in the Olive congregation from 1933 until 1949. In recent years he has also served as treasurer of the congregation.

NOAH WEAVER, 1865-1938   Deacon   Salem

Born March 29, 1865. Ordained deacon in the Salem Mennonite congregation, November 24, 1912, by David Burkholder. (He succeeded Isaiah Christophel, who was killed by lighting August 28, 1912.) Served in the Salem congregation about fourteen years. Removed to California in 1926. Died December 30, 1938.

NORMAN P. WEAVER, 1903-   Preacher, Bishop   Maple Grove, U.P.

Born in Elkhart County, Indiana, May 10, 1903. Married (1) Mabel Weldy of St. Joseph County, Indiana, October 17, 1925. Three children. Ordained preacher in the Nappanee congregation, August 29, 1943, by Ray F. Yoder, at the request of the district mission board. Ordained bishop in the Maple Grove congregation, Upper Peninsula of Michigan, November 19, 1953, by Clarence Troyer. (He was chosen by vote of the congregations in the Upper Peninsula.) Married (2) Florence Troyer of the Howard-Miami congregation, Kokomo, Indiana, December 22, 1956.

SAMUEL E. WEAVER, 1880-1935   Preacher   Forks

Born at Nappanee, Indiana, February 26, 1880, son of Emanuel Weaver, 1849- 1920, of Holmes County Ohio and his wife Magdalena Yoder 1854-1920. (Samuel was the brother of William B. Weaver, preacher and author). Married (1) Fannie Stahly of Lagrange County Indiana, in August 1902. One son. (She died in 1903). Married (2) Laura Johns (niece of D. J. Johns) of Lagrange County, Indiana, August 25, 1904. Four children. Ordained preacher in the Forks Amish Mennonite congregation, by congregational vote, June 12, 1904, by D. J. Johns. He preached his last sermon at Forks on June 4, 1916, and was released by the congregation at his own request on July 23, 1916. Samuel suffered with poor health. He was, however, an effective minister and served as secretary of the Indiana-Michigan Amish Mennonite Conference. Died November 16, 1935, at the early age of 55. Burial in Bontrager Cemetery, Lagrange County. He received the B.A. degree from Goshen College, 1911. His widow reports that he was especially interested in church and Sunday-school work from his childhood, although unable to attend Sunday school for several years on account of poverty. As a young man he served the Sunday school either as teacher, assistant superintendent, or superintendent. During his ministry he was sent as a delegate to the Eastern Amish Mennonite and Western Amish Mennonite Conferences. He was chosen as delegate to the General Conference a number of times and served on the resolutions committee.

VIRGIL C. WEAVER, 1907-   Preacher   Yellow Creek

Born in Harrison Township, Elkhart County, Indiana, November 19, 1907, brother of Bishop Ivan Weaver and great-grandson of Preacher John Weaver, 1821-1907. Married Mary Hoover of Harrison Township, Elkhart County, in 1942. Five children. Ordained preacher in the Yellow Creek congregation, by lot, October 6, 1935, by D. A. Yoder. Served faithfully and effectively as pastor of the Yellow Creek congregation until February 1942. He is an outstanding dairy farmer, specializing in Guernsey cattle.

WILLIAM B. WEAVER, 1887-   Preacher   Prairie Street

Born at Nappanee, Indiana, January 24, 1887, brother of S. E. Weaver, 1880-1935. Married Fanny A. Stoltzfus of Hartford, Kansas, May 30, 1915. Eight children. Ordained preacher in the Prairie Street Mennonite congregation, by congregational vote, September 13, 1914, by J. K. Bixler. Supplied the Barker Street pulpit from January 1913 to September 1914. Served the Prairie Street congregation following his ordination, from September 1914 until September 1920. He then transferred to the Central Conference of Mennonites and served the Danvers congregation from the year 1922. Has been a member of the Congo Inland Mission Board for decades, and also of the Board of Bluffton College. Received the B.A. degree from Goshen College, and the M.A. degree from Northwestern University. Ordained elder (bishop), September 11, 1927, by Emanuel Troyer. He accepted Christ the first year in which he taught school, in 1905, when he was eighteen years of age. Served as Professor of History in Goshen College, 1914-22. William's grandfather, David Weaver, removed from Weaverland, Lancaster County, Pennsylvania, to Holmes County, Ohio, making the journey in a Conestoga wagon. His father, Emanuel Weaver, left Holmes County, Ohio, with his parents when he was sixteen years old, in 1865, and located on a farm near Nappanee, Indiana. In 1891, when he was four years of age, the family removed to Lagrange County, one-half mile from the village of Emma. Here he was raised, and taught school for six years, 1905-11. He was then a student at Goshen College, 1911-14, after which he began his teaching and preaching career.

NEWTON S. WEBER, 1897-   Preacher   Fort Wayne

Born at Waterloo, Ontario, October 10, 1897, brother of Lewis S. Weber, missionary and bishop in South America. Married Nellie Agnes Burkholder of Augusta County, Virginia, April 14, 1923. Four children. Ordained preacher at Waterloo, Ontario, by lot, March 25, 1921, by Bishop Jonas Snider. Held various pastorates in Ontario and in the United States, and served as superintendent of the Fort Wayne Mennonite Mission, 1934-40. Was a member of the General Mission Board in that period, and vice-president of the Indiana-Michigan Mennonite Mission Board, 1938-40. Attended Toronto Bible College for four months.

ALFRED WEIDMAN, 1894-   Preacher   Pigeon

Born January 3, 1894, nephew of Deacon Menno Wideman. Ordained preacher in the Pigeon (Berne) congregation, November 8, 1917, by Menno Esch. Withdrew from the Mennonite Church in 1924 and united with the Missionary Church Association. About 1954 he united with the Assembly of God Church. Was living near Elkton, Michigan, in 1959.

See also WIDEMAN

AMOS WELDY, 1873-1947   Deacon   Berea

Born at Wakarusa, Indiana, April 27, 1873, brother of Preacher Henry Weldy of the Holdeman congregation and of Levi Weldy of the Mennonite Brethren in Christ (now United Missionary) Church. United with the Mennonite Church in 1892. Married (1) Amanda Hartman (1873-1907) (daughter of Adam and Nancy [Brenneman] Hartman) on January 6, 1895. Two children. Married (2) Mary Kohli (1877-   ) (daughter of Isaac and Christina [Shank] Kohli) on November 21, 1908. Two children. Moved to Daviess County, Indiana, in 1921. Ordained deacon in the Berea Mennonite congregation, by congregational vote, October 30, 1921, by J. K. Bixler. Served almost twenty-six years. Died September 11, 1947. He was the great-grandson of Bishop Abraham Weldy of Westmoreland County, Pennsylvania, who in turn was the son of immigrant John Weldy.

HENRY WELDY, 1862-1934   Preacher   Holdeman

Born in Elkhart County, Indiana April 23,1862, son of Abraham Weldy, 1827-1909, of Tuscarawas County, Ohio, and his wife, Nancy Yoder. Married Alma Dolman (1866-1947) on July 15, 1883. Seven children, including Cornelius S. of the Holdeman congregation. United with the Holdeman Mennonite Church in 1886. Was a farmer in Locke Township, three and one-half miles southwest of Wakarusa, until 1915, when he removed to Olive Township. Ordained preacher in the Holdeman congregation, February 3, 1889, by Henry Shaum. He also preached at Teegarden, Indiana (at least fourteen years), and at the Madison Union Chapel—every four weeks at Teegarden and every other Sunday in the forenoon and every other Sunday in the evening at the Madison Union Chapel. He promoted the books and periodicals of the Mennonite Publishing House, Scottdale, Pennsylvania. He was a conservative in church discipline and a missionary-minded preacher. Served as a trustee of the North Union Cemetery. Died February 24, 1934. Burial at North Union. He preached in both English and German.

JACOB I. WELDY, 1871-1953   Deacon   Holdeman

Born December 31, 1871, son of John K. and Susan (Mumaw) Weldy. United with the Holdeman congregation in 1892. Married Rhoda Landis (1876-1949) on September 21, 1895. Five children, including Professor Dwight Weldy of the Goshen College music department. Ordained deacon in the Holdeman congregation, February 8, 1913, by David Burkholder. Served until January 1, 1951, when he asked to be released because of his age. Taught in many singing schools. Died April 25, 1953. Burial in Olive Cemetery.

PAUL F. WELDY, 1916-   Deacon   Berea

Born at Wakarusa, Indiana, October 17, 1916, son of Deacon Amos Weldy. Married Corona Mae Haarer of Midland, Michigan, April 9, 1939. Six children. Ordained deacon in the Berea Mennonite congregation, by lot, August 10, 1947, by Edd P. Shrock. Farmer and electrician.

SILAS L. WELDY, 1877-1955   Preacher   Holdeman

Born in Locke Township, Elkhart County, Indiana, November 27, 1877, brother of Deacon J. I. Weldy. Married Elnora Metzler of Wakarusa, October 8, 1899. Two children, as well as a foster son, Walter Weaver. Converted to Christ at the age of eighteen. Ordained preacher in the Holdeman congregation, by lot, December 20, 1908, by David Burkholder. Served as secretary and field evangelist for the district mission board, and was an active evangelist. Served the Pleasant Valley congregation in De Kalb County, Indiana, for about five years, during the first World War era. Served the Holdeman congregation from 1908 until his death in 1955, although less active after 1949. His sight largely failed in his last years. Was a member of the Indiana-Michigan Mennonite Mission Board, 1915-32. Served for a decade on the executive committee of the Sunday School Conference, now the Christian Workers' Conference. Was a man of much prayer. It is said that in the last week of his life he prayed for every family, and each individual by name, of the Holdeman congregation. Died May 27, 1955. Burial at Olive.

CHRISTIAN G. WENGER, 1846-1906   Preacher   Caledonia

Born in Lancaster County, Pennsylvania, December 22, 1846. Married Lavina Nagel (1853-1935) on February 27, 1872. Eleven children. Was superintendent of the Caledonia Sunday School for twenty years. Ordained preacher in the Caledonia Mennonite congregation, February 28, 1886, by J. P. Speicher. (John F. Funk and Peter Keim were also present.) Preached in a number of the congregations of Elkhart County in 1889, such as Yellow Creek, Salem, Nappanee (North), Nappanee (West), Holdeman, and Olive. John F. Funk spoke hopefully of the future of this gifted preacher in his diary. There is a tradition that the lot fell on the other nominee, who refused to serve, whereupon Wenger was ordained. He served until June 1897, when he and John F. Funk became involved in a serious dispute. Wenger then united with the Dutton, Michigan, Undenominational Church; later he joined the United Brethren Church. Died September 17, 1906, in his sixtieth year. Burial in Caledonia (village) Cemetery.

JOHN C. WENGER, 1910-   Deacon, Preacher, Bishop   North Goshen, Olive
    Born at Honey Brook, Chester County, Pennsylvania, on Christmas Day, 1910.
Junior College diploma, Eastern Mennonite School, 1931; B.A., Goshen College, 1934;
Th.D., University of Zurich, 1938; and M.A., University of Michigan, 1942. Married
Ruth D. Detweiler, R.N., of Sellersville, Bucks County, Pennsylvania, April 3, 1937.
Four children. Ordained deacon in the North Goshen congregation, by congrega-
tional vote, May 2, 1943, by D. D. Miller. Ordained preacher in the same church,
July 9, 1944, by Paul Mininger. Served the Olive congregation as acting pastor,
1949-50. Ordained bishop in the Olive congregation, May 6, 1951, by Paul Mininger.
Member, Mennonite Board of Education, 1935-39; Publication Board, 1945- ;
Executive Committee, Indiana-Michigan Mennonite Conference, 1947- . Moderator,
Mennonite General Conference, 1959. Teacher in Goshen College and Goshen College
Biblical Seminary.

WAYNE J. WENGER, 1919-   Preacher   Bethany, Caney Creek
    Born at South English, Iowa, October 21, 1919, first cousin to Linden Wenger,
secretary of the Virginia Mennonite Conference. Married E. Mae Schrock (daughter
of Bishop T. E. Schrock of Clarksville, Michigan) on August 12, 1945. Six children.
Ordained preacher in the Bethany Mennonite congregation, Imlay City, Michigan,
April 21, 1946, by Edwin J. Yoder, at the request of the district mission board.
Served in the Bethany congregation from April 1946 until August 1952, when he
transferred to the Caney Creek congregation in Kentucky. Completed two years of
college. Joined the Conservative Mennonite Church, 1961.

PAUL E. WHITMER, 1876-   Preacher   Goshen College
    Born at North Lima, Ohio, January 2, 1876, son of David L. and Anna (Otto)
Whitmer. Married Fannie H. Yoder on September 9, 1908. Two sons. B.A. degree.
Oberlin College, 1907; B.D., Oberlin, 1908; M.A., University of Chicago, 1917. Ordained preacher at North Lima, November 17, 1901, by I. J. Buchwalter. Professor of
English and Bible, Goshen College, 1908-16; Dean, Goshen College, 1913-16; Professor of Bible, Bluffton College, 1917-21. Transferred from the Mennonite Church
to the General Conference Mennonite Church, 1925. Now retired at Bluffton, Ohio.

JOHN WICKEY, 1922-   Preacher   Smith School, Kentucky
    Born at Centreville, St. Joseph County, Michigan, October 24, 1922. Married Eva
Mae Kauffman of Clarksville, Michigan, January 10, 1948. Four children. Licensed
for Smith School, June 27, 1958, by Lee J. Miller. Ordained preacher at Shore, by vote
of the Shore Church, August 2, 1959, again by Lee J. Miller. Serves the Smith School
Mennonite congregation of the Indiana-Michigan Conference in Butler County,
Kentucky. This is an outpost of the Shore congregation.

WILLIAM WICKEY, 1929-   Preacher   South Colon
    Born in Lagrange County, Indiana, April 9, 1929. Married Florence Miller on
January 1, 1953. Two children. Ordained preacher at South Colon, November 18,
1956, by Lee J. Miller. On his father's side William's family was Swiss Amish, and
lived in Adams County, Indiana. In 1907 the Wickey family moved to Alpena, Michigan, to a newly formed Amish settlement, which later became extinct when the members moved away. In the spring of 1911 the Wickey family returned to Adams County,
only to move to St. Joseph County, Michigan, the fall of 1911.

MENNO WIDEMAN, 1868-1923   Deacon   Pigeon
    Born July 20, 1868. Ordained deacon in the Pigeon (Berne) congregation, by lot,
July 5, 1897, by Amos Cressman. (Peter Ropp was ordained preacher in the same
service.) Died April 26, 1923.
See also WEIDMAN

PETER B. WIEBE, 1928-   Preacher, Bishop   Yellow Creek

Born at Plum Coulee, Manitoba, April 7, 1928. Came from the Mennonite group known as Bergthal. Married Rheta Mae Hostetler of Holmes County, Ohio, August 13, 1950. Three children. Attended Goshen College and its Biblical Seminary, where he completed the B.D. curriculum in 1952. Ordained preacher in the Yellow Creek congregation, by congregational vote, October 14, 1951, by Ray F. Yoder. Ordained bishop in the same congregation, again by congregational vote, January 31, 1954, by Ray F. Yoder. Served the Yellow Creek Church, 1951-59, when he removed to Hesston, Kansas, to become pastor of the College congregation there. Served as a member of the Peace Problems Committee, 1955-59, and of the General Council of Mennonite General Conference, 1958-59. Was an active and energetic pastor who devoted all his energies to the building of the church. The Yellow Creek congregation grew rapidly during his years of service. Conducted twenty-three series of evangelistic meetings, 1951-59. He writes: "Converted when a child; had very early convictions for the ministry; contacts with churches across our land have given me a real burden for our church and an appreciation for her position."

JACOB H. WISLER, 1833-1908   Deacon   Blosser, Nappanee (North), Prairie Street

Born in eastern Ohio in Mahoning or Columbiana County, October 17, 1833, nephew of Bishop Jacob Wisler. Removed to Indiana about 1848. Married (1) Anna Troxel (daughter of Preacher Peter Troxel of Wayne County, Ohio) on May 13, 1858. (She died in 1866.) Two children. Married (2) Sarah Kilmer (1844-1912) on January 26, 1868. Four children. United with the Mennonite Church in 1865. Ordained deacon in the Blosser meetinghouse, June 12, 1872. Served in the "Christophel district" from 1872 until about 1890, when he transferred to the North Main Street Mennonite Church, Nappanee. Here he served until soon after 1900, when he removed to Elkhart and served there as deacon until his death. Died November 21, 1908, at the age of 75. Burial in Olive Cemetery.

JACOB WISLER, 1808-1889   Preacher, Bishop   Yellow Creek

Born in the Deep Run community of Bucks County, Pennsylvania, October 31, 1808, eighth child of Christian Wisler, who died in 1830, and Susan (Holdeman) Wisler, 1774-1838. Removed with his parents to eastern Ohio about the year 1820. Married (1) Mary Hoover (1818-1860) (daughter of David L. Hoover, 1781-1833, of Lancaster County, Pennsylvania, and Esther [Lehman] Hoover, 1787-1851, of Franklin County, Pennsylvania) on November 19, 1827. Seven children. Married (2) Catherine Knopp (1819-1888) of eastern Ohio. (She was his housekeeper before his first wife died.)

Jacob was ordained preacher in 1833, likely by Bishop Jacob Nold, and almost certainly in the Midway meetinghouse, in Ohio. In 1848 he removed to Elkhart County, Indiana, because, so it is reported, the members of his congregation in eastern Ohio felt that it was not appropriate for their minister to be engaged in the threshing business. He then decided that he would need to move to Indiana where land was cheaper. Bishop Abraham Rohrer of Medina County, Ohio, came to Elkhart County in 1851, after the death of Bishop Martin Hoover, the previous October, and ordained Jacob to the office of bishop. He therefore became the first active bishop of the Mennonite Church in Northern Indiana.

Jacob was a goodhearted and earnest Christian. He felt that the church had no need of making any particular changes. He therefore preferred one-part, rather than four-part, singing. He had a fondness for the German language, which was the traditional language of his brotherhood. He did not see any reason why Mennonites needed to adopt such new institutions as the Sunday school, nor could he see why evening services were a necessity under ordinary circumstances. On almost every point of difference between himself and such other leaders as Daniel Brenneman and John F. Funk, Wisler stood for the traditional Mennonite position. After an unhappy period of tension with out-of-state committees, reconciliations, and fresh tensions, a final division came between the Indiana Conference, in which Preacher John F. Funk was the dominant figure, and Jacob Wisler and his supporters, in January 1872. Since that date the two groups have been separate. Wisler died May 1, 1889, at the age of 80. Burial in East Cemetery of the Yellow Creek (frame) meetinghouse. His tombstone has an English inscription.

HENRY WISMER   Preacher   Caledonia

Lived about ten miles from Grand Rapids. Ordained preacher in the Caledonia congregation, April 30, 1866, by John M. Brenneman of Ohio. Served only seven years, and left the church in 1873 because it did not sanction prayer meetings and "experience meetings." United with Daniel Brenneman's Reformed Mennonites (now United Missionary Church).

PETER WITMER, 1848-1924   Deacon   Leo

Ordained deacon in the Leo Amish Mennonite congregation, by lot (three nominees), May 8, 1883. Served for some time as a deacon. Was the father of David Witmer of the Leo Church. Burial in Leo Cemetery.

PAUL A. WITTRIG, 1905-   Preacher   Bethany

Born at Noble, Iowa, December 21, 1905. Married Effie M. Wyse of Wayland, Iowa, July 11, 1928. Four children. Ordained preacher in the Prairie Street meetinghouse, May 15, 1938, by D. A. Yoder, at the request of the district mission board. Served in the Bethany congregation at Imlay City, Michigan, from May 1938 until 1959. Transferred to Colorado Springs, Colorado. Before serving as a preacher in the Bethany congregation, he had been a banker at Elkhart, Indiana. While at Imlay City he was a letter carrier for the post-office department. Served as business manager at Hesston College for one year.

ALBERT WYSE, 1879-1961   Deacon   Midland

Born at Archbold, Ohio, January 28, 1879. Married Abbie L. Baer of Iowa County, Iowa, December 20, 1900. Ten children. Ordained deacon at Midland, December 4, 1919, by J. K. Bixler, at the request of the district mission board. Served the Midland congregation since that time as deacon. He is the father of Monroe B. Wyse, formerly controller of Eastern Mennonite College, of Preacher Lester A. Wyse of the Ohio and Eastern Mennonite Conference, and of Preacher Ora C. Wyse of the Upper Peninsula, Michigan. Died August 15, 1961. Burial near Midland.

LESTER A. WYSE, 1909-   Preacher   Pleasantview

Born at Archbold, Ohio, January 29, 1909. Married Miriam E. Johns (daughter of Preacher Ira S. Johns) on March 15, 1931. Four children. Ordained preacher in the Pleasantview congregation, near Brethren, Michigan, May 7, 1944, by Edwin J. Yoder, at the request of the district mission board. In June 1949 he secured his conference letter for transfer to the Ohio and Eastern Mennonite Conference, where he is serving as a preacher at Hartville, Ohio.

ORA C. WYSE, 1919-   Preacher   Naubinway

Born at Midland, Michigan, January 3, 1919. Married Esther E. Thomas of Sandusky, Michigan, August 25, 1940. Four children. Ordained preacher in the Midland congregation, December 16, 1945, by F. F. Bontrager, at the request of the district mission board. Served the Naubinway congregation since that date.

CLARENCE R. YODER, 1903-   Preacher   Midland

Born at Thomas, Oklahoma, July 30, 1903. Married (1) Herma Yoder on September 20, 1926. Married (2) Delilah Miller of Mio, Michigan, May 9, 1929. Five children. Ordained preacher in the Midland congregation, by congregational vote, May 10, 1936, by F. F. Bontrager. Served as preacher in the Midland congregation since that date.

DANIEL YODER, 1853-1924   Preacher   Yoder, Adams County

Daniel Yoder began to serve as preacher in the Yoder congregation of the Amish Mennonite Church in Adams County sometime in the 1880's. The exact date of his ordination has been lost. He served until the year 1907 when he removed to Allen County, Ohio, and attended the Leo congregation. In 1908 the Indiana-Michigan Amish Mennonite Conference delegated the bishops and Daniel Yoder to care for the congregation in Adams County. Both Reuben R. Ebersole, later a Mennonite preacher, and Frances Zook, later Mrs. D. S. Oyer, taught school in Adams County. D. S. Oyer reported that Preacher Daniel Yoder went to church barefooted, and had little influence in the community. His own children united with the Missionary Church Association, rather than with his Amish Mennonite Church. He was a brother to Eli Yoder, the Leo bishop. His body is buried in the Leo Cemetery.

DAVID A. YODER, 1883-   Preacher, Bishop   Holdeman, Olive

Born in Elkhart County, Indiana, October 14, 1883. Accepted Christ the spring of 1896 and was baptized by John F. Funk on Sunday, April 4, 1896, in a baptismal class of twenty-six persons, which also included Silas Weldy, later a preacher at Holdeman. Married Frances Ferguson on March 17, 1906. Three children. Ordained preacher at Holdeman, by lot, July 14, 1907, by David Burkholder, with the understanding that he would be available to be used wherever he would be sent. There were three brethren in the lot: S. C. Hartzler, Menno Weaver, and D. A. Yoder. In January 1908, he was placed in the Olive congregation to serve as preacher there, because William H. Hartman, who had been ordained at Olive, did not feel able to take up the ministry. Ordained bishop in the Yellow Creek (frame) meetinghouse, by lot, September 1, 1910, by David Burkholder. J. S. Hartzler was in the lot with him on this occasion, but was in absentia (in India). Brother Yoder has been one of the most active leaders in the Indiana-Michigan Mennonite Conference. He served for almost a lifetime as bishop at the Holdeman Church (from 1914) and likewise in the Prairie Street congregation. He also cared for many other churches for longer or shorter periods. He served for about forty years as an active member of the Mennonite Board of Education, about half of that time as president, whereupon he was made a life member. He has the status of a retired bishop in the Olive congregation, and is bishop emeritus of the Prairie Street congregation. He taught school for a number of years as a young man. Very few bishops in the history of the conference have been living fifty years after their ordination.

DONALD E. YODER, 1930-   Preacher, Bishop   Forks

Born in Lagrange County, Indiana, December 16, 1930, nephew of Deacon Malvin P. Miller of the Forks congregation. Married Bonnie Lou Miller on September 25, 1955. One daughter. Ordained preacher in the Forks congregation near Middlebury, Indiana, by lot, July 12, 1953, by E. C. Bontrager. Has served effectively since that date. Is currently chairman of the Christian Workers' Conference. Received a B.A. degree from Goshen College and a Th.B. degree from the Seminary, 1954. Is much interested in trying to help youth spiritually through a church camping program. Chosen bishop by vote of the Forks Congregation, and ordained July 30, 1961, by E. C. Bontrager.

EDWIN J. YODER, 1889-   Preacher, Bishop   Maple Grove

Born at Topeka, Indiana, December 2, 1889, son of Daniel J. and Emma C. (Burkholder) Yoder. Educated in the public schools of Topeka; at Purdue University, 1911-12; and at Goshen College, 1912-13. Married (1) Mollie Mae Stoltzfus of West Liberty, Ohio, January 22, 1913. Five children. (She died in 1932.) Married (2) Mary E. Shumaker of West Liberty, Ohio, March 13, 1934. Ordained preacher in the Maple Grove congregation, by vote of the church, November 1, 1925, by Jonathan Kurtz. Ordained bishop at the Maple Grove Church, again by congregational vote,

November 3, 1935, by D. D. Miller. Has been very active in the missionary program of the Indiana-Michigan Conference. Has served on the conference Examining Committee; as vice-president of the Mennonite Board of Missions and Charities; as president of the Indiana-Michigan Mennonite Mission Board; as mission superintendent for the district mission board; as business manager of Goshen College; and as endowment custodian of the Mennonite Board of Education. The Yoder family comes from Fairfield County, Ohio; they settled in Indiana in 1856. The Burkholder family of his mother comes from Wayne County, Ohio. E. J. Yoder has been very helpful in gathering information for this history. Preacher Joseph Yoder of the Barker Street congregation was his great-uncle.

ELIAS YODER, 1857-1935   Preacher, Bishop   Leo

"Eli" Yoder was ordained preacher about 1880 or 1881. Soon thereafter he was ordained bishop and served until about the year 1906. In his later years he had no responsibility in the Leo congregation, but was allowed to preach elsewhere by request.

FLOYD M. YODER, 1920-   Preacher   Fairview

Born at Nappanee, Indiana, November 23, 1920, grandson of Ezra Bleile. Married Irene Faye Miller of Fairview, Michigan, December 16, 1944. Three children. Accepted Christ during evangelistic meetings conducted in the North Main Street, Nappanee, Mennonite Church. Ordained preacher in the Fairview congregation, by lot, August 10, 1952, by Menno Esch.

HAROLD A. YODER, 1915-   Preacher   Middlebury

Born at Middlebury, Indiana, February 1, 1915. Married Erma Sigler of White Pigeon Michigan, December 5, 1936. Two children. Ordained preacher at Middlebury, by lot, September 22, 1946, by Paul Mininger. Is currently (1961) supplying the pulpit at the Kalamazoo Mennonite Church.

HERBERT L. YODER, 1929-   Preacher   Wawasee Lakeside Chapel

Born at West Liberty, Ohio, June 8, 1929. Married Dorothy Jean Beason of Bellefontaine, Ohio, December 31, 1948. Four children. Studied in Goshen College and its Biblical Seminary. Licensed to preach in 1953, and again in 1954. Ordained preacher in the Wawasee Lakeside Chapel, Syracuse, Indiana, December 18, 1955. Both the licenses and the ordination by Edwin J. Yoder of the Maple Grove congregation, which assumed basic responsibility for the Wawasee Lakeside Chapel.

JOHN J. YODER, 1919-   Preacher   Clinton Brick

Born at Kokomo, Indiana, September 22, 1919. Married Millie Eash on November 28, 1940. Four children. Ordained preacher at Farmerstown, Ohio, May 23, 1951. Transferred to the Indiana Conference where he was received as a member in June 1956. Served as assistant minister, and as pastor from December 6, 1959, in the Clinton Brick congregation. Took some work in the Goshen College Biblical Seminary.

J. OTIS YODER, 1914-   Preacher   Midland

Born at Brandon, Colorado, September 21, 1914. Married Isabelle King of West Liberty, Ohio, June 23, 1939. Two children. Ordained preacher at the Midland Mennonite Church, by lot, July 24, 1938, by F. F. Bontrager. Served at Midland, 1938-41. Is now Professor of New Testament at Eastern Mennonite College. Has a Th.B. from Eastern Mennonite School; a B.A. from Goshen College; a B.D. from Faith Theological Seminary; and a Th.D. from Northern Baptist Theological Seminary, 1954. About 1945 he wrote: "Bishop Enos Hartzler of Marshallville, Ohio, has been a very real inspiration to me by his fatherly concern in the church."

JOHN YODER   Preacher   Nappanee (West)

Weaver's History of Elkhart County, 1916, Volume I, pages 385, 386, lists John Yoder as an early preacher in the W. Market Street Amish Mennonite Church. This is confirmed in an essay by David Burkholder of the Nappanee Mennonite Church.

JOHN M. YODER, 1878-   Preacher   Zion

Born in St. Joseph County, Michigan, October 11, 1878. (His parents were members of the Barker Street congregation.) Married Nannie Hershey of Shelby County, Missouri, September 20, 1908. Seven children, including Preacher Jesse L. of the Conservative Mennonite Conference. Licensed in August 1913, by J. K. Bixler, for the work at Homestead, Benzie County, Michigan. Transferred to Montcalm County in June 1914, and labored where the Zion congregation later developed. Conducted preaching services in a schoolhouse. Ordained preacher in Montcalm County, July 26, 1914. Removed to Shelby County, Missouri, in March 1920. Moved to Parnell, Iowa, in March 1951.

JONAS C. YODER, 1833-1914   Preacher, Bishop   Pretty Prairie

Born near Allensville, Pennsylvania. Removed with his parents to Logan County, Ohio, at the age of twelve. Removed to Northern Indiana in 1862 and became affiliated with the Pretty Prairie congregation; the Herald of Truth in 1871 speaks of Jonas Yoder "of Pretty Prairie." The Mennonite Cyclopedic Dictionary reports that he was ordained preacher in Northern Indiana (that is, at Pretty Prairie) about 1863, and bishop a year or two later. In 1872, according to the Herald of Truth, he was still at Pretty Prairie, but by 1887 he had returned to Logan County, Ohio, where he did his lifework. The year of his return to Ohio is not known.

JOSEPH YODER, 1822-1908   Preacher, Bishop   Maple Grove, Townline,
                                                                              Barker Street

Born at Lewistown, Mifflin County, Pennsylvania, August 21, 1822. Ordained preacher in Fairfield County, Ohio, in 1852. Was serving as a preacher at Haw Patch (Maple Grove) in 1867 (is reported to have come to Indiana about 1853). Is said to have been ordained bishop in 1876. Was one of the founders of the Townline Conservative Mennonite congregation in that year and had the bishop oversight of Townline, 1876-83. As early as 1871, however, his address was Bristol, and his "home congregation" was evidently Barker Street. In 1886 the Herald of Truth reported that Joseph Yoder's new address was Goshen; this was further clarified the next year when it was reported that he was living on the Elkhart Prairie, a tract of land lying southeast of Goshen. In 1888, however, the Herald of Truth speaks of "Joseph Yoder of the Amish Mennonite Church at the Town Line." Married (1) Lydia Kurtz (1823-1887) on August 30, 1842. Five children. Married (2) Barbara Orendorf of near Flanagan, Illinois. Probably somewhere around the turn of the century he removed to Gridley, Illinois, for a number of years. In 1906 he settled at Wayland, Iowa, where he died February 21, 1908, at the advanced age of eighty-five years and six months. Burial in the Wayland Amish Mennonite Cemetery east of the meetinghouse. He was a bit too conservative for the Amish Mennonites of the Maple Grove, Clinton Frame, and Forks congregations. This explains his preference for the Townline congregation which is now a part of the Conservative Mennonite Conference. He was a brother of E. J. Yoder's paternal grandfather. He wrote numerous articles for the Herald of Truth.

LEVI W. YODER, 1876-1947   Preacher   Nappanee (West)

Born at Orrville, Ohio, October 26, 1876, son of Stephen Yoder. Married (1) Clara Alice Troyer. (She and an infant daughter died in 1914.) Married (2) Edith Buzzard on December 28, 1916. Taught school in Lagrange County as a young man, then kept store in the village of South West until shortly before his death. Ordained preacher in the West Market Street Amish Mennonite congregation, June 16, 1911, by J. P. Smucker. (Simon Smucker was ordained deacon in the same service.) Served until the year 1930, when he transferred his membership to the Mennonite Brethren in Christ denomination (now United Missionary Church). Was survived by five children, including Mrs. Q. J. Everest of South Bend. Died June 11, 1947, at Wakarusa. Burial in South Union Cemetery.

MELVIN A. YODER, 1910-   Deacon   Midland
    Born in McPherson County, Kansas, May 1, 1910, brother of J. Otis Yoder. Married Luella May Short of Wauseon, Ohio, December 22, 1933. Five children. Ordained deacon in the Midland congregation, by lot, August 29, 1944, by F. F. Bontrager. Has served in the Midland Church since that date. Factory worker and carpenter.

MENNO J. YODER, 1874-1957   Deacon, Preacher   Emma
    Born in Indiana, February 9, 1874. Married (1) Martha E. Smith (1876-1936), also of Indiana, in October 1900. Five children. Married (2) Lizzie Frey in February 1937. Ordained deacon in the Emma congregation, by lot, October 16, 1902, by John Nice of Illinois. (O. S. Hostetler was ordained preacher in the same service.) Ordained preacher at the Emma Church, by lot, May 13, 1923, by D. J. Johns. (O. S. Hostetler was ordained bishop in the same service.) Was severely injured in an automobile accident in his late years, but recovered. Died September 20, 1957. Burial in Yoder Cemetery, near the Yoder School, in Lagrange County.

NOAH Z. YODER, 1887-1918   Preacher   Fairview
    Born in Juniata County, Pennsylvania, November 24, 1887. Married (1) Lydia Hertzler. Four children. Married (2) Mary Waltz. Three children. Ordained preacher near Concord, Tennessee, in 1895, by John F. Funk of Elkhart, Indiana. Removed from Tennessee to Fairview, Michigan, in 1906, where he served in the ministry until his death, which occurred October 13, 1918, at Fairview.

RAY F. YODER, 1893-   Preacher, Bishop   Salem
    Born at Wakarusa, Indiana, February 21, 1893, son of Eli Yoder (1858-1942) and Elizabeth (Freed) Yoder (1860-1947). Married Clara E. Smeltzer of Wakarusa, Indiana, February 20, 1913. Nine children. United with the Holdeman Mennonite Church, November 17, 1907. Transferred his membership to the Salem congregation, November 14, 1914. Ordained preacher at Salem, by vote of the congregation, upon the recommendation of the conference Executive Committee, February 6, 1918, by D. A. Yoder. Ordained bishop in the Yellow Creek meetinghouse, by lot, July 4, 1947, by D. D. Troyer. Has been one of the strong leaders of the Indiana-Michigan Conference. Served on the Executive Committee of conference, 1931-42, and on the Executive Committee of the Sunday School Conference from about 1931 to 1943. Was moderator of the Indiana-Michigan Mennonite Conference, 1948-50. Has exerted influence for conservatism in his congregation and conference.

RICHARD W. YODER, 1929-   Preacher   Nappanee
    Born at Midland, Michigan, November 8, 1929. Took college and seminary work at Goshen, completing the Th.B. degree in 1956. Licensed to preach, September 16, 1956, by Homer F. North, bishop of the Nappanee congregation. Ordained preacher, in the Nappanee meetinghouse, by vote of the congregation, November 17, 1957, by Homer F. North. Married Loretta A. Shrock of the state of New York, July 5, 1958. One daughter. Became pastor at Nappanee, November 20, 1960.

SAMUEL YODER   Preacher, Bishop   Nappanee (West)
    In giving a brief history of the West Market Street Amish Mennonite Church, Abraham E. Weaver in his Standard History of Elkhart County, Indiana, 1916, I, 385, indicates that the first bishop and preacher of the Nappanee Amish Mennonite Church were "Samuel Yoder as bishop and John Ringenberg as minister." David Burkholder, first pastor and bishop of the North Main Street Mennonite Church, Nappanee, wrote in an essay which has been preserved in the Mennonite Historical Library, Goshen College: "It would not be out of place to state here that our Amish Mennonite brethren held meetings there too in the same schoolhouse on the intervening Sunday. Their ministers were John Ringenberg, Samuel Yoder, and Samuel Hochstetler, and later on Jonathan Smucker." The possibility of course remains that Burkholder got this

information from the Weaver Elkhart County history. It is very doubtful, however, if he would have written an error for the period in which he himself was a living participant. It is therefore entirely likely that this name is not a mistake. At this writing his grave has not been found, and his birth and death dates are unknown. But there is more evidence.

The **Herald of Truth** contains a record of funerals conducted by Samuel Yoder and John Ringenberg in Union Township, Elkhart County, February and March 1867; they again preached at another funeral in May 1867. In that same year Samuel Yoder and John Ringenberg went by team to Howard and Miami counties, to the home of Absalom Miller, who served as deacon in the Howard-Miami congregation, and held meetings in the homes of Benjamin Schrock and Daniel Miller, both of whom were preachers, and later bishops in the same congregation. Again in 1868 Samuel Yoder and John Ringenberg preached funeral sermons.

SAMUEL YODER, 1835-1925   Preacher   Mikesell, Prairie Street

Born in Columbiana County, Ohio, May 3, 1835, son of Samuel and Margaret (Holdeman) Yoder. His widowed mother later married Jacob Freed and came to Elkhart County, Indiana, with her family in 1851. They lived one and one-half miles south of Wakarusa. On April 22, 1858, Samuel married (1) Elizabeth Woods (1840-1903) in Grundy County, Illinois. Eight children. He first farmed in Elkhart County, but later removed to St. Joseph County, six or seven miles southwest of the town of South Bend. He had a forty-acre farm in section 24 of Warren Township. He preached for a small group of Mennonites in a nearby schoolhouse. John M. Brenneman of Ohio ordained Samuel as a preacher for this little congregation on January 11, 1867. Samuel's second wife was Susan (Alsbaugh) Lehman, a widow of Cullom, Illinois, and the mother of Preacher L. J. Lehman. The fall of 1885 Samuel Yoder removed to Prairie Street, Elkhart, and preached in the Prairie Street congregation for the next forty years. Died March 12, 1925, in his ninetieth year. Burial in Prairie Street Church Cemetery on Hively Avenue.

SANFORD C. YODER, 1879-   Preacher, Bishop   Goshen College

Born near Iowa City, Iowa, December 5, 1879. Married Emma Stutsman, also of near Iowa City, September 23, 1903. Three children. Ordained preacher at Chappell, Nebraska, June 8, 1911, by Joseph Schlegel. Ordained bishop in the East Union Mennonite congregation, Kalona, Iowa, by lot, September 21, 1913, by Christian Warey. Was pastor at Chappell, Nebraska, 1911-13; of the East Union congregation, Kalona, Iowa, 1913-24; served as president of Goshen College, 1923-40; also served for many years as bishop of the Goshen College congregation, although the active responsibilities of the office have now been turned over to John H. Mosemann, the pastor of the congregation. Served also for many years on the Committee of Arrangements of Mennonite General Conference; as assistant moderator, 1919; as moderator, 1921; and as moderator of the Western District Amish Mennonite Conference. Devoted servant of the Mennonite Board of Missions and Charities. Served on the executive committee, 1918-49, as secretary, 1921-44, and as president, 1944-48. Has the B.A. degree from the State University of Iowa; the M.A. (Theol.) from the Winona Lake School of Theology; the B.D. and D.D. from the Northern Baptist Theological Seminary; the LL.B. from the Hamilton College of Law; and the S.T.D. from Gordon Divinity School. Is Director of Bible Correspondence for Goshen College Biblical Seminary. Author of numerous books. Is a man of deep personal piety, a wise and sane church leader, and a tenderhearted shepherd. He writes: "I was converted under the preaching of A. I. Yoder. **Jacob's Ladder,** by J. E. Hartzler, helped me more than any religious book I read while in my early Christian life."

SILAS YODER, 1868-1943   Preacher   Clinton Frame

Born at Goshen, Elkhart County, Indiana, May 7, 1868, son of Levi and Martha (Magdalena) Honderich Yoder. Married Abbie Sunthimer, of Elkhart County, in 1891.

Three children, including Orus R. Yoder, M.D., Medical Superintendent of the Ypsilanti State Hospital, Ypsilanti, Michigan. Ordained preacher at Clinton Frame, April 9, 1905, by Jonathan Kurtz. Transferred to the Middlebury Mennonite Church about the year 1925. Died March 1, 1943. He was a brother of Samuel A. Yoder of the Goshen College congregation, and therefore an uncle of Samuel's son, Preacher Raymond M. Yoder. He was also a brother of the wife of David Yontz.

SIMON S. YODER, 1878-1943   Deacon, Preacher   Forks, Middlebury

Born in Lagrange County, Indiana, May 5, 1878. Married Sarah Troyer on May 14, 1899. Three children. Taught school over twenty years. Was a brother of O. S. Hostetler's wife. Ordained deacon in the Forks congregation, by lot (four nominees), May 17, 1903. Transferred to the Middlebury congregation two or three years later. Ordained preacher at Middlebury, December 22, 1907, by D. J. Johns. In the up-heavals in the Indiana-Michigan Conference, 1923-24, Simon withdrew from the conference, and transferred to the Central Conference of Mennonites. In 1941 he returned to the Indiana-Michigan Conference. Died September 3, 1943.

WILBUR YODER, 1909-   Preacher, Bishop   Middlebury

Born at Middlebury, Indiana, October 8, 1909. Married Suzanne Troyer, who had been born at Shipshewana, Indiana, on November 23, 1929. Three children. Ordained preacher in the Middlebury congregation, by lot, December 20, 1936, by D. D. Miller. Ordained bishop in the same congregation, by congregational vote, August 30, 1959, by Paul M. Miller. He is especially gifted in the field of evangelism and has held many series of evangelistic meetings. He reports that A. J. Metzler of Scottdale, Pennsylvania, has been particularly helpful to him in his Christian life and understanding.

AMOS D. YONTZ, 1910-   Deacon   Benton

Born at Goshen, Indiana, September 10, 1910, son of Deacon David Yontz. Married Ferne Anna Leinbach, who had been born in Alberta, Canada, on April 8, 1939. Three children. Ordained deacon at the Benton Church, by congregational vote, January 30, 1949, by Edwin J. Yoder. Served at Benton until March 1960. He is an outstanding farmer in Elkhart County.

ANDREW J. YONTZ, 1864-1938   Preacher   Maple Grove

Andrew was an older brother of Deacon David Yontz of the Clinton Frame congregation. Andrew and David were the sons of Heinrich and Catharina (Lutken) Jantz of the Mennonite Karolswalde Colony, Kreis Ostrog, Volhynia, then a territory of Russia. Heinrich and Catharina Jantz obtained a Russian passport bearing the date, September 26, 1874, to emigrate to America. They were the parents of fifteen children. They brought along to America a sort of expanded German church letter entitled, **Birth, Baptism, and Marriage Certificate,** signed by Tobias Unruh, elder of the Mennonite congregations at Karolswalde, and bearing the church seal of the Ostrog, Volhynia, congregations. These documents are now in the possession of Deacon Amos Yontz.

Andrew was first married to Catharine Hartzler (1869-1914) (sister of J. S. Hartzler). One daughter, Viola. On October 25, 1914, he married Sarah Haynes Holman. They adopted a son, Herbert. Andrew was ordained preacher in the Maple Grove congregation, September 7, 1903. Served about twelve years. In 1915 he united with the Church of the Brethren, the church of his second wife. Died in 1938. Burial in Maple Grove Mennonite Cemetery.

DAVID YONTZ, 1872-1958   Deacon   Clinton Frame

Born about ninety miles from Warsaw, Poland, October 31, 1872. For his family background see the paragraph under his brother, Andrew J. Yontz. Came to America with his parents in 1874. Married Emma Yoder of Goshen, Indiana, February 8, 1898. Four children, including Deacon Amos D. Yontz. Ordained deacon in the Clinton Frame congregation, by vote, January 8, 1925, by D. A. Yoder. Served faithfully for a whole generation. Died January 11, 1958. Burial in Elkhart Prairie (Alwine) Cemetery.

EMERSON YORDY, 1917-   Preacher   Maple Grove, U.P.
    Born in Nebraska, August 27, 1917. Married Rhoda Handrich of Fairview, Michigan. Six children, two of whom are deceased. Licensed as a minister, June 1, 1958, by Norman Weaver. Ordained preacher in the Maple Grove Mennonite congregation at Gulliver, Michigan, September 27, 1959, by Norman Weaver. Resigned April 11, 1960, and removed to Oregon about eleven days later.

HOMER E. YUTZY, 1926-   Preacher   Gay, Petoskey
    Born at Plain City, Ohio, July 19, 1926. Married Elizabeth G. Williams on November 29, 1952. Four children. Ordained preacher at Gay in the Upper Peninsula of Michigan, October 18, 1953, by Clarence Yoder. Gay did not prove to be a successful mission field, and in 1959 Homer accepted the call of the Petoskey congregation to become their pastor succeeding Ivan Weaver who had moved to Elida, Ohio. He was installed at Petoskey, May 10, 1959, by Ivan Weaver.

HOWARD J. ZEHR, 1916-   Preacher, Bishop   Prairie Street
    Born in Tazewell County, Illinois, March 24, 1916. Married Edna Good on June 21, 1942. Four children. Received the Th.B. degree from Goshen College Biblical Seminary, 1940. Ordained preacher at Freeport, Illinois, April 19, 1942. Ordained bishop at Freeport, September 5, 1948. Served at Freeport, 1941-50; at Peoria, Illinois, 1950-52; at Fisher, Illinois, 1952-58; and at Prairie Street congregation, Elkhart, Indiana, since January 15, 1958; formal installation, February 2, 1958.

JOHN D. ZEHR, 1922-   Preacher, Bishop   Yellow Creek
    Born at Manson, Iowa, July 16, 1922. Married Ruth Lais of Hubbard, Oregon, August 12, 1945. Four children. Studied at Goshen College Biblical Seminary, 1946-49, and received the Th.B. degree. Served at Los Angeles, California, 1950-58. Ordained preacher at Manson, Iowa, June 23, 1946, by Simon Gingerich of Wayland, Iowa. Became assistant minister in the Yellow Creek congregation in August 1958. Installed pastor at Yellow Creek, April 24, 1960, by J. C. Wenger, moderator of conference. Ordained bishop at Yellow Creek, by vote of the congregation, September 18, 1960, by Russell Krabill and J. C. Wenger.

DANIEL E. ZOOK, 1907-   Preacher   Bowne
    Born at White Cloud, Michigan, February 3, 1907, son of Deacon Eli Zook and grandson of Bishop J. P. Miller. Married Edna M. Yoder of Alto, Michigan, February 7, 1925. Ten children. Ordained preacher in the Bowne congregation, by lot, July 5, 1940, by T. E. Schrock. Has served faithfully since his ordination. Farmer.

ELI ZOOK, 1870-1924   Deacon   White Cloud, Bowne
    Born in Howard County, Indiana, November 9, 1870. Removed to Illinois and united with the Hopedale congregation, 1897. Married Fanny E. Miller (daughter of Bishop J. P. Miller) on January 27, 1898. (Eli S. Miller performed the ceremony.) Two children. Ordained deacon in the White Cloud congregation, November 24, 1900, by P. Y. Lehman. Served at White Cloud, 1899-1910. Lived one year at Elmira, Michigan. Removed to the Bowne congregation in 1911, where he served until his death. Died September 9, 1924. Burial at Bowne. He was the son of Jacob Zook (1842-1913) of Holmes County, Ohio, who removed to Howard County, Indiana, in 1851; his first wife was Mary Schmucker, and his second wife, Rebecca Mast.

J. KORE ZOOK, 1894-   Preacher   Bethel
    Born at Belleville, Pennsylvania, February 7, 1894. Married Ruth Gladys Cooprider of McPherson, Kansas, May 18, 1919. Eight children. Ordained preacher in the Manitou Springs, Colorado, congregation, by congregational vote, November 19, 1925, by J. A. Heatwole. Served at Manitou Springs, 1925-29; at Roseland, Nebraska,

1929-33; at **Morrison, Illinois, 1933-37; in the Bethel** congregation, Ashley, Michigan, 1937-54; and in the Oak Terrace congregation, Blountstown, Florida, 1957-59. He is now living in Goshen, Indiana. He writes: "I was led into a deeper experience through the ministry of Brother [C. F.] Derstine."

* * *

SUPPLEMENT

IRVIN M. DETWILER, 1932-   Preacher   East Goshen

Born in Montgomery County, Pennsylvania, March 29, 1932. Married Althea Alderfer of Montgomery County, Pennsylvania, June 27, 1953. Two children. Received B.D. degree from Goshen College Biblical Seminary in 1961. Ordained preacher in the East Goshen congregaton, by congregational vote, July 23, 1961, by Paul M. Miller.

ONEY L. HATHAWAY, 1914-   Preacher   Anderson

Born at Palmyra, Marion County, Missouri, October 21, 1914. United with the Pea Ridge Mennonite Church in 1928. J. M. Kreider baptized him. Married Cleo Miller of Yoder, Kansas, on December 25, 1941. Five children (four living). Ordained preacher at the Pea Ridge Church February 20, 1949, by Nelson E. Kauffman and J. R. Shank, to serve the Berea Church near Birch Tree, Missouri. Plans to begin serving the Anderson congregation, August 1961.

HAROLD G. KREIDER, 1924-   Preacher   Waterford

Born at Palmyra, Missouri, May 3, 1924. Married Roberta Showalter of Yoder, Kansas, April 21, 1946. Three children. Studied at Hesston College, 1948-49, and at Goshen College, 1959-. Ordained preacher at the Pea Ridge Mennonite Church, September 3, 1950, by J. R. Shank, Nelson E. Kauffman, and Simon Gingerich, to serve at Palmyra and Hannibal. Served at Palmyra, 1950-52; as assistant pastor, Hannibal, 1952-56; and as pastor, 1956-59. Served as a minister of the Waterford congregation after entering Goshen College.

J. PAUL LAUVER, 1923-   Preacher   Marion

Born at Carlos Casares, Argentina, January 12, 1923, son of Missionary William G. Lauver. Received B.A. degree from Goshen College in 1944, and Th.B. in 1945. Married Lois M. Swihart of Howe, Indiana, October 14, 1945. Four children. Ordained preacher at the Maple Grove Mennonite Church, Belleville, Pennsylvania, November 4, 1945, by Aaron Mast. Served as a missionary in Puerto Rico, 1945-57. Is taking an extended furlough because of the health of his mother-in-law. Served as a minister in the Marion congregation from 1958, and as pastor since 1960.

FRED SLABACH, 1922-   Deacon   Clinton Frame

Born in Oscoda County, Michigan, September 29, 1922. Married Lillian Esther Riegsecker of Elkhart County, Indiana, April 21, 1946. Six children. Farmer and factory worker. Ordained deacon by lot in the Clinton Frame congregation by Vernon E. Bontreger on August 27, 1961.

DANIEL W. STAUFFER   Preacher   "Eagle Lake"

In February 1872 Preacher Michael W. Shank visited the Amish Mennonite settlement near Eagle Lake in Starke County, Indiana. The German **Herold der Wahrheit** refers to Daniel Stauffer as a preacher and brother. The English **Herald of Truth** calls him Preacher D. Stouffer. In November 1870 Daniel Brenneman visited [Bishop] Jonas D. Troyer in Starke County, and also D. Stauffer; he also baptized D. Stauffer and wife. Daniel W. and Elizabeth Stauffer wrote a letter to the **Herald of Truth**, which was published in March 1871; their address was Grovertown in Starke County. Did John M. Brenneman perhaps ordain the man? The possibility remains that Stauffer never was a preacher. M. W. Shank refers to him in his German letter as "Pr. D. Stauffer." In the next sentence he calls him "Br. Stauffer." It is possible that Shank wrote Br. [Brother] both times, and that John F. Funk misread it as Pr. [Preacher] the first time.

Concluded on page 258

VI

Other Mennonite Bodies

Reformed Mennonite Church, 1812

A century and a half ago a layman of Lancaster County, Pennsylvania, named Francis Herr, 1747-1810, began to meet with a small group of strict and exclusive Mennonites which have been variously known as Herrites or New Mennonites, but officially as Reformed Mennonites. Francis seems to have been expelled from the Mennonite Church about the year 1798. He eventually began to hold meetings in his dwelling house, having singing and prayer, and exhorting those who came to hear him while remaining seated. After Herr's death in 1810 a man named David Buckwalter became the more or less recognized leader of the meetings and in the course of time the son of Francis, a man named John Herr, 1781-1850, who had never been a member of the Mennonite Church, was chosen as the pastor and bishop of the tiny schismatic group. This choice occurred in Herr's own home May 30, 1812, and the church was formally established. John Herr was at that time a young man thirty years of age. One of the members who had been a Mennonite, Abraham Landis, was selected to baptize John. John in turn rebaptized Landis, also Abraham Groff, who served as the first deacon of the group. Landis was also chosen as a minister in a short time, and his brother, John Landis, became an additional minister of the group. The movement later spread to Ohio and to Ontario.

In the course of time the Reformed Mennonites established a few small congregations in Indiana and Michigan. They seem to have migrated to these states largely from the province of Ontario. In 1860, a small congregation was established at Valparaiso in Porter County in Northern Indiana. At the present time the Valparaiso Reformed Mennonite Church has a membership of approximately twenty-four.

Two congregations of Reformed Mennonites were also established in the state of Michigan. In 1868 the Shelby congregation was formed in Oceana County, Michigan, near the village of Shelby, thirty miles north of Muskegon. The meetinghouse of the group was built three miles east of the town. Formal organization of the Shelby congregation seems to have taken place in 1888, and the meetinghouse, which is a frame structure with a seating capacity of approximately 160, was built in the year 1893. Ministers in the church have been Ambrose Bearss, Eli Near, Al Near, Jesse Fogelsonger, and Omar Near. The membership of the group at the present time is fifty-two. The other congregation of Reformed Mennonites in Michigan was established at Rochester, eight or ten miles northeast of Pontiac, in Oakland County, possibly twenty miles north of Detroit. This congregation was established in the neighborhood of 1900, and died out in the 1930's because the members moved to other locations. The Reformed Mennonite minister, who is listed in the *Mennonite Yearbook* as living at Hudson, Michigan, serves the Reformed Mennonite congregation at Archbold, Ohio, and lives just across the Michigan line.

The Reformed Mennonite Church strongly emphasizes that its members are the true followers of Menno Simons, and seeks to uphold all the Biblical principles for which Menno Simons stood, including shunning. Actually the Reformed Mennonites are much like the Mennonite Church prior to its "Great Awakening" in the latter nineteenth century. The total membership of the Reformed Mennonites in the United States is 620, found in twenty-four congregations; in Canada six additional congregations with 214 members bring the total membership for North America to 834. The only organ which the church ever had was *Good Tidings* published at Lancaster, Pennsylvania, 1922-32, with Jacob Kreider serving as editor.

Stauffer Mennonites, 1845

The Stauffer Mennonite Church takes its name from a preacher in the Lancaster Mennonite Conference named Jacob Stauffer, *c.*1811-1855, who in 1845 led a small conservative schism from the Lancaster Mennonite Conference. He and his followers worshiped in the Pike meetinghouse not far from the village of Hinkletown in Lancaster County, Pennsylvania.

In the spring of 1887 a group of Stauffer Mennonites decided to found a Utopia in Osceola County, Iowa. The leader of the church in Osceola County, Iowa, was Bishop Jesse S. Bowman of Ontario. In the spring of 1888 Bishop Bowman was followed from Canada by his assistant minister, Josiah Martin, 1845-1918, and by Deacon Elias Bowman. The Iowa experiment did not work out well, and in 1896 Preacher Josiah Martin removed to South Haven, Van Buren County, Michigan. In 1899 Preacher Josiah Martin and his followers located at Stanton in Montcalm County, Michigan, about forty miles northeast of Grand Rapids. Preacher Josiah Martin's son, Elam C. Martin, 1876-1928, who had been ordained in Iowa in 1903, also moved to Stanton, Michigan, and served as preacher of the tiny Stauffer Mennonite group there. Elam C. Martin was ordained bishop in the Pike

Stauffer Mennonite Church in 1921, although he continued to live at Stanton, Michigan, for two more years before his permanent removal to Pennsylvania. Elam died March 5, 1928, at the age of fifty-two; burial in the Pike Cemetery. The Stauffer Mennonites never had more than eight members in Michigan at any one time, there was some moving in and out, and the group always worshiped in private homes. After the removal of Elam Martin to Pennsylvania in 1923 the group disintegrated and the few remaining members, affiliated themselves with the Wisler (Ramer) Mennonite Church. *The Mennonite Encyclopedia* has a good article on the Stauffer Mennonite Church, written by the leading historian of the Lancaster Mennonites, Ira D. Landis.

Church of God in Christ, Mennonite, 1859

The so-called "Holdeman" Mennonite Church is properly known as the Church of God in Christ, Mennonite, and was founded by a Mennonite layman from Wayne County, Ohio, in the year 1859. John Holdeman, 1832-1900, was a man who felt the inner call to preach, but not being ordained by his congregation, he launched forth on his own initiative in the year 1859. John Holdeman was a man of some ability, a good preacher, and a writer. One of the leaders in his church wrote in *The Mennonite Encyclopedia:* "He served the church, which he named the 'Church of God in Christ, Mennonite,' as pastor, evangelist, elder, moderator of general conferences, and first editor of its official periodical, *Botschafter der Wahrheit* [Messenger of Truth], from June, 1897, until his death in 1900."

The Holdeman Mennonites have no congregations in the state of Indiana, and but two in Michigan, Newark and Harrison. The Newark Church of God in Christ, Mennonite, located two miles west and four miles south of Ithaca, was established in Gratiot County in the 1880's by families bearing such names as Brown, Diller, Peters, Eicher, and Gable. The meetinghouse of the group was built in the year 1902, and was replaced by a larger building in 1920, which in turn was remodeled and enlarged in the year 1947 and again in 1954. The ministers in order of ordination from 1893 to 1951 were Fred C. Fricke, 1893; Peter Litwiller, 1893; Charles Peters, 1905; H. J. Mininger (a brother of Bishop Jonas Mininger of the Franconia Conference), 1909; August Peters, 1911; Frank F. Haynes, 1924; Glen Litwiller, 1937; Francis Peters, 1937; Harry H. Harms, 1937; Reno Hibner, 1948; and Newell Litwiller, 1951. The Newark congregation has 285 members.

In the year 1897 the Mennonite leader, John F. Funk, visited the Holdeman congregation "near St. Johns, Michigan," and was entertained

24

in the homes of "Father Peters," Preacher Peter Litwiller, Preacher Fricke, etc. Naturally these brethren insisted vigorously on the apostasy of the Mennonite Church of which Funk was a member. In fact, the principles of their church compelled them to refrain from eating with Funk. Funk held services in the schoolhouse on the evening of December 13, 1897, where the Holdeman Mennonites usually held their services. They in turn were disappointed when he did not invite them to participate in conducting the meeting.

The second Holdeman congregation in Michigan is known as the Harrison Church of God in Christ, Mennonite, congregation. It was organized in the year 1912. For a number of years this congregation held its services in the Amble schoolhouse, seven and one-half miles northeast of Harrison in Clare County, between Saginaw and Cadillac. The membership of the congregation is sixty. A new house of worship was dedicated in January 1952. The minister of the congregation is Wilbert Koehn.

The Mennonite Brethren Church of North America, 1860

Two of the best books on the history of the Mennonite Brethren group are J. H. Lohrenz: *The Mennonite Brethren Church*, Hillsboro, Kansas, 1950; and A. H. Unruh: *Die Geschichte der Mennoniten-Brüdergemeinde, 1860-1954*, Winnipeg, Manitoba, 1954.

A religious awakening came to the Mennonites of South Russia, beginning in the year 1845. This awakening came about partly through Moravian influence, and occurred in the village of Gnadenfeld. The Lutheran settlement, south of the Mennonite colony called Chortitza, called a revivalist preacher, Edward Wüst from Germany. Wüst served the Lutheran Church in South Russia, 1845-59. He was a powerful man, with deep convictions, and an able speaker. He preached repentance, conversion to Christ, and holy living. Wüst had many followers among the Mennonites who called themselves simply Brethren. Groups of Brethren began to raise a protest against certain practices in the Mennonite colonies of South Russia which they considered inconsistencies; these Brethren demanded church discipline. When they were refused the privilege to hold separate communion services, they nevertheless met in December 1859 and held their own communion service. The leaders of the old church demanded that they should desist from any further private communion services, and they refused to comply.

On January 6, 1860, a number of brethren met in the colony known as Molotschna, in a village called Elisabeththal, and drew up a memorandum to the elders of the Russian Mennonites in which they announced their withdrawal from the church and justified their step. Eighteen persons signed. The leaders of this movement were Abraham Cornelsen, Johann Claasen, and Heinrich Hübert. The elders of the church were very unhappy about this development and ordered the group to desist from their course, which they refused to do. Johann Claasen persisted until he secured government recognition for the new church body. The Mennonite Brethren Church also arose in the Chortitza settlement.

The emphases of the new Mennonite Brethren Church were repentance from sin, conversion to faith in Jesus Christ, an earnest prayer life, family worship, holy living, nonresistance, the rejection of the oath, the practice of foot washing, simplicity of life, immersion, the practice of church discipline, the giving of happy testimonies, Christian assurance, hearty congregational singing, and the institution of Sunday schools on Sunday afternoons. On May 30, 1860, the Mennonite Brethren Church in Russia elected Heinrich Hübert as elder, and Jacob Becker as preacher. In the years 1874 to 1880 a large emigration of Mennonite Brethren occurred from Russia to Kansas, Nebraska, Minnesota, and Dakota. A second migration to America occurred in the years 1923 to 1929, but this time the major settlements were made in the Canadian provinces of Manitoba, Saskatchewan, Alberta, and British Columbia; also in Paraguay in South America.

The Mennonite Brethren have an active interest in missions. By 1957, for example, they were supporting 137 missionaries. The church was also giving a quarter of a million dollars annually for foreign missions. Their periodicals are the *Zionsbote,* the *Mennonitische Rundschau; The Mennonite Observer,* and the *Christian Leader.* A publication center of the church is Hillsboro, Kansas. An educational institution of the church is Tabor College, also at Hillsboro, established in the year 1908.

The Mennonite Brethren have no congregations either in Indiana or in Michigan at the present time. Earlier there had been three small congregations in the state of Michigan. In 1906 a number of Mennonite Brethren families from Corn, Oklahoma, moved to Gladwin County northwest of Saginaw, Michigan. First they held only Sunday school, later church services, and finally in 1907 a congregation was organized at Nolan. Pastors who served there were H. F. Janzen and P. E. Penner. The work was discontinued in the year 1919.

A second congregation was established at Gladwin in Gladwin County, seven miles south of Nolan. This congregation was established in 1914 when a group of German Baptists asked to join the Mennonite Brethren Conference. A congregation was organized with P. E. Penner as pastor. His successors were Ewald Roloff and D. F. Strauss. In 1924 the Gladwin congregation had fifty-six members. It outlasted the Nolan

Church, but also finally dissolved. Several members lived as far away as Comins in Oscoda County.

Mennonite Brethren members began to settle in Detroit, Michigan, after the first World War. In 1923 there were about twenty members in the city. These members began to hold Sunday school and preaching services. Preacher D. F. Strauss of the Gladwin congregation visited them and preached for them. But the work was not permanent. In the course of time it completely disintegrated and all services were discontinued.

The Mennonite Brethren have approximately 25,000 baptized members in North America, about half of which are located in the United States, and half in Canada.

The General Conference Mennonite Church, 1860

The General Conference Mennonite Church with a membership of over 50,000 baptized members in North America is the second largest Mennonite group. The formal date of origin of the General Conference is May 28, 1860, at West Point, Iowa. The chief leaders in the organization of the General Conference Mennonites were John H. Oberholtzer, 1809-1895, of Eastern Pennsylvania, and Daniel Krehbiel, 1812-1888, of West Point, Iowa. The General Conference Mennonites hold to the same basic doctrines as the other bodies of the denomination, such as nonresistance, believers' baptism, nonconformity to the world. By background about two thirds of the group is of Dutch ancestry, which lived for almost a century in Russia (a part of the group lived more than a century there); the other third is made up of families of Swiss ethnic origin. The General Conference Mennonites in Eastern United States, especially in Eastern Pennsylvania, are made up of congregations which withdrew from the Franconia Conference in 1847, largely in Bucks and Montgomery counties in Southeastern Pennsylvania.

We turn now to the congregations of the General Conference Mennonite Church which are located in Indiana and Michigan.

FIRST MENNONITE CHURCH, 1838

Berne, Indiana

The background of this congregation was given in chapter one. The first Swiss Mennonite settlers of 1838 organized the Baumgartner Mennonite congregation near Berne. In 1852 a group of Swiss Mennonites from the Jura area, including Preacher Peter S. Lehman, 1821-1899, settled at Berne and organized a new church in Berne instead of uniting with the older Baumgartner congregation. In 1853 Lehman was ordained as elder (bishop) and given the oversight of the Baumgartner and Berne Mennonite congregations. In 1858 a small schism occurred when a number of members united with the vigorous Evangelical Association which had been formed by Jacob Albright in Pennsylvania in 1800. At the same time another small group withdrew from the Berne Church to unite with the "New Manist" Church (a nickname for the Apostolic Christian Church; another was "New Amish"). But the Berne congregation prospered and grew, and developed into one of the largest congregations of Mennonites in North America. The first meetinghouse was built in 1860, in size twenty-eight by thirty feet. About 1860 the Baumgartner congregation also erected a house of worship. These meetinghouses were plain and austere; the benches of the Berne congregation lacked backs, for example. The singing was strictly a cappella, without accompaniment of any sort. All the women wore prayer veils ("caps"). These veils were generally black, but had to be white for the communion services. The men shaved the upper lip, for historically the mustache savored of the military. Another tiny schism occurred in 1869 when several families withdrew to form a congregation which later united with the "Mennonite Church" (the largest body, with which chapters one to five of this book are concerned).

One of the momentous days in the history of the Berne congregation was August 23, 1868. On that day seventeen men were in the lot for preacher, and the book which contained the lot (a slip of paper designated the one, in whose book the presiding minister found it, as called to the ministry) was chosen by Samuel F. Sprunger, 1848-1923. Each nominee chose a copy of the hymnbook, the *Ausbund,* and in Sprunger's copy was the slip: "Lord, Knower of all hearts, indicate which one Thou hast chosen" (translated from the German). "Sammie," as he was known then, was immediately ordained. He went to the new Wadsworth Mennonite School in Ohio for further training. When he returned to his home church for a visit on Good Friday, 1871, he startled everyone by: (1) no longer wearing a "plain coat" (the garb of the group); (2) arising to give testimony to the sermon, contrary to the historic custom; and (3) venturing to speak in high German rather than in the beloved Swiss dialect which had always been employed in the services. When Sprunger graduated from Wadsworth in 1871 (academy course), he returned to Berne to take up his ministerial work. The majority refused to hear him; so he and his small group of followers met every other Sunday for services. On the alternate Sundays he preached for the Baumgartner congregation. In 1886 all three groups merged (Sprunger's Church in Berne, the Baumgartner Church, and the Berne Church).

When the Berne Church built its second house of worship in 1879 (forty by sixty feet in size), another tiny schism occurred, led by a conservative preacher, Peter M. Neuenschwander of Switzerland (where he had been ordained as a preacher at seventeen). His group died out about 1945.

Under the leadership of S. F. Sprunger the Berne congregation prospered greatly. He was an earnest and dynamic leader. Sunday school was started in 1874. The 1879 house of worship was remodeled in 1886 and again in 1899. The present building (eighty-five by one hundred and fifty-eight) was erected in 1912; the main auditorium seats 2,000. The cost was $56,519.20.

Singing has always been stressed in First Mennonite, Berne. There is an adult choir, a young people's choir, and a junior choir. The church also has a choral society which presents "The Creation" each June, and the "Messiah" each December. The well-known men's chorus was organized in 1898, and the ladies' chorus in 1912. The annual giving of the congregation is about $115,000.00.

The year 1886 was not only the year of the mergers; it was also the time of the great revival. Over one hundred persons, mostly young people, took Christ as their Saviour and Lord. With great power the Holy Spirit smote down sin and self-sufficiency as people were convicted and converted. The joy of the Lord surged through the members of the church. There was an eagerness to witness to the Lord Jesus Christ. After a Sunday night prayer meeting, for example, a large group of radiant believers left the church building and walked down the middle of Main Street, singing the praises of the Saviour. When they came to the railroad some turned north, and some south; some went east, and some west. The whole town simply had to hear the songs of joy and praise! The revival extended through the months of July and August of 1886.

Down through the decades many cultural changes took place, and a few adaptations were made in religious practice. A small organ was placed in the church building in 1902, but the first time the organ music was heard, one woman wept during the entire service. She felt that "worldliness" was entering the church. In 1914 a pipe organ displaced the smaller organ. Individual communion cups were adopted in 1914, also. Through the years all dress regulations and restrictions were abandoned. English was slowly introduced into the services, and German gradually given up, in the period from 1915 to 1930. Open communion was not adopted until 1935.

S. F. Sprunger served as pastor, 1871-1903, and as interim pastor, 1911-13; he was succeeded by: J. W. Kliewer, 1903-11; P. R. Schroeder, 1912-28; C. H. Suckau, 1928-43; J. P. Suderman (interim), 1944-45; Olin

A. Krehbiel, 1945-57; and Gordon J. Neuenschwander (interim, 1957-58), 1958-   .

The congregation has been a member of the General Conference Mennonite Church since 1872. The membership in 1960 was 1,341, by far the largest Mennonite congregation of any branch in Indiana and Michigan.

In July 1957 a ground-breaking ceremony was held for a new educational wing, 120 x 130 feet in size, which cost $600,000.00. Dedicatory services were held on June 14, 1959. Erland Waltner, president of the General Conference Mennonite Church, and president of Mennonite Biblical Seminary, Elkhart, Indiana, preached the dedicatory sermon.

First Mennonite Church

Nappanee, *ca.*1854

The second General Conference Mennonite congregation in Indiana is the First Mennonite Church of Nappanee, Indiana, originally the West Market Street Amish Mennonite Church. As early as 1853 Amish settlers were gathering in private homes in the southwest corner of Elkhart County for worship services. Visiting ministers from Ohio and Pennsylvania preached for them. The congregation then chose two of its members as ministers, John Ringenberg and Tobias Hochstetler. Soon (probably in 1854 when the Amish of Elkhart-Lagrange, and of the Howard-Miami settlements divided) the Nappanee Amish Church also divided. Ringenberg and wife with five or six other families organized a new Amish Mennonite congregation, while Hochstetler remained "Old Order" Amish. At first the Ringenberg congregation worshiped in various schoolhouses, but later only in the Culp schoolhouse which was located along County Road 7, a half mile north of the east edge of the present town of Nappanee. Here the Amish Mennonite congregation of Ringenberg worshiped one Sunday and the Mennonite congregation of which David Burkholder was later pastor, on the alternate Sunday. In 1867, when Nappanee built a new schoolhouse, the Amish Mennonite congregation donated $250.00 toward the cost of the building with the understanding that they would have the privilege of using it for their services. This arrangement continued until the year 1878 when the Amish Mennonites built their first meetinghouse, thirty-four by forty feet, on West Market Street, on a lot now within the town of Nappanee. This building is a part of the present house of worship of the First Mennonite Church. It was heated by two stoves and lighted by oil lamps. Besides John Ringenberg, the first ministers were Bishop Samuel Yoder, and Preachers John Yoder and Samuel Hochstetler. (The names of these ministers are found in an unpublished manuscript by Bishop David Burkholder, as well as in Abraham E. Weaver's *Standard History of Elkhart County, Indiana,* I, 385, 386.)

In 1875 Preacher Jonathan P. Smucker moved into the Nappanee area from the Amish Mennonite congregation near Eagle Lake, Starke County, and reorganized the weak congregation. There were thirteen "charter" members in 1875. Smucker served as a minister for twenty years until he moved east of Goshen in 1895. About two years after he came to Nappanee he was ordained as an Amish Mennonite bishop. The West Market Street congregation was in fellowship with the Haw Patch, Clinton Frame, and Forks congregations east of Goshen. The Sunday school was begun about 1880 and became "evergreen" about 1890. Young people's Bible meeting was begun in 1898. The women's sewing circle was organized in 1907. In 1910 the building was remodeled, which included the turning of the meetinghouse at right angles. A basement was put under the entire building, and a new front built on the structure. The lawn was leveled and seeded and the first circle of trees planted. Jacob Bleile was ordained preacher in 1885, but four years later he transferred to the Mennonite congregation on North Main Street. Eli A. Bontrager was ordained preacher in 1900, but moved to Fairview, Oscoda County, Michigan, in 1902. J. H. McGowen was ordained deacon in 1885, in the same service in which Jacob Bleile was ordained preacher, and he himself was ordained preacher in 1888 by J. P. Smucker. All of these ministers from Ringenberg through McGowan served without pay. In 1911 Levi W. Yoder was ordained preacher and Simon Smucker was ordained deacon.

The fall of 1923 witnessed a complete reorganization of the Nappanee congregations. Fifteen members withdrew from the West Market Street congregation and united with other denominations; fifty members withdrew to unite with the North Main Street congregation and remain in the Indiana-Michigan Mennonite Conference; while fifty-six members withdrew from the North Main Street congregation, of which thirty-five united with the West Market Street congregation. Twenty-five additional members united with the West Market Street Church in 1924. Ezra S. Mullet, formerly of the North Main Street Mennonite Church, was called as pastor of the West Market Street Church and served, 1923-43. He was succeeded by I. R. Detweiler, 1943-44; Jacob J. Enz, 1944-48; Rollin W. Moser, 1948-51; Earl Salzman, 1951-58; and Gordon R. Dyck, 1959. The summer of 1926 the congregation voted to unite with the General Conference Mennonite Church, and soon was known as the First Mennonite Church of Nappanee. About 1926 a piano was bought for $300.00, and in 1949 an organ was installed at a cost of $3,000.00. The 1878 church building, which was rebuilt in 1910, was remodeled in 1926 and again in 1955. The seating capacity is 250. The present membership is 169.

SILVER STREET MENNONITE CHURCH, 1892

The Silver Street Mennonite Church originated in the year 1892 as a schism from the Clinton Frame Amish Mennonite Church. The actual division occurred June 22, 1892, when about fifty dissatisfied members met in the Clinton Frame meetinghouse to discuss their situation. They decided to withdraw and thenceforth held their meetings in the old Union Chapel, which was located on the lot where the Union Cemetery is located, southwest of the Clinton Frame meetinghouse. Bishop Benjamin Schrock, who was a retired minister in the Clinton Frame congregation, was chosen as the first pastor of the new group. This new group withdrew from the Clinton Frame congregation because they considered the discipline of that congregation too strict. The new group invited "Father" Joseph Stuckey and Peter Schantz of Illinois to hold meetings in June 1892. The result of the meetings was that twenty-two new members were added to the church, eleven by baptism, and eleven by confession and letter. On June 28, 1892, communion services were held, and the entire membership of seventy-two persons participated.

The summer of 1892 the congregation built a meetinghouse at a cost of $2,468.48. The Clinton Frame congregation paid the new group $1,000.00 as its equity in the old meetinghouse. The new congregation dedicated their "Silver Street Mennonite Church" free of debt on October 29, 1892. Following the dedication services evangelistic meetings were again held for ten days and seventeen additional persons were received into the church, making a total membership of eighty-seven. During these meetings the congregation also chose John C. Mehl as pastor. He was installed October 27, 1892. In 1899 the Ladies' Aid was formed. Pastors since Benjamin Schrock and J. C. Mehl have been Menno A. Niswander, 1906; Alvin K. Ropp, 1911; Allen Yoder, 1913; Harry Yoder, 1935; Robert W. Hartzler, 1942; H. E. Nunemaker, 1946; William Klassen, 1953; Daniel Graber, 1954; and Donald R. Emmert, 1959-   .

Two daughter congregations have been established from the Silver Street Church: Topeka, 1893; and Eighth Street, Goshen, 1913. The high point in the membership of the Silver Street Church was reached in 1924, when there were 250 members, during the pastorate of Allen Yoder. The 1960 *Handbook of Information* of the General Conference Mennonite Church gives the present membership of the Silver Street Church as 119.

The Silver Street church building is located on County Road 34, the

"Silver Street Road," about a fifth of a mile west of County Road 35, which means that it is about four fifths of a mile north of the Clinton Frame meetinghouse and one fifth of a mile west. It is located in Section 8, Clinton Township, Elkhart County, Indiana.

TOPEKA MENNONITE CHURCH, 1893

As early as 1893 a number of Amish Mennonite families living in the vicinity of Topeka, Indiana, affiliated with the new Silver Street Mennonite Church. J. C. Mehl, pastor of the Silver Street congregation, drove to Topeka every four weeks and preached for this small branch of his congregation. In 1897 the congregation at Topeka purchased the Eden Chapel building one and one-half miles west of Topeka and moved it one mile east, where they used it as their house of worship for about thirty years. The deed for this property was granted by John King on September 17, 1898, to Christian Z. Greenawalt, Rufus A. Kauffman, and Henry Hostetler, as trustees of "The Topeka Branch of the Silver Street Mennonite Church of Elkhart County, Indiana." The land consisted of 126 square rods. The trustees paid King $75.00 for this plot of land. It is located in Section 36 of Eden Township, Lagrange County, Indiana. Four years later, in December 1901, John C. Lehman was ordained to become the first resident pastor of the Topeka congregation. He removed to Topeka in November 1902, formally organized the congregation, established the Sunday school, and served until 1918. Ernest Hostetler was ordained in 1918 as the assistant to J. C. Lehman, and served until 1926. The present house of worship, in the town of Topeka, was completed in 1927. Pastors who succeeded Mehl, Lehman, and Hostetler were Earl Salzman, 1926-41; Wilmer S. Shelly, 1941-47; Esko Loewen, 1947-53; Orlin F. Frey, 1953-56; Martin H. Schrag, 1956-57; and Roy W. Henry, 1957-60. The Topeka congregation was greatly strengthened in 1930 when ninety members who had withdrawn from the Maple Grove congregation in 1924, and who had claimed possession of the old 1879 brick meetinghouse southwest of Topeka, merged with the Topeka Central Conference Mennonite Church.

When William B. Weaver wrote his *History of the Central Conference Mennonite Church* in 1926, he listed the membership of the congregation as ninety-nine. Today's membership is 213.

ZION MENNONITE CHURCH, 1895

The Zion Mennonite Church is located at Goodland, Indiana, in Newton County, not far from the Jasper County line. This congregation was established by a minister named D. D. Augspurger who had been ordained as a preacher in the East Washington Church, Illinois, who had then moved to Aurora, Nebraska, but who settled in the vicinity of Goodland, Indiana, in 1895. He immediately organized a Sunday school three miles south of his home; this was in the month of April 1895. He also started preaching services. For three years Augspurger and his small congregation worshiped in a schoolhouse. In the year 1898 they built a meetinghouse.

Augspurger served as pastor until the year 1908 when he ordained Jacob Sommer, his son-in-law, as his successor. Sommer in turn served as pastor, 1908-10. Later ministers were Peter D. Nafsinger, 1911-26, and Aaron Egli, 1926-45. The pastor since 1945 is Dale Schertz, and the membership is forty-nine.

EIGHTH STREET MENNONITE CHURCH, 1913

The first daughter of the Silver Street Church was Topeka, 1893. In 1913 a second daughter congregation was established out of the Silver Street congregation. Early in that year a number of Silver Street members who were living in Goshen began to consider the formation of a Central Conference Mennonite Church in the city of Goshen. On February 28, 1913, a total of twenty persons met in the home of A. K. Ropp, the Silver Street pastor, who had removed to Goshen in December 1911. In this meeting it was decided to establish a new congregation. The group purchased a dwelling house at 616 South Fifth Street, which was remodeled so that it could be used for church purposes. This building was dedicated for the use of the congregation on April 20, 1913, with Valentine Strubhar conducting the dedication services. A. K. Ropp became the pastor of the congregation. There were fifteen charter members. By November 1913 the membership had increased to thirty. In 1915 there were fifty-five members, and in 1918 seventy-three.

The congregation soon established a fine array of activities. Sunday school began with the founding of the congregation. Christian Endeavor was organized in 1914, as was a Ladies' Aid.

Ministers who have served the congregation are A. K. Ropp, 1913-17; L. E. Blauch, 1917-19; W. W. Miller, 1919-20; Eugene Augspurger, 1920-21; William B. Weaver, 1921-22; I. R. Detweiler, 1923-30; G. T. Soldner, 1930-36; A. E. Kreider, 1936-37; G. S. Stoneback, 1937-43; A. E. Kreider, 1943-46; and Robert W. Hartzler, 1946- .

In 1919 the congregation decided to build a house of worship, which was located on South Eighth Street in Goshen. It was dedicated May 2, 1920, with John F. Funk of the "Mennonite Church" participating in the service. In 1956-57 the congregation spent $200,000.00 remodeling and enlarging the church, especially adding better facilities for the Christian

Education program of the congregation. This enlarged house of worship was dedicated October 13, 1957. Under the ministry of Robert W. Hartzler, who has served longer than any other man as pastor, the congregation has prospered, and now has a membership of 362.

WARREN STREET MENNONITE CHURCH, 1923

Middlebury, Indiana

The Warren Street congregation, Middlebury, Indiana, originated in 1923 when Preacher Simon S. Yoder, who had originally been a deacon in the Forks congregation of the Mennonite Church, but who had been a minister in the Lawrence Street congregation of the Mennonite Church in Middlebury, withdrew from the Indiana-Michigan Conference, taking about one hundred members with him. The Warren Street congregation was without conference affiliation from the time of its formation in November 1923 until 1926, when it united with the Central Conference Mennonite Church. There were eighty-one members in 1926.

Pastors who served the Warren Street congregation are S. S. Yoder, 1923-31; Lee Lantz, 1931-34; E. A. Sommer, 1936-42; Ernest J. Bohn, 1943-45; Alvin J. Regier, 1945-47; Harold Thiessen, 1948-55; and Elmer A. Wall, 1955-60. The present membership of the congregation is sixty-four. In 1961 the congregation installed a pastor and an associate pastor: Raymond Mark Yoder and Bernhard Wiebe (a Bergthal Mennonite studying at Goshen College) respectively.

COMINS MENNONITE CHURCH, 1924

The Comins Mennonite Church is located in Oscoda County, in the northern part of the lower peninsula of Michigan, about five miles north of Fairview. The founder of the work was F. F. Stutesman, who was formerly a member of the Fairview congregation of the "Mennonite Church." Stutesman organized a union Sunday school after the Methodists had allowed their Sunday school to die out. In 1924 Stutesman went to Middlebury, Indiana, and interviewed Preacher Emanuel Troyer, field secretary of the Central Conference of Mennonites. Troyer in turn went to Comins and held revival services the fall of 1924. The summer of 1925 Troyer and Allen Yoder went to Comins and organized a Central Conference congregation. The Central Conference of Mennonites which was in session August 29 to September 1, 1925, accepted the application of the Comins congregation for admission into conference.

The Comins Mennonite Church erected a house of worship in 1925 which was dedicated November 1 with Allen Miller, Emanuel Troyer, and Allen Yoder in charge. In 1926 the membership of the congregation was twenty-six. Pastors have been: Harvey Nunemaker, 1927-31; Frank Mitchell, 1931-41; Paul Kreft, 1942-45; LaVerne Rutschman, 1946-47; Amos Eash, 1947-48; Joseph Atherton, 1949-55; Archie Kliewer, 1955-60; and Rudolph Martens, 1960- . The membership is ninety-eight.

McKINLEY MISSION CHAPEL, 1951

The McKinley Mission Chapel was begun in 1951 under the sponsorship of the Home Mission Board of the Central Conference of Mennonites. The building was built in 1951, and the first service was held, on July 1 of that year. On that date Lowell O. Troyer was also licensed as a minister. A year later, July 6, 1952, he was ordained to the ministry. He is the only minister who has served in this congregation. In 1954 the Home Mission Board also built a parsonage in McKinley beside the Chapel. McKinley is on the Star Route of the mail service from Mio, in Oscoda County, Michigan. The present membership at McKinley is seven.

HIVELY AVENUE MENNONITE CHURCH, 1958

Hively and Pleasant Plain Avenues

Elkhart, Indiana

The Hively Avenue congregation held its first worship service February 2, 1958, in the home of Pete R. Classen, M.D., of Elkhart, with thirteen adults in attendance. On May 4, 1958, the group began to worship in the Mishawaka Road School. It was organized as a congregation on August 31, 1958. Walter Gering assumed the pastorate of the new congregation April 19, 1959. The present membership of the congregation is thirty-nine. A brick building, twenty-four by ninety-six feet in size, was built, 1960-61, and was first used on March 5, 1961. Eventually it is to be an educational wing.

The chief impetus for the establishment of the Hively Avenue Mennonite Church was the location of *Mennonite Biblical Seminary* on the south side of Elkhart in 1958. Prior to this time the Mennonite Biblical Seminary had been attached to Bethany Biblical Seminary in Chicago. But in 1958 the Mennonite Biblical Seminary was located at Elkhart, new buildings were erected, and the plant was dedicated September 28, 1958. The Mennonite Biblical Seminary (General Conference Mennonite) and the Goshen College Biblical Seminary (Mennonite Church) are organized as the "Associated Mennonite Biblical Seminaries."

FORT WAYNE, 1960

Leonard C. Wiebe graduated from Mennonite Biblical Seminary in 1960. On March 6, 1960, he started holding services in Fort Wayne, Indiana. He is located in a spacious home at 4226 Meyers Road, which also serves as a place of meeting. At this writing no house of worship has been built, and there are no members in the proposed congregation. The work is sponsored by the First Mennonite Church of Berne. The work is listed, however, in the 1960-61 *Handbook of Information,* General Conference Mennonite Church. Attendance averages thirty, including eighteen to twenty adults.

Wisler Mennonite Church, 1872

The first tiny cluster of Mennonite families to settle in Elkhart County, Indiana, came in the year 1845, and brought with them the aged Bishop Martin Hoover, c.1760-1850. Because of his advanced age Bishop Hoover never did very much church work in Indiana. In 1848 Preacher Jacob Wisler, 1808-1889, removed from Columbiana County, Ohio, to Elkhart County, Indiana. He was ordained bishop in 1851 by Abraham Rohrer of Medina County, Ohio. Wisler had some trouble getting along well with Preacher Joseph Rohrer who removed from Stark County, Ohio, to Elkhart County about 1850. Also Deacon Joseph Holdeman tended to be critical of Bishop Wisler. In 1864 Preacher Daniel Brenneman removed from Fairfield County, Ohio, to Elkhart County, and was soon quite critical of the bishop. Wisler found himself in the midst of brethren with quite diverse views as to the exact nature of the discipline which should be exercised in the Mennonite Church. In his diary for 1866 John F. Funk reported that "great disorder" prevailed in the Indiana Conference of that year; there were "dissensions among the brethren," he wrote. In April 1867 Funk himself also removed from Chicago to Elkhart County, and was at that time thirty-two years of age.

The chief issues, 1867-72, appear to be trivial to most Mennonites today. Wisler desired to keep the church as nearly as possible the way he had known it in his Bucks County, Pennsylvania, boyhood, as well as in Columbiana, Ohio. This meant a preference for German services, no regular evening meetings, no bass singing, and especially no Sunday schools. Funk, on the other hand, who had been an active Sunday-school worker with D. L. Moody in Chicago, had little patience with such an "ultraconservative" position. On June 28, 1867, because of the vast amount of criticisms which had been brought against him, Bishop Wisler agreed to desist from preaching until the church should reinstate him. On August 17 of that year the Yellow Creek congregation voted to keep Wisler inactive ministerially. But the next day Bishop Isaac Hoffer of Williams County, Ohio, autocratically restored Wisler to office, and suspended Preacher Daniel Brenneman and his supporters. This led to a gathering of outstanding Mennonite leaders from various parts of North America, October 11, 12, 1867. This group required Bishop Hoffer to make a confession to the congregation and to ask for forgiveness and patience for his imprudent behavior. Bishop Wisler was instructed to repent, to acknowledge his mistakes, to ask the church for forgiveness, and to seek to be more prudent in the future. The decisions of the special conference were signed by five Ontario ministers, three from Pennsylvania, two from Virginia, four from Ohio, and two from Illinois.

A year later Bishop Dilman Moyer of Ontario, accompanied by Bishop Joseph Hagey, succeeded in resolving the difficulties in the Elkhart County Mennonite Church. All the parties involved forgave one another and the church was fully unified; however, Wisler's restoration to full bishop oversight was made dependent upon the initiative of the ministry.

Bishop Wisler was naturally quite unhappy with the way in which he had been treated, for he felt that he was simply seeking to uphold the historic faith and practice of the church. On the other hand, Brenneman and Funk were determined to bring about various innovations, especially the Sunday school. Deacon Joseph Holdeman was also chronically dissatisfied with Wisler's administration. The outcome of all this was that on March 2, 1869, Wisler and his supporters withdrew from the Mennonite Church and made their own preaching appointments. On May 11, 1869, nine deeply concerned Ontario Mennonite leaders addressed an earnest appeal to the Elkhart County Church and its leadership, pleading that they might resolve their difficulties and again be a united church. They reported that divisions are not only human but carnal; "and the Spirit of Christ has never been the cause of any. He, if we follow Him aright, always leads us together, and unites us with God and with one another in brotherly love." They reported that if the Elkhart County Church was not able to achieve unification, "it is our fear that this might provide an occasion to bring confusion into all the congregations of America and into Canada." They also pleaded that the matter should not be carried to the Ohio Conference but should be settled locally. In July 1869 a committee of five leaders from Ontario and Ohio again labored in vain to try to reconcile the contending elements in the Elkhart County Church.

It was not until August 5, 1870, that peace was made. The leader who accomplished this seemingly impossible task was the able bishop, John M. Brenneman, of Allen County, Ohio. The preachers, Daniel

Brenneman, John M. Christophel, John F. Funk, and J. A. Beutler; and the deacons, Martin Ramer and H. B. Brenneman, expressed their willingness to accept Wisler, whereupon a counsel of the church was taken and Wisler was reinstated by a vote of 171 to 20. "Many hearts thrilled with joy and praised God that the church was once more united into one."

The difficulty was bound to reappear, however. The occasion was as follows. In 1870 the Indiana Conference approved Sunday schools as an institution of the church. The spring of 1871 Bishop Wisler accepted the complaints of those members who were not favorable toward the Sunday school, contrary to the action which the conference had taken. Wisler was also accused of giving his own opinion, namely, that the Sunday school was "not necessary." Funk, however, took Wisler's objections seriously, and trouble was not long in coming. The fall of 1871 a new committee of six leaders was called to Elkhart County to attempt once more to make peace. These leaders were from Allen County, Ohio; Williams County, Ohio; Branch County, Michigan; Putnam County, Ohio; Whiteside County, Illinois; and Greene County, Ohio. The outcome of this meeting was that Wisler was relieved of his bishop oversight, but was allowed to continue as a minister. During the fall of 1871 Wisler became more and more unhappy about the decision which had been made, and finally he made it known that he did not intend to submit. The final break came on January 6, 1872, when it was publicly announced in the Yellow Creek Church that Bishop Jacob Wisler, and Preachers John Weaver and Christian Bare, were no longer "brethren in the Old Mennonite Church." Wisler's followers seemed to have numbered about one hundred members. Various efforts were made in the years following the division to reunite the two branches of the Mennonite Church in Elkhart County, but without success.

The Elkhart County so-called Wisler Mennonites alternated with the Indiana Conference Mennonites, represented by John F. Funk, in the use of the Yellow Creek, Blosser, and Shaum meetinghouses. About 1877 the Wisler group also built a new meetinghouse on Section 21 of Madison Township, St. Joseph County, on the Elkhart County line about midway between the New and Osborne County roads; the deed was not given until 1891, however. In 1891 the Wisler group also built a new Blosser meetinghouse to replace the old log church building. The 1891 Blosser meetinghouse was renovated in 1947. The Wisler Mennonites seem to have given up the use of the Shaum meetinghouse about 1888, when a new meetinghouse was built. The Wisler Mennonites purchased from the Funk group the 1861 Yellow Creek (frame) meetinghouse in 1912. They renovated and enlarged this building, 1953-54.

The following persons served as ministers in the Elkhart County Wisler Mennonite Church from its founding in 1872 until 1907; Bishop Jacob Wisler, Preacher Christian Bare, Deacon John Troxel, Preacher John Weaver, Deacon Tobias Ramer, Deacon David B. Martin, Preacher Martin A. Hoover, Bishop Christian Shaum, Deacon David Newcomer, Deacon Elias Z. Martin, Deacon Joel Snider, Deacon David Wisler, Preacher Martin Ramer, Preacher Henry Schrock, Bishop John W. Martin, Deacon Isaac Martin, and Preacher Christian Z. Weaver.

Old Order Mennonites, 1907

The Wisler Mennonites of Indiana and Ohio were organized into the *Ohio and Indiana Mennonite Conference* in the home of Preacher Henry Beery, Wayne County, Ohio, by Bishop Jacob Wisler in 1872. Bishop John W. Martin of Elkhart County, Indiana, withdrew from the Ohio and Indiana (Wisler) Mennonite Conference in its session in the County Line meetinghouse, St. Joseph County, Indiana, May 17, 1907. The leader of the conference in 1907 was Bishop Henry Hursh of Ohio. John W. Martin was followed in his schism by ten preachers and four deacons, while only eight ordained men were left in the Ohio and Indiana Wisler Conference after the division. The issue in the division was ostensibly the telephone, with Martin taking the more rigid position that it was not to be permitted, while Hursh was inclined to follow the traditional position of leaving the matter to the individual conscience. It is likely that personal attitudes were the chief cause of the division, rather than whether or not to forbid the use of the telephone. Bishop Martin took all the ordained men of the Elkhart County Wisler Church with him into his *Old Order* group, except the aged Preacher John Weaver, 85. However, two thirds of the Wisler laity of Elkhart County remained loyal to the *Wisler* Conference which was led by Bishop Hursh of Ohio.

Ordained men who have served in the *Wisler* Mennonite Church since 1907 have been Deacon Levi A. Ressler (brother of India missionary, J. A. Ressler), Preacher Christian L. Ressler, Bishop Martin Ramer, Bishop William Ramer, Deacon John M. Weaver, Preacher Noah W. Wenger, Deacon Jacob H. Bechtel, Preacher Paul Hoover, and Deacon William Henry Bechtel. The present membership of the Wisler Mennonite Church of Elkhart County is 183.

Those who have served in the ministry of the *Old Order* Mennonite Church since 1907 are Deacon Isaac M. Brubaker, Bishop Joseph E. Martin, Preacher Henry E. Martin, Deacon Menno Ramer, Bishop William G. Weaver, Preacher Enos S. Martin, and Deacon Ralph Martin.

25

Preacher Harvey Horst, originally of Stark County, Ohio, moved from Virginia to Elkhart County in 1947. The present membership of the Old Order congregation in Elkhart County is 102.

The *Wisler* Mennonites have tolerated various changes during the life of their group. For example, they allow the use of automobiles, telephones, etc. The *Old Order* group, however, attempt as nearly as possible to maintain the way of life which obtained in 1872 when the Wisler Mennonite Church was founded. They therefore drive with horse and buggy, and shun various modern inventions. Neither group, however, allows the Sunday school. In 1947 Bishop Joseph E. Martin, son of the former Bishop John W. Martin, withdrew from his Old Order group because of various difficulties in discipline and administration, and remained independent for three years. In 1950 he and his followers, which constituted about one third of the Old Order group, affiliated with the more progressive Wisler Mennonite Church. Locally the Old Order group is oftentimes spoken of as Martin Mennonites, because their founder was John W. Martin; while the more progressive group is known as the Ramer Mennonites, because the only two bishops of the group have been father and son, Martin Ramer and William Ramer.

It was actually both branches of the Wisler Mennonites who cooperated in purchasing the equity of the "Mennonite Church" in the 1861 Yellow Creek meetinghouse in the year 1912. The Yellow Creek Mennonite Church (affiliated with the Indiana-Michigan Mennonite Conference) built the Yellow Creek (brick) meetinghouse in 1912, while the Wisler and Old Order groups then alternated in the use of the Blosser and Yellow Creek meetinghouses. In 1959 the Old Order group assumed the sole ownership of the Blosser meetinghouse, and the Wisler group took the 1861 Yellow Creek meetinghouse, which had been enlarged 1953-54 by the addition of a north wing, twenty-two by forty-two feet in size. During the fall of 1959 the Old Order group then built a new Yellow Creek (frame) meetinghouse a short distance west of the 1861 meetinghouse, but on the north side of the road. The Old Order group also purchased the old benches in the 1861 meetinghouse. The Old Order Mennonites held their first service in their new Yellow Creek meetinghouse on Sunday, March 6, 1960.

In an article on the Wisler division, published in *The Mennonite Quarterly Review*, April and July issues, 1959, the author wrote:

"It is nothing short of a tragedy that the Wisler division occurred. The fear of Preacher David Sherk in 1868 that an Elkhart County division might involve the entire American Mennonite Church was in some sense realized, for the 1872 division in Indiana and Ohio was followed by a similar division in Ontario in 1889, by one in the Lancaster Con-

ference of Eastern Pennsylvania in 1893, and by another in Rockingham County, Virginia, in 1901. The loss of the conservative wing of the
brotherhood in the years 1872 to 1901 hastened the cultural accommodation of the larger body of the Mennonite Church, by depriving it of the
needed checks on a too rapid cultural change. On the other hand, the
present writer is inclined to fear that such an excessive preoccupation
with the endeavor not to permit change, as obtains in the more conservative factions of the Old Order Mennonites, does not lead to true spirituality nor to unity in the church. Looking back over the history of the
Wisler schism one's heart must bleed for a man being expelled from his
church for trying to maintain the doctrine and practice which he had
known from his boyhood. If only Brenneman and Funk would have
been more patient with Wisler it is possible that the unity of the church
could have been maintained. And it is certain that the newer agencies
for which they contended would ultimately have come anyhow. The
most indefensible—if not rash—act of Funk was the expulsion of Jacob
Wisler on Saturday, January 6, 1872. The fact that Daniel Brenneman
was expelled in 1874, and that Funk had to be relieved of his bishop oversight in 1902, would indicate that Wisler was probably not the only
leader at fault in the sad years, 1866-72."

Wisler Mennonites in Emmet County, Michigan

The division between the Mennonites of the Indiana-Michigan Conference, and the Mennonites of the Wisler Conference, did not occur in
Emmet County, Michigan, until 1886. In that year Jacob Wisler ordained
Jonathan Gehman to the ministry. For many years Gehman's Wisler
congregation at Brutus in Emmet County was far stronger numerically
than the congregation which remained with Funk and the Indiana Conference.

Deacon Joel Snider who was ordained in 1886 at Brutus soon moved
to Elkhart County, Indiana, and was succeeded by Joseph K. Detweiler,
who was ordained about 1890 but was soon silenced. L. J. Burkholder
was of the opinion that Preacher Abraham W. Detweiler followed Wisler
in 1886. If so, he must have returned to the "Mennonite Church," for
Funk disciplined him in 1896. May he have united with the Wisler
group late in life? Owen Snider was ordained as preacher in 1896, several years after Gehman's death, which occurred in 1893, but about 1904
Snider became mentally ill. An Ontario young man, Daniel G. Brubacher, was ordained preacher at Brutus, December 7, 1901, and as bishop,
September 4, 1911; both ordinations were performed by John W. Martin of Indiana. Henry Brenneman was ordained preacher in 1907. The

Wisler congregation at Brutus alternated in the use of the meetinghouse with the Indiana Conference congregation. The Wisler Mennonites at Brutus also followed John W. Martin in his Old Order Mennonite schism from the Wisler Conference in 1907. The Mennonite congregation at Brutus, which was affiliated with the Indiana-Michigan Conference, grew progressively weaker until 1919 when only three members were left. In 1920 the Indiana-Michigan Mennonite Mission Board placed Clyde X. Kauffman as preacher at Brutus. Immediately Wisler Old Order members began to transfer to the conference congregation of Clyde X. Kauffman. Internal dissensions also contributed to the decline of the Old Order congregation. Deacon Jonas Brubaker moved to Alberta. David B. Horst was ordained deacon September 4, 1911, but resigned in 1917 and moved out of the state. Christian Leinbach was ordained deacon in 1918, but was silenced about 1926. He removed to Pennsylvania. Henry G. Martin succeeded Leinbach as deacon, but also removed to Pennsylvania in 1939; he was ordained October 17, 1927. Bishop Brubacher held a few services at Brutus during 1939, then removed to Ontario, but in 1950 he settled with his son Paul at Elverson, Pennsylvania. At this writing there is only one Old Order Mennonite left at Brutus, Michigan.

WISLER MINISTERIAL LIST

Indiana and Michigan

The letters OO mean Old Order and refer to the John W. Martin group of 1907, while W means Wisler and refers to those who followed Henry Hursh in 1907 and remained in the Wisler Conference.

CHRISTIAN BARE, 1816-1904   Preacher   Elkhart County
     Born in Rockingham County, Virginia, May 6, 1816. Married Esther Shank (1815-1906) in Columbiana County, Ohio, October 16, 1837. Seven children. Ordained preacher in Putnam County, Ohio, in 1856. Moved to Elkhart County in 1857. Followed Bishop Wisler in 1872. Died September 24, 1904, at the age of eighty-eight years, four months, and eighteen days. Preached German. Tall, slim, smooth-shaven, long hair. Earnest and able preacher. Burial in Yellow Creek East Cemetery.

JACOB H. BECHTEL, 1870-1948   Deacon   W   Elkhart County
     Born in Elkhart County, April 13, 1870. Married (1) Elizabeth Shaum (1871-1896) on November 27, 1892. Three children, including Deacon William Henry. Married (2) Leah Lehman (1859-1960) (who reached the advanced age of 101 years) on January 30, 1898. Two children. Ordained deacon, October 2, 1926, by Bishop Moses G. Horst. Died May 12, 1948, at the age of seventy-eight years and twenty-nine days. Burial in Yellow Creek West Cemetery.

WILLIAM HENRY BECHTEL, 1895-   Deacon   W   Elkhart County
     Born in Elkhart County, September 19, 1895. Married Effie Weaver (1896-   ) on October 12, 1919. Seven children. Ordained deacon at Yellow Creek, May 23, 1948, by Bishop William Ramer.

HENRY BRENNEMAN, 1863-1943   Preacher   OO   Emmet County
Ordained preacher June 9, 1906. Outlived the Brutus congregation.

DANIEL G. BRUBACHER, 1870-1961   Preacher, Bishop   OO   Emmet County
Born near Kitchener, Ontario, December 2, 1870. Married Anna D. Eby (1871-   )
on February 20, 1898. Five children. Ordained preacher at Brutus, December 7,
1901, by Bishop John W. Martin. Ordained bishop, September 4, 1911, by Martin.
Moved to Ontario in 1939, and to Elverson, Pa., in 1950. Died Aug. 13, 1961.

JONAS BRUBACHER, 1843-1915   Deacon   OO   Emmet County
Born in Waterloo County, Ontario, November 16, 1843. Ordained deacon at
Brutus in 1896. Married Magdalena Gingerich (1847-1922). Nine children. Removed
to Alberta in 1911, where he died February 4, 1915.

ISAAC M. BRUBAKER, 1860-1936   Deacon   OO   Elkhart County
Born in Snyder County, Pennsylvania, December 1, 1860, son of Deacon Abraham
Brubaker, 1814-1883. United with the Yellow Creek congregation about 1904. Ordained in the County Line meetinghouse, St. Joseph County, Indiana, 1911. Married
Catharine Brubaker (daughter of Bishop Daniel Brubaker of Snyder County, Pennsylvania) on October 16, 1881. Two daughters. Moved to Lancaster County, Pennsylvania, in 1920. Died February 5, 1936. Burial in the Pike Mennonite Cemetery
near Ephrata.

ABRAHAM W. DETWEILER, 1828-1912   Preacher   OO   Emmet County
Born in Ontario, May 8, 1828. Moved to Caledonia in Kent County, Michigan,
in 1864, and from thence to Brutus in 1879. Married Barbara Koch. The Maple
River congregation at Brutus was first called Detweilers. Did his lifework in the
"Mennonite Church." May have become Old Order in his late years (LJB). Died
August 15, 1912.

JOSEPH K. DETWEILER, 1860-1940   Deacon   Emmet County
Born September 8, 1860, son of Preacher Abraham W. Detweiler. Married Elizabeth Leinbach (1860-1943). Followed Joel Snider as deacon, possibly about the year
1890, but served only a short time. Moved to Kingman, Alberta, about 1910, where
he died November 9, 1940.

JONATHAN GEHMAN, 1856-1893   Preacher   OO   Emmet County
Ordained preacher at Brutus about 1886 by Bishop Jacob Wisler. Served seven
years. Had moved to Brutus from Elkhart County, Indiana. Married Mary Baer
(1858-1931).

MARTIN A. HOOVER, 1834-1895   Preacher   Elkhart County
Born in Wayne County, Ohio, September 20, 1834, son of Abraham and Christiana
(Martin) Hoover. Removed with his parents to Clinton Township, Elkhart County,
Indiana, in 1853. Married (1) Margaret Musser (daughter of Martin and Susanna
[Shirk] Musser) in 1860. Ten children. Married (2) Elizabeth (Good) Hartman.
Three children. Ordained preacher in Harrison Township (to which he had removed
in 1870) the fall of 1875. Was a large man, six feet in height, and stout. Died Novem-
ber 26, 1895. Burial in Yellow Creek West Cemetery.

PAUL HOOVER, 1904-   Preacher   W   Elkhart County
Born in Elkhart County, November 20, 1904, grandson of Preacher Martin A.
Hoover. (Paul's mother was a daughter of Bishop Christian Shaum.) Married Myrtle
Good (daughter of Benjamin and May [Royer] Good) on November 6, 1929. Seven
children. Ordained preacher at Yellow Creek, May 18, 1931, by Bishops Moses G.

Horst and William Ramer. Building fund treasurer of the proposed MCC mental hospital, Oaklawn Psychiatric Center, Elkhart, Indiana.

DAVID B. HORST, 1873-   Deacon   OO   Emmet County
    Born in Elgin County, Ontario, August 20, 1873. Married Mary Martin (1875-1934). Ordained deacon at Brutus, September 4, 1911, to succeed Jonas Brubacher. This date also marked the ordination of Daniel Brubacher as bishop at Brutus. John W. Martin of Elkhart County officiated. Horst resigned in 1917 and moved to Florida, and in 1921 to Ontario.

HARVEY HORST, 1874-   Preacher   W, OO
          Mahoning County, Rockingham County, Elkhart County
    Born at North Lawrence, Stark County, Ohio, December 10, 1874, son of Jonas B. Horst, 1835-1926, and Mary (Hursh) Horst, 1842-1888. Married Susanna (Witmer) Horst (daughter of John L. and Lydia [Witmer] Witmer) on December 14, 1899. Six children. Ordained a Wisler preacher in the Pleasantview congregation in Mahoning County, by the unanimous vote of the congregation, May 31, 1908, by Henry Hursh. Moved to Virginia in 1928, where he united with the Old Order group. Located in Elkhart County, Indiana, in 1947.

CHRISTIAN LEINBACH, 1878-1946   Deacon   OO   Emmet County
    Born in Harrison Township, Elkhart County, August 13, 1878, son of Isaac and Catharine (Bare) Leinbach. United with the Yellow Creek Wisler Mennonite congregation in May 1895. Married Fanny Martin on November 27, 1901. Seven children. Ordained deacon the spring of 1918 by Bishop John W. Martin, for the Old Order congregation at Brutus. (Martin was his father-in-law.) Was silenced eight years later for becoming involved in the congregational troubles at Brutus. Moved to Lancaster County, Pennsylvania, where he died June 26, 1946. Burial in Bowmansville Cemetery.

DAVID B. MARTIN, 1829-1902   Deacon   Elkhart County
    Born in Waterloo County, Ontario, February 13, 1829. Came to Elkhart County, Indiana, in early life. Married Elizabeth Eyman (1839-1884). Four children. Was a deacon in the "Mennonite Church," by 1869. Transferred to the Wisler Church late in life. Died June 19, 1902. Burial in Yellow Creek East Cemetery.

ELIAS Z. MARTIN, 1843-1909   Deacon   OO   Elkhart County
    Son of Deacon Henry Martin, 1807-1873, and his wife Anna Zimmerman of Lancaster County, Pennsylvania, and brother of Bishop John W. Martin. Came to Elkhart County in 1866. Married Barbara Wenger (1842-1903) (daughter of Christian and Mary [Wenger] Wenger, and sister of the well-known Martin D. Wenger, who worked as an editor for John F. Funk). Three children. Ordained deacon at the Wisler Church about 1884. Followed his brother John when he withdrew from the Wisler Conference in 1907. Died June 20, 1909.

ENOS S. MARTIN, 1916-   Preacher   OO   Elkhart County
    Born in Harrison Township, Elkhart County, May 13, 1916, son of Preacher Henry E. Martin. (His mother, Elizabeth [Schrock] Martin, was a daughter of Preacher Henry Schrock.) Married Esther Martin (1912-   ) (daughter of Abram and Mary [Ramer] Martin) on March 28, 1937. Two foster children. Ordained preacher at Yellow Creek, June 19, 1951, by Bishop Aaron Sensenig of Lancaster County, Pennsylvania. Served until 1959.

HENRY G. MARTIN, 1874-1944   Deacon   OO   Emmet County
    Born in Perth County, Ontario, April 19, 1874, son of Wisler deacon, Levi P. Martin, 1844-1919, of Ontario, and his second wife, Barbara Gingerich. United with the Wisler Mennonite Church in Waterloo County, Ontario, in 1893. Married Matilda

Kilmer (daughter of John and Harriet [Snider] Kilmer) on September 15, 1903. Eight children. Ordained deacon in the Brutus congregation, October 17, 1927, by Daniel G. Brubacher. (The sixth and last deacon of the dying congregation.) Moved to Lancaster County, Pennsylvania, in 1939 (upon the expiration of the congregation), where he died April 10, 1944. Burial in Churchtown Cemetery. (His brother, Isaac G. Martin of Elmira, Ontario, furnished much data on the history of the Brutus congregation.)

ISAAC MARTIN, 1854-1911   Deacon   OO   Elkhart County

Born in Lancaster County, Pennsylvania, December 18, 1854, son of Christian and Elizabeth (Wenger) Martin. Married Margaret Lechlitner (daughter of David and Susanna [Holdeman] Lechlitner) on April 6, 1876. Twelve children. Ordained deacon on Whit Sunday, May 26, 1901, by Bishop John W. Martin. Died May 7, 1911. Burial in Olive Cemetery.

JOHN W. MARTIN, 1852-1940   Preacher, Bishop   OO   Elkhart County

Born at Goodville, Lancaster County, Pennsylvania, November 29, 1852, son of Deacon Henry Martin, 1807-1873, and Anna Zimmerman. Married (1) Susanna Eberly (1857-1893) (daughter of Preacher Levi Eberly of Williams County, Ohio) on December 7, 1876. Eleven children. Married (2) Catharine L. Weaver (1847-1916) on October 30, 1895. Married (3) Barbara (Hunsberger) (Bechtel) Jones (1853-1943) on October 6, 1918. Ordained preacher May 17, 1896, and bishop May 20, 1899. Leader of the 1907 schism from the Ohio and Indiana Mennonite Conference. Was able to preach in either German or English. A man of strong convictions and a firm will. Died December 9, 1940, at the age of 87. Burial in West Cemetery at Yellow Creek.

JOSEPH E. MARTIN, 1888-   Preacher, Bishop   OO, W   Elkhart County

Born in Elkhart County, Indiana, October 28, 1888, son of Bishop John W. Martin. Married Mary Shaum (1892-   ) (daughter of Joseph and Barbara [Berkey] [Markley] Shaum) on June 1, 1913. Seventeen children. Ordained preacher in the County Line meetinghouse, St. Joseph County, Indiana, May 25, 1924, by his father. Ordained bishop in the Yellow Creek meetinghouse, May 19, 1934. Withdrew from the Old Order group in 1947. United with the Wisler body in 1950. Was most helpful in assembling the history of the Wisler Mennonites.

RALPH MARTIN, 1928-   Deacon   OO   Elkhart County

Born in Elkhart County, Indiana, November 27, 1928, son of Reuben L. and Ella (Hunsberger) Martin and grandson of Deacon Isaac Martin. Married the former Lucy G. Weaver (daughter of Eli and Barbara [Gehman] Weaver) on September 13, 1949. Five children. Ordained deacon at Yellow Creek, June 15, 1954, by Bishop William G. Weaver.

MARTIN RAMER, 1858-1928   Preacher, Bishop   OO, W   Elkhart County

Born in Elkhart County, Indiana, December 4, 1858, son of Deacon Tobias Ramer. Married Lydia Ann Shaum (1865-1947) (daughter of Joseph and Elizabeth [Gable] Shaum) November 9, 1884. Ten children. Ordained preacher ca. May 21, 1887, and bishop, November 6, 1911, at Yellow Creek. The vote he received for bishop in 1889 was rejected when John W. Martin was ordained. Followed Martin in 1907 when he withdrew from the Wisler Conference, but six months later was reunited with the majority of the congregation which had remained with the conference. Died September 29, 1928, in his seventieth year.

MENNO RAMER, 1880-1959   Deacon   OO   Elkhart County

Born in Elkhart County, Indiana, April 8, 1880, son of Samuel and Lydia (Reed) Ramer, and nephew of Bishop Martin Ramer. Married Martha Martin (daughter of Deacon Isaac Martin) on December 10, 1910. Ten children. Ordained deacon at

Yellow Creek, October 27, 1935, by Bishop John W. Martin. Died December 25, 1959, at the age of 79.

TOBIAS RAMER, 1824-1887   Deacon   Elkhart County

Born February 29, 1824. Was serving as a deacon at Yellow Creek by 1869. Was later a deacon in the Wisler group. Married Esther Hoover. Four children survived him, one of whom was Martin who became a bishop. Died of palsy at his home three miles southwest of Wakarusa, October 21, 1887. Services by Christian Bare, Christian Shaum, and the aged Jacob Wisler.

WILLIAM RAMER, 1890-   Preacher, Bishop   W   Elkhart County

Born in Elkhart County, Indiana, September 26, 1890, son of Bishop Martin and grandson of Deacon Tobias Ramer. Married Mary Weaver (1891-   ) (daughter of John B. and Lydia [Blosser] Weaver) on September 23, 1917. (Mary was a granddaughter of Preacher John Weaver.) Three children. Ordained preacher at Yellow Creek, May 19, 1919, by Bishop Moses G. Horst of Medina County, Ohio. Ordained bishop, May 20, 1929, by Bishops Moses G. Horst, Moses Horning, and Daniel Witmer.

CHRISTIAN L. RESSLER, 1879-1958   Preacher   W   Elkhart County

Son of Deacon Levi A. Ressler and nephew of Bishop and Missionary J. A. Ressler of the Mennonite Church. Married Anna Zimmerman (1882-   ) (daughter of Christian and Esther [Nolt] Zimmerman). Eight children. Ordained preacher for the Yellow Creek congregation, which remained with the Wisler Conference, on July 21, 1907. Sold his property on December 3, 1917, and moved out of the state. Later he was a member of the "Mennonite Church," and finally of the Conservative Mennonite Church. Died February 25, 1958. Burial at North Lawrence, Ohio.

LEVI A. RESSLER, 1848-1930   Deacon   W   Elkhart County

Born October 19, 1848, father of Preacher Christian Ressler and father-in-law of Deacon John M. Weaver; also brother of India missionary J. A. Ressler. Married Fanny Kreider. Ordained deacon July 21, 1907. (His son was ordained preacher the same day.) Died December 8, 1930, at the age of 82.

HENRY SCHROCK, 1862-1946   Preacher   OO   Elkhart County

Born in St. Joseph County, Indiana, May 5, 1862. Married Sarah Metzler (1867-1939). Six children. Ordained preacher in 1894. Died September 11, 1946. Burial in South Cemetery at the Olive meetinghouse.

CHRISTIAN SHAUM, 1828-1903   Preacher, Bishop   Elkhart County

Born in Northampton County, Pennsylvania, August 30, 1828, son of Bishop John Shaum, and brother of Bishop Henry Shaum of the Mennonite Church. Moved as a small child, with his parents to Wayne County, Ohio. Married Susanna Weldy (1833-1901) on April 20, 1854. Six children. Taught school several years. Did his lifework in Elkhart County. Ordained preacher May 23, 1881, and bishop May 21, 1882. It is said that he liked to fish, one of his favorite places being Mud Lake south of South West. His obituary in the Gospel Herald describes him as "a man of large charity . . . wielded a strong influence for good in a wide circle." Died February 16, 1903, in his seventy-fifth year. Burial in East Cemetery at the Olive Church.

JOEL SNIDER, 1847-1898   Deacon   Emmet County, Elkhart County

Born in Waterloo County, Ontario, August 31, 1847, son of Abraham and Magdalene (Bauman) Snider (Schneider in German). Married Mary Reed (1852-1947) on October 5, 1873. Two children. Came to Indiana at the age of eleven. United with the Wisler Mennonite Church about 1875. Ordained deacon at Brutus in 1886. Moved to Elkhart County, Indiana. Died instantly January 24, 1898, at the age of 50. (Was kicked by a horse.) Lived a mile and a half south of the Yellow Creek meetinghouse. Burial at Yellow Creek.

OWEN SNIDER, 1854-1917   Preacher   Emmet County

Born in Waterloo County, Ontario, April 3, 1854, brother of Deacon Joel Snider. Married Mary Eby (1854-1920) of Waterloo County (sister of Bishop Daniel Brubacher's wife). Ordained preacher at Brutus, Michigan, in the year 1896. Became mentally ill, perhaps eight years later, and had to be given institutional care at Traverse City, Michigan. Died September 26, 1917. Burial at Brutus.

JOHN TROXEL, 1826-1907   Deacon   Elkhart County

Born in Ohio, December 30, 1826, son of Preacher Peter and Anna (Clingaman) Troxel. Married (1) Elizabeth Meyers (niece of Bishop Jacob Wisler and daughter of Henry and Mary Meyers) in 1851. Six children. Married (2) Elizabeth Keller (1841-1900) in 1886. Eight children. Ordained deacon in the "Mennonite Church" by the year 1867, perhaps as early as 1864. Followed Jacob Wisler in the division of 1872. Died March 7, 1907. Burial in Olive East Cemetery.

CHRISTIAN Z. WEAVER, 1848-1939   Preacher   OO   Elkhart County

Born in Lancaster County, Pennsylvania, October 27, 1848, son of Preacher John Weaver. United with the Mennonite Church in 1867. Came with his parents to Elkhart County in 1868. Married (1) Fanny Wenger (1849-1920) (daughter of Christian and Mary [Wenger] Wenger) on October 31, 1869. Six children. Married (2) Leah (Berkey) Imhoff (1852-1932). Ordained preacher May 21, 1903. Died March 8, 1939, at the age of 90. Burial in Yellow Creek West Cemetery.

JOHN WEAVER, 1821-1907   Preacher   W   Elkhart County

Born in Lancaster County, Pennsylvania, September 2, 1821, son of David and Christiana (Buckwalter) Weaver. Married (1) Mary Zimmerman (1824-1879). Twelve children. Married (2) Elizabeth Lehman (1839-1907) on October 16, 1888. Moved from Lancaster County to Elkhart County the spring of 1868 and threw himself on the side of Jacob Wisler in his controversy with some of the Elkhart County ministers. Ordained preacher in Lancaster County, in 1856, by Bishop George Weber. Withdrew from the Indiana Conference in 1872 and followed Wisler. Labored hard to avert the 1907 schism of John W. Martin, but in vain. Died September 2, 1907, on his eighty-sixth birthday anniversary.

JOHN M. WEAVER, 1873-1952   Deacon   OO, W   Elkhart County

Born in Elkhart County, October 26, 1873, son of Christian Z. Weaver. Married (1) Sarah L. Ressler on December 8, 1895. Married (2) Anna Leona Schrock (daughter of Preacher Henry Schrock) on January 22, 1911. One daughter. Ordained deacon, May 21, 1920, by Bishop John W. Martin. Transferred to the Wisler group. Died February 10, 1952, at the age of 78.

WILLIAM G. WEAVER, 1922-   Preacher, Bishop   OO   Elkhart County

Born near Wakarusa, Indiana, March 8, 1922, son of Eli and Barbara (Gehman) Weaver, and grandson of Preacher Christian Z. Weaver. Married Annetta Martin (1922-) (daughter of Elias and Amanda [Ramer] Martin) on November 2, 1944. Eight children. United with the Old Order Mennonite Church in 1940. Ordained preacher in the Yellow Creek (frame) meetinghouse, June 5, 1950, by Bishop Aaron Sensenig of Lancaster County, Pennsylvania. Ordained bishop, June 2, 1953, by Bishops Aaron Sensenig, Addison Gingerich, and Daniel Brubaker.

NOAH W. WENGER, 1895-1931   Preacher   W   Elkhart County

Born near Wakarusa, Indiana, December 24, 1895, brother of Preacher David W. Wenger, 1884-1947, of Orrville, Ohio. Married Anna Ramer (sister of Bishop William Ramer, and daughter of Bishop Martin and Lydia [Shaum] Ramer) on January 5, 1919. Four children. United with the Wisler group the spring of 1917. Was drafted in July 1918 and taken to Camp Taylor, Kentucky, later to Chillicothe,

Ohio. Ordained preacher, November 2, 1925, by Moses G. Horst. His ministry was short. He preached his last sermon (from I Corinthians 1), which lasted an hour and a half, on March 15, 1931. He became ill with appendicitis, and soon died of heart failure on March 20, at the early age of 35. An immense crowd attended the funeral services which were held simultaneously in the Yellow Creek (frame) meetinghouse and in the Yellow Creek (brick) meetinghouse.

DAVID WISLER, 1830-1902   Deacon   Elkhart County
   Born in Columbiana County, Ohio, June 8, 1830, son of Bishop Jacob Wisler. Moved to Elkhart County the spring of 1848 with his parents. Married Christene Shank (1834-1896) (sister of Preacher Michael W. Shank, 1833-1905, and aunt of Preacher Jacob Shank). Nine children. Lived on the farm northwest of the Holdeman meetinghouse where Mervin Hahn now resides. The date of his ordination is not known; possibly around 1885 when Deacon Tobias Ramer, 1824-1887, was approaching the end of his service. Was called Davie, but his tombstone and the **Pictorial and Biographical Memoirs of Elkhart and St. Joseph Counties,** 1893, give his name as David. Died September 22, 1902, at the age of 72. Burial in West Cemetery, Yellow Creek (frame) meetinghouse.

JACOB WISLER, 1808-1889   Preacher, Bishop   Columbiana County, Elkhart County
   Born in Bucks County, Pennsylvania, October 31, 1808, son of Christian Wisler (died 1830) and Susan (Holdeman) Wisler, 1774-1838. Moved about 1820, with his parents to Columbiana County, Ohio, to that section which later (1846) became Mahoning County. Married (1) Mary Hoover (1818-1860 (daughter of David L. Hoover, who was originally of Lancaster County, Pennsylvania, and his wife Esther [Lehman] Hoover, originally of Franklin County, Pennsylvania) on November 19, 1827. Seven children. Married (2) Catharine (Ketty) Knopp (1819-1888). Ordained preacher in 1833, probably at the Midway meetinghouse in Columbiana County, Ohio, and likely by Bishop Jacob Nold. Ordained bishop in 1851, in all likelihood in the Yellow Creek meetinghouse, by Bishop Abraham Rohrer of Medina County, Ohio. Removed to Elkhart County the spring of 1848 and farmed on Section 19 of Harrison Township, where Russell Blosser now farms. Is said to have moved to Elkhart County because the members of his congregation in Ohio objected to his operating a threshing rig; he therefore moved to Indiana where land was cheaper. It was announced at Yellow Creek on January 6, 1872, that he was no longer a member of the "Mennonite Church." Thereupon he organized the **Ohio and Indiana Mennonite Conference.** Died May 1, 1889, at the age of 80. Burial in East Cemetery of the Yellow Creek (frame) meetinghouse.

HISTORICAL NOTE

   Because the Mennonites have always married within the church historically, and since the number of members in the Wisler congregations is limited, there is considerable intermarriage. One example may suffice. Bishop Joseph E. Martin and wife have the following ordained relatives: Deacon Jacob Bechtel is married to Mrs. Martin's sister Elizabeth. Deacon William Henry Bechtel is Mrs. Martin's nephew. Preacher Henry Brenneman was married to Mrs. Martin's aunt. Preacher Levi Eberly was Mr. Martin's maternal grandfather. Preacher Paul Hoover is the son of Mrs. Martin's first cousin. Bishop John W. Martin was his father. Preacher Henry E. Martin is his brother. Deacon Elias Martin was his uncle. Bishop John Shaum was his wife's grandfather. Bishop Christian Shaum was his wife's uncle. Deacon Christian Leinbach was married to his sister Fanny. Bishop Martin Ramer was married to his wife's sister. Bishop William Ramer is his wife's nephew. Bishop Christian Z. Weaver was married to his wife's aunt. Although Deacon Ramer is no relative of Bishop Martin, three of Ramer's sons are married to three of Martin's daughters.

United Missionary Church, 1874

The only sizable church which originated as a schism from the Mennonites of Indiana is the body now known as the United Missionary Church. This group consisted originally in Indiana of the followers of Daniel Brenneman who was expelled from the Mennonite Church in 1874. Here is the story.

Daniel Brenneman was born near Bremen, Fairfield County, Ohio, June 8, 1834. At about twenty-two years of age he was deeply convicted of sin, yielded himself to God, and was brightly converted. He accepted water baptism and united with the Mennonite Church. Indeed, his baptism, his marriage, and his ordination as preacher, all occurred in less than one year's time. The spring of 1864 Daniel Brenneman and family removed to Elkhart County, Indiana, when he was almost thirty years of age.

In the Mennonite Church of Fairfield County, Ohio, Daniel Brenneman had known of no particular opposition to English preaching, nor was there any objection to the fine singing which obtained in the church there. But when he got to Elkhart County he found that Bishop Wisler took a dim view of English preaching, and also insisted that only one-part music be sung. Brenneman wrote as an aged man: "It seemed to be very difficult and withal quite uncalled for, for me to refrain from using the strong bass voice which God had given me, to good advantage in rendering our singing more attractive and edifying. . . ." Furthermore as Brenneman began to accept invitations to preach English sermons at funerals and other occasions, this also was displeasing to the bishop. Even more grievous in the judgment of Bishop Wisler was the way Funk and Brenneman favored the Sunday-school work which was just then being adopted in various areas of the Mennonite Church. Brenneman came safely through the Wisler division of 1872, only to get involved in a serious difficulty himself. The story is as follows.

In Canada a powerful revival broke out, in which Preacher Solomon Eby of Port Elgin felt that he was for the first time really converted. This occurred in the year 1869. In 1873 Daniel Brenneman and his friend, Preacher John Krupp of the Pleasant Hill Mennonite Church in

Branch County, Michigan, decided to go to Ontario to see for themselves the character of the revival which was still in progress in that province. Upon returning to Indiana the brethren Krupp and Brenneman were strictly interrogated about this new revival in Canada. Brenneman was rather reserved in expressing himself, for he feared that the Mennonites of Indiana were not in a position to accept the type of revival which was in progress. John Krupp, however, felt free to speak warmly about his appreciation for the revival. Brenneman decided that the best course for him was to visit Ontario again. This he did. On this occasion there were some thirty applicants for baptism and when the bishop in charge refused to baptize persons who were warm advocates of the revival movement, Brenneman himself consented to baptize them, although he was not a bishop, and at that time ministers baptized only in cases of emergency. Brenneman returned from Ontario near the end of the year 1873, only to learn that John Krupp had been expelled from the church. Meanwhile Krupp had begun to hold revival meetings in Elkhart County, accompanied by Samuel Sherk, a "New Mennonite" preacher (Daniel Hoch's group of Ontario). The meetings of Krupp and Sherk were held in February and March of 1874 in the Jones schoolhouse on the southwest corner of Section 5 of Harrison Township, Elkhart County. The Jones schoolhouse was located on the Bashor Chapel Road one mile east of what is now Highway 19. This schoolhouse stood on the northeast corner of the intersection, across the road from the present (abandoned) Jones schoolhouse.

Daniel Brenneman was quite unhappy with the expulsion of John Krupp in 1873, and refused to acknowledge that this had been justly done. Finally after the emotional excesses of the Krupp and Sherk meetings, the Mennonite ministry of Elkhart County met on April 25, 1874, and drew up the following document:

"At a conference held at Yellow Creek meetinghouse in Elkhart County, Indiana, on the 25th day of April, 1874, the conduct of Daniel Brenneman toward the church during the past several months was taken into consideration, and the ministers present came to the following conclusion:

"That because Daniel Brenneman in the first place left the church and united himself with and supported a man who had been placed under censure, thus working in direct opposition to his own church and bishops,

"And secondly, because he began to teach and practice customs which we hold unscriptural (I Timothy 2:11, 12; I Corinthians 14:34, 35) and which never have been sanctioned in the church,

"And thirdly, because he according to the Scriptures walked disorderly, causing dissension and offense in the church, both at home and abroad,

"We do hereby decide and determine that according to II Thessalonians 3:6, 7, and Romans 16:17, 18, he can no longer be held as a brother in the church, having of his own accord left the church and refused the admonitions and exhortations given him, and withdrawn himself from the rules and regulations which the Gospel, the church, and conference require of every faithful laborer in the vineyard of the Lord.

"It is, however, distinctly understood that in this conclusion the conference is led only by the most solemn convictions of duty both toward God and the church, having no feelings of ill will toward the erring brother, but hereby pray and admonish him to return, acknowledge his error, and labor with us again in the vineyard of the Lord. And that as soon as he shall acknowledge his error, reconcile himself with this and other churches where he has been [a] cause of offense we shall willingly and heartily welcome him back again."

This was signed by Bishops John M. Christophel and Jacob A. Beutler; by Preachers Christian Christophel, Henry Shaum, J. M. Culbertson, Martin E. Kreider, and John F. Funk; and by Deacons Jacob H. Wisler, Henry B. Brenneman, Henry Christophel, David Martin, and Joseph Holdeman.

In an account written in 1918 Brenneman wrote:

"It has been in a measure painful to me in writing this defense of the truth, to be necessitated to mention the names of those who have gone to their long home. Yet in giving a statement of facts I do not wish to assume the position of casting needless reflections upon the character of anyone, but would much rather put the most lenient construction possible upon the face of these bygone events. I feel much rather to cast the mantle of charity over the whole matter as far as I am personally concerned. As the name of Bishop Wisler needs to be mentioned in order to bring out a clear conception of the facts in the case, allow me here to say in his behalf that in the after-years of his life, when difficulties between us were no longer called for on account of our different convictions of Christian obligation (our church relationship having been severed), there was no longer a spirit of antagonism manifested on his part toward me.

"We frequently met each other on the streets of Goshen, and very seldom if ever did he allow such opportunity to pass without shaking hands, bidding the time of day, and courteously inquiring as to our welfare. Thus was indicated that one could yet be on good terms as friends, though differing in sentiment and understanding of the Scriptures. And if he and I shall sometime meet on the beautiful golden streets of the New Jerusalem, we can again shake hands and forever be mutually gratified to see eye to eye more clearly.

"After being expelled from church fellowship we were left as sheep outside the sheepfold with the door seemingly relentlessly fastened against us, the hand of fellowship sternly denied us, and by some held as 'heathens and publicans.' Under these trying circumstances the question, What shall we do? confronted us. As for the popular churches we had no inclination to go that way. Then aside from these were the minor churches. The Dunkards, though they taught many things in unison with our understanding of the Scriptures—and one of their ministers said to me, 'We thought you would go with us'—yet we thought the general tenor of their preaching more of the letter than of the Spirit. And understanding as we did from the Bible that 'the letter killeth, but the Spirit maketh alive,' we could not make up our minds to seek shelter there. The Quakers were another people whose nonresistant principles we could admire, yet they discarded all the ordinances of God's house, and hence we could not endorse this idea. Then there were right in our midst the Evangelical Association who 'showed us no little kindness' in this that when other churches were closed against us, they threw open theirs and invited us in, supposing, as we thought, we might possibly seek shelter with them. But here were the barriers: warfare was tolerated, infant baptism practiced, and secret lodge men admitted to their church as members. Then also we knew of the Free Methodists as being a plain people opposed to secret lodges; yet withal, they sanctioned warfare, baptized infants, and discarded feet washing as a command. Hence we failed to see a place where in every sense we might feel ourselves at home, contented, and satisfied."

The consequence was that the only course Daniel Brenneman could see was to establish his own denomination, which he proceeded to do, and named it the *Reformed Mennonite Church.*

In the course of time, by a series of mergers, a church arose known as the Mennonite Brethren in Christ. Let us trace briefly the history of this movement.

In 1838 a Brethren in Christ leader named John Wenger led a small schism from the group then known as "River Brethren." In 1848 Daniel Hoch of Ontario led a revivalist schism from the Mennonite Church which took the name *New Mennonites.* In 1857 William Gehman of Eastern Pennsylvania led a schism from the General Conference Mennonite Church, which group became known as the *Evangelical Mennonites.* In 1860 John Swank led a small schism from the followers of John Wenger which had left the River Brethren in 1838. In 1872 Solomon Eby of Ontario led a schism from the Mennonite Church which was known as the *Reforming Mennonites*. As was noted above, Daniel Brenneman led his Reformed Mennonites out of the Indiana Mennonite Church in 1874. The Brenneman and Eby groups united as *Reformed Mennonites* in 1874. In 1875 the Reformed Mennonites merged with Hoch's New Mennonites to form the *United Mennonites*. In 1879 the United Mennonites merged with William Gehman's Evangelical Mennonites to form the *Evangelical United Mennonites*. In 1883 the Evangelical United Mennonites merged with the so-called *Swankite* Brethren in Christ followers of John Swank to form the *Mennonite Brethren in Christ*. The Mennonite Brethren in Christ Church retained that name from 1883 until 1947 when at Potsdam, Ohio, the name *United Missionary Church* was adopted. (The Pennsylvania Conference refused to adopt the new name, however, and in 1952 withdrew from the United Missionary Church completely, and in 1959 adopted the name, *Bible Fellowship Church*.)

Two good histories of the denomination have been written. In 1920 Jasper A. Huffman wrote the *History of the Mennonite Brethren in Christ Church*, which was published by the Bethel Publishing Company, New Carlisle, Ohio. In 1958 Everek R. Storms wrote the *History of the United Missionary Church*, which was published by the Bethel Publishing Company, Elkhart, Indiana. Useful also for obtaining information about the United Missionary Church are the *Michigan Conference Journal* and the *Indiana Conference Journal*, which Journals contain the proceedings of the district conferences of the two states. A valuable historical booklet was also issued by the United Missionary Church in 1955 with the title on the cover, *75 Years of Progress for God*, with the title page on the inside reading, *An Historical 75th Anniversary Publication*. Useful also is the *United Missionary Church Yearbook & Directory*, the last issue available was for the years 1958-59. Perhaps most valuable of all for solid information about the church is, *The Constitution and Manual of the United Missionary Church*, published by the General Board and Publications Board of the General Conference, 1959 (Bethel Publishing Company, 1819 South Main Street, Elkhart, Indiana).

The General Conference of the United Missionary Church meets triennially, and is currently led by Kenneth Geiger, general superintendent; Ward M. Shantz, vice-general superintendent; Ira L. Wood, secretary; and Ancel L. Whittle, treasurer. The General Board of the denomination is made up of district conference representatives, and meets at least semiannually. There are four organizations which serve the General Board: the Church Extension Board, the United Missionary Society, the Publications Board, and the Co-ordinating Educational Board. There are at present seven district conferences in the United Missionary Church, each of which is led by a district superintendent, and each of which meets annually. Ontario has approximately 2,400 members, Indiana has almost 3,000 members, Michigan has over 2,000 members, Ohio has 1,000 members, Nebraska has 800 members, the Canadian Northwest has 500 members, and Washington has 500 members, making a total of about 200 congregations and well over 10,000 members. The Indiana Conference includes about thirty-five congregations and mission points, mostly in Northern Indiana and Southern Michigan. The Michigan Conference has over forty congregations and over 2,000 members.

The United Missionary Church is one with the Mennonite Church in basic beliefs on the fundamental doctrines of God, Christ, sin, salvation, the church, etc.; and including such distinctive practices as believers' baptism, the washing of the saints' feet, the rejection of the oath, opposition to lodge membership, abstention from beverage alcohol and tobacco, and the shunning of the theater. The group, however, holds to a mild interpretation of nonresistance, and has adopted two doctrines which are rather new to the Mennonite Church: immersion and the second work of grace.

VII

Other Amish Mennonite Bodies

The Old Order Amish

Elkhart and Lagrange Counties, Indiana

By far the largest settlement of the Old Order Amish in the states of Indiana and Michigan is the thirty congregations found in Elkhart and Lagrange counties in Northern Indiana. From 1841, when the Amish settled in Northern Indiana, until 1854, when the progressive portion of the Amish seceded to form the so-called Amish Mennonites, the two bodies have a common history. One of the 1841 settlers who came from Somerset County, Pennsylvania, to Clinton Township, Elkhart County, Indiana, was Joseph ("Sep") Borntreger, 1811-1908. "Sep'" had been ordained as a deacon in Pennsylvania in 1839. He had therefore been serving in that office for fifteen years when the 1854 division occurred, and was forty-three years of age. When "Sep" was ninety-six years of age, his son, Preacher John ("Hans") E. Borntreger, 1837-1930, wrote in German *A History of the First Settlement of the Amish Mennonites and the Establishment of their First Congregation in the State of Indiana, together with a Brief Account of the Division which Occurred in this Church.* Hans was a boy of fifteen when the 1854 division occurred, but of course had often heard his father rehearse the circumstances of that unfortunate schism. Hans listed the causes as four: (1) The Amish Mennonites, he declared, tolerated costly clothing and worldly adornment. (2) The Amish Mennonites permitted the holding of worldly offices. (3) The Amish Mennonites permitted their members full freedom to enter into business. (4) The Amish Mennonites succumbed to "the wisdom of this world." (Just what he meant by this fourth charge is not entirely clear; perhaps he referred to the fact that the Amish Mennonites allowed their young people, at least in the course of time, to attend high schools and colleges.)

The first service of the Amish in Northern Indiana was held in the home of Daniel S. Miller the fall of 1841, in Lagrange County. During the winter few or no services were evidently held, for the first service of 1842 was held on Easter, March 27, in the home of Preacher Joseph Miller in Elkhart County when the congregation numbered about fourteen members. Services were held thereafter every two weeks. The first congregation had some members in Clinton Township, Elkhart County,

385

26

and others in Newbury Township, Lagrange County. About 1843 the original congregation was divided into the Clinton and Lagrange congregations. In the course of time it was necessary to divide and subdivide the Clinton congregation until in 1960 the Amish Almanac, *Der Neue Amerikanische Calender,* lists seven congregations in Elkhart County. Meanwhile the Lagrange congregation of 1843 was divided in 1866 to form the new daughter congregation, Yoder. In 1876 the Forks congregation produced another daughter, North Barrens. In 1882 the Yoder congregation divided to form the new Clearspring congregation. In 1901 the Yoder congregation produced another daughter, Honeyville. And so the dividing and subdividing went on as the Amish spread out across the western half of Lagrange County. The Amish Almanac of 1960 lists twenty-three congregations in Lagrange County.

It would be possible to form a fairly complete ministerial list of bishops, preachers, and deacons in the Old Order Amish Church, by using three sources: (1) The German History of Hans E. Borntreger; (2) The Mennonite Yearbook and Directory, 1905-60; and (3) The German Almanac of J. A. Raber, Baltic, Ohio, *Der Neue Amerikanische Calender,* 1930-60.

Undoubtedly the three most influential bishops of the Elkhart and Lagrange County congregations were: (1) Joseph Miller, 1808-1877. He was born in Somerset County, Pennsylvania, in November 1808. He came to Elkhart County, Indiana, in 1841 as an Amish preacher. He settled first in Clinton Township, Elkhart County, but in 1846 removed to Lagrange County where he served in the congregation which was then called Lagrange, but which was later known as Forks. He was ordained to the office of bishop in 1848 and served faithfully for twenty-nine years until his lamented death on October 12, 1877. In 1949 Bishop Eli J. Bontreger wrote of Joseph Miller: "To a very large extent he was intrumental in forming the policies and practices of the Amish churches in Indiana." (2) The second influential figure among the Amish of Northern Indiana was Bishop David S. Kauffman, 1835-1918, originally of the Forks congregation. He was ordained preacher in the Forks Amish Church in November 1873, and bishop in the North Barrens congregation, May 20, 1877. It is thus evident that the ministry of Joseph Miller and David S. Kauffman covered the period from 1841 until 1918. Eli J. Bontreger, one of the most intelligent and influential leaders who ever served in the Amish Church, in speaking of conditions in a certain congregation, wrote: "The conditions there are not satisfactory at all, due mostly to the fact that the church policy of our former highly respected and revered bishop, David S. Kauffman, as practiced by us all these years, is being ignored." (3) The third influential leader among the Amish, not only in Indiana and Michigan, but throughout the United States, was Bishop Eli J. Bontreger, 1868-1958. He was ordained preacher in the North Barrens congregation, May 13, 1894, and bishop, June 18, 1901. By May 16, 1944, Bishop Bontreger had baptized 366 persons, had married 149 couples, had preached 2,418 times, including 226 communion sermons and 118 funeral sermons. He had also ordained thirty ministers and eleven bishops. He also figured that by that time he had traveled by rail over 372,000 miles, and by auto over 38,000 miles, in connection with his trips to do church work. Around the turn of the century the Amish of Northern Indiana created their so-called Amish Aid Plan, which was a mutual fire insurance company. The Federal Land Banks desired that a constitution and bylaws be written for this organization, although they were completely satisfied with its method of operation. Bishop Bontreger therefore wrote such an instrument, and took it to the Federal Bank at Louisville, Kentucky, where with a few slight changes it was approved. Eli J. Bontreger wrote an autobiographical sketch, *My Life Story,* in August 1943, and with supplements from a number of different years thereafter. The final mimeographing was done in 1955.

One of the finest students of Amish faith and culture is Professor John A. Hostetler, now a teacher of sociology in the University of Alberta. Professor Hostetler takes a sympathetic interest in both the Mennonites and the Amish, and is a successful writer dealing with their culture and history. He wrote the article, "Old Order Amish," for *The Mennonite Encyclopedia.* While a student at Goshen College, 1947-49, he attended many Amish services in Northern Indiana. He has a good ear for the Pennsylvania German dialect, which he thoroughly understands, and has the eyes of a keen observer. He recognizes that the Amish are earnest and devout Christians and strict nonresistants, he understands the origin and symbolism of their plain clothing, and is able to write effectively. Following is his account of an Amish baptismal service which he attended:

"This service was held in a large barn near Middlebury, Indiana. The barnyard was packed full of black buggies. When we arrived, the service was about to begin. Women sat on one side of the barn floor, and the men and boys on the other, each group facing the other. Except for the two long rows of benches in the middle, the seating space was almost full. To the right, directly back of the women, was the alfalfa haymow. A curtain of binder canvas was tacked along the side to prevent the stubble from scratching their backs and to improve the general appearance. To the left was the long granary, on the side of which hung the large-brimmed black hats of the men.

"It was a beautiful September morning. The sun shone brightly into the faces of the audience through the entrance of the large swinging doors, which were propped open on the bank of the barn. The clear blue sky and the warm sunlight were symbols of the special occasion of the morning, a baptismal service. Although this was a regular worship service, it was also a meeting of special interest and anticipation to all loyal members of the church. As the song leader began singing the first syllable of the first song, the ministers, bishops, and deacons retired to a room in the house to discuss ministerial matters, to counsel with the baptismal applicants for the last time, and to agree on the order of the service for the day.

"Between hymns there was deep silence in the audience. The horses could be heard below, munching on some timothy hay. The owner of the farm, while waiting for another hymn to be announced, sensed that it was getting too warm and began to unlatch, with some difficulty, a second barn door on the side where the women were seated. To help facilitate a breeze the owner walked to the other end of the barn floor and pushed open the roller door leading to the straw shed. Now that the ventilation was taken care of he again took his seat near the middle of the barn floor.

"After several hymns were sung by the congregation, the applicants for baptism, on this occasion six girls from ages sixteen to eighteen, came marching up the barn bank single file and took their seats provided for in the center section near the ministers' bench. Both young and old gazed at the sight—six young women in the bloom of youth ready to make their vows with God and the church, to say no to the world, the flesh, and the devil, and to say yes to Jesus Christ and His church here on earth. In spite of the many necks stretching here and there to see the applicants, their new dresses, and the expression on their faces, the congregation managed to continue their singing. Each applicant sat with bowed head, as though she were in deep meditation and prayer for the lifelong vow she was about to make. None dared to risk a view at the audience or gaze about. This was a solemn occasion. All were of the same mind, and with folded hands in their laps they all sat in a straight row. Their clothing was strictly uniform—black caps [prayer veils], black dresses, white capes, and long white aprons. This garb, together with the pink complexion and sincerity of expression on their faces, added an element of simplicity and beauty to the occasion, which comes to an Amish member only once in a lifetime.

"The ministers now entered the scene and gently took off their hats as they entered the barn. All seven, including several visiting deacons and bishops for this special service, offered the handshake with all who were nearby as they leisurely made their way to the ministers' bench. The last minister to come in stacked the seven hats on one end of the bench. Each took his seat, the one who was to make the opening address at the head of the bench, and the visiting bishop who was to bring the longer message, next in line. As soon as the ministers were seated, the congregation discontinued the hymn at the first convenient stopping place.

"The minister on the far end of the bench took his position in front of the large beams which held up the frame structure of the barn. With folded hands beneath his full-grown white beard he began to preach in a low tone, gradually building up to an audible and even flow of words. Translated from the German his message was along this line: 'Dear brothers and sisters and all who are assembled here, first of all I wish you the grace of God and the accompanying power of the Holy Ghost. As Peter says, "Blessed be the God and Father of our Lord Jesus Christ, which according to his abundant mercy hath begotten us again unto a lively hope by the resurrection of Jesus Christ from the dead, to an inheritance incorruptible, and undefiled, and that fadeth not away, reserved in heaven for you." '

"In this introductory sermon he reminded the congregation of the purpose of the meeting, namely, to listen once more to the Word of God. He brought to their attention some Scripture teachings and pointed out the importance of obeying the commandments of the Bible. 'Work out your own salvation with fear and trembling.' Before he brought his half-hour introduction to a close he mentioned the importance of baptism and gave his word of encouragement and warning to the applicants. At first he called them sisters, but quickly corrected himself and called them the young daughters, because, after all, they were not yet baptized, and it would be improper to call one a brother or sister who had not been baptized, even though they were approaching the very hour of baptism. After a few words of apology for his weakness he informed the congregation that he did not wish to take the allotted time away from the brother who was to bring the morning message. He asked the members to pray for the minister and quoted a favorite verse from the psalmist, 'O come, let us worship and bow down; let us kneel before the Lord our maker.' The entire body then knelt together for a season of silent prayer. When the ministers began to rise to their feet, the entire audience also stood up.

"All remained standing after prayer while the deacon read a chapter from the Gospel of John. Before doing so he took the liberty to make a few remarks, and admonish the applicants for baptism to be obedient to the church and to the Lord. The entire chapter was read, as is the custom among Amish churches, in a singsong, almost chanting, fashion. After the last verse of the chapter was read the deacon concluded, 'Thus far does the Scripture reading extend.' Thereupon all the people sat down.

"The time had now come for the visiting bishop to begin the main sermon. He began with the usual greeting in German, 'Grace be with you and peace from God our Father. We have been admonished many times in this morning hour by the brother.' He then reminded all present of the importance of the occasion, which was the observance of the ordinance of baptism, and said that it was a time when not only the applicants should profit from the experience, but all who were already members should think back to the time when each had made his own vow, and thus renew his covenant with God.

"At this point in the service a dish of crackers and cookies was passed up and down the aisle for the benefit of babies and youngsters who had by this time become fidgety and noisy. After the introductory remarks the bishop began to preach his main sermon and related the Old Testament story from Adam to Abraham, and then the New Testament history from John the Baptist to the end of Paul's missionary journeys. The earnestness with which he spoke produced drops of sweat on his face so that every few minutes it was necessary to reach to his inside coat pocket and draw out a handkerchief with which to wipe his forehead. He held the white cloth in his hand and waved it through the air as he illustrated points of Scripture. The sermon consisted of a continuity of thought between the events in the narrative and was delivered rather systematically.

"After having preached for an hour the bishop addressed the applicants for baptism. At this point the deacon left the service and returned with a small pail of water and a tin cup. The bishop reminded the class that the vow they were

about to make was not made to the church, but to God. He requested the applicants to kneel if it was still their desire to become members of the body of Christ.
All six knelt down. The bishop then asked a few simple questions and each
applicant answered accordingly:

1. " 'Are you able to make the beautiful confession of the Ethiopian eunuch,
that you believe that Jesus Christ is God's Son?' Each responded, 'Yes, I believe
that Jesus Christ is God's Son.'

2. " 'Do you recognize the group with which you are about to unite as the
Christian church and congregation?'

3. " 'Do you renounce the devil and the world with all its sinful ways, as
also your own flesh and blood, and do you desire to serve Christ Jesus alone who
died for us on the cross?'

4. " 'Do you promise to fulfill the ordinances of the Lord and the church,
to faithfully observe them, to be diligent in church attendance, and not absent
yourself therefrom even though life and death should be involved?'

"After the applicants had responded satisfactorily to the preliminary questions the bishop asked the congregation to rise for prayer. He read simple and
impressive prayers from the German prayer book, *Christenpflicht*.

"Following the prayer the congregation was seated. The bishop with the
assistance of one of the deacons proceeded with the ordinance of baptism. The
deacon called for one of the older women to assist, whereupon the deacon's wife
immediately came forward. The three stood at the head of the line of the
applicants and the deacon's wife began to untie the ribbons of the prayer veil
of the first applicant. She removed it completely, whereupon the bishop laid
his hands on her head and proceeded with the baptismal ceremony. The deacon
poured a small quantity of water on each head three times as the bishop repeated, 'Father, Son, and Holy Spirit.' The deacon's wife then placed the black
prayer veil on the head of each one baptized, but left the ribbons untied as she
proceeded to untie the prayer veil of the next applicant in line. This process
was repeated until all six were baptized.

"As I looked upon the young women who had just sealed their vows in baptism, water was dripping from their heads and noses. But they paid no attention,
for they were in deep meditation. The pure white aprons were saturated with
water, and the fringes were soiled with the moisture and dirt of the barn floor.
High overhead inside the barn the pigeons were flapping their wings as they
flew from one end of the barn to the other. A gentle breeze brought from the
open door of the straw shed a cloud of fine particles of chaff and dust. High in
the clear blue heavens an airplane overhead roared in the distance, a symbol of
earthly wisdom, progress, and evil.

"The act of baptism was complete. The bishop and the sister began again
at the head of the line, this time extending the right hand of fellowship to the
new members. The bishop took the hand of the kneeling newly baptized member and greeted each, 'In the name of the Lord and the church I offer you my
hand, arise!' The new member stood up and the bishop then turned to the
deacon's wife who greeted the new member with the holy kiss. All remained
standing until the last one was greeted and the bishop then permitted them to
be seated. A few tears were brushed aside, and a few began to tie their prayer veil

ribbons. They were now considered full members of the church. The bishop resumed his preaching position and admonished the congregation to be helpful to the new members.

"At this point four of the unmarried girls left the service to prepare the noon meal. The ones who had just been baptized were then instructed to be faithful to the church and to the ministry. The bishop referred to the story of the terrible idolatry committed by Israel while Moses was up in the mountain to pray. The moral he drew from the story was that young people sometimes hold parties and do sinful things while their parents are away from home. He stated that if Satan can get young people that is what he desires. He concluded the long sermon and the baptismal service, which lasted for one and three-quarter hours, with the reading of Romans 6. After taking his seat he asked the ministers present to bear testimony to the sermon. In this case these remarks were made by three of the seven ministers on the ministers' bench, and consisted of a brief statement of approval to what had been said in the sermon and a few additional remarks as in their judgment seemed suitable. The first brother heartily approved of the day's sermon and wished for the new members a rich spiritual nature, and added that he hoped they would keep their promises to the end. The church, he remarked, had received a fresh growth with the addition of these new members. He added, 'I hope that they may faithfully persevere to a saved end.' The second brother said that he was entirely in harmony with what had been done and that he with his great weakness could add nothing to what had already been said. The third brother added additional admonitions for the new members. In tears and with heaviness of heart he said that it was only a short time ago when it was his privilege to sit in the audience and listen, but now he had been called to preach and he requested the members to remember the ministry in prayer.

"After the testimonies were completed the bishop again took his place before the audience and made a few closing remarks. He said that he was thankful that the sermon could be received as God's Word and requested that the congregation give the honor to God and not to man. He thanked the audience for being quiet and attentive. As a guest speaker he again admonished the congregation to be obedient to its ministers, and also requested the ministry to visit other congregations; this, he said, strengthens and builds up the church. Not desiring to part without turning to God in thanksgiving, the bishop once more asked the congregation to kneel for a closing prayer. Except for three or four mothers who were holding sleeping babies, all knelt while the minister read in a rather chanting style from the prayer book. At the conclusion of the prayer the congregation stood for the benediction which was pronounced from memory. At the mention of the name of Jesus all the members practiced genuflection. The congregation then sat down for the announcement as to the place for the next worship service of the congregation. After the singing of a closing hymn the service was completed." (This account reproduced by permission of Professor John A. Hostetler.)

Readers desiring to know more of the life and culture of the Amish should read Dr. Hostetler's *Amish Life*, as well as the monograph by Joseph W. Yoder, *Rosanna of the Amish,* the Yoder Publishing Company, Huntingdon, Pennsylvania, 1940. Another valuable source of information was compiled by L. D. Christner, of Topeka, Indiana, in 1949, *Old Order Amish Church Districts in Indiana,* printed by Waddell Printing Company, Lagrange, Indiana.

About 1904 an Amish scholar of Iowa, S. D. Guengerich, made a list of all the Amish congregations that he could learn of in Indiana, and gave for each its location, the person by whom organized, the first settlers, the first ministers, the ministers in 1904, their addresses, the number of families in the congregation, and the number of members. He listed six congregations of Amish in Northern Indiana with 232 families, and 539 members. The present (1961) membership has increased about sixfold, there being over 3,000 members in the thirty congregations of Elkhart and Lagrange counties.

Adams County, Indiana

Eva F. Sprunger in her fine history of the Mennonite Church in Adams County, Indiana, *The First Hundred Years,* 1938, reproduced a letter written by Preacher David Baumgartner, 1765-1853, which he wrote from Adams County, Indiana, to his friends in Switzerland in 1849: "At the present time there are sixteen families that belong to our church. Every three weeks we hold divine worship. Christian and I alternate in giving exhortations. There are also an equal number of Amish people near here, also some Reformed Church people and some Lutherans."

Very little seems to be known of the Amish who were living near David Baumgartner in 1849. The article on Adams County in *The Mennonite Encyclopedia* reports that Henry Egli and family removed from Butler County, Ohio, to Adams County, Indiana, in 1850. Other early settlers included the following heads of families: John Hirshe, Philip Hirshe, Dan Kauffman, Joseph Kauffman, Minister Joseph Schwartz, and Deacon John Schwartz, both of the ordained men having come to Adams County from Stark County, Ohio. J. A. Raber, who issues the Amish Almanac, *Der Neue Amerikanische Calender,* for 1960, lists six congregations of Old Order Amish in Adams County: North, North Middle, East, East *(sic),* West Wabash, and South Wabash. These congregations have a membership of something like 400 *in toto.* The Amish of Adams County, in contrast with the Amish for the rest of Indiana, speak Swiss German, rather than Pennsylvania German. A family history which has data on a number of ministers who have served in the Old Order Amish Church in Adams County is the book by Anna D. Schwartz, *Descendants of Johannes Schwartz,* Berne, Indiana, 1949. Amish of Adams County, Indiana, are perhaps the most conservative of any in the state; even having backs on buggy seats, to lean against while riding, has been considered by some leaders as "worldly."

Howard and Miami Counties, Indiana

The division of 1854 in Northern Indiana, in the Clinton and Forks congregations, was paralleled by a similar division in the Howard and Miami counties Amish congregation in the same year. The leader of the group which became Amish Mennonite was Preacher, later Bishop, Benjamin Shrock, 1819-1895, who later served in the Elkhart County congregations, especially Clinton Frame. The leader of the Old Order Amish congregation in Howard and Miami counties in 1854 was Preacher "Hans" (John) Schmucker, 1816-1872, who was ordained to the office of bishop about 1854. Later bishops in the Howard-Miami Amish settlement were Cornelius E. Hochstedler, 1847-1910; Noah C. Bontrager; David S. Slabaugh; and Andrew Swartzentruber.

Following the division of 1854 the Old Order Amish congregation thrived for a time, while the Amish Mennonite group life almost disintegrated. The Amish Mennonite preacher, Joseph Kennedy, transferred his membership to the German Baptist Church (now known as the Church of the Brethren), and Bishop Benjamin Shrock, 1819-1895, removed to Elkhart County, leaving the Amish Mennonite group without any pastoral oversight. After a time, however, the Amish Mennonite group began to thrive, and a decline set in in the life of the Old Order Amish. The low point was reached, through emigration to other communities and through transfers to the Amish Mennonites, in 1892 when but six families and seventeen members remained in the Howard-Miami Old Order Amish Church. In the latter years of the nineteenth century, however, Amish people began to move into the Howard-Miami area again, and a number of young people united with the Old Order Amish congregation. This growth resulted in the formation of two congregations in 1908, the South congregation being the Amish living in Howard County, and the North congregation being those who resided in Miami County. But the story of the Amish congregations in Howard and Miami counties in the twentieth century is rather dismal. In the period from 1900 to 1948 a tabulation of withdrawals from the Amish congregations in those two counties reveals that sixty-five former Amish united with either the Conservative or the Beachy Amish Mennonites, 218 former Amish united with the Howard-Miami Mennonite Church, 184 Amish moved to other communities, and seventeen simply dropped their church membership. The 1960 *Mennonite Yearbook and Directory* indicates that the North congregation (Miami County) has twenty-eight members, while the South congregation in Howard County has fifty-six members.

Marshall, Elkhart, and Kosciusko Counties, Indiana

Between the years 1848 and 1852 about ten families settled in Marshall County, near Nappanee. Among the earlier settlers were three brothers named Hochstetler: David H. and Susan (Yoder) Hochstetler and five children, Manasses and Fanny (Yoder) Hochstetler and one child, and Samuel H. and Elizabeth (Miller) Hochstetler. Other settlers included John C. and Catherine (Mast) Schlabach and two children. The four Hochstetlers and the Schlabach family all came from Somerset County, Pennsylvania. Other settlers included Valentine and Mary (Schrock) Yoder, Jacob Schmucker and family (he was a Swiss immigrant who had first located in Fulton County, Ohio), Solomon Miller, Elias Yoder, Jonas Yoder, Sr., and John and Rachel (Hochstetler) Borkholder from Holmes County, Ohio. (Borkholder was the son of a Mennonite orphan who had been reared by an Amish family.)

When Amish scholar, S. D. Guengerich of Iowa, made his list of Amish congregations in Indiana about 1904, he indicated that the Marshall County congregation had been organized in 1853 by Levi Miller and Joseph Miller. (It is not known who Levi Miller was, but Joseph Miller was the bishop of the Clinton congregation in Elkhart County.)

In the 1929 *Mennonite Yearbook* of the General Conference Mennonites, E. S. Mullett wrote a history of the West Market Street congregation of Nappanee. He also set 1853 as the date of organization of the Marshall County Amish congregation. Mullett also indicated that the first two preachers were John Ringenberg, 1827-1871, and Tobias Hochstetler. (The identity of Tobias Hochstetler is not entirely clear. The only man by this name in the 1912 Hostetler genealogy was Tobias Hochstetler, 1818-1887, whose first wife died in Locke Township, near Nappanee, in 1857, while he himself died at Berlin, Ohio, in 1887. It is entirely possible that this is the man who led the Old Order Amish schism of about 1854 in Marshall County, and whose name was forgotten by the present generation of Old Order Amish in that county.) It is definitely known that John Ringenberg is the man who led the Amish Mennonite schism from the Old Order Amish, with five or six other families, and who served as a minister in what became the West Market Street Amish Mennonite Church, Nappanee.

The first bishop which the present generation of Amish know of was David H. Hochstetler, 1818-1885, who served in the Marshall County Church until about 1876 when he with a considerable number of other Old Order Amish families moved to Newton County, Indiana.

The next bishop in the Marshall County Amish Church was Moses Borkholder, 1838-1933, who was ordained preacher April 27, 1862, and bishop, October 20, 1878. For almost fifty-five years Moses Borkholder was the leader of his people. He was twice married, and had a very large family, so that at his death in his ninety-fifth year he was the ancestor of 565 descendants.

When S. D. Guengerich made his list of Amish congregations in Indiana about 1904, he recorded that the Marshall County congregation consisted of fifty-eight families with 132 members. Beginning in 1906 it became necessary to divide the Marshall County Old Order Amish congregation into two groups because of its size. Seven subsequent divisions in the next fifty years have produced a total of nine congregations south, southeast, and west of the town of Nappanee. These nine congregations can be arranged in three tiers running north and south. East and southeast of Nappanee in the easternmost tier are two districts, Milford, and south of it the Southeast Church. Nappanee itself is in the North District which extends northward from the town. South of Nappanee in the middle tier of three congregations is the East District, and south of the East District are the North Millwood and South Millwood churches. The westernmost tier of three congregations consists of the Northwest Church, south of it the West Church, and south of the West District is the Hepton Church. The 1960 *Mennonite Yearbook and Directory* indicates nine congregations in Marshall and Kosciusko counties with a total membership of 747.

The Marshall-Kosciusko and Elkhart-Lagrange Amish settlements were parallel from the beginning; neither is a daughter of the other. However, both groups are similar in many ways, and operate with almost identical standards. In the years between the departure of Bishop David H. Hochstetler and the ordination of Moses Borkholder as his bishop-successor, Bishop John L. Miller ("Leff" John) of the Clinton congregation, who had been a bishop from 1866, served in the Marshall County congregation. Later Amish bishops from east of Goshen who served in the Marshall Church were David S. Kauffman who became a bishop in 1877, and Eli E. Bontreger who was ordained bishop in 1887. In 1867 Preacher David S. Miller of Marshall County moved to Lagrange County and affiliated with the, Yoder congregation.

Allen County, Indiana

The first-known Amish settlers in Allen County, Indiana, were the Graber brothers, sons of immigrant Daniel Graber. The immigrant father migrated from Alsace to America and settled in Holmes County, Ohio. He had nine children. He was a strict member of the Amish Church and dressed his sons in knee breeches and frock coats with buttons. The Graber brothers migrated from Stark County, Ohio, to Allen County, Indiana, in November 1852. Peter Graber, 1811-1896, served as preacher and bishop in the Amish Church in Allen County, where he remained all his days; his wife was Anna Miller, 1819-1890. His brother John Graber, 1816-1877, was also a preacher, but lived for a number of years in Daviess County, Indiana, before he died. The third brother Jacob Graber, 1821-1904, was first a deacon, and then a "confirmed deacon," or bishop. He located in Daviess County in 1869.

In April 1853 a party of Amish numbering fifty-two persons, including children, made the long journey by ox team from Stark County, Ohio, to Allen County, Indiana; there were twelve teams in this group. The Allen County Amish settlement is the only one in Indiana and Michigan which is made up primarily of Alsatian Amish immigrants. Prominent names in the present Amish congregations of Allen County, and in the Mennonite and Evangelical Mennonite groups, are Egli, Gerig, Graber, Lederman, Liechty, Lugbill, Miller, Neuhouser, Ramseyer, Richer, Schlatter, Sommer, Stalter, Stoll, Stuckey, Witmer, and Yoder.

In the Amish General Conferences, known as *Diener-Versammlungen*, which convened from 1862 to 1878, there were seven ordained men who attended from the Allen County Amish settlement in the first six years: Andrew Gerig and Joseph Gerig, 1864, Jacob Graber, 1864, John Graber, 1862, Peter Graber, 1867, John Klopfenstein, 1865, and Michael Miller, 1865. In 1876 an eighth man attended, Christian Lugbill, whose name was listed by the secretary as Luggenbill. Christian Lugbill was the first minister ordained in what is now the Leo Mennonite Church, 1875.

No records are available for the date of organization of the first Amish congregation in Allen County, but it is known that the three Graber brothers did not find it possible to work permanently with the two Gerig ministers, Andrew and Joseph. (Joseph P. Gerig, 1824-1892, was ordained to the ministry about 1850 before he left France. He served in the Allen County Amish congregation from 1854 until the Defenseless Amish Mennonite congregation was organized about ten years later.) The Amish settlement in Allen County is located in the northeast quarter of the county about twelve miles northeast of Fort Wayne. The Amish members receive their mail at such post offices as Leo, Grabill, Harlan, and Woodburn. Partly through growth, and partly through minor disagreements in church discipline, the Amish of Allen County are now organized in six congregations: the South Schmucker congregation, the North Graber congregation, Spencerville, the East Wagler congregation, the West Graber congregation, and Lengacher. The total membership in these six districts is probably about 500.

Daviess and Martin Counties, Indiana

The history of the Amish in this area was written by Joseph Stoll in 1959, *The Amish-Mennonites in Daviess County, Indiana.*

The first Amish brother to purchase land in Daviess County was Peter Gingerich, who made his purchase on December 25, 1868. Other early settlers were Bishop Jacob Graber, 1821-1904, who came in 1869 from Allen County, Indiana; Peter Stoll, 1869; Preacher John Graber, 1816-1877, a brother of Bishop Jacob Graber, who also settled in Daviess County, and was ordained bishop four months before he died; Deacon John S. Wagler, who came from Lorraine, France, and first settled in Ontario, located in Daviess County in 1871 (his son Peter Wagler was ordained as bishop); John Raber and Manasseh Raber, who both came from Ohio to Daviess County, but were not close relatives; Christian Richer, who had been born in Europe, and who settled in Daviess County in 1874. The first ordination in the colony was Joseph Wittmer, 1844-1915, who was chosen as preacher in 1871, and as bishop in 1882. Recent bishops who have served the church were ordained as follows: Amos G. Wittmer, 1924; John L. Graber, 1932; Amos Yoder, 1940; Peter Yoder, 1941; and Fred W. Knepp, 1957.

When S. D. Guengerich made his catalog of Amish congregations in Indiana about 1904, he indicated that the Amish in Daviess County consisted of sixty families with 140 members. Today there are five congregations of Amish in Daviess and Martin counties with 400 members. The following names are found in these five congregations down through the years: Amann, Ashleman, Bacher, Brandenberger, Eicher, Gingerich, Graber, Grabill, Kauffman, Kemp, Knepp, Lichty, Lengacher, Mast, Miller, Overholt, Raber, Richer, Stoll, Stutzman, Swartzentruber, Wagler, Wagner, Wittmer, and Yoder.

Newton and Jasper Counties, Indiana

Old Order Amish families from Ohio began to move to the vicinity around Rensselaer, in Jasper County, in 1872, but soon moved to a new location near Mount Ayr in Newton County. This original group of Ohio Amish families was joined about four years later by Bishop David H. Hochstetler of Marshall County with a goodly number of other Amish families from the same county. Almost forty years later, in 1914, another group of Amish families from Daviess County moved to a new location near Parr in Jasper County.

For a number of years the Amish settlement in Newton and Jasper counties prospered; at their high point there were about sixty families with possibly 175 members. Until 1914 there was only one congregation, but the Daviess County group had its own congregation from that date.

Only four bishops have served in the Newton-Jasper Amish settlement: David H. Hochstetler, his son Valentine ("Wallie"), David Miller, and Albert Anderson, who was ordained in 1925 but who moved to the Elkhart-Lagrange Amish settlement about twenty-five years later. The congregation was gradually weakened as members moved away, while others united with the Burr Oak Mennonite Church. When Bishop Anderson moved away about 1950, only ten families remained. By 1957 the number had dwindled to three families without a preacher. The last Amish families moved out of Newton County in 1960.

Other Amish Settlements in Indiana

Brown County

The Brown County Amish settlement was begun about 1896 when Adam D. Hochstetler of Fayette County, Illinois, removed to Brown County. When he had loaded up a freight car to move, his wife died, but he and his children moved to Brown County anyhow. The next year, 1897, a number of Amish families from Northern Indiana under the leadership of Preacher David J. Hochstetler, 1839-1929, moved to Brown County. Included in the short-lived Amish settlement in Brown County were David J. Hochstetler's sons, Adam who preceded him to Brown County, Levi, Joseph, and a son-in-law Daniel Stutzman: each with their respective families. David J. Hochstetler led this migration of Northern Indiana Amish to Brown County because he wished to have Sunday-school privileges for his family and congregation, and the Amish of Northern Indiana were not favorable to the Sunday school. While the group lived in Brown County, Preacher David Hochstetler's son, Samuel D. Hochstetler, was ordained preacher November 3, 1902. Most of the families moved out of Brown County and returned to Northern Indiana in 1910. The high point of the Brown County Amish settlement saw fourteen families there. Preacher Samuel D. Hochstetler and family remained in Brown County until 1911 and worshiped with the "English" in their Sunday school.

Pike County

In 1903-4 Bishop Joseph Wittmer, 1844-1915, an immigrant from France, who had lived in Daviess County, led a movement of a number of Daviess County Amish families to Pike County. The settlement there lasted only until 1914, and consisted of fourteen families at its highest point. Some Amish then returned to Daviess County, while others moved elsewhere. Leading families in the settlement were Aschleman, Gingerich, Grabill, and Wittmer.

Jay County

In the year 1937 a few Amish families began to settle in Jay County, Indiana, in the Portland area. They were joined about 1945 by Preacher Alvin Yoder who moved there from Calhoun County, Michigan. The Jay County Amish settlement ended in 1958, when the members moved to the state of Missouri.

The Portland, Indiana, newspaper, *The Commercial Review,* in reporting that the last Amish families planned to move out of Jay County the spring of 1958, commented: "Within the next few months the entire group—whose kindly faces, beards, severe clothing, 'old-fashioned' equipment, and friendly attitude toward other county residents distinguished their stay here—will be gone from the Jay County scene."

De Kalb County

About 1950 a few Amish families moved into the area of Ashley, Indiana. Their preacher was Ora Graber who by 1960 had moved away. In the latter year there were still three Amish families living in De Kalb County.

Sullivan County

Amish families began to move into Sullivan County in 1955. This small group has as its minister in 1960, Preacher Amos Stoll.

Orange County

A number of Amish families began to move into the Paoli area in 1956. Their minister is Bishop Henry M. Miller.

*   *   *

It is entirely possible that there were temporary Amish settlements in other counties in Indiana which did not come to the attention of the writer. One illustration would be the case of Amish Preacher Joseph Kinsinger. Kinsinger came from the Palatinate in Germany and settled in Butler County, Ohio, in the year 1850. In 1861 he was ordained as a preacher in the Butler County Amish Church. In 1868 Kinsinger removed to Wayne County, Indiana, where he is said to have established a congregation. He died in 1894 and his body was buried at Germantown, Indiana, which would indicate that he was likely living in either Shelby or Decatur County when he died. Germantown is in Decatur County, close to the Shelby County line, about six miles northeast of Geneva, Indiana, and about one mile south of St. Paul which lies either on or close to the Shelby-Decatur County line. (See "Kinsinger" in *The Mennonite Encyclopedia,* II, page 177; also Grubb, *Mennonites of Butler County, Ohio,* page 30.)

The Amish in Michigan

Newaygo County

The Amish began to settle in Newaygo County in the White Cloud area about the year 1895. This settlement seems to have lasted for about twenty-five years. Eventually the Amish of the area either united with the White Cloud Mennonite Church or moved to other areas. Typical Amish names in the Newaygo County settlement, which was located near Diamond Loch, were Chupp, Fry, Hochstetler, Kauffman, Miller, Schmucker, Schrock, Stutzman, Troyer, and Yoder. Included in the settlement was a preacher, Daniel Miller from Lagrange County, Indiana. John F. Funk visited the Amish settlement at Diamond Loch in December 1897. He reports that Preacher Daniel Miller allowed him (Funk) to preach the sermon in the morning worship service, December 5. "Good attention and a fair attendance. There are several families here, about nine miles away from the others. Land is more hilly here. Meeting was held at house of David Yoder."

Alpena County

There was a small settlement of Amish in Alpena County established about the year 1897, and which lasted only a few years. Some of these members removed to Oscoda County and helped to establish the Amish settlement there in the year 1900. The Alpena County settlement was located near the town of Alpena.

Oscoda County

In the year 1900 a number of Amish families moved to the area around Mio from Alpena County, Michigan, and from Geauga County, Ohio. The congregation was organized in 1901. At that time the ministers consisted of Emanuel Schlabach, David Nissley, Jacob Gascho (bishop, 1909-), Yost Yoder, and David D. Schlabach who was ordained to the office of bishop in 1903. Since that time the following have served as bishops: Jacob Gascho, ordained in 1908, and Levi S. Troyer (1870-1954), ordained preacher in 1910 and bishop in 1939. Other ministers were Daniel Miller, Samuel Weaver, and Benjamin Schlabach. A total of about sixty Amish families over the years settled in Oscoda County. For a time there were two congregations: one near Fairview, and one in Elmer Township. The numerical high point was reached about 1905. But in recent years, especially since the death of Bishop Levi S. Troyer, the Amish have been moving away. In 1956 the membership was twenty, and by 1960 it had dwindled to fourteen. The services are in charge of a lay brother named Ezra Kauffman who has been delegated with the responsibility of conducting the worship services. The few members who are left are evidently moderating in their Amish beliefs somewhat, for it was the Beachy Amish who held communion there November 6, 1960. The group had always been fairly progressive; a Sunday school was held every other Sunday, alternating with the preaching services, in the 1920's.

Ogemaw County

The Amish began to move into Ogemaw County in 1908 and the settlement lasted for twenty-five years. A number of the early families came from Nobles County, Minnesota. Included in the settlement were such names as Bender, Eash, Gascho, Gerber, Jantzi, Kropf, Miller, and Swartz. Some of the families came from Oscoda County, Michigan, while others were from Elkhart County, Indiana. The bishops of the group were Joseph N. Gerber and Jacob Gascho. Other ministers who served were John B. Gerber, Klaus Jantzi, Jacob Swartz, and Solomon Jantzi. At its high point there were about twenty families in the settlement. Beginning in 1925 the families began to move away, mostly to Ontario, and by 1933 the congregation had died out.

Midland County

The Amish began to move into Midland County about the year 1909, and settled about fourteen miles north of Midland. These settlers came from the Elkhart-Lagrange Amish settlement in Indiana. The only person to serve as bishop for the group was Peter Yoder, 1925-28. The last family moved away in 1930. A number of those who remained united with the Midland Mennonite Church. One of the Amish bishops, in discussing the transfer of an Amish member to the Mennonites, said to Eli A. Bontrager, the Mennonite preacher: "Well, 's iss besser als nichs" (Well, it is better than nothing).

Arenac County

Amish families began to move into the Au Gres area of Arenac County in 1905. In the course of time the Au Gres Amish moderated in their Amish views, and in 1911 were organized by S. J. Swartzendruber, and became affiliated with the Conservative Amish Mennonite Conference. In 1960 it was reported that there was still one Amish member who considered himself a member of the Oscoda County Amish congregation.

Saint Joseph County

The Amish began to locate in Saint Joseph County, Michigan, in the Centerville and Mendon areas in the year 1911. By 1960 three congregations had developed which are known as West, Middle, and East.

27

These three congregations have a membership of about 170. There are three bishops in the group: William P. Miller of the West District, and David S. Bontrager and William J. Bontrager of the East District. The ministers are Alva Bontrager, Ervin J. Yoder, and Deacon Henry Miller of the West congregation; William D. Hochstetler, Reuben S. Bontrager, and Deacon Samuel N. Bontrager of the Middle District; and Alva Bontrager of the East congregation. The Saint Joseph County Amish are the only active congregations of that faith in the state of Michigan in 1960.

Calhoun County

A number of Amish families from Lagrange and Daviess counties, Indiana, and from Saint Joseph County, Michigan, began to settle in the vicinity of Homer in the southeastern part of Calhoun County in 1941. Regular services were started on December 1 of that year. The minister for the group was Alvin J. Yoder, and Henry N. Miller of Middlebury had the bishop oversight. The settlement lasted for less than a decade.

Hillsdale County

A number of Amish families settled near the town of Jerome in the spring of 1945. The settlement also received a few settlers from Daviess County, Indiana. Amos Stoll was the resident minister of the group and Albert Graber of Middlebury had the bishop oversight of the congregation. By 1949 the membership was thirty-nine. This settlement, however, did not prove to be permanently attractive to the few families who were living there.

A second Amish settlement was made ten years later, about 1955, by Swiss Amish from Allen County, Ohio. The minister of this group in 1960 was Levi R. Graber, whose address was Camden. In contrast with all the other Amish of Indiana and Michigan, except those in Adams County, these Swiss Amish employ the Swiss dialect in their services.

*   *   *

All the major Amish settlements in Indiana and Michigan are treated in *The Mennonite Encyclopedia* except the Marshall County settlement. A student in Goshen College named Allen K. Yoder made a careful investigation of the history of the Marshall County Amish and got much information from Jacob Borkholder, Sr., who in December 1958 was in his ninety-fifth year.

Evangelical Mennonite Church

The founder of the Evangelical Mennonites was Henry Egly, 1824-1890. He was born in Baden, Germany, and came to Butler County, Ohio, with his parents in 1839. In 1851 he settled at Linn Grove, French Township, Adams County, Indiana. He had been ordained as deacon in the year 1850 in Ohio, he became a preacher in 1854, and was ordained as bishop in 1858. As a result of illness, coupled with much meditation and prayer, and from which illness he felt that he was divinely healed, he came to realize deeply the need of personal faith and genuine conversion. It is said that he was excommunicated by the Old Order Amish in 1865. The next year he set up a new church which was simply nicknamed "Egly Amish" and was so known for many years. The group officially adopted the name Defenseless Mennonite Church in 1908, but forty years later changed it to the Evangelical Mennonite Church. The chief congregations of the group historically were the one at Linn Grove in Adams County; Grabill in Allen County; Edna Mills in Tippecanoe County; and Woodburn in Allen County. A number of other churches in Indiana and Michigan have been established more recently.

In 1911 the Defenseless Mennonites in co-operation with the Central Conference of Mennonites set up what is now known as the Congo Inland Mission. In the course of time directors for this mission were added from the General Conference Mennonite Church, and the Central Conference of Mennonites also merged with the General Conference Mennonite Church. At the present time the control of the Congo Inland Mission is vested about as follows: one half in the General Conference Mennonite Church, and one fourth each in the Evangelical Mennonite Church and Evangelical Mennonite Brethren. The annual budget of this mission now runs at about $280,000.00. At the end of 1959 the Congo Inland Mission was able to report over 22,000 church members, with seventy missionaries on the field plus fifty-four children. This is one of the most successful Mennonite missions anywhere, if not the most successful. Since 1953 the Evangelical Mennonite Brethren and the Evangelical Mennonite Church have been affiliated in what is known as the Conference of Evangelical Mennonites. The organ of the Evangelical Mennonites is *The Evangelical Mennonite.*

Two ministers of the Evangelical Mennonite Church who do not have pastorates because of other work are Dr. Milo A. Rediger, born 1913, who has been affiliated with Taylor University, Upland, Indiana, since 1943, where he serves as vice-president and academic dean; and Alvin G. Becker of Woodburn, Indiana, who is also widely known because of his promotional work for the Northern Bible Society.

In 1889, the year before his death, Bishop Henry Egly visited John F. Funk, Mennonite publisher of Elkhart, Indiana. Egly desired to have a hymnbook printed. Funk commented in his diary: "They seem to be warm and devoted Christians." After identifying the visitor as the "originator of the Egly Church," Funk added: "They are positive Mennonites and we cannot discard them."

Following are the chief congregations of the Evangelical Mennonite Church in Indiana and Michigan.

BERNE

French Township, Adams County, Indiana

This was the original congregation of the "Egly Amish," and it was formed in the year 1866. The first meetinghouse of the group was built five years later. In 1881 the 1871 meetinghouse was replaced, which building was in turn remodeled in 1937, and again in 1947. Outstanding in the life of this church was the revival of 1880 which resulted in seventy-five converts. The Indiana-Michigan Amish Mennonite Conference held its sessions in the Egly meetinghouse in 1900.

Ministers who have served in the Berne congregation of French Township have been Henry Egly, Joseph Egly, Chris Egly, Moses Rupp, David Schindler, C. N. Stucky, Eli Lantz, Emanuel M. Becker, Henry Klopfenstein, and N. J. Schmucker. E. G. Steiner is the present pastor, and the membership is 285.

GRABILL EVANGELICAL MENNONITE CHURCH

Cedar Creek Township, Allen County, Indiana

The Grabill Evangelical Mennonite Church was also established in 1866, and the first meetinghouse was built in 1875. In 1912 a new meetinghouse was built in the town of Grabill. The 1912 church building was remodeled in 1937. Ministers who have served in the Grabill congregation are Richard Diemer, Reuben Cantrell, Jerry H. Sauder, Aaron Sauder, David Sauder, and Don W. Klopfenstein. The last-named is the present pastor, and the membership is 139.

EDNA MILLS

Lafayette, 26th and Kossuth Streets, Indiana

Amish Mennonites must have settled in the area of Edna Mills in Clinton County, Indiana, soon after 1840. For example, the 1874 *Lagrange County Atlas*, page 20, indicates that J. J. Bontrager was born there in the year 1843. Edna Mills is located in Clinton County, but is also close to the counties of Tippecanoe and Carroll, both to the north of Clinton County. It is said that the Amish Mennonites who settled in the area of Edna Mills moved there from Bluffton, Ohio, and from Adams County, Indiana. The first minister was Christian Zimmerman, 1825-1899, an immigrant from Baden, Germany. His wife was Christina Schlatter of France who was born in 1828 and who died in 1897. Both are buried in the Egly Amish Cemetery nine tenths of a mile south of the bridge at the east edge of Edna Mills. In 1865 Preacher Christian Zimmerman and another ordained brother named Jacob Ehresman, 1806-1894, both of Rossville in Clinton County, attended the Amish General Conference in Wayne County, Ohio. Bishop Henry Egly was another attendant. The second minister who served in the Edna Mills congregation was Christian Gerber, 1847-1931; and the third was John Zimmerman, 1832-1909. The Egly Amish of the Edna Mills community, some ten miles east of Lafayette, worshiped in private homes until 1885 when they erected a meetinghouse four miles northwest of Edna Mills about a hundred rods west of the Carroll County line, in Perry Township, Tippecanoe County. The Egly Amish worshiped in this meetinghouse from 1885 until the 1940's.

In 1940 a number of interested Evangelical Mennonites began to hold services in the city of Lafayette. In 1941 the Lafayette Evangelical Mennonites began to build a church building, and the first services were held in this new building in April 1942. The congregation was organized formally on August 2, 1942, with twenty-four charter members. This building was enlarged in 1951 to provide more room for Sunday-school purposes. The country meetinghouse near Edna Mills was sold and converted into a dwelling. In 1959 the person living in the former Egly meetinghouse was a German Baptist named Loran Jessup, and his address was Route 4, Lafayette, Indiana.

Ministers who have served since Christian Gerber are Elmer Klopfenstein, Samuel Ehresman, John Rediger, Levi Mellinger, Eli J. Oyer, Reuben C. Cantrell, Eli G. Steiner, Paul McCoy, Owen L. Haifley, and Floyd Greiner. The annual budget of the Lafayette congregation is about $10,000. The membership is sixty-two. This congregation also established an outpost called the Lafayette Gospel Center, and Stanley I. Rupp serves as its pastor.

WOODBURN EVANGELICAL MENNONITE CHURCH

Maumee Township, Allen County, Indiana

The Woodburn congregation originated in the year 1893. Three years later the first meetinghouse was built. The 1896 meetinghouse was remodeled and enlarged in 1926, and again in 1949. Preachers who have served in the Woodburn congregation are Andrew M. Gerig, 1896-1917; Eli J. Oyer, 1921-36; Harold I. Fraker, 1936-44; Emanuel M. Rocke, 1944-51; and Charles L. Rupp, 1951- . In the period between 1917 and 1921 the congregation had no regularly appointed pastor, but the interim minister was Deacon Andrew S. Yaggy, assisted by various ministers.. Forrest Yoder is the present pastor, and the membership is 149.

HIGHLAND BETHEL MENNONITE CHURCH

Ridgewood Drive and Leo Road, Fort Wayne, Indiana

The Fort Wayne congregation is the third Evangelical Mennonite Church to be established in Allen County. The work was begun in 1937 when a church building was built. The first services were held in this new house of worship December 19, 1937. It was not until November 19, 1944, however, that the congregation was formally organized. At that point there were twenty-one charter members. In 1949 a new brick building structure was started, one block from the older house of worship; the completed house of worship was dedicated September 17, 1950. The pastors who have served this church are Milo Rediger, Paul Rupp, and Maurice L. Klopfenstein. Kenneth Becker is the present pastor, and the membership is eighty-five.

BROOK SIDE MENNONITE

Saint Joe Road, Fort Wayne, Indiana

The Brook Side Evangelical Mennonite Church was established in Fort Wayne in the year 1958. By the close of 1960 the membership was about thirty, and Paul McCoy was serving as pastor.

ADRIAN

Adrian, Michigan

A basement church was built in 1947 at Adrian, Michigan, the congregation was organized on October 23, 1949, and the superstructure of the church building was built in 1953. Virgil Oyer is the present pastor, and the membership is twenty-five.

MIDLAND MENNONITE CHURCH

899 Poseyville Road, Midland, Midland Township, Midland County, Michigan

The work of the Evangelical Mennonite Church in Midland, Michigan, was begun, 1952-53. The congregation was formally organized

January 25, 1953. By 1955 there were twenty-eight members in the congregation. Ministers who have served are Virgil Oyer, Owen L. Haifley, and Charles L. Rupp. The last-named is the present pastor, and the membership is forty-five.

Central Conference Mennonite Church

The Central Conference Mennonite Church originated in the Rock Creek Amish Mennonite Church of Illinois, which was often known as the Yoder Church after its outstanding bishop, Jonathan Yoder, 1795-1869. Later the congregation officially took the name, North Danvers Mennonite Church. In this congregation Joseph Stuckey, 1825-1902, served as a capable bishop and strong leader. "Father Stuckey," as he was known, was ordained to the office of bishop in 1864. He was deeply loved by his people. In 1872 he refused to excommunicate an Amish brother who wrote a German poem entitled, "The Joyful Message." This poem taught the doctrine of universalism, that all people would ultimately be saved. Evidently Bishop Stuckey considered the brother a rather harmless individual and believed that he did not merit excommunication. The other Amish bishops of the state thereupon broke fellowship with Bishop Stuckey, so that he more or less stood alone as far as conference affiliation was concerned. Nevertheless he traveled widely in various areas of the Amish Mennonite Church and exerted considerable influence. The Stuckey group began to hold conferences in 1899 which were of the nature of Bible study meetings, rather than district conferences in the full sense of the term. The Central Conference Mennonite Church was formally organized in 1908 when twelve congregations affiliated themselves together as a distinct branch of the Amish Mennonite Church. The group did not use the term Amish, however, but spoke of themselves only as Mennonites.

Six congregations of Central Conference Mennonites were established in Indiana and Michigan. These are Silver Street in Elkhart County, 1892; Topeka in Lagrange County, 1893; Zion, Goodland, in Newton County, 1895; Eighth Street Mennonite Church, Goshen, Elkhart County, 1913; Middlebury, Elkhart County, 1923; and Comins, Oscoda County, Michigan, 1924. These congregations were all treated under the General Conference Mennonite Church with which they are now affiliated; therefore their history will not be given here.

The General Conference Mennonite Church and the Central Conference Mennonite Church merged in the year 1945. Since there was already a Middle District Conference in the General Conference Mennonite Church, this merger created the odd situation that the General

Conference Mennonite Church then had both a Central Conference and a Middle District Conference. This situation was rectified in 1957, when there was a complete merger of the Middle District and Central Conference to form the new Central District of the General Conference Mennonite Church.

Conservative Mennonite Conference

INDIANA

TOWNLINE MENNONITE CHURCH

Section 32, Newbury Township, Lagrange County, Indiana

The meetinghouse of the Townline congregation stands six and one-half miles southwest of Shipshewana, and four miles west of the village of Emma. It is on the line between Newbury and Eden townships.

When the Amish Mennonites settled the Elkhart-Lagrange Amish community in 1841, they came predominantly from two areas: Somerset County, Pennsylvania, and Holmes County, Ohio. About 1845 the first division occurred between those Amish which came from Pennsylvania, and those which came from Ohio. This schism was healed in 1847 through the efforts of a mediation committee from the state of Ohio. It is said that a similar division occurred the next year, 1848, in Holmes County, Ohio, with the main issue being the new practice of baptizing persons as they knelt in a stream of water, rather than in private homes or barns.

In 1854 there was a division in the Elkhart-Lagrange Amish community, similar to the one in Holmes County, Ohio, in 1848. Here also the Amish Mennonites introduced baptism in streams, rather than in private homes, as had been the Amish custom prior to that time. The Clinton Frame congregation was formed in 1854 as was the similar Haw Patch congregation (now Maple Grove, Topeka), Howard-Miami, etc. The Townline congregation was created in 1876, largely by Amish Mennonite families who withdrew from the Forks Amish Mennonite congregation, which had been formed in 1857. Names in the Townline congregation were Bontrager, Eash, Hostetler, Miller, Schrock, Weirich, Yoder, and Zook. The total number of members who formed the Townline congregation was about seventy-five. Two leaders, John P. King and Chris Yoder, came from Logan County, Ohio, to Indiana and organized the new Townline congregation on March 25, 1876. The name Townline really means Township line. There were no essential differences between the older Forks and the new Townline congregation in doctrine, piety, or practice. It is true that there had been some petty criticisms of the Forks preacher, Joseph Bontrager, but nothing of significance. Bontrager affiliated with the new congregation and served as its first minister. The bishop oversight for the Townline congregation was assumed by Joseph Yoder, formerly a preacher in the Haw Patch congregation, but ordained bishop in the Barker Street congregation, 1876.

Some six months after Townline was organized the congregation decided to choose a young minister to assist Joseph Bontrager. The choice of the Townline congregation was John M. Hostetler, who was ordained October 19, 1876. On that date the first communion services were also held. The meetinghouse was built in 1877, and the deed indicates that the land was formally transferred to the trustees November 1, 1877. The meetinghouse cost $600.00. A number of visiting bishops also helped the Townline congregation, including Peter Stuckey of Fulton County, Ohio, and Eli Yoder of Allen County, Indiana. The most dominant figure in the history of the Townline congregation was Jonathan ("Joni") J. Troyer, who was ordained deacon in the Townline congregation in 1883, preacher, 1886, and bishop, 1895. He served as bishop for thirty-five years until his death in 1930, although he was partially retired the last three years of his life. Under his jurisdiction Sunday school was held in the Townline congregation as early as 1890.

One of the surprising things in the history of the Townline congregation was its slow growth. While the neighboring Amish Mennonite congregations, Forks, Clinton Frame, and Haw Patch, prospered, the Townline congregation did not. By 1890 the congregation still had only about 125 members. By 1900 the membership had dropped to seventy. In 1907 the congregation was further weakened when a sizable portion of the Townline members moved to Shelbyville, Illinois, to follow the so-called "sleeping" preacher, John D. Kauffman, 1847-1913, where they formed the Mt. Hermon Amish Mennonite congregation. (Kauffman preached while in a trance, which was possibly the result of self-hypnosis.) In 1914 the congregation had forty members. It has sometimes been remarked facetiously that the coming of the automobile accounts for the growth of the Conservative Amish Mennonite congregations. That is, a number of Old Order Amish families transferred their membership to the Townline congregation where the automobile was permitted. In 1922 Townline had 100 members and in 1927, 150 members. In 1927 a basement was dug just west of the Townline meetinghouse and the meetinghouse erected on the foundation walls which were then built. Sixteen feet was also added to the Townline meetinghouse in 1927. In 1952 the Townline meetinghouse was furnished with new benches and new pulpit furniture. In 1956 a new front was placed on the south end of the

meetinghouse. Through the formation of several daughter congregations the membership of the Townline congregation in 1959 was only
117.

GRINER CONSERVATIVE MENNONITE CHURCH

Section 27, Middlebury Township, Elkhart County, Indiana

In 1921 the Townline congregation purchased the Griner church
building (which is located on what is now State Highway 13 two miles
south of Middlebury) from the Lutherans for $1,000.00 A portion of
the Townline congregation then formed a daughter congregation to meet
in the new Griner Conservative meetinghouse. This new congregation
was organized in 1922. Services then alternated between Townline and
Griner Sunday by Sunday, until 1935 when each congregation began to
meet weekly. In 1959 the membership of the Griner congregation was
234, with Sam. T. Eash continuing to serve as bishop, to which office he
had been ordained in 1927.

CUBA CONSERVATIVE MENNONITE CHURCH

Section 32, Springfield Township, Allen County, Indiana

The Cuba congregation is located twelve miles northeast of Fort
Wayne, near Harlan. The congregation first met in a schoolhouse in
Defiance County, Ohio, but by 1929 had begun to meet in a schoolhouse
in Allen County, Indiana, one mile north of the present church building.
The congregation was organized in the year 1924 by Bishop S. J. Swartzendruber of Pigeon, Michigan. The meetinghouse was built in 1948. The
1959 membership of the Cuba congregation was 209. In 1960 the congregation built a splendid church cabin at a cost of $18,000.00.

PLEASANT GROVE CONSERVATIVE MENNONITE CHURCH

Section 21, Clinton Township, Elkhart County, Indiana

The Pleasant Grove meetinghouse stands one and one-eighth miles
south, and one-half mile west, of the Clinton Frame meetinghouse, on
the Rock Run Road (C.R. 38). It is two miles north of Millersburg,
and one and one-half miles west. The Pleasant Grove congregation is a
more recent daughter of the Townline and Griner congregations. The
meetinghouse was built 1947-48. The first service was held in the new
Pleasant Grove meetinghouse on August 15, 1948. This new church
building was erected to relieve the crowded conditions in the Townline
and Griner congregations. Clarence A. Yoder was ordained bishop in
1950 and continues to serve the Pleasant Grove congregation. The 1959
membership was 240.

AUSTIN CONSERVATIVE MENNONITE CHURCH

Mann Avenue, Austin, Jennings Township, Scott County, Indiana

The Conservative Mennonite work was begun in Scott County in 1952 in charge of Jesse P. Zook. Austin is thirty-five miles north of Louisville, Kentucky. Jesse had taken the two-year Christian Workers' Course at Eastern Mennonite College, Harrisonburg, Virginia. The Conservative Mennonites built their meetinghouse in Austin in 1953. By 1959 the membership of the Austin congregation was fourteen.

CHRISTIAN MISSION CHURCH

Berne, Monroe Township, Adams County, Indiana

The Conservative Mennonites began mission work in Adams County in 1954, under the leadership of William J. Stutzman and his wife Sarah. Sarah's sister and her large family were living at Berne without the opportunity to attend worship services in the Conservative Mennonite Church. The small group is worshiping in a former schoolhouse. The 1961 membership was thirty-five, and the attendance sixty.

BETHEL CONSERVATIVE MENNONITE CHURCH

Section 21, Union Township, Elkhart County, Indiana

The Bethel meetinghouse is located on County Road 50, four tenths of a mile west of C.R. 9, and three and one-half miles northeast of Nappanee. The Bethel congregation is composed largely of Old Order Amish families who had transferred to the Conservative Mennonite Church. The Bethel meetinghouse was built, 1954-55, at a cost of $20,000.00. The formal opening was held on February 6, 1955, with J. C. Wenger preaching the sermon. Homer D. Miller was ordained preacher in the Old Order Amish Church in 1948, transferred to the Conservative Mennonite congregation in 1954, where his ministry was soon recognized, and in 1957 he was ordained bishop to have the oversight of the Bethel congregation. The 1959 membership at Bethel was eighty-nine.

The Conservative Amish Mennonites of Elkhart and Lagrange counties held their services in German almost exclusively from 1876 until 1947. During the next decade the transition was made almost entirely to the English language, so that by 1957 there was almost no German left in the services. Following the church services each Sunday there is much conversation in the Pennsylvania-German dialect, however. Services are now held in the several congregations each Sunday morning. In the Townline congregation the old German hymnal was used for many years, *Eine Sammlung von schönen Lieder,* with its English supplement.

(Translated this title reads, *A Collection of Beautiful Songs*.) In 1941 the *Church Hymnal, Mennonite*, was adopted at Townline. Midweek meetings have been held since 1946. Revival meetings are held annually. Summer Bible school was adopted in 1948. An excellent account of the Conservative Mennonite churches in Northern Indiana was written by Ora Troyer and published in the *Mennonite Historical Bulletin* for April 1959. Bishop Sam. T. Eash also gave a valuable historical address on July 29, 1951, in a historical meeting held on the lawn of Irvin Yoder, several miles east of Goshen; this address was available to the present writer, who was also present at the meeting.

MICHIGAN

PIGEON RIVER CONSERVATIVE MENNONITE CHURCH

Windsor Township, Huron County

The Pigeon River Conservative Mennonite meetinghouse is located near the village of Pigeon, several miles south of Saginaw Bay. In the year 1900 Amish Mennonite families from Croghan, New York, came to Huron County and made their homes there. Included in this group was Michael S. Zehr who was later ordained preacher. These families were joined in 1901 by a number of other Amish Mennonite families from Ontario. In that year Sunday school started. In 1902 the first communion service was held, in charge of Bishop Jacob M. Bender of Ontario. In 1904 the first meetinghouse was built, thirty-two by forty feet in size. The cost was about $1,000.00. The dedication date was set for November 10, 1904. During the night prior to this date the church building caught fire from oily rags in nail kegs which had been placed in the anterooms for people to lay their outer garments on while in the worship service. These oily rags became ignited and burned holes through the floor so that piles of nails were found in the basement the next morning amid the ashes from the fire. Fortunately the fires went out of themselves, and after cleaning up the interior of the auditorium the dedication service was held as scheduled. The 1904 meetinghouse was enlarged in 1909. It was replaced by a new house of worship in 1957.

In the year 1904 Bishop Solomon J. Swartzendruber moved to Huron County from Iowa. He was the leading figure in 1910 in establishing an association of Conservative Amish Mennonite congregations into a conference which took the name officially, *Conservative Amish Mennonite Conference*. (In 1954 the name was changed to Conservative Mennonite Conference.) At the first conference in 1910, which was held November 24, 25, at Pigeon, Michigan, only three ministers were present besides the two Pigeon Amish Mennonite ministers, S. J. Swartzendruber and M. S. Zehr. In addition to these two ministers, others who have served in the Pigeon River Conservative Mennonite congregation were: Jacob Yoder, Dan. Shetler, Edwin Albrecht, Raymond Byler, Emmanuel Swartzendruber, Willard R. Mayer, and Earl J. Maust. The last three are the present officers of the congregation. The 1959 membership was 264.

RIVERSIDE CONSERVATIVE MENNONITE CHURCH
Whitney Township, Arenac County

The Riverside meetinghouse is located one mile east and five miles north of the town of Au Gres, Michigan, about sixty miles north of Saginaw. This congregation was formed by Old Order Amish families who moved to Arenac County from Ogemaw and Oscoda counties, Michigan. At an early date these Amish families (unorganized as a congregation) began to hold Sunday school services in the Riverside and Santiago schoolhouses. The congregation was organized by S. J. Swartzendruber, of the Pigeon (Michigan), A.M. Church, in 1911. Ministers from the Pigeon River congregation began to come to the Riverside congregation periodically to preach for them. In the course of time Deacon Jacob Swartz was also authorized to preach. Noah Miller was ordained preacher in 1918. In 1924 Peter Swartz was ordained preacher, and in 1944, bishop. In 1937 Peter Swartz's son, Levi K. Swartz, was also ordained preacher. Elmer Jantzi was ordained preacher in 1953. Deacon Noah Swartzendruber of Delaware moved to the Riverside congregation in 1940. The 1959 membership was ninety-three.

FLINT CONSERVATIVE MENNONITE CHURCH
2128 East Williamson Avenue, Flint, Michigan
Burton Township, Genesee County

The Conservative Mennonites built their first mission building in Flint in 1929 and ordained Noah Swartzendruber to take charge of the work. He was later succeeded by Edwin Albrecht, then Andrew Jantzi, and in 1948 by Jesse L. Yoder, who was ordained preacher on August 9, 1949. The 1959 membership of the Flint congregation was thirty-seven.

FAIRHAVEN CONSERVATIVE MENNONITE CHURCH
Sebewaing, Fairhaven Township, Huron County

Fairhaven is an outpost of the Pigeon River Conservative Mennonite Church. It was established in the year 1938. In 1945 the group purchased the town hall, and three years later remodeled it. The minister

of the congregation is Loren L. Dietzel, who was ordained preacher
December 27, 1953. In 1955 he wrote: "We are working as a mission
outpost and have our membership at Pigeon River. There are ten
families assisting as teachers and workers. Our main outreach is summer
Bible school. We have forty children from our church and twice that
number from non-Mennonite homes. Possibly half of these have no
church home." As late as 1959 no resident membership had been established: the Fairhaven members were reckoned as members at Pigeon
River.

MENNONITE GOSPEL MISSION

Vassar, Tuscola County

This is another outpost of the Pigeon River congregation which
resulted from an investigative tour which was made in 1938. It was decided to begin mission work at Vassar. The first convert was made the
next year, 1939. Emmanuel Swartzendruber was placed in charge of the
work. In 1945 Orie Kauffman took charge. The meetinghouse was built
in 1950. Elam C. Bender, the present preacher, was ordained in 1956.
The membership in 1959 was sixteen.

MOUNT MORRIS CONSERVATIVE MENNONITE CHURCH

1478 West Mount Morris Road,

Mount Morris Township, Genesee County

Mount Morris was established as a Conservative Mennonite Mission
in the year 1953. The parsonage was built in 1955. The minister is
Raymond Swartz, ordained preacher in 1953. The 1959 membership was
twelve.

RIVERVIEW CONSERVATIVE MENNONITE CHURCH

Mottville Township, St. Joseph County

The Riverview meetinghouse is located on Highway 131 south of
White Pigeon. The congregation was organized November 13, 1952. A
basement meetinghouse was built the previous year, and the superstructure added in 1954. The Riverview congregation tends in some respects to
bear a closer resemblance to the Mennonite churches of Northern Indiana than to the Conservative Mennonite churches. The Executive Committee of the Conservative Mennonite Conference placed E. B. Peachey
in charge as the original bishop of the congregation. In 1955 Orie Kauffman, the resident minister, was ordained to the office of bishop. The
1959 membership was 184. Many of the members were formerly members
of the Townline or Griner congregations.

CUMBER CONSERVATIVE MENNONITE CHURCH

Cumber, Sanilac County

The most recent outpost of the Pigeon River Conservative Mennonite Church is the mission in Cumber, which was established in 1955. The pastor is Luke D. Yoder, who was ordained preacher in 1957. As recently as 1959 there were no resident members at Cumber.

MINISTERIAL LIST

Conservative Mennonite Conference

Indiana and Michigan

Note: It is rather arbitrary to list the ministers of the Townline and associated congregations as Conservative Mennonites prior to the formation of the Conservative Amish Mennonite Conference in 1910. As a matter of fact the Townline congregation worked closely with the Pretty Prairie, Barker Street, and Leo congregations in Indiana, as well as with the Amish Mennonites of Logan County, Ohio. On the other hand, the Haw Patch (Topeka), Clinton Frame, Forks, and West Market Street (Nappanee) Amish Mennonite congregations formed a second circle which worked closely together. The chief congregations which formed the Indiana-Michigan Amish Mennonite Conference in 1888 and the following years were the latter circle: Haw Patch, Clinton, Forks, Nappanee, and Pretty Prairie. Barker Street became very weak and was ultimately cared for co-operatively by the Mennonite and Amish Mennonite Conferences. Leo did not affiliate with the Amish Mennonite Conference until 1905. Townline remained independent, from its founding, until it was identified with the Conservative Amish Mennonite Conference.

Name	Office & Ordination	Congregation
Edwin Albrecht, 1899-	Preacher 1926, Bishop 1953	Pigeon River, Flint, Cuba
Elam C. Bender, 1928-	Preacher 1956	Vassar
Fred S. Bontrager, 1898-	Deacon 1934	Old Order Amish, Griner
Joseph J. Bontrager, 1830-1921	Preacher 1867	Forks, Townline (Kansas, Montana)
Calvin Borntrager, 1936-	Preacher 1956	Townline
Raymond Byler, 1914-	Preacher 1940, Bishop 1958	Pigeon River, Florida
Menno Coblentz, 1898-1959	Preacher 1932, Bishop 1942	Cuba, Florida
Loren Dietzel, 1913-	Preacher 1952	Fairhaven
Daniel J. Eash, 1881-	Deacon 1929	Townline
Samuel T. Eash, 1891-	Preacher 1923, Bishop 1927	Townline, Griner
John M. Hostetler, 1839-1914	Preacher 1876	Townline
Andrew Jantzi, 1912-	Preacher 1943	Flint, Florida
Elmer Jantzi, 1925-	Preacher 1952	Riverside
Louis D. Kauffman, 1915-	Preacher 1953	Griner
Orie Kauffman, 1909-	Preacher 1947, Bishop 1955	Vassar, Riverview
Edwin J. Knepp, 1929-	Preacher 1953	Pleasant Grove
Noah Kropf, 1883-	Deacon 1911	Townline (Forks Mennonite)
Earl J. Maust, 1898-	Preacher 1930	Pigeon River
Willard R. Mayer, 1926-	Preacher 1953, Bishop 1956	Pigeon River
Albert H. Miller, 1919-	Preacher 1956, Bishop 1960	Griner
Alpha H. Miller, 1925-	Deacon 1960	Townline
Christian J. Miller, 1890-	Preacher 1918	Townline (Old Order Amish)
Eli D. Miller, 1909-	Preacher 1948, Bishop 1956	Townline
Homer D. Miller, 1924-	Preacher 1948, Bishop 1957	(Old Order Amish) Bethel
Jacob E. Miller, 1903-	Preacher 1955	Bethel

Jonas D. Miller, 1904-	Preacher 1937	Townline, Ohio, Griner, Riverview
Manasses R. Miller, 1879-	Preacher 1924	Townline, Griner
Menno D. Miller, 1878-1950	Deacon 1915, Preacher 1915	Midland, Cuba
Noah C. Miller, 1865-1940	Preacher 1918	Riverside
Noah S. Miller, 1870-	Deacon 1920	Townline, Iowa
Menno S. Schrock, 1900-	Preacher 1935	(Old Order Amish) Pleasant Grove
Daniel J. Shetler, 1864-1938	Preacher 1912	Pigeon River
David Showalter, 1918-	Preacher 1951, Bishop 1955	Austin, Kentucky
William Stutzman, 1921-	Preacher 1957	Berne Mission
Levi K. Swartz, 1904-	Preacher 1937	Riverside
Peter Swartz, 1881-1950	Preacher 1924, Bishop 1944	Riverside
Raymond Swartz, 1920-	Preacher 1953	Mount Morris
Emmanuel Swartzendruber, 1893-	Preacher 1934, Bishop 1944	Pigeon River
Noah Swartzendruber, 1897-	Deacon 1929	Flint, Riverside
Solomon J. Swartzendruber, 1856-1932	Preacher c.1887, Bishop c.1890	Pigeon River
Jephtha S. Troyer, 1878-	Preacher 1913	Townline, Shore Mennonite
Jonathan J. Troyer, 1841-1930	Deacon 1883, Preacher 1886, Bishop 1895	Townline
Christian S. Yoder, 1845-1908	Deacon 1886	Townline
Clarence A. Yoder, 1917-	Preacher 1948, Bishop 1950	Pleasant Grove
Irvin C. Yoder, 1931-	Preacher 1960	Riverview
Jacob S. Yoder, 1863-1924	Preacher 1906	Pigeon River
Jesse L. Yoder, 1923-	Preacher 1949, Bishop 1958	Flint
John Yoder, 1916-	Preacher 1953	Cuba
John J. S. Yoder, 1884-	Preacher 1926	Townline, Griner, Townline
Joseph Yoder, 1822-1908	Preacher 1852, Bishop 1876	(Maple Grove A.M.) Townline, Barker Street (Iowa)
Luke D. Yoder, 1929-	Preacher 1957	Cumber
Michael S. Zehr, 1872-1944	Preacher 1905	Pigeon River
Noah Zehr, 1895-	Preacher 1933	Cuba, Griner, Riverview
Jesse P. Zook, 1926-	Preacher 1953	Austin

Missionary Church Association

A fine history of this group was written by Walter H. Lugibihl and Jared F. Gerig, *The Missionary Church Association*, Berne, Indiana, 1950. Of great value also is the *Missionary Church Association Directory of Officers, Churches, Ministers, and Missionaries*, 1959; also the annual *Conference Report and Directory*.

The Missionary Church Association originated in a schism from the Defenseless Mennonite Church. The long-time leader of the M.C.A. was J. E. Ramseyer, 1869-1944, who was dismissed from the Defenseless Church in 1896 for being rebaptized (immersed). He served as president of the M.C.A. from 1900 until his death in 1944. The founding date of the

M.C.A. was August 29, 1898, at Berne, Indiana. The leadership of the M.C.A. was originally sufficiently German that the conference minutes were kept in German from 1898 until 1907. The original German name of the church was *Missions Gemeinde Verein.*

In addition to the usual Christian doctrines of God existing eternally in three persons, Father, Son, and Holy Spirit; the fall of man; the Saviourhood of Jesus Christ; the Holy Spirit as the One who sanctifies; the church as the body of Christ, etc., the Missionary Church Association holds to the usual Mennonite doctrines of a brotherhood church, believers' baptism, and the like. The issues in 1898 are said to have been four or five. The history of the church lists the issues as follows: "the baptism with the Holy Spirit subsequent to the new birth, the second coming of our blessed Lord for His waiting saints, and the resurrection of the just before the great tribulation, which precedes the thousand years of peace on earth, and water baptism by immersion." The article on the Missionary Church Association in *The Mennonite Encyclopedia* lists an additional issue, that of divine healing.

True to its name, the M.C.A. has been very active in the field of missionary work both in the United States and abroad. The chief missions abroad of the M.C.A. are Sierra Leone, West Africa; Ecuador; Jamaica; Dominican Republic; Haiti; and the Hawaiian Islands. In co-operation with the Christian and Missionary Alliance the M.C.A. also carries on mission work in countries such as India, Japan, and Colombia. The M.C.A., with less than 10,000 members, has missionaries in sixteen different countries.

The goal of the M.C.A. has been to reach a total of 10,000 members by the year 1960; at this writing it appears that the goal was not met, although the membership does run over 7,000. Indiana has a total of nineteen congregations in twelve cities. The membership of these congregations runs from twenty-eight to 302, with an average of 114 per congregation. The total membership for Indiana in 1960 was 2,161. The congregations are located in the following cities and towns: Angola, Auburn, Berne (two churches), Decatur, Fort Wayne (seven churches), Grabill, Monroe, Mooresville, Bluffton, Peru, Woodburn, and Yoder.

The M.C.A. carries on work in sixteen locations in Michigan: Bad Axe, Battle Creek, Detroit, East Detroit, Elkton, Farwell, Flint, Jackson (three churches), Loomis, Midland, Rhodes, Roseville, Royal Oak, Sturgis, and Wayne. There are sixteen congregations with resident membership varying from fourteen to 180 members; the average membership of these sixteen congregations is sixty, and the total membership in 1960 was 969.

The organ of the M.C.A. is *The Missionary Worker.* The head-

28

quarters of the M.C.A. is Ramseyer Memorial Hall, 3901 South Wayne Avenue, Fort Wayne, Indiana. Fort Wayne is also the home of the M.C.A. institution, Fort Wayne Bible College, which was originally located at Bluffton, Ohio, and was established there in 1895. J. E. Ramseyer served as president of this institution from 1912 until his death in 1944.

Beachy Amish Mennonite Churches

The so-called Beachy Amish Mennonites are named for Moses M. Beachy of Salisbury, Pennsylvania, who served as a bishop in the Old Order Amish Mennonite Church from the year 1916 until his death in 1946. About the year 1927 his congregation was no longer recognized as being fully in agreement with the regular Old Order Amish congregations, and his followers were nicknamed "Beachy Amish."

A small Beachy Amish congregation was established in Miami County, Indiana, near the town of *Amboy*, in 1939. The first minister was Levi Sommers. In 1948 Ezra Miller and Enos Miller were ordained preachers, and one year later Ezra Miller was ordained bishop. In 1946 this Miami congregation of Beachy Amish converted a former brick schoolhouse into a meetinghouse. The group had eighteen charter members in 1939, by 1956 there were forty-nine members, and in 1959 the membership was sixty-seven.

The *Odon* congregation of Beachy Amish was established in 1948 in Daviess County, Indiana. The ministers who have served are Jacob D. Gingerich, bishop; William Yoder, and Ben S. Wagler. In 1959 the membership of the Odon congregation was 165.

In Northern Indiana the schism from the Old Order Amish was led by Bishop David O. Burkholder, 1886-1959, the son of the patriarchal Moses Borkholder, 1838-1933. Moses Borkholder was a preacher in the Old Order Amish Church of Marshall County, near *Nappanee*, Indiana, from 1862, and bishop from 1878, until his death in 1933. His son David O. Burkholder was ordained preacher in 1915 and bishop in 1917. In 1940 he withdrew from the Old Order Amish and organized what is now the Maple Lawn Amish Mennonite congregation on April 28, 1940. There were twenty-four charter members. The other ministers in the congregation have been Jacob L. Mast, 1898- , ordained preacher 1941; Irvin D. Miller, 1919- , ordained preacher 1947; and Steve Yoder, 1924- , ordained preacher 1952, and bishop 1954. The membership in 1959 was ninety-five.

A daughter congregation of Maple Lawn was established about five and one-half miles east of Goshen on State Road 4 in 1947. It is now known as the Fairhaven Amish Mennonite Church, but is listed in *The Mennonite Encyclopedia* as the Clinton Amish Mennonite Church. The Fairhaven congregation was organized on Ascension Day, 1947. The first meetinghouse was dedicated December 7, 1947. In 1951 the membership had reached 107, and in 1959 it was 173. Ministers who have served are Bishop David A. Bontrager, Moses J. Bontrager, Eli A. Miller, and Deacon Andrew J. Yoder. These so-called Burkholder Amish are in fellowship with the Beachy Amish congregations of the United States. They do not have a conference.

There is also a congregation of Beachy Amish in *Centerville,* Michigan, known as Oak Grove. It was established about the year 1954, and the following are serving as ministers: Bishop Clarence Miller, Moses Yoder, and Deacon Reuben E. Bontrager. There are thirty-two members in the congregation.

The Beachy Amish, including those known locally as Burkholder Amish, are intermediate in discipline between the stricter Old Order Amish and the less strict Conservative Mennonites. In many respects the Beachy Amish may be described as basically Old Order Amish who allow the use of electricity, tractors, automobiles, and meetinghouses. Their services are generally conducted in the German language, Amish garb is worn, and the singing is in unison, not four parts.

Woodlawn Amish Mennonite Church

Section 11, Clinton Township, Elkhart County, Indiana

The founder and leader of the Woodlawn Amish Mennonite congregation is Elam S. Hochstetler, 1902- , who is descended from a long line of respected Amish leaders. Jacob Hochstetler, 1704-1776, was the immigrant who came to America in 1736. Elam is descended from his son John Hochstetler, who died in 1805. John's son was Daniel Hochstetler, who died about 1844. Daniel's son in turn was Jonas D. Hochstetler, 1811-1875, who was ordained preacher in the Elkhart-Lagrange Amish Church the spring of 1844. Preacher Jonas in turn was the father of David J. Hochstetler, 1839-1929, who was ordained as an Amish preacher, June 16, 1863. Preacher David in turn was the father of Bishop Samuel D. Hochstetler, 1872-1954, who was ordained preacher in the Amish Church of Brown County, Indiana, November 3, 1902, and bishop in the Elkhart County Amish Church, November 23, 1923. Bishop Samuel D. Hochstetler's son is Elam S. Hochstetler, founder of the Woodlawn Amish Mennonite Church. This church is located north of the Fish Lake Road in Section 11 of Clinton Township, Elkhart County.

Elam S. Hochstetler was ordained preacher in the Elkhart County

Amish Church in 1939, and bishop in 1954. He was a man of rather progressive views, with more vision than characterized many of his Amish fellow ministers, and he had deep convictions for Bible study, and for a "clean life" which does not make use of beverage alcohol or tobacco. He also had a vision for doing mission work. At the same time he was less rigidly opposed to modern farm machinery such as tractors. Moreover, he saw no need to "shun" members who transferred to a less strict church of the Mennonite faith. This view of not practicing "avoidance" toward those who united with a more progressive Mennonite or Amish Mennonite congregation was held by Elam's grandfather. The consequence of Bishop Elam Hochstetler's progressive views led to a breaking of fellowship between the other Amish leaders of Northern Indiana and himself. The final break in fellowship came the summer of 1956. The next year the congregation of Elam Hochstetler began to permit the use of automobiles. In 1959 the congregation decided to build a meeting-house. The first use of the basement church was on June 7, 1959, and the first service in the main auditorium of the first floor was held December 20, 1959. It is located four miles north of Millersburg, and a half mile east. In 1960 the group decided by vote that the majority favored the name "Woodlawn" for the new congregation. By late in 1960 the membership of the Woodlawn Amish Mennonite congregation was 168. The Woodlawn congregation is exploring the possibility of merging with the Burkholder Amish Mennonites of Northern Indiana, which in turn are recognized as in fellowship with the Beachy Amish churches of the United States. Elam S. Hochstetler also has the bishop oversight of the fourteen former Old Order Amish members at Fairview, Oscoda County, Michigan.

Non-Conference Conservative Mennonites

In 1957 the Pleasant View Conservative Mennonite Church, of Daviess County, Indiana, was established near the town of Montgomery. This congregation is recognized as in fellowship with those former Conservative Amish Mennonite congregations which do not recognize the jurisdiction of the Conservative Mennonite Conference. These congregations have only one bishop in the United States, Roman H. Miller of Hartville, Ohio. The ministers of the Pleasant View [Non-conference] Conservative Mennonite Church are Andrew J. Overholt and Deacon Elmo E. Stoll. In 1959 there were thirty-five members.

VIII

Related and Similar Groups

Brethren Bodies

The Church of the Brethren

A Christian body which is truly almost a twin denomination to the Mennonites is that of the Church of the Brethren, formerly known as German Baptists. The Church of the Brethren holds to the historic fundamentals of the Christian faith: belief in God, Father, Son, and Holy Spirit; the creation of all things by God; the fall of original man into sin; the revelation of God through the patriarchs and prophets, and supremely through Christ; the atonement for human sin made by Jesus Christ on the cross; the resurrection of the Lord Jesus from the dead; the establishment of the church by the gift of the Holy Spirit on the day of Pentecost; and the personal return of Jesus in glory. The German Baptists also hold to the distinctive views taught by the Mennonite Church: the baptism of believers only; the necessity of church discipline; the doctrine of Biblical nonresistance; the rejection of all oaths; the importance of "heart religion"; the importance of the imitation of Christ in personal discipleship; separation of church and state; the sinfulness of living a life of wealth and luxury; the necessity for the excommunication of backsliders; freedom of conscience, with no state coercion in matters of faith; the practice of a "free ministry," that is, avoiding making the ministry a profession, supported by a salary; tension between church and world, the doctrine of "nonconformity to the world"; the washing of the saints' feet, as well as the sacraments of baptism and the Lord's Supper; the practice of the holy kiss; and the rejection of personal adornment, together with plainness of attire.

On only two points did the Church of the Brethren deviate from the Mennonites: (1) trine, or as they prefer—triune, baptism, by forward action; and (2) the practice of holding a love feast in connection with the Lord's Supper. The Church of the Brethren also holds simply to the New Testament as its creed, refusing even to write a human creed. It was this characteristic of the Church of the Brethren which greatly impressed Benjamin Franklin. Franklin, who was well acquainted with one of the early members of the German Baptists, or "Dunkers," was on one occasion in conversation with a German Baptist. The man reported to Franklin that the Church of the Brethren was being greatly slandered and charged with all sorts of ridiculous practices, of which the group was not guilty. Franklin replied that this is commonly the case with new sects and that the way to bring such abuse to an end was to publish their articles of belief and their standards of discipline. The man replied that they had considered this plan, but as they looked back over their brief history they observed that they had not held truth perfectly at the beginning, and that as they went along in the life of the church the Lord gave them further light, so that they felt that their principles were improving, and that their errors were diminishing. This brother continued by saying that they felt that if they should attempt to put down in writing what they believed at a given point, time would prove that perhaps they had not even at that time attained to a full understanding of God's Word. This attitude greatly impressed Franklin and he commented: "This modesty in a sect is perhaps a singular instance in the history of mankind, every other sect supposing itself in possession of all truth, and that those who differ are so far in the wrong; like a man traveling in foggy weather, those at some distance before him on the road he sees wrapped up in the fog, as well as those behind him, and also the people in the fields on each side, but near him all appears clear, though in truth he is as much in the fog as any of them."

Many fine books and source materials are available for a study of the life and doctrines of the Church of the Brethren. Perhaps the following dozen works would be of help to the interested reader: Rufus D. Bowman: *The Church of the Brethren and War, 1704-1941;* Martin G. Brumbaugh: *A History of the German Baptist Brethren in Europe and America,* second edition, Brethren Publishing House, Elgin, Illinois, 1910; George N. Falkenstein: *History of the German Baptist Brethren Church,* New Era Publishing Company, Lancaster, Pennsylvania, 1901; John S. Flory: *Flashlights from Brethren History,* Brethren Publishing House, Elgin, Illinois, 1932; John S. Flory: *Literary Activity of the German Baptist Brethren in the Eighteenth Century;* H. R. Holsinger: *History of the Tunkers and the Brethren Church,* Pacific Press Publishing Company, Oakland, California, 1901; *The Brethren Encyclopedia,* by Henry Kurtz, 1867; Floyd E. Mallott: *Studies in Brethren History,* Brethren Publishing House, Elgin, Illinois, 1954; J. E. Miller: *The Story of Our Church,* Elgin, Illinois, 1941; *Classified Minutes of the Annual Meetings of the Brethren. A History of the General Councils of the Church from 1778 to 1885,* The Brethren's Publishing Company, Mt. Morris, Illinois, and Huntingdon, Pennsylvania, 1886; Lawrence W. Schultz and Medford D. Neher: *A Mural History of the Church of the Brethren,* The Shaw Printing Company, Dixon, Illinois, 1953; Otho Winger: *History and Doctrines of the Church of the Brethren,* Elgin.

The Church of the Brethren originated in the village of Schwarz-enau, Germany, east of the present city of Cologne, on the Eider River, in 1708. The natural leader of the group was Alexander Mack, 1679-1735. The original eight members of the denomination, five men and three women, cast lots as to who should perform the first baptism; and the secret was carried with them to the grave. In the course of time almost all the Church of the Brethren members migrated to Eastern Pennsylvania. They came in several groups. (1) The first group was led by Peter Becker, 1687-1758, and consisted of twenty families with 126 souls. They settled at Germantown, Pennsylvania. The date of this migration was 1719. Becker's body was buried in the Harley Cemetery, near Harleysville, Montgomery County, Pennsylvania. Becker's daughter Mary married Rudolph Herley, son of the immigrant who bore the same name. (2) The second migration of the Brethren to America occurred under the leadership of Alexander Mack in 1729. This time there were thirty families and 126 souls. (3) The third migration was in 1733 and was led by John Naas. There was a fourth tiny movement from Schwarzenau in the year 1737 to Denmark. There they won a few converts, and a small group called the Assembly of Christ still exists in the Scandinavian countries of Norway and Sweden, as well as North Germany, with a total membership of about 185. This group strongly resembles the Church of the Brethren in America, stating: "We speak when the Bible speaks, and we are silent when the Bible is silent." They differ with their American brethren in having somewhat more "holiness" influence, speaking in tongues, for example.

The Church of the Brethren has prospered numerically in America, having some 61,000 members in the Southeastern Region consisting largely of Maryland, Virginia, and West Virginia; some 54,000 members in the Eastern Region of Pennsylvania; another 54,000 in the Central Region of Illinois, Indiana, and Ohio; 17,000 members in the Western Region embracing such states as Colorado, Iowa, Kansas, etc.; and 15,000 members in the Pacific Coast Region consisting largely of the churches in California and Western Canada. The organ of the Church of the Brethren is entitled *The Gospel Messenger,* and the publication center as well as the headquarters of the denomination are located at Elgin, Illinois. The seminary of the group is Bethany Biblical Seminary, currently located in Chicago.

Indiana has 111 congregations with 19,250 baptized members, while Michigan has twenty-four congregations with 3,000 baptized members. The chief mission fields of the group are India, where the baptized membership is approaching 10,000; and Nigeria, where the Church of the Brethren has almost 5,000 members.

One of the chief leaders in the Church of the Brethren, not only in the Central Region, but also throughout the denomination, was President Otho Winger, 1877-1946, "undoubtedly the most forceful personality produced by the Indiana Church of the Brethren." Winger was born near Somerset, Indiana, October 23, 1877. He united with the Church of the Brethren when in his eleventh year. He studied at the Brethren School, Manchester College, and at Indiana University, where he received both the B.A. and M.A. degrees. He began to teach at Manchester College in 1907, and in 1911 was elected president, a position he held for thirty years. "With tremendous energy and deepest dedication he now threw himself into the job of building a college." Winger was called to the ministry when nineteen years of age. After serving briefly as a licentiate, he was advanced to the second degree, that is, made a regular minister in the Church of the Brethren. Later, in 1910, he was ordained to the office of elder. "Otho Winger was a forceful preacher. He preached many dedication sermons, baccalaureate sermons, harvest meeting sermons, and gave many commencement addresses. His preaching was direct, and forceful, and was well received." *The History of the Church of the Brethren in Indiana* continues: "He was an indefatigable worker, working unbelievable hours for many years. He had a brilliant mind, was alert, alive, vigorous, and forceful. He loved people and gave himself to them unreservedly. His great strength lay in his forceful and winsome personality, his prodigious energy, his devotion to his task, and his great faith. No one of his generation excelled him in the impact he made on the church of his day. In every way he was a great man."

The Brethren first settled in Union County, Indiana, in the years 1804-9. In the latter year their first congregation was organized. In Northern Indiana the first settlement was begun in what is now West Goshen in 1830, with the first meetinghouse built there in 1859. The Turkey Creek congregation was begun in 1838, its first meetinghouse being the one now known as Maple Grove, and which was built in the period 1851-54.

As similar as are the Mennonites and Church of the Brethren, it is amazing how much tension sometimes existed between the two groups over the mode of baptism. Fortunately this struggle has greatly diminished in recent years. One factor also points to the brotherly relations which obtained in the two bodies, that is, they often settled in the same communities.

The Old German Baptist Church

The German Baptist Church, as the Church of the Brethren used to be known, continued as an undivided body until 1881. In that year the beginnings were laid for a three-way division. The main body continued as the German Baptist Brethren until the year 1908, when the name "Church of the Brethren" was adopted. The Old German Baptist Church seceded in 1881 in order to maintain a stricter church discipline. A small directory of the congregations and ministers of this group was published in 1959 by Willis A. Hess, Waynesboro, Pennsylvania: *The Old German Baptist Church, April, 1959; Directory of Officials.*

The Old German Baptists resemble in many respects the Old Order Amish, although not related to them organically. Many of the Old German Baptist men wear beards and plain garb. The women wear large capes. The main body of the group, however, does not object to its members' driving automobiles. In Indiana there are approximately 1,100 baptized members of the Old German Baptist Church, distributed as follows: three congregations in Carroll County, totaling 377 members; Madison County, 105 members; Kosciusko County, 62 members; Cass County, 33 members; Clinton County, 190 members; Wabash County, 202 members; Miami County, 8 members; and Elkhart County, 122 members. The church in Elkhart County is known as the Yellow Creek congregation, and consists of 122 members, served by five ministers (four of whom are elders) and four deacons. They have two meetinghouses, commonly known as the East and West meetinghouses. One is west of Goshen, a third of a mile west of the Model School, on County Road 32, not far from the southeast corner of Section 7 of Elkhart Township. The West meetinghouse of the Old German Baptist Church is two miles west of the village of South West, near the southwest corner of Section 29 of Harrison Township, on County Road 40, two miles east of Wakarusa.

There is no organized congregation of the Old German Baptist Church in Michigan; there are living in that state only eight members with no ordained brethren. The organ of the group is *The Vindicator,* Covington, Ohio, with Lester Fisher as editor.

Old Order German Baptist Church

This small body of German Baptists insists on driving only with horse and buggy, and does not permit the use of automobiles. It originated in two small schisms from the Old German Baptist Church in the years 1913 and 1921. There are in all of Indiana possibly forty members of this group, with only two living in Elkhart County, Deacon Earl Crist and his wife, who live on Highway 19 near Wakarusa. They removed to Elkhart County from Miami County.

The Old Brethren Church

This small body of German Baptists separated from the Old German Baptist Church in 1913, on the issue of maintaining a greater degree of congregational government. There are in all of Indiana possibly eighty-five members, in two main bodies: (1) the Old Brethren German Baptists, 1913, who drive horse and buggy. They are represented in Elkhart County by the group of Elder Daniel P. Graybill of Route 5, Goshen, who lives near the village of Foraker; and by (2) the Old Brethren Church, 1929, which seceded from the preceding one because they wished to allow the use of automobiles. They are represented locally by the group of Elder Edward Royer, also of Route 5, Goshen, who lives in the village of South West. There is also a dissident elder in Carroll County, who separated from the Old Brethren German Baptists about 1953, but only four or five members adhere to his group, two of them being two women of Elkhart County. The elder's name is Solomon Lavy of Route 1, Camden, Indiana.

The Dunkard Brethren Church

The Dunkard Brethren Church originated in the year 1926 under the leadership of a conservative elder named B. E. Kesler, Sr. Benjamin Elias Kesler, 1861-1952, was a native of Franklin County, Virginia. He became a minister in the Church of the Brethren in the year 1884. Kesler, in addition to being a Brethren elder, also taught school for thirty years. He reached the advanced age of ninety-one years and four months.

Within two decades two small schismatic groups had withdrawn from the Dunkard Brethren, but these two tiny bodies merged in 1948 under the name, "Conservative German Baptist Brethren Church."

Those who are interested in the Dunkard Brethren can secure the booklet, *Dunkard Brethren Church Polity, 1957.* They also publish minutes of their district conference meetings.

The Dunkard Brethren Church is represented by three congregations in Indiana: Goshen, with seventy-five members in Elkhart County; Peru with twelve members, and Plevna with fifty-five members, Peru and Plevna being in Miami County. There are nine members of the church living in Ionia County, Michigan, but they hold their church membership in the state of Ohio.

The organ of the Dunkard Brethren is the *Bible Monitor,* published at Taneytown, Maryland.

The Brethren Church

The Brethren Church is the progressive group which seceded from the German Baptists in the years 1881-83. The organ of this group is *The Brethren Evangelist,* Ashland, Ohio, which is also the center of its educational institutions, Ashland College and Ashland Theological Seminary. The publication headquarters of the denomination are also located at

Ashland, the Brethren Publishing Company. The yearbook information of the Brethren Church (Ashland group) is found in one issue of *The Brethren Evangelist*, entitled *The 1959-60 Brethren Annual Number*.

An unfortunate division occurred within the Brethren Church in the year 1939. The one group maintained its headquarters at Ashland, Ohio, while the other group has its headquarters at Winona Lake, Indiana, where it established Grace Theological Seminary and Grace College.

The Ashland group has a membership in the United States of 18,200, with thirty-one congregations and over 7,000 members in Indiana, and one congregation with twenty-five members in the state of Michigan.

The Ashland group of the Brethren Church has recently issued a fine instrument for the indoctrination of its young people, Albert T. Ronk *et al.*, *Our Faith, A Manual of Brethren History, Bible Doctrine, and Christian Commitment*, Ashland, Ohio. Here we find such traditional doctrines of the Brethren Church as triune immersion, the Lord's Supper, the love feast, feet washing, anointing with oil, nonresistance, and the rejection of the oath.

The Brethren Church

As was indicated in connection with the Ashland group, a severe break occurred in the 1881 Brethren Church in the year 1939. Perhaps one cause was a doctrinal struggle over modernism. However, the Ashland group would regard the introduction of two new emphases on the part of some of the ministers in the church as basic causes of the 1939 division. These two new emphases were the doctrine of eternal security, and dispensational theology. Two of the chief leaders in what became the so-called "Grace group" were Louis S. Bauman, 1875-1950, of Long Beach, California, and President Alva J. McClain of Grace Theological Seminary, Winona Lake, Indiana. Both were staunch Fundamentalists.

The membership in the United States of the Brethren Church, Grace group, is approximately 25,000 baptized persons, with seventeen congregations totaling 1,800 members in the state of Indiana, and six congregations with 500 members in the state of Michigan.

The organ of the Brethren Church, with headquarters at Winona Lake, is *The Brethren Missionary Herald*, Winona Lake, Indiana. A fine history of the Church of the Brethren and the Brethren Church was written by Homer A. Kent, Sr., entitled *250 Years . . . Conquering Frontiers: A History of the Brethren Church*, the Brethren Missionary Herald Company, Winona Lake, Indiana, 1958.

On the historic doctrines of the Church of the Brethren and the Brethren Church, the Winona Lake and Ashland groups, both of which are officially known as the Brethren Church, stand together.

The Brethren in Christ

Another group of devout Christians who in many respects resemble the Mennonites is the body originally known as River Brethren, but whose official name since 1862 has been Brethren in Christ. In the year 1942 A. W. Climenhaga, then dean of Messiah Bible College, Grantham, Pennsylvania, wrote a *History of the Brethren in Christ Church*. It was published by the E. V. Publishing House, Nappanee, Indiana. This book contains some information on the history of the Brethren in Christ both in Indiana and in Michigan. Available also are the *Minutes of the Annual General Conference of the Brethren in Christ Church;* the eighty-fifth sessions were held in 1955.

The chief founder of the Brethren in Christ was Jacob Engel, 1753-1832, who was born in Switzerland, who emigrated with his parents to America in 1754, where they settled in Lancaster County, Pennsylvania, not far from Marietta and the Susquehanna River. Jacob Engel's parents died when he was still a boy and he was placed under the guardianship of Jacob Schock. Jacob Engel united with the Mennonite Church.

The event which led ultimately to the founding of the Brethren in Christ Church was a spiritual awakening which Engel experienced at the age of eighteen. In the year 1778 he and a man named Witmer are said to have immersed each other in a river. They pledged to each other never to reveal which one performed the first baptism. Finally in 1785 Jacob ventured to immerse eleven persons, after which the newly organized group met for a love feast and communion service. Soon Jacob Engel was chosen as the first overseer or bishop of the group.

The Brethren in Christ hold to principles remarkably similar to the Mennonites, including such doctrines as believers' baptism, nonresistance, nonconformity to the world, and the necessity of an earnest life of Christian discipleship. They practice the washing of the saints' feet, and observe the salutation with the holy kiss. In size, however, the Brethren in Christ are much smaller than the Mennonites, for they have only between 7,000 and 8,000 baptized members.

The first Brethren in Christ members to settle in Indiana came from Ontario to Elkhart County about the year 1838. The next year they began to meet together for services under the leadership of Elder Daniel Stump. The body of Daniel Stump is buried in the Union Center Cemetery, Elkhart County, likely the Daniel Stump who was born in 1790 and who died in 1877. Stump served as the first overseer of the Brethren in Christ in Indiana. He was succeeded by Martin Hoover, 1813-1896, grandson of the Mennonite bishop, Martin Hoover, c.1760-1850. (Martin Hoover, the Brethren in Christ overseer, was in turn the father-in-law of Preacher Michael M. Shirk, 1832-1912.) The third Indiana Brethren in

Christ overseer was John A. Stump, grandson of Elder Daniel Stump. The present overseer is Carl G. Stump.

The Brethren in Christ have three main congregations in Indiana, all of them with less than fifty members: the Union Grove meetinghouse was built in 1885, renovated in 1905, and again in 1951. It is located in Union Township on the southwest corner of the intersection of County Roads 15 and 50. The Locke church building was purchased from the United Brethren for the use of the group of members who constituted a sort of outpost from the Union Grove congregation, and who began the work in Locke in 1910. In 1915 the Locke house of worship was also renovated. Locke is located two miles north of the intersection of Indiana Highway 19 with Federal Highway 6 in Nappanee, one-half mile west. The third congregation of the Brethren in Christ in Indiana is the Christian Union congregation near Garrett in De Kalb County. A few Brethren in Christ families began to locate in De Kalb County in the 1840's and worshiped in a schoolhouse. In the year 1882 the Church of the Brethren and the Brethren in Christ united in building the Christian Union meetinghouse. In 1908 the 1882 building was replaced by the present brick structure, in which year the Church of the Brethren withdrew to build their own house of worship. These three Brethren in Christ congregations have a total of about 125 baptized members.

The Brethren in Christ began to settle in Michigan in the last quarter of the nineteenth century. The two original settlements were made at Sandusky where a house of worship was built at Ship Center, and at Yale. The group at Sandusky took for its name the Mooretown Church, and the location is in Sanilac County in the "thumb" of Michigan. Yale is about twenty-one miles south of Sandusky and is located in St. Clair County, about twenty-five miles northwest of Port Huron.

For many years the overseer for Michigan was Elder Henry Schneider, Jr., who on June 7, 1960, wrote in a private letter what he remembered of the growth of the Brethren in Christ Church in the state of Michigan. Elder Schneider says that he was ten years of age when his parents removed from Canada to Michigan. At that time, so far as he knows, there were only two Brethren in Christ churches in the state, one at Mooretown Center, and another near Yale. It was in the year 1888 that the Schneider family removed to Michigan. About 1891 a minister named T. A. Long held services in a schoolhouse at Carland, northwest of Owosso, in Shiawassee County, about twenty-five miles west of Flint. As a result of the revival a church was organized, and the next year a house of worship was built at Carland. Henry Schneider, Sr., and Charles Baker were elected deacons of the new congregation. About the year 1908 Henry Schneider, Jr., was ordained as a Brethren in Christ minister. He and Jonathan Lyons, who was ordained bishop the same time Schneider was elected to the ministry, went to Merrill in Saginaw County, about twenty miles west of Saginaw, and held meetings in a schoolhouse. Later the meetinghouse was torn down at Yale and shipped to Merrill and built there. The name of the congregation at Merrill is the Bethel Brethren in Christ Church. The date of moving the meetinghouse was about 1915. The next congregation was established at Gladwin in Gladwin County, about fourteen miles west of the shore of Saginaw Bay. The meeting-house of the Mt. Carmel congregation at Gladwin was built about 1924. In 1936 the Brethren in Christ went to Hillman in Rust Township, Montmorency County, in the northern part of the lower peninsula, about twenty-five miles west of Alpena. Here they started work by holding a tent meeting in 1936. The church building was erected in 1942. The next congregation to be established was the one at Leonard in Oakland County, about thirty miles north of Detroit. Here the first house of wor-ship was built in 1941. The Brethren in Christ also started work in De-troit about the year 1936. In the course of time this house of worship was sold to the colored people of the community and a new meetinghouse was built in Dearborn about the year 1959.

It is thus evident that the Brethren in Christ from their entry into Michigan about seventy-five years ago moved westward from Port Huron and around the city of Saginaw and northward to the town of Hillman. These seven permanent congregations have a total membership of about 150 members: not a single congregation has a total of fifty members.

There is also a congregation of about thirty-five members located in Cassopolis, Cass County, about twenty miles northeast of South Bend, In-diana. The name of the Brethren in Christ congregation at Cassopolis is Bethel. The official organ of the Brethren in Christ Church is the *Evan-gelical Visitor,* published by the Evangel Press, Nappanee, Indiana.

Bishop C. N. Hostetter of Grantham, Pennsylvania, long-time presi-dent of Messiah College, reports in his article on the Brethren in Christ in *The Mennonite Encyclopedia* that the Brethren in Christ Church is "aggressively missionary in interest and program." The chief mission fields are in India and in Rhodesia, South Africa. The colleges of the Brethren in Christ are Messiah College, Grantham, Pennsylvania, and Upland College, Upland, California. The Brethren in Christ are a mem-ber of the Council of Mennonite and Affiliated Colleges, and of the Men-nonite Central Committee.

Two small schisms from the Brethren in Christ occurred in the mid-dle of the nineteenth century in Eastern Pennsylvania. In 1843 a con-servative faction withdrew, now known as the Old Order Brethren in Christ, or "Yorkers." In 1853 another schism occurred, which group is now known as "Brinser" or "United Zion's Children." Various efforts have been made for a reunion of the United Zion's Children with the Brethren in Christ, but to this date slight differences in church polity have prevented this merger.

The Society of Friends

Another body of nonconformist Christians is that known as the Society of Friends, commonly called Quakers. The Friends originated in England under the ministry of George Fox, 1624-1691, who began his spiritual reformation in the year 1647. Those who are interested in the doctrines of the Friends should consult the article "Friends, Society of" in the *Encyclopaedia Britannica,* as well as such books as Howard Brinton, *Friends for 300 Years,* Harper and Brother, 1952. Other useful sources are the annual *Minutes of the Indiana Yearly Meeting of Friends;* the annual *Friends Directory: A Friends World Committee Publication;* and the *Handbook of the Religious Society of Friends,* 1952.

A number of distinctive doctrines and practices characterize the Quakers. Perhaps their most distinctive doctrine is that of the Inner Light, the doctrine that the light of Christ is found in every man by the gracious work of the Holy Spirit, which light if followed is sufficient to bring him to heaven. The Quakers also reject the clergy as an institution in the church, holding that all Christians are "ministers" in the same sense. Quakers also reject all outward ceremonies and sacraments. One of their more noteworthy historic practices is that of the silent meeting, in which no one is especially appointed to speak, in which each worshiper sits in silent meditation and prayer before God, and in which each person, man or woman, is free to speak forth as he feels prompted by the Holy Spirit. Friends hold that the Bible is truly inspired of God, yet subordinate to the inner Holy Spirit which is the possession of every child of God. Historically Quakers were also noted for "plain speech" in which they retained such archaic forms as *thee,* rather than the supposedly more polite form *you.* Quakers also hold to nonresistance or pacifism, refusing historically to participate in warfare. They also reject the oath. Quakers have also been famous for plain dress, that is, they resisted the fashions of the world and in the course of time by retaining the older conventions developed a religious garb, similar to the Mennonites and the Church of the Brethren. On these last three points, nonresistance, the rejection of the oath, and plain dress, Quakers and Mennonites stood on common ground.

Of the 195,000 Friends in the world, almost 123,000 live in the United States. It was William Penn who brought large numbers of Quakers from England, where they were severely persecuted, to Pennsylvania, his "holy experiment," in which he sought to operate a political govern-ment while retaining the principle of Christian nonresistance. Fifteen thousand Friends had been imprisoned in England before the enactment of the Toleration Act in 1689, and at least 450 had died in prison. In colonial America one of the more outstanding Quakers was John Wool-man, 1720-1772, of Pennsylvania, who served as a sort of prophet in the Society of Friends. In the nineteenth century one of the outstanding Friends was John Greenleaf Whittier, 1807-1892, the Quaker poet.

Friends have been known for their activity as abolitionists, that is, those who favored the abolition of human slavery, for prison reforms, and for world peace. These concerns are common to all Quakers, which in the course of time became divided into the so-called Hicksite (Liberal) Friends, led originally by Elias Hicks; the Wilburite (Conservative) Friends, led by John Wilbur; and the Gurneyite (Orthodox) Friends, led by Joseph John Gurney.

There are two major groups of Friends in the state of Indiana and four smaller bodies. The Indiana Yearly Meeting of Friends, which is affiliated with the Five Years Meeting, was established in the year 1821. There are in this conference about seventy-five meetings (congregations), with approximately 12,000 members. This is the group to which D. Elton Trueblood, the well-known Quaker writer, belongs. The Western Five Years Meeting which was organized in 1858 has about seventy-six meet-ings in the state of Indiana, with approximately 12,700 members. There are no significant differences between these two bodies. Both groups em-ploy pastors, but they are not ordained in the ordinary sense of the word, because of the Quaker doctrine that each member of the body of Christ is a minister in the same sense. These pastors are chosen because of their particular gifts and their ability to give leadership to the Quaker meet-ings.

The Friends General Conference, which was organized in 1900, has three meetings in Indiana with about 400 members. The Friends World Committee of 1938 also has three meetings in the state of Indiana with approximately seventy-five members. The Central Yearly Meeting, organ-ized in 1926, has nine meetings in the state of Indiana with a total of about 465 members. The Western Conservative Meeting has two congre-gations in Indiana with about fifty members. These four groups all prac-tice the old silent meeting of historic Quakerism. The Central Yearly Meeting teaches the doctrine of entire sanctification as set forth in the *Teachings of Evangelical Friends as Gleaned from George Fox's Journal and Friends Disciplines,* by J. Edwin Newby: messages given at Central Yearly Meeting, 1952.

Along with other minority groups many bodies of Friends have felt the pressure to conform at least in part to general Christendom. The outcome in the Indiana Yearly Meeting has been to discard plain dress and plain speech, to introduce music into the service, and to employ pastors. This pattern was adopted as early as 1887.

The Quakers are world-renowned for the excellent work of the American Friends Service Committee, with headquarters at 20 South Twelfth Street, Philadelphia 7, Pennsylvania. In the first World War the Friends Service Committee rendered much help to the needy and war-torn countries of Europe by sending conscientious objectors to those countries as relief workers, especially to France, Serbia, and Poland. They also helped to feed the starving people of Russia in the Volga River area and rendered splendid service in Germany by feeding undernourished children.

In contrast with Indiana with its 25,000 Quakers, Michigan has only 1,325. Nine meetings with about 865 members are affiliated with the Ohio Yearly Meeting of 1813, which is conservative theologically and which has adopted water baptism. Four congregations ("meetings") with about 200 members belong to the Indiana Yearly Meeting. Ten meetings with 261 members are affiliated with the Friends World Committee.

Undoubtedly the most outstanding member of the Society of Friends in the twentieth century was the famous Rufus M. Jones, 1863-1948, accurately described in the *Encyclopaedia Britannica* as a "teacher, writer, and humanitarian." Included in the more than fifty books which Jones wrote may be mentioned: *Studies in Mystical Religion,* 1909; *The Quakers in the American Colonies,* 1911; *Spiritual Reformers in the 16th and 17th Centuries,* 1914; *The Later Periods of Quakerism,* 1921; *A Small-town Boy,* 1941; *Finding the Trail of Life,* 1926; *The Trail of Life in the Middle Years,* 1934.

Historically the Mennonites and Quakers have always enjoyed cordial relations. European Quakers visited the Mennonite colonies in South Russia early in the nineteenth century. In the later years of that century Philadelphia Quakers used to visit the Mennonites of the Franconia Conference occasionally; this was true even after the first World War. Although a smaller body than the Mennonites, the Society of Friends has exerted an influence for social justice and for righteousness out of all proportion to its size.

The Apostolic Christian Church

A brief account of the life and faith of this small Christian body may be found in the article of President Tilman R. Smith in *The Mennonite Encyclopedia,* "Apostolic Christian Church of America." A longer history is that of Herman Rüegger, *Apostolic Christian Church History,* I, Chi-

29

cago, 1949. A sort of small directory or yearbook was published in a revised form in 1959 by Orel R. Steiner of Oakville, Iowa, *Apostolic Christian Churches and Ministers in America.* The following information is taken from the Steiner directory.

There are eight congregations of Apostolic Christian Church members in the state of Indiana. The *Bluffton* congregation is located five miles east and two miles south of that town in Wells County, Indiana. In this congregation there are 300 families with 644 members. The *Bremen* congregation is located on North Baltimore Street of that town in Marshall County. The Bremen congregation has sixty-eight families with ninety-three members. The *Francesville* congregation in Pulaski County is located in that town on State Road 421 and has eighty-five families with 187 members. The *LaCrosse* congregation in Starke County is also located on State Road 421 and has sixty-five families with 106 members. The *Leo* congregation in Allen County, on the Leo-Grabill Road, has ninety-five families with 155 members. The *Milford* congregation in Kosciusko County is located at the north edge of the town along State Road 15. In this congregation there are 111 families represented, with 161 members. The *Remington* congregation in Jasper County is located four miles south of the town, and one mile east on U.S. Highway 24; it has forty-five families represented with eighty-five members. The *Wolcott* congregation in White County is located along the south side of the city. In this congregation there are thirty-seven families represented with seventy-five members. The total for Indiana is therefore a little over 800 families represented in these eight congregations with 1,506 members.

There are three congregations of the Apostolic Christian Church in Michigan with a total of 237 members. These congregations are the *Alto* Church in Kent County, located two miles east of Alto, with nineteen families and thirty-three members; the *Bay City* congregation in Bay County, three miles west of Kawkawlin, with eighty families and 160 members; and the Detroit congregation, located at 26741 Five Mile Road, with thirty-nine families represented, and forty-four members.

The Apostolic Christian Church was founded in Switzerland in the year 1835, by Samuel Fröhlich, 1803-1857. Fröhlich emphasized an earnest and emotional conversion from sin to Christ, baptism by immersion, the complete avoidance of the religious services of other denominations, and a severely nonconformed Christian life. He introduced baptism by immersion. In Switzerland the denomination is commonly known as Neu-Täufer, while in America the nickname of the group is "New Amish." The first migration of the Apostolic Christian Church members to America occurred in 1846. In recent years the Apostolic Christian Church has somewhat modified its earlier rigid stand against other

Christian bodies. The women members of the church wear a prayer veiling in times of worship. The group also holds to the doctrine of nonresistance, but permits its members to serve as noncombatant soldiers when drafted into the armed forces. There has been only one major division in America, and that over the issue of retaining the German language, in 1907. Both groups now use the English language, but have not yet reunited. The two groups number respectively 7,300 and 4,500 members in the United States.

There is a very similar body in the Balkan States, especially in Hungary and Jugoslavia with 70,000 members; these Christians are commonly called Nazarenes. Those who are interested in reading further on any aspect of the Apostolic Christian Church should consult the literature listed in *The Mennonite Encyclopedia.*

Appendixes

1
List of Mennonite Settlements and Congregations in Indiana and Michigan, 1860

The dates when certain ministers began to serve are conjectural. All membership figures are estimates. Congregations, 7; estimated membership, 385.

INDIANA

HAMILTON COUNTY

Arcadia, 1838—Possibly 2 to 4 members, unorganized. No ministers.

ELKHART COUNTY

Possibly 350 members in the county. Jacob Wisler, bishop.

Yellow Creek, 1845—   West of Goshen ministers: Preachers Jacob
Olive, ca.1850—   Christophel, Daniel Moyer, Joseph Rohrer,
Holdeman, ca. 1850—   Benjamin Hershey, Jacob Freed, John Snyder,
Christophel, ca.1850—   Christian Bare, and Daniel Brundage. Deacons
    John Eyer, David Good, and Benjamin Hoover.
Clinton Brick, ca.1850—Preacher John Nusbaum & Deacon John Nusbaum, Jr.
Frisians, 1853—R. J. Smid, bishop.

ALLEN COUNTY

Gar Creek, 1854—Possibly 4 members, not organized. No ministers.

OWEN COUNTY

Bower, ca.1852—   Possible ministers: Preacher William Silvius; and Deacons Elias Mishler and John Royer. Perhaps 20 members.

DE KALB COUNTY

Pleasant Valley, ca.1850—Possibly 6 members, unorganized. No ministers.

MICHIGAN

KENT COUNTY

Caledonia, ca.1852—Possibly 3 or 4 members, unorganized. No ministers.

2
Indiana Amish Mennonite Churches, 1860

All membership figures are estimates. Congregations, 5; estimated membership, 150.

HAW PATCH [Topeka]   40   CLINTON [Later: Clinton Frame]   35
Eden Township, Lagrange County   Clinton Township, Elkhart County
  *Isaac Smucker   *Jonas D. Troyer
  Joseph Yoder   John Smiley
  David F. Hertzler
  †George Z. Boller

FORKS   25
  Newbury Township, Lagrange
  County
    Christian S. Plank
    Christian Miller
  LOCKE [Later: W. Market St., Nap-
    panee]   15

Locke Township, Elkhart County
  *Samuel Yoder
  John Ringenberg
HOWARD-MIAMI   35
  Howard & Miami Counties
    *Benjamin Schrock
    Joseph Kennedy

3
Indiana Mennonite Conference, 1910

Meets annually on the second Thursday and Friday of October. Membership figures taken from the 1908 *Mennonite Yearbook and Directory*. Congregations, 17; membership, 1,271.

Bishop District of David Burkholder, J. K. Bixler, and D. A. Yoder.

YELLOW CREEK   110
  South West, Ind.
    Jonas Loucks
    J. W. Christophel
    †N. S. Hoover
SALEM   80
  Foraker, Indiana
    John H. Bare
    †Isaiah Christophel
OLIVE   55
  Jamestown, Ind.
    *D. A. Yoder
    (William H. Hartman)
    †Jonas Brubaker
  N. Main St., Nappanee   100
  Nappanee, Ind.
    *David Burkholder
    E. S. Mullett
    †Franklin B. Maust
HOLDEMAN   170
  Wakarusa, Ind.
    *J. K. Bixler
    Henry Weldy
    Silas Weldy

    †Abram Culp
    †Samuel Smeltzer
FT. WAYNE   29
  Ft. Wayne, Ind.
    B. B. King
    †Frank J. Martin
TEEGARDEN   3
  Teegarden, Ind.
    Pulpit supplied from Holde-
    man
PRAIRIE STREET   80
  Elkhart, Ind.
    John F. Funk
    George Lambert
    Samuel Yoder
    †Jacob H. Wisler
    †George L. Bender
GOSHEN COLLEGE   77
  Goshen, Ind.
    J. S. Hartzler (Menn.)
    †A. S. Landis (Menn.)
    I. W. Royer (A.M.)
    I. R. Detweiler (A.M.)

Bishop District of John Garber:

CLINTON BRICK   95
  Goshen, Ind.
    Amos Nusbaum
    †Jacob C. Hershberger
    †Daniel H. Coffman
SHORE   180
  Shipshewana, Ind.

    Amos S. Cripe
    Josiah J. Miller
    †J. J. Mishler
EMMA   70
  Emma, Ind.
    O. S. Hostetler
    †Menno J. Yoder

Bishop District of Jacob P. Miller:

BOWNE 81
  Clarksville, Mich.
    Isaac Weaver
    †J. W. Mishler
UNION 71
  White Cloud, Mich.
    *Jacob P. Miller
    T. U. Nelson
    †Eli Zook
DETWEILER 15
  Brutus, Mich.
    Christian W. Detweiler
    †John N. Reinbold

CALEDONIA 10
  Caledonia, Mich.
    Pulpit supplied by Bowne
BARKER STREET (Mich.) 25
  Vistula, Ind.
    Harvey Friesner
PLEASANT HILL [ca. 2]
  Bronson, Mich.
    †Daniel F. Beery
PLEASANT VALLEY 18
  Hudson, Ind.
    Eli Stofer

4

Indiana Amish Mennonite Conference, 1910

Meets annually on the first Thursday and Friday of June. Membership figures taken from the 1908 *Mennonite Yearbook and Directory.* Congregations, 11; membership, 1,068.

MAPLE GROVE A.M. 174
  Topeka, Ind.
    *Jonathan Kurtz
    A. J. Yontz
PRETTY PRAIRIE A.M. 5
  Lagrange, Ind.
AMISH MENNONITE 64
  Leo, Ind.
    A. S. Miller
FORKS A.M. 208
  Middlebury, Ind.
    *D. D. Miller
    Samuel E. Weaver
    †Joseph Y. Hooley
AMISH MENNONITE 200
  Kokomo, Ind.
    *E. A. Mast
    Niles M. Slabaugh
    †Noah W. King
AMISH MENNONITE 10
  Linn Grove, Ind.
CLINTON FRAME A.M. 190
  Goshen, Ind.
    *D. J. Johns

    D. D. Troyer
    Silas Yoder
    †Ira S. Johns
MIDDLEBURY A.M. 32
  Middlebury, Ind.
    A. J. Hostetler
    Simon S. Yoder
W. MARKET ST. A.M. 100
  Nappanee, Ind.
    James H. McGowen
GOSHEN
  (See Mennonite Conference)
FAIRVIEW A.M. 70
  Fairview, Mich.
    E. A. Bontrager
    Menno Esch
    N. Z. Yoder
    †Menno S. Steiner
UNION 15
  Chief, Mich.
    J. S. Horner
    †Harvey W. Sarver

5

Indiana-Michigan Mennonite Conference, 1960

ORGANIZED ca.1853

The conference meets annually the first week of June.

EXECUTIVE COMMITTEE

Moderator _____ John C. Wenger, 1410 S. Eighth St., Goshen, Ind. (1962)
Assistant Moderator ____ Russell Krabill, 409 Middlebury, Goshen, Ind. (1961)
Secretary _____ Galen Johns, R. 4, Box 280, Goshen, Ind. (1962)
Fourth Member _____ T. E. Schrock, R. 1, Clarksville, Mich. (1962)
Fifth Member _____ Howard J. Zehr, 1300 Prairie St., Elkhart, Ind. (1961)
Treasurer _____ Malvin P. Miller, R. 1, Ray, Ind. (1961)

Membership 9,479; Independent Congregations 46;
Dependent Congregations 48

Note: The code numbers assigned to the bishops and overseers may be used to determine the bishop oversight for any congregation by referring to the number listed after the congregational name. The bishops and overseers are also listed in the congregations in which they have pastoral responsibilities in addition to bishop oversight.

EXPLANATION OF SYMBOLS

*Bishop   **Without official duties in congregation
†Deacon   §Regional overseer or director of zone
¶Licensed   ‡Sponsored by district mission board
#Missionary   ††Sponsored by local board or local congregation
¶¶Retired   ‡‡Sponsored by Mennonite Board of Missions and Charities
***On leave of   §§Sponsored by individuals
  absence

BISHOPS AND OVERSEERS

*Beachy, Ezra (1)
*Bontrager, Earley C. (2)
*Bontrager, Floyd F. (3)
*Bontreger, Vernon E. (4)
*Graber, J. D. (5)
*Handrich, Harvey (6)
*Hooley, Orvin H. (7)
*Horner, Anson G. (8)
*Kauffman, Amsa H. (9)
*Kauffman, Nelson E. (10)
*King, Donald (11)
*Krabill, Russell (12)
*Leinbach, Etril J. (13)
*Miller, Ivan (14)
*Miller, Lee J. (15)
*Miller, Paul M. (16)
*Miller, S. J. (17)
*Miller, Samuel S. (18)
*Mosemann, John H. (19)
*Myers, Harold D. (20)

*Neuhouser, J. S. (21)
*North, Homer F. (22)
§Schrock, Oscar (23)
*Schrock, T. E. (24)
*Shrock, Edd P. (25)
*Slaubaugh, Tobias (26)
*Stahly, Ralph (27)
*Steiner, John S. (28)
*Troyer, Clarence (29)
*Weaver, Norman (30)
*Wenger, John C. (31)
*Yoder, D. A. (32)
*Yoder, Edwin J. (33)
*Yoder, Ray F. (34)
*Yoder, S. C. (35)
*Yoder, Wilbur (36)
§Yutzy, Homer (37)
*Zehr, Howard J. (38)
*Zehr, John D. (39)

ANDERSON (1933) (21) 33
Ft. Wayne, Ind.
  *J. S. Neuhouser
‡BEAN BLOSSOM (1945) (25) 52
Morgantown, Ind.
  Charles Haarer
BELMONT (1929) (10) 138
Elkhart, Ind.
  Neil Beachy
  *S. Jay Hostetler#
  A. L. Buzzard¶¶
BENTON (1944) (33) 100
Benton, Ind.
  Irvin Nussbaum
  †Amos D. Yontz**
BEREA (1921) (26) 236
Montgomery, Ind.
  *Tobias Slaubaugh
  David J. Graber
  †Paul F. Weldy
  *Edd P. Shrock**
‡BETHANY (1918) 27
Imlay City, Mich.
  Samuel Hostetler
BETHEL (1920) (16) 127
Ashley, Mich.
  Herman Weaver
BON AIR (1947) (8) 65
2443 N. Apperson Way,
Kokomo, Ind.
  Clayton Sommers
BOWNE (1866) (24) 97
Clarksville, Mich.
  *T. E. Schrock
  Daniel E. Zook
‡BURR OAK (1918) (8) 53
Rensselaer, Ind.
  Henry J. Stoll
††CADY (1945) (11)
Midland, Mich.
††CALIFORNIA (1956) (2)
California, Mich.
  ¶¶Malvin P. Miller
‡CALVARY (1941) (13) 33
Pinckney, Mich.
  ¶Melvin Stauffer
‡CANEY CREEK (1952) (25) 4
Hardshell Station,
Lost, Creek, Ky.
  Wayne J. Wenger

‡CEDAR GROVE (1951) (30) 26
Manistique, Mich.
  Leonard E. Schmucker
††CLARION (1957) (37)
Boyne Falls, Mich.
CLINTON BRICK (1854) (9) 186
Goshen, Ind.
  *A. H. Kauffman
  John J. Yoder
CLINTON FRAME (1854) (4) 245
Goshen, Ind.
  *Vernon E. Bontreger
  Galen I. Johns**
  Gordon Schrag**
  †Norman D. Kauffman***
††COLD SPRINGS (1948) (6) 22
Mancelona, Mich.
  Willard L. Bontrager
‡CRUMSTOWN (1933) (27) 40
North Liberty, Ind.
  William R. Miller
  ¶Calvin R. Kaufman
DETROIT MENNONITE (1926) (5) 30
15800 Curtis Ave.,
Detroit 35, Mich.
  Henry Wyse
  †David E. Plank
EAST GOSHEN (1942) (16) 222
Goshen, Ind.
  *Paul M. Miller
  Ray Keim
  Howard H. Charles**
  John E. Beachy**#
  Claude Beachy**
‡‡EAST SIDE MENNONITE (1955)
  (5) 11
2709 N. Washington St.,
Saginaw, Mich.
  ¶Melvin Leidig
††ELMWOOD (1953) (33) 32
S. Town St.,
Kendallville, Ind.
  Lewis B. Miller
EMMA (1901) (14) 215
Topeka, Ind.
  *Ivan Miller
  Amos O. Hostetler
  †Orvan Bontrager
  *Oscar S. Hostetler¶¶

††ENGLISH LAKE (1949) (18) ___ 26
San Pierre, Ind.
    Emanuel S. Birkey
††FAIRHAVEN (1954) (17).
Ft. Wayne, Ind.
    Martin Brandenberger
    Arthur Cash°°
FAIRVIEW (1904) (6) _____ 382
Fairview, Mich.
    °Harvey Handrich
    Floyd M. Yoder
    †Otis Bontrager
    °Menno Esch¶¶
    Moses S. Steiner¶¶
‡FERNLAND (1937) (30) _____ 23
Germfask, Mich.
    Bruce Handrich
FIRST MENNONITE (1903) (16) 125
1213 St. Mary's Ave.,
Ft. Wayne, Ind.
    John R. Smucker
‡FIRST MENNONITE (1954) (12) 43
2311 Kessler Blvd., N. Dr.,
Indianapolis, Ind.
    Cleo A. Mann
FIRST MENNONITE (1941) (32)
    (35) _____ 202
New Bremen, N.Y.
    Donald Jantzi
††FISH LAKE (1950) (39) _____ 22
Walkerton, Ind.
    James L. Christophel
FORKS (1857) (2) _____ 222
Middlebury, Ind.
    °E. C. Bontrager
    Donald E. Yoder
    †Malvin P. Miller
GOSHEN COLLEGE (1903) (19)
    (35) _____ 646
S. Main St.,
Goshen, Ind.
    °John H. Mosemann
    °S. C. Yoder
    J. Robert Detweiler
    I. E. Burkhart
    C. L. Graber
    Ernest E. Miller
    †Levi C. Hartzler
    °Ezra Beachy°°
    °Wilbur Hostetler°°

°J. N. Kaufman°°
Leland Bachman°°
Royal H. Bauer°°
Harold S. Bender°°
J. Lawrence Burkholder°°
Samuel M. King°°
J. Robert Kreider°°
Millard Lind°°
Chester Raber°°
J. B. Shenk°°
Floyd W. Weaver°°
J. Kore Zook°°
Lee Kanagy#
John Litwiller#
Don McCammon#
Peter Sawatsky#
David Shank#
‡GRAND MARAIS (1948) (29) ___ 5
Grand Marais, Mich.
    Willard Handrich
‡HEATH STREET MENNONITE (1952)
    (24) _____ 16
Battle Creek, Mich.
    †Harold Christophel
HERRICK (1952) (3) _____ 11
Clare, Mich.
    °Floyd F. Bontrager
HOLDEMAN (1851) (31) _____ 236
Wakarusa, Ind.
    Simon Gingerich
    ¶Kermit Derstine
    †Manford Freed
HOPEWELL (1918) (18) _____ 277
Kouts, Ind.
    °Samuel S. Miller
HOWARD-MIAMI (1854) (8) ___ 321
Amboy, Ind.
    °Anson G. Horner
    Niles M. Slabaugh
    Emanuel J. Hochstedler
    †John W. Horner
    †Paul J. Myers
††HUDSON LAKE (1950) (31) ___ 30
New Carlisle, Ind.
    Daniel H. Stoltzfus
††KALAMAZOO (1960) (13)
Milwood Road,
Kalamazoo, Mich.
    °Etril J. Leinbach

††Lake Bethel (1956) (14) ___ 23
Lagrange, Ind.
Titus Morningstar
Leo (1861) (17) _____ 305
Leo, Ind.
*S. J. Miller
Virgil Vogt
†Ben Graber**
‡Liberty (1946) (24) _____ 25
Clarke Lake, Mich.
Oscar Leinbach
††Lighthouse (16)(ca.1950) ___ 8
Goshen, Ind.
Locust Grove (1943) (27) _____ 55
Elkhart, Ind.
*Ralph Stahly
Aden Horst**
Locust Grove (1941) (7) _____ 135
Sturgis, Mich.
*Orvin H. Hooley
†LeRoy Rhinesmith
Maple Grove (1854) (33) _____ 204
Topeka, Ind.
*Edwin J. Yoder
Ellis B. Croyle
C. Norman Kraus**
‡Maple Grove (1942) (30) ___ 27
Gulliver, Mich.
*Norman Weaver
Maple River (1879) _____ 54
Brutus, Mich.
Earl Hartman
Clyde X. Kauffman
Royal A. Buskirk**
Marion (1944) _____ 113
Howe, Ind.
Paul Lauver
†John Mishler
*Willard Sommers**
Middlebury (1903) (16) (36) 444
Middlebury, Ind.
*Wilbur Yoder
†Earl Miller
Harold A. Yoder**
John I. Byler**
Midland (1913) (11) _____ 126
Midland, Mich.
Clarence R. Yoder
†Albert Wyse

†Melvin A. Yoder
Erie Kindy**
Moorepark (1947) (13) _____ 75
Moorepark, Mich.
*Etril J. Leinbach
‡Morgantown (1952) (25) _____ 8
Morgantown, Ky.
Cledus Slaubaugh
‡Mt. Pleasant (1951) (25) _____ 11
Martinsville, Ind.
Charles Haarer
‡Naubinway (1943) (29) _____ 17
Naubinway, Mich.
Ora C. Wyse
††New Bethel (1949) (21) _____ 18
Ossian, Ind.
Orvil J. Crossgrove
‡‡Ninth Street Mennonite
(1950) (5) _____ 47
1119 N. Ninth St.,
Saginaw, Mich.
Leroy Bechler
North Goshen (1936) (12) ____ 336
501 N. Eighth St.,
Goshen, Ind.
*Russell Krabill
†Vernon U. Miller
*Paul Mininger**
†Henry B. Weaver¶¶
North Main Street (1867)
(22) _____ 369
Nappanee, Ind.
*Homer F. North
Richard Yoder
†Ezra P. Bleile
†Clyde L. Hershberger
†Alvin R. Miller
‡Oak Terrace (1953)
(23) _____ 42
Blountstown, Fla.
Oscar Schrock
Olive (1850) (31) _____ 267
Jamestown, Ind.
*J. C. Wenger
Elno Steiner
†Andrew J. Miller
*D. A. Yoder¶¶
Clarence A. Shank¶¶
Calvin Pletcher¶¶

††Osceola (1951) (22) 30
Osceola, Ind.
  Maurice Long
Petoskey (1950) (37) 40
Petoskey, Mich.
  Homer Yutzy
Pigeon (1894) (11) 96
Pigeon, Mich.
  °Donald E. King
Plato (1949) (14) 94
Lagrange, Ind.
  Willis C. Troyer
  ¶Dean Brubaker
  †John Ray Miller
Pleasant View (1936) (28) 160
Goshen, Ind.
  °John S. Steiner
  ¶Daniel Zehr
  †M. John Kauffman
  Walter Funk°°
‡Pleasantview (1904) (13) 29
Brethren, Mich.
  Warren C. Shaum
Prairie Street (1871) (38) 299
1316 Prairie St.,
Elkhart, Ind.
  °Howard J. Zehr
  °J. D. Graber°°
  R. R. Smucker°°
  †Harold S. Alexander°°
††Providence (1953) (26)
Washington, Ind.
  °Tobias Slaubaugh
‡Rexton (1948) (29) 28
Rexton, Mich.
  Joe J. Swartz
††Roselawn (1949) (38) 63
Elkhart, Ind.
  Verle Hoffman
Salem (1889) (20) (34) 185
Foraker, Ind.
  °Harold D. Myers
  °Ray F. Yoder
  Francis E. Freed
Santa Fe (1960) (8)
Peru, Ind.
‡Seney (1946) (29) 7
Seney, Mich.
  Victor V. Miller

Shore (1865) (15) **345**
Shipshewana, Ind.
  °Lee J. Miller
  Percy J. Miller
  Arnold Roth
  †Homer J. Miller
††Smith School (1959) (15) __ 6
Jetson, Ky.
  John Wickey
‡Soo Hill (1952) (30) 10
Escanaba, Mich.
  Paul Horst
South Colon (1954) (24) 51
Colon, Mich.
  William Wickey
  Harold Mast
South Bend 16
  South Bend, Ind.
‡Stutsmanville (1957) (29)
Harbor Springs, Mich.
‡Sunnyside (1947) (10) 51
Sunnyside Ave.,
Elkhart, Ind.
  D. Richard Miller
††Talcum (1952) 20
Talcum, Ky.
  John Mishler
††Toto Mennonite Gospel
Mission (1948) (20) 36
North Judson, Ind.
  Jency L. Hershberger
Tri-Lakes (1960) (28)
Mottville, Mich.
††Walnut Hill Chapel (1956)
(12) 10
911 N. Sixth St.
Goshen, Ind.
  ¶Marvin Miller
Waterford (1959) (35) 81
2904 S. Main St.,
Goshen, Ind.
  Virgil Brenneman
  Harold Kreider
‡Wawasee Lakeside Chapel
(1947) (9) 32
Syracuse, Ind.
  Herbert L. Yoder
‡Wayside (1948) (29) 28
Brimley, Mich.
  Ralph O. Birkey

†† WELLINGTON MENNONITE MISSION (1955) (6) _____ 21
Lachine, Mich.
  Harold Sharp
WHITE CLOUD (1899) (7) _____ 53
White Cloud, Mich.
  Edward D. Jones
  †Lowell H. Burkholder
WILDWOOD (1939) (29) _____ 32
Curtis, Mich.
  *Clarence Troyer
  Lloyd R. Miller

YELLOW CREEK (1845) (39) ___ 318
Goshen, Ind.
  *John David Zehr
  ¶Lawrence Klippenstein
  †Abram Hartman
ZION (1914) (11) _____ 25
Vestaburg, Mich.
  Erie E. Bontrager
  †Neil C. Buskirk
—Ellrose D. Zook, Mervin Swartzentruber, Editors: *Mennonite Yearbook and Directory,* Volume Fifty-Two, 1961. Statistical Data as of October 1, 1960. Slightly revised.

6

Declaration of Commitment in Respect to Christian Separation and Nonconformity to the World

The Position of the Mennonite Church as Adopted by the Mennonite General Conference at Hesston, Kansas, August 26, 1955

Introduction

From its very inception in Switzerland (1525) and Holland (1533-34) the Mennonite Church has earnestly held to the principle of Christian separation and nonconformity to the world. The term "world" is here employed to designate that sphere in which Satan is obeyed, for he is recognized in Scripture as the head of a house or empire. That which conforms to Satan is in Scripture spoken of as the world. This position of Christian nonconformity to the world is based on the fact that God calls His children to a life of holiness, and to conformity to the character of Jesus Christ, delivering them "from this present evil world." In reference to those who do not know Christ, the divine summons is, "Come out from among them, and be ye separate, saith the Lord, and touch not the unclean thing; and I will receive you, and will be a Father unto you, and ye shall be my sons and daughters, saith the Lord Almighty." The Apostle John commands, "Love not the world, neither the things that are in the world. If any man love the world, the love of the Father is not in him." Peter writes, "But as he which hath called you is holy, so be ye holy in all manner of conversation [conduct]; because it is written, Be ye holy; for I am holy." And Paul commands, "Be not conformed to this world: but be ye transformed by the renewing of your mind, that ye may prove what is that good, and acceptable, and perfect, will of God." The inspired writers of the New Testament all recognize that God has called His saints "out of darkness into his marvellous light," and therefore they ought to "shew forth the praises" of God. Gal. 1:4; II Cor. 6:14-18; I John 2:15; I Pet. 1:15, 16; Rom. 12:2; I Pet. 2:9.

We recognize that in human strength we cannot live a life which pleases

God and glorifies the Lord Jesus Christ. We are also humbly aware that neither legalism nor formalism is the answer to our need. We therefore call upon God for the quickening and sanctifying influence of His blessed Holy Spirit to renew us in heart and life, creating in us more perfectly the image of the blessed Son of God.

We believe that union with the Lord Jesus, with its ensuing nonconformity to the world, is not a matter of ecstasy or mere emotion, but that it is a devotion of love and faith which calls for a resolute discipleship in life, a holy obedience to the precepts of the Word of God, lived in the power of the indwelling Holy Spirit. Furthermore, Christians are called upon by Christ to "make disciples of all nations." They are not to withdraw from all contact with society, but are to labor actively to bring all people to the obedience of the faith. It is also our understanding that a Christian separation and nonconformity to the world apply to all of life including the areas hereinafter specified.

1. Christian Love

We believe that both the letter and the spirit of the New Testament enjoin upon us a life of absolute love and nonresistance. The Saviour commanded that if anyone strike the right cheek, we should turn to him the other also. Christians are to love their enemies, bless them who curse them, do good to those who despitefully use them and persecute them. They are to be perfect in love, even as their heavenly Father is perfect. The command of the apostle is, "Recompense to no man evil for evil. . . . Dearly beloved, avenge not yourselves, but rather give place unto [God's] wrath: for it is written, Vengeance is mine; I will repay, saith the Lord. Therefore if thine enemy hunger, feed him; if he thirst, give him drink: for in so doing thou shalt heap coals of fire on his head. Be not overcome of evil, but overcome evil with good." Our Lord indicated that because His kingdom is not of this world, His servants do not fight. Paul states that although we walk in the flesh, "we do not war after the flesh: (for the weapons of our warfare are not carnal)." "The servant of the Lord must not strive; but be gentle unto all men." Christians are not to render "evil for evil"; on the contrary they are to bless their abusers. They shall follow the Lord Jesus who in His innocent suffering did not strike back but simply committed Himself to the care of God the righteous Judge. Matt. 5:38-48; Rom. 12:17-21; John 18:36; II Cor. 10:3, 4; II Tim. 2:24; I Pet. 2:21-23; 3:8, 9; I Thess. 5:15; I John 2:9; 3:10, 14, 15; 4:8, 20. (See also our statements, *Peace, War, and Military Service*, 1937; and *A Declaration of Christian Faith and Commitment*, 1951, which set forth in greater detail our position as a Mennonite Church.)

We take these Biblical commands at face value and seek humbly by the help of God to apply them to every area of life, and at all times, without exception. Hence we seek to live in peace in all human relationships, avoiding strife and violence, and we reject every form of military service and military training. But we stand ready to aid the needy of the world, to build rather than to destroy, to feed the hungry and clothe the naked, and even at the risk of life and safety to do all in our power to show love to the helpless and suffering. And we are ready to carry on this Christian ministry and witness regardless of what it may cost us. For we understand that the Lord desires every disciple to take upon himself the cross of personal suffering for Christ's sake as God's way of overcoming evil.

2. *Attitude Toward Possessions*

We understand the Scriptures to teach that the end of life for the Christian is not the amassing of wealth but Christian service and evangelism. Our Lord gave stern warnings on the dangers of money-seeking and avarice. Furthermore, whatever may come to us through honest toil and effort is not ours, to be used selfishly, but is God's and we are but His stewards. Therefore we invoke His sanctifying power to deliver us from the materialistic age in which we are living, and to enable us to first give our own selves to the Lord. And we call upon all members of the church to practice lives of self-denial and frugality, to live simply rather than in luxury, and to use the things of this world in the full realization that we do not really belong to this world, but are strangers and pilgrims on the earth.

Although it is not wrong to own property or to save money for emergencies and for old age, yet we protest against the evident wealth-seeking on the part of many professing followers of Christ. And we urge all our members to practice "graduated giving," that is, increasing the percentage returned to the Lord as the income becomes greater. Only thus will the church be able to help its pastors with Scriptural support; only thus can the church carry on its ministry of evangelism and nurture; and only thus can the Gospel be carried to all nations in obedience to the command of the Lord of the church. Psalm 50:10-12; Luke 16:9; Acts 5:14; I Thess. 4:10-12; II Thess. 3:10-12; I Cor. 4:12; 10:24; Eph. 4:28; Matt. 6:19-21, 24; Luke 12:15; 12:21-31, 33, 34; 18:23-27; I Cor. 16:2; II Cor. 8:1-5; 9:6, 7.

3. *Courtship and Marriage*

In contrast with people of the world the children of God are to be pure and holy in life. The Word of God calls particular attention to this in connection with the securing of a life companion. Christians shall keep their bodies unstained by sin so that they may be fit tabernacles for the Holy Spirit. The child of God shall in holiness and honor obtain a life companion, "not in the lust of concupiscence." The apostle also calls upon Christians to follow the Golden Rule of love and not to take advantage of a brother in this matter, "because that the Lord is the avenger of all such" (I Thess. 5:3-7).

So beautiful in God's sight is the loving union of husband and wife that it is made in the New Testament the symbol of the relationship which obtains between Christ and the church. The home God meant is a home of love, of kindness and gentleness, of much joy and happiness, of comradeship, of prayer and devotion to the Lord. It is a home which has family worship. It is a home where husbands love their wives, and where wives love and co-operate fully with their husbands. Marriage is intended by God to be the lifelong union of one man and one woman in the Lord. Christians shall enter into this relationship only with those of like precious faith. No one shall put away his companion except for unfaithfulness which is unrepented of. If a couple separates for incompatibility, they shall either be reconciled or remain unmarried. As a church we call upon all Christians to make their homes Christian, and to resist the current blight of broken homes, divorces, and remarriages. Matt. 5:31, 32; 19:3-12; Mark 10:2-12; Luke 16:18; Rom. 7:2, 3; I Cor. 7; Eph. 5:22-31; Col. 3:18, 19; Titus 2:4, 5; I Pet. 3:1-7.

4. Dress and External Appearance

The Lord Jesus taught His followers not to be worried and anxious about food and clothing, for God cares for His own. The New Testament writers recognize that the heart of Christianity lies not in externals but in the new birth, union with Christ, and Holy Spirit sanctification. But because Christians have been delivered from the world and its sin they cannot any longer follow the fashions and dictates of a sensuous and sensate culture. Christians are not to fashion themselves after this wicked world, but are to be transformed by the renewing of their minds. The apparel of the Christian should therefore be simple, modest, neat, and becoming for those professing godliness. The Apostle Peter calls upon Christian women not to conform to current fashions by occupying themselves in the preparation of elaborate coiffures, nor shall they wear rings or bracelets of gold. For their real "beauty" is that of the heart and spirit, not in external conformity to the worldly forms of adornment. Similarly Paul entreats Christian women to wear clothing which is expressive of their genuine modesty, with proper reserve and Christian discretion. The hair should be worn long, and not arranged according to the current fashions. No jewelry ought to be worn, either of gold or pearls. Neither should there be a display of wealth by the purchase of expensive clothing. Rather let the "adornment" consist of those good works which characterize those who truly are filled with the love of God.

We therefore feel that we are on Scriptural ground when we appeal to all Christian women to dress simply and plainly, avoiding all forms of rings and jewelry, short hair and fashionable coiffures, immodest dresses, and anything which would violate the principles of Christian holiness, purity, modesty, and economy. Likewise Christian men should dress simply and plainly, wearing no rings or jewelry, and scrupulously avoid conforming to worldly fashions. It is not consistent with a profession of faith and holiness to wear flashy or costly clothing, and jewelry. Matt. 6:28-34; Gal. 6:15; Rom. 12:2; I Pet. 3:1-6; I Tim. 2:9, 10.

5. The Clean Life

Since the body of the Christian is the temple of the Holy Spirit, it is sinful and wrong to do anything to the body which would weaken or damage it. Christians are to make their bodily members "instruments of righteousness" in the service of a holy God. It is a violation of Scriptural principles for a Christian to become a slave to anything. The inspired Apostle Paul declared that food has its place, but he would not be brought under the power of anything.

Inasmuch as both the tobacco and drink habits enslave those who have them, and inasmuch as alcohol and tobacco are both costly and injurious to the body, and inasmuch as their use gives an unworthy testimony on the part of men and women of God, we appeal to all Christians "by the mercies of God" to voluntarily adopt the "clean life" by making no use of tobacco in any form and by a complete abstention from the use of beverage alcohol. If this is done out of love for Christ and His cause, and in awareness of the dangers which are involved in the use of alcohol and tobacco, and in consideration of the principle of Christian stewardship, we see no reason to fear the charge of legalism or meritorious asceticism. We also protest the production, manufacture, and sale of both alcohol and tobacco. I Cor. 6:12, 19; Rom. 6:13, 19; Rom. 12:1, 2; I Cor. 8:13; Rom. 14:21; I Cor. 10:31.

6. Worldly Organizations

In the complex world in which we are living there are a number of factors which the nonconformed Christian must take into account when facing the question of uniting with various organizations which bid for membership and support. One consideration is that kingdom concerns fill much of life, leaving too little time and energy for other legitimate concerns at the best. One must therefore seek to invest time and energy only in the best projects. The rearing of a family in the nurture and admonition of the Lord is also a major consideration. One dare not be away from one's family unnecessarily if one takes his obligations seriously as a parent. Another consideration is the "unequal yoke" of II Corinthians 6. As earnest disciples of Jesus we want to remain aloof from any organizational connection which would handicap us in giving a Christian witness or which would make us unwilling participants in an activity or program which we feel is sub-Christian or worldly. Finally, we must raise the question of the propriety of "strangers and pilgrims" entering too deeply into the organizations of our society when many members of those organizations are hostile to the radical type of Christian discipleship for which we as a church stand.

It is not proposed in this *Declaration* to make an exhaustive list of all organizations, dividing them into the legitimate and the inadvisable. But we do wish to call attention to our 1941 statement, *Industrial Relations*, which points out that we can take no part in any social or industrial strife between classes such as labor and capital. We therefore urge all our members to seek employment in such places of labor as do not require labor union membership or who honor church membership cards on the basis of contracts as between unions and our Committee on Social and Economic Relations. In any case, those members employed in institutions having labor unions and no agreement with our church shall register with the union a statement that they are nonresistant Christians and as such will take no part in strife or other activities unbecoming for a nonresistant Christian.

We also reaffirm our agelong opposition to secret and oath-bound fraternities and lodges, holding that the principle of organized secrecy is wrong in itself, that the swearing of oaths is prohibited the Christian by the plain word of our Lord, that the hierarchical titles of the lodge are unbecoming to a humble follower of Christ, that Christians ought not be unequally yoked with non-Christians, and that in many cases lodges erroneously offer salvation to their members on other grounds than the shed blood of Jesus Christ. Lodge membership is therefore a test of membership in the Mennonite Church. John 18:20; Matt. 5:33-37; Jas. 5:12; Matt. 23:8-12; II Cor. 6:14-18; John 14:6; Acts 4:12.

7. Recreation

We recognize that man is so constituted by God that he needs rest and refreshment. We are not unaware of the improvement in health, the correction of physical handicaps, and enhancement of physical and mental efficiency which can come only through a proper use of recreation and leisure time. But we are gravely concerned at the overemphasis on sports in our culture, and at the ruination of wholesome recreation by commercialization, and by a professionalism which makes central in the lives of a few persons what ought to be peripheral in the lives of many. Again, we want to have no part in any activity which would becloud the Christian testimony and witness of those who are "strangers and pilgrims" in this world. We therefore give our testimony against

30

playing cards, pool, the dance, theater-attendance, mixed bathing, the reading of filthy literature, and the like. We urge that Christian people seek refreshment of body and mind only through wholesome activities, clean games, good reading, retirement to God's great out-of-doors, good music, and other forms of recreation which give no questionable witness, which do not spoil one's taste for God's Word and prayer, and which truly build people up rather than weaken them. We protest against the evil influences of many radio and television programs, and call attention to the fact that television can bring many of the undesirable aspects of the theater into the home. I Thess. 5:22; I Cor. 10:13; I Pet. 2:11; Rom. 14:21; I Cor. 8:13; 6:12.

8. Simplicity of Worship

Although the Christian Church was initially a spiritual body of genuine saints, possessing a lively awareness of their separation unto God and their nonconformity to the world, it was but a few centuries until the church became a respectable institution in the world, and ultimately a worldly institution lacking its original faith and power. Along with its new wealth and prestige the church lost its real character. In the Middle Ages the worship of the church was strongly ritualistic, the ministers of the Gospel were transformed into "priests" to intercede with God for the "laity," and the houses of worship lost every vestige of simplicity. The triumph of the world over the church was well-nigh complete.

Our Mennonite brotherhood has sought to return to the type of apostolic church faith and life which are reflected in the Acts and Epistles of the New Testament. We have, therefore, conceived of the church basically as a brotherhood rather than as a hierarchy of clergy and laity. We have conceived of the house of worship as a plain meetinghouse rather than as a costly and ornate edifice of worship. We have had a quiet type of piety in our worship services rather than a demonstrative meeting. We have sung a cappella hymns rather than to employ either organ or piano. Our ministers have been preachers who have proclaimed God's Word in simplicity and clarity.

We encourage our district conferences and congregations to take steps to maintain the simplicity of the apostolic church and to try to regain it in so far as it has been lost. We reaffirm our desire to be a body of redeemed and regenerated pilgrims whose houses of worship, service, preaching, singing, and piety are all made to conform to the spirit and letter of the New Testament. We therefore call upon God to guide us as a church, to sanctify us in the power of the Holy Spirit, and to give us grace and wisdom to resist every effort to conform to a Christendom which has been partially secularized. We request our members to earnestly seek to maintain our Biblical heritage by rejecting every tendency toward worldliness, legalism, or other aberration. We encourage our schools to continue to regain and perpetuate and propagate the "Anabaptist Vision." And we humbly ask God for forgiveness and healing in respect to the carnality, materialism, and worldliness with which our congregations are now struggling. Matt. 23:8; I Cor. 14; Col. 2:16-23; Heb. 11:13, 14, 16; I Pet. 2:5, 9, 11; I John 2:15, 16.

9. Speech

Inasmuch as speech is recognized in God's Word as being the index to the "abundance of the heart," we are concerned that our people may truly be Christian in their use of the tongue. We understand Christianity to involve absolute truthfulness, the avoidance of all flattery, an insistence on holiness and purity of language, the use of the lips to edify the saints and warn sinners, the propriety of praising God, the elimination of all gossip on the part of Christians, the avoidance of oaths as well as such "minced oaths" as are but substitutes for holy names and words, and the like. Since Americans are known abroad as not being as restrained in speech as is proper, we caution our members to be on their guard against conforming more or less unintentionally to the modes of speech in our land. We urge all Christian people to give earnest heed to the plain teaching of the Scriptures on the type of speech which ought to characterize the saints of God. Special warning ought to be given in reference to the sinful way in which people often ruin the good name of others by careless gossip. We plead for intercessory prayer and brotherly admonition to completely displace gossip within the fold of the body of Christ. Matt. 12:34; Eph. 4:25; Col. 3:9, 10; Rev. 22:14, 15; Psalm 12:2, 3; Eph. 4:20; 5:4; Prov. 25:11; Matt. 18:15; I Pet. 4:11; Heb. 2:12; I Pet. 4:15; Matt. 5:34-37; 23:16-22; Jas. 1:19; Titus 3:2; Jas. 4:11.

10. Adopting Resolution

We, the Mennonite General Conference, assembled at Hesston, Kansas, this 26th day of August, 1955, do hereby adopt this *Declaration of Commitment in Respect to Christian Separation and Nonconformity to the World.* We urge our ministers to teach these doctrines and to keep our members aware of the issues which face nonconformed Christians as they seek to live a holy life in this era. We implore God for His renewing grace to cleanse our brotherhood of all sin and worldliness. We call upon all our members to be satisfied with nothing less than a vital union with the Lord Jesus Christ. We dedicate ourselves afresh to the preaching of the Gospel of Christ and the whole counsel of God. We humbly call the attention of all Christians to those areas of this statement which we regard as neglected Bible truths in our day. May the Holy Spirit sanctify us wholly so that we may not be ashamed before our Lord at His coming.

Bibliography

I. MANUSCRIPTS AND UNPUBLISHED MATERIALS

Anderson, Tillie, *Burr Oak History*, 1958
Anonymous, *History of Bethel Mennonite Church*, n.d.
—————————, *Moorepark History*, 1958
—————————, *Osceola History*, n.d.
—————————, *Sunnyside History*, 1949
—————————, *Toto History*, n.d.
Beechy, Winifred Nelson, *White Cloud History* (published in *Mennonite Historical Bulletin*, July 1952)
Birky, Darlene, *English Lake History*, 1958
Birky, Elsie G., *English Lake History*, n.d.
Birky, Joyce, *Hopewell History*, 1958
Birky, Lester, *Hopewell History*, 1959
Bixler, Jacob K., Berea (Daviess County) Historical data, 1928
Bontrager, Eli J., *My Life Story* (mimeographed), 1955
Bontrager, Floyd F., Herrick historical data
Bontrager, Warren, *Biography of Eli A. Bontrager*, n.d.
Brenneman, John M., Memorandum books of preaching trips
Burkholder, David, *Nappanee Church History*
Christophel, Allen B., *Yellow Creek History* (In *Christian Monitor*, August 1932)
Christophel, W. W., *Christophel Genealogy*
Coffman, John S., Diaries (copious extracts kindly furnished by Barbara Coffman)
Delagrange, Betty Lou, *Biography of S. J. Miller*, 1955
Eash, Sam T., *History of Townline Conservative Church*, 1951
Emmert, Patricia, *Maple Grove History*, 1954
Frey, Mabel A., *Biography of Christian Miller*
Funk, John F., Diaries, papers, memorandum books, and letters
Gingerich, Kay, *Hopewell (Kouts) History*, 1960
Good, Clara, *Hopewell History*, 1948
Graber, Gerry, *Leo History*, 1952
Graber, Harry L., *Leo History*, 1953
Graber, Harvey, *Spiritual Awakening in the Old Order Amish Church*, 1956
Graber, Irvin, *The Proper Use of the Ban*, 1950
Hartman, Dean, *Olive History*, 1952
Hertzler, Asa M., *Long Green, Maryland, Church History*
Hochstetler, Miriam, *Biography of Homer F. North*, 1953
Hochstetler, Russell, *History of Pleasant View (Ind.) Mennonite Church*, 1960
Holoway, Jay, *North Main Street (Nappanee) History*, n.d.
Hooley, Carl, *Roselawn History*, n.d.
Hoover, Ira, *Yellow Creek History*, n.d.
Hoover, Samuel, *et al.*, *Hoover Family History*
Hostetler, John A., *Amish Preaching*, 1949
Hughes, Willis, *Biography of C. A. Shank*, 1952
Johns, D. J., *Conference Ministerial List and Data*
Kauffman, Edith, *Middlebury History*, n.d.
Kauffman, Eunice, *Biography of G. J. Lapp*
Kauffman, Milo F., *Rise and Development of Sunday Schools in the Mennonite Church in Indiana*, 1931. M.A. in Rel. Ed. thesis.

Kauffman, Phyllis, *History of Bethany Christian High School,* 1959
Kaufman, Wilma, *Organization and Expansion of the Townline Congregation,* 1956
Kolb, Phoebe M., *Biography of A. C. Kolb*
—————, *Biography of H. A. Mumaw*
Krabill, Russell, *Biography of D. A. Yoder,* 1944
—————, *North Goshen Church History Book,* n.d.
Lambright, Janet, *Biography of Percy J. Miller,* 1954
Lehman, David, *Indianapolis History,* 1957
Leininger, Mrs. C. W., *Prairie Street Mennonite Sewing Circle, c.*1945
Litwiller, Doris, *History of Bethany Christian High School,* 1957
Long, Sharon Kay, *Osceola History,* 1957
Mann, Dean, *Pleasant View History (Indiana),* 1953
Mann, John E., *Prairie Street (Elkhart) History,* n.d.
Martin, Allen F., *Prairie Street (Elkhart) History,* n.d.
Martin, Allen R., *Hopewell History,* 1959
Martin, Jason, *John Fretz Funk: Mennonite Leader 1865-1900*
Mensch, Jacob B., Travel Notes, 1867-97
Miller, Bonnie Lou, *Biography of D. D. Miller,* 1952
Miller, Eileen, *Crumstown History,* n.d.
Miller, Gail, *Moorepark History,* 1951
Miller, Kenneth, *Shore History,* n.d.
Miller, Margaretha, *Emma Church History,* n.d.
Osborne, Herbert L., *Fort Wayne History,* n.d.
Oyer, D. S., *Homestead History,* n.d.
Oyer, John S., *History of Goshen College Mennonite Church* (in *The Parish Messenger,* 1961)
Phinezy, Dorothy, *Fair Haven History,* 1957
Questionnaires to Ordained Men
Raber, Chester, *Detroit History,* 1951
Reiff, Marianna, *Prairie Street (Elkhart) History,* 1935, copied by Phoebe Kolb
Rodman, Jerry, *Sunnyside History,* n.d.
Schlabach, Theron, *Biography of Ira S. Johns,* 1957
Schrock, Lyle, *Topeka History,* n.d.
Shenk, Charles B., *Biography of J. S. Coffman*
Short, Bertha Emmert, *Midland History,* 1960
Slagel, Gene, *History of the Bethel Mennonite Church,* Ashley, Michigan, n.d.
Smeltzer, Lois, *Olive History,* n.d.
Smucker, Jonathan P., Memorandum books
Steiner, Elno, *History of the Indiana-Michigan Mennonite Mission Board,* 1951
—————, *Mission Sunday Schools in the Indiana-Michigan Mennonite Conference,* 1951
Stoltz, Gary L., *The Topeka (G.C.) Mennonite Church,* 1959
Strauss, Jane, *Osceola History,* 1955
Stuckey, Earl, *Salem, Michigan, Congregation History,* 1960
Swartz, Merlin L., *The Historical Background of the Conservative Mennonite Conference,* 1960
Troyer, Clyde O., *Fairview Amish Church History,* 1959
Troyer, Nancy Jane, *Bon Air History,* 1957
Troyer, Ora, *History of the Conservative Mennonite Churches in the Northern Indiana Area,* 1957
Tyson, Vivian, *Yellow Creek History,* 1956
Weldy, Loren, *Holdeman History,* n.d.
Weldy, Paul, *Biography of Silas L. Weldy,* 1954
Wenger, Mary Lois, *Christophel History,* 1960

Wicker, Betty Jean, *The Ninth Street Mennonite Church*, Saginaw, n.d.
Yancey, Virginia, *Conservative Mennonite Church, Lewis County, New York*, 1960
Yoder, Allen K., *A History of the Amish South and West of Nappanee, Indiana*, 1958-59
Yoder, Charles, *Middlebury History*, n.d.
Yoder, Edna, *Walnut Hill Chapel History*, 1958
Yoder, Keith, *Fish Lake History*, 1956
Yoder, Leona V., *Biography of D. D. Troyer*
Yoder, Marie, *Salem Mennonite Church History*
Yoder, Orville, *Elmwood History*, Kendallville, Indiana, 1958
Yoder, Silvanus, *Mennonite Aid Association*
Yoder, Tillie, *Glimpses of the Amish Church of Howard and Miami County*, 1949

II. PERIODICAL FILES

Bethany Bulletin, 1955-
Brethren Annual Number, The Brethren Evangelist, 1886-
Christian Living, 1954-
Evangelical Visitor (Brethren in Christ Church organ)
Friends Directory, Friends World Committee
General Conference Mennonite Church, Handbook of Information
Gospel Herald, 1908-
Gospel Witness, 1905-8
Handbook of Information, The General Conference Mennonite Church
Handbook of the Religious Society of Friends, 1952
Herald of Truth, 1864-1908
Mennonite Community, 1947-53
Mennonite Historical Bulletin, 1940-
Mennonite Yearbook and Directory, Mennonite Church, 1905-
Michigan Mennonite Bible School Bulletin
Missionary Church Association Directory
The Gospel Evangel, formerly *The Rural Evangel*, 1920-
United Missionary Church Yearbook and Directory
Yearbook, Church of the Brethren
Yearbook of the Goshen College Mennonite Church

III. REPORTS

Brethren in Christ Church, Minutes of the Annual General Conference
Evangelical Mennonites, *Report of Inaugural Conference*, 1953
Indiana-Michigan Mennonite Christian Workers' Conference (formerly Sunday School Conference)
Indiana-Michigan Mennonite Conference, Minutes of, 1930-
Indiana-Michigan Mennonite Mission Board ("District Board")
Mennonite Board of Missions and Charities ("General Board")
Michigan Conference Journal, United Missionary Church
Minutes of Indiana Yearly Meeting of Friends
Missionary Church Association, Conference Report and Directory
Reports of the Conservative Amish Mennonite Conference: I, 1910-24; II, 1925-37; III, 1938-50
The Brethren Annual, The Brethren Missionary Herald
United Missionary Church Conference Journal (Indiana) and *Proceedings* (Michigan)

Verhandlungen der Diener-Versammlungen, 1862-78
Women's Missionary and Service Auxiliary

IV. BOOKS, BOOKLETS, AND PUBLISHED ARTICLES

Anderson, Emil V., *Taproots of Elkhart History,* 1949
Atlas of Elkhart County, Indiana, 1874
Atlas of Elkhart County, Indiana, 1915
Atlas and Plat Book of Elkhart County, 1929
Bartholomew, Henry S. K., *Pioneer History of Elkhart County,* 1930
───────────────────, *Stories and Sketches of Elkhart County,* 1936
Battle, J. H., *Counties of Warren, Benton, Jasper, and Newton,* 1883
Bender, D. H., *A Brief Sketch of My Life,* 1943
Bender, Harold S., *Conrad Grebel, c.1498-1526,* 1950
───────────────, *Mennonite Encyclopedia,* 4 vols., 1955-59
───────────────, *Two Centuries of American Mennonite Literature,* 1929
Blanchard, Charles, ed., *Counties of Clay and Owen,* 1884
───────────────────, *Counties of Howard and Tipton,* 1883
Blosser, Mrs. Lawrence, *History of the Union Center Church of the Brethren, 1859-1959*
Bodurtha, A. L., ed., *History of Miami County,* 1914
Borntreger, Hans E., *Erste Ansiedelung der Amischen Mennoniten,* 1907
Borntreger, John E., *Borntraeger Genealogy,* 1923
Braght, T. J. van, *Martyrs Mirror,* 1950
Brenneman, Daniel, *Thoughts in Rhyme,* 1911
Brunk, Harry A., *History of Mennonites in Virginia 1729-1900,* 1959
Burkholder, L. J., *Brief History of the Mennonites in Ontario,* 1935
Butler, G. W., *The Manual of Elkhart,* n.d.
Cassel, Daniel K., *History of the Mennonites,* 1888
Christner, Levi E., *Old Order Amish Church Districts of Indiana* [1949]
Christophel, Alta Kurtz, *Kurtz Genealogy,* n.d.
Climenhaga, A. W., *History of the Brethren in Christ Church,* 1942
Coffman, Centennial Memorial of J. S., 1949
Constitution and Guiding Principles of the Congo Inland Mission, 1956
Constitution and Manual of the United Missionary Church, 1959
Constitution, Conservative Mennonite Conference, 1957
Constitution of the Conference of the Mennonite Brethren Church of North America, 1936
Constitution of the Evangelical Mennonite Church, 1957
Constitution of the General Conference Mennonite Church, 1956
Constitution of the Mennonite General Conference, 1959
Counties of Lagrange and Noble, 1882
Deahl, Anthony, *Historical and Biographical Record of Elkhart County*
Doctrines and Discipline of the United Missionary Church
Eby, Benjamin, *Kirchen-Geschichte der . . . Mennoniten,* 1853
Elkhart and St. Joseph Counties: Pictorial and Biographical Memoirs, 1892
Esch, Carolyn W., and Hartzler, Levi C., *Mennonite Board of Missions and Charities, 1906-1956,* 1956
Esch, Henry D., *Year Book of the Pigeon River Congregation,* 1942
Ford, Ira, *et al., History of Northeast Indiana,* 2 vols., 1920
Gingerich, Melvin, *Mennonites in Iowa,* 1939
───────────────, *Service for Peace,* 1949
Gnagey, Elias, *Gnaegi Genealogy*
Gongwer, Robert L., *Centennial Memorial, Holdeman Mennonite Church,* 1951
Goshen College Bulletin: Golden Anniversary Alumni Directory, 1951

Graber, J. D., *The Church Apostolic,* 1960
Gratz, Delbert L., *Bernese Anabaptists,* 1953
Haines, J. F., *History of Hamilton County,* 1915
Hamilton, L. H., *Standard History of Jasper and Newton Counties,* 1916
Hartzler, John E., *Education Among the Mennonites in America,* 1925
Hartzler, J. S., *Mennonites in the World War,* 1922
Hartzler, J. S., and Kauffman, Daniel, *Mennonite Church History,* 1905
Heatwole, L. J., *Mennonite Handbook of Information,* 1925
Hege, Christian, and Neff, Christian, *Mennonitisches Lexikon,* I, 1913-24; II, 1937; III, 1958
Hershberger, Guy F., *The Mennonite Church in the Second World War,* 1951
——————, *The Recovery of the Anabaptist Vision,* 1957
——————, *The Way of the Cross in Human Relations,* 1958
——————, *War, Peace, and Nonresistance,* 1953
History of Elkhart County, Indiana, 1881
Holdeman, John, *History of the Church of God,* 1938
Holsinger, H. R., *History of the Tunkers and the Brethren Church,* 1901
Hoover, David M., *Hoover Genealogy,* 1936
Hoover, Mrs. George E., *Family History of Christian Schmucker,* 1957
——————, *Family History of William A. Hoover,* 1960
Horsch, John, *Infant Baptism,* 1917
——————, *Mennonites in Europe,* 1950
——————, *Principle of Nonresistance,* 1951
Hostetler, Harvey, *Hochstetler Genealogy,* 1912
Hostetler, John A., *Amish Life,* 1957
——————, *Annotated Bibliography on the Amish,* 1951
——————, *God Uses Ink,* 1958
——————, *Mennonite Life,* 1957
Huffman, Jasper A., *History of the Mennonite Brethren in Christ Church,* 1920
Johns, Ira S., *et al., Minutes of the Indiana-Michigan Conference* [1929]
Kauffman, Amsa H., *The Clinton Brick Mennonite Church,* 1854-1954
Kauffman, Daniel, *Mennonite Cyclopedic Dictionary,* 1937
Kaufman, Edmund G., *Development of the Missionary and Philanthropic Interest Among the Mennonites,* 1931
Kent, Sr., Homer A., *250 Years . . . Conquering Frontiers,* 1958
Knox and Daviess Counties, History of, 1886
Krehbiel, H. P., *General Conference of the Mennonites,* I, 1898; II, 1938
Loucks, Aaron, *John Fretz Funk,* n.d.
Lugibihl, Walter H., and Gerig, Jared F., *The Missionary Church Association,* 1950
Mack, Sr., Alexander, *Rites and Ordinances,* 1939
Mallott, Floyd E., *Studies in Brethren History,* 1954
Manual of Doctrine and Government of the Brethren in Christ Church, 1959
Maple Grove Mennonite Church, 1854-1954
McDonald, D., *History of Marshall County, Indiana, 1836-1880,* 1881
McDonald, Daniel, *History of Marshall County,* 1908
Menno Simons, Complete Writings of, Verduin-Wenger, 1956
Miami County, History of, 1887
Miller, Ernest E., *Daniel D. Miller,* n.d.
Miller, Harry D., *Miller Family History,* 1795-1927
Miller, Henry D., *Descendants of John C. Miller,* 1952
Mumaw, Catherine, *Shaum Genealogy,* 1915
Newby, J. Edwin, *Teachings of Evangelical Friends,* 1952
Old German Baptist Church, Directory of Officials, 1959
Oyer, Dean Noah, 1931

Pannabecker, Ray P., *75th Anniversary Publication, Indiana Conference, United Missionary Church* [1955]

Pictorial and Biographical Record of La Porte, Porter, Lake, and Starke Counties, 1894

Pigeon River Congregation Yearbook, 1942

Royse, Willard L., *Standard History of Kosciusko County,* 1919

Rutt, Harvey S., *History of Chester Township, Wayne County, Ohio, and Shaum and Holdeman Genealogies,* 1930

Schwalm, V. F., *et al., History of the Church of the Brethren in Indiana,* 1952

Schwartz, Anna D., *Descendants of Johannes Schwartz,* 1949

Smith, C. Henry, *Mennonite Immigration to Pennsylvania,* 1929

——————————, *Mennonites of America,* 1909

——————————, *The Mennonites,* 1920

——————————, revised by Krahn, Cornelius, *The Story of the Mennonites,* 1950

Snyder, Wilden L., *Elkhart County Plat Book,* 1959

Sprunger, Eva F., *The First Hundred Years,* 1938

Stauffer, Ezra, *Weber-Weaver Genealogy,* 1953

Stauffer, Ezra N., *Stauffer Genealogy,* 1917

Steiner, M. S., *John S. Coffman, ca.*1903

Stoll, Joseph, *The Amish Mennonites in Daviess County,* Indiana, 1959

Storms, Everek R., *History of the United Missionary Church,* 1958

Stutzman, Leon K., *Bontrager Genealogy,* 1953

Troyer, Glenn, *et al., Mennonite Church History of Howard and Miami Counties, ca.*1917 (contains 1916 Constitution, Rules and Discipline of the Indiana-Michigan Conference)

Troyer, Hiram B., *Descendants of Michael Troyer,* 1953

Umble, John S., *Elkhart Institute Memorial,* n.d.

——————————, *Goshen College, 1894-1954,* 1955

——————————, *Mennonite Pioneers,* 1940

——————————, *Ohio Mennonite Sunday Schools,* 1941

Umble, John S., *Elkhart Institute Memorial,* n.d.

Warkentin, A., *Who's Who Among the Mennonites,* 1937

Warkentin, A., and Gingerich, Melvin, *Who's Who Among the Mennonites,* 1943

Weaver, Abraham E., *History of Elkhart County,* 2 vols., 1916

Weaver, Cora, *John Weaver Genealogy,* 1953

Weaver, Edwin L., *Holdeman Descendants,* 1937

Weaver, Martin G., *Mennonites of Lancaster Conference,* 1931

Weaver, William B., *History of the Central Conference Mennonite Church,* 1926

——————————, *Thirty-five Years in the Congo,* 1945

——————————, *Twenty-five Years of Mission Work in Belgian Congo,* 1938

Weber, Harry F., *History of the Mennonites of Illinois, 1829-1929,* 1931

Weiss, Lister O., and Weiss, Edna M., *Bauer Genealogy,* 1952

Wenger, J. C., "Documents on the Daniel Brenneman Division of 1874," *M.Q.R.,* 1960, 48-56

——————————, *Glimpses of Mennonite History and Doctrine,* 1959

——————————, *History of the Mennonites of the Franconia Conference,* 1937

——————————, *Introduction to Theology,* 1954

——————————, "Jacob Wisler and the Old Order Mennonite Schism of 1872 . . ." *M.Q.R.,* 1959, 108-31, 215-40

——————————, *Mennonite Handbook, Indiana-Michigan Conference,* 1956

——————————, *Separated unto God,* 1955

Wenger, Jonas G., *et. al., Wenger Genealogy,* 1903

31

Yoder, J. W., *Rosanna of the Amish,* 1940
Yoder, Ora M., *Shore Mennonite Church* [1952]
Yoder, Raymond M., *Clinton Frame Sketches,* 1944
————————, *Indiana Literaries,* 1936
Yoder, Sanford C., *The Days of My Years,* 1959
Yoder, Silvanus, *Peter Schrock Genealogy,* 1923
Zimmerman, David N., *Zimmerman Genealogy* [ca.1956]

Index

The pages indicated give the more important treatments of the items listed.

Miller, Deacon Andrew J., 305
Miller, Preacher Andrew S., 305
Miller, Preacher C. Nevin, 306
Miller, Preacher Christian C., 306
Miller, Preacher D. Richard, 306
Miller, Bishop Daniel C., 306
Miller, Bishop D. D., 306, 307
Miller, Deacon Earl, 307
Miller, Bishop Eli S., 307
Miller, Preacher Ernest E., 307
Miller, Deacon Harvey A., 307
Miller, Preacher Henry, 308
Miller, Bishop Henry A., 308
Miller, Deacon Homer J., 308
Miller, Preacher Isaac A., 308
Miller, Bishop Ivan M., 308
Miller, Bishop Jacob P., 308, 309
Miller, Preacher John Ray, 309
Miller, Bishop Joseph (Amish), 386
Miller, Preacher Joseph D., 309
Miller, Preacher Josiah J., 309
Miller, Bishop Lee J., 309
Miller, Preacher Lewis B., 309
Miller, Preacher Lloyd R., 309
Miller, Deacon Malvin P., ix, 310
Miller, Bishop Paul M., 310
Miller, Preacher Percy J., 310
Miller, Bishop S. S., 310
Miller, Deacon Vernon U., 310
Miller, Preacher Victor V., 311
Miller, Preacher W. W., 311
Miller, Preacher William R., 311
Miller, Preacher Yost C., 311
Mininger, Bishop Paul E., 311
Ministerial meetings, District, 28
Ministerial support, 53
Ministers' meetings (December), 49
Mishler, Preacher Elias, 311
Mishler, Deacon James J., 311, 312
Mishler, Preacher John F., 312
Mishler, Deacon John J., 312
Mishler, Deacon Joseph W., 312
Mishler, Bishop Michael, 312
Mishler, Preacher Samuel, 312
Mission Board, Indiana - Michigan Mennonite, 47, 48
Missionary Awakening, 47, 48
Missionary Church Association, 416-418
Missionary concern, Loss of, 13

Missions, vii
Missions, Concept of, 13, 27
Montcalm County, Michigan, 154
Montmorency County, Michigan, 160, 206
Moorepark congregation, 244
Morgan County, Indiana, 235
Morgantown, Kentucky, 257
Morningstar, Preacher Titus L., 312
Morrell, Preacher David, 312
Mortality, Infant, 16
Mosemann, Bishop John H., 312, 313
Mount Morris, Michigan, Conservative Mennonite Church, 414
Mount Pleasant congregation, 235
Moyer, Preacher Daniel, 313
Moyer, Deacon John, 313
Mullett, Preacher E. S., 313, 314
Mumaw, Preacher Amos, 314
Münsterite theocracy, 5
Münsterites, 3
Myers, Bishop Harold D., 314
Myers, Deacon Paul J., 314

Nappanee A.M. Church, 178-181
Nappanee (GCM) congregation, 359-361
Nappanee Mennonite congregation, 79-87
Naubinway congregation, 253
Nazarenes, 435
Nelson, Preacher T. U., 314, 315
Neuhouser, Bishop Joseph S., 315
New Bethel congregation, 235
New Bremen congregation, New York, 255, 256
Newaygo County, Michigan, 155, 400
Newcomer, Deacon Dwight, 315
Newcomer, Deacon Henry, 315
Newton County, Indiana, 397
Noble County, Indiana, 238
Nofsinger, Preacher Christian V., 315
Nold, Jacob, 8
Non-Conference Conservative Mennonites (Hartville, Ohio, group), 420
Nonresistance, vii, 2
North Goshen congregation, 215, 216
North, Bishop H. F., 315, 316
Nonresistance, 12

Spiritual life, 52
Springer, Preacher John C., 330
Springer, N. P., viii
Sproal, Preacher Nobert, 10, 330, 331
Stahl, Deacon George, 331
Stahly, Bishop Ralph, 331
Starke County Amish Mennonites, 20, 196-199
Starke County, Indiana, 233
State church, 1
Statistics, Mennonite, 55
Stauffer, Daniel W., 350
Stauffer, Preacher Melvin, 350
Stauffer Mennonite Church (1845), 352, 353
Steiner, Preacher Elno W., 331
Steiner, Bishop John S., 331
Steiner, Deacon Menno, 331
Steiner, Preacher M. S., 27, 331, 332
Steiner, Preacher Moses S., 332
Steiner, Preacher Peter D., 332
Stemen, Henry, 7
Stofer, Preacher Eli, 332
Stoll, Preacher Henry J., 332
Stoltzfus, Preacher Daniel H., 332
Stutsmanville congregation, 247, 248
Suffering church, Concept of, 13
Sullivan County, Indiana, 399
Summer Bible Schools, viii, 44
Summer, Bishop George H., 332
Sunday school conferences, 28
Sunday schools, Adoption of, 43
Sunnyside, Indiana, congregation, 220
Sunnyside, Michigan, congregation, 206
Swartley, Preacher Willard, 258
Swartz, Preacher Joseph J., Jr., 332, 333
Swiss Brethren, 1
Swope, Wilmer D., viii

Talcum congregation, 257
Taufgesinnten, 6
Teachers' meetings, 29
Teegarden outpost, 127, 128
Tennessee, Amish Mennonites in, 202
Tennessee, Mennonites in, 131
Tippecanoe congregation, 232
Topeka (GCM) congregation, 362
Torture of Anabaptists, vii

Toto congregation, 233, 234
Townline Conservative Mennonite Church, 408-410
Transubstantiation, 4
Troxel, Deacon John, 333
Troyer, Bishop Clarence, 333
Troyer, Bishop D. D., 333
Troyer, Deacon John M., 333
Troyer, Bishop Jonas D., 333, 334
Troyer, Preacher Nathaniel O., 334
Troyer, Preacher Seth, 334
Troyer, Preacher Willis C., 335
Tuscola County congregation, 152-154
Tuscola County, Michigan, 152, 414
Two Kingdoms, Concept of, 12

United Missionary Church (1874), 379-384
Unity problems, Elkhart County Amish, 20
Unruh, Preacher Cornelius, 335

Vassar, Michigan, Conservative Mennonite Church, 414
Virginia, 7
Virginia Mennonite names, 9
Vogt, Preacher Virgil V., 335
Voluntarism in faith, 2

Walnut Hill congregation, 221, 222
War, Civil, 21-23
War I, World, 38-41
War II, World, 45-47
Warey, Bishop Christian, 335
Warren Street (GCM) congregation, 364
Waterford congregation, 223
Wawasee Lakeside Chapel, 232, 233
Wayside congregation, 254
Weaver, Preacher Floyd W., 335
Weaver, Deacon Henry B., 335
Weaver, Preacher Herman, 335, 336
Weaver, Preacher Isaac, 336
Weaver, Bishop Ivan K., 336
Weaver, Preacher J. J., 336
Weaver, Preacher John, 336
Weaver, Deacon M. C., 337
Weaver, Deacon Noah, 337
Weaver, Bishop Norman P., 337
Weaver, Preacher S. E., 337

The Author

J. C. Wenger was born in Chester County, Pa., in 1910. He was graduated from Sellersville, Pa., High School in 1928, and from the Junior College Department of Eastern Mennonite School in 1931. He holds the B.A. degree from Goshen College, the M.A. from the University of Michigan, and the Th.D. from the University of Zurich (Switzerland). In 1937 he married Ruth D. Detweiler, R.N., of Telford, Pa. They have two sons and two daughters.

He was ordained as a Mennonite deacon in 1943, as a preacher in 1944, and as a bishop in 1951. He has served as president of Mennonite Publication Board, as moderator of the Indiana-Michigan Mennonite Conference, and as moderator of Mennonite General Conference. He has been a member of the Indiana Historical Society, Mennonite Historical and Research Committee since 1937, and is the author of many articles in the *Mennonite Encyclopedia*. He is also a member of the Mennonite Historical Society (Goshen College), Mennonitischer Geschichtsverein (Germany), American Society of Church History, American Society for Reformation Research, American Theological Society, and Evangelical Theological Society.

It is his hope that this volume will enhance the sense of mission on the part of Mennonites, and that it will present a true and sympathetic portrait of them to the wider society.